PROGRAMMING WITH MANAGED EXTENSIONS FOR MICROSOFT® VISUAL C++® .NET

Richard Grimes

PUBLISHED BY
Microsoft Press
A Division of Microsoft Corporation
One Microsoft Way
Redmond, Washington 98052-6399

Library of Congress Cataloging-in-Publication Data
Grimes, Richard, 1964-
Programming with Managed Extensions for Microsoft Visual C++ .NET / Richard Grimes.
p. cm.
Includes index.
ISBN 0-7356-1724-4
1. Microsoft Visual C++. 2. C++ (Computer program language) 3. Microsoft .NET. I. Title.

QA76.73.C153 G7428 2002
005.26'8--dc21 2002071751

Printed and bound in the United States of America.

1 2 3 4 5 6 7 8 9 QWE 8 7 6 5 4 3

Distributed in Canada by H.B. Fenn and Company Ltd.

A CIP catalogue record for this book is available from the British Library.

Microsoft Press books are available through booksellers and distributors worldwide. For further information about international editions, contact your local Microsoft Corporation office or contact Microsoft Press International directly at fax (425) 936-7329. Visit our Web site at www.microsoft.com/mspress. Send comments to *mspinput@microsoft.com.*

Acquisitions Editor: Danielle Bird
Project Editor: Sally Stickney
Technical Editor: Jim Fuchs

Body Part No. X08-81826

For my wife, Ellinor, and my children, Jennifer and Thomas.
Now you'll get back your husband and father.

Contents at a Glance

Table of Contents

Acknowledgments

As with any technical book, there are many people who have contributed to this book other than those beneath the byline. First I have to mention Danielle Bird, acquisitions editor at Microsoft Press, who helped to get this book started and smoothed its development. The ink would never have found its way to the paper without the steady hand of project editor, Sally Stickney, or without my copy editor, Holly Viola, who ensured that my English became an English that you could read and understand. On the technical side, I am indebted to Jim Fuchs, my technical editor at Microsoft Press, and to Christophe Nasarre, for reviewing the manuscript and pointing out when my code would fail to compile or produce results that I did not expect. I am also grateful to Ronald Laermans, Mike Hall, and Jeff Peil from the Visual C++ team at Microsoft for answering my questions about the C++ compiler.

Finally, no book would issue from my PC without my wife. Ellinor provides love, support, and copious quantities of tea while I write.

Richard Grimes
Kenilworth, United Kingdom
June 2002

Introduction

The most immediately obvious feature of .NET is the runtime, which Microsoft calls the common language runtime. The concept of a runtime is not new to Microsoft technologies—Visual Basic applications have always carried around the baggage of the Visual Basic runtime, and Microsoft's foray into Java brought about the Microsoft Java Virtual Machine (JVM). But unlike the Visual Basic runtime and the JVM, the .NET runtime is not constrained to a specific language. Both Microsoft and third-party companies have produced several languages that can produce code to run under the .NET runtime. Some, such as C#, are new languages, and others use the syntax of existing languages. Microsoft Visual C++ .NET is an existing language that has been extended to produce .NET code, and these extensions are called the Managed Extensions for C++.

The Managed Extensions allow C++ classes to take advantage of .NET garbage collection and memory protection. More important, they enable C++ code to access the .NET Framework class library and libraries written by any of the other .NET-enabled languages; and other languages can use managed libraries written in C++. No longer do C++ developers need to use myriad technologies such as COM, DLL exported functions, and template libraries to get access to the libraries they need to create a fully featured application; just about all the necessary library code is available as .NET classes in the .NET Framework class library.

The Managed Extensions essentially define a subset of the C++ language—it looks like C++, and it smells like C++, but it is really .NET. You might be asking yourself, "If .NET allows me to choose between a multitude of languages, why should I use C++ to write my .NET code?" C++ has always been a systems language, and it gives you the power and flexibility to produce truly innovative solutions. This ethos has been carried over to the Managed Extensions, in which you have not only the complete features of the .NET runtime and class library but also the full power of the unmanaged language. Indeed, C++ is the only language in which you can mix .NET code and unmanaged code in the same source file. The compiler also allows you to seamlessly access all your unmanaged libraries: static-link libraries, template libraries, COM objects, and DLLs. This easy access means that you can reuse all your existing code and, in the few cases in which the .NET Framework class library does not have suitable classes, use existing unmanaged libraries. Again, no other language gives you these facilities, so no other language can be regarded as *the* .NET systems language.

The Contents of This Book

This book is organized to take you end-to-end through the development process. I start by describing the basic features of the language, and then I progress through .NET features such as interop, delegates, and GUI applications. The last two chapters of the book focus on the project management and debugging features, respectively, of Visual Studio .NET. You do not need Visual Studio .NET to develop .NET code in C++, but as you'll see from Chapter 6 and Chapter 7, your work will be far easier if you use it. A more detailed description of the contents of each chapter follows.

Chapter 1

In this first chapter, I cover the basic features of the Managed Extensions. I start by explaining how to develop managed types and how these differ from unmanaged types, both in their declaration and their use. I cover how to use managed arrays, interfaces, and exceptions. C++ written with the Managed Extensions follows the .NET model rather than the C++ model in terms of inheritance and casts, so I conclude this chapter by describing how .NET differs from unmanaged C++ in these respects.

Chapter 2

One of the reasons for using C++ is that it allows you to use existing unmanaged code in your .NET projects. The Managed Extensions compiler has a technology quaintly called *It Just Works!* (IJW). This technology allows you to use unmanaged libraries in managed projects and to intermingle managed and unmanaged classes. In this chapter, I tell you how to use IJW and give some insights into how it works.

.NET also has an attribute-based technology called *platform invoke* that allows any .NET-enabled language to access code exported from a DLL. I explain how you can use platform invoke and describe how you can customize the marshaling it performs. A variation of platform invoke is COM interop, which is the final subject of this chapter. COM interop allows managed code to use COM objects as if they were .NET objects, and it allows unmanaged code to use .NET objects as if they were COM objects. I go over how COM interop works and how you can register classes and generate the attributes required by COM interop.

Chapter 3

Function pointers are useful in unmanaged projects because they allow function binding to be performed at run time rather than at compile time. C++ virtual functions and COM interfaces are based on function pointers, and function pointers also enable you to define notification systems. .NET has its own version of function pointers—called *delegates*—that are type-safe, eliminating one big disadvantage of unmanaged function pointers: namely, casting between function pointer types.

In this chapter, I show you how to use delegates with C++, how this approach compares with unmanaged function pointers, and how you can use delegates with unmanaged code. I also explain how to make asynchronous calls through delegates (using a system-provided thread) and talk about how to write multithreaded code with .NET. Finally, I clarify how .NET uses delegates to implement a formal notification mechanism called *.NET events*.

Chapter 4

The .NET Framework augments Windows with a new graphics library called *GDI+*. This is an unmanaged library, but the .NET Framework comes with .NET wrapper classes. The windowing technology in .NET is called *Windows Forms*. You can draw on a form with GDI+, and you can use a form as a container for controls. In this chapter, I explain how you can create GUI applications in C++ with Windows Forms and describe how to implement such applications using Win32 windows. I also show how to handle Windows messages through .NET events and how to bypass this mechanism to get the most control over a window's behavior.

I also go over how to use managed resources and native resources efficiently in a managed class so that resources are released when your application no longer needs them. Finally, I define "managed" resources and explain how to add a managed resource to your application, and discuss how to localize resources.

Chapter 5

In this chapter, I delineate how .NET code is stored in executable files. I start by explaining the format of .NET assemblies and describing how they are implemented as Win32 portable executable (PE) files. I then discuss how you can get information about .NET metadata and code within an assembly by using COM objects the .NET Framework supplies. The .NET runtime is implemented with unmanaged code, and Microsoft has designed the runtime so that unmanaged code can get access to the runtime through COM objects. In this chapter, I explain how to use these objects to access and configure the runtime from unmanaged code and how to instruct the runtime to run managed code.

A managed application can be configured through an XML file associated with the application. The runtime reads the configuration file when the application starts so that it can get information about the facilities that the application requires. One of the big advantages of the runtime is that it will load only the libraries that your application was specifically built to use. You can configure the rules that the runtime uses to locate those libraries via the configuration file. Your code can also access the information in a configuration file, and in this chapter, I show you how to do this and how to extend configuration files and the API to read them.

Finally, I describe code access security and demonstrate how to use it in your code. I also show the default permissions that are required by .NET code written with Managed Extensions for C++.

Chapter 6

Visual Studio .NET is a mixed managed and unmanaged application that integrates various application-development tools. In this chapter, I explain how you can use the environment to develop your projects. I cover the facilities of the editor and the tools that are provided to allow you to manage your projects. I talk about the Visual Studio .NET project wizards and the types of C++ projects that you can develop. I conclude the chapter with examples of the types of managed projects that you can develop and describe how to customize the code provided by the project wizard.

Chapter 7

The last stage of your development cycle is typically the testing stage: you need to test the project to ensure that it works the way you intend it to, and when it does not work as expected, you will need to debug the code to determine where the problem lies. Although the testing stage often comes at the end of a development cycle, you can save yourself a lot of effort by writing code up front that provides diagnostic information. In this chapter, I describe the facilities that the .NET Framework offers to allow you to diagnose problems in your code and explain how you can collect this diagnostic information.

Visual Studio .NET has an integrated managed and native code debugger, so once you have identified a problem you can step through your code to pinpoint the source. I explain how to use the debugger and its various facilities. I also talk about the special issues you need to consider when debugging multithreaded code and applications that consist of more than one process. Finally, I show you how to profile code. Visual Studio .NET does not provide a code profiler, but the .NET Framework has support for providing profiling information through a user-supplied COM object. I give an example of such a profiling object.

Appendix A

The .NET Framework class library is very comprehensive, and you'll find code in it to perform just about any task you could do previously with the C runtime library (CRT) or the standard C++ library. In this appendix, I present, in a series of tables, the .NET code that is equivalent to the most useful CRT functions and standard library classes. The intention of this appendix is to provide a starting point for when you ask the inevitable question, "How do I do *this* in .NET?"

Appendix B

This appendix is a personal list of further resources. This list is not exhaustive, and I am sure that it is not the best list of .NET resources. However, I have provided the resources that were particularly useful to me, and I hope that you'll benefit from them too.

System Requirements

The first five chapters require only the C++ compiler (version 13). The .NET Framework SDK is a free download from Microsoft (*msdn.microsoft.com/netframework*). The C++ compiler supplied as part of the Framework SDK does not produce optimized code, nor does it provide extensions like the unmanaged ATL Attribute Provider, but it is a fully featured C++ compiler that can be used for both managed and unmanaged C++ development. If you want to learn about the .NET Framework, the C++ compiler is the place to start.

The last two chapters use features of Visual Studio .NET. Visual Studio .NET includes the full optimizing C++ compiler, and it also comes with unmanaged libraries: the complete CRT library, the standard C++ library, and the combined ATL (ActiveX Template Library) and MFC (Microsoft Foundation Class) libraries, all of which you can access from .NET code (*msdn.microsoft.com/vstudio*). Visual Studio .NET also provides code wizards to create the initial files of your application, tools to manage your projects, a fully featured editor, and an integrated debugger. If you intend to develop projects larger than a handful of classes, you should use Visual Studio .NET.

Support

Every effort has been made to ensure the accuracy of this book. Microsoft Press provides corrections for books through the World Wide Web at the following address:

http://www.microsoft.com/mspress/support/

To connect directly to the Microsoft Press Knowledge Base and enter a query regarding a question or issue that you might have, go to:

http://www.microsoft.com/mspress/support/search.asp

If you have comments, questions, or ideas regarding this book, please send them to Microsoft Press using either of the following methods:

Postal Mail:

Microsoft Press
Attn: Programming with Managed Extensions
for Microsoft Visual C++ .NET Editor
One Microsoft Way
Redmond, WA 98052-6399

E-Mail:

MSPINPUT@MICROSOFT.COM

Please note that product support is not offered through the above mail addresses. For support information regarding C++, Visual Studio .NET, or the .NET Framework, visit the Microsoft Product Standard Support Web site at:

http://support.microsoft.com

1

Managed Types

The Managed Extensions for C++ are extensions to the C++ compiler and linker to allow them to create .NET code. The Managed Extensions use C++ keywords and syntax, but they follow .NET rules for types and facilities. So, in effect, you have a language within a language. In some cases, .NET has concepts that are not available in standard C++, and in other cases, it has items that have similar names to items in C++ but with totally different behavior. To extend the language for these new facilities and to distinguish between .NET and native C++ items, some new keywords have been added to the language. These new keywords , some new syntax, two new pragmas, and a compiler switch constitute the Managed Extensions, which colloquially gives us managed C++.

The Managed Extensions are *extensions*—that is, you can continue to use native C++, and the standard rules of C++ will still apply to that code. Indeed, all of your existing code works with code compiled for .NET: native C++, static libraries, and template libraries.

New Keywords in Visual C++ .NET

To allow you to distinguish between code written for the .NET runtime and code that will not be managed by the runtime, Microsoft has introduced extensions to the C++ language with the keywords in Table 1-1.

In addition, the compiler and linker have new switches for compiling .NET code; these will be explained in more detail in Chapter 6. The most important new compiler switch is */clr*. This switch tells the compiler to compile all code to Microsoft intermediate language (MSIL), regardless of whether the code is managed by the .NET garbage collector.

Table 1-1 New Keywords in C++ to Support Managed Code

Keyword	Description
`__abstract`	Indicates that the class is abstract—that is, not all methods have an implementation, and to use the class, you must derive from it.
`__box`	Used to box a value type. Boxing creates an object with the value of the value type that has been boxed. (See the section "Boxing" later in this chapter for more detailed information about boxing.)
`__delegate`	Declares a delegate type. Delegates are essentially type-safe function pointers.
`__event`	Declares an event, a notification mechanism as part of a class. This keyword indicates that the class can generate the event, and it adds code to store the delegates invoked when the event is raised.
`__gc`	Identifies that a class is managed by the .NET garbage collector or that a pointer points to a managed object.
`__identifier`	Used when the name of a type or member is a keyword in C++ and indicates to the compiler to ignore the C++ meaning of the word.
`__interface`	When combined with the *__gc* keyword, the *__interface* keyword allows you to declare a managed interface.
`__nogc`	Used to indicate that the type is not managed by the .NET garbage collector or to indicate that a pointer points to a non–managed object.
`__pin`	Used on a pointer to *pin* the object it points to. This pinning means that for the scope of the pointer the object will not be moved in the managed heap during garbage collection.
`__property`	Indicates that a method is the get or set method for a property.
`__sealed`	Used on a class to indicate that the class is complete and cannot be extended through class derivation.
`__try_cast`	This cast operator performs a run-time type check and throws a managed exception if the cast fails.
`__typeof`	Operator used to obtain the *Type* object for a particular type.
`__value`	Indicates that the type is lightweight and is created on the stack rather than on the managed heap.

When you use the */clr* compiler switch, you also should have the following *#using* statement somewhere in the project:

```
#using <mscorlib.dll>
```

This statement has two functions. First, it gives access to the metadata in the identified assembly, which means that you can use the public types defined in the assembly. Second, *#using* indicates to the linker to generate metadata in the output assembly to identify the assemblies that the output assembly uses. Every assembly must use the types in *mscorlib*, and that's why you must include the previous *#using <mscorlib.dll>* statement. Notice that the name given in the *#using* statement is the name of the *file* that contains the metadata, not the name of the assembly.

The complete name of an assembly contains the culture, version, and public key token, as well as the short assembly name. If available, all of this information for an assembly that your assembly depends upon must be added to the dependent's manifest. If you are likely to use an assembly that will be installed in the global assembly cache (GAC)—a container for shared assemblies—then it is important that the correct, full name of the assembly is placed in the assembly that you are creating. There can be several versions of an assembly in the GAC, so the .NET Fusion technology uses metadata in the dependent assembly to determine which version to load. (Fusion is the system that handles locating and binding to assemblies.) The *#using* statement does not look in the GAC for a metadata container, so you have to give the name of (and possibly the full path to) a copy of this assembly outside of the GAC. The system assemblies (*mscorlib*, *System*, *System.Windows.Forms*, and so on) are installed in the GAC, but there are copies of their DLLs in the .NET Framework folder in the %SYSTEMROOT% folder. The *#using* statement checks this folder automatically.

The *#using* statement takes the name of the metadata container in either angle brackets or quotes; it does not matter which you use. If you specify a path, the compiler will use this information to locate the metadata. The exception is the *mscorlib* assembly. If you provide a path to the mscorlib.dll file, the compiler will ignore your path information.

The search order is:

1. The full path specified in *#using*
2. The current working folder
3. The .NET Framework folder in %SYSTEMROOT%
4. The folders mentioned on the command line with the */AI* compiler switch
5. The folders mentioned in the LIBPATH environment variable

The .NET Fusion technology uses specific rules (probing) to locate assemblies at run time (which I will explain in Chapter 5). The *#using* search order is not the same as the Fusion probing rules.

Note that I have been careful to say that *#using* takes the name of a file that contains metadata rather than saying that you must provide an assembly.

Metadata can be found in assemblies, modules, and .obj files, and you can specify any of these files with *#using*. If you provide the name of an assembly, the details of the assembly will be added to the manifest of the assembly you are creating, so Fusion will be able to probe for, and bind to, the assembly at run time. Provide the name of a module when you intend to use types in the imported module in your assembly and you want the module to be part of your assembly. As a consequence, the manifest of the assembly you are creating will have metadata for the module. Finally, you can use an .obj file in the *#using* directive. Whenever you compile a source file, the .obj file will have metadata for the types in the .obj file. If you want to use the types in an .obj file, the file will also have to be linked to the assembly that you are creating. In this respect, *#using* is similar to *#include* for native C++. When you specify a library assembly with *#using*, you will get access to only the public types defined in the assembly. (I'll explain how to declare public types later in this chapter.) If you use *#using* on an .obj file, you will have access to both public and private types.

Executables are assemblies in .NET and can export types. However, don't be tempted to use *#using* on an executable. Although the C++ compiler will compile the code, the .NET runtime will complain when your code runs because when it loads the assembly, the runtime will see that the assembly is not a library assembly (a DLL) and will throw a *BadImageFormatException* exception.

To compile C++ to MSIL, the compiler must be invoked with the */clr* switch. The *#using <mscorlib.dll>* statement and the */clr* switch go hand in hand—if you have one, you have to use the other. This switch tells the compiler that the code should be compiled as MSIL. All managed code will be compiled as MSIL, but most native (nonmanaged) code will also be compiled as MSIL. This means that if you have classes that will be created on the unmanaged C++ heap, the code will still be MSIL and will be run by the .NET runtime. There are exceptions (which I will outline later), but essentially all code will be compiled to MSIL.

MSIL and Native Code

The C++ compiler will compile the code in all C++ functions—managed and nonmanaged classes—to MSIL, with a few exceptions. The first case is when you specifically identify that you do not want code to be MSIL, and you do this with a pragma. One gripe often made about .NET is that assemblies have metadata and IL that can be readily viewed with the IL disassembler and hence your algorithms are an open secret. One way that you can get around this problem is to compile the code to native x86.

```
#pragma unmanaged
char Encrypt(char cClear, char cKey)
{
   return cClear ^ cKey;
}
#pragma managed
```

The code that encrypts a string can pass each character to *Encrypt*. The following code shows a simple use of this function. This code assumes that no data is lost when the characters in the managed string *strClear* are converted from the 16-bit Unicode characters that *System::String* uses internally to the 8-bit *char*.

```
// encrypt.cpp
// strClear is the string to encrypt.
// strKey is the key to encrypt the data.
// bEncrypted is an array with the encrypted data.
// Create an array to hold the encrypted data.
Byte bEncrypted[] = new Byte[strClear->Length];
int posKey = 0;
for (int pos = 0; pos < strClear->Length; pos++)
{
   // String::Chars[] returns the character
   // at the specified position.
   bEncrypted[pos] = Encrypt(strClear->Chars[pos],
      strKey->Chars[posKey]);
   posKey++;
   if (posKey == strKey->Length) posKey = 0;
}
```

You could use code such as this if you wanted to encrypt data before passing the byte array to a stream—for example, *FileStream* to write to a file or *NetworkStream* to pass the data to a socket. My simple encryption algorithm XORs each character of the cleartext with the corresponding character in the secret key. Because I do not want my secret algorithm to be widely known, I have compiled it as native code. When a snooper uses ILDASM to view my assembly, he will see the following code:

```
.method public static pinvokeimpl(/* No map */)
int8 modopt([Microsoft.VisualC]Microsoft.VisualC.NoSign
SpecifiedModifier)
   modopt([mscorlib]System.Runtime.CompilerServices.CallConvCdecl)
Encrypt(
   int8 modopt(
      [Microsoft.VisualC]Microsoft.VisualC.NoSign
SpecifiedModifier) A_0,
   int8 modopt(
      [Microsoft.VisualC]Microsoft.VisualC.NoSign
SpecifiedModifier) A_1) native unmanaged preservesig
```

```
{
   .custom instance void
      [mscorlib]System.Security.SuppressUnmanagedCode
SecurityAttribute::
         .ctor() = ( 01 00 00 00 )
  // Embedded native code
  // Disassembly of native methods is not supported.
  // Managed TargetRVA = 0x1000
} // end of method 'Global Functions'::Encrypt
```

I will explain the *modopt* modifier in Chapter 2. In essence, the C++ compiler has generated a managed function that wraps the unmanaged function. Because ILDASM cannot disassemble x86 machine code, the snooper does not get to see my secret algorithm.

Of course, a determined hacker could access the native code referenced in the managed function and use an x86 disassembler to get the assembly code for the algorithm, as shown here:

```
Encrypt:
00401010  push   ebp
00401011  mov    ebp,esp
00401013  movsx eax,byte ptr [cClear]
00401017  movsx ecx,byte ptr [cKey]
0040101B  xor    eax,ecx
0040101D  pop    ebp
0040101E  ret
```

It is interesting to compare this with the IL that would be generated if the method had been compiled to IL, as shown here:

```
.maxstack  2
IL_0000:  ldarg.0
IL_0001:  ldarg.1
IL_0002:  xor
IL_0003:  conv.i1
IL_0004:  br.s IL_0006
IL_0006:  ret
```

In this simple example, it is clear in both cases what the algorithm does. In a more complicated algorithm—one that makes library calls, makes Boolean checks, or performs loops—there will be a marked difference between the disassembled x86 and IL. The main difference will be that without symbols there will be no indication in the disassembled x86 about the procedure calls that are made, whereas in IL, metadata identifies the calls.

The compiler will check the code that you are compiling to see whether the code can be compiled to MSIL. This check is important if you are compiling existing C++ code. If a function contains code that cannot be compiled to MSIL, the entire function will be compiled to x86 native code. The cases when this compilation to x86 native code happen are:

- Functions that have *__asm* blocks
- Functions that have *varargs* parameters[1]
- Functions that call *setjmp*
- Functions with intrinsics such as *_ReturnAddress* and *_AddressOfReturnAddress* that directly access the machine code.
- Functions with variables that are aligned types (using *__declspec(aligned)*)

With these rules taken into account, most code will compile to MSIL and the remaining code will compile to native x86.

C++ Primitive Types

The .NET Framework defines value types for all the primitive types used in C++. (Value types will be explained later in this chapter, in the section "Managed Types and Value Types.") You can continue to use C++ types, and the compiler will ensure that the correct .NET type is used. These types are shown in Table 1-2. All of these types are defined in the *System* namespace, and I have given the corresponding value from *System::TypeCode* enumeration. If you use the C++ equivalent type (other than *void**, *std::time_t*, and *std::wstring*<>), the compiler will use the equivalent .NET type. If your code uses *void**, *std::time_t*, or *std::wstring*<> and you want to pass the values to .NET code, you will have to change your code to the equivalent .NET type.

I have included the basic types in the .NET Framework for which there are no equivalents in C++ or the C++ standard library: *DBNull* and *Decimal*, which are used to represent a NULL value in a database and a decimal value with 29 significant digits, respectively. In addition, I have listed the nearest equivalent in C++ terms for three types: *DateTime*, to hold a time; *String*, which is a string type that holds a Unicode string; and *Object*, which is the top class in all class hierarchies in .NET and hence an *Object** is used in the situations when a *void** is typically used in C++.

---

1. In fact, there is an equivalent of *varargs* in .NET, and C++ can call such methods. However, the current version of C++ cannot compile methods that have *vararg* parameters.

Table 1-2 Primitive .NET Value Types and Their Equivalent C++ Types

.NET Type	Size (Bits)	*TypeCode*	C++ Equivalent Types
Boolean	8	0x03	*bool*
Char	16	0x04	*wchar_t*
Byte	8	0x06	*unsigned char*
SByte*	8	0x05	*char*
Int16	16	0x07	*short*
UInt16	16	0x08	*unsigned short*
Int32	32	0x09	*int*
UInt32	32	0x0a	*unsigned int*
Int32	32	0x09	*long*
UInt32	32	0x0a	*unsigned long*
Int64	64	0x0b	*__int64*
UInt64	64	0x0c	*unsigned __int64*
Single	32	0x0d	*float*
Double	64	0x0e	*double*
DateTime	—	0x10	*std::time_t*
DBNull	—	0x02	—
Decimal	—	0x0f	—
Object	—	0x01	*void**
String	—	0x12	*std::wstring<>*

* If you use the */J* compiler switch, a C++ *char* is compiled as a *Byte*.

Notice that *int* and *long* have the same underlying .NET Framework type: *Int32*. Thus, the same code will be generated for *int* as for *long*, and this behavior might appear to imply that a method cannot be overloaded on *long* and *int*. However, the C++ compiler will use a special modifier (*Microsoft::VisualC::IsLongModifier*) to indicate that the type is *long* rather than *int*, so the runtime will treat methods overloaded with the *long* and *int* parameters as being different.

Each of the .NET types for primitive types derives from *System::ValueType*. These .NET types have methods to convert to other primitive types, to compare values, to create a value from a string, and to convert to a formatted string; and they each have a method named *GetTypeCode* that returns a *TypeCode* enumerated type. This *TypeCode* is used to identify the particular type, so you can pass a primitive type through a *ValueType* pointer and use the *TypeCode* to identify which type is being passed. Here are some examples:

```
// Use a .NET primitive type.
Int32 i32 = 99;
// Convert to a string.
String* s = i32.ToString();
// Use as a C++ primitive type.
int i = i32;
```

The compiler will automatically convert C++ primitive types to the .NET primitive types, so you can assign an *int* to an *Int32* and vice versa. To call the other conversion methods (for example, *ToSingle* and *ToDecimal*), the call must be made on a managed interface and this requires that the type be boxed. I'll cover boxing in the section "Boxing" later in this chapter. This interface is called *IConvertible*.

The *System::Convert* class can be used to convert from one primitive type to another. You can use the generic *ChangeType* method, which takes *Object** pointers to the value you want converted and the type you want to convert the value to, but since most primitive types are value types, this operation will involve boxed values. The *Convert* class also has overloaded methods to convert between specific types:

```
int i = 0;
// true is nonzero.
bool b = Convert::ToBoolean(i);
String* s = Convert::ToString(i);
```

In addition, most .NET types will have a *ToString* method to get a string version of the object.

Managed Types and Value Types

.NET languages are described as *consumers* or *extenders*. A consumer language can merely use existing .NET types whereas an extender—such as C++—can create new types. .NET defines two different sorts of types, depending on where instances of the type are allocated and how they are used. Reference types are created on the garbage collector managed heap, where allocation and deallocation is cheap but heap cleanup during garbage collection is expensive. Reference types are usually passed to methods by reference. Value types are typically created on the stack and are passed to methods by value.

Garbage collected reference types appear to solve the problem of leaking memory—your code merely has to allocate the objects, and the garbage collector does the deallocation. However, garbage collection is more important than merely solving memory leaks within client code. In a distributed application, memory allocation is extremely important because objects can be accessed across process or machine boundaries, which introduces the issue of which code has the responsibility to perform the cleanup. Furthermore, when data is passed from one context to another by value, the data has to be serialized into a form that can be transmitted and then deserialized at the other end in the form that the receiving code expects to get. In both cases, memory allocation has to be performed, and this brings into question how long these memory buffers should exist and who has the responsibility of releasing them.

In synchronous code, the issues were straightforward because both sides of the call know when a buffer is no longer being used. COM provided rules about who had the responsibility of managing memory based on parameter attributes, and this strategy worked well in most cases. However, when you passed variable-length buffers out of a method, the code got a little messy and involved using a global memory manager. (Allocations are performed with *CoTaskMemAlloc,* and memory is freed with *CoTaskMemFree.*) With asynchronous COM code, memory management started to get more complicated and required a final clean-up call to be made when it was clear that the call was completed. .NET makes asynchronous calls easy (as you will see in Chapter 3), and you can decide to ignore any return values from the call, in which case the final clean-up call is not made, but because memory is allocated on the managed heap, this lack of a clean-up call is not a problem. When I cover asynchronous methods in Chapter 3, you'll see the great power of using managed types.

If your application uses many small objects with short lifetimes, individually allocating these objects on the heap can be a significant performance hit. For this reason, the .NET Framework provides value types. Value types are short-lived, small objects that are usually created on the stack. Allocating them is cheap: when you declare a value type variable, the stack pointer is merely moved to provide space. Deallocation is also cheap and is automatic—when the variable goes out of scope, the stack pointer is moved to indicate that the space is now available. Furthermore, accessing the data members involves direct access, so a dereference is not required. Because value types are normally created on the stack, their lifetime is short (except, of course, for those created in the entry point method).

Managed Objects

In C++ you identify that a class is managed by the garbage collector by using the *__gc* modifier. This modifier can be used on classes and structs, and it can be used on pointers to explicitly specify that the pointer is to a managed object. All *__gc* class members are private by default; *__gc* struct members are public. This scheme follows the usual C++ meaning of these types, and I will refer only to classes in the following discussion.

Here is an example of a managed type:

```
__gc class DataFile
{
   System::String* name;
public:
   DataFile(System::String* n) : name(n){}
   // Other members omitted
};
```

This class is named *DataFile*. I have used the C++ *public* keyword to indicate that the constructor can be accessed by any code outside of the class, and I have used the default member access to indicate that the *name* field can be accessed only by code within the class. The *name* field is a managed string, and in this example I have given the fully qualified name, including its namespace. I will return to *System::String* and to namespaces in the section "Managed Strings" later in this chapter.

The *name* field is initialized in the initializer list of the constructor, and the syntax here is similar to native C++: the pointer of the *name* field is initialized with the pointer *n*, but it does not mean that a constructor is called. Because the string is a reference type, all that occurs is an assignment of the reference. This behavior is important because when an instance of *DataFile* is created with this constructor, the *name* field is initialized with a reference to a managed string.

Instances of this class can be created only on the managed heap, as shown in the following code:

```
// strFile is a managed string initialized elsewhere.
DataFile* df = __gc new DataFile(strFile);
```

You cannot create instances of a *__gc* class on the stack. If you attempt to create a stack-based instance, the compiler will issue an error (C3149). Notice that I have explicitly used the *__gc* modifier on the *new* operator to indicate that the managed operator is used. You do not have to use this syntax. If you omit this modifier, the compiler will still use the managed *new* operator because the class that is being created is managed.

If you omit the *__gc* modifier from the class declaration or you use the *__nogc* modifier, a native C++ class will be created, as shown here:

```
// Must compile with /EHsc to enable unmanaged exception handling
__nogc class natDataFile
{
   std::wstring name;
public:
   natDataFile(std::wstring n) : name(n){}
   // Other members omitted
};
```

This code can exist in the same source file as *DataFile*, and as you'll see in Chapter 2, you can use pointers to native C++ objects in *__gc* classes and pointers to *__gc* objects in native C++ objects. I will leave the details until Chapter 2, but note that you cannot use a *raw* *__gc* pointer as a data member of a native C++ object. The reason is that the native object will not be allocated on the managed heap and the pointers to the object will not be managed. (You can explicitly identify them as *__nogc* pointers.) This arrangement means the garbage collector will not be able to identify when the native object is destroyed and thus when the reference to the managed data member is freed. Instead, the native class must manage the reference itself and tell the runtime when the reference should be treated as being freed. I'll explain how to do this in Chapter 2.

All *__gc* classes look similar to native C++ classes, but they are subject to the .NET rules of reference types. Some of these rules are similar to C++; others apply more restrictions. The most significant restriction is that .NET allows only single-implementation inheritance, which means you cannot derive a class from more than one other class.

Methods on Managed Types

Managed types can have methods, and methods contain code. There are several types of methods that can be called—for example, the metadata devices, properties, and events are really descriptions of methods that can be called (respectively, to get or set a property value; and to add or remove a delegate from an event and to raise that event). Methods can be called on a type (static methods) or on an instance. The default is for a method to be an instance method, but this can be changed with the *static* keyword. Methods are called with a special calling convention named *__clrcall*. You do not specify this (because the compiler will not recognize the keyword), and the only time that you will see this mentioned is in the error that is generated if you attempt to apply a different calling convention on a class method. However, you can apply other calling conventions to global functions, as I'll explain in Chapter 2. Note also that *__gc* class methods cannot be marked using the C++ *const* or *volatile* keywords.

Class methods can be overloaded. The .NET specification allows methods to be overloaded by return type as well as parameters, but this has not been carried over to the Managed Extensions. Instead, the normal C++ rules apply: methods can be overloaded only on the parameters. There is an exception to this C++ rule: if you define a static operator named *op_Explicit* or *op_Implicit* to perform conversions between managed types, the operator can be overloaded on the return value. Native C++ methods can have default values for parameters so that the method can be called without mentioning the parameter. Default parameters are not legal in .NET. A method on a *__gc* type with a default parameter will not compile and will generate the error C3222.

Methods can be implemented inline in the class, or you can separate the declaration and the implementation into separate header and .cpp files. The concept of inlining is redundant for several reasons. First, if a method is public, it could be used by another assembly unknown to the compiler at compile time, so the method must be available as a single item. Second, inlining code is actually performed by the JIT compiler. The first time a method is called, the JITter will analyze the code, and it can decide to optimize the JITted method by compiling small methods as inline code. This decision is not yours to make; it is purely the choice of the JITter, so the C++ *inline* keyword has no effect.

The method parameters can be an instance of any .NET type, and they can be *in*, *out*, or *in/out*. By default a parameter is an *in* parameter, which means that it is passed from the calling method to the called method via the stack. If the parameter is an instance of a *__gc* reference type, the parameter will be passed via a pointer, so it is possible that the called method can change the instance by accessing its members through the pointer. It is the pointer that is treated as an *in* parameter.

The parameter is *in/out* if it is passed in both directions, that is, initialized in the calling method and then used in the called method before being reinitialized and passed back to the calling method. To use an *in/out* parameter in managed C++, the parameter should be passed by reference, which means that a C++ reference or a pointer to a *__gc* reference type pointer should be used, as shown here:

```
void UseDataFile(DataFile __gc*& file)
{
   if (file == 0)
      file = new DataFile(S"Default.dat");
   // Use file here.
}
void PassDataFile()
{
   DataFile __gc* df; // Initialized to zero automatically
   UseDataFile(df);
   // Use df here.
}
```

UseDataFile takes a reference to a *DataFile __gc** variable, and if this value is zero, the method creates an instance. Because the parameter is a reference, the variable in the calling code, *PassDataFile*, will be initialized with this new object, so this method can call the members of the new object. In this code, I have explicitly called the pointer *DataFile __gc*&* but because the class is a *__gc* type, it is perfectly acceptable to omit the *__gc* modifier and call the parameter *DataFile *&*

C++ references are fine, but in this situation I think that the call to *UseDataFile* is confusing because it is not obvious that an instance can be returned; hence, I prefer to use the equivalent syntax using pointers and the address-of operator.

```
void UseDataFile(DataFile __gc* __gc* file)
{
   if (*file == 0)
      *file = new DataFile(S"Default.dat");
   // Use file here.
}
void PassDataFile()
{
   DataFile __gc* df; // Initialized to zero automatically
   UseDataFile(&df);
   // Use df here.
}
```

Again, it is acceptable to omit the *__gc* modifier on the pointer declarations. Although it appears that *PassDataFile* calls the address-of operator, the address is not obtained in this call. The compiler recognizes the use of *&* here to mean that the parameter is passed as *in/out*. The same IL will be generated whether you use a reference or a pointer, but if the code is in the same C++ file, you cannot mix the two—the C++ compiler will refuse to allow you to pass a pointer to a method that requires a reference. If you call *UseDataFile* (either version) from C#, the parameter should be passed using the *ref* modifier. The runtime does not distinguish between parameters passed as *in/out* or passed as *out* within the same context. However, some languages do make a distinction; C#, for example, uses the *out* and *ref* modifiers. The preceding examples pass the parameter as *in/out*. To indicate that the parameter should be passed as an *out*-only parameter, you should use the *[Out]* attribute of the *System::Runtime::InteropServices* namespace. When it sees the *[Out]* attribute, the compiler adds the [out][2] metadata attribute to the parameter.

In a similar way, by default a value type is passed as an *in* parameter. Value types, of course, are not passed through a pointer. To pass a value type as *in/out*, you have to use a managed pointer, and to pass the parameter as an *out* parameter, you have to apply the *[Out]* attribute.[3]

```
void PassValueTypes(int inParam, int __gc* inoutParam,
   [Out] int __gc* outParam);
```

.NET classes can have virtual methods, so the runtime determines, from the type of this pointer when a method is called, which particular implementation of the method will be called. In fact, the runtime can call a virtual method virtually or nonvirtually, and the compiler decides which. When your code calls a

2. Note that the attribute you add in C++ has an uppercase O whereas the metadata attribute that is applied has a lowercase o.

3. In this code, I have explicitly used *__gc* on the pointer because *int* is a primitive C++ type, and without *__gc* an unmanaged pointer will be used. It is interesting to note that in MSIL a managed pointer is identified with & whereas an unmanaged pointer is identified by a *.

method on a type that is declared as virtual, the C++ compiler will always call those methods virtually. Virtual methods are usually identified with the C++ *virtual* keyword. Additionally, .NET classes can be abstract—that is, you do not intend that instances of the class should be created and you do intend that it should be used only as a base class. There are two ways to do this. The first way is to use the *__abstract* keyword on the class declaration, as shown here:

```
// abstract.cpp
__gc __abstract class FileBase
{
protected:
   Stream* stm;
public:
   // Get a stream to read/write to the disk.
   virtual Stream* GetStream(){ return stm; }
   // Other methods omitted
};
```

Because *FileBase* has the *__abstract* modifier the class is abstract, even though the method has an implementation. The compiler puts the *abstract* metadata attribute on the class in the assembly so that code in other languages is also aware that the class cannot be created. A class derived from *FileBase* can override the *GetStream* method, or the derived class can leave the method as-is and allow client code to access the method through the pointer to an instance of the derived class. This pattern is useful for providing partial implementations of classes, and the documentation should indicate the extra code that should be implemented.

You do not have to use the *__abstract* keyword. If one or more virtual methods have no implementation, the compiler will generate the metadata to indicate that the class is abstract (although it is useful to use *__abstract* because it gives a visual clue in your code what your intentions are).

```
// abstract.cpp
__gc class FileBase2
{
protected:
   Stream* stm;
public:
   // Get a stream to read/write to the disk.
   virtual Stream* GetStream() = 0;
   // Other methods omitted
};
```

In this case, I have used the C++ syntax to identify a pure virtual method. In C++, any class that has a pure virtual method is abstract. The compiler also adds the metadata attribute abstract to the method to indicate that it has no implementation, and the pure virtual syntax is the only way that you can get this attribute applied. To use *FileBase2*, you not only have to derive a class from it, but you also have to implement the pure virtual methods. In this case, the pure virtual methods indicate an *interface* that derived classes should support. This system was how the C++ bindings for COM interfaces were implemented in versions of Visual C++ prior to the .NET Framework SDK and Visual Studio .NET. The new version of the compiler introduces a new keyword, *__interface*, that enforces the semantics of interfaces, which I will explain in the section "Managed Interfaces" later in this chapter. .NET allows multiple interface inheritance, but unlike native C++, abstract classes are not treated as interfaces. So, the rule is that a class can derive from at most one class and from any number of *__interfaces*. Methods that are used to implement interfaces are virtual (but you do not have to mark them as such).

The antithesis of *__abstract* is *__sealed*. This keyword can be applied to virtual methods and to classes. When applied to an overridden virtual method, it indicates that the method is complete; the implementation cannot be overridden in a derived class. It is nonsensical to make a method both virtual and sealed because virtual implies that the method can be overridden, but sealed prevents overriding. However, the compiler does allow this usage. When one method is sealed, the class is marked as sealed in its metadata. If you apply the *__sealed* keyword to a class, all the methods are considered to be sealed. Think carefully when you apply the *sealed* keyword to a class because the keyword means that another developer cannot extend your code, and do you know about all uses other developers might have for your code? The only reason that I can think of for using *sealed* on a class is to prevent other developers from accessing protected members.

Constructors

Constructors are used to initialize a newly created instance of a class. In managed C++, constructors of *__gc* classes are declared in the same way as in native C++: the name of the class is used as if it is a method without a return type. In metadata, a constructor has the special name of *.ctor*. Constructors can be overloaded, but like methods, they do not permit you to define default values for parameters. You are able to pass *in/out* and *out* parameters to constructors, although returning a value from a constructor goes against the reason to call the constructor—which is to construct the object.

Classes can also have a *static constructor* (also known as a *type constructor*). A static constructor of a .NET class created with C++ is called just before the first access is made to a member. The static constructor is called by the runtime and thus you are not able to pass any parameters to it. This arrangement means that only one, parameterless static constructor is allowed on each class.

In metadata, a static constructor is named *.cctor*. If your class has a static field and you initialize this inline, the compiler will generate a static constructor with the code to initialize the field; if you define a static constructor, the compiler will put the initialization code before your code.

```
public __gc class Data
{
   static Data()
   {
      Console::WriteLine(S"we are called {0}", str);
   }
public:
   static String* str = S"the Data class";
};
```

In this code, there is a static member named *str*; this member is initialized to a string within the class. (Contrast this behavior to native C++, where only constant static integral members can be initialized like this.) The class also has a static constructor that prints out the value of the static field. This class is fine because the compiler will inject code before the call to *WriteLine* to initialize the string to the specified value.

```
ldstr "the Data class"    // Initialize the string...
stsfld string Data::str   // ... and store it in the
                          // static field.
ldstr "we are called {0}" // Load the format string.
ldsfld string Data::str   // Load the parameter,
                          // and call WriteLine().
call void [mscorlib]System.Console::WriteLine(string, object)
```

Finally, it is worth pointing out that because reference types are created on the managed heap and the garbage collector tracks the pointers that are used, you cannot define a copy constructor on a class. If you want to make an exact copy of an object, you should implement *ICloneable* and call the *Clone* method.

Operators

Managed types can implement .NET operators, but I will leave the details until much later in the chapter, in the section "Managed Operators." In this section, I will make a few comments about C++ operators. Class instances are created using the operator *new*. For a *__gc* managed class, this operator is defined by the runtime, so you cannot create your own operator *new* on the class. Similarly, because objects are removed from the heap by the garbage collector, you cannot implement operator *delete*, and because the garbage collector manages pointers, you cannot define operator *&*

Your access to a managed object should be through its members. You cannot change the pointer to the object, and you cannot increment a whole object pointer. Thus, the C++ *sizeof* and *offsetof* operators do not work. There are cases when you might need to know the size of an unmanaged type represented by a .NET value type or the position of a member within that class (for example, if you are defining custom interop marshalling). In this case, you can use *Marshal::SizeOf* and *Marshal::OffsetOf* (in the *System::Runtime::InteropServices* namespace). However, these do not work on managed objects.

Value Types

I mentioned earlier that value types are typically small, short-lived objects and they are usually created on the stack. In managed C++, you can define a value type as a class or a struct. The important point is that the value type is marked with *__value*, as shown here:

```
__value class Point
{
public:
   int x;
   int y;
};
```

You cannot create a value type directly on the managed heap. Typically, they are created on the stack.

```
Point p = {100, 200};
```

This example shows an initializer list used for the value type. The compiler will generate code to pass 100 to the first member (*x*) and 200 to the second member (*y*). If an initializer list is not used, the members will be initialized to their default values, which is zero for primitive types. A value type can also implement constructors (including a static constructor), but if you define a constructor, you cannot use an initializer list to initialize an instance.

```
__value class Point
{
public:
   int x;
   int y;
   Point(int i, int j) : x(i), y(j) {}
   // Default constructor to define the default value of this type
   Point() : x(-1), y(-1) {}
};
void Useit()
{
   Point p(100, 200);
}
```

A value type is implicitly sealed; you do not have to apply the *__sealed* modifier. A value type cannot derive from a *__gc* type. Thus, the only methods that you can override in the value type are the methods of *System::ValueType*, which is the base class of all value types. Methods inherited from *System::ValueType* are virtual, but other than these, it makes no sense to define new virtual methods on a value type.

Value types are typically used as records of data—much as you would use a struct in C. By default, the items are sequential—that is, in memory the fields appear in the order that they are declared, but the amount of memory taken up by each member is determined according to the *.pack* metadata for the method. (The default is a packing of eight.) You can change this behavior with the *[StructLayout]* pseudo custom attribute (in the *System::Runtime::InteropServices* namespace). This attribute can take one of the three members of the *LayoutKind* enumeration: if you use *Auto* (the default for reference types), the runtime determines the order and amount of memory taken up by each member (this amount will be at least as large as the size of the member); if you use *Sequential* (the default for value types), just the order is defined, the actual space taken up is determined by the size of the member and the packing specified. The final value you can use is *Explicit*, which means that you specify the exact layout of members—their byte location within the type and the size of each member—and you do this with the *[FieldOffset]* attribute. The *[StructLayout]* pseudo custom attribute adds the auto, explicit, or sequential metadata attribute to the type.

Here is an example of using *LayoutKind::Explicit*:

```
// union.cpp
[StructLayout(LayoutKind::Explicit)]
__value class LargeInteger
{
public:
   [FieldOffset(0)] int lowPart;
   [FieldOffset(4)] int highPart;
   [FieldOffset(0)] __int64 quadPart;
};
```

The first two members are 32-bit integers. Thus, the first member appears at offset 0 within the type and the second member appears at offset 4. However, notice that I have also intentionally put the third member (*quadPart*) at offset 0. There are no unions in .NET, but by using *[StructLayout(LayoutKind::Explicit)]* and *[FieldOffset]* like this you can simulate a union. Here, the *quadPart* member will be a 64-bit integer. The lower 32-bits can be obtained through the *lowPart* member, and the higher 32-bits through the *highPart* member.

Value types are typically small, which usually means that they contain primitive types. There are no restrictions to the types that you can use. A value type can contain pointers to *__gc* types, which will be allocated on the managed heap. If the value type does not contain *__gc* pointers, it can be created on the unmanaged heap by calling *__nogc new*. (Of course, you have to remember to delete these allocated members.) Value types cannot be created directly on the managed heap. There are two cases when a value type will appear on the managed heap: when it is in a managed array or when it is a member of a *__gc* type.

Enumerations

Enumerations are value types and have similar characteristics (allocated on the stack, implicitly sealed). However, enumerations do have some distinct differences. For a start, enumerations are derived from *System::Enum* (derived from *System::ValueType*), which gives access to methods to convert enumerated values to other types, to get the names and values of members, and to create an enumerated value from a string. Further, you cannot provide implementations of methods on enums.

Enumerated values are integral types. You can specify the underlying type that will be used. The syntax looks like inheritance, but you do not specify an access level.

```
// enums.cpp
__value enum Color : unsigned int {RED=0xff0000,
   GREEN=0xff00, BLUE=0xff};
```

Here I have defined a new enum named *Color* that has 32-bit values. The enumeration has three items, and I have explicitly given them values. If you omit a value, the item will have the incremented value of the previous item (or zero for the first item). Of course, the items in the enum are not members in the same sense as other value types. The items are named values for the enum. Thus, an instance of *Color* can be initialized using an integral value or the named value.

```
Color red = Color::RED;
Color white = (Color)0xffffff;
Color cyan = (Color)(Color::BLUE | Color::GREEN);
Color gray = (Color)0x010101;
```

Here I have qualified the name of the enumerated value with the name of the enum; this means that there is no ambiguity. It is possible to omit the enum name (to get a *weak* enumerator name), and the compiler will search for an appropriate value. If the compiler finds another symbol with the same name, you might not get the result you expect. For example:

```
Color red = RED;
```

This will initialize *red* with a value of 0xff as long as *RED* is not defined as a symbol. If you define another enum, then there will be a problem.

```
__value enum UKTrafficLight {RED, AMBER, GREEN};
```

Then the compiler will complain because it does not know whether *RED* refers to *Color* or *UKTrafficLight*. Further, if you declare a variable with the same name

```
int RED;
```

the compiler will attempt to convert the integer variable to an enum, and because no implicit conversion exists, you will get an error. I find this error dangerous because as I have shown previously, you can assign an integral value to an enum variable as long as you cast to the enum type. (See the earlier *white* and *cyan* examples.) The error caused by using a weak enumerator name indicates that an explicit cast will solve the problem, but in fact it makes the problem worse. It is always better to use qualified names for enumerators. The compiler allows you to define anonymous enums and will generate a name for you. However, an anonymous enum implies that you will use weak enumerator names.

Normally, when you call *System::Object::ToString* on an object you will get the string version of the value of the object returned. *ToString* called on an enum does a little more work. First *ToString* checks to see whether the *[Flags]* attribute has been applied. The documentation says that the members of such an enum can be combined with the bitwise *OR* operator, but C++ still treats the value as the underlying integral type and (as I showed earlier) you have to cast to the enum type. However, without the *[Flags]* attribute, *ToString* expects the enumerated value to be a single item from the enum. If this is the case, the enum item name will be returned. If I call *ToString* on the *red* variable I mentioned earlier (I'll mention how in a moment), the string "RED" will be returned. If *ToString* cannot find a single item that matches (for example, *white*, *cyan*, and *gray* defined earlier), a string is returned that represents the number. When *ToString* sees the *[Flags]* attribute, the method will attempt to build a string made up of a comma-separated list of the names of the items in the enum that constitute the value. If the number cannot be represented completely by the items in the enum, the string representation of the number is returned. So if *Color* had the *[Flags]* attribute, the formatted string for *white* will be "RED, GREEN, BLUE" whereas *gray* will return 65793 (if the default formatting is used).

Boxing

Value types can have methods, and you access these through the dot operator just like any other member of the value type. Value types also derive from *System::ValueType* (directly, or in the case of enums, indirectly through *System::Enum*). However, if you look up *ValueType*, you'll see that it is a *__gc* type and not a value type, which means that its members should be accessed through a *__gc* pointer and not a value type instance. .NET allows you to convert a value type to a *__gc* object through a process named *boxing*. Boxing is explicit in C++ (unlike other languages supported by .NET) because the operation is not without a performance issue, so you have to specify that a boxed value is being used rather than the value. When you box a value type, the runtime creates an object on the managed heap that has an exact copy of the value type being boxed. The type of this object on the heap is called the *boxed type*. Here is an example using the *Color* enum declared in the last section:

```
Color cyan = (Color)(Color::GREEN | Color::BLUE);
__box Color* boxedCyan = __box(cyan);
Console::WriteLine(boxedCyan->ToString());
```

Here I have used the *__box* operator on the *cyan* value to get a pointer to an object of type *__box Color*. This object is on the managed heap, so I can call *ToString* using pointer syntax, and I can access any of the other public members defined on the value type. If the value type overrides a method in *ValueType*, then I have the choice of accessing the method through the value type (with the dot operator) or through the boxed type (through the -> operator).

Primitive types are value types, and they implement methods that allow you to convert instances to other types. These methods are part of the *IConvertible* interface, and to get access to this interface, you have to box the object first, as shown here:

```
Int32 i = 42;
__box Int32* b = __box(i);
IConvertible* cvt = b;
Double d = cvt->ToDouble(new NumberFormatInfo);
Console::WriteLine(d);
```

Note that if a value type is boxed, a copy of its fields are made. The boxed object is a clone of the value type but located on the managed heap. Consider the *Point* class I showed earlier.

```
Point p1(100, 200);
__box Point* p2 = __box(p1);
p2->x = 300;
Trace::Assert(p1.x != p2->x);
```

When a change is made to a member of the boxed object, it affects the value on the managed heap, not the value type, which is why I have performed an assert. (See Chapter 7 for a description of asserts.) In this case, the assertion is *true* because *p1.x* is not equal to *p2->x*. This behavior is one reason why it is important that the C++ team has decided to provide boxing through an operator. If you intend to call a method of *System::Object* on the boxed object, you can make the type of the pointer *Object**; however, I would advise against this practice because you cannot specify that the pointer is a boxed type. (You cannot use *__box Object** because you can box only value types.)

You will have to box a value type whenever you pass a value type to a method that takes an *Object** pointer. The most frequent occasion when you will box a value type is when you pass value types to *Console::WriteLine* or when you put value types into a collection. *Console::WriteLine* has many overloads, some of which take value types, so the following statement will compile and run because there is an overload that takes an *Int32* parameter:

```
Console::WriteLine(999);
```

If I want to pass a format string to print the integer in hex, I could try this:

```
// Does not compile
Console::WriteLine(S"{0:x}", 999);
```

This statement will not compile because no overload exists that takes a *string* and an *Int32*. The nearest version takes a *string* and an *Object** pointer, so you can get the line to compile by boxing the value type.

The *System::Collection* namespace has various general-purpose classes. These classes are generic, so they contain *Object** pointers. Thus, you have to box value types to create an object on the heap. If you have many items that you want to put into a collection, boxing each one is inefficient. (Value types exist precisely to avoid having many small items on the heap.) The alternative is to use an array.

Once a value type has been boxed, you can obtain a managed pointer to the value type from the boxed object, and you can initialize a value by dereferencing the pointer. (Pointers to value types obtained through the address-of operator (&) are *__nogc* pointers.)

```
// Implicit conversion from pointer to boxed type
// to a managed pointer to a value type
Point __gc* p3 = p2;
// Dereference pointer to initialize a value type.
Point p4 = *p2;
Point p5 = *p3;
```

Dereferencing a pointer to a boxed value is called *unboxing*. If the type of the boxed value is a boxed type, no cast is required during unboxing. If the object type is *Object*, you have to cast to the appropriate value type. For example, *System::Enum* has a method named *Parse* that you can use to pass either the name of an item in the enum or an absolute value, as shown here:

```
Color red;
Object* o = Enum::Parse(__typeof(Color), S"RED");
red = *static_cast<__box Color*>(o);
```

Parse takes the type of the boxed object to return, but the method actually returns an *Object** pointer. I know that the type of the object is *__box Color*, so I can use *static_cast<>* to get a pointer, and then I can dereference this pointer to unbox the object and initialize the value type.

Reference types can have value types as members, and the memory for the value type will actually be allocated on the heap. However, this memory behaves like a stack frame insofar as the lifetime of the value type depends on the lifetime of the reference type object. Contrast this behavior to a reference type pointer within a reference type: the lifetime of this referred-to object might depend on the lifetime of the containing object, but there could be other pointers to the same object and those pointers could also have an effect on the lifetime of this object.

Managed Pointers

Reference types are accessed through managed pointers. There are a couple of types of managed pointers, depending on what they point to, and the rules for these differ significantly from the rules applied to unmanaged pointers. Managed pointers must point to an object. You cannot initialize them to some arbitrary section of memory because unlike C pointers, managed pointers are strongly typed and can be initialized only with a pointer to the specified type. You can use casts to fool the compiler like this:

```
int* p = reinterpret_cast<int*>(0x1000000);
String* s = reinterpret_cast<String*>(p);
```

This code is perverse, and you should avoid ever getting into the position of writing such code. Here I am using *reinterpret_cast<>* to initialize an unmanaged pointer with a value. (The compiler does not even allow direct initialization of unmanaged pointers.) Then I cast the unmanaged pointer to a *String** pointer. At run time, the code that uses this *String** pointer will throw an exception. If you have a managed array (which I will describe in the section "Managed Arrays" later in this chapter), the pointer is to the array object and not to the memory that the array uses. In general, if you have a managed pointer to an object, you cannot perform pointer arithmetic.

When you declare a managed pointer, the compiler will generate code that initializes the pointer to zero, so it is redundant to do this operation yourself. In general, an untyped pointer to a reference type (for example, a member of a collection, or if you want to write a generic algorithm) is an *Object** pointer. For unboxed value types, the equivalent is *Void __gc **. However, be wary of pointers to value types because when you cast from an address of a value type to a *Void __gc**, you get a managed pointer but you do not get a boxed object.

```
// pointers.cpp
// Don't do this!
__gc class BadCast
{
   Queue* q;
public:
   BadCast()
   {
      q = new Queue;
      int i = 99;
      q->Enqueue(reinterpret_cast<Object*>((Void __gc*)&i));
   }
   int Pop();
};
```

In this case, the address of the *local* variable is obtained, cast to a managed pointer, and then cast to an *Object** pointer so that it can be put in *Queue*. This code will compile and run, but it has an inherent problem. The lifetime of the value type is determined by the stack frame, but the array's lifetime is determined by the lifetime of the instance of *BadCast*. Take a look at *Pop*:

```
// pointers.cpp
int BadCast::Pop()
{
   return *reinterpret_cast<int __gc*>(q->Dequeue());
}
```

This code obtains the first item in *Queue* and treats the item as a pointer to an *int*. However, the original address was the address on the stack, which will now have changed—the original *int* had been lost well before this method was called. The value returned from *Pop* will be some random value. The message is clear: be wary of pointers to value types; in most cases, they refer to an address on the stack frame and should be considered only temporary.

If a *__gc* type has a data member (*__value* or *__gc* types), the member will be allocated on the managed heap, and the lifetime of the member will be determined by the lifetime of the containing object. You can create a pointer to such a member, but again you have to be careful because the pointer is not to a whole object, but only to part of the object, so it is called an *interior pointer*.[4]

4. The ECMA specification talks about object references (O types) and managed pointers (& types). An object reference is equivalent to what I call a whole object pointer, and what the ECMA spec calls a managed pointer is what I call an interior pointer. In both cases, they point to memory on the managed heap, which is why I call them, collectively, managed pointers.

An interior pointer can be a stack variable, passed as a method parameter or returned from a method. However, interior pointers cannot be stored as fields in a *__gc* or *__value* class, in a static variable or in an array, in order to guarantee that the lifetime of the pointer is not longer than the item it points to. In general, any *__gc* pointer to a *__value* type will be an interior pointer and the compiler will issue an error if you try to store the pointer as described earlier. Interior pointers are special in that the runtime allows certain limited pointer arithmetic to occur, but this code will not be verifiable by the runtime. (Verifiable code is covered in Chapter 5). Interior pointers can be incremented or decremented, or you can subtract one interior pointer from another to get the offset between the two members. Subtraction of interior pointers in IL gives the number of bytes between the pointers, but the C++ compiler inserts code to divide this by the size of the item pointed to by the interior pointers so that the result mirrors the behavior in C++.

Of course, you always have to be careful when you get free access to memory.

```
// pointers.cpp
// Don't do this!
__gc class BadInteriorPointers
{
   __int64 x;
   __int64 y;
   String* s;
public:
   BadInteriorPointers()
   { x=1; y=2; s=S"Test"; }
   void KillMe()
   {
      Dump();    // Initial values
      __int64 __gc * p = &x;
      *p = 3;
      Dump();    // Changed x
      p++;
      *p = 4;
      Dump();    // Changed y
      p++;
      *p = 5;
      Dump();    // Oops! Changed s
   }
   void Dump()
   {
      Console::WriteLine(S"{0} {1} {2}", __box(x), __box(y), s);
   }
};
```

Here I have two 64-bit integers and a *__gc String* member. The *Dump* method just prints out the values of these members to the console. I call this method in the *KillMe* method and then obtain an interior pointer to the first item. After that, I write a value through this pointer, which will change the value of the member *x*. The next code changes member *y*, and then I do something that is fatal to this code: I increment the pointer again so that some of the memory that the pointer points to is the memory occupied by the string pointer *s*. (I have used 64-bit integers for *x* and *y* so that the interior pointer will be *__int64 __gc**, and thus incrementing the pointer after it points to *y* will make the pointer refer to memory other than the packing between members.) No exception will be thrown when I change the memory pointed to by this interior pointer, but when I access the member *s* through the pointer (and hence treat it as a *String** pointer), an exception will occur. Here are the results that I get:

```
1 2 Test
3 2 Test
3 4 Test

Fatal execution engine error.
```

The error is so serious that I cannot catch this error, and there is no automatic stack dump.

Pinning Pointers

Managed pointers are managed by the garbage collector so that when copies are made—or the pointer is assigned to zero—the garbage collector knows that references are created or lost. When a pointer is passed to native code, the garbage collector cannot track its usage and so cannot determine any change in object references. Furthermore, if a garbage collection occurs, the object can be moved in memory, so the garbage collector changes all managed pointers (including interior pointers) so that they point to the new location. Because the garbage collector does not have access to the pointers passed to native code, potentially a pointer used in native code could suddenly become invalid. The runtime does not allow managed pointers to be passed to native code; instead, a pinned pointer must be used. (I will come back to pinning pointers in Chapter 2, where I will cover interop in more depth.)

When a managed pointer is pinned, the garbage collector is informed and this pinned pointer represents an extra object reference; in addition, pinning a pointer tells the garbage collector that during the lifetime of the pointer the object will be pinned in memory, which means that the garbage collector cannot move the object. Note that the lifetime of the pointer is the entire method where the object is used, not just the scope of the C++ pinned pointer (although if you assign a pinning pointer to zero, the object will no longer be pinned).

An interior pointer will always be a *__gc* pointer even if the member pointed to is a *__value* type with no *__gc* pointers. To convert an interior pointer to a *__nogc* pointer, you must pin the pointer, as shown here:

```
// pinning.cpp
#pragma unmanaged
void print(int* p)
{
   printf("%ld\n", *p);
}
#pragma managed

__gc struct Test{int i;};

void main()
{
   Test* t = new Test;
   int __pin* p = &t->i;
   print(p);
}
```

In this example, I have a function that is compiled to native code (it could be a method called through platform invoke, for instance), and I want to pass an interior pointer to this function. To do this, I create a pinning pointer, *p*, and assign it to the interior pointer. During the lifetime of the pinning pointer, the entire object, *t*, will be pinned.

Passing by Reference and by Value

When you pass parameters to a method, a copy of those parameters are made on the stack. If the parameter is a *__gc* type, the parameter will be a pointer to the instance. If the parameter is a *__value* type, a bitwise copy is made of *__value* type members and copies are made of object reference members. If a change is made to a *__value* type or to its *__value* type members, the change is made to the copy on the stack and will not affect the original.

This code will work fine for calls within the same application domain. (An application domain, or, as more commonly called by its class name, an AppDomain, is a unit of code isolation used within a .NET process. More details are given in Chapter 5.) However, if you pass the value across application boundaries, the type must be serializable. The simplest way to do this is to apply the *[Serializable]* attribute to the type, as shown in the following code:

```
[Serializable]
__value struct Point
{
   int x; int y;
};
```

This attribute instructs the runtime, when an instance of this type is passed across context boundaries, to serialize all members that are not marked with *[NotSerialized]* and transmit these to the new context where a new (uninitialized) instance will be created on the stack and initialized with the serialized data. Again, if you make changes to the value instance, the change will be made to the copy on the stack in the method.

A *__value* type can be passed by reference, in which case you have to pass a pointer to the object (a C++ pointer or a C++ reference).

```
void MirrorX(Point& p)
{
   p.y = -p.y;
}
```

This code will work if the call is made within the same process, although it is interesting that even though the parameter is accessed through the C++ reference (a pointer) the type still has to be serializable. This code cannot be called across a process boundary because .NET remoting does not support passing pointers to value types via remoting. The reason is that if you want to pass a parameter by reference, it must be derived from *MarshalByRefObject*, and of course value types cannot be derived from this class (or any class).

A reference type is usually passed by reference, so if, in a method, you change the parameter's members through the pointer, the original object will be changed. This works fine for calls within the same application domain, but if the call is made outside of the domain (either in the same process or in another process), the *__gc* type must derive from *MarshalByRefObject*, which will mean that the object will be created and will live in one domain, but it can be accessed by code in other domains.

You can also pass *__gc* types by value, in which case you have to apply the *[Serialization]* attribute. The object will be serialized only if remoting is used—that is, if the call is made into another application domain.

Properties

Both *__gc* types and *__value* types can have properties. Strictly speaking, a property is not really a member of a type. It is a description—metadata—that identifies methods on the type that can be called through property access. Data members of a type are called *fields* by .NET and can have any type that you choose, including arrays. Fields have the disadvantage that they allow the data member to be read and written, and they have no mechanism to perform validation. On the other hand, properties are implemented using methods, which means that you can determine whether a property is read-only, write-only, or read/write by the methods that you implement. Furthermore, the property methods can perform validation on the values passed to them or returned from them, so they can take evasive action if the values are invalid.

Properties are implemented with *get_* and *set_* methods. The *get_* method is used to return the property, so its return type should be the same as the property. The *set_* method is used to initialize the property, so the method should not have a return type and its last parameter should be the same type as the property. To tell the compiler to generate the *.property* metadata, you use the *__property* modifier on the property methods.

```
__gc class GrimesPerson
{
   String* name;
public:
   __property String* get_Name()
   {
      if (name == 0) name = S"the man with no name";
      return name;
   }
   __property void set_Name(String* n)
   {
      if (n == 0)
         throw new ArgumentException(S"name cannot be null");
      name = n;
   }
};
```

This class has a string property named *Name*. The name of the property is the name after the *get_* or the *set_*. In this case, the property methods change the private field name, but this behavior is an implementation detail of my class. The property could generate a name dynamically, or it could read the name from a database or a file. The choice is entirely yours.

The metadata for the property looks like this:

```
.property specialname instance string Name()
{
  .get instance string GrimesPerson::get_Name()
  .set instance void GrimesPerson::set_Name(string)
}
```

The European Computer Manufacturer's Association (ECMA) spec says that the property can also have a method marked with *.other*, but there is no way that you can define these methods in C++, nor is it clear how such methods are called other than directly through their name.

Code that uses the property treats the property as if it is a data member. The compiler will convert the property access to one of the methods mentioned in the *.property* metadata, for example:

```
GrimesPerson* me = new GrimesPerson, *you = new GrimesPerson;
me->Name = S"Richard";
you->set_Name(S"Ellinor");
Console::WriteLine(S"{0} and {1}", me->Name, you->get_Name());
```

I hope that you agree that the syntax used with the *me* variable is more readable than the syntax used with the *you* variable.

Properties can be static or instance members, they can be virtual, and an abstract class can have pure virtual implementations for either access method.

```
__property static String* get_SurName()
{
   return S"Grimes";
}
```

The access methods cannot differ by the static specifier, but they can differ by the virtual specifier and the member accessibility.

When you declare a property, you do not automatically add storage to a type. (As I mentioned previously, this decision is an implementation detail.) This behavior, coupled with the fact that properties can be pure virtual, means that properties can be members of interfaces. Thus, any class that implements the interface must implement the property. The interface can mention only one of the accessor methods, but any class can implement both accessors, meaning that the other accessor can be accessed only through an object reference.

Properties can have indexes, which means that they look (in code) similar to arrays. To add an index, you have to add a parameter to the *get_* and *set_* methods. The last parameter of the *set_* method, of course, is the value that you are passing to the property. The index can be any type that you want.

```
// properties.cpp
public __gc class FileStore
{
public:
   __property StreamReader* get_Document(String* name)
   {
      return File::OpenText(name);
   }
   // Other members
};

void main()
{
   FileStore* fs = new FileStore();
   StreamReader* stm = fs->Document[S"readme.txt"];
   Console::WriteLine(stm->ReadToEnd());
   stm->Close();
}
```

Here the *Document* property is indexed with a string parameter. To call this property, I give the name of the property followed by the index value in square brackets. Properties with parameters can be overloaded.

```
__property StreamReader* get_Document(String* name);
__property StreamReader* get_Document(int i);
```

In this case, there are two properties, one indexed with a file name and the other indexed with an integer (which might be an index into some other list maintained by the object). This declaration will result in two *.property* metadata descriptions.

However, note that not all languages support indexed properties. As it stands, the *FileStore::Document* property can be accessed in C# only through the accessor methods directly.

```
// C#
FileStore fs = new FileStore();
StreamReader sr = fs.get_Document("readme.txt");
```

This code is quite ugly and is not what C# developers expect to see. In C#, indexed properties are called *indexers*. C# does not allow access to indexed properties through indexer syntax unless you add the *[DefaultMember]* attribute to your class identifying the indexed property.

```
[DefaultMember("Document")]
public __gc class FileStore
{
public:
   __property StreamReader* get_Document(String* name);
};
```

Now the C# code will look like this:

```
// C#
// puser.cs
FileStore fs = new FileStore();
StreamReader sr = fs["readme.txt"];
```

Because no name is specified, the C# compiler looks for the default value and accesses the specified property. This syntax means that only one indexed property can be accessed in this way. All others have to be accessed directly through their accessor methods. The converse is a little odd: C# can define indexers, but by default the C# compiler calls the property *Item*. The C# developer can change the name of the property using the *[IndexerName]* attribute.

In C++, a property with an integer index looks as if it is an array field. Indexed properties can have more than one index, and in this case, the syntax looks like native C++ array syntax because the calling code has to enclose each parameter with square brackets, so for this code:

```
// arrayprop.cpp
__gc class Multiplier
{
public:
   __property int get_Value(int x, int y)
   { return x*y; }
};
```

the calling code looks like this:

```
Multiplier* m = new Multiplier;
int i = m->Value[5][6];
Console::WriteLine(i);
```

Of course, you can use any type for the indexes. C# can handle indexed properties with more than one index as long as they are treated as indexers—that is, the property is the default member. The C# code for accessing *Multiplier::Value* looks like this:

```
// C#
Multiplier m = new Multiplier();
int i = m[5,6];
Console.WriteLine(i);
```

I regret to admit that, in my eyes, this syntax looks better than the syntax in C++.

Delegates and Events

I will cover delegates and events in more depth in Chapter 3, so in this section, I will just introduce the syntax and explain a little about what they are. Delegates are simply type-safe function pointers. When defined, a delegate can be initialized with the address of a static or an instance method, but the method *must* have the same signature as the delegate or a run-time exception will be thrown. This restriction protects you from some of the nastier bugs in Win32 that occur when the wrong method is imported from a DLL using *::GetProcAddress* and cast to an inappropriate function pointer.

Delegates are declared in C++ using the *__delegate* keyword on the signature of the method that can be called through the delegate. The declaration can be within a class or outside of a class.

```
// delegates.cpp
public __delegate int CallMethod(String*);

public __gc class ActiveClass
{
public:
   __delegate void ActionStarted(String*);
};
```

The compiler generates a class from the declaration, so if the delegate is declared within a class, the delegate class will be nested within that class. For the preceding code, the compiler will generate a class named *CallMethod* and another class named *ActiveClass::ActionStarted*. The IL for *CallMethod* looks like this:

```
.class public auto ansi sealed CallMethod
   extends [mscorlib]System.MulticastDelegate
{
   .method public specialname rtspecialname instance void
      .ctor(object __unnamed000,
         native int __unnamed001) runtime managed forwardref
   {}
   .method public newslot virtual instance int32
      Invoke(string __unnamed000) runtime managed forwardref
  {}
   .method public newslot virtual instance
      class [mscorlib]System.IAsyncResult
      BeginInvoke(string __unnamed000,
         class [mscorlib]System.AsyncCallback __unnamed001,
         object __unnamed002) runtime managed forwardref
   {}
   .method public newslot virtual instance int32
      EndInvoke(class [mscorlib]System.IAsyncResult __unnamed000)
         runtime managed forwardref
   {}
}
```

I will go into more depth about these methods in Chapter 3, but the points pertinent to this discussion are that the class derives from *MulticastDelegate* and that the methods are empty, but they are marked as *forwardref* and *runtime*. The modifiers *forwardref* and *runtime* mean that the methods are not declared in this class because they are implemented by the runtime. The base class *MulticastDelegate* holds a linked list of delegates. Delegates are combined into this list with a static method named *Combine* that takes two delegates as parameters. This method creates a new delegate whose linked list is the combination of the lists from the two delegates. In a similar way, there is a static method named *Remove* that will create a new delegate whose linked list is the difference between the lists of the two delegates passed as its parameters.

A delegate is created by passing a function pointer to the constructor of the compiler-generated delegate class, so given this class

```
// delegates.cpp
__gc class Caller
{
public:
   int CallMe (String* s)
```

```
    { Console::WriteLine(s); return s->Length; }
    static int CallMeToo(String* s)
    { Console::WriteLine(S"static: {0}", s); return s->Length; }
};
```

I can create a delegate that calls either the instance method or the static method.

```
Caller* c = new Caller;
CallMethod* m1 = new CallMethod(c, &Caller::CallMe);
int i = m1(S"Hello");
CallMethod* m2 = new CallMethod(0, &Caller::CallMeToo);
int j = m2(S"Hello");
```

The variable *m1* is created using an instance of *Caller*, which is passed as the first parameter to the delegate class constructor. The second parameter indicates the method to call: the instance method *CallMe*. The delegate is invoked by treating it as if it is a function pointer, so I call *m1*, passing it a string parameter, and under the covers, the C++ compiler calls *CallMethod::Invoke*, which will go through the linked list the delegate class holds and call *Invoke* on each one. In this case, there is only one delegate in the list, and thus *Caller::CallMe* is called. The variable *m2* is created from a static method, so the first parameter is zero because there is no object to call. The delegate is invoked in the same way.

This code might look a little redundant, but be aware that because *CallMethod* is a class, an object reference could be passed as a method parameter, even to another process. And of course, the delegates can be combined, as shown in the following code:

```
CallMethod* m3;
m3 = dynamic_cast<CallMethod*>(Delegate::Combine(m1, m2));
int k = m3(S"Hello, again");
```

Delegate is the base class of *MulticastDelegate*. When the combined delegate is invoked, the *m1* delegate is called first, and then the *m2* delegate is called. So what value is returned in *k*? Well, it is the value returned from *m2*. The rule is that when a multicast delegate is invoked, the result from the last delegate added to the delegate is returned. In this code, I have called *Delegate::Combine* directly. Because this method returns a *Delegate**, I have to cast the pointer to my typed delegate. The C++ compiler allows you to use the += and -= operators on delegates, which it will translate as calls to *Combine* and *Remove*. The advantage of these operators is that the cast is not required in your code.

```
CallMethod* m3;
m3 += m1;
m3 += m2;
int k = m3(S"Hello, again");
```

If you want to get the return value from all the delegates, you can call the inherited member *GetInvocationList*, which will return an array of delegates. You can then call each member in the array in any order that you want.

```
Delegate* d[] = m3->GetInvocationList();
IEnumerator* e = d->GetEnumerator();
while (e->MoveNext())
{
   CallMethod* m = dynamic_cast<CallMethod*>(e->Current);
   int i = m(S"another call");
}
```

Another interesting thing that you can do with delegates is use them as fields to another class, as shown here:

```
// events.cpp
public __gc class Worker
{
public:
   CallMethod* m;
   void AddMethod(CallMethod* m1)
   {
      m += m1;
   }
   void DoSomething()
   {
      // Do some work here.
      m(S"something was done");
   }
};
```

The methods in the *Worker* class can be called as shown in the following code:

```
Worker* w = new Worker;
w->AddMethod(m1);
w->AddMethod(m2);
w->DoSomething();
```

This code represents a notification mechanism. The *Worker* class could perform some work in *DoSomething* and then inform the delegates *m1* and *m2* when that work has completed. Events are a formalization of this notification mechanism. They are declared in C++ with the *__event* keyword.

```
public __gc class Worker
{
public:
   __event CallMethod* m;
   void DoSomething()
```

```
    {
        // Do some work here.
        m(S"something was done");
    }
};
```

When you use the *__event* keyword, the compiler adds a private member for the delegate, three methods to the class, and the *.event* metadata. The methods have the name of the event prefixed with *add_*, *remove_*, and *raise_*. These methods are used to combine a delegate with the delegate field, to remove a delegate from that field, and to invoke the delegate. For this event, the compiler will add this metadata:

```
.event specialname CallMethod m
{
  .addon instance void Worker::add_m(class CallMethod)
  .removeon instance void Worker::remove_m(class CallMethod)
  .fire instance int32 Worker::raise_m(string)
}
```

In general, you should make the event public, in which case the compiler will make the delegate field private so that access to the field will be only through the methods added by the compiler. The *add_* and *remove_* methods will be made public, so external code can add delegates, but the *raise_* method will be protected. This scheme fits in with the idea that events are used for notifications because it means that the notification can be generated only by the class containing the event (and derived classes). The C++ compiler allows you to use the += and -= operators on the event to add and remove events. The compiler translates calls to these operators to calls to the *add_* and *remove_* methods. Note that although the += operator is made on what appears to be a delegate field (admittedly one marked with *__event*), the code generated does not call *Delegate::Combine* on that field. Instead, it calls the *add_* method on the class that contains the field.

```
Worker* w = new Worker;
w->m += m1;
w->m += m2;
w->DoSomething();
```

If you want to perform some special processing in the *add_*, *remove_*, and *raise_* methods, you can provide implementations and inform the compiler. To do this task, you should not declare *__event* on a delegate field; instead, you should decorate the methods with the *__event* keyword. So that the compiler knows which methods are used to add and remove the delegates and which method is used to raise the event, you should use the convention of prefixing the event name with *add_*, *remove_*, and *raise_*.

```
public __gc class Worker
{
   CallMethod* m1;
public:
   __event void add_m(CallMethod* d)    { m1 += d; }
   __event void remove_m(CallMethod* d) { m1 -= d; }
   __event int raise_m(String* s)       { return m1(s); }
   void DoSomething()
   {
      // Do some work here.
      m(S"something was done");
   }
};
```

I have added a private delegate field to hold the delegates that are added to the event. It is important to give this a name different from the event (that is, the name after the *raise_* prefix). Chapter 4 shows a real-life example of providing custom event methods: the *Control* class. The problem with the default implementation of events provided by the compiler is that for each event, the class will have a delegate field. An instance will have storage for each delegate even if no clients have provided event handlers. The *Control* class stores all delegates in an instance of *EventHandlerList*, which allocates only sufficient memory for the delegates added to the object that can generate events.

Events can be declared as static, and the compiler-generated methods and the delegate field will also be static, in which case the event is treated as a notification mechanism for the type—that is, when the event is raised, all delegates added through all instances of the type are informed. Furthermore, events can also be virtual. If you write the individual event methods, you must ensure that you are consistent with the static and virtual keywords.

Attributes

Metadata is vital to .NET code. All types are described in metadata within the assembly where they are defined. Code that uses those types has metadata that describes exactly which code they will call. The runtime uses this information when executing your code, and if the exact method (in the exact assembly) you ask to be executed cannot be found, the runtime will throw an exception.

Compilers generate metadata when they compile your code. They also read the metadata in the assemblies that you use (which you specify in C++ with *#using*). In some cases, you might decide that you want the compiler to apply a particular .NET metadata to your type. To do this task, you use an attribute, such as the *[Serializable]* attribute that I introduced earlier. If you add this attribute to a type, the compiler will add the *serializable* metadata to the type, which you can view in ILDASM.

```
[Serializable]
__gc struct Square
{
   int x;
   int y;
   int w;
   int h;
};
```

For the purpose of this discussion, I will make this type a *__gc* type, which means that objects are passed through object references. A type this size would normally be a *__value* type, in which case the data is always passed by value. The *[Serializable]* attribute is a *pseudo* custom attribute because strictly speaking it is not a custom attribute—a custom attribute is used to extend metadata, whereas *[Serializable]* applies existing metadata that can be added to the class.

The syntax that you see here is the standard syntax for custom attributes.[5] Custom attributes are implemented by *__gc* classes derived from *System::Attribute*. These classes can have constructors, fields, and properties, and you can pass data to a constructor to initialize the attribute. If an attribute class has a constructor with parameters, the parameters are passed through positional, unnamed parameters.

```
[CLSCompliant(true)] __gc class Test{};
```

This custom attribute indicates that the class is compliant with the Common Language Specification (CLS), meaning that its public members use types that can be used by any .NET language. The value of *true* is passed to the constructor of the class *CLSCompliantAttribute*. The convention is that the name of a custom attribute class has the suffix *Attribute*, but the C++ compiler allows you to call it either with or without the suffix.[6] Named, optional attribute parameters are implemented through properties or public fields, for example:

```
[ObjectPooling(true, CreationTimeout=10000)]
__gc class MyComp : public ServicedComponent{};
```

The *[ObjectPooling]* attribute in *System::EnterpriseServices* is used to indicate the properties of object pooling that should be used for this class. The first

5. The astute reader will notice that pseudo custom attributes are not the only way to add metadata to a type. The *__abstract* keyword adds the *abstract* metadata, *__sealed* adds the *sealed* metadata, and *__value* adds the *value* metadata to a type. Furthermore, *__event* and *__property* are used to identify code that will be used to create the *.event* and *.property* metadata. Pseudo custom attributes allow other languages to add metadata to their types.

6. There are a few cases in which you *must* use the suffix. The most obvious is *[GuidAttribute]* in *System::Runtime::InteropServices*, which is used to apply a COM GUID to a type. You can also use GUIDs in your code, and for this you can use *System::Guid*. To avoid the compiler mistaking one for the other, you should use the complete attribute name.

parameter is not optional, and it indicates that object pooling is enabled. *CreationTimeout* is a property and is used to indicate the maximum amount of time that a client should wait for an object until an exception is thrown. There is no constructor that takes the timeout as a value, so if you want to specify this value, you have to do it through the property. If you omit this parameter, a default value is used. The syntax looks a little odd. It looks like you are calling a constructor and naming one of the parameters. In fact, the information that you give in a custom attribute is stored in metadata as a list of instructions. So in effect, this attribute says: "create for me an instance of *ObjectPoolingAttribute* by calling the constructor that takes a *Boolean* and pass *true* for this parameter, and then give the *CreationTimeout* property a value of 10000". I'll come back to this issue in a moment.

If you want to apply multiple attributes to an item, you can either use a pair of square brackets for each attribute or use one pair of square brackets and give the attributes in a comma-separated list. Attributes can be placed on any item that can generate metadata, before any other modifier that can be applied to the item. However, there are some cases when the compiler will not know where you intend the attribute to be applied. Here's one example:

```
[Test] int MyMethod();
```

When the compiler sees this code, it will not know whether the attribute should be applied to the return value or to the method. (The compiler does not allow the attribute to be applied between the return type and the method name.) In this case, the attribute will be applied to the method. If you want to apply the attribute to the return value, you'll need to specify a target specifier.

```
[returnvalue: Test] int MyMethod();
```

Table 1-3 lists the target specifiers that you can use. Some attributes appear redundant, for example:

```
[delegate: Test] __delegate void delOne();
[method: Test] __delegate void delTwo();
```

In this example, the *[Test]* attribute is applied to both the *delOne* and *delTwo* delegates. However, in your C++ code it is more readable to use the *delegate* target because the *__delegate* directive actually declares a delegate class (which the compiler will generate) and not a method.

Table 1-3 Target Specifiers Used to Specify the Item an Attribute Should Be Applied To

Target Specifier	Description
assembly	For attributes applied to anonymous blocks that will generate assembly metadata.
class	For attributes applied to a C++ class.
constructor	The attribute is applied to a constructor.
delegate	The attribute is applied to the delegate (as opposed to the return value); this is the same as using the *method* target.
enum	The attribute is applied to the enum.
event	The attribute is applied to the *.event* metadata. If you want the attribute to be applied to the *add_*, *raise_*, or *remove_* method, use the *method* target.
field	The attribute is applied to the field.
interface	The attribute is applied to the managed interface.
method	The attribute is applied to a global or member method; the *add_*, *raise_*, or *remove_* methods of an event or the *get_* or *set_* methods of a property.
module	For attributes applied to anonymous blocks that will generate module metadata.
parameter	The attribute is applied to a method parameter.
property	The attribute is applied to the property (as opposed to the *get_* or *set_* methods, in which case you should use the method target); this is the same as using the *returnvalue* target.
returnvalue	The attribute is applied to the return value of a method or to a property.
struct	The attribute is applied to a struct.

Another situation in which the target specifier is vital is when you want to apply an attribute to an assembly or to a module. In .NET, the unit of deployment and versioning is the assembly. An assembly can be made up of one or more code and resource files. Code and embedded resources can be in files called *modules*. To specify that an attribute should be applied to the assembly rather than to a module, you should use the assembly or module target specifier, as shown in this example:

```
[assembly: ApplicationName("My COM+ Application")];
```

This code gives the name of the COM+ application that the assembly is used for. When the assembly is registered with RegAsm (or a *ServicedComponent* type defined in the assembly is used for the first time), this string will be used as the name of the COM+ application.

It is interesting to look at the metadata generated for a custom attribute. Let's go back to the *ObjectPooling* example given earlier. The metadata for the class looks like this:

```
.class public auto ansi MyComp
  extends [System.EnterpriseServices]
    System.EnterpriseServices.ServicedComponent
{
  .custom instance void [System.EnterpriseServices]
    System.EnterpriseServices.ObjectPoolingAttribute::.ctor(bool)
       = ( 01 00 01 01 00 54 08 0F  // .....T..
           43 72 65 61 74 69 6F 6E  // Creation
           54 69 6D 65 6F 75 74 10  // Timeout.
           27 00 00 )               // '..
}
```

The custom attribute is applied through the .custom directive. This gives the name of the constructor that is used to create the attribute (whenever that is—I will cover this issue in a moment) followed by binary data that gives the information about the data that will be passed to the constructor. This data starts with 0x0001 (all attribute data appear to start with this value) followed by one byte (0x01), which is the serialized value of *true*. Next it gives the number of properties or fields that should be set (0x0001), and after this the properties and fields are listed in the order that they were declared. The binary data has an identifier to indicate whether the item is a property (0x54) or a field (0x53) and then the name of the property. This name is made up of a single byte string prefixed with the number of characters in the string. The property name is then followed by the value of the property (0x00002710).

The name of the property is stored as single-byte characters, but if you pass a string for the value of a parameter of an attribute (either positional parameters or named parameters), the data is stored as a serialized managed string—that is, as Unicode characters. It makes no difference whether you provide the string value as ANSI (""), as Unicode (L""), or through managed string syntax (S"") in your code because the compiler will always store it as a serialized managed string.

As I mentioned before, the attribute is stored in metadata as a list of instructions used to create the attribute, but the question is: when is this attribute object created? A custom attribute is not necessarily created when an object instance is created. Custom attributes are created only when code attempts to access the attributes on an item. This action is performed by calling the static method *Attribute::GetCustomAttribute* to get a specified attribute on an assembly, module, class member, or method parameter; or by calling the instance method *MemberInfo::GetCustomAttributes* to get a list of custom attributes on any item. *System::Type* derives from *MemberInfo*, so you are likely to get the custom attributes for an object through the *Type* object.

When one of these methods is called, the runtime will create the attribute object using the instructions in the *.custom* directive. If you call *GetType()->GetCustomAttributes* twice on one object, two attribute objects will be created. Note also that *GetCustomAttributes* returns *custom* attributes; pseudo custom attributes are not returned by this method because they represent standard metadata. Pseudo custom attributes such as *[Serializable]* can be obtained through reflection (in this case, *Type::IsSerializable*). For more information on reflection see Jeffrey Richter's *Applied Microsoft .NET Framework Programming (Microsoft Press, 2002)*.

MemberInfo::GetCustomAttributes returns an array of *Object* pointers. There are several ways that you can determine the type of each member. First, you could perform a *dynamic_cast*<> for the attribute type that you are interested in, and if the cast succeeds, the attribute has been applied to the item. Note that the type that you will cast to is the full name of the attribute class; you can use the abbreviated name (without the *Attribute* suffix) in square brackets only when you are applying an attribute. Second, you can test the type object against the type object obtained from the class; the type object returned from *GetType* and *__typeof* is a static object for each type. Finally, you could compare the name of the type object returned from *GetType()->ToString*, but remember that if the attribute is in a namespace, the scope resolution operator will be the dot, not ::, thus:

```
Test* t = new Test;
Object* attrs[] = t->GetType()->GetCustomAttributes(false);
IEnumerator* e = attrs->GetEnumerator();
while (e->MoveNext())
{
   if (e->Current->GetType()->ToString()
          ->Equals(S"System.ObsoleteAttribute")
   {
      Console::WriteLine(S"this class is obsolete");
   }
}
```

Here's another assembly attribute:

```
[assembly: AssemblyVersion("1.0.*")];
```

This attribute is interesting because the information is a request to the compiler and the information in the attribute is not placed in the assembly as a custom attribute. Instead, the compiler interprets the information and uses it to create information that it puts in the assembly's *.ver* metadata. In this case, the compiler creates a version of the form 1.0.*xx.yy*, where *xx* is the build number that the compiler will create from the number of days since the first day of the year 2000, and *yy* is the revision number that the compiler will create from the number of seconds since midnight modulo 2.

Creating your own attribute classes is straightforward: you derive from *System::Attribute* and apply the *[AttributeUsage]* attribute to indicate where the attribute can be used. In addition, *[AttributeUsage]* also allows you to indicate whether the attribute can be used more than once on the same item and whether the attribute is inherited when it is applied to a *__gc* type and that type is the base for another type. Any mandatory parameters should be constructor parameters, whereas optional parameters can be passed through fields or properties. The attribute classes in the .NET Framework class library often accommodate optional parameters through overloaded constructors, but I think it is clearer to use constructors only for mandatory parameters. Whatever you decide on this issue, you should ensure that all constructors initialize fields and properties to a suitable default value.

You are restricted to the types that you can use for constructor parameters, fields, and properties on attribute classes. The acceptable types are listed below the following code. Because integers are allowed, you can also use enumerated values. You are also allowed to use arrays of the types given in this list, in which case when you apply the attribute, you should use an initializer list.

```
[AttributeUsage(AttributeTargets::All)]
__gc class UsersAttribute : public Attribute
{
public:
   String* names[];
};

[Users(names = { S"Paul", S"John", S"George" } )]
__gc class ThisClass
{
public:
};
```

Here are the types that can be used for constructor parameters, fields, and properties of attribute classes:

- *bool*
- *char*
- *unsigned char*

- *wchar_t*
- *short*
- *unsigned short*
- *int*
- *unsigned int*
- *__int64*
- *float*
- *double*
- *Object **
- *String **
- *char **
- *wchar_t **

Managed Interfaces

The new C++ compiler supports a new keyword named *__interface*. This keyword is supported for both managed and unmanaged code, so for a managed interface, you have to use *__gc*. Interfaces add metadata that describe behavior. They do not contain implementation. Indeed, all interfaces are implicitly abstract (you can use *__abstract* on an interface, but it is not necessary), and all members are implicitly pure virtual (again, you can use =0 on methods, but it is not necessary). Interfaces can contain methods, properties, and events, and all members are implicitly public. They cannot contain any implementation and cannot contain any storage, so they cannot contain fields. However, interfaces can contain *__value* enums because these do not represent storage. They are named values. Furthermore, interfaces cannot contain constructors, destructors, or operators, and because they are used to generate *vtables*, they cannot contain static members. Finally, *__gc* interfaces cannot derive from classes, but they can derive from other *__gc* interfaces. .NET supports multiple interface inheritance.

```
// interfaces.cpp
__gc __interface IPrint
{
   void Print();
   __property unsigned get_Pages();
   __property void set_Pages(unsigned);
   __event OnPrinted* printed;
};
```

This interface has a property named *Pages*, a method named *Print*, and an event named *OnPrinted*. The intention is that the interface will be implemented by a class that can print documents, and when the print job has completed, it informs interested parties by raising the *OnPrinted* event.

```
__delegate void OnPrinted(String*);

__gc class PrintedDoc : public IPrint
{
   unsigned pages;
   String* doc;
public:
   PrintedDoc(String* s, unsigned p) : doc(s), pages(p){}
   void Print()
   {
      for (int i = 1; i <= pages; i++)
         Console::WriteLine(S"printing page {0}", __box(i));
      printed(doc);
   }
   __property unsigned get_Pages() { return pages; }
   __property void set_Pages(unsigned num) { pages = num; }
   __event virtual OnPrinted* printed;
};
```

Because the event is a member of the interface, it is declared as virtual. The *PrintedDoc* class needs to declare the event as virtual so that the generated methods are also virtual.

Here is a class that uses an instance of *PrintedDoc*:

```
__gc class Book
{
   ArrayList* chapters;
public:
   Book()
   {
      chapters = new ArrayList;
      PrintedDoc* doc;
      doc = new PrintedDoc(S"Chapter1.doc", 90);
      doc->printed += new OnPrinted(0, Notify);
      chapters->Add(doc);
      doc = new PrintedDoc(S"Chapter2.doc", 67);
      doc->printed += new OnPrinted(0, Notify);
      chapters->Add(doc);
      doc = new PrintedDoc(S"Chapter3.doc", 87);
      doc->printed += new OnPrinted(0, Notify);
      chapters->Add(doc);
   }
```

```
    static void Notify(String* doc)
    {
        Console::WriteLine(S"{0} printed", doc);
    }
    void PrintAll()
    {
        IEnumerator* e = chapters->GetEnumerator();
        while(e->MoveNext())
        {
            IPrint* doc = dynamic_cast<IPrint*>(e->Current);
            if (doc != 0) doc->Print();
        }
    }
};
```

The *PrintAll* method iterates through the collection of documents and prints each one. The collection contains *Object** pointers, so I cast to *IPrint** because the *only* behavior that I want to get from the entry is its printable behavior. The collection could contain items other than *PrintedDoc*, but as long as those items implement *IPrint*, they will still be printed in *PrintAll*.

This feature of interface programming—defining behavior—is often overlooked. Types can derive from more than one interface, which means that a type can have more than one behavior, so you can choose which behavior you want from an object—a document could be both printable (rendered on paper) and persistent (saved to persistent storage, such as to disk).

```
__gc class Document : public IPrint, public IPersistent
{ /* other members */ };
```

An interface can derive from one or more interfaces.

```
__gc __interface IOne
{
    void One();
};
__gc __interface ITwo
{
    void Two();
};
__gc __interface IThree : IOne, ITwo
{
    void Three();
};
```

A class that derives from *IThree* must implement the three methods *One*, *Two*, and *Three*, and it is treated as if it derives from *IOne*, *ITwo*, and *IThree*. A pointer to this class can be implicitly converted to any of the interfaces, and an *IThree** pointer can be implicitly converted to an *IOne** or *ITwo**. If you have an *IOne** pointer on a class that implements *IThree*, there is no implicit conversion from *IOne** to *ITwo**, but because the class implements both interfaces, you can explicitly cast between these interfaces with *static_cast<>*.

One issue you might come across with multiple interfaces is if your class implements two interfaces that have a method with the same signature.

```
// interfaces2.cpp
__gc __interface IOarsman
{
   void Row();
};
__gc __interface IArgumentative
{
   void Row();
};
__gc class Rower : public IOarsman, public IArgumentative
{
public:
   void Row(){ Console::WriteLine(S"pull oar or shout?"); }
};
```

Both interfaces have a method named *Row*. The class implements both interfaces and hence implements *Row*. Because interfaces represent different *behaviors*, you do not necessarily intend to have a single implementation of *Row*. As it stands, I can create an instance of *Rower* and call *Row* through a pointer to *Rower*, to *IOarsman*, or to *IArgumentative*.

The C++ compiler allows you to specify that a method implementation is for a specific interface.

```
__gc class Rower : public IOarsman, public IArgumentative
{
public:
   void IOarsman::Row(){ Console::WriteLine(S"pull oar"); }
   void IArgumentative::Row(){ Console::WriteLine(S"shout"); }
};
```

Now a user of the class can specify which version of *Row* should be called. To specify the version the user must obtain the appropriate interface pointer and call the following method:

```
IOarsman* o = new Rower;
o->Row();
```

Providing an explicit interface implementation such as this on a class has a side effect: you can call these methods only through interface pointers; you cannot call these methods through a pointer to the class.[7] This side effect is useful, and classes in the .NET Framework use explicit interface implementation even when the class implements only one interface, to prevent the methods being called through a class pointer. For example, classes can be passed by value if they are serializable. I have already mentioned one way to indicate this: simply apply the *[Serializable]* attribute to the class, and all fields not marked as *[NotSerialized]* will be serialized. If you want to customize the way that serialization works, you can implement *ISerializable* on your class.

```
// serialize.cpp
__gc class MyFile : public IDisposable
{
   FileStream* f;
public:
   MyFile(String* name)
   {
      f = new FileStream(name, FileMode::OpenOrCreate,
                         FileAccess::ReadWrite);
   }
   FileStream* GetStream()
   { return f; }
   void Close()
   { if (f != 0) f->Close(); }
   void Dispose()
   { Close(); }
};
```

This class encapsulates a *FileStream* object, and the constructor takes a string with the name of the file and opens the file for read/write access. Client code can call *GetStream* to get access to this stream to read or write data through the *GetStream* method. I have indicated that the class implements *IDisposable*, which indicates to users of the class that it holds a resource that should be released as soon as possible by calling the *Close* method.

I might decide that I want to serialize this object and store it somewhere (perhaps in a database). The intention being that when I deserialize the object, it will be initialized in such a way that I can call *GetStream* to get access to a stream on the original file and use the object as if it had never been serialized.

---

7. The compiler is rather coy about this:

```
Rower* r = new Rower;
r->IOarsman::Row();
```

will result in an error telling me that the method call will fail at run time, rather than telling me that the code is just plain wrong.

The first approach is to add *[Serializable]* to the class and attempt to serialize the object with the following code:

```
// Create the file.
MyFile* f = new MyFile(S"data.txt");
// Write to the file using a StreamWriter.
StreamWriter* sw = new StreamWriter(f->GetStream());
sw->Write(S"this is data");
sw->Close();

// Now serialize the object.
SoapFormatter* sf = new SoapFormatter();
Stream* txt = File::Create(S"MyFile.soap");
sf->Serialize(txt, f);
txt->Close();
f->Close();
```

This code will fail. The reason is that the *SoapFormatter* will attempt to serialize the *FileStream* object, which is not serializable. Let's take another approach and instead of serializing the fields in the class, let's serialize the name of the file. To do this, the class needs to turn off standard serialization and implement custom serialization. This task is done by implementing *ISerializable*.

The *ISerializable* interface is interesting: it has just one method named *GetObjectData*, which is called by the formatter to ask the object to serialize itself. This method is passed a *SerializationInfo* object that acts like a collection of name-value pairs. This object can be used to store enough information to identify the file that the *FileStream* object is based on. The interesting point is that if you implement this interface, you also have to implement a constructor that takes the same parameters as *GetObjectData*. This constructor is called by the formatter when an object is deserialized. Interfaces cannot declare constructors, so the only way that you know about this is to read the documentation. Here is the class with custom serialization:

```
[Serializable]
__gc class MyFile : public ISerializable, public IDisposable
{
   FileStream* f;
public:
   MyFile(String* name)
   {
      f = new FileStream(name, FileMode::OpenOrCreate,
                         FileAccess::ReadWrite);
   }
   FileStream* GetStream()
   { return f; }
   void Close()
   { if (f != 0) f->Close(); }
```

```
   void Dispose()
   { Close(); }
protected:
   MyFile(SerializationInfo* info, StreamingContext context)
   {
      String* machine = Environment::MachineName;
      if (!info->GetString(S"__MachineName")->Equals(machine))
         throw new Exception(S"must be on the same machine!");
      if (info->GetString(S"__FileName") == S"<null>")
         throw new Exception(S"file has no name!");
      f = new FileStream(info->GetString(S"__FileName"),
         FileMode::Open, FileAccess::ReadWrite);
   }
   void ISerializable::GetObjectData(
      SerializationInfo* info, StreamingContext context)
   {
      info->AddValue(S"__MachineName", Environment::MachineName);
      info->AddValue(S"__FileName", f==0 ? S"<null>" : f->Name);
   }
};
```

I have made the new constructor protected so that users are not tempted to call it. I have also made the *GetObjectData* protected, but for added safety, I have identified that the method should be called only on an *ISerializable* interface pointer so that the user of this class is not tempted to call this method unless he specifically wants to serialize the object.

There is one final property that I ought to mention about interfaces: default implementation. A class can derive from another class and one or more interfaces. If the base class has a member that has the same signature as a member of one of the interfaces it implements, that member can be used to provide the interface member, even if the base class does not implement the interface, as shown in this example:

```
__gc class Base
{
public:
   virtual void f()
   { Console::WriteLine(S"default impl"); }
};

__gc __interface ITest
{
   void f();
};

__gc class Test : public Base, public ITest
{
};
```

Base does not implement *ITest*, but it does provide an implementation of a method that has the same signature as an interface method (including the implicit virtual). The *Test* class derives from *Base* and gets the implementation of *ITest::f* from this base class.

Managed Strings

In .NET, strings are managed objects. The *System::String* class encapsulates most of the actions that you will want to do on a string: compare strings; test for substrings and individual characters; create new strings by concatenating strings; split up existing strings; add padding spaces or trim them; and insert, replace, or remove substrings. However, it is important to realize that a *System::String* is immutable. If you call any of its methods that change a string, you do not get back the original string modified; instead, you get a completely new string. For example, if you call *ToLower* on a string, you do not affect the string that you are calling. Instead, you get a new string that has the lowercase characters.

If you want to create a string buffer that can be modified, you should use a *StringBuilder* object (in the *System::Text* namespace), which has methods to insert, remove, and replace substrings in a buffer and add the string representations of various primitive types to the end of the buffer.

The *String* class holds data as Unicode characters. Each one is a *Char* data type. You can access each character through the *Chars* indexed property, as shown here:

```
String* str = S"Hello";
// Get the fourth character.
Char c = str->Chars[3];
```

The *String* class implements the *Chars* property so that the first character in the string is at index zero. Also notice the syntax for declaring a literal string. The S prefix indicates that the string is a managed string. The *String* class has constructors that take an unmanaged pointer to a *char* buffer (*String(SByte*)*) and an unmanaged pointer to a wide *char* buffer (*String(Char*)*), which will convert the strings to the managed string. However, to do so requires the compiler to generate extra code, so if possible, you should always use managed string literals.

For example, this code:

```
String* str = L"Hello";
```

generates this IL:

```
ldsflda valuetype $ArrayType$0xe68a7113
 '?A0xcfbb78fe.unnamed-global-0'
newobj instance void [mscorlib]System.String::.ctor(char*)
stloc.0
```

The first line loads the address of a static, global field named *?A0xcfbb78fe.unnamed-global-0*. This array is passed to the *String* constructor that takes an unmanaged pointer to a wide *char* buffer. The constructor string (in this case) is stored as the local variable 0. The static field looks like this:

```
.field public static valuetype $ArrayType$0xe68a7113
   '?A0xcfbb78fe.unnamed-global-0' at D_00008030
```

The type of the field is *$ArrayType$0xe68a7113*, another compiler-generated name that looks like this:

```
.class private explicit ansi sealed $ArrayType$0xe68a7113
   extends [mscorlib]System.ValueType
{
   .pack 1
   .size 12
   // Other items omitted
}
```

The type has no code and no members. It merely indicates that the type takes up 12 bytes—the size of the literal string in Unicode characters. The static field *?A0xcfbb78fe.unnamed-global-0* is stored in the initialized data section of the PE file at location 0x8030.

```
.data D_00008030
   = bytearray (48 00 65 00 6C 00
                6C 00 6F 00 00 00) // H.e.l.l.o...
```

A similar data item and field will be created if you initialize the string with an ANSI string. So in both of these cases, you will have a static field initialized with data in the initialized data section of the PE file and this field is then passed to the constructor of *System::String*. Compare this to the situation when the literal is a managed string. The IL generated is this:

```
ldstr "Hello" /* 70000001 */
stloc.0
```

In other words, the string is stored in the user strings section (*#US* stream[8]) of the metadata section of the PE file (this is part of the PE *.text* section), which is loaded as a managed string and pushed onto the stack all in one IL statement. The value in comments after the string literal is the metadata token for the literal (which you can view by using the */token* switch of ILDASM). The token is actually a 1-based index into a table. The top byte (0x70) indicates that the metadata table is the string table. Consider this code:

8. This is the 'user string' metadata stream held within the PE file; items in this stream are identified by metadata tokens. MSIL is composed of opcodes and metadata tokens. The various metadata streams are documented in the ECMA spec, "Partition II Metadata," Chapter 23, "Metadata Physical Layout."

```
String* s1 = S"Hello";
String* s2 = S"Hello";
```

The two references are initialized with the same literal string. The IL looks like this:

```
ldstr "Hello" /* 70000001 */
stloc.1
ldstr "Hello" /* 70000001 */
stloc.0
```

As you can see, the compiler has noticed that the same literal is used for both, so the metadata *#US* stream has only one copy. Furthermore, the object references will be the same (*Object::Equals* will return *true*) because when the first string is created, the runtime will *intern* the managed string. The next time a string with the same metadata token is loaded, the runtime will return the same interned object.

You have to be wary about comparing strings—especially if, like me, you write some code in C#.[9] There are several ways to compare strings: some compare string references, some compare the actual strings, and some compare both. The C++ == operator, when used with string references, tests to see if they are the same reference—that is, the operator is the same as in unmanaged C++. You get a comparison of the references and not a comparison of what the objects contain. Be careful here because in C# the operator == for *System::String* checks both the references for equality, and if they are not the same object, the operator checks the value of the objects for equality. Thus, the code

```
// Managed C++
String* s1 = S"X";
String* s2 = S"XX";
// Get substring so we do not get the interned string
String* s3 = s2->Substring(0, 1);

if (s1 == s3) Console::WriteLine(S"same");
else          Console::WriteLine(S"not the same");
```

will indicate that the strings are not the same because the comparison of the string references fails. The C# code

```
// C#
string s1 = "X";
string s2 = "XX";
// get substring so we do not get the interned string
string s3 = s2.Substring(0, 1);

if (s1 == s3) Console.WriteLine("same");
else          Console.WriteLine("not the same");
```

9. My thanks to Jeroen Frijters for clarifying some of my confusions over the string comparison methods.

indicates that the strings are the same. The reason is because == in C# actually calls the *String::op_Equality* method, which calls the static *String::Equals(String*, String*)* method. You can call this method in C++ explicitly.

```
if (String::Equals(s1, s3))
   Console::WriteLine(S"same");
else
   Console::WriteLine(S"not the same");
```

The == operator first checks to see whether the references are the same (which is a quick check for equality), and if they are not, it checks to see whether either is a null pointer. If this check fails, the operator calls the instance method *String::Equals(String*)*, which does the more costly comparison of the values of the strings. It is better to call the static *Equals* rather than the instance *Equals* because the former is potentially faster if you are likely to compare strings that could be the same object reference.

String::Equals does a case-sensitive comparison. If you want to do a case-insensitive comparison, call the static *String::Compare* overload that takes two strings and a *Boolean*. A value of *true* for the *Boolean* does a case-insensitive comparison. However, be wary of this method (and the associated *CompareOrdinal* and *CompareTo*) because the return value is not a *Boolean*; it is an integer with a similar meaning as the integer returned from the CRT *strcmp*. So if the strings are the same, *CompareTo* will return zero, which, of course, C++ will treat as a *Boolean false*.

You cannot pass a managed string to a C++ standard library or a CRT function. Instead, you can use the *Marshal::StringToHGlobalUni* method in the *System::Runtime::InteropServices* namespace to convert a managed string to a Unicode native string allocated on the *LocalAlloc* heap. After using the string, you must free the string with a call to *FreeHGlobal*. For better performance, Visual C++ provides the following function to give access to the internal buffer of *wchar_t* characters in a managed string:

```
// From vcclr.h
inline const System::Char * PtrToStringChars(
   const System::String *s)
{
   // Pin to avoid one-instruction GC hole in reinterpret_cast.
   const System::String __pin*pps = s;
   const System::Byte __pin*bp
      = reinterpret_cast<const System::Byte*>(s);
   if (bp != 0)
   {
      unsigned offset = System::Runtime::CompilerServices::
         RuntimeHelpers::OffsetToStringData;
      bp += offset;
   }
```

```
    return reinterpret_cast<const System::Char*>(bp);
}
```

Each managed string has a character buffer at a fixed offset from the beginning of the object. The *OffsetToStringData* property has this offset value, so the function pins the object and obtains a pointer to the first byte of the string object. The function then increments this byte pointer by the standard offset, which will give access to the character buffer. The function returns a *Char_gc** pointer because the pinning only lasts as long as the scope of the function. The code that uses *OffsetToStringData* has to pin the return value before passing it to an unmanaged function, as shown here:

```
String* s = S"hello";
const Char __pin* p= PtrToStringChars(s);
_putws(p);
```

Managed Arrays

In .NET, arrays are managed types—that is, each array is an object and is allocated on the managed heap. The syntax to declare a managed array is slightly different from the syntax for declaring native arrays, and similarly the syntax to access the array, and to use the array as parameters for methods or return types from methods, is different than that of native arrays. If you come from a C++ background, you have to be careful with managed arrays because a native array variable is essentially a pointer into memory and the square brackets are used to perform memory arithmetic and dereference the pointer. With managed code, you should not normally access memory directly, and the .NET Framework classes actively prevent this access. This restriction means that some of the tricks that you are used to performing with native arrays and pointers you will not be able to perform with managed arrays. However, although some of these tricks are useful (for example, using negative indexes), the extra checks performed by the runtime mean that you gain enormously by having the safety of index validation and garbage collection that ensures that your code does not leak memory.

Declaring a one-dimensional array is straightforward:

```
// arrays.cpp
String* names[] = __gc new String*[3];
names[0] = S"Richard";
names[1] = S"Thomas";
names[2] = S"Grimes";
```

The first line allocates an array of *String** pointers. The type of this variable is *String*[]*, which is not the same as *String*** (which is the type you would use to return a *String* reference as an in/out parameter). You can test the type of the array with this code:

```
Type* t = names->GetType();
while (t != 0)
{
   Console::WriteLine(t->ToString());
   t = t->BaseType;
}
```

The output actually shows the type of the variable as *System.String[]*, which is the IL format that the runtime uses. This code also shows that the base class of the variable is *System::Array*. Thus, an array can be accessed through a typed array variable (*String[]*), a pointer to *Array*, or to *Object*, so all three of these declarations are allowed:

```
String* a1[] = names;
Array* a2 = names;
Object* a3 = names;
```

Of course, when you have an *Array** pointer, you do not get the advantage of using the square bracket syntax, but it is possible to cast between the types. The *Array* class is abstract, so if you want to create an instance, you use the static method *CreateInstance*, which allows you to identify the type of the *Array* you want created. Our string array could be created like this:

```
Array* a = Array::CreateInstance(__typeof(String), 3);
String* names2[] = dynamic_cast<String*[]>(a);
names2[0] = S"Richard";
names2[1] = S"Thomas";
names2[2] = S"Grimes";
```

CreateInstance creates an array of the specified type, and the *__typeof* operator returns the static *Type* object for the type (the same object that is returned from *GetType* when called on an instance).

When the array is created, the items are assigned to zero (for primitive types and *__gc* types) or the default constructor is called (for *__value* types), so you do not have to worry about the random values that occur in native C++. The runtime does not create the objects in the array when you declare it, so you have to allocate each item, as I have shown in the preceding code. The index of the array is always zero-based. If you use an index outside of the range 0 <= *index* < *names->Length*, where the *Length* property is one less than the value given in the declaration, a run-time exception of *IndexOutOfRangeException* will be thrown.

In this example, I have called the overloaded version of *CreateInstance* that creates a single-dimension array—a vector. There are overloads that can create multidimensional arrays and can specify the lower bounds of the array, for example:

```
int dims __gc[] = {3};
int idx __gc[] = {1};
Array* a = Array::CreateInstance(__typeof(String), dims, idx);
```

Here I have declared two *int* arrays, and to indicate that I want a managed array rather than a native array, I have to explicitly mention that the array is a *__gc* array. The *dims* array is used to specify the size of each dimension, and because this declaration has a single value, the array that I want created should have a single dimension of three items. The *idx* array gives the lower bound of each dimension. Here I have decided that the index of the first dimension should be 1-based (like default arrays in Visual Basic 6).

This code will compile, and it will work at run time. However, if I attempt to use *dynamic_cast<>* to cast the *Array** variable to a *String*[]* variable, I will get a zero pointer. I can use *static_cast<>* and the cast will succeed, but when I try to access indexes out of the range 0 through 2, I get an *IndexOutOfRangeException* exception:

```
String* names3[] = dynamic_cast<String*[]>(a);

names3[1] = S"Richard";
names3[2] = S"Thomas";
names3[3] = S"Grimes";
```

The reason is that the runtime sees that I want to use square brackets to access the array, and when I use *dynamic_cast<>*, the runtime check determines that the indexes of the dimensions make them incompatible with square bracket syntax. When I decide that I know better than the runtime by using *static_cast<>*, the cast succeeds, but whenever I access an item, the runtime performs an index bounds check, and it always assumes that the lower bound is zero. If you want to access an array with a lower bound other than zero, you have to use the methods on the *Array* class: *GetValue* and *SetValue*.

In the previous example, I used an initializer list for the *dims* and *idx* arrays. You can create arrays of value types and *__gc* types with an initializer list, for example, using this *__gc* class:

```
__gc struct Person
{
   unsigned short age;
   String* name;
   Person(String* n, unsigned short a) : name(n),age(a){}
};
```

I can create the following arrays:

```
String* names[] = { S"Richard", S"Ellinor" };
Person* people[] =
   { new Person(S"Richard", 37), new Person(S"Ellinor", 38) };
```

You still have to allocate the members of the array using *__gc new*. *String** arrays are an exception because when you give a string literal, the compiler will generate the code to use it to initialize a managed string.

As I indicated earlier, managed arrays can contain value types and pointers to *__gc* types. An array of value types will actually contain the values. You will get a contiguous buffer of memory containing the items. If you obtain an interior pointer to this buffer, you can access the items through pointer arithmetic.

```
// System::Char array can be initialized with characters or
// with unsigned short values. In this example, I ensure that the
// last item is zero.
Char c __gc [] = {'R', 0x0069, 0x0063, 'h', 'a', 'r', 'd', 0};
Char __gc* p = &c[0];
for (int i = 0; i < c->Length-1; i++, p++)
   Console::Write(__box(*p));
```

The second line gets an interior pointer to the first item in the array, and then, in the *for* loop, I dereference the pointer to get the item and then increment the pointer with each loop. This code, naturally, prints *Richard* at the console. If you want to pass this array to unmanaged code, you have to pin the array first. If you pin a single item in an array, the entire array is pinned.

```
Char __pin* p2 = &c[0];
// Pass this to _putws; this is the reason why the last
// item is zero.
_putws(static_cast<wchar_t*>(p2));
```

The syntax for allocating and accessing a one-dimensional array is not too different than the syntax for unmanaged arrays. The syntax to allocate and access multidimensional arrays looks quite different to native C++.

```
// multiarray.cpp
String* books[,] = new String*[3,2];
books[0,0] = S"Professional ATL COM Programming";
books[0,1] = S"1-861001-40-1";
books[1,0] = S"Professional Visual C++ 6 MTS Programming";
books[1,1] = S"1-861002-39-1";
books[2,0] = S"Developing Applications with Visual Studio .NET";
books[2,1] = S"0-201-70852-3";
```

This code creates a *String* array with two columns and three rows. C++ does not support initializer lists for multidimensional arrays, so I have to initialize each item individually. Note that the array is a rectangle—that is, there are six elements arranged as two columns and three rows.

In native C++, you can interchange pointer and square bracket syntax. *a[n]* is equivalent to **(a+n)*, so you can treat an array of three rows and two columns as an array of three rows where each item is a single-dimensional array with two items. Furthermore, arrays are allocated from contiguous memory, so you can play tricks with indexes (for example, for an array *int[4][2]*, item [2][2] is the same as item [3][0]). When you use the square bracket syntax with managed arrays, you are restricted to the dimensions that you used when you declared the array. If you use an index out of this range, you'll get an exception at run time. C++ does not allow you to cast between an *Array** and a multidimensional array in square bracket syntax, so you cannot allocate using *CreateInstance* and then have the convenience of accessing the elements with the square bracket syntax.

The memory for a multidimensional managed array is allocated as a contiguous block of memory, and you can take advantage of this layout with interior pointers. For example, I can allocate an array of integers like this:

```
// Create a multidimensional array.
int i __gc[,] = new int __gc[5,5];
for (int j=0; j<=i->GetUpperBound(0); j++)
{
   for (int k=0; k<=i->GetUpperBound(1); k++)
   {
      // Initialize the elements.
      i[j,k] = (j*10) + k;
   }
}
```

Here I use the inherited *GetUpperBound* to get the highest value of the index of the specified dimension, which for an array allocated using the square bracket syntax is one less than the size of the dimension given in the array declaration. I can then obtain an interior pointer to the array like this:

```
// Get an interior pointer to the first element.
int __gc* p = &i[0,0];
// Obtain all the elements.
for (int j = 0;
     j < (i->GetUpperBound(0) + 1)*(i->GetUpperBound(1) + 1);
     j++, p++)
{
   Console::WriteLine(S"{0}={1}", __box(j), __box(*p));
}
```

This code will print out all the items in the array without an index check. If I miscalculate the size of the array, I will obtain memory that does not belong to the array. As I mentioned earlier, you must be careful when you use interior pointers. Because you could have free access to the managed heap, such code is not verifiable.

When you have an array, you can call any of the inherited members from *System::Array*. *Array* implements *IEnumerable*, so you can call *GetEnumerator* to return an *IEnumerator* interface.

```
IEnumerator* e = i->GetEnumerator();
while (e->MoveNext())
{
   Console::WriteLine(e->Current->ToString());
}
```

The class has various methods that allow you to search for items in a one-dimensional array. The static methods *IndexOf* and *LastIndexOf* take the array and an object. *IndexOf* returns the index of the first element that matches the object, and *LastIndexOf* returns the index of the last element that matches the object passed to the method. (You can also pass the range of indexes to search.) The method calls *Equals* on the items in the array, which is usually implemented as a bitwise test for value types and a test of identity equality (the references are to the same physical object) for *__gc* types. These methods return the index of the first item that is found (the array can contain several references to the same object) or *GetLowerBound(0)*–1. (Usually the lower bound is zero, but it is better to explicitly check the value because in the future C++ might support arrays with lower bounds that are not zero.)

Now consider this code:

```
// checkcmd.cpp
__gc struct Item
{
   int i;
   Item(int j) : i(j){}
   // Other methods omitted
};

void main()
{
   String* args[] = Environment::GetCommandLineArgs();
   Item* items[] = new Item*[args->Length - 1];
   for (int j = args->GetLowerBound(0) + 1;
         j <= args->GetUpperBound(0); j++)
   {
      items[j-1] = new Item(Int32::Parse(args[j]));
   }
```

```
    int i = Array::IndexOf(items, new Item(42));
    if (i < args->GetLowerBound(0))
       Console::WriteLine(S"42 must be on the command line!");
    // Other code...
}
```

The intention is to take the parameters passed to the command line and use each one to create an *Item* object. My code needs to have at least one item initialized with the value of 42. As it stands, this code will always print the error message regardless of the items put on the command line. The reason is that the search is performed by passing a new instance of *Item* initialized to the value of 42 to *IndexOf*. The default implementation of *Object::Equals* will check for object identity, so even if a user types 42 at the command line, the object created from that command line argument will *always* be a different object from the one passed to *Equals*.

If *Item* were a *__value* type, this problem would not occur because the default implementation of *Equals* for a *__value* type is a bitwise comparison. If I performed the same search on the *String* array (args)*, looking for the string "42", the problem would not occur because *String::Equals* does a string comparison. I could implement *Item::Equals* to perform a comparison of the fields of the objects, but I might have other code that relies on *Equals* to be an identity check. The solution is to implement *IComparable* and to use *Array::BinarySearch*.

```
// checkcmd.cpp
__gc struct Item : IComparable
{
   int i;
   Item(int j) : i(j){}
   int CompareTo(Object* obj)
   {
      Item* item = dynamic_cast<Item*>(obj);
      if (i == item->i) return 0;
      if (i > item->i) return 1;
      return -1;
   }
};
```

BinarySearch will go through each item in the array and check for the *IComparable* interface on each. (If none of the items implement this interface, an exception is thrown.) *BinarySearch* then calls *CompareTo* on each item, passing the object with which to make the comparison. If the return value is zero, the objects are considered to have the same value. The change to the call to search the array looks like this:

```
int i = Array::BinarySearch(items, new Item(42));
```

You can also sort one-dimensional arrays with the *Sort* and *Reverse* static methods. *Reverse* takes an existing array and reverses the order of items in the array or within a range in the array. *Sort* is more interesting—it uses a quick sort algorithm to sort the items in the array or items within a range of the array. The items should implement *IComparable*, in which case *CompareTo* will be called on each item to perform the sort; or if the items do not implement this interface (or the implementation is not suitable), a separate comparer object (that implements *IComparer*) can be used:

```
// checkcmd.cpp
__gc struct ItemComparer : IComparer
{
   int Compare(Object* x, Object* y)
   {
      Item* item1 = dynamic_cast<Item*>(x);
      Item* item2 = dynamic_cast<Item*>(y);
      if (item1->i == item2->i) return 0;
      if (item1->i > item2->i) return 1;
      return -1;
   }
};
```

IComparer::Compare should return zero if the parameters are equal (using whatever criteria the comparer decides *equals* means; in this case, the state held by the objects). If the first object is greater than the second object, *IComparer::Compare* returns a number greater than zero, and if the first object is less than the second object, it returns a number less than zero. The array can be sorted like this:

```
Array::Sort(items, new ItemComparer);
for (int k = items->GetLowerBound(0);
         k <= items->GetUpperBound(0); k++)
{
   Console::WriteLine(S"item {0} = {1}",
                      __box(k), __box(items[k]->i));
}
```

You can pass arrays as method parameters, either as an *Array** pointer, as a pointer to one of the interfaces that it implements (*IList*, *IEnumerable*), or as a typed array. Passing an *IList* or *IEnumerable* pointer allows you to write generic routines that can be used with a whole range of containers. Declaring the method parameter as a typed array means that you can use the square bracket syntax in the method.

```
// arrayparams.cpp
void TimesTwo(int i __gc [])
```

```
{
   for (int j = i->GetLowerBound(0); j <= i->GetUpperBound(0);
      j++)
      i[j] *= 2;
}
```

Note that it is always a good idea to test the array size in the method. Methods can also return arrays using the standard C++ syntax, but the current version of the Visual C++ compiler allows only this syntax for managed code. (Unmanaged code must use pointers.)

```
// arrayparams.cpp
int CreateArray(int size) __gc[]
{
   int i __gc[] = new int __gc [size];
   for (int j = i->GetLowerBound(0); j <= i->GetUpperBound(0);
      j++)
      i[j] = j;
   return i;
}
```

The .NET Framework class library has an attribute named *[ParamArray]*, which is used on an array parameter to indicate that languages can treat the method as having a variable number of parameters, similar to the ... syntax in unmanaged C++. One overload of the *Console::WriteLine* uses this attribute.

```
[ParamArray]
static void WriteLine(String* format, Object* arg __gc[]);
```

If this method is called in C#, the language allows any number of parameters to be placed after the format string and the language will generate an object array to pass to the method. You can write a similar method in C++ using *[ParamArray]*, but note that if you call this method in C++, you will have to construct the array in your code. You might wonder how you can call *WriteLine* in C++ and pass more than four parameters. In this case, C++ will call another method that has a method signature that looks like this in IL:

```
.method public hidebysig static vararg void WriteLine(
   string format, object arg0, object arg1,
   object arg2, object arg3) cil managed;
```

This method truly does have a variable number of arguments because it has the *varargs* metadata attribute; in the implementation, the method obtains the parameters through the *System::ArgIterator* class. Clearly, C++ can call methods with the *varargs* attribute, but at present the only way to write such a method is if you write it in IL. C# neither has the facility to write, nor attempts to call, *varargs* methods.

Exceptions and Managed Code

.NET finally removes the need for old-style C error reporting mechanisms. C code typically used function return values to report errors,[10] with the associated problem of maintaining a list of what each error value means. This system persisted into C++ through COM programming, where *HRESULT*s were the main error-reporting mechanism. In .NET, method return values are just that—they are intended to return results. Errors are reported through exceptions.

All .NET exceptions should be instances of *System::Exception* or derived classes; there is no concept of throwing a primitive type or throwing a C++ reference. *System::Exception* looks like this:

```
[Serializable]
__gc class Exception : public ISerializable
{
public:
   Exception();
   Exception(String*);
   Exception(String*, Exception*);
   Exception(SerializationInfo*, StreamingContext*);
   virtual String* get_HelpLink();
   virtual void set_HelpLink(String*);
protected:
   int get_HResult();
   void set_HResult(int);
public:
   virtual Exception* get_InnerException();
   virtual String* get_Message();
   virtual String* get_Source();
   virtual String* get_StackTrace();
   virtual Exception* GetBaseException();
   virtual void GetObjectData(SerializationInfo* info,
                              StreamingContext* ctx);
};
```

You have seen *ISerializable*. Because *Exception* implements *ISerializable* (and has an appropriate constructor), exceptions can be serialized. When you call a remote object via .NET remoting and that object throws an exception, the exception is serialized and passed via the remoting channel to the calling code, where it is rethrown.

Exceptions can be created based on other exceptions. This arrangement means that if your code catches an exception that it cannot handle, it can create a new exception based on the exception it has caught and add its own description string. This system allows code to build up a list of exceptions, each of which can be accessed through the *InnerException* property.

10. And even static variables to hold the last reported error.

```
// Get Exception* e from somewhere.
while (e != 0)
{
   Console::WriteLine(e->Message);
   e = e->InnerException;
}
```

Managed C++ uses the same keywords as native C++ to guard code that can generate exceptions.

```
StreamReader* txt;
try
{
   txt = File::OpenText(S"file.txt");
}
catch(FileNotFoundException* fnfe)
{
   Console::WriteLine(S"cannot find file");
   throw new Exception(S"cannot process file", fnfe);
}
catch(Exception* e)
{
   Console::WriteLine(S"some other reason");
   throw;
}
```

If the file data.txt does not exist, a *FileNotFoundException* will be thrown. This exception is caught by the first *catch* clause, which prints out a diagnostic message and then throws a new exception based on the caught exception. The second *catch* clause behaves like the unmanaged C++ *catch(...)* to catch all exceptions not caught by the earlier *catch* clause. Clearly, you should arrange exception handling so that the more generic exceptions are caught lower down in the list of handlers, and the C++ compiler will warn you if you catch an exception type that is higher in the inheritance tree than other exceptions caught lower in the catch handler list. Managed C++ allows you to use exception specification on methods, but there is no concept of exception specifications in .NET, so they are ignored. However, I find exception specifications a great documentation device.

```
__gc class Test()
{
public:
   Test() throw()
   {}
   void f(int x) throw(ArgumentException*)
   {
      if (x < 0)
         throw new ArgumentException(S"x must be >= 0");
```

```
        // Use x.
    }
};
```

Earlier I deliberately ignored the issue of throwing *__value* types as exceptions. You can throw *__value* types as long as you box the value first, as shown here:

```
try
{
    throw __box(42);
}
catch(Object* o)
{
}
```

Notice that to catch the exception, the catch handler catches an *Object** pointer. I do not like this code because the exception is not based on *System::Exception*, which means that you lose the ability to nest exceptions. Another drawback is that because most code will have an exception handler for *Exception**, most code will miss your boxed *__value* type exception, which means that your exception will propagate up the stack. It is best not to throw exceptions like this.

Constructors cannot return values, so if a constructor does not succeed, the only way that you can inform the caller is to throw an exception. If you throw an exception from the constructor of a managed class, the instance will not be created. Thus, the caller will get a *null* pointer. It is important that if a class's constructor could throw an exception, you check the pointer returned to make sure that it is not *null*.

```
FileInfo* info;
try
{
    info = new FileInfo(strFileName);
}
catch(Exception*)
{
    // Handle the exception.
}
if (info != 0)
{
    Console::WriteLine(S"{0} is {1} bytes",
                        info->Name, __box(info->Length));
}
```

In this code, information about a file *strFileName* can be obtained through a *System::IO::FileInfo* object. If the variable *strFileName* is the empty string, the constructor of this class will throw an *ArgumentException* exception and the *info* variable will be zero.

Once caught in a catch handler, the exception will not propagate further. To propagate the exception outside of this guarded block, you need to rethrow it, using either a new exception or the same one.

```
StreamReader* txt;
try
{
   txt = File::OpenText(S"file.txt");
}
catch(Exception* e)
{
   Console::WriteLine(S"some other reason");
   throw;
}
```

The handler in this example prints out a diagnostic message, but because it does not want to handle the exception, the code rethrows the exception by calling *throw* with no parameter. Managed C++ does not support rethrowing an exception outside of a *catch* handler, and if you try to do so, the exception will be treated as a generic exception and will be caught as an *SEHException*.

```
void ThrowException()
{
   throw;
}
void Test(Object* o)
{
   try
   {
      try
      {
         if (o == 0)
            throw new NullReferenceException;
         // Use o here.
      }
      catch(Exception*)
      {
         ThrowException();
      }
   }
   catch(SEHException* e)
   {
   }
```

```
    catch(NullReferenceException* e)
    {
    }
}
```

In this code, a separate method is used to rethrow the exception. However, although the exception would appear to be a *NullReferenceException*, it will actually be thrown as an *SEHException*. If the exception is rethrown from the original *catch* handler, it will be rethrown as the original type *NullReference-Exception*.

It is usually a good idea to rethrow exceptions if the method returns values. The reason can be seen in this code:

```
void Errant(int& i)
{
    i = 99;
    throw new Exception("ignore my results");
}
void CallErrant()
{
    int j = 0;
    try
    {
        Errant(j);
    }
    catch (Exception*)
    {
    }
    Console::WriteLine("j has the value {0}", __box(j));
}
```

The code calling *Errant* passes a parameter by reference. The method initializes this reference and then throws an exception. Because *Errant* has thrown an exception, any results from this method are suspect—something exceptional has happened. This code is bad because it catches the exception and then attempts to use the results.

You can also define a *finally* handler. This is code that is called whenever code guarded by *try* is left, regardless of whether this is due to an exception, a call to return from the method, or the end of the *try* block being reached. Managed C++ reuses the *__finally* keyword from Win32 structured exception handling.

```
StreamReader* txt;
try
{
    txt = File::OpenText(S"file.txt");
    Console::WriteLine(txt->ReadToEnd());
}
```

```
catch(FileNotFoundException* fnfe)
{
   Console::WriteLine(S"cannot find file");
   throw new Exception(S"cannot process file", fnfe);
}
catch(Exception* e)
{
   Console::WriteLine(S"some other reason");
   throw;
}
__finally
{
   if (txt != 0) txt->Close();
}
```

This code ensures that the file is closed when it is no longer being used. If an exception is thrown during the call to *OpenText*, the *txt* reference will be zero but the *__finally* clause will still be executed, hence the reason for the check on this pointer. If the file is successfully opened but an exception is thrown when reading the file, the *catch* handler will be executed first before the *__finally* clause is executed. If the file is successfully opened and the call to read from the file succeeds, *__finally* is still called. This means that the file is always closed correctly.

The alternative is to call *Close* outside of the guarded block, but this arrangement means that if an exception is thrown, *Close* will not be called (because the exception handlers rethrow the exception). Instead, the reference to the object will be lost when the stack frame is unwound, and eventually the garbage collector will do a collection, which will result in a call to the *Finaliser* on the *StreamReader* object, which will eventually call *Close*.

This behavior of the stack unwinding differs from unmanaged C++. If you have stack instances of *__nogc* classes, the destructors of these objects will be called when the stack frame is unwound. .NET objects do not really have destructors, so although the local reference to the object will disappear when the stack is unwound, the objects created by code in that stack frame will not necessarily be destroyed. This destruction occurs when the garbage collector decides to perform garbage collection.

You can specify a generic function to catch unhandled unmanaged exceptions with the *_set_se_translator* method. .NET has an equivalent of this method through the *AppDomain::UnhandledException* event. As the name suggests, this event will catch any exception thrown from any thread that is running in the application domain that has not been caught. The event is really a case of post-mortem handling. There is little chance of allowing your process to continue running, but it does at least allow you to prevent the standard exception handling from generating a dialog that might frighten your users. If an exception is thrown by the main thread of your process, it will be passed to the JIT debugger before being passed to the unhandled exception handler. These concepts are described in Chapter 3 and Chapter 7.

Unmanaged Exceptions

If you call unmanaged code, for example, through platform invoke (PInvoke), that code might throw an exception. This exception will be propagated as a native structured exception. Your code can catch these exceptions. The .NET Framework tests the type of exception that is thrown and attempts to create a suitable .NET Framework exception object. If there is not a suitable .NET Framework exception, *SEHException* is used. This exception class does very little work for you. It does have a member named *ErrorCode*, but this merely returns 0x80004004 (*HRESULT E_FAIL*). You can call *Marshal::GetExceptionCode*, which will return the SEH exception code, and *Marshal::GetExceptionPointers* to get the Win32 *EXCEPTION_POINTERS* structure, which enables you to determine the code that threw the exception and the state of the CPU registers. Be aware that this method returns an *IntPtr*, so you are responsible for extracting the information out of an unmanaged structure. More details will be given in Chapter 2 (in the section "Exceptions").

Your code can throw and catch native C++ exceptions.

```
try
{
   f();
   throw 42;
}
catch(int x)
{
}
catch(Exception* e)
{
}
```

The compiler will generate both .NET and native C++ handling for this code. If method *f* is managed and throws an exception, the exception will be caught by the final exception handler. If *f* does not throw an exception, the native exception will be thrown (through a method named *_CxxThrowException* that the compiler adds to your assembly). By default, the */GX-* switch is used when the compiler is invoked from the command line—that is, unwind semantics are not enabled, so code such as this example will have to use one of the */EH* switches. Because the Standard Template Library (STL) can catch and throw exceptions, you must use one of the */EH* switches if you use STL in your unmanaged code.

Implementing .NET Types

So far in this chapter, I have explained the basic features of .NET, how they relate to C++, and how to implement them in managed C++. In this section, I will look at details of implementing hierarchies of .NET objects in C++.

Namespaces

Both C++ and .NET use namespaces for expressing logical grouping. Declaring a namespace is straightforward, as shown here:

```
namespace RTG
{
   namespace Diagnostics
   {
      __gc class Log {};
   }
}
```

This code declares a class with the .NET name of *RTG.Diagnostics.Log*. Note that I say this is the *.NET name* of the class: if you get the type object of the class and call *ToString*, you'll get *RTG.Diagnostics.Log* with dots separating the items in the name.

```
Type* t = __typeof(RTG::Diagnostics::Log);
Console::WriteLine(t->ToString());  // prints RTG.Diagnostics.Log
Console::WriteLine(t->Namespace);   // prints RTG.Diagnostics
Console::WriteLine(t->Name);        // prints Log
```

The *Log* class is declared in the *RTG::Diagnostics* namespace. To declare aggregated names like this, you have to use this nested syntax; you can declare types in the outer declared namespaces.

```
namespace RTG
{
   __gc class Utility{};
   namespace Diagnostics
   {
      __gc class Log{};
   }
}
```

Now I have two namespaces, *RTG* and *RTG::Diagnostics*. To use a class, you have to use the C++ name.

```
RTG::Diagnostics::Log* log  = new RTG::Diagnostics::Log;
```

This requirement is true of the classes that you define and of .NET Framework classes. C++ provides several ways to reduce your typing—for example, you can use the *using* statement to indicate the default namespace for the compiler to check for items, as shown here:

```
using namespace RTG;
using namespace RTG::Diagnostics;
```

Again, the name is the C++ name for the namespace, not the .NET name. Incidentally, you cannot split namespaces, so although I have used *using* on the namespace *RTG*, I cannot refer to *Log* as *Diagnostics::Log*. C++ allows you to define namespace aliases.

```
namespace interop = System::Runtime::InteropServices;

void main()
{
   int bytes = interop::Marshal::SystemDefaultCharSize;
   Console::WriteLine(S"characters on this system are {0} bytes",
      __box(bytes));
}
```

Here I have defined *interop* as an alias for a .NET namespace, which saves me typing a long line to access the static property *Marshal::SystemDefaultCharSize*, but it also protects me because I am using the fully qualified name. C++ also allows you to group classes from different namespaces in a new namespace.

```
namespace Utility
{
   using interop::Marshal;
   using System::Type;
}
```

Now I can call *Marshal* and *Type* through the new namespace *Utility*. However, I think this strategy is confusing, especially for .NET Framework classes.

Namespaces are logical groupings. They do not give an indication of the actual location of the code. Namespaces can span assemblies—for example, most of the classes in the *System* namespace are in the *mscorlib* assembly, but other types in the namespace are implemented in other assemblies. For example, the *System::Uri* class is implemented in the *System* assembly, so if you want to use this class, you have to make sure that you have an appropriate *#using* statement. If you compile code and you get errors that certain types are *undeclared identifiers*, you have two possible reasons: either the compiler cannot find the type from the namespaces mentioned in the *using* namespace statements you have given (test this possibility by using the fully qualified name for the type), or you do not have the metadata for the type. In the latter case, you have to check the documentation to determine the assembly in which the type is implemented. Consider this example:

```
#using <mscorlib.dll>

void main()
{
   System::Uri* url =
      new System::Uri(S"http://www.microsoft.com");
   System::Console::WriteLine(S"The host is {0}", url->Host);
}
```

This code will not compile. The compiler will give errors indicating that *Uri* is an undeclared identifier. Because I use fully qualified names, the problem must be due to metadata. In fact, the *Uri* class is implemented in the *system* assembly, so the errors will go away if I add this line to the source file:

```
#using <system.dll>
```

Inheritance

.NET supports only single implementation inheritance, which means that any *__gc* classes that you define can have only one *__gc* base class (although it can *implement* more than one *__gc* interface). All class derivation in .NET is public; there is no concept of private or protected inheritance as there is in unmanaged C++. However, you still have to explicitly specify that you are deriving from a base class or implementing an interface through public inheritance.

```
// bases.cpp
__gc __interface IInterface
{ };
__gc class BaseWithItf
   : public IInterface  // Interfaces only supported through
                        // public inheritance
{ };
__gc class DerivedWithItf
   : public BaseWithItf // Base classes only supported through
                        // public inheritance
{ };
```

Class hierarchies are useful because they allow you to put common code in base classes. These base classes can be concrete or they can be abstract through the *__abstract* keyword or through C++ pure virtual syntax, which still results in an abstract .NET class.

If the base class has no constructors, the compiler will generate a default constructor (one without parameters) that calls *System::Object*. The compiler will add code in the derived class constructors to call the default base class constructor. (The default base class constructor will be called first, before the call to

System::Object.) You can choose to call a nondefault constructor in the same way that you do in unmanaged C++.

```
// bases.cpp
__gc class Base
{
   int m_i;
public:
   Base()       : m_i(0){}
   Base(int i) : m_i(i) {}
};

__gc class Derived : public Base
{
public:
   Derived(int i) : Base(i){}
};
```

If a derived class overrides a base class method, the derived class can call the base class version of the method as long as the derived class has a suitable access. To call the base class version of the method, you call the method qualified with the base class name. Visual C++ introduces a new keyword for calling a method on the immediate base class: *__super*, shown here:

```
__gc class Base
{
public:
   void f() {}
};

__gc class Derived : public Base
{
public:
   f()
   {
      __super::f();
      // Same as calling Base::f();
   }
};
```

This keyword is more useful for unmanaged Active Template Library (ATL) attribute-injected code, and the keyword will allow you to call only the immediate base class, but it is a syntax that you might see in managed code.

The C++ rules of converting derived class pointers to base class pointers apply to *__gc* classes: the conversion is implicit. However, if you have a base class pointer, you must cast it to get a derived class pointer. I'll cover the C++ cast operators in the section "Cast Operators" later in this chapter. Of course, managed arrays are .NET objects. As I mentioned earlier, a pointer to an array is typed according to the items in the array. A pointer to an array of a derived class can be cast to an array pointer of the base type. However, assigning a member of the array uses the runtime type. For example:

```
void CreateControls(Control* ctrls[])
{
   ctrls[0] = new Button;
   ctrls[1] = new TextBox;
   ctrls[2] = new Control;
}
```

This code uses the *System::Windows::Forms* classes. The *Button* and *TextBox* class both derive from *Control*, so the code in *CreateControls* looks fine because a *Button** or a *TextBox** can be implicitly converted to a *Control**. The compiler is happy. However, a *Button*[]* can also be converted to a *Control*[]*, so calling code could do this:

```
// calling code
Button* buttons[] = new Button*[3];
CreateControls(buttons);
```

The compiler is still happy: this code creates an array of *Button** and passes this array to *CreateControls* where there is an implicit conversion to a *Control*[]*. The runtime type of each element of the array is *Button**, so in *CreateControls*, a run-time error will occur when attempting to put a *TextBox** and even a *Control** into the array.

.NET allows you to derive from a type in another assembly, and that assembly can be written in any .NET language. Indeed, other languages can derive from the non *__sealed* classes you write in C++. Of course, for other languages to be able to do this derivation, the type has to be accessible outside of the assembly.

Exporting and Importing Types

You can create executable assemblies and library assemblies—also known as EXEs and DLLs. A DLL is useful only if the types are visible to code outside of the assembly. There are three categories of types in .NET: *public* types, which are visible outside of an assembly, *private* types, which are accessible only within the assembly, and *nested* types (types nested within other types), in which the visibility is controlled by its enclosing type.

Visibility

In C++, you specify that a type is a public or private type by applying either the *public* keyword or the *private* keyword, as shown here:

```
public __gc class A{};
private __gc class B{};
__gc class C{};
```

The default visibility is private, so in the previous code, only the type *A* is visible outside of the assembly. When I say *visible*, I do not mean that you will never be able to "see" a private type. The visibility of a type is a .NET attribute accessible through reflection; for a public non-nested type, *Type::IsPublic* is *true*, whereas for a private non-nested type, *Type::IsNotPublic* is *true*. Thus, if you use ILDASM to look at an assembly, you'll be able to see any private types in the assembly. The C++ linker uses .NET visibility when determining which code to put in the final assembly. All public types will be linked, but only private types used by a public type (directly or indirectly) will be linked. So, if you view your assembly with ILDASM and see that a private type is not in the assembly, it is because it is not used in your code.

Private types will not be accessible outside of the assembly when called using metadata. You use *#using* to import metadata from an assembly, but only public types will be imported. Note that I said only public types from the *assembly* can be imported using the *#using* statement. Modules (usually housed in .netmodule files) are part of an assembly, so if you specify a module with *#using*, all types in the module are available to the code in the file in which the *#using* statement resides. Similarly, if you specify an .obj file with *#using*, you'll get access to all types in the file, which will be linked into the final assembly.

Because private types are available through reflection, if you are willing to write the reflection code, you will have access to it. For example, here's the code for a library DLL:

```
//compile with cl /clr /LD lib.cpp
#using <mscorlib.dll>
private __gc class B
{
public:
   void f()
   { System::Console::WriteLine(S"called B"); }
};
public __gc class A
{
   // Reference an instance of B so that the optimizer does
   // not remove the type from the DLL.
   A(){B* b = new B;}
};
```

On the surface, this code implies that only type *A* is accessible outside of the assembly. However, the following code accesses the type through reflection:

```
// Compile with cl /clr libuser.cpp.
#using <mscorlib.dll>
using namespace System;
using namespace System::Reflection;

void main()
{
   AppDomain* ad = AppDomain::CurrentDomain;
   Object* obj;
   obj = ad->CreateInstanceAndUnwrap(S"lib", S"B");
   Type* t = obj->GetType();
   MethodInfo* m;
   BindingFlags bf = (BindingFlags)(BindingFlags::Instance
                                    | BindingFlags::Public);
   m = t->GetMethod(S"f", bf);
   m->Invoke(obj, 0);
}
```

The *CreateInstanceAndUnwrap* method on the application domain will load the specified type in the specified assembly. The name used is the display name of the assembly. Because in this example I have not given the library assembly a version or a culture and I have not signed the assembly, the display name is simply the name of the DLL without the extension. (I will explain in detail how to apply a version, a culture, and a public key to an assembly in Chapter 5.) *CreateInstanceAndUnwrap* accesses the type whether or not it is public, and once an instance has been created, it is relatively easy to access the members of the class. Note that the *BindingFlags* used in *GetMethod* refers to the member, not the type.

What you cannot do is call the type through a typed pointer. You cannot use a *B** pointer because the metadata for this type is not available. (Only metadata from public types can be imported from a library assembly through *#using*.)

I am not suggesting that you regularly call code in this manner. The point I am trying to make is that even though the type is private, it is still accessible if you are willing to write the code.

Member Access

Visibility of a type is only part of the information needed to determine if you can access members of the type. .NET defines six[11] levels of access on members of a class. All levels are available to C++ code. Member access is specified using the C++ *public*, *protected*, and *private* keywords. Clearly there are not enough keywords for the number of access levels, so C++ uses a combination of these three keywords. Table 1-4 shows these combinations.

11. The ECMA spec actually gives seven levels, but the level that I have left out of Table 1-5, *privatescope*, is not put on class members by the C++ compiler.

Table 1-4 Member Access Specifiers in C++

Access Level	Metadata Attribute	Assembly Accessibility	External Accessibility
public public	*public*	*public*	*public*
public protected	*famorassem*	*public*	*protected*
public private	*assembly*	*public*	*private*
protected protected	*family*	*protected*	*protected*
protected private	*famandassem*	*protected*	*private*
private private	*private*	*private*	*private*

If the access level has a repeated keyword, you can omit the second word. Thus, *public* can be used instead of *public public*. As you can see, there are only six of the possible nine combinations. In fact, the order that you give the keywords in the access level is unimportant: the most restrictive accessibility always determines the visibility to code outside the assembly.

Consider this code:

```
public __gc class Base
{
protected protected:
   void f(){}
protected private:
   void g(){}
};
```

This class can be used as a base class for a class within this assembly or within another assembly. This ability is controlled by the *public* keyword on the type. If I had used the *private* keyword on the type, only classes within this assembly would be able to derive from this class. The member *f* is marked as *protected protected* (or simply, *protected*), which means that code within the same assembly as this class can access this member as long as that code is part of a class that derives from this class. The *protected protected* keywords also mean that if a class in another assembly derives from this class, that class can also access this member. This type of access is why the metadata for this access level is named *family*: any code that is part of the family can access this member. The member *g* is marked as *protected private*, which means that only code in a class derived from this class that is in the same assembly as this class can access this member. This type of access is why this access level is named *famandassem* (in the same family *and* in the same assembly).

C++ has keywords that bend the C++ rules of member accessibility. These keywords, such as the *friend* keyword, are not allowed in managed C++. Friends are not allowed, and you cannot change the accessibility with the *using* directive.

However, you can change accessibility by deriving from a class—a member of a derived class can have a wider accessibility than the member it overrides.

Finally, access levels are applicable only to code used through normal binding. If you decide to call code through reflection, you can access nonpublic members.

Nested Types

You can define a type within an existing type. The new type is a nested type. Nested types do not have a visibility; they take the visibility of the enclosing type, which means that a nested type cannot be more accessible than the type that it is defined in. Because a nested type is a member of its enclosing type, you can apply a member access specifier to the nested type. Thus, you can make the nested type less accessible than its enclosing type.

All *__gc* and *__value* types can have *__gc* types, *__value* types, enums, and delegates as nested types. Managed interfaces cannot be a nested type, neither in a *__gc* or *__value* type, nor in another managed interface; managed interfaces cannot have a nested *__gc* or *__value* type, other than an enum. The name of a nested type is scoped by the enclosing type, not the assembly, so two enclosing types can have nested types with the same name.

```
public __gc class Outer
{
public:
   __gc class Inner
   {
   public:
      __value enum VALUES {One, Two};
   };
protected protected:
   __gc class Inner2
   {
   };
};
```

In this example, there is a public class named *Outer*, which is visible to code outside of this assembly. Within this class is another class named *Inner*, which is also visible outside of the assembly, but because it is a public member of the class, it is also accessible outside of the assembly. The *Outer* class also has a member named *Inner2*, which is declared as *protected protected*, so it too is visible outside of the assembly (it gets this visibility from its enclosing type's visibility), but *Inner2* is accessible only by code derived from the enclosing type (within the same assembly or in another assembly).

In C++, the name of the nested type is scoped by the C++ resolution operator, ::. Thus, *VALUES* is named *Outer::Inner::VALUES*, and code outside of the enclosing type must use this qualified name. However, metadata uses a different naming scheme. The code

```
Type* t = __typeof(Outer::Inner::VALUES);
Console::WriteLine(t->ToString());
```

will print

```
Outer+Inner+VALUES
```

at the command line. If you are likely to access members through reflection, you should be aware that metadata uses + as the scoping operator. Furthermore, MSIL uses a forward slash as the scoping operator for nested types, so the MSIL for the previous code looks like this:

```
ldtoken Outer/Inner/VALUES
call class [mscorlib]System.Type
   [mscorlib]System.Type::GetTypeFromHandle(
      valuetype [mscorlib]System.RuntimeTypeHandle)
callvirt instance string [mscorlib]System.Type::ToString()
call void [mscorlib]System.Console::WriteLine(string)
```

The accessibility of a nested type is given by the accessibility of the member within the enclosing type. Thus, *VALUES* has the metadata *nested public* applied to it because it is a *nested* member of *Inner* and it is a *public* member of this type. If you test the metadata of a nested type, you should test the appropriate *IsNested* metadata.

```
Type* t = __typeof(Outer::Inner::VALUES);
Console::WriteLine(S"IsPublic {0}", __box(t->IsPublic));
Console::WriteLine(S"IsNotPublic {0}", __box(t->IsNotPublic));
Console::WriteLine(S"IsNestedPublic {0}", __box(t->IsNestedPublic));
```

This code gives *true* for *IsNestedPublic* but *false* for the other two tests.

Nested types can derive from the outer type, but in C++, the nested type must be defined outside of the class.

```
public __gc class OuterClass
{
public:
   __gc class InnerClass; // Forward reference
};

public __gc class OuterClass::InnerClass : public OuterClass
{
};
```

A nested type has access to all the members of the enclosing type. Thus, a nested type has access to private and protected static members, and if a nested type has an instance of the enclosing type, it has access to instance members too. However, the converse is not true: the enclosing type does *not* get access to protected and private members of nested types.

A *__gc* type can define a *__nogc* type as a nested type, but although *you* can access the nested type in *your* C++ code, it will not be visible nor accessible to any other code.

Using Types from Other Languages

When you import metadata from another assembly, you have no indication about the language that was used to write the code. This ability to use code written in other languages is one of the significant features of .NET. However, different languages have different keywords, so a C# developer can export a type that has the same name as a C++ keyword. C++ has a mechanism to use such types, to identify that the compiler treats them as types and not as the C++ keyword. For example, I could define this class in C#:

```
// C#
public class friend
{
   private string name;
   public friend(string n) {name = n;}
   // Other members
}
```

The problem is that *friend* is a C++ keyword, so the following code will not compile:

```
friend* f = new friend;
```

The C++ compiler will interpret the type name as the C++ *friend* keyword and will issue errors indicating that the use is incorrect. To get around this problem, C++ has the *__identifier* keyword, shown here:

```
__identifier(friend)* f = new __identifier(friend);
```

Now the C++ compiler treats these instances of the word *friend* as being the name of a type. The code will compile.

You can use *__identifier* anywhere a symbol is used, so you can use it on type names and members of types. You can also use it on type declarations within your own code.

Casts and Conversions

Much of the code you will write will be through typed pointers. However, some of the time you will get a generic pointer or a pointer to a base class. If this is the case, you will need to convert the pointer to a more specific pointer so that you can access the functionality that you require. .NET is strongly typed: object references are to a specific object of a specific type. You will not be able to call an object through a reference other than one in its class hierarchy.

Cast Operators

The most generic cast is a C-style cast. The C++ compiler will warn you whenever you use a C-style cast on object references. The reason for the warning is that no compile-time check is performed. If you attempt to cast to a pointer of another object type, at run time .NET will throw an exception. C-style casts are so simple and tempting to use, but .NET is the ideal reason to banish them in favor of C++ casts. Because C-style casts are so dangerous, the compiler will warn you (warning message C4303) when you use them on managed pointers. You should take this opportunity to use an appropriate C++ cast.

There are two types of casts that you'll perform. The first case is when you absolutely, utterly, and definitely know the type of the object and that the cast will succeed, in which case no run-time check is required. The other case is when you are not so sure, in which case you are happy for .NET to perform a type check for you.

The C++ *dynamic_cast*<> operator is used to convert pointers of related types. The runtime will check the type of the object to see whether the pointer that you request is to the object type or to a base class. If the cast fails, *dynamic_cast*<> will return 0. If you use *dynamic_cast*<>, you should ensure that you check the return value.

Managed C++ has a new operator named *__try_cast*<>. This operator behaves like *dynamic_cast*<>, except if the cast fails, an exception of type *InvalidCastException* is thrown. In terms of implementation, the only difference between *dynamic_cast*<> and *__try_cast*<> is that the former uses the IL *isinst*, whereas the latter uses *castclass*.

If you are sure that you know the runtime type of an object, you can use *static_cast*<>. This operator will convert between pointer types with no check at run time. (In the intermediate language, the object reference being cast is merely copied into the reference it is being cast to.) If the object being cast is a *__value* type, you can use *static_cast*<> only to convert it to a *System::Void** pointer.

Finally, C++ provides *reinterpret_cast*<> to convert between unrelated pointers. In general, this operator should not be used for object references. The C++ compiler will issue warning C4669 if you use this cast on a *__gc* pointer, which you should use as an indication that you should change the cast operator. This operator is useful for casts on pinned pointers, where your intention is usually to get an unmanaged pointer access to managed memory.

The *const* modifier is a C++ism, so although you can use it on your variables and method parameters, it has no effect on the .NET code generated. You use *const* to get the compiler to perform checks on how you use pointers.

```
void UseDataObject(const Data* pdata)
{
   pdata->x = 88;  // Error: object cannot be modified
}
```

In this code, I have decided that the method cannot modify the object passed to it. Making the object constant (prefixing the pointer with *const*) tells the compiler to check to see whether I make any attempt to modify the object. This code will not compile, but it is perfectly fine in terms of .NET. (If the parameter was declared *Data* const pdata*, the *pointer*, rather than the object, is constant.) When C++ sees *const*, it applies *Microsoft::VisualC::IsConstModifier* to the parameter, although interestingly, it is applied to the parameter in the same way whether *const* is used to make the pointer constant or to make the object constant. C++ allows you to cast away the effect of *const* using the *const_cast<>* operator.

Conversion Operators

The Common Language Specification defines two operators with the special names *op_Explicit* and *op_Implicit*. These operators are used for the conversion of one type to another type. *op_Explicit* is used when the conversion will lose data, and *op_Implicit* is used when no data is lost during the conversion. In most cases, in C++ code you will have to explicitly call these operators. Other CLS languages (such as C#) will call *op_Explicit* when a cast operator is used, and *op_Implicit* when it is not used.

These conversion operators are always static members of a class and either take an instance of the class as a parameter or return an instance of the class, depending on whether you are converting to another type or from another type. (Of course, conversion from another type can also be achieved with a constructor that takes a parameter of that type.) These operators are interesting because you can overload them based only on the return type.

Managed Operators

As I mentioned earlier, operators are used by CLS-compliant languages to implement certain language features. Languages are not required to implement nor are they required to call the operators if they exist (as can be seen with the conversion operators and C++). Operators are static members of a class, and they return the result of the operation, which is an instance of the class.

Operators defined on *__value* types behave as you would expect: the compiler will convert the use of the C++ operator into the appropriate method call. Operators on *__gc* types typically have to be called directly in C++ (through a method call), but other languages might allow you to use language operators.

Unary Operators

Unary operators have a single parameter. Because operators are static, the ++ and — are equivalent to the prefix ++ and — operators—that is, they return the new value. Table 1-5 lists the unary operators available in managed C++.

Table 1-5 Unary Operators

Operator	Description
op_Decrement	Decrement the object, equivalent to ++.
op_Increment	Increment the object, equivalent to --.
op_LogicalNot	Used for *Boolean* types to reverse the value.
op_UnaryNegation	Make the item negative (+).
op_UnaryPlus	Unary +.

Binary Operators

Binary operators take two parameters that are being combined with the operator. For example:

```
// operators.cpp
__value struct Complex
{
   int x; int y;
   Complex(int i, int j) : x(i), y(j) {}
   static Complex op_Addition(Complex lhs, Complex rhs)
   { return Complex(lhs.x + rhs.x, lhs.y + rhs.y); }
   String* ToString()
   {
      return String::Format(S"({0} + {1}j)", __box(x), __box(y));
   }
};

void main()
{
   Complex c1(1,2);
   Complex c2(2,3);
   Complex c3 = c1 + c2;
   Console::WriteLine(S"{0} + {1} = {2}",
      c1.ToString(), c2.ToString(), c3.ToString());
}
```

Table 1-6 lists the binary operators available in managed C++.

Table 1-6 Common Binary Operators

Operator	Description
op_Addition	Add two objects.
op_Assign	Create a new object with the value of another one.
op_BitwiseAnd	Perform a bitwise AND (&) on two objects.
op_BitwiseOr	Perform a bitwise OR (|) on two objects.
op_Division	Divide one object by another.
op_Equality	Test the value of two objects for equality.
op_ExclusiveOr	Perform a logical XOR (^) on two objects.
op_GreaterThan	Test to see if one object is greater than another.
op_GreaterThanOrEqual	Test to see if one object is greater than or equal to another.
op_Inequality	Test the value of two objects for inequality.
op_LeftShift	Left-shift the value the specified number of places.
op_LessThan	Test to see if one object is less than another.
op_LessThanOrEqual	Test to see if one object is less than or equal to another.
op_LogicalAnd	Perform a logical AND (&&) on two objects.
op_LogicalOr	Perform a logical OR (||) on two objects.
op_Modulus	Return the remainder after dividing one object by another (%).
op_Multiply	Multiply one object by another.
op_RightShift	Right-shift the value the specified number of places.
op_Subtraction	Subtract one object from another.

Creating and Destroying Objects

All *__gc* types must be created with *__gc* new. All *__gc* types can have a C++ destructor.[12] The C++ compiler will implement this as the method with the special name of *__dtor* that has the special purpose of being called when the operator *delete* is called. If your class does not have a destructor, you cannot call *delete* on that type. The destructor on a *__gc* type does not have the same meaning as a destructor on a *__nogc* type, and correspondingly, calling *delete* on a *__gc* type does not mean the same as calling *delete* on a *__nogc* type.

When you create an instance of a *__gc* type with *__gc new*, the instance is created on the managed heap and your code will get a pointer to that object, which represents a reference to the object. While you use that pointer, the garbage

12. *__value* types cannot have destructors.

collector knows that a *reference* is held to the object. When that pointer goes out of scope or if you assign zero to it, the garbage collector knows that the reference no longer exists to that object. If you copy the pointer in some way (pass the pointer to a method or do a pointer assignment), you have made another reference to the object. The lifetime of an object depends on the extant references and the amount of time until the garbage collector decides to perform garbage collection. (You can explicitly tell the garbage collector to perform garbage collection by calling *System::GC::Collect*.)

When the garbage collector determines that an object on the heap is no longer reachable from any pointer in your code, the object is a candidate for collection. In most cases, the garbage collector will merely reuse the object's memory. However, if the object implements *Object::Finalize*, there is some code that the object needs to have run just before the object is freed. During the collection, the garbage collector will identify such objects and schedule them to be called on a separate thread (the finalizer thread). This thread will go through each of these objects (in no specific order) and call its *Finalize* method. This action delays the final demise of these object still further.

In C++, you cannot define a *Finalize* method on an object; instead, you declare a destructor. When the compiler sees that your class has a destructor, it generates two methods, a public method named *__dtor* and the protected override of *Finalize*. Whatever way you declare your destructor, the compiler will always make *__dtor* virtual. This method is called when your code calls the *delete* operator or when your code calls the destructor directly—for example, with this class:

```
__gc class Test
{
public:
   void f(){}
   ~Test(){/* dtor code */}
};
```

I can call this code:

```
Test* t = new Test;
t->f();
delete t;
t->~Test();
t->__dtor();
t->f();
```

Notice that after I call *delete* on the pointer, the pointer is still valid. Indeed, it still remains valid after I call the destructor using C++ syntax and through the compiler-generated method. Unlike native C++, *delete* does not affect the pointer. In Managed C++, *delete* merely calls the destructor code. Of course, the code that you have in your destructor might invalidate the state of the object, so calling other methods on the object will have inherent dangers, but the object itself is still valid.

The compiler places the code that you write in your destructor into the generated *Finalize* method. Thus, this code will be called when the object is eventually called by the finalizer thread. The *__dtor* method looks like this:

```
virtual void __dtor()
{
   System::GC::SuppressFinalize(this);
   Finalize();
}
```

This code calls the *Finalize* method (which contains the code that you put in the destructor). When this method is called, it means that your cleanup code has already been called, so you do not want the garbage collector to do this again. This is why *__dtor* calls *SuppressFinalize*. Because the object still exists after the destructor has been called (and indeed, unless you assign the pointer to zero, a reference will still exist to the object), you can still access the object. If the object relies on resources that might have been released in the destructor, you will need to reinitialize these resources before object methods can be called, but because *SuppressFinalize* has been called, the garbage collector will not now call the *Finalize* method. The solution to this issue is to call *ReRegisterForFinalize* in the method that reinitializes these resources. It is a good idea not to allow objects to be used like this. Indeed, as you will see in Chapter 4, objects that hold onto resources should implement an interface called *IDisposable*, and once disposed, such an object should throw an *ObjectDisposedException*.

If your class has a base class that also has a *Finalize* method (for example, if it was written in C++ with a destructor), the destructor for your class will call the base class *Finalize* after your class's *Finalize* has been called.

This behavior of the destructor, prolonging the lifetime of your objects, is a problem, and you should try to avoid it where possible. To do so often requires rethinking the problem to avoid holding onto resources for the lifetime of the object. Instead, retain the resources only as long as you need them. Another trick that you can employ—which I will investigate further in Chapter 2—is that destructors on unmanaged classes are called just as you will expect them to be. So you can create temporary objects on the stack, and when the object is destroyed, its destructor is called. You can write unmanaged classes that hold managed pointers as data members—obtained in the constructor and released in the destructor, but I will leave details about that for Chapter 2.

Like native C++, when a *__gc* class is created, an appropriate constructor is called on the base class. (This will be the default constructor, but you can specify another constructor.) The default constructor on *System::Object* will be called before any code that you specify in your class's constructor is called. If your class has virtual methods and a base class constructor calls these methods, there will be no problems even though officially the object has not been called yet. The reason is that the object's members will be initialized to zero before any constructors are called, so they will have valid values. Indeed, in contrast to native C++, the vtable for an object is created before a constructor is called, so it is safe to call virtual methods.

Entry Points

When you compile your code, the compiler will assume that you will use the CRT, in which case the entry point will be *mainCRTStartup*. This function calls your *main* function, passing the command-line arguments. The command-line arguments will be available through a *char** pointer or *wchar_t** pointer array depending on whether the code was compiled with the *UNICODE* symbol defined. These parameters are always unmanaged, so if you want to use them in your code, you will have to convert these strings to managed strings. (*System::String* has two constructors that take a *char** pointer or a *wchar_t** pointer parameter.) Because *main* is the function that you are used to using in traditional C programs, you can expect to get the same parameters. For example, the following are all valid signatures for the entry point of a managed console process:

```
void main();
int main();
int main(int argc, char* argv[]);
int wmain(int argc, wchar_t* argv[]);
int main(int argc, char* argv[], char* envp[]);
int wmain(int argc, wchar_t* argv[], wchar_t* envp[]);
```

Also, you can link with setargv.obj, and the command-line arguments will be treated as file specifications with the wildcards * and ? expanded.

If you will not use the CRT and do not have any global native C++ objects, you do not need to initialize the CRT and you can make *main* your entry point.

```
cl /clr mycode.cpp /link /entry:main
```

The code that loads the application will assume that the *main* function takes no parameters, so you do not have access to the traditional parameters of the C *main* function: *argc* and *argv*. If you want to get the command line, you can call *Environment::CommandLine* to get the command line as one string, and *Environment::GetCommandLineArgs* to get an array of the command-line arguments. In both cases, the first argument will be the command name that you used to start the process. You can call *Environment::GetEnvironmentVariables* to get a dictionary (a name-value associative container) of the environment variables.

Command-line processes can return an integer to the operating system that is often used as an error level.[13] You can return a value back from your managed entry point, or you can call the managed *Environment::Exit* with the error level.

Your assembly can be a GUI application, which means that the PE file must be marked as such so that a console is not created when it is run, and your application must have a *WinMain* entry point. I will leave a more detailed description until Chapter 4, but here I will simply say that if you add *WinMain* to your code, the compiler will use this function as the entry point and the linker will ensure that it uses the */SUBSYSTEM:WINDOWS* switch. If the assembly is a library, your code does not need an entry point—the assembly is loaded by the .NET Fusion technology and not the *LoadLibraryEx* function.[14] So you do not need a *DllMain*. By default, you'll get a *_DllMainCRTStartup* function to initialize the CRT. If you do not need the CRT, you can use the */noentry* linker switch to remove the *_DllMainCRTStartup* function.

Summary

.NET is touted as having a *common language runtime*. In fact, the runtime will execute only one language, Microsoft intermediate language, but the assemblies that contain the MSIL can be created by any .NET language and any .NET language can use types in .NET assemblies. The Managed Extensions for C++ allow you to use C++ to write .NET code—code that implements and uses .NET types.

Managed C++ extends the language with new keywords that allow you to specify that a class is a .NET class and allow you to add metadata to the class and its members. Code that does not have these new keywords will be native C++, and instances of these types will not be managed by the .NET garbage collector, although in most cases, their code will be compiled to MSIL.

Managed C++ gives you all the .NET features that are available to other .NET languages, but it has all the power of a language that has always been regarded as the language of choice for power programming. The significant point about C++ is that it allows you to compile both managed and unmanaged types and to use native code all in the same project. This ability will be the topic of Chapter 2.

---

13. If you forget to return a value from the entry point, the compiler will automatically return zero. I don't recommend that you use this facility.

14. In fact, if your library assembly has a *DllMain* it will be called but only when the assembly is first loaded, when it is passed a value of *DLL_PROCESS_ATTACH*.

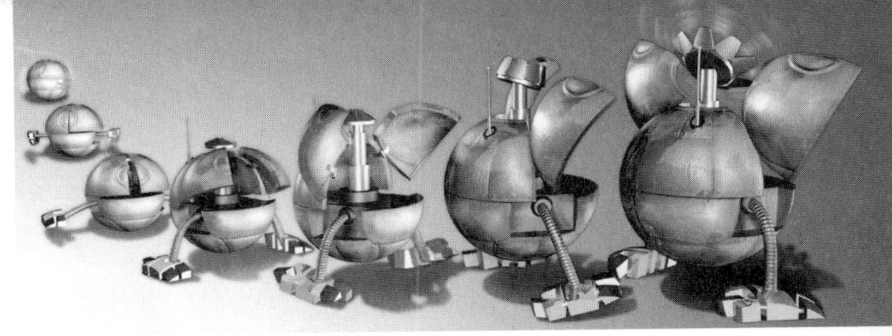

2

Interop

The current shipping version of .NET is built upon Win32, and the Microsoft .NET Framework classes make calls through to Win32 to perform their work. You, too, will sometimes need to make calls to Win32 or to your own native code exposed as COM objects, as C functions exported from a DLL, or as code in a static-link library. The .NET Framework supplies most of the facilities that you'll want to use, but some features have not found their way into the .NET Framework and you'll have to access native code to use them.

Native code runs outside of the control of the .NET runtime, so when you make calls to native code, you have to take into account that pointers are not tracked, memory is not garbage collected, and the .NET context is not available. Thus, object references cannot be passed to native code; instead, they have to be marshaled into a form that is suitable for native code. Collectively this process is named *interop*, and it allows you to call code outside of the embracing arms of .NET.

You might have your own libraries, and these could be written in a variety of languages and provided as COM, DLL-exported functions, static-link libraries, or even C++ template libraries. If this code is provided by a third party, you'll often have little choice other than to access that code through interop. If these libraries are written by your company, an argument is needed to port such code over to .NET. However, porting is not always a viable solution because you'll multiply the amount of effort that you'll put into testing and debugging the code—not only do you have to test your new code, but you also have to test your ported code. Furthermore, the .NET Framework is based on different paradigms than most Win32 code, and there is rarely a one-to-one equivalence. It is almost always better to use this code in the environment where it was originally designed and access it through interop.

When you execute code through interop, the native code has direct access to memory. This access is not tracked by the garbage collector, and code access security is not applied; code access security gives code permissions based on evidence provided by the code, which includes the code's source location. (See Chapter 5 for more details about code access security.) You get the advantage of increased performance because the .NET Framework does not make checks on native code (run-time type checks, code access checks, bounds checks on array indices, and so on), but you risk the associated danger that because these run-time checks are not performed, the code can modify memory that it does not own.

You can use interop in several ways, as described in the following list. I'll cover each approach in detail in the rest of this chapter.

- **It Just Works! (IJW)** This technology is available only through the Managed Extensions for C++. With IJW, you use native code directly. You do not need to add any other code; the compiler generates all the code to call to make the transition to native code.
- **Platform invoke** This technology is accessed through custom attributes, and it allows you to access code exported as C functions from a DLL.
- **COM interop** This technology allows you to access COM objects as if they were .NET objects and .NET objects as if they were COM objects.

COM interop allows you to use .NET types from unmanaged code as if they were COM objects. The .NET code will run in an apartment in the native process—the client code does not have to be compiled with a .NET-specific library. Of course, if the .NET code runs on the same machine as the client, you have to make sure that the code and the .NET Framework are deployed on the client machine. If the code is accessed remotely[1] or if it is installed as part of a COM+ application on a remote machine, the client machine need know nothing at all about .NET.

If you want to have more control in your native client, you can decide to create your own application domain and call .NET code from there. This strategy really makes sense only if you want to have more control over how application domains are created and over their run-time properties. I will cover the details of creating application domains and calling .NET components in those domains in Chapter 5.

---

1. Through sockets, SOAP, or ASP.NET, but not through .NET remoting, which requires the runtime on the client.

It Just Works!

Try this: Take any C++ application for which you have the source code, and in the make file, add the */clr* switch to the rule for C++ files. Compile the project. Now look at the application using ILDASM. You'll see that the code has compiled even though it knows nothing about .NET. You'll also see that the code will compile (mostly) to Microsoft intermediate language (MSIL) even though the code does not have managed types. The application will also run. You have not had to make any changes to your code to make it compile to MSIL and to be linked into a .NET assembly.

The compiler has ensured that IL calls native code from static-link libraries and functions imported from DLLs without any additions to the source code. You do not have to worry about the security aspects of accessing memory directly because the compiler marks your assembly in such a way that ensures that the user of the assembly must be explicitly deemed as being safe to use such code. (This process sounds dangerous, but as I'll explain in Chapter 5, it is not.) The compiler does all of this work for you; there is nothing else for you to do because It Just Works!

Let's take a closer look at how IJW achieves all of this.

Native C++ Classes

I mentioned in Chapter 1 that the compiler will attempt to compile all C++ to MSIL. (There are exceptions, which I listed in that chapter.) When the compiler comes across a type definition that is either marked explicitly as *__nogc* or a type not marked as *__gc,* the compiler knows that instances of this type are not managed by the garbage collector. Instances of this type can be created on the stack, can be passed either by value or by reference to native code, and can be created with the unmanaged *new* operator and deleted with the unmanaged *delete* operator. If you use the *new* or *delete* operators with these types, the compiler will add the unmanaged *new* and *delete* operators to the assembly—either the operators provided by the standard library or, if you define your own, your custom operators. If you provide custom operators as C++ source code, the compiler will attempt to add them as MSIL; if you use the standard library *new* operator, this operator will be added to your assembly as native code.

Although these native classes are compiled as MSIL, they are not *managed*. Thus, the normal rules of C++ apply: you must ensure that when the instance is no longer needed, you delete it, and that any memory held by the instance (or any COM pointers) should also be freed (most likely in the class destructor). Indeed, the destructor of a *__nogc* class created on the stack is called when the variable goes out of scope, just as you would expect with native C++, so you can use the destructor of a *__nogc* class to manage resources. The methods in these unmanaged classes can call any code in the .NET Framework and use managed types. They can also have managed types for parameters and return values. There is no issue here with the garbage collector because the managed pointers (and hence the lifetime of the reference they represent) passed to the methods are created on the stack, as are the pointers for managed types created in the methods. Because this code is MSIL, the runtime controls the stack. Unmanaged classes can have *__value* types or *__nogc* pointers to *__value* types as data members (as long as they follow the guidelines I give later in the section "Native Types") because the garbage collector does not track *__value* types. However, because the garbage collector cannot track pointers held as data members in unmanaged types, unmanaged types cannot have managed pointers as data members. I will return to this issue in the section "Managed Pointers in Unmanaged Types."

Unmanaged C++ is normal C++, so you can use multiple inheritance and you can define copy constructors, destructors, and conversion operators. However, if you use metadata from an assembly, those managed types will be available to your code (as long as your code can be compiled to MSIL). So long as you do not use managed types as data members, you can write unmanaged types that have managed types as function parameters and return values. For example, imagine that you have a method that looks like this:

```
// envvars.cpp
void DumpStrings(String* s[])
{
   for (int i = 0; i < s->Length; i++)
   {
      Console::WriteLine(s[i]);
   }
}
```

This code could be a global function or a member of a managed class. The method takes an array of strings and prints out each one. I could call the method like this:

```
String* str[] = {S"one", S"two", S"three"};
DumpStrings(str);
```

There is nothing new here; I have merely created a managed array of strings and passed it to the method. Now what happens if you have an array of unmanaged strings? The first issue is what is meant by *an array of unmanaged strings*. This term usually means an array of string pointers. Although the process of converting an unmanaged string pointer to a managed string pointer is straightforward (you simply pass the unmanaged string pointer to the constructor of *System::String*), there is the problem that an unmanaged array cannot be used in place of a managed array. Another interpretation of *an array of strings* could be a contiguous buffer that contains the actual characters of the strings; such a buffer is actually an array of characters. The Win32 function *::GetEnvironmentStrings* returns a buffer in this format. The buffer contains the current environment variables in the format *Name=Value*, where *Name* is the name of the variable and *Value* is its value. Each string is *NULL* terminated; the end of the array is identified by an empty string.

With this information, I can use the following class to convert such a buffer to an array of managed strings:

```
// envvars.cpp
__nogc class EnvVars
{
   typedef String* StrArray [];
   LPTSTR pv;
   int count;
public:
   EnvVars()
   {
      pv= static_cast<LPTSTR>(::GetEnvironmentStrings());
      LPTSTR str = pv;
      count = 0;
      while (true)
      {
         if (*str == 0) break;
         while (*str != 0) str++;
         str++;
         count++;
      }
   }
   ~EnvVars()
   {
      ::FreeEnvironmentStrings(pv);
   }
   operator StrArray()
   {
      String* strs[] = new String*[count];
      LPTSTR str = pv;
      for(int i = 0; i < count; i++)
      {
         strs[i] = new String(str);
         while (*str != 0) str++;
         str++;
      }
      return strs;
   }
};
```

The first point to make is that the class is *__nogc* and hence does not have any managed data members. The class is designed to convert the unmanaged buffer returned from *::GetEnvironmentStrings*. (This buffer is allocated in the constructor and freed in the destructor.) I want to use this class whenever a *String*[]* is expected, so I define a *typedef* for this type named *StrArray* and then declare a conversion operator. The conversion operator creates an array of the appropriate size and initializes each member with a managed string. The conversion from the unmanaged string to the managed string is performed using the *System::String* constructor.

Now I can pass an instance of *EnvVars* wherever a *String*[]* parameter is expected:

```
EnvVars vars;
DumpStrings(vars);
```

or I can even pass a temporary variable:

```
DumpStrings(EnvVars());
```

It is interesting to take a look at the code that the compiler generates for this class. Take a look at the method generated for the conversion operator:

```
.method public static string[] modopt(
   [mscorlib]System.Runtime.CompilerServices.CallConvThiscall)
   EnvVars..P$01AP$AAVString@System@@(
      valuetype EnvVars* modopt(
         [Microsoft.VisualC]Microsoft.VisualC.IsConstModifier)
         modopt([Microsoft.VisualC]
            Microsoft.VisualC.IsConstModifier) A_0)
    cil managed
```

The .NET Framework has specific naming rules about conversion operators on .NET types (*op_Explicit* and *op_Implicit*), which I covered in Chapter 1. Because this is not a .NET type, I have not followed these rules, so the compiler has treated the operator as an ordinary method. Also, because I have not given this method a name, the compiler has generated one. This method is named *EnvVars..P$01AP$AAVString@System@@()* and (like all methods on *__nogc* types) is declared as a static method at global scope, so to allow this method to have access to the *this* pointer of the object, a parameter of *EnvVars** is passed as the first parameter.

Native Types

In the previous section, a *__nogc* type that had data members was declared. Those data members were native types. In fact, you can use .NET types as data members as long as you follow some rules. Basically, an instance of a *__nogc* type can be passed to native (non-MSIL) code in which the garbage collector has no knowledge of what is happening to the instance. This arrangement could mean that the instance is copied or even deleted; therefore, *__nogc* types cannot hold managed types because the garbage collector will not be able to determine when object references are created or released. So there is an absolute rule that *__nogc* types cannot contain *__gc* pointers.

A *__nogc* type can contain a *__nogc* pointer to a *__value* type because a *__nogc* pointer means that the type is created on the unmanaged heap, so the memory is not the responsibility of the garbage collector. In practice, this also means that the *__value* type cannot have *__gc* pointers. The compiler does not warn you when you declare such a *__value* type in a *__nogc* type, but it will generate an error when you use *__nogc new* to create an instance of the *__value* type to initialize the *__nogc* pointer.

The default layout for a *__value* type is *LayoutKind::Auto*, which means that the runtime determines the format the type has in memory, how many bytes are taken up by each member, and the order of the members. Such a type cannot be an embedded data member in a *__nogc* type because the runtime will not have control over the enclosing object. Thus, if you want to have an embedded *__value* type in a *__nogc* type, you have to declare the *__value* type as *LayoutKind::Explicit* or *LayoutKind::Sequential*, as shown here:

```
__value struct A
{ int i; };
__value struct B
{ String* s; };
[StructLayout(LayoutKind::Sequential)]
__value struct C
{ int i; };
__nogc struct Unmanaged
{
   A __nogc* a; // OK
   B __nogc* b; // Compiles, but you cannot initialize it
   A p;         // Error, wrong layout
   C c;         // OK
};
```

If this code is compiled, you will get the rather unhelpful error C3265: "cannot declare a managed 'p' in an unmanaged 'Unmanaged'". Clearly, this message is not the complete reason because I was able to declare the member *c* in the unmanaged type. In this case, *managed* refers not to the garbage collector but to the fact that the layout specified indicates that the runtime manages its format in memory.

It is also worth pointing out that there is a bug in the current version of Visual C++ that requires the custom attribute *[StructLayout]* to be used on the classes of members of *__nogc* types. Even if the type has a sequential layout (ILDASM reports the *sequential* attribute on the type), the compiler will issue the C3265 error. This means that types such as *Int32*, *IntPtr*, and *GCHandle* (described in the section "Managed Pointers in Unmanaged Types") cannot be members of a *__nogc* type.

Implementation in Assemblies

When the compiler sees a *__nogc* type, it will compile it as MSIL, subject to the guidelines I gave in Chapter 1. However, the type will not be a class in .NET terms, so let's take a deeper look into what the compiler is actually doing.

An instance method of a native C++ class is called with *thiscall* calling convention[2]—that is, when the method is called, the first parameter will be the *this* pointer to the instance on which the call is made. The method can then use this pointer to access the other members of the instance. Members of .NET types (*__value* and *__gc* types) are called using *__clrcall*, the .NET runtime calling convention.[3] Consider this class:

```
__nogc class Test
{
   int x;
   int y;
public:
   Test(int i) : x(0), y(i) {}
   void f(int i){ y = i; }
};
```

The *Test* class is unmanaged, and so it cannot be created on the managed heap. In .NET, *__value* types are not created on the managed heap, and thus the C++ compiler declares the *__nogc* type *Test* as a *__value* type.

```
.class private sequential ansi sealed Test
       extends [mscorlib]System.ValueType
{
   .pack 1
   .size 8
   .custom instance void [Microsoft.VisualC]
    Microsoft.VisualC.DebugInfoInPDBAttribute::.ctor() =
       ( 01 00 00 00 )
}
```

The type has no methods! It has been declared merely to allocate the memory required by the data members of the type. The *.size* directive gives the number of bytes required, but it "flattens" out the memory. There are no explicit data members. To allow the class's methods to be called with *thiscall*, the compiler makes the *__nogc* class's methods global and simulates the calling convention by passing a pointer to the class as the first parameter.

2. You cannot declare a method with this calling convention; the compiler uses it automatically.

3. Again, you do not declare this.

```
.method public specialname static valuetype Test* modopt(
   [mscorlib]System.Runtime.CompilerServices.CallConvThiscall)
   Test.__ctor(valuetype Test* modopt(
      [Microsoft.VisualC]Microsoft.VisualC.IsConstModifier)
      modopt([Microsoft.VisualC]
         Microsoft.VisualC.IsConstModifier) A_0,
      int32 y) cil managed
{
   IL_0000:  ldarg.0
   IL_0001:  ldc.i4.0
   IL_0002:  stind.i4
   IL_0003:  ldarg.0
   IL_0004:  ldc.i4.4
   IL_0005:  add
   IL_0006:  ldarg.1
   IL_0007:  stind.i4
   IL_0008:  ldarg.0
}

.method public static void modopt(
   [mscorlib]System.Runtime.CompilerServices.CallConvThiscall)
   Test.f(valuetype Test* modopt(
      [Microsoft.VisualC]Microsoft.VisualC.IsConstModifier)
      modopt([Microsoft.VisualC]
         Microsoft.VisualC.IsConstModifier) A_0,
      int32 i) cil managed
{
   .maxstack  2
   IL_0000:  ldarg.0
   IL_0001:  ldc.i4.4
   IL_0002:  add
   IL_0003:  ldarg.1
   IL_0004:  stind.i4
   IL_0005:  ret
}
```

The names of these global methods are *Test.__ctor* and *Test.f*. In .NET terms, they are not members of the *Test* class. The constructor is used to initialize an existing instance of the *Test* class, which is why *Test.__ctor* has a pointer to a *Test* as the first parameter. Similarly, the *Test.f* method takes a pointer to a *Test* as its first parameter, which is in effect the *this* pointer. In both cases, the second parameter of the method is the data that the method will use. The IL in these methods loads the *Test** parameter onto the stack first so that the methods can access the members of the object. Because this parameter is a pointer, the runtime can perform pointer arithmetic with it. The *f* method uses the second parameter to initialize *Test::y*, the second member of the class, so the IL increments the *this* pointer by 4 bytes before storing the second parameter into the memory that the incremented pointer points to.

These methods are public; however, because they are global methods, the process to access them is not straightforward since *#using* imports only types. (I'll show you how to access these methods in the section "Global Methods.") These public static methods are effectively inaccessible to code outside the assembly, and furthermore, the type that is used for the first parameter, *Test*, is marked as *private* and so cannot be accessed outside the assembly.

I could have declared the *Test* class as a nested class within a *__gc* type. Again, the compiler will make the methods public global methods, but even if I give the *__nogc* class public access, the compiler will change the access to *nested assembly*. The reason for this change is that if the *__gc* type is public, *#using* can import the *__gc* type. If the *nested assembly* access was not applied, it would mean that code from outside the assembly would be able to access the unmanaged type.

Inheritance and Native Classes

The previous example shows that native C++ classes are implemented as value types, but value types are always sealed, so how is native class inheritance implemented? The C++ compiler will create a separate value type for each class in the hierarchy. These classes have no relationship in .NET terms. When an IL unmanaged pointer is cast, no type check is made, so a pointer to an instance of one unmanaged type can be passed when a pointer to the type's base class is needed, as shown in this example:

```
__nogc class TestChild : public Test
{
public:
   TestChild(int i) : Test(i) {}
};
```

The constructor needs to initialize the base class part of the instance, and the constructor does this by calling the base class constructor. When the constructor is called, it is passed a pointer to a *TestChild*. The IL generated by the compiler passes this pointer to *Test.__ctor* with no type check because it knows that in C++ terms the two types are related.

Native Virtual Methods

Native virtual methods are called at run time through a vtable. Each class will have a vtable that is initialized with pointers to the class's virtual methods. Each object will have a pointer to its vtable. When a virtual method is called through a pointer at run time, the vtable is obtained and the appropriate function pointer is located and invoked. It does not matter whether the pointer is the same type as the object or if the pointer is a base class pointer. To implement this behavior in IL, the C++ compiler creates a new value type that represents the vtable and adds a pointer to the vtable as the first data member of the value types that the compiler generates for your classes. (This pointer is essentially a vptr.) When your code makes a call to a virtual method, the IL accesses the vtable through this vptr and locates the method pointer. This pointer is then called with the MSIL opcode *calli*.

C++ Run-Time Type Information

If you use native code that calls *dynamic_cast*<>, run-time type information (RTTI) will be used to determine whether the cast is allowed. By default, RTTI is not enabled for compiling to MSIL, so you have to enable RTTI by using the */GR* switch. The compiler will add a value type named *_TypeDescriptor* and create static instances of this type, one instance for each unmanaged type that has RTTI. An address to the appropriate instance is stored in the vtable for the object. The cast at run time is performed by a function named *__RTDynamicCast*, which is added to your assembly as a native function. This function compares the values stored in the vtable for each object against the address of the static instances of the *_TypeDescriptor* objects to determine the object's type. This mechanism is the same as that used with native C++.

Templates

You cannot write templated code with managed types because .NET does not currently support generic programming. You can write templated code with unmanaged types, and those types will be compiled as MSIL. The mechanism is the same as with nontemplated classes: the compiler generates a value type to hold the data members, and the methods are added as global methods to the module.

Here's a very simple templated class:

```
// strtemp.cpp
template <typename charType>
class String
{
public:
   charType* ptr;
   String(charType* s)
   {
      ptr = new charType[strlen(s) + 1];
      strcpy(ptr, s);
   }
   ~String()   { delete [] ptr; }
   int strlen(){ return strlen(ptr); }
   static int strlen(charType* s)
   {
      int len = 0;
      while (s[len] != 0) len++;
      return len;
```

```
    }
    static void strcpy(charType* dest, charType* src)
    {
        while (*src != 0)
        {
            *dest = *src;
            dest++; src++;
        }
        *dest = *src;
    }
    void strrev()
    {
        int len = strlen();
        for (int i = 0; i < len/2; i++)
        {
            charType c = ptr[i];
            ptr[i] = ptr[len-i-1];
            ptr[len-i-1] = c;
        }
    }
};
```

If I use this class like so:

```
String<char> string("Hello");
string.strrev();
puts(string.ptr);
String<wchar_t> wstring(L"Hello");
wstring.strrev();
_putws(wstring.ptr);
```

the compiler will generate two value types, *String<char>* and *String<unsigned short>*, to hold the data members of the unmanaged types. For each type there will be a global member equivalent to the member in the C++ templated class—for example, the *strcpy* for the specialization based on *wchar_t* looks like this:

```
.method public static void modopt(
    [mscorlib]System.Runtime.CompilerServices.CallConvCdecl)
    'String<unsigned short>.strcpy'( unsigned int16* dest,
        unsigned int16* src) cil managed;
```

The important point is the name of the method, *String<unsigned short>.strcpy*. The specialization based on *char* has a similar method, named *String<char>.strcpy*. In other words, the unmanaged type is treated as part of the name of the method, but apart from that, there is nothing special about the global method.

CRT and Static-Link Libraries

The C run-time library (CRT) is provided through static-link libraries. These libraries either contain the actual CRT code that will be statically linked or are an import library for the DLL version of the CRT. You do have the source for the library, which will be loaded when you debug CRT code, but the actual build process links to the CRT static-link libraries. All .NET code is compiled as multithreaded, but you do have the option of using the CRT through static-linking the multithreaded CRT library or through the MSVCR70.dll library, so your code can be compiled with */MD* or */MT* (or the debug versions */MDd* or */MTd*). Code compiled with */clr* cannot be compiled with the single-threaded CRT, so you cannot use */ML* or */MLd*. Take a look at the following code:

```
#include <stdio.h>
void main()
{
   puts("Called Me");
}
```

ILDASM shows that the assembly has the following members:

```
.vtfixup [1] int32 fromunmanaged at D_0000904C // 06000001
.class private explicit ansi sealed $ArrayType$0x26c5351f
   extends [mscorlib]System.ValueType
.field public static valuetype $ArrayType$0x26c5351f
   '?A0x077cbc20.unnamed-global-0' at D_00009040
.method public static pinvokeimpl(/* No map */)
   unsigned int32  _mainCRTStartup() native unmanaged preservesig
.method public static int32 modopt(
   [mscorlib]System.Runtime.CompilerServices.CallConvCdecl)
   main() cil managed
.method public static pinvokeimpl(/* No map */)
   int32 modopt([mscorlib]
      System.Runtime.CompilerServices.CallConvCdecl)
   puts(int8 modopt(
        [Microsoft.VisualC]
              Microsoft.VisualC.NoSignSpecifiedModifier)
        modopt([Microsoft.VisualC]
              Microsoft.VisualC.IsConstModifier)* A_0)
   native unmanaged preservesig
```

From the discussion of strings in Chapter 1, you'll recognize the first two members as being, respectively, the declaration for the storage needed for the literal string and the actual instance that is initialized from the initialized data section of the PE file.

Let's return to the other members of the assembly. The first is the entry point *_mainCRTStartup*, which is added to initialize the CRT and global class instances. Your C++ entry point code is provided in *main*, which is called by *_mainCRTStartup*. Finally, there is *puts*, which is the CRT function you call. It does not matter whether you link to the static version of the CRT or the DLL version. You will get a method declared in your assembly with the same signature as *puts*. The calls to *modopt* indicate that the function has the *__cdecl* calling convention and that the parameter is a *const char** pointer. These modifiers are optional and are not used by the runtime other than to distinguish between two signatures where one has a *modopt* and the other does not. (You can use these modifiers to overload a C++ function with *long* and *int*. Both functions will give an *int32* parameter, but the compiler will add *IsLongModifier* to the *long* parameter through *modopt*.)

The manifest for the assembly (which contains global information about the assembly) gives a single *.vtfixup* directive. This directive indicates that at the specified location (here, 0x904c) is a table of method metadata tokens. (In this example, the value in square brackets indicates that there is just one token, 0x6000001. I will explain metadata tokens in Chapter 5.) The runtime will read this data and create a method pointer to the methods identified in the table. In this example, the *.vtfixup* directive has the *fromunmanaged* attribute, which means that the runtime will generate a thunk to convert the unmanaged call to a managed call. The fixup is for the method with the metadata token 0x06000001, which identifies the *main* function. (The fixup is required when *_mainCRTStartup* calls *main*.) The *_mainCRTStartup* function is unmanaged and is provided by the CRT.

C++ Standard Library

You can use the C++ standard library, but be aware that you cannot use it with managed types. So you can neither put managed objects directly into Standard Template Library (STL) containers, nor write stream operators for managed types. If you want to integrate managed objects and native objects, you have to write wrapper classes, either managed wrappers around your native types so that they can be put into a managed container or a native wrapper so that a managed type can be put into an STL container. STL code can generate C++ exceptions, so if your code uses STL, you have to enable exception handling with the */EH* switch.

Managed Pointers in Unmanaged Types

I mentioned earlier that an unmanaged type cannot contain a managed pointer because the garbage collector will not be able to track the managed pointer. However, there are cases when it is useful for an unmanaged type to treat a managed type as a "data member," and to do this, the unmanaged type must explicitly handle the lifetime of the managed object.

The .NET Framework has a class named *GCHandle* that represents a reference on a managed object. A *GCHandle* is a value type that has *sequential* layout and does not have managed members, but because of the bug I mentioned earlier (the compiler ignores the *sequential* layout attribute), *GCHandle* cannot be a member of a *__nogc* type. A *GCHandle* can be converted to an *IntPtr*—in other words, as a platform specified integer—which can be converted to an *int*, and hence, a *GCHandle* can be stored indirectly in a *__nogc* type.

GCHandle does not have an accessible constructor; instead, you initialize an instance by calling the *Alloc* method. This method is overloaded, and both versions take an object reference from which the *GCHandle* will be initialized. The value in the *GCHandle* instance acts like a pinning pointer: while the value exists, the object will be pinned, so it will not be moved in memory or collected. However, unlike a pinning pointer, you must take explicit steps to unpin the object by calling *GCHandle::Free*, as shown in this example:

```
// filewriter.cpp
__nogc class FileWriter
{
public:
   FileWriter(String* name)
   {
      StreamWriter* sw = File::AppendText(name);
      GCHandle h = GCHandle::Alloc(sw);
      IntPtr ptr = GCHandle::op_Explicit(h);
      writer = ptr.ToInt32();
   }
   ~FileWriter()
   {
      StreamWriter* sw = GetStream();
      sw->Close();

      GCHandle h = GCHandle::op_Explicit(IntPtr(writer));
      h.Free();
   }
   void Write(String* s)
   {
      StreamWriter* sw = GetStream();
      if (sw) sw->Write(s);
   }
private:
   int writer;
   StreamWriter* GetStream()
   {
      GCHandle h = GCHandle::op_Explicit(IntPtr(writer));
      return static_cast<StreamWriter*>(h.Target);
   }
```

```
   // Prevent copying, see later
   FileWriter(const FileWriter&){}
   operator=(const FileWriter&){}
};
```

This unmanaged class wraps a *StreamWriter* object; the object is created in the constructor, and it is released in the destructor. Because this class is unmanaged, it can be created on the stack. Therefore, it allows you to hold onto the managed resource only as long as the stack frame survives.

The constructor takes a managed string as a parameter. This arrangement is fine because the managed string reference lives only as long as the stack frame of the method call. The constructor uses this reference to create a *StreamWriter* object. The constructor then creates a *GCHandle* based on this object—which effectively pins the object. The handle is first converted to an *IntPtr* and then converted to an *int* so that the handle can be stored in the unmanaged type.

The instance of the unmanaged *FileWriter* class must release its managed resources when it is destroyed. The first action the object performs is to close the file. The object then unpins the *StreamWriter* object by converting the integer to an *IntPtr*, converting the *IntPtr* to a *GCHandle*, and then calling *Free*. The private method *GetStream* returns the *StreamWriter* object by accessing the *GCHandle::Target* property, which is the object that has been pinned.

You might decide to hold more than one managed type in an unmanaged class. However, the code to access these objects and their *GCHandle* structures would get rather messy. To help out, the C++ team has provided the unmanaged template *gcroot*<> in gcroot.h, as shown here:

```
template <class T> struct gcroot
{
   gcroot();
   gcroot(T t);
   gcroot(const gcroot& r);
   ~gcroot();
   gcroot& operator=(T t);
   gcroot& operator=(const gcroot &r);
   operator T () const;
   T operator->() const;
};
```

The template parameter, *T*, is a managed pointer type. The class will always create a *GCHandle* for the managed object passed to the constructor; the copy constructor and assignment operator also create new handles based on the object that the *gcroot*<> instance wraps. This arrangement is so that if an instance of a class that uses a *gcroot*<> is copied, there will be two separate *GCHandle* structures for the same object. This duplication is needed because if both instances of *gcroot*<> had the same handle, destroying one of the instances would invalidate the other instance of *gcroot<>*. (In the preceding *FileWriter* example, I have ignored this issue by making the copy constructor and assignment operator private.)

The *gcroot<>* template has conversion operators that return the object wrapped by the handle and an *operator->* so that you can treat the *gcroot<>* as a smart pointer class. The *FileWriter* class using *gcroot<>* looks like this:

```
// filewriter2.cpp
__nogc class FileWriter
{
   gcroot<StreamWriter*> writer;
   FileWriter(const FileWriter&){}
   operator=(const FileWriter&){}
public:
   FileWriter(String* name)
   {
      writer = File::AppendText(name);
   }
   ~FileWriter()
   {
      writer->Close();
   }
   void Write(String* s)
   {
      writer->Write(s);
   }
};
```

I think you'll agree that this code is far clearer than the previous version.

Global Methods

Managed C++ allows you to write global methods. Other languages supported by the .NET Framework insist that all methods (even static methods) are part of a class. This code, when compiled as a DLL:

```
#using <mscorlib.dll>
void f()
{
   System::Console::WriteLine(S"Called f()");
}
```

will have the following global methods:

```
.module test.dll
.method public static void modopt(
   [mscorlib]System.Runtime.CompilerServices.CallConvCdecl)
   f() cil managed;
.method public static pinvokeimpl(/* No map */) int32
   __DllMainCRTStartup@12(void* A_0, unsigned int32
```

```
    modopt([mscorlib]
       System.Security.Permissions.SecurityAction) A_1,
    void* A_2) native unmanaged preservesig;
```

The compiler adds the call to *_DllMainCRTStartup@12* to initialize the CRT and global C++ unmanaged objects. This function is marked as the Win32 entry point and is called by the system when the DLL is loaded into a process or unloaded from a process, or when a thread is created or destroyed in a process in which the DLL is loaded. If your code does not use the CRT or does not have global C++ objects, you don't need *DllMainCRTStartup*. You can remove this function by passing */noentry* to the linker.

The method *f* is marked as public and static, so how can you call it? I want to cover two situations: calling a global method from unmanaged code and calling it from managed code. In Win32, the usual way to export a function from a DLL is as a C entry point, by mentioning the function in the *EXPORTS* section of the .def file or by using *__declspec(dllexport)*, as shown here:

```
// expfunc.cpp
extern "C" __declspec(dllexport) void func()
{
   System::Console::WriteLine(S"Called func()");
}
```

I have also used *extern "C"* so that the name of the exported function is not mangled. The modifier adds the following metadata to the method:

```
.vtentry 1 : 1
.export [1] as func
```

Neither of these directives is documented in the ECMA specification, but it is easy to speculate that the *.export* directive indicates that the function is exported with the name *func* and the ordinal *1*. (You can confirm this information with DUMPBIN.) When you compile C++ code for a DLL, the compiler conveniently creates an import library, so assuming *func* is exported from expfunc.dll, I can write this unmanaged code:

```
// usefunc.cpp
// Do not use /clr.
#pragma comment(lib, "expfunc.lib")
extern "C" void func();
void main()
{
   func();
}
```

When this code is run, the message *Called func()* is printed at the command line. Stop a moment and think about what is happening. This message is printed using the *System::Console* class, yet the DLL is loaded from an unmanaged client. The client does nothing to initialize the .NET runtime. (DUMPBIN shows that only test.dll and kernel32.dll are imported.) If you take a look at expfunc.dll with DUMPBIN, you'll see that the assembly imports the runtime shim DLL (a shim is a thin piece of code that accepts a version number and other startup parameters from the host and starts the common language runtime), mscoree.dll, so when expfunc.dll is loaded, the .NET runtime is initialized so that the managed code can run. Isn't managed C++ wonderful?

You can call *func* from managed code in three ways. First, because the function is exported from a DLL, you can use platform invoke (described in the next section) to call the method. Second, you can link to the import library and call the method through IJW. In both cases, this process will involve treating the method as an unmanaged method. It seems like overkill to have an extra managed/unmanaged transition when calling the method—it would be far better to treat the method as a managed method (which indeed it is).

The problem is that a global method does not appear to have a class and imported methods can be called only as instance or static methods of a class. However, global methods are members of a class: they are members of the module that they are compiled into. If you create a DLL, the module will have the name of the DLL file (in this example, expfunc.dll). Unfortunately, .NET does not allow you to access the module directly, which is a pity. Your only recourse is to use reflection, the third way to get access to the function, as shown here:

```
// reffunc.cpp
Assembly* assem = Assembly::LoadFrom(S"expfunc.dll");
Module* module = assem->GetModule(S"expfunc.dll");
MethodInfo* info = module->GetMethod(S"func");
info->Invoke(module, 0);
```

Note that even if *func* were declared in a namespace, the fully qualified name would still be *func* because I exported it with *extern "C"*.

The *#using* directive will be able to ascertain the global methods exported from the assembly, so it would be nice if the C++ compiler would allow you to call global methods in an imported assembly. This feature is on my wish list for the next version of the compiler.

Platform Invoke

The Windows API is essentially a C API with functions exported from DLLs. Win32 code loads these DLLs either by static linking or dynamic linking. When you link to a library such as User32.lib or Kernel32.lib, you are actually linking with an import library for the DLL. When you statically link to an import library, the linker adds information about the DLL and the functions that you import in a section of the PE file called the *import address table* (IAT, which you can view with *DUMPBIN /imports* or the Platform SDK tool Depends). The linker forwards calls to each imported API to its entry in the appropriate IAT. When Windows loads the PE file, it determines the DLLs that the file uses, and as it loads each DLL, the loader goes through the entries in the IAT and stores the actual address of the function in the DLL, a process known as *performing fix-ups*. In C++, a method call to an imported function appears the same as if the function was linked from a static-link library.

To dynamically link a DLL, your code must call *::LoadLibraryEx* and then use *::GetProcAddress* to get the address of the exported function. The *::GetProcAddress* function returns a *void**, so you have the added complication of casting this pointer to an appropriate function pointer and then calling the function through this pointer. (In a way, COM interfaces are a simple way to cast an array of such *void* pointers to an array of function pointers through which those interface methods can be called.)

The problem with DLLs is that no version information is passed to *::LoadLibraryEx* nor is there any present in the import library. So both mechanisms of loading DLLs could load the wrong version of a DLL. A process could get around this problem by passing an absolute path to *::LoadLibraryEx* and then testing the version resource of the loaded DLL, but the *VERSIONINFO* API is far from straightforward to use. COM inproc servers were the first big effort from Microsoft to solve this issue with DLL versioning (in which a central repository—the system registry—is used to associate class names with the DLLs that implement them), but this technology also had its problems with versioning. The .NET solution is far more robust, and I'll cover this issue in Chapter 5. Whichever way a DLL is loaded, its entry point function (usually named *DllMain*) is called. Furthermore, when a new thread is created or destroyed in the process, the entry point function of each DLL is also informed (although this behavior can be turned off with *::DisableThreadLibraryCalls*).

Functions can be exported from a DLL through a module definition file (*.DEF*) or by applying the *__declspec(dllexport)* to the function. To keep the number of possible clients as wide as possible, DLL functions are typically exported as C functions, so they have the C calling convention (*__cdecl*) and the names are not C++ mangled (*extern "C"*). Of course, the DLL does not have any information about the exported functions, so the client must know the types of the parameters and what they are used for. (This restriction can be regarded as an advantage of DLLs.)

DllImport

Platform invoke is used to call functions exported from a DLL. The mechanism involves supplying a prototype of the function that you want to call decorated with the *[DllImport]* attribute. This attribute has the name of the DLL that exports the function and, optionally, the name of the exported function. The platform invoke mechanism is essentially a managed version of dynamic linking. When you call a method marked with *[DllImport]*, the runtime will load the DLL (if the DLL is not already loaded) and then locate the exported function and run it, marshaling parameters you pass to the function and marshaling back any return values. If your DLL has an entry point, the runtime will call this function, and once the runtime has loaded the DLL, the entry point will also be called whenever an operating system thread is created or dies. Although the documentation does not explicitly say so, in the current version of .NET, all threads are operating system threads. Furthermore, the runtime appears to use an algorithm similar to *::LoadLibraryEx* to locate DLLs mentioned in *[DllImport]*: you can give an absolute or a relative path, but if no path is specified, platform invoke looks in the current folder and in the folders mentioned in the *PATH* environment variable. However, although the evidence appears to suggest that platform invoke uses *::LoadLibraryEx* to load the DLL, this is not the mechanism that platform invoke actually uses. You can verify this statement by putting a breakpoint on *::LoadLibraryEx*. When you debug the process, you will see that the breakpoint will be hit when the process loads (to load required DLLs such as *ole32.dll* and *kernel32.dll*). However, the breakpoint will not be hit when an imported function is called through platform invoke.

To use platform invoke, you use the *[DllImport]* pseudo custom attribute in *System::Runtime::InteropServices*. The following code shows some simple examples:

```
// Imported function as part of a type
__nogc struct Win32
{
   [DllImport("user32")]
   static unsigned MessageBeep(unsigned uType);
};

// Imported function declared globally
[DllImport("kernel32")]
extern unsigned GetLogicalDrives();
```

The attribute is given the name of the DLL (with or without the extension), and this name can have an absolute or a relative path. I do not recommend that you use an absolute path with *[DllImport]* because you will not be able to guarantee that the same path will exist on the deployment machine.[4] The

4. Microsoft makes a big noise about *XCOPY deployment*—that is, you can deploy an application merely by copying the files that constitute the application. You can bet that users will take this to heart and will regularly copy .NET applications from folder to folder on the same machine or between machines.

imported function can be a static member of a type (*__gc*, *__nogc*, or *__value* type), but it should have no implementation. If you declare the function outside of a type, you should declare it as *extern*. The linker recognizes that the *[DllImport]* attribute was used, so it does not complain that there is no implementation in the project when this attribute is applied to an *extern* function or a *static* member of a type.

The declaration of the imported function should have a .NET signature using .NET data types as close as possible to the unmanaged types. The signature is the managed method that will be called by managed code. If there is no direct mapping between an unmanaged type and an existing .NET type, you can define a new type or you can specify metadata that gives information about how a parameter should be marshaled. In these examples, I have assumed that the exported function has the same name as the managed signature, but you might decide to use a different name, in which case you should use the *EntryPoint* field of *[DllImport]* to specify the actual name. Table 2-1 gives the fields of the *[DllImport]* attribute.

Table 2-1 The Fields of the *[DllImport]* Attribute

Field	Description
CallingConvention	The calling convention of the method that specifies how parameters are put on the stack and how the stack is cleaned up after the method is called.
CharSet	The default character set of the function. This field specifies how *System::String* and *System::Text::StringBuilder* parameters are marshaled and might be used to determine the entry point name.
EntryPoint	The name of the function exported by the DLL. If *ExactSpelling* is *false*, *CharSet* is used to determine whether the entry point name is appended with *A* or *W*.
ExactSpelling	If this field is *true*, the *EntryPoint* is the name regardless of the *CharSet* used.
PreserveSig	If this field is *true*, the function is treated as a COM method, so failure *HRESULT* values are converted to managed exceptions and the managed method will return the final parameter as the return value of the method.
SetLastError	If this field is *true*, platform invoke calls *::GetLastError* when the method has completed to determine whether an error occurred in the method. The error value can be accessed in managed code through *Marshal::GetLastWin32Error*.

The name of the entry point is actually created from the *EntryPoint*, *CharSet*, and *ExactSpelling* fields. (If you do not specify *EntryPoint*, the name of the managed method will be used.) If *ExactSpelling* is *true*, you are making the assertion that you know exactly the spelling, and platform invoke will use the name that you suggest. If this field is set to *false*, platform invoke will consult the *CharSet* field—even if the method has no string parameters—and will use the value to determine the entry point name suffix. If the character set is *CharSet::Ansi*, platform invoke will first look for an exported function with *EntryPoint*; if this function is not exported, platform invoke will append an *A* to *EntryPoint* and attempt to find this name. The process for *CharSet::Unicode* is the reverse: first platform invoke will append a *W* to *EntryPoint*, and if this function cannot be found, platform invoke will look for *EntryPoint*. If the *CharSet* is set to *CharSet::Auto*, the native character set for the current operating system (which you can determine by the value returned from *Marshal::SystemDefaultCharSize*) will be used.

If you know the ordinal of the method that you want to call, you can use this ordinal instead of the name of the function, as shown in the following code. However, you do not get the advantage of .NET choosing the best version for the default character set supported by your operating system (*CharSet::Auto*).

```
__nogc struct Win32
{
   [DllImport("user32", EntryPoint="#451")]
   static unsigned MessageBeep(unsigned uType);
};
```

The *CallingConvention* field is interesting. The default for the C++ compiler is to compile all global functions as *__cdecl* (*/Gd*), and C++ non-*static* member functions will be compiled as *thiscall*. You can change the calling convention of global functions using *__cdecl*, *__fastcall*, or *__stdcall*. The latter convention is the standard calling convention for Windows API functions and is the default setting for *[DllImport]*. The *__cdecl* and *__stdcall* calling conventions differ only by the name decoration that is used on the exported function: functions exported with *__declspec(dllexport)* with the *__cdecl* calling convention will have no prefix or suffix, whereas exported functions with the *__stdcall* calling convention will have the function name prefixed with an underscore and appended with @ followed by the number of bytes (in decimal) consumed by all the parameters.

It is possible to use platform invoke to import an unmanaged class. However, you can import the class only as individual functions. For example, the following class is declared and exported from an unmanaged DLL:

```
// expclass.cpp
class __declspec(dllexport) MyClass
```

```
{
   int x;
public:
   MyClass(int y)
   {
      x=y;
      return;
   }
   int GetX(){return x;}
};
```

Using the DUMPBIN tool (which is a wrapper for the linker—you can use *LINK /DUMP* in place of *DUMPBIN*), I get the mangled names shown in Table 2-2.

Table 2-2 C++ Decorated ("Mangled") Name for the Members of *MyClass*

C++ Decorated Name	Class Member
??0MyClass@@QAE@H@Z	*MyClass::MyClass(int)*
?GetX@MyClass@@QAEHXZ	*MyClass::GetX*

Bearing in mind that a class should be called through *thiscall* (and hence the first parameter is the *this* pointer of the object), the class can be used like this:

```
// useclass.cpp
__nogc class TestClass
{
public:
   int x;
   [DllImport("expclass",
              EntryPoint="??0MyClass@@QAE@H@Z",
              CallingConvention=CallingConvention::ThisCall)]
   static void ctor(TestClass*, int);
   [DllImport("expclass",
              EntryPoint="?GetX@MyClass@@QAEHXZ",
              CallingConvention=CallingConvention::ThisCall)]
   static int GetX(TestClass*);
};
```

The unmanaged *TestClass* is used to provide the storage that will be initialized by the constructor and accessed by the other methods in the class. I have also taken the opportunity to add the prototypes of the methods that will be called through platform invoke. In each case, the first parameter is a pointer to an object instance (or at least, memory that is the same size as the exported class). Here's code that uses it:

```
// useclass.cpp
void main()
{
   TestClass t;
   // Construct the object.
   TestClass::ctor(&t, 42);
   // Access a function.
   Console::WriteLine(TestClass::GetX(&t));
   // Access the data member directly.
   Console::WriteLine(t.x);
}
```

First I create an instance of *TestClass*, which I then initialize by calling the exported constructor of *MyClass*, passing the instance of the object as the first parameter and then the constructor parameter as the second parameter. This method will initialize the object, and the data member can be accessed either through *TestClass::x* or through the imported method *GetX*.

If the class has virtual methods (or derives from a class with virtual methods), it will have a vtable, which means that each object will contain a 32-bit pointer as its first member. You will have to explicitly allocate storage for such a member. Also note that if the exported class has a destructor, you will have to call this method explicitly in the code that imports the class. All in all, this would involve writing a lot of code and would be very difficult to debug. In general, you should not import unmanaged classes through platform invoke; other mechanisms are far better (for example, as a COM class, or just include the code and use the class through IJW).

Platform Invoke Under the Covers

The implementation details of platform invoke are not included in the ECMA specifications for .NET, so I will give only a brief overview about what is happening. Basically, every call your IL makes to unmanaged code occurs through a thunk created by the compiler. This thunk does the necessary transition from managed to unmanaged contexts and marshals any parameters that are passed. When the call returns from the unmanaged function, the thunk is responsible for unmarshaling the return value and any *out* parameters and doing the transition from unmanaged to managed contexts. This thunk is not visible in ILDASM, and it is not visible in the debugger. Indeed, when you step into a call to an unmanaged function (for which you have source code and symbols) in the debugger, the execution point will appear immediately in the unmanaged function. Even if you single-step through disassembly view in the debugger, the thunk code will be hidden from you.

The *GetX* method shown in the previous section is imported through this MSIL:

```
.method public static
pinvokeimpl("expclass" as "\?GetX@MyClass@@QAEHXZ" thiscall)
int32  GetX(valuetype TestClass* __unnamed000)
   cil managed preservesig
{
}
```

From this MSIL, you can see that the fields of the pseudo custom attribute *[DllImport]* are used to provide values for the *pinvokeimpl* modifier and other attributes applied to the method. The *pinvokeimpl* modifier gives details about the platform-specific description of where the implementation is located (in this case, a DLL named *expclass.dll*) and the name of the implementation. If you give an absolute or relative path to the DLL, this path will appear in the first parameter of *pinvokeimpl.*

Platform Invoke and Parameters

When you use platform invoke, you provide a managed signature of the method, which your MSIL will call. The parameters of this method should match as closely as possible to the parameters of the unmanaged function that will be called. In most cases, you need do no more, and the platform invoke thunk will marshal the parameters. However, there are some situations when extra attention will have to be given.

Return Values and Exceptions

From the first version of Windows, all developers have had to adhere to the strict rule that exceptions should not be allowed to leak out of a code module. The reason is that until .NET it was not possible to guarantee that the client would be able to catch the exception. Of course, .NET means that library code *can* throw exceptions (and Microsoft encourages you to throw exceptions when they are appropriate), but you should do so only if the code throwing the exception is managed and exported from an assembly. Clearly, developers will have to learn new habits.

An unmanaged function exported from a DLL should not throw exceptions (there might be cases when this can happen, and I'll cover this later in the section "Exceptions"), and instead, the function will use return values to return errors. For example, an unmanaged function could look like this:

```
HRESULT GetNumber(int* p);
```

This method will return a number through the pointer parameter and will return an error *HRESULT* if it cannot obtain the result. The managed signature might look like this:

```
[DllImport("dllexp", PreserveSig=false)]
extern int GetNumber();
```

The runtime interprets the last parameter as a return value, so in the managed signature, this value will be returned from the method. The *PreserveSig* field indicates whether the signature that you give corresponds to the unmanaged function. If the unmanaged function returns an error value, the runtime will convert this value to a managed exception. If there isn't a suitable exception type in the .NET Framework, the runtime will throw a *COMException* containing the *HRESULT*.

This arrangement might initially appear convenient, but it has problems. In particular, the unmanaged function must return 0 (*S_OK*) for the runtime to treat the call as being successful, and most Win32 APIs use the convention of returning non-zero to indicate that a method is successful (*TRUE*). Furthermore, if a method returns a success code (for example *S_FALSE*), these codes are ignored. It usually makes better sense to handle error values yourself and set *PreserveSig* to *true*.

Strings

Managed strings are immutable, so they can be passed as *in* parameters via interop, as shown here:

```
[DllImport("kernel32", CharSet=CharSet::Auto)]
extern bool DeleteFile(String* file);
```

In managed code, the method is passed a managed string, and the thunk will convert this string to an unmanaged buffer according to the *CharSet* field. In this example, the runtime is asked to determine the default character set of the operating system.

The *System::String* type is implemented internally as a buffer of Unicode characters, so if a managed string is passed to a method that takes an ANSI string, a conversion must occur. The runtime will allocate a buffer large enough for the ANSI string using *CoTaskMemAlloc*, convert the Unicode string to an ANSI string, and then pass this buffer to the function. When the unmanaged function returns, the runtime will do the necessary cleanup and call *CoTaskMemFree*. If the managed string is to be passed to a method that takes a Unicode string, the runtime will get an interior pointer to the string's buffer and pass this pointer to the function.

If an unmanaged function returns a string, the function will return the string by writing to a string buffer allocated by the caller. For example, the

Win32 *::GetCurrentDirectory* is passed a caller allocated buffer and the API will fill that buffer with the name of the current folder. If a *System::String* is passed to a Unicode method, you get the same behavior as you would if the caller had been unmanaged—that is, a pointer to a buffer allocated in the caller is passed to the called method. To take advantage of this behavior, you need to allocate a managed string of sufficient size to the function, as shown in the following code:

```
// strings.cpp
// This technique only works with Unicode parameters.
[DllImport("kernel32", EntryPoint="GetCurrentDirectory",
          CharSet=CharSet::Unicode)]
extern unsigned GetCurrentDirectoryUnicode(unsigned, String*);
```

This function can be called by code like this:

```
// strings.cpp
// Get the required size.
unsigned size = GetCurrentDirectoryUnicode(0, 0);
// Allocate a string big enough.
String* strReply = new String(' ', size);
// Now get the string.
GetCurrentDirectoryUnicode(strReply->Length, strReply);
Console::WriteLine(strReply);
```

This technique works because the Win32 API takes a *LPWSTR* parameter and there is no indication about the direction of data flow, so platform invoke will assume that the data is going from the caller to the function. Since the function is Unicode, platform invoke will pass an interior pointer to the actual data in the *System::String* (which holds the string as a Unicode character array). In this code, the *strReply* string is initialized with spaces, which platform invoke assumes is the data to be sent to the API, but in fact, it merely serves to allocate enough space for the returned data.

However, this technique will not work when the ANSI version is called because the runtime will convert the *String* parameter to an ANSI and pass this intermediate buffer to the API. This intermediate buffer will be discarded when the unmanaged function returns because platform invoke assumes that the data is passed to the function via the *String* parameter and not returned through it. The solution is to use the .NET Framework class *StringBuilder*, which can be used to construct mutable string buffers. This class can be used for methods that return strings, as shown here:

```
// strings.cpp
// This technique works with both Unicode and ANSI parameters.
[DllImport("kernel32", CharSet=CharSet::Auto)]
extern unsigned GetCurrentDirectory(unsigned, StringBuilder*);
```

This function can be called by the following code:

```
// Get the required size.
unsigned size = GetCurrentDirectory(0, 0);
// Allocate a string big enough.
StringBuilder* sbReply = new StringBuilder(size);
// Now get the string.
GetCurrentDirectory(sbReply->Capacity, sbReply);
Console::WriteLine(sbReply->ToString());
```

This time the *Capacity* property of the *StringBuilder* is passed to the unmanaged function because at this point the object will not be initialized, so *Length* will return zero. If the call to the unmanaged function is successful, the value of *StringBuilder::Length* will correctly return the length of the string. Contrast this behavior to the previous example, where calling *String::Length* after calling the unmanaged function will return the size of the string that you originally allocated.

Arrays

Arrays are ordered containers of items of the same type. In unmanaged C++, an array is implemented as a contiguous block of memory. Consider this unmanaged function:

```
void PassIntArray(int size, int* array);
```

The idea is that an array of integers is passed to the function; the size of the array is passed as the first parameter, and a pointer to the first item in the array is passed as the second parameter. In C and C++, if an array is passed to a function, the actual data is passed by reference—that is, the buffer for the array is allocated in the calling function and then a pointer to this buffer is passed to the function. This arrangement was a problem with RPC (and hence, COM) because access to the data from the called function could involve a network call. So IDL (used to defined RPC proxies) used attributes to define the data direction flow and hence allow the proxy to copy data. In .NET, the *[In]* and *[Out]* attributes are suggestions to the marshaler and are not necessarily acted upon, so you cannot use these attributes to specify how parameters are marshaled. Instead, you use the *[MarshalAs]* pseudo custom attribute, which adds the *marshal* attribute to the parameter's metadata in the assembly. Thus, the managed signature for the *PassIntArray* function will be:

```
[DllImport("dllexp")]
static void PassIntArray(int size,
   [MarshalAs(UnmanagedType::LPArray, SizeParamIndex=0)]
      int array __gc[]);
```

The *[MarshalAs]* attribute indicates that the parameter is a C-type array and that the number of members in the array is given by the first parameter of the method. (*SizeParamIndex* is 0-based.) The marshaler used by the managed/unmanaged thunk will create an unmanaged array based on the metadata provided. The marshaler knows that the array holds *int* values, and it knows that the size of the array is given by the *size* parameter; the marshaler can then copy the data from the managed array to the unmanaged array. The parameters are very non-.NET-like. The *array* parameter contains its own size, so why does the managed signature have to have the extra parameter for the array size? Well, the marshaler needs to know which of the unmanaged parameters takes the size of the array (if at all), and the only way that this determination can be done is by the managed signature having a parameter for the array size.

Structures

In the .NET signature for a method called through platform invoke, you can use the .NET primitives types in place of the C primitives. However, if the unmanaged function takes a struct as a parameter, you have to ensure that a buffer big enough to take the structure is passed. If you want to read the fields of this structure, it makes sense to allocate a structure that has members equivalent to the unmanaged type. Here you have two options: if the data is to be used in your code only, you can use an unmanaged structure; if the data is to be used outside of your assembly, you can define a *__value* type to take the data.

If you declare an unmanaged type as a parameter of your managed type, the managed type becomes inaccessible. Consider this:

```
__nogc struct POINT{int x; int y;};
public __gc class Square
{
public:
// Other members omitted
   __property void set_Position(POINT p) {};
};
```

The *Square* class has a property named *Position* that is initialized with an unmanaged type *POINT*. This code can be used within the same assembly, but when you attempt to compile code in another assembly that uses *Square*, you will get the error that the type *POINT* is inaccessible (error C3376) because the metadata for the unmanaged type indicates that it is *private*.

The solution in this example is to make the *POINT* structure a *public __value* type, but this strategy means that you have a new type. In the example, I have defined a new unmanaged type, but I could have used the Windows *POINT*, so redefining the structure as a managed type will result in an error unless you prevent the name conflict by defining the new type in a namespace.

Defining a *__value* type to represent an unmanaged struct is straightforward. The most important point to remember is that the *__value* type is at least as large as the struct. Of course, you also have to ensure that the members in the *__value* type are in the same position in the record as the members of the unmanaged struct; otherwise, you will get nonsensical values when you read the values. I mentioned in Chapter 1 the mechanism that you use to do this ordering: the *[StructLayout]* attribute.

.NET does not guarantee the positioning or order of members within a type unless you tell it specifically to do so. To do this positioning, you use the *LayoutKind::Explicit* value in *[StructLayout]* and apply the *[FieldOffset]* attribute on each member to indicate the position of the member with respect to the start of the *__value* type. You have to be careful and keep a running count of the size of each member. If the unmanaged struct has a *union*, you can simulate this union in your *__value* type by using *[FieldOffset]* to allow members to overlap as described in Chapter 1.

Structures can contain embedded instances of other structures, in which case you have to ensure that the right amount of storage is reserved. So, you can define *__value* type and add an instance of this storage to your enclosing structure, or you can simply add suitable members to the enclosing structure. If a structure contains a pointer to an instance of a structure, you need to declare this pointer as being a *__nogc* pointer because you cannot pass *__gc* pointers to unmanaged code.

```
// Unmanaged
struct Inner { int i; };
struct Outer { Inner* inner; };
// Managed
__value struct Inner { int i; };
__value struct Outer { Inner __nogc* inner; };
```

If *Outer* is passed as a method parameter (as opposed to a pointer to *Outer*), the structure will be passed by value to the unmanaged code. However, access to the *Inner* instance will be by reference because the copy of *Outer* placed on the stack will be a shallow copy. In general, you cannot put a *__gc* pointer in a structure to be passed to unmanaged code; the exception is strings. Here is an example:

```
// Unmanaged
struct Person{ TCHAR* name; USHORT age; };
// Managed
__value struct Person
{
   String* name;
   unsigned short age;
};
```

The *CharSet* field used on the declaration of the method will determine whether an intermediate buffer is created so that the string can be converted from Unicode to ANSI. Some structures hold the actual string rather than a pointer to a string buffer. In this case, a fixed amount of memory has to be allocated, as shown here:

```
// Unmanaged
struct Person{ USHORT age; TCHAR name[50]; };
// Managed
__value struct Person
{
   unsigned short age;
   [MarshalAs(UnmanagedType::ByValTStr, SizeConst=50)]
   String* name;
};
```

This time the marshaler knows that it has to allocate an array of characters and embed this in the structure (*UnmanagedType::ByValTStr*). The type of the characters is determined by *CharSet*, and the size of the character array is given by *SizeConst*.

Other Win32 Types

When you access Win32 APIs, you will use Win32 types. In most cases, these Win32 types correspond directly to the C++ primitive types that you are used to using. However, there are some types that you will have to be wary of.

The first Win32 type I want to cover is *BOOL*. Win32 defines this type as a *long* with *FALSE* defined as 0 and *TRUE* as 1. If an unmanaged function returns a *BOOL*, the managed signature can return a *bool*. .NET will convert 0 to a value of *false* and 1 to a value of *true*. However, COM methods return an *HRESULT*, which means that the top bit of the return value determines whether the value is a success code (0) or a failure code (1). The value of *S_OK* is 0, so you must *not* convert an *HRESULT* to a *bool* in the managed signature. If you use *PreserveSig=false*, the return value will be automatically converted to an exception for failure values.

Some APIs return a *HANDLE* type or some equivalent type (for example, *FILE** for CRT file functions). These handle types are meant to be opaque—that is, you are to treat them as a mere number and the API will interpret what that number means. In this case, you have two options: either you treat the *HANDLE* parameter as an *unsigned int* or as an *IntPtr*. *IntPtr* is a general purpose *__value* type that can be used to hold pointers. The nice thing about *IntPtr* is that it will hold the pointer in a buffer according to the operating system: a 32-bit buffer for a 32-bit operating system and a 64-bit buffer for a 64-bit operating system. The type has conversion operators that allow you to copy between the various formats: *void**, *__int64*, or *int*. Although this type might seem wonderful—you simply use *IntPtr* and the compiler will ensure that the parameter is assigned with the correct pointer type—there is a problem: you cannot return a .NET type from a method that is used for interop. For example, if you were to call the Win32 kernel event API through interop, you could define the following methods:

```
struct Win32Events
{
   [DllImport("kernel32", CharSet=CharSet::Auto)]
   static int CreateEvent(IntPtr sec, bool bManual, bool bInit,
      String* name);
   [DllImport("kernel32", CharSet=CharSet::Auto)]
   static int OpenEvent(unsigned access, bool inherit,
      String* name);
   [DllImport("kernel32")]
   static bool SetEvent(IntPtr handle);
   [DllImport("kernel32")]
   static bool ResetEvent(IntPtr handle);
   [DllImport("kernel32")]
   static bool CloseHandle(IntPtr handle);
};
```

I said that you can treat handles as *unsigned int*, and yet in this code, I convert the handle returned from these methods to a *signed int*. Why? For a handle to be totally opaque, it should just be a jumble of bits that mean nothing to the caller who receives that handle. It makes no sense to treat a handle as signed. However, some languages can accept only signed types, so *IntPtr* can be initialized only with a signed *Int32*. I don't like this behavior, but if I want to use an *IntPtr*, I have to accept this restriction. Using these definitions, I can write code like this:

```
IntPtr h(Win32Events::CreateEvent(IntPtr::Zero, true,
   false, S"EVENT"));
Win32Events::SetEvent(h);
Win32Events::CloseHandle(h);
```

Some .NET Framework classes are built over Win32, and these classes usually give access to the Win32 handle so that you can pass it to Win32 via interop. For example, the *System::IO::FileStream* class is the .NET Framework class used to read and write to files, and the Win32 file handle is accessible through a property named *Handle*. Similarly, the *System::Windows::Forms::Control* class is a managed wrapper around a Win32 window, and the *HWND* is accessed through a property named *Handle*. In each case, the property is an *IntPtr*, so the data the property holds is an opaque handle. However, the property is a member of a managed type, so if you pass such a handle to an unmanaged function, you must ensure that the managed object that provides the handle lives as long as the unmanaged code has access to the handle. If the managed object is garbage collected, its finalizer is typically used to free the unmanaged resource. In many cases, you do not have to worry about this detail because most functions are called synchronously, so the stack frame that calls the unmanaged function will exist (and hence the object references defined on that stack frame) until the unmanaged method returns. Some Win32 APIs are designed to be called asynchronously (for example, the file APIs, which use an *OVERLAPPED* structure), and in this case, the API will return immediately, and the caller has the responsibility of checking to see whether the action has completed, which could be in another stack frame.

To prevent such a wrapper-managed object from being garbage collected, you can pass a *HandleRef* instead of an *IntPtr* or an *unsigned* for the *HANDLE* parameter. This *__value* type is initialized with the handle and a pointer to the object that wraps it. Platform invoke will ensure that the *HandleRef* (and the object it refers to) will not be garbage collected while the call is active.

Of course, such code is quite unnecessary when you have IJW, which leads me to the next section.

Calling Win32 APIs Using IJW

Why bother to declare the Win32 methods you want to call in your code using *[DllImport]* when there are header files that have already done this? As I mentioned earlier, the Windows header files have the prototypes for all the Win32 functions, and the static-link libraries contain the information that the linker uses to create the import address table. As we have seen, IJW will create a wrapper function that will take into account the transition from managed to unmanaged code, so calls to Win32 should be as simple as adding an *#include* statement for the appropriate header files, linking to the appropriate import library, and calling the method.

Calling a Win32 function is not that simple. The first problem you will get is a name clash. Try compiling this code:

```
#using <mscorlib.dll>
using namespace System;
#include <windows.h>
void main()
{
}
```

You will get a series of errors caused by an ambiguous symbol *IServiceProvider*. The reason for this name clashing is that ServProv.h is included through Windows.h, and this header file holds a definition for *IServiceProvider*, a COM interface. There is also a .NET interface *System::IServiceProvider*, and I have indicated that I want to access the members of the *System* namespace without using fully qualified names, which means that the compiler can also access these types, and hence the name clash. In this simple case, the solution is to make sure that the names the compiler sees when processing the header file do not clash, as shown here:

```
#using <mscorlib.dll>
#include <windows.h>
using namespace System;
void main()
{
}
```

Here the compiler will see the name of the managed interface as *System::IServiceProvider* when it is processing Windows.h, but I have the convenience of not using fully qualified names in the *main* function. Although this arrangement will work in most cases, it will cause problems if I want to use the *IServiceProvider* COM interface in *main* because the compiler will not know whether I want to use the managed or the COM interface. It makes sense in this case to simply remove the *using namespace* line and use fully qualified names throughout.

Now consider this code:

```
#using <mscorlib.dll>
#using <system.windows.forms.dll>
#include <windows.h>

void main()
{
   System::Windows::Forms::MessageBox::Show(S"Hello");
}
```

This code will not compile. The compiler will complain that *MessageBoxA* is not a member of the *System::Windows::Forms* namespace. The reason for this error is that the preprocessor has gone through your code making the text substitutions that the Windows header files has told it to do.

```
#ifdef UNICODE
#define MessageBox  MessageBoxW
#else
#define MessageBox  MessageBoxA
#endif
```

The preprocessor is dumb; it makes no distinction between the Win32 function name and the .NET class; it merely makes a text substitution. The only solution to this problem is to undo the effect of the preprocessor, as shown here:

```
#undef  MessageBox
```

If you choose to use the Win32 method in your code, you will have to ensure that you use the appropriate version for the character set you are using, rather than rely on the *MessageBox* macro.

With a simple example such as this, it is easy to say that name clashes are simple to remove. However, with a large project, this simple solution will not be the case. The name clashes occur because .NET Framework classes have been used in the same translation unit as Win32 functions. To a certain extent, you can avoid this situation by separating your code so that the files that call Win32 functions do not call .NET Framework classes, in which case there is no need to have a *#using* statement in those files (not even for mscorlib.dll). However, if you use a precompiled header for the Win32 headers, you will have to ensure that you turn off precompiled headers for the files that have .NET Framework classes. I'll return to precompiled headers in Chapter 6.

Calling Win32 functions initially looks inviting, but the function prototypes that you include through the Windows headers will use unmanaged types, so the compiler will ensure that you use these types. This restriction means that either your code uses unmanaged code or, if your code has data in managed types, you'll have to convert between the two types, as shown here:

```
String* name = WindowsIdentity::GetCurrent()->Name;
IntPtr ptrName = Marshal::StringToCoTaskMemAnsi(name);
LPCTSTR strName;
strName = static_cast<LPCTSTR>(static_cast<void*>(ptrName));
// Call ANSI version of MessageBox
::MessageBoxA(NULL, strName, NULL, MB_OK);
Marshal::FreeCoTaskMem(ptrName);
```

You have several options about how to convert from managed strings to unmanaged strings. These options are listed in Table 2-3.

Table 2-3 .NET Framework Classes and Visual C++ Methods to Obtain Unmanaged Strings

Convert To	Use	Explanation
Wide Char String	*PtrToStringChars*	Get an interior pointer to a managed string.
	Marshal::StringToCoTaskMemUni *Marshal::StringToHGlobalUni*	Create a new buffer with the converted string. This requires that you free the buffer when you have finished with the buffer.
ANSI String	*Marshal::StringToCoTaskMemAnsi* *Marshal::StringToHGlobalAnsi*	Create a new buffer with the converted string. This requires that you free the buffer.

If you know that the function requires a constant wide character string (*wchar_t const **), you should use *PtrToStringChars* because that function is quicker than the methods in *Marshal* and does not involve a separate buffer that you will need to remember to free later.

If the API returns data through a string buffer, you have two options. The first option is to create an unmanaged buffer using either *Marshal::AllocCoTaskMem* or *Marshal::AllocHGlobalMem*, pass this buffer to the API by casting the returned *IntPtr*, and then remember to free the buffer afterwards, as shown in the following code:

```
String* GetDir()
{
   DWORD len = ::GetCurrentDirectory(0, 0);
   IntPtr dir = Marshal::AllocCoTaskMem(len * sizeof(TCHAR));
   LPTSTR strDir = static_cast<LPTSTR>(static_cast<void*>(dir));
   String* str = 0;
   if (::GetCurrentDirectory(len, strDir) != 0)
   {
      str = new String(strDir);
   }
   Marshal::FreeCoTaskMem(dir);
   return str;
}
```

If the API you are calling uses wide characters, you can allocate the buffer using a *String* or *StringBuilder*, as shown here:

```
String* GetDir()
{
   DWORD len = ::GetCurrentDirectoryW(0, 0);
   String* str = new String(' ', len);
   wchar_t __pin* strDir = PtrToStringChars(str);
   if (::GetCurrentDirectoryW(len, strDir) == 0) return 0;
   return str;
}
```

A managed string can be created from a *char** or a *wchar_t** pointer, so your second option is to simply allocate unmanaged buffers and use these buffers to create the managed string, as shown here:

```
String* GetDir()
{
   DWORD len = ::GetCurrentDirectory(0, 0);
   TCHAR* strDir = new TCHAR [len];
   String* str = 0;
   if (::GetCurrentDirectory(len, strDir) != 0)
   {
      str = new String(strDir);
   }
```

```
    delete [] strDir;
    return str;
}
```

If a Win32 function takes a structure as a parameter, it is almost always simpler to use the Win32 structure rather than go through the effort of declaring a managed value type and marshaling this type to the unmanaged function.

Typically, Win32 structures that return data either have pointers to buffers that you allocate or have fixed-sized string buffers. In the latter case, to initialize such a parameter from a managed string, you will have to convert the managed string to an unmanaged string and use *strcpy* or *wcscpy* to initialize the buffer. Of course, if the string contains wide characters, you avoid a lot of effort by using *PtrToStringChars*. If the structure takes a string buffer allocated by you (for example, *SHFILEOPSTRUCT* used by *SHFileOperation*) either to pass data to a function or to receive data from the function, you have to use one of the string conversion routines given in Table 2-3.

Some Win32 APIs (for example, *::LookupAccountSid*) require that you allocate a buffer and pass it to the API, and then the API will fill the buffer with data. This type of API raises the question of how you should allocate the buffer: should you use the CRT *malloc* or the C++ *new* operator; should you use one of the Win32 heap or *HGLOBAL* APIs; or should you use the managed methods in the *Marshal* class?

The methods in the *Marshal* class are a managed wrapper around the unmanaged APIs, and their purpose is to allow languages that do not have direct access to unmanaged code to be able to allocate unmanaged buffers. If you access such a buffer beyond its bounds, you will get an unpredictable result: the memory pointers you use are unmanaged, so there are no bounds checks. If you forget to free this memory, you'll get a memory leak. There are no diagnostic classes in the .NET Framework that allow you to determine such problems, so unless you are writing in C# or a similar language, it is best to avoid the memory allocation APIs in *Marshal*.

The CRT memory allocation method *malloc* is integrated with the CRT debugging functions. You can use these functions to detect leaked memory. The debug version of *malloc* will allocate the memory with guard blocks, and the CRT debugging APIs can check for changes in these guard blocks for an indication that the buffer was written to outside of its bounds. The debug version of the unmanaged operator *new* is also integrated with the CRT debugging mechanism, so you can also catch leaks allocated with this operator.

ATL 7 provides a header file named atldbgmem.h that provides additional support, which is great for unmanaged code. However, this file uses the preprocessor to redefine operator *new* with the placement operator *new*, and because there is no managed placement operator *new*, you cannot use this file with code that will use the managed *new* operator. However, because this file has some interesting code, it is worth taking a look at and learning from the coding techniques in the file. In particular, near the bottom of atldbgmem.h is a series of definitions, as shown in this example:

```
#define HeapCreate(flOptions, dwInitialSize, dwMaximumSize) \
   ATL::_AtlHeapCreate(flOptions, dwInitialSize, \
                       dwMaximumSize, __FILE__, __LINE__)

#define HeapFree(hHeap, dwFlags, lpMem) \
   ATL::_AtlHeapFree(hHeap, dwFlags, lpMem, __FILE__, __LINE__)
```

These methods are called as if the developer were using a private Win32 heap. The actual implementation of the methods will create buffers on the CRT heap, which means that these allocations will be tracked. ATL provides definitions for the private heap API and for the virtual memory API. If you want to use these macros in your code, you will have to make a copy of this header file and remove the definitions of *new*. The advantage of using macros such as these is that you get diagnostics about your memory usage in your debug builds, but in the release build, you can have the advantage of the appropriate Win32 memory allocator.

Marshaling

You can apply the *[DllImport]* pseudo custom attribute to static methods in a class or to global *extern* methods. When you apply this attribute, the compiler adds the *pinvokeimpl* modifier, which specifies the code that implements the method. You can use the *[MarshalAs]* pseudo custom attribute on the parameters and the return value of a method with the *[DllImport]* attribute and on fields of *__value* types. The *[MarshalAs]* attribute gives the .NET marshaler information about how to marshal the item. *[MarshalAs]* is a pseudo custom attribute because there is .NET metadata named *marshal* that is set with this attribute. For example, for this code:

```
[DllImport("dllexp")]
static void PassIntArray(int size,
   [MarshalAs(UnmanagedType::LPArray, SizeParamIndex=0)]
      int array __gc[]);
```

the compiler generates this IL:

```
.method public static pinvokeimpl("dllexp" winapi)
   void  PassIntArray(int32 size,
                      int32[]  marshal([ + 0]) 'array')
   cil managed preservesig forwardref
```

The square brackets in the *marshal* attribute indicate that the data type is an array, and the + *0* value indicates that the size is given by the first parameter (parameter zero).

You can define custom marshaling code by defining a class that implements *ICustomMarshaler* and mentioning it in the *MarshalType* field of the *[MarshalAs]* attribute. Custom marshaling occurs on *parameters* and not on the *method*, which means that the method must have the same number of parameters as the unmanaged function. One trick that the .NET Framework uses is to hide the platform Invoked method and provide wrapper methods that call the hidden method; such wrapper methods can have whatever parameters you want.

For example, let's return to the Win32 *::GetEnvironmentStrings* API that I showed earlier. This function returns a buffer with each environment string in the form *name=value*. This buffer is read-only and is allocated by the system. After you have finished using the buffer, you should release it by calling *::FreeEnvironmentStrings*. Because environment strings are name-value pairs, it makes more sense to access them through an associative container such as *NameValueCollection*. I have chosen to use a wrapper class for this function:

```
// envvars2.cpp
__gc class EnvStrings
{
   [DllImport("kernel32", CharSet=CharSet::Unicode)]
   [returnvalue: MarshalAs(UnmanagedType::CustomMarshaler,
                           MarshalType="StringArrayMarshaler")]
   static NameValueCollection* GetEnvironmentStrings();
   NameValueCollection* vars;
public:
   __property NameValueCollection* get_Var()
   {
      if (vars != 0) return vars;
      vars = GetEnvironmentStrings();
      return vars;
   }
};

void main()
{
   EnvStrings* env = new EnvStrings;
   IEnumerator* en = env->Var->AllKeys->GetEnumerator();
   while (en->MoveNext())
   {
      Console::WriteLine(S"{0}={1}",
         en->Current,
         env->Var->Item[en->Current->ToString()]);
   }
}
```

Here I define a class named *EnvStrings* that has a property that gives access to the *NameValueCollection* of environment strings. The Win32 *::GetEnvironmentStrings* function returns an *LPVOID* parameter. I want to marshal this parameter so that it is converted into a *NameValueCollection*. To do this conversion, the return value is marked with the *[MarshalAs]* attribute, which mentions the marshaler class *StringArrayMarshaler*. I have used the *MarshalType* field to give the name of the class. (This field should be the fully qualified name, but in this case, the class is declared in the same assembly as the code that will use the class, so there's no need to specify the fully qualified name.) I could have used the *MarshalTypeRef* field instead, in which case I would pass the *Type* object of the marshaler class rather than the name. The marshaler class looks like this:

```
// envvars2.cpp
public __gc class StringArrayMarshaler : public ICustomMarshaler
{
   [DllImport("kernel32", CharSet=CharSet::Unicode)]
   static bool FreeEnvironmentStrings(const wchar_t*);
   const wchar_t* buffer;
   // Make ctor private so that instances are only created
   // by calling GetInstance().
   StringArrayMarshaler(){}
public:
   static ICustomMarshaler* GetInstance(String* pstrCookie)
   { return new StringArrayMarshaler; }
   void CleanUpManagedData(Object* ManagedObj) {}
   int GetNativeDataSize()
   { return 0; }
   IntPtr MarshalManagedToNative(Object* ManagedObj)
   { return IntPtr::Zero; }
   Object* MarshalNativeToManaged(IntPtr pNativeData)
   {
      buffer = static_cast<const wchar_t*>(
                  static_cast<void*>(pNativeData));
      const wchar_t* pv = buffer;
      NameValueCollection* arr = new NameValueCollection;
      while (*pv)
      {
         String* name = new String(pv);
         int idx = name->IndexOf('=');
         String* value = name->Substring(idx + 1);
         name = name->Substring(0, idx);
         arr->Add(name, value);
         while (*pv) pv++;
         pv++;
      }
```

```
        return arr;
    }
    void CleanUpNativeData(IntPtr pNativeData)
    {
        FreeEnvironmentStrings(buffer);
        buffer = 0;
    }
};
```

The marshaler class implements *ICustomMarshaler* and also implements a static method named *GetInstance*. This example demonstrates deficiency with the way that the runtime uses some interfaces because the documentation says that any class that implements *ICustomMarshaler* must also implement *GetInstance*, but static methods are not allowed as members of *__gc __interfaces*. It would be nice if the .NET Framework had a custom attribute that indicated a noninterface method that must be implemented by a class that implements the specified interface, which a compiler could check.

When the system sees a custom marshaling class that contains a parameter marked with *[MarshalAs]*, the system calls the *GetInstance* method on that class, passing a marshaling cookie. This cookie can be specified via the *MarshalCookie* field of *[MarshalAs]*. The *GetInstance* method can use the value of this cookie to determine how the marshal class will work (and pass appropriate information to the marshaler class's constructor), or indeed, whether to create an instance of a totally different class.

Because this particular marshaler is used only to marshal data from the native to the managed worlds, only two methods are implemented: *MarshalNativeToManaged*, which is called when the parameter is marshaled and is expected to return the managed object initialized by the parameter; and *CleanUpNativeData*, which gives the marshaler an opportunity to release any native buffers allocated by the native function. In this code, I use *MarshalNativeToManaged* to access the string buffer and then iterate through the strings, separating them into name-value pairs and inserting them into the collection. The following *[MarshalAs]* pseudo custom attribute adds the *marshal* attribute to the method:

```
.method private static pinvokeimpl("kernel32" unicode winapi)
        class [System]
           System.Collections.Specialized.NameValueCollection
        marshal( custom ("StringArrayMarshaler",""))
        GetEnvironmentStrings() cil managed
           preservesig forwardref
{
}
```

The *custom* modifier mentions the name of the class and the cookie (in this case, an empty string).

Exceptions

Unmanaged code can throw software exceptions (typically C++ exceptions) or structured exceptions. Structured exceptions are purposely thrown with the Win32 *::RaiseException* function, but they might also be thrown by the system due to faults in the unmanaged code. When you guard managed code with a *try-catch* block, the runtime will catch any exceptions thrown by native code, and it will attempt to translate the exception into a managed exception. So, if native code tries to dereference a *NULL* pointer, the managed code will catch this error as a *NullReferenceException*.

If there is no managed exception that corresponds to the native exception, the runtime will throw an *SEHException*. This class is underwhelming—the only members in addition to those provided by *Exception* are *CanResume* and *ErrorCode*. If native code throws an exception, can you guarantee that this exception has not been caused by writing over vital memory? My advice is to ignore whatever *CanResume* returns and assume that you should not resume execution. *ErrorCode* is not much better; it always returns *0x80004005 (E_FAIL)*.

So how do you make any sense about exceptions that have been thrown by native code? The *Marshal* class has two static methods that you can use to get more information: *GetExceptionCode* and *GetExceptionPointers*. Logically, these methods should have been part of *SEHException* because you will access them only if you catch a native exception. Indeed, these two methods will return meaningful information only if they are called in a catch handler.

GetExceptionCode and *GetExceptionPointers* are essentially wrappers around the Win32 functions *::GetExceptionCode* and *::GetExceptionInformation*. The value returned by *GetExceptionCode* makes a lot more sense than *SEHException::ErrorCode* because the value actually corresponds to the exception that was thrown. The Win32 exception codes are defined in winbase.h using symbols defined in winnt.h (do a search for *STATUS_ACCESS_VIOLATION* to see where the exception code symbols are defined), but user code can define its own exception codes and pass a code through the first parameter of *::RaiseException*. Here's some code used to handle native exceptions in managed code:

```
// exceptions.cpp
try
{
   CallNativeCode();
}
catch (Exception* /* ignore exception */)
{
   switch(Marshal::GetExceptionCode())
   {
```

```
    case EXCEPTION_ACCESS_VIOLATION:
        Console::WriteLine(
            S"access attempted through an invalid pointer");
        break;
    case EXCEPTION_INT_DIVIDE_BY_ZERO:
        Console::WriteLine(
            S"code has attempted to divide by zero");
        break;
    case EXCEPTION_INT_OVERFLOW:
        Console::WriteLine(
            S"number too big to fit into an integer");
        break;
    default:
        Console::WriteLine(S"some other native exception");
    }
}
```

You can get a further list of exception codes[5] through the Exceptions dialog in Visual Studio .NET (through the Debug menu or the *Debug.Exceptions* command). The codes in the example above are listed under the Win32 Exceptions node.

You can use *Marshal::GetExceptionPointers* to get more detailed information about the native exception that was thrown. This method returns an *IntPtr* that holds the address of an unmanaged *EXCEPTION_POINTERS* structure. This structure is documented in winnt.h, which will be included through windows.h. However, note that the preprocessor will attempt to redefine the symbol *GetExceptionCode* as the intrinsic *_exception_code*, which will cause errors in your code. To remove these errors, you can simply add the following line of code after winnt.h is included:

```
#undef GetExceptionCode
```

The *EXCEPTION_POINTERS* structure is declared as follows:

```
// winnt.h
typedef struct _EXCEPTION_RECORD
{
    DWORD ExceptionCode;
    DWORD ExceptionFlags;
    struct _EXCEPTION_RECORD *ExceptionRecord;
    PVOID ExceptionAddress;
    DWORD NumberParameters;
    ULONG_PTR ExceptionInformation[EXCEPTION_MAXIMUM_PARAMETERS];
} EXCEPTION_RECORD;
typedef EXCEPTION_RECORD *PEXCEPTION_RECORD;
```

5. Exceptions thrown by native C++ will have an exception code of 0xe06d7363.

```
typedef struct _EXCEPTION_POINTERS
{
   PEXCEPTION_RECORD ExceptionRecord;
   PCONTEXT ContextRecord;
} EXCEPTION_POINTERS, *PEXCEPTION_POINTERS;
```

The first member of *EXCEPTION_POINTERS* is platform independent, and the second member gives the state of the CPU and is platform dependent. SEH exceptions can be nested, so *EXCEPTION_RECORD* acts as a linked list with a pointer to the next item in the list. The members in which you are perhaps the most interested are the *ExceptionAddress* and *ExceptionInformation* members. *ExceptionAddress* will give you the address in the native code where the exception was thrown, as shown here:

```
// exceptions.cpp
EXCEPTION_POINTERS* pointers;
pointers = static_cast<EXCEPTION_POINTERS*>(
   static_cast<void*>(Marshal::GetExceptionPointers()));
void __nogc* address =
   pointers->ExceptionRecord->ExceptionAddress;
Console::WriteLine(S"the exception was thrown at 0x{0:x}",
                   __box((int)address));
```

If the call to *RaiseException* passed parameters for the exception, the *NumberParameters* will give the number of parameters and *ExceptionInformation* will be an array in which each item points to an exception parameter.

The *ContextRecord* member of *EXCEPTION_POINTERS* is a *CONTEXT* structure that holds information about the state of the CPU at the point that the exception occurred. Again, winnt.h has definitions for this structure, but because this information is CPU-specific, there are versions for Alpha and x86 (32-bit and 64-bit) CPUs.

COM Interop

.NET interop would be only half complete if it did not include interop with COM. Before .NET, COM was the only effective way to develop components, and it is still used by many parts of Windows. (The shell uses COM-like interfaces for its UI elements, and APIs such as DirectX are accessible through COM.) In spite of the claims from some .NET commentators, COM will not disappear while .NET exists. The reason is that most of the access to the .NET runtime from native code is through COM: profiling code, debugging code, access to metadata, and hosting the runtime. I will come back to these APIs in Chapter 5 and Chapter 7.

.NET and COM Objects

With COM interop, a COM object can be used in managed code as if it is a .NET object, and a .NET object can be used in native code as if it is a COM object. This particular piece of programming magic requires marshaling code and type information. Unmanaged code requires type information in the form of type library (*ITypeInfo*) data to determine the methods (and the types of the parameters) implemented on a .NET object so that the type library marshaler can perform inter-apartment marshaling and so that tools such as Visual Basic 6 can generate client code. Managed code requires type information in the form of metadata for *all* code that the managed code accesses. Most COM servers have type libraries, and all .NET assemblies have metadata, so it makes sense for Microsoft to provide tools to generate metadata from type libraries and to generate type libraries from metadata. If a type library is not available for a COM server, you can generate the metadata in managed code using custom attributes.

When .NET code calls a COM object, a managed/native transition will occur when a method is called, and a corresponding transition will occur when the method returns. If the COM method has parameters that are COM types, the .NET code will have to pass a .NET equivalent (most likely a COM interface pointer that resides in the .NET context), and there must be marshaling to convert from the .NET type to a COM type. A COM object will call a .NET object through a COM interface, so there will be managed/native transitions during the method call, and the parameters will require marshaling through these transitions.

The lifetime of a .NET object is determined by the .NET garbage collector, which during a collection will use the references to an object to determine whether the memory assigned to an object can be freed. Clearly, any COM code that has access to a .NET object represents such a reference. The identity of .NET objects are defined in terms of object references: two object references are to the same object if the result of passing the references to *Object::ReferenceEquals* returns *true*. Any code that gives access to COM objects must take this condition into account.

On the other hand, the lifetime of a COM object is determined by the number of reference counts on the object; these reference counts are changed through the methods of *IUnknown*. .NET objects do not have reference counts, so when native code calls the reference counting methods of *IUnknown*, these methods must ultimately result in events that affect the object references tracked by the garbage collector. The identity of a COM object is defined in terms of *IUnknown*: two interface pointers point to the same object if the absolute value of the *IUnknown* interface obtained on one interface pointer is identical to the absolute value of the *IUnknown* interface obtained on the other interface pointer.

.NET objects are created through the managed *new* operator, and the .NET type loader will use .NET Fusion and the metadata in the calling code to locate the assembly that contains the type and then create a new instance of the type. COM objects are created through calls to *::CoCreateInstanceEx*, which uses the CLSID of the object to search the system registry for the COM server; for inproc servers, *::CoCreateInstanceEx* uses the registered path for the server. If the server does not have a path, *::CoCreateInstanceEx* uses the Win32 module loading rules (in other words, the same DLL location rules as used by *::LoadLibraryEx*) to locate the DLL and load it. The actual COM object is created by a class factory that is intimately involved with the COM object because only the class factory knows how to create and initialize the COM object, and only the COM object knows how to destroy itself and free the resources it uses.

Clearly, .NET must supply a class factory that can be used to create .NET objects that are accessible through COM. The native "face" to the .NET runtime is the file mscoree.dll, which exports *DllGetClassObject*. *DllGetClassObject* can access the class factories for all .NET classes. When a .NET object is registered as accessible by native code as a COM object (I'll explain how in a moment), the *InprocServer32* registry key will specify mscoree.dll as the server DLL and will have registry keys that identify the .NET class, the name of the .NET assembly that contains the class, and (optionally) an absolute path to the assembly.

Note that I specifically said the *InprocServer32 registry key* because .NET does not support local (EXE) servers; it only supports giving access to .NET objects through COM for library assemblies. .NET does support out-of-process activation, but this ability requires the use of a surrogate. If you use out-of-process activation, however, you do not need to derive the .NET class from *MarshalByRefObject* even though the object will be accessed from another AppDomain. If you access a .NET object in another AppDomain through .NET remoting, the remote .NET class must derive from *MarshalByRefObject*.

> **Note** If a class is accessed through COM+, the class has to be derived from *ServicedComponent*, which is derived from *MarshalByRefObject*.

Interfaces

COM objects are always accessed through interfaces; COM only knows how to marshal interfaces. A COM interface pointer is effectively a pointer to a vtable. The vtable holds a series of "slots," each of which contains a function pointer to a member of the interface. The COM contract implicit in interfaces is that when a COM client obtains a COM interface (through *::CoCreateInstanceEx*,

IUnknown::QueryInterface, or some other COM API), the vtable will have the correct number of slots (one for each member of the interface), and each of these slots will have a valid function pointer associated with the member in the same position in the interface. Put simply, the client is *guaranteed* that when it calls an interface member through an interface pointer it will make the call through a valid function pointer. In effect, COM interface marshaling transposes the vtable of a C++ object from one context (apartment) to another.

The ECMA specification for .NET does not mention how interface references are implemented. The ECMA specification says that interface methods are virtual and are called with the *callvirt* opcode (although as with other virtual methods, they can also be called non-virtually). The *callvirt* opcode calls the method based on the run-time type of the object rather than the compile-time class visible in the method metadata token, but the specification gives no indication how this is achieved. If you step into a call through an interface reference, you will find that the interface is implemented through a vtable—just as COM interfaces are. This information is important because it means that the order that you declare members in an interface is significant. Normally, when you use .NET interfaces, you will not be aware of this order because .NET type safety ensures that you can use an interface reference only on an object that implements that *specific* interface. However, as you'll see later (the section ".NET COM Attributes"), when you manually declare interfaces used in COM interop, the runtime cannot perform such stringent type checks, and consequently you have the responsibility to ensure that the interfaces are declared correctly.

COM is based on interface programming—that is, all access to a COM class is through the interfaces that the class implements. The .NET designers decided to follow the example of Visual Basic and Common Object Request Broker Architecture (CORBA) and to prefer access via class members rather than via interfaces. The .NET designers also bowed to the Java model and allowed the developer to use interface programming as a secondary approach. Interface programming is a great model because developers select the *behavior* that they want; when you access an object through its class, you have a mishmash of all the behaviors implemented by the object. Because .NET gives preferences to accessing an object through class members, it has some incompatibilities with pure-COM interface programming. How do you handle code that expects access to class-based methods with a mechanism that expects methods to be members of interfaces?

Visual Basic 6 could use COM objects through class (as opposed to interface) methods if such objects implemented *IDispatch*. *IDispatch* uses late binding—that is, the method is determined at run time based on an identifier passed to *IDispatch::Invoke*. Of course, this system means that there is an extra performance issue of carrying out this dispatch, and there is the implicit possibility that the identifier will be invalid, so the method will not be able to be called. Earlier bound, vtable-based interfaces *always* guarantee that if the interface pointer is valid, *all* of the methods in the interface will be valid.

The problem with the .NET approach, from the COM point of view, is that an external class can access the public members of another class even in the case when those methods are not members of interfaces. You can understand that a one-to-one mapping could be performed between .NET interfaces and COM interfaces, but how do public non-interface methods fit into this scheme? To address this problem, .NET has a concept of a "class" interface. This interface is an amalgamation of all the public methods on the class—methods on interfaces and non-interface methods and the accessor methods for properties.[6] This interface is provided as a named implementation of *IDispatch*. The interface takes the name of the class prefixed with an underscore (for example, the class interface for *MyObject* is *_MyObject*). Depending on the attributes that you use on your managed class, you can indicate that the class interface is implemented solely through *IDispatch* or through a dual interface.

Versioning in COM is performed through interfaces; early bound interfaces are immutable, which preserves the layout of the interface vtable. If a COM coclass changes, its COM name (its CLSID) must also change, and the changes are expressed through the coclass implementing a new interface. Old clients are supported because the old interfaces are supported. If a .NET class changes, the class interface will also change, and hence the vtable will change, which will break clients that are early bound to this interface. For this reason, the default for .NET classes accessed through COM interop is *not* to allow the class interface to be accessible through a dual interface (and be early bound) but to allow the class to be accessible through late-bound clients (by explicitly calling *IDispatch::GetIDsOfNames* and *IDispatch::Invoke*). The message is clear: for versioning to work with .NET classes accessible through COM interop, those classes should implement interfaces.

Note also that .NET interface inheritance does not have the same meaning in COM as it does in .NET: COM interfaces can have only a single base interface. If a .NET interface inherits from more than one .NET interface, this relationship cannot be reflected in the COM world. COM clients do not use the inheritance relationship between interfaces. If you want to cast from one COM interface to another, you use *IUnknown::QueryInterface*. Thus, a .NET class that implements an interface that has two base interfaces will appear to a COM client as a class that implements three interfaces: the relationship has been "flattened."

---

6. Interfaces contain only methods, so public fields of a .NET class are not accessible through COM interop.

COM Callable and Runtime Callable Wrappers

When you create a COM object in .NET code through COM interop, you will get an object reference. (If you use IJW, you will be able to use unmanaged COM pointers.) The object reference will be to a managed wrapper around the COM object. This object will implement managed interfaces equivalent to the COM interfaces that are requested. This wrapper is called by code running under the runtime, so it is known as the *runtime callable wrapper* (RCW). There will be an RCW for each COM object accessed through COM interop.

The RCW is a .NET object, so everything that you expect on a .NET object will be available. If you use reflection on an RCW, you will get information about the methods on the COM class[7] in addition to some extra methods provided by the RCW. (The RCW derives from *MarshalByRefObject*.) The RCW gets this information from the type library and does not appear to call *IDispatch::GetTypeInfo*.

The RCW provides a method stub for each interface method. The method stub performs the transition from managed to unmanaged context and marshals the parameters. When the method completes, the stub catches any exceptions thrown by the COM method and checks the *HRESULT* for failure values. The stub then translates these values to managed exceptions. If the method has a parameter marked as *[out, retval]*, the RCW will use this parameter as the return value to the method.

When COM code calls a .NET object through COM interop, the code will get a wrapper object named a *COM Callable Wrapper* (CCW). The CCW implements the interfaces supported by the .NET object as well as the class interface. The vtables for these interfaces are tear-off interfaces: they are created dynamically by *IUnknown::QueryInterface* of the CCW. The methods in the tear-off do the transition from unmanaged to managed context and marshal the parameters. If the .NET object throws an exception, the CCW will convert this exception to an appropriate *HRESULT* and to a COM error object.

COM Servers

COM servers accessed through COM interop can be inproc (DLL), local servers (EXE), hosted by a surrogate (DllHost.exe, with or without COM+), or remote. The RCW is the "interface" to COM on the local machine that will load the appropriate proxy to allow the RCW to access the COM object.

.NET types can be accessed through COM interop only if they are implemented in DLLs—that is, the .NET assembly will be accessed in-process or via a surrogate; .NET will not load the assembly as a local server. When a COM client releases its last reference count on a CCW, the .NET object becomes available for collection. COM clients expect that in-apartment objects will be released as

7. The *class*: you will get all the members on the class even if you call reflection on an interface reference.

soon as the last reference count is removed. (Out-of-apartment objects will not necessarily go away immediately because the stub manager will actually hold references to the object, and the stub manager, not the client, ultimately decides when the object is no longer being accessed.) However, the occurrence of garbage collection will depend on the state of the managed heap. Rest assured: when the .NET assembly unloads from memory, a garbage collection will be triggered, and the COM client process will not be allowed to terminate until all the finalizers of the .NET objects have completed.

Tools

So far I have mentioned wrappers and the registration of .NET objects as COM objects, but I have not mentioned how this process happens. The .NET Framework SDK provides tools to help you do this.

Exporting Types

If you want to use a .NET class from a COM client, you need to register the .NET class so that the object is co-creatable. You also need to provide type information so that the COM client has interface information. To register a COM class, you use a tool named RegAsm (and optionally, another tool named GacUtil), and to generate the type information, you use TlbExp.

The TlbExp tool will generate a type library (.tlb) based on the metadata in an assembly that you supply. You can then use this type library in a tool such as Visual Basic 6 or pass the name of the library to the *#import* directive in Visual C++ to generate the C++ bindings for the interfaces the type library describes. Type libraries are used by the COM type library marshaler to describe the types being marshaled and typically are bound as a resource to the code that uses the interfaces.

When a .NET object is registered, its *ThreadingModel* is given as *Both*, which means that if the object is accessed inproc (in other words, if it is not hosted in a surrogate or in COM+), COM marshaling will not be used. This lack of COM marshaling means that a proxy will not be required, so type information is not strictly required. Furthermore, the .NET class could implement interfaces for which there are standard proxies for the equivalent COM interface. Bear in mind that although *Both* COM objects can be created in any apartment type, cross-apartment access to such an object will require interface marshaling. However, .NET components accessed through COM interop on a machine that has the runtime installed do not have to use type library marshaling and do not need a type library to be registered or even generated.

In some cases, you will want to generate type information, if only for the convenience of having the type information. The TlbExp tool is used like this:

```
TlbExp myassem.dll
```

This command will generate a type library named myassem.tlb from the metadata in myassem.dll. This tool uses the facilities in the *TypeLibConverter* class, which is a public class in *System::Runtime::InteropServices*, so you can call the class in your own code.

You can influence the type information generated by this tool by using custom attributes. I will cover these attributes in the sections ".NET COM Attributes" and "Using .NET Types from COM." If you need to have a type library for an assembly (for example, if the types will be used by Visual Basic 6 or scripting languages), it makes sense to bind the type library to the PE file of the assembly so that the type library is always associated with the types it describes. The .NET Framework SDK has an example named TlbGen. This tool takes the name of an assembly and generates a type library from the metadata in the assembly. The tool then binds the type library resource to the assembly and, because this operation will alter the size of the assembly (and hence the hash generated for the assembly), the tool will re-sign the file if you indicate that the assembly should have a strong name.

The RegAsm tool searches the metadata of the assembly passed to it for public *__gc* types that are not *__abstract*. For each suitable type that it finds, the tool will generate COM registration information. If the metadata does not have CLSIDs, this tool will generate a CLSID for the class; it will do the same for ProgIDs. Note that the tool ignores interfaces; in COM, interfaces are registered to specify the proxy-stub code used to marshal the interface. The CCW implements *IMarshal*, which means that the interfaces are custom marshaled and the CCW provides the proxy-stub code used to marshal the interfaces on the object.

You too can have the facilities of RegAsm because the *RegistrationServices* class has static members to register an assembly (*RegisterAssembly*), unregister an assembly (*UnregisterAssembly*), or register a specific type (*RegisterType-ForComClients*).

After you have run this tool on an assembly, each public *__gc* type will have an *InprocServer32* key specifying mscoree.dll as the server and the key will have the additional values shown in Table 2-4.

Table 2-4 The *InprocServer32* Registry Values for a .NET Class Accessed Through COM Interop

Value	Explanation
Assembly	The full name of the assembly
Class	The fully qualified name of the .NET class
CodeBase	Gives the full path to the assembly file
RuntimeVersion	The version of the runtime that the class was written for
ThreadingModel	The COM threading model of the class, always set to *Both*

The whole point of the COM registration values is to provide definitive information about the location of the server that provides the object. However, the registry values for a class registered with RegAsm will give only an absolute path to mscoree.dll. The intention is that .NET assembly location rules will be used to try to avoid the common Win32 problem of loading the wrong DLL. Fusion will search for the assembly in this order:

1. The folders specified in the *DEVPATH* environment variable (Clearly, this variable should be used only on development machines.)
2. The global assembly cache
3. The current folder
4. A subfolder of the current folder that has the short name of the assembly

In general, the assembly should be in the same folder as the client that uses it. One side effect of this policy is that if you try to create an instance of the object in OleView, you will get the *HRESULT* of *COR_E_TYPELOAD* because the runtime will not find the assembly in the same folder as OleView. To solve this problem, and if you decide that the types in the assembly are so useful that you want to allow other COM clients to access them, you have to either make the assembly shared or make it more accessible. To make the assembly shared, you put it in the GAC; to make the assembly more accessible, you specify a codebase. The codebase can be specified in the machine or the application config file, or if you use the */CodeBase* switch with RegAsm, a value named *CodeBase* will be added to the registry value for the object. To use this switch, the assembly must be signed, and if you sign the assembly, it makes more sense to add the assembly to the GAC, in which case the *CodeBase* value is not needed.

Importing Types

To use a type in .NET, you have to import metadata in the source file so that the compiler has the information it needs to access the type. To get metadata for a COM object and its interfaces, either you can declare the metadata yourself (which I will explain in the next section) or you can use TlbImp, which will create metadata based on a type library. The output from this tool is an assembly (an *interop assembly*) that contains only metadata. Creating an interop assembly is straightforward, as shown here:

```
tlbimp mylib.tlb /out:mytypes.dll
```

This command will create an assembly named *mytypes* with the metadata for the types defined in the type library. (You too can convert a type library to an interop assembly through the *TypeLibConverter* class.) You can use this metadata in an assembly with the *#using* directive. Now, imagine that another user of the types uses TlbImp to create another import assembly named *yourtypes*. In .NET, the assembly is the boundary of versioning, so the types defined in *mytypes* and *yourtypes* will be different. This difference means that if you have a third assembly that uses types in the assemblies that use *mytypes* and *yourtypes*, you will suffer type mismatches. The solution is to ensure that you create only one interop assembly from a type library, and whenever you use the COM types, you always use that official interop assembly.

Such an assembly is called the *primary interop assembly* (PIA) and is created by calling TlbImp with the */primary* switch and providing a key file. The key file is used to sign the PIA to prove that it is the official interop assembly. When you install Visual Studio .NET, you will get a folder under Program Files\Microsoft.NET named *Primary Interop Assemblies* that contains PIAs for standard Windows type libraries. You are most likely to use these PIAs if you are creating an interop assembly because a type library often references other type libraries that define the types the library uses. (In particular, the type library *stdole.tlb* is usually referenced.) TlbImp will locate these referenced type libraries and add their definitions to the interop assembly. Of course, this generates the possibility of the problem I mentioned earlier, namely having several assemblies with different definitions of the same COM type. To get around this issue, you should use the */reference* switch of TlbImp to specify a PIA that will be checked first for a type before attempting to add the type from a type library.

When you think about it, an interop assembly is an odd beast—after all, what use is metadata if the data is not associated with code? However, on closer inspection, interop assemblies do make sense because the metadata contains information that indicates where the code resides, namely in a COM server. This information is added through attributes.

.NET COM Attributes

The TlbImp tool will read the types in a type library and generate .NET metadata from those types. This metadata will have custom attributes that indicate to the runtime the COM types that the metadata refers to. The .NET code that uses the interop assembly will call the managed types to access the COM types, and the metadata information is used by the RCW to make the COM calls. When you call methods on the RCW, your code calls managed code with managed parameters, so the RCW will need to marshal those parameters. Again, this information is given via custom attributes.

Let's look at an example. Here is a type library definition:

```
[object, dual, uuid(347DEDAC-205E-3987-9AF3-DBB1A0ADAFF2)]
interface ITest : IDispatch
{
   [id(1)] void Method();
   [id(2)] void MethodTwo();
};
```

```
[uuid(E5AD6A74-6A89-357A-A571-0D38CBE92ABE), version(1.0)]
coclass Test
{
   [default] interface ITest;
};
```

TlbImp will generate metadata equivalent to the following pseudo managed C++:

```
[ GuidAttribute("347DEDAC-205E-3987-9AF3-DBB1A0ADAFF2"),
   ComImport]
__gc __interface ITest
{
   [DispId(1)] void Method();
   [DispId(2)] void MethodTwo();
};
[ GuidAttribute("E5AD6A74-6A89-357A-A571-0D38CBE92ABE"),
   ComImport ]
public __gc __abstract class TestClass : public ITest
{
public:
   TestClass();
   void Method();
   void MethodTwo();
};
[ GuidAttribute("347DEDAC-205E-3987-9AF3-DBB1A0ADAFF2"),
   CoClass(__typeof(TestClass)), ComImport ]
public __gc __interface Test : public ITest
{
};
```

The *[GuidAttribute]* attribute is used to indicate the COM GUID of the specified item. (Names of items in COM are GUIDs.) *ITest* is a managed interface that is implemented by the *TestClass* class. (This class is abstract, and I'll come back to it in a moment.) TlbImp also generates an interface named *Test*. That interface is the .NET equivalent of the *coclass* in COM. In fact, if you create instances of the *TestClass* in managed C++, the *Test* class can be used by other .NET languages. For example, a C# program can create the COM object with this code:

```
// C#
Test test = new Test();
test.Method();
```

At this point, I should say *do not try this at home* because you cannot create an instance of an interface. However, this *TestClass* interface is special because it is marked with the *[CoClass]* custom attribute and the *[ComImport]* pseudo custom attribute. The *[ComImport]* attribute indicates that the interface is the result of importing type information, and the *[CoClass]* custom attribute indicates an "interface" to the class's class factory. Together, these attributes tell the C# compiler to treat the code as a request to create an instance of the class specified as the parameter to the *[CoClass]* attribute through a COM class factory.

The implementation of the *TestClass* constructor and the other methods in the class are marked as *runtime managed internalcall* in the assembly, which means that the method is not provided in the class, but instead is provided by the runtime. I cannot simulate this behavior in C++, so the only way that you can import a managed version of a *coclass* is through TlbImp.[8] However, although the imported interface methods are also marked *runtime managed internalcall*, the runtime appears to ignore this information. Furthermore, the RCW ignores .NET rules when you tell it to perform interface programming. Thus, the COM object *Test* implements *ITest*, but I can define the following interface in my assembly that imports the interop assembly for *Test*:

```
[GuidAttribute("347DEDAC-205E-3987-9AF3-DBB1A0ADAFF2")]
__gc __interface IAnotherInterface
{
   [DispId(2)] void MethodTwo();
   [DispId(1)] void Method();
};

void main()
{
   IAnotherInterface* test;
   test = dynamic_cast<IAnotherInterface*>(new TestClass);
   test->Method();
}
```

Note that I have defined a new interface with a totally different name, but the GUID is the same as the *ITest* GUID. The cast to this interface will succeed because under the covers the runtime treats the cast to the interface type as a call to *IUnknown::QueryInterface*. However, notice that in my new interface I have switched the declarations of *Method* and *MethodTwo*. I mentioned in the "Interfaces" section earlier in this chapter that the runtime makes managed interface calls through vtables, so the call to *Method* in the *main* method is actually an instruction to make a call to the second method of the interface, which the RCW will interpret as a call to the unmanaged *ITest::MethodTwo*. Thus, it is vitally important that if you define the managed interface version of a COM interface in your assemblies, you take care to ensure that you preserve the order of the methods.

---

8. I can make a method *runtime internalcall* using *[MethodImpl]* in *System::Runtime::CompilerServices*, but creating a type with such a method will throw a run-time exception.

But why go to the bother of defining an interface when TlbImp will do it for you? When you use TlbImp on a type library, it will convert the interface method signatures from COM to .NET—that is, TlbImp will hide the *HRESULT* return value that all marshalable methods must return and it will convert failure *HRESULT* values to exceptions. If the COM method has a parameter marked as *[out, retval]*, the managed method will use this parameter as the return value. Some COM methods use the method return value to return success *HRESULT* values. The classic example is an enumerator interface that returns *S_FALSE* from a call to *Next* to indicate success (in other words, no exceptions were thrown), but the interface had no more data to return. If you have such a method, the value of the success *HRESULT* is important to you, but that value is thrown away by the RCW. To overcome this problem, you can redefine the interface by marking the method with the *[PreserveSig]* custom attribute and declaring the method as returning an *unsigned int* value.

Interfaces Defined by the .NET Framework

If your interfaces are not described by a type library, you can declare them yourself as managed interfaces, as shown in the previous section. You might have to use the *[MarshalAs]* attribute to ensure that the parameters are marshaled from the managed types to the COM types expected by the COM object. In particular, if the COM interface has parameters that are COM interfaces, you need to indicate how the interface should be marshaled. If the COM interface expects an *IUnknown* or an *IDispatch* pointer, you can use *Unmanaged-Type::IUnknown* or *UnmanagedType::IDispatch*. If the interface is a custom interface, you should use *UnmanagedType::Interface*, which indicates that the proxy used to marshal the parameter is determined from the *[GuidAttribute]* of the managed interface.

Furthermore, if the parameter of the COM interface is a *SAFEARRAY**, the equivalent parameter on the managed interface will be a managed array. The *[MarshalAs]* attribute indicates that the parameter should be marshaled as a *SAFEARRAY* by *UnmanagedType::SafeArray*, and the field *SafeArraySubType* indicates the COM type of the data in the *SAFEARRAY*.

Finally, the *System::Runtime::InteropServices* namespace also declares some managed versions of unmanaged COM interfaces. (These are interfaces with the prefix *UCOM*.) However, you are unlikely to use these interfaces unless you access objects through monikers or access the type information of a COM object.

Using COM Types in .NET

If your .NET code uses COM components, you have the choice between using COM interop or IJW. If you use COM interop, you have the advantage of using managed types. Managed types are particularly useful for late binding code because the .NET reflection API is less complicated to use than COM automation, particularly the code to access type information. The RCW will hold a reference count to the COM object and will do so until the RCW has been collected. Consider the following code:

```
TestClass* test = new TestClass;
test->Method();
test = 0;
// COM object still survives
```

Assigning the object reference to zero will remove the reference, so the object will be a candidate for collection. But you cannot guarantee when the collection will occur. You could add a call to *GC::Collect* after this code, but the collection could take time, and it is usually best to make this call only when you know that any performance hit will not affect the behavior of your application. Instead, the *Marshal* class provides a static method to tell the RCW to release its reference count. Consider this code:

```
TestClass* test = new TestClass;
ITest* testPtr = dynamic_cast<ITest*>(test);
testPtr->Method();
Marshal::ReleaseComObject(test);
test = testPtr = 0;
```

Here I have called *ReleaseComObject* on the object reference, but I could have called the method on the interface reference to get the same effect. The interesting thing about this call is that I have two references to the .NET object (through *test* and *testPtr*) and yet only one call to *ReleaseComObject* is needed to release the COM object. After this call, do not be tempted to call the RCW; if you do, you will get a *NullReferenceException* because the RCW will not have a pointer to the COM object. This behavior is why I have assigned the object and interface references to zero. The *ReleaseComObject* method is useful if the COM object holds onto scarce resources and the object is accessed in-apartment.

If you access COM objects through IJW, you might want to pass an interface pointer from a .NET object to the COM object. Such a .NET object must be visible to COM code, which means that the object derives from a managed interface imported through TlbImp. For example, imagine that you have these COM interfaces:

```
// See comobj.cpp.
interface ICallback : IDispatch
{
```

```
   HRESULT CallMe();
};
interface IInformer : IDispatch
{
   HRESULT InformYou(ICallback* p);
};
```

A COM object could implement *IInformer*, and when the object is called with *InformYou*, it might do some work and then inform the caller by calling *ICallback::CallMe*. If you have a managed version of *ICallback* (defined in a namespace, say *managedItfs*), you can create a managed class to handle the call back. However, if you create the *Informed* object through IJW, you have the problem of getting a native interface on the managed object. You can get the interface by calling *Marshal::GetComInterfaceForObject*, as shown here:

```
// usecomobj.cpp
// This class implements managedItfs::ICallback.
CallbackObj* x = new CallbackObj;
IntPtr itf = Marshal::GetComInterfaceForObject(
   x, __typeof(managedItfs::ICallback));
// Create the object through IJW.
IInformer* informed;
hr = ::CoCreateInstance(__uuidof(Informed), NULL,
   CLSCTX_ALL, __uuidof(informed), (void**)&informed);
// Cast to the unmanaged interface to keep the compiler happy.
informed->InformYou(static_cast<ICallback*>(
                     static_cast<void*>(itf)));
informed->Release();
```

GetComInterfaceForObject obtains the COM interface on the managed object based on the *[GuidAttribute]* applied to the managed interface. The method returns an *IntPtr*, so you have to cast the *IntPtr* first to a *void** to get the encapsulated value and then cast to the unmanaged interface type before finally passing the interface to the COM object.

Marshal also has *GetIUnknownForObject* and *GetIDispatchForObject*, which you can call to get the *IUnknown* and *IDispatch* interfaces implemented by the RCW for a .NET object. The method *GetITypeInfoForObject* will return the *ITypeInfo* based on a *Type* object returned from the RCW. In some cases, COM methods pass object pointers through a *VARIANT*, and you can convert an object to a COM *VARIANT* by calling *GetNativeVariantForObject*.

If you have an unmanaged interface pointer obtained through IJW, you can convert the pointer to a managed interface pointer using *GetObjectForIUnknown*, *GetObjectForNativeVariant*, or *GetTypedObjectForIUnknown*, depending on how the interface pointer was marshaled and the .NET format that you want to use.

If you use COM interop, a *VARIANT* parameter will appear in the managed interface as *Object __gc**. If you pass an object reference through this pointer, the object will be marshaled as *VT_UNKNOWN*. This type of marshaling might not be your intention. You might decide that you want the object passed as an *IDispatch* pointer (*VT_DISPATCH*), in which case you can create an instance of *DispatchWrapper*, passing your object to the constructor, and then pass this instance to the COM method. Similarly there are wrapper classes, *CurrencyWrapper*, *ErrorWrapper*, and *UnknownWrapper*, that explicitly marshal an object as *VT_CY*, *VT_ERROR*, and *VT_UNKNOWN*, respectively.

Using .NET Types from COM

If your .NET types are likely to be used by COM clients through COM interop, you can apply some .NET custom attributes to improve the access to those objects. In general, you do not need to apply the *[GuidAttribute]* attribute because the TlbExp tool (and RegAsm) will generate a unique GUID for the type. You can see this GUID by calling *Marshal::GenerateGuidForType*. Similarly, a ProgID will be generated for you (which you can view with *GenerateProgIdForType*) but this ID might not be of a suitable format, so you can use *[ProgId]* to specify your own ProgID.

You can also use the *[DispId]* attribute to give the DISPID of an interface method. Bear in mind that the class interface will have methods inherited from *System::Object* and the interface will automatically give *ToString* a DISPID of 0 (the default method). You can use the *[ClassInterface]* attribute to indicate how the class interface should be supplied to the client. (The class interface has all class public members, including members that are not part of an interface.) The choices are given by the *ClassInterfaceType* enumeration; the default is *AutoDispatch*, which means that the class interface is available only through *IDispatch*. *AutoDispatch* is the safest option because if the .NET class changes, no interface will change, so existing clients with an old type library will still be able to access the object. Of course, this means that your clients must use automation, which is a pain to do in C++ and creates performance issues.

The *[ClassInterface]* attribute can also take *AutoDual*, but this member of the *ClassInterfaceType* enumeration is not recommended because it will provide a dual interface with all the public members of the class. If the class changes, this interface will change, and hence it will have a new IID. Older clients querying for the IID of the previous class interface will get an error. Finally, you can use *None* for the *[ClassInterface]*. I actually prefer this option for this reason: COM objects are designed for interface programming, so they should be accessed only through interfaces. It goes against the principles of interface programming to provide a class interface because there is no grouping of members according to their behavior. The class interface groups members only by their implementation—that is, they are the members implemented by a particular class.

You can also determine how other interfaces are exposed to COM. The *[InterfaceType]* attribute takes a *ComInterfaceType* value of either *InterfaceIsDual*, *InterfaceIsIDispatch*, or *InterfaceIsIUnknown*. The first value indicates that the interface will be available through *IDispatch* or through a dual interface (and hence will allow early binding), the second value means that it will be available only through *IDispatch*, and the last value supports only early binding.

TlbExp will make all public members visible through the type library; RegAsm will register all public classes as co-creatable. This behavior might not be your intention. You might decide that only a few types defined in your assembly should be visible through the type library, or you might have a class that is not co-creatable (that is, the class is creatable only as a return value from another class). To hide types from the type library, you can use the *[ComVisible(false)]* attribute. Types with this attribute will not be put in the type library, and they will be ignored by RegAsm.

With COM, you have to specify explicitly how parameters are marshaled: are they *in* parameters or *out* parameters, or will the data be passed in both directions? The .NET attributes *[In]* and *[Out]* are only suggestions to the runtime for pure .NET methods. However, for COM interop, they are obeyed by the runtime, and they are used by TlbExp to determine the COM attributes that will go in the type library.

Exceptions

Throwing exceptions is the accepted .NET way of indicating errors. In COM, *HRESULT* values and error objects are the accepted mechanism. Indeed, COM developers are taught from an early age never to allow an exception to be thrown by a COM method. Thus, the two mechanisms are incompatible, so the CCW tries to ensure that .NET exceptions are treated in a way acceptable to COM. The .NET Framework SDK lists the *HRESULT* values that correspond to the managed exceptions in the header file CorError.h. It is important to point out that the .NET runtime facility code is *0x13*, so any *HRESULT* that has *0x8013* as the top *WORD* will be a failure *HRESULT* from .NET. To get additional information, you should access the error object through the *::GetErrorInfo* API, as shown here:

```
// ptr is a COM interface pointer to a managed object.
HRESULT hr = ptr->Method();
if (FAILED(hr))
{
   printf("Method failed with: %08x\n", hr);
   CComPtr<IErrorInfo> error;
   hr = GetErrorInfo(0, &error);
   if (hr == S_OK)
```

```
   {
      CComBSTR bstr;
      error->GetDescription(&bstr);
      printf("Exception: %S\n", bstr.m_str);
      bstr.Empty();
      error->GetSource(&bstr);
      printf("Assembly: %S\n", bstr.m_str);
      bstr.Empty();
      error->GetHelpFile(&bstr);
      printf("Help file: %S\n", bstr.m_str);
      DWORD dw;
      error->GetHelpContext(&dw);
      printf("Help ctx: %ld\n", dw);
   }
}
```

The *Exception::Message* property is accessible through *IErrorInfo::GetDescription*, whereas *GetSource* returns the name of the assembly that contained the type that threw the exception.

You get the "outer" exception only through *IErrorInfo*; the *Exception::InnerException* is effectively thrown away. This behavior is a pity because COM has a perfectly usable mechanism through *IErrorRecords* that allows multiple error records to be passed to another apartment, but sadly, COM interop does not use this interface.

The astute reader will notice that *System::Exception* has a property named *HelpLink* that is expected to be a URL to a description of the error. This URL can be to a page or to an anchored item on the page. *IErrorInfo* splits the error location into two parts: a help file and a help context. During the translation of an *Exception* to an error object, the runtime examines *HelpLink*, and if this property contains a numeric anchor, the anchor is used as the help context and the URL without an anchor is used as the help file. If the anchor is missing or if the anchor is not numeric, the help file will merely return the entire string in *HelpLink*.

Marshaling .NET Objects

The CCW for a .NET object accessed through COM interop will implement the following interfaces:

```
IConnectionPointContainer
IDispatch
IManagedObject
IMarshal
IProvideClassInfo
ISupportErrorInfo
IUnknown
_Object
```

IManagedObject is described in mscoree.tlb, and *_Object* is described in mscorlib.tlb. If the .NET object is serializable, the serialized state is returned from *IManagedObject::GetSerializedBuffer*. The *GetObjectIdentity* method returns a *BSTR* with a GUID that represents the identity of the .NET object and two integers that represent the identity of the AppDomain and the CCW. The *_Object* interface is described in mscorlib.tlb and is *System::Object* accessible through COM interop.

It is interesting that the CCW implements *IMarshal* because this implementation means that the CCW manages its own marshaling, so the interfaces supported by the object do not have to have proxy-stub information in the system registry. When a CCW interface is unmarshaled, the system calls *IMarshal::GetUnmarshalClass*. This call will return the CLSID of an object with the ProgID of *CCWU.ComCallWrapper*.

The .NET Framework has an attribute named *[AutomationProxy]*, and the .NET Framework documentation states that you can use this attribute on your .NET classes to indicate that the class will be marshaled with the automation marshaler. My tests, however, indicate that whether I use this attribute or not I still get *CCWU.ComCallWrapper* used as the class to unmarshal the object.

Threading

COM objects can run only in a COM apartment. If you attempt to call a COM API or access a COM object through an interface pointer without initializing a COM apartment, you'll get an error: *CO_E_NOTINITIALIZED*. .NET code clearly has to initialize an apartment before you can call a COM object through COM interop, so how does this initialization happen? Well, like most things in .NET, the initialization is done automatically. When a COM call is made, the runtime will initialize an apartment automatically. A native thread initializes itself in an apartment by calling *CoInitializeEx*, and the parameter of this API determines which apartment type: the thread is either initialized in a new STA apartment, or it is initialized in the process MTA apartment. In .NET, there are two ways to specify the apartment that a .NET thread runs: attributes and the thread object. When you create a new thread, you can set the apartment membership through the *Thread::ApartmentState* property, but you can set this property only once.

If you do not specify the apartment type that should be used, the runtime will assume an MTA; before any COM call is made, the runtime will ensure that an apartment is initialized. This initialization happens whether you access the COM object through COM interop or IJW. Thus, if you call *::CoCreateInstanceEx*, the initialization will succeed whether or not you call *CoInitializeEx*. Of course, if the object you access is an inproc object and is marked as being *Apartment* threaded, the object will always run in an STA. If you call this object from .NET code, the call will be from an MTA apartment, so the calls to the object will be marshaled to the STA apartment through a COM proxy. This code is not very efficient, so to call the COM object from the apartment for which it is best designed, you should specify the apartment type before making the COM call, as shown here:

```
Thread::CurrentThread->ApartmentState = ApartmentState::STA;
IMyInterface* pItf;
::CoCreateInstanceEx(__uuidof(MyObject), NULL, CLSCTX_ALL,
   __uuidof(pItf), (void**)&pItf);
// Use pItf.
```

COM+ Interop

It is worth pointing out here that COM+ Component Services is .NET Component Services (now known as .NET Enterprise Services). Regardless of what you might read from any other self-appointed commentator (including this one), you can be assured that Microsoft will *always* support both COM and COM+. You can be assured that code written for COM and COM+ will always work with .NET.

Summary

Interoperation with unmanaged code and COM is vitally important for the .NET Framework, and interop is also important for your code. If you need to use code that is not part of the .NET Framework, you must import this code from somewhere else, and this is where interop comes in.

The term *interop* is wide, and in this chapter, I have covered the three cases where interop is used: platform invoke, COM interop, and IJW. Platform invoke is an attribute-based technology; the developer uses attributes to instruct the compiler to import code from DLLs and can optionally indicate to the compiler to add metadata that tells the runtime to use a custom marshaler. COM interop is also attribute based, but unlike platform invoke, COM interop is two-way: COM clients can access .NET objects through COM interop, and .NET code can access COM objects through COM interop. The .NET Framework SDK provides the tools and classes to allow you to generate interop assemblies and type libraries and to register .NET objects with COM. Finally, managed C++ can access native code (C++ classes or native static-link libraries) directly. This access does not need any other code, and for this reason, the technology is called *It Just Works!* IJW is a great technology because you can write managed code that uses existing code: if that code is provided through a C++ library, the native C++ will be compiled to MSIL, but the data will be *unmanaged* and hence allocated on the C++ or CRT heap or on the stack. Such types behave as C++ types but can interoperate seamlessly with managed code that uses .NET types.

If you need to interoperate with native code, C++ is the best language to use. I will come back to interoperation later in this book because this technology is so important. In Chapter 4, I will show how to interoperate with GDI, and in Chapter 5, I will show how to interoperate with .NET application domains, and I will explain the security aspects of interoperation. However, there is one aspect of interop that I have not covered in this chapter: callbacks. Callbacks to native code and COM use delegates and events, which are the topic of the next chapter.

3

Delegates and Events

This chapter is all about indirect calls to methods. Methods can be *instance* methods or *static* methods, but they have one thing in common: they are code implemented in a .NET type. Usually when you call a method, you know the class where the object is implemented. Indeed, .NET *requires* the class to be known because this knowledge ensures the type safety of the call. Sometimes you will want to call a method of a particular type, and in native C++, you will normally make this call through a function pointer of some kind. In .NET, you make the same type of call through a delegate.

I will explain what delegates are and how .NET type safety is guaranteed through delegate calls. Delegates are the basic building blocks of many features in .NET, so once I have given the details about how to use delegates themselves, I will show the application of delegates: asynchronous calls, notifications through events, and calling threads.

Delegates as Type-Safe Function Pointers

One source of errors with native code using dynamic-link libraries (DLLs) was caused by the incorrect use of function pointers. A pointer to a function in a DLL can be obtained by calling *::GetProcAddress*, but because this API is general purpose, it returns a *void** pointer that you have to cast to an appropriate function pointer so that the compiler will set up the stack correctly to make the function call. Casts are always dangerous, and the worst cast is one that casts a *void** pointer because the compiler has no knowledge about the type pointed to before the cast and cannot ensure that the cast is correct.

Objects are accessed through pointers. These pointers point to the memory allocated for the object, which essentially means the data that the object contains.

This statement is true for .NET objects (where the object is created on the managed heap) and for C++ objects (which are usually created on the C++ heap). When you call a method, you do so through a typed pointer, and the compiler uses the type of the pointer to determine the method to call. In .NET, the type information is associated with the intermediate language (IL) through metadata.

Objects can have virtual methods, and when a virtual method is invoked, the runtime will locate the method based on the type of the object that the pointer points to, rather than the type of the pointer. In native C++, this locating is done through a vtable, and under the covers, the current version of the runtime appears to use a vtable also. To confirm this, I created an object, pinned the pointer, and then dumped the memory pointed to by the pinned pointer. The first item in this dumped memory is a pointer to a structure that, among other things, contains a vtable.[1]

Thus, when you make a call to an object method through a typed pointer in .NET, information is added to the code that the runtime uses to ensure that the correct method is called at run time. This check is performed at compile time for native C++ code; the compiler checks the type of the pointer and the type of the method.

Function Pointers with Unmanaged Code

Native C++ allows you to declare pointers to methods that are members of a class. This type of pointer is a C++ *pointer to member*. Let's see how the compiler handles this pointer for native C++ compiled to MSIL. Consider this class:

```
// fnptr.cpp
__nogc class Test
{
public:
   void f(int i){ Console::WriteLine(S"called f"); }
};
typedef void (Test::* FUNC)(int);
```

This code defines an unmanaged class and a *typedef* for a pointer to member that takes an integer as a parameter and returns no value. The method uses the .NET Framework class *Console* to print a message to the console, so the code should be compiled with the */clr* switch. As I mentioned in Chapter 2,

1. Obviously, this is an implementation detail and might change with other versions of the runtime. However, it is interesting that this pointer is not merely a pointer to a vtable. The structure appears to hold information such as the number of methods and the size of the object.

the compiler creates a *__value* type for the unmanaged class to hold its data members, and the methods will be added as public static global methods to the module.

I can use the class like this:

```
// fnptr.cpp
Test __nogc* test = new Test;
FUNC ptr = &Test::f;
(test->* ptr)(42);
```

It is interesting to examine how C++ calls methods through the pointer to member. In this code, I first get a pointer to the method of a specific signature (*ptr*), but this pointer is for the class and it is not for a specific object instance. The pointer to member is associated with an instance only when the call is actually made. This arrangement does not seem to be very C++-like to me, C++ is all about abstraction and encapsulation, but there is no encapsulation here.

Now let's design a class to invoke a method that has the same signature as *FUNC*, as shown in the following code:

```
// fnptr.cpp
template<typename T>
class Caller
{
public:
   typedef void (T::* FUNC)(int);
   Caller(void* obj, FUNC f) : m_obj(obj), m_f(f){}
   void Invoke(int i)
   {
      T* obj = static_cast<T*>(m_obj);
      (obj->*m_f)(i);
   }
   void operator()(int i) { Invoke(i); }
private:
   void* m_obj;
   FUNC m_f;
};
```

The method pointer is invoked by calling the *Invoke* member, and for convenience I have declared an *operator* function (but this function is convenient only if you call it through a stack instance). Clearly this class will work only with classes that have a method of the form *void f(int)*. If you want a class like this for another function type, you have to change the *typedef* and *Invoke* (and *operator*). However, because I have written it as a template, I can use the class for any class that has a method with the same signature. The code to use this class looks like this:

```
// fnptr.cpp
Caller<Test> caller(test, &Test::f);
caller.Invoke(42);
caller(42);
```

This syntax is much easier to use than the previous code with pointer to member syntax. It is also better C++ because the *Caller* class encapsulates the object that is being called and the function pointer that is called on the object. Bear this class in mind when I cover delegates later.

Let's return to the code to call a method through a *member to pointer*, as shown here:

```
Test __nogc* test = new Test;
FUNC ptr = &Test::f;
(test->* ptr)(42);
```

The compiler will generate IL to access the function through the pointer, as shown in the following code:

```
.locals (int32 V_0,              // Pointer to member
         valuetype Test V_1)  // The object
ldc.i4.1    // Test has no data, so to have a 'this' pointer,
            // we have to allocate memory (one byte).
call void* modopt(
   [mscorlib]System.Runtime.CompilerServices.CallConvCdecl)
   new(unsigned int32)
stloc.1     // Save the Test instance in V_1.
ldsfld int32** __unep@?f@Test@@$$FQAEXH@Z
stloc.0     // Get the address of Test::f, store it in V_0.
ldloc.1     // Load the 'this' pointer to pass to the method.
ldc.i4.s 42 // Load the parameter to pass to the method.
ldloc.0     // Load the function pointer, and call the method.
calli unmanaged thiscall void modopt([mscorlib]
   System.Runtime.CompilerServices.CallConvThiscall)(int32)
```

The *ptr* variable is initialized with the address of the function. There is no MSIL opcode for loading the address of a native method, so the compiler will calculate this address and put it in a global static field:

```
.field public static int32** __unep@?f@Test@@$$FQAEXH@Z
 at D_000060F0
.data D_000060F0 = bytearray (60 10 40 00)
```

The value stored at location *D_000060F0* is the address of the unmanaged function (the PE header for this file indicates that the function will load at virtual address 0x00400000), so this is why the field name starts with *__unep*, (unmanaged entry point). The stack is constructed with the parameters to be sent to the function followed by the pointer to the unmanaged function. The *this* pointer is always treated as the first parameter, which is why it is the first on the stack. The method is called with the *calli* opcode. Notice that the metadata for the method that is called is marked as being *__thiscall*, which means that the first parameter will be the *this* pointer, which is passed as a 32-bit integer.

If you change the *Test* class from a *__nogc* type to a *__gc* type, you'll find that the compiler will issue an error. You cannot take the address of a method in a managed class.

Function Pointers and Global Functions

Global functions are usually compiled as MSIL, but they are not members of a class, so they are not called with a *this* pointer. Consider this method:

```
String* GetDate()
{
   return DateTime::Now.ToString();
}
typedef String __gc* (__cdecl *Date)(void);
```

This function will be compiled as MSIL, but because it is not a member of a class, the calling convention used will be the default, *__cdecl*. (You can change this calling convention with the */Gd*, */Gr* or */Gz* switches.) The function uses .NET Framework code, and it returns a .NET Framework class, but because the calling convention is one of the unmanaged calling conventions, you can call it through an unmanaged function pointer.

Calling the method is simple, as shown here:

```
// global.cpp
Date date = GetDate;
Console::WriteLine(date());
```

The MSIL generated for this call is similar to the MSIL generated for calling methods on unmanaged classes: the compiler stores the address of the global method in the *.data* section, and this address is accessed through a global field. Because this method is global, there is no *this* pointer, so the MSIL merely loads the field that holds the address of the unmanaged entry point and then executes *calli*.

```
.locals (method unmanaged cdecl string modopt(
   [mscorlib]System.Runtime.CompilerServices.CallConvCdecl)
   *() V_0)
ldsfld int32** __unep@?GetDate@@$$FYAP$AAVString@System@@XZ
stloc.0
ldloc.0
calli unmanaged cdecl string modopt(
   [mscorlib]System.Runtime.CompilerServices.CallConvCdecl)()
```

```
call void [mscorlib]System.Console::WriteLine(string)
ldc.i4.0
ret
```

The only notable differences between this and the MSIL I showed earlier are that this time the function has a typed variable and the local field is marked as *method unmanaged cdecl*. You can call static methods on *__nogc* classes in the same way, and the compiler will generate essentially the same code.

Delegates

Methods on managed types are called with the *__clrcall* calling convention. You cannot declare a function pointer as using this calling convention, so you cannot obtain the address of a method member of a class using C++.[2] Instead, .NET provides a mechanism called a *delegate* that you can use. A delegate works in a similar way to calling through a C++ pointer to member in that you have a method pointer and an object through which the method pointer will be invoked. However, unlike C++, a delegate encapsulates the two. You declare a delegate like this:

```
// delegates.cpp
__delegate void Caller(int);
```

This delegate can be declared at global scope, or it can be a nested member of another type. The compiler will generate a class that looks like this (in which I have converted the MSIL to pseudo C++):

```
__gc __sealed class Caller : public MulticastDelegate
{
public:
   Caller(Object* obj, int meth);
   virtual void Invoke(Int32 i);
   virtual IAsyncResult* BeginInvoke(
      Int32 i, AsyncCallback* cb, Object* state);
   virtual void EndInvoke(IAsyncResult* ar);
};
```

This class derives from *MulticastDelegate*, but ignore that for a moment because I want to concentrate on its base class, *Delegate*. *Delegate* has the following three members that I want to explain:

---

2. However, as you'll see in a moment, MSIL has an opcode named *ldftn* that places the address of a method pointer as an unmanaged *native int* on the stack. Also, the platform invoke marshaler can get an unmanaged pointer to a class member, and I'll show you how to do this later.

```
.field private native int _methodPtr
.field private object _target
.field private class System.Reflection.RuntimeMethodInfo _method
```

These members are initialized with the parameters passed to the delegate constructor and represent the function pointer, the object, and the type information about the method. As you can see, there are parallels with the *Caller<>* class that I showed earlier. Between them, *_methodPtr* and *_method* give enough information for the runtime to make a call on the appropriate method of the *_target* object.

As I mentioned in Chapter 1, the delegate is invoked synchronously by calling the *Invoke* method; the delegate is invoked asynchronously with *BeginInvoke*, and cleanup is performed with *EndInvoke*. The parameters of *Invoke* and *BeginInvoke* depend on the parameters of the method being invoked, whereas the return value of *Invoke* and *EndInvoke* depend on the return value of the method. Thus, the delegate class has to be generated by the compiler for a specific method signature.

Using the delegate is simple:

```
// delegates.cpp
// Class to call
__gc class CallMe
{
public:
   void Call(int i)
   { Console::WriteLine(S"You called me with {0}", __box(i)); }
};
// Code to call the delegate
CallMe* called = new CallMe;
Caller* caller = new Caller(called, &CallMe::Call);
caller->Invoke(42);
caller(42);
```

The parameters of the constructor are the object to call and the address of the method to call. Note that the compiler allows you to use the syntax for getting a pointer to member through the address-of operator (as I have used here), and it also allows you to get the address of the method as if it is a C function pointer (that is, without the address-of operator). If the method is overloaded, the compiler will use the delegate type to determine which method is used to initialize the delegate.

The IL generated to initialize the delegate looks like this:

```
.locals (class Caller V_0,
          class CallMe V_1)
ldnull
stloc.1
ldnull
stloc.0
newobj instance void CallMe::.ctor()
stloc.1
ldloc.1
ldftn instance void CallMe::Call(int32)
newobj instance void Caller::.ctor(object, native int)
stloc.0
```

The important opcode here is *ldftn*, which gets the address of the specified method and returns it as an unmanaged pointer. The .NET Framework equivalent of *native int* is *IntPtr*, but the compiler will not convert the address of a managed method to an *IntPtr*. The following code will not compile because the compiler refuses to convert the managed method to an integer:

```
IntPtr fnPtr(&CallMe::Call);
```

Clearly, the compiler specifically looks for code that initializes a delegate with the address of a managed method and calls *ldftn* in this situation. I will show how you can do this in the section "Delegates and Interop" later in this chapter. In the example I gave earlier, I showed calling an instance method on a *__gc* type; however, you are not restricted to just instance methods or *__gc* types. If the *Call* method was *static*, the only change to the code to initialize the delegate is that the method is not called on an instance, so the first parameter to the delegate constructor should be zero.

The method that is invoked can be an interface method implemented by the object, but note that the compiler will not allow you to pass the address of the interface method as the method parameter to the delegate constructor.

```
__gc __interface ICallback
{
   void Call(int i);
};
__gc class CallMe : public ICallback
{ /* Methods as before */ };

// Code to call it
CallMe* called = new CallMe;
// This code will not compile.
Caller* caller = new Caller(called, &ICallback::Call);
```

The last line will not compile because the compiler expects the method address to be an implementation of a method, and an interface does not implement methods.

The type implementing a method can be a *__value* type, but the type must implement an interface that has the method, as shown here:

```
// delegates.cpp
__value class CallMeVal : public ICallback
{
public:
   void Call(int i);
};

// Code to call it
CallMeVal called;
Caller* caller = new Caller(__box(called), &CallMeVal::Call);
```

Because *__value* methods called through a delegate have to be part of an interface, you cannot call *__value* type *static* methods through a delegate.

Be aware that when you initialize a delegate you pass the address of the method that will be called when the delegate is invoked. The address of this method is determined statically, when the code is compiled. Virtual methods are called through a vtable, determined by the type of the object that is called; however, delegates bypass this mechanism, so in effect, virtual methods are not called virtually when called through a delegate. Consider this code:

```
// delegates.cpp
__gc class Base
{
public:
   virtual void Callback(){Console::WriteLine(S"called Base");}
};
__gc class Derived : public Base
{
public:
   virtual void Callback(){
      Console::WriteLine(S"called Derived");}
};
__delegate void Del();
```

Here I have declared a delegate and two classes that implement a method that has the same signature: the *Derived* class derives from *Base*. Here's some code that uses these classes:

```
Derived* d = new Derived;
Del* d1 = new Del(d, &Base::Callback);
Del* d2 = new Del(d, &Derived::Callback);
d1();
d2();
```

The first delegate is initialized with the address of the *Callback* method on the base class, so when the delegate is invoked, it is this method that is called. It makes no difference that the method is declared as *virtual* because the vtable of the object passed to the delegate constructor is not used.

Dynamic Creation of Delegates

I have shown the usual way to create and invoke a delegate: use *new* on the delegate class, and call the *Invoke* method either directly or indirectly. The developer must know the signature of the method so that she can declare a delegate. In some situations, the type of the method will not be known at design time—for example, if your code is a scripting engine. The *Delegate* class provides methods that allow you to dynamically create a delegate and invoke it, based on type information. The class contains a *static* member named *CreateDelegate* that you can use to create delegate instances. If the method you want to invoke is *static*, you call the version of *CreateDelegate* that has a *Type* pointer and a *MethodInfo* pointer that you use to indicate the type of the delegate to create and the method to invoke, as shown here:

```
// dynamdel.cpp
// Indicate the method to invoke; this is a static method.
MethodInfo* mi;
mi = __typeof(TestClass)->GetMethod (S"StaticMethod");
MyDelegate* d;
// Create a delegate.
d = static_cast<MyDelegate*>(
      Delegate::CreateDelegate(__typeof(MyDelegate), mi));
```

The *Delegate* class has a read-only property named *Method* that returns a *MethodInfo* object for the delegate. The class also contains an overload that takes the *Type* object of the class that implements the *static* method and a string with the method name, which saves you a little typing, as the following code shows:

```
// dynamdel.cpp
MyDelegate* d;
d = dynamic_cast<MyDelegate*>(
   Delegate::CreateDelegate(
      __typeof(MyDelegate), __typeof(TestClass), S"StaticMethod"));
```

If the method to invoke is an instance method, you have to provide the object that implements the method. There are two overloads that perform this task, and they differ only by a single parameter. Here's the first overload version:

```
// dynamdel.cpp
TestClass* test = new TestClass;
MyDelegate* d;
d = dynamic_cast<MyDelegate*>(
   Delegate::CreateDelegate(__typeof(MyDelegate), test, S"Method"));
```

The second version of the overload takes a Boolean that indicates whether the case of the string should be ignored. The *Delegate* class has a read-only property named *Target* that returns the object that implements the invoked method.

As you can see, all of these overloads take the type of the delegate to create. This arrangement limits the usefulness of *CreateDelegate*; I would have hoped that there would be an overload that would dynamically create the delegate class based on the type information of the method. Sadly, such an overload does not exist.

Invoking a delegate involves calling the *Invoke* method on the delegate class. You can also invoke a delegate at run time using the *DynamicInvoke* method.

Delegate Parameters

The parameters of a delegate can be primitive types or they can be .NET types, and they can be passed by value or by reference. Consider this example:

```
__delegate int Pass_integers(int i1, Int32 i2);
```

This delegate takes two parameters and returns an integer. Both of the parameters are passed by value, and so they are *in* parameters. Notice that the two parameters are 32-bit integer values, so they represent the same type of data.

Now consider these delegates:

```
__delegate void Pass_Int32Ptr(Int32*);
__delegate void Pass_intPtr(int*);
```

The usual intention of passing an integer by reference is to treat it as an *out* parameter; however, as you will see in the section on asynchronous programming, the compiler will treat these two delegates differently in terms of the code it generates. The compiler will treat the parameter as *in/out* for *Pass_Int32Ptr*, but the compiler will treat the parameter as an *in* parameter only for *Pass_intPtr*; that is, *Pass_intPtr* is treated as if it has a pointer passed as an *in* parameter rather than the parameter being used to return an *int*. I think this behavior is counterintuitive. Notice that I specifically mentioned that the compiler treats these two delegates differently for the *code generated for asynchronous calls* because you can still use these parameters as *out* parameters for synchronous calls.

Normally, you can treat the primitive types as being synonymous with the corresponding .NET Framework *__value* types. However, this behavior is not the case with respect to pointers, especially when one is used as a parameter to a delegate. Closer inspection of the pointer types used in these two delegates reveals the difference: *Pass_Int32Ptr* takes an *int __gc** pointer, whereas *Pass_intPtr* takes an *int __nogc** pointer. Because the two differ by the pointer type, a method used to initialize one delegate type cannot be used to initialize the other delegate type. When passing a pointer to a primitive type, it is *always* a good idea to specify the pointer type explicitly, and in most cases, this will mean declaring the pointer as a *__gc* pointer because *__nogc* pointers cannot be used with remoting.

A *__value* type is usually passed by value, but if you pass a *__gc* pointer to a *__value* type, the pointer will be passed by reference. Managed objects are always passed through a *__gc* pointer, as shown here:

```
__delegate void Pass_String(String* s);
```

This parameter is an object, so it is passed by reference, but bear in mind that *System::Strings* are serializable and immutable, so they should be treated as read-only parameters by the method that is invoked.

Now consider this example:

```
__gc class [Serializable] MyObject{};
__delegate void Pass_SerObject(MyObject* o);
```

When you invoke a delegate synchronously, the method is called in the context in which the delegate was created. So if a delegate is created in one context and then passed to a second context and invoked, it means that the parameters passed to the method will be marshaled from the context in which the delegate was invoked, rather than from the context in which the delegate was created. In this example, the *MyObject* class is a managed class, and it is marked as serializable. If there is no marshaling (the delegate is invoked in the same context as the one in which the method is called), the parameter is passed by reference, so the method can change the state of the object through the parameter. If the call is across a context boundary, then because the object is marked with *[Serializable]*, a clone of the object is passed to the invoked method. This means that if the invoked method changes the state of the object, the original object is unaffected.

```
__gc class MyObject2 : public MarshalByRefObject {};
__delegate void Pass_ByRefObject(MyObject2* o);
```

In this example, the class is derived from *MarshalByRefObject*, which means that the object will be context bound—it can execute only in the context in which it was created—so .NET remoting will be used if a cross-context call is made. In this case, if the invoked method changes the state of the object through the parameter, the original object is affected. This is also the effect if the delegate invocation does not involve a context change.

Multicast Delegates

When you use the *__delegate* keyword, the compiler will generate a sealed class that derives from *MultiCastDelegate*. As the name suggests, this class is a container for multiple *Delegate* instances. *MultiCastDelegate* has a private member named *_prev* that is the pointer to a delegate that is the next in a linked list. When a delegate is invoked, the runtime invokes every delegate in this list. *Delegate* has a *static* member named *Combine* that is used to combine two *Delegate*s as a new *Delegate*, as shown in the following code:

```
MyDelegate* d = new MyDelegate(0, &TestOne::StaticMethod);
d = dynamic_cast<MyDelegate*>(
   Delegate::Combine(d, new MyDelegate(0, &TestTwo::StaticMethod)));
d = dynamic_cast<MyDelegate*>(
   Delegate::Combine(d, new MyDelegate(0, &TestThree::StaticMethod)));
```

First I create one delegate, and then I combine it with two other delegates. *Combine* does this task by calling a protected member named *CombineImpl* on the first delegate, passing the second delegate to this method. If a delegate passed to *Combine* is single cast (derives from *Delegate*), an exception will be thrown by *Delegate::CombineImpl*. *Single cast* means that you cannot combine the delegate with another one.[3] If the delegate is *multicast*, *MulticastDelegate::CombineImpl* is called, and this method will clone a new delegate from the parameter passed to *CombineImpl* and iterate through the linked list of delegates, adding them to the cloned delegate. Finally the linked list of delegates of the delegate on which *CombineImpl* was called is added to the end of the linked list of the clone. This arrangement is summarized in Figure 3-1.

3. All delegates in the current version of .NET are multicast, but earlier in the beta cycle, C++ did allow you to declare single cast delegates.

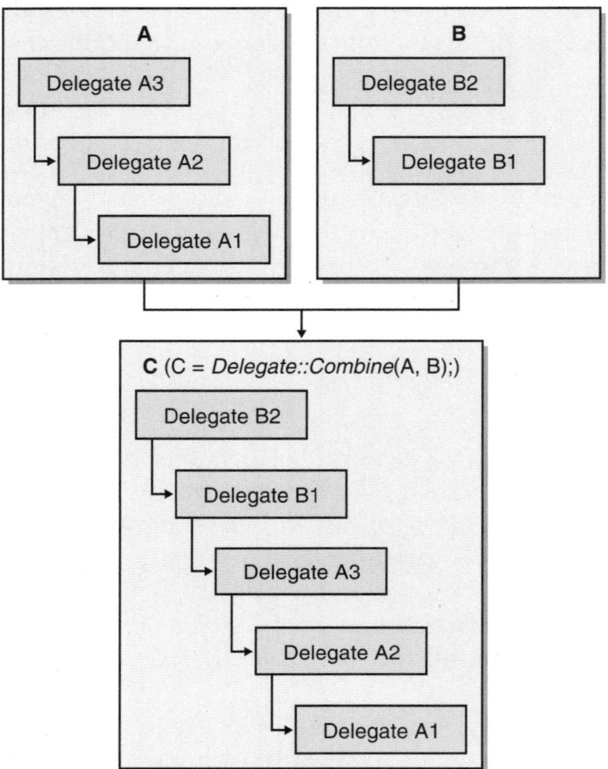

Figure 3-1 The effect of combining two delegates with *Delegate::Combine*

In effect, the *static Combine* method returns a *Delegate* with the second delegate first in the list, and then the first delegate after that. This arrangement would appear to imply that the delegates are invoked in the reverse order that they are combined, but this appearance is not so. Calling *GetInvocationList* returns an array of the delegates in the linked list, but if you look through the IL for this method, you will see that it adds the delegates in reverse order; presumably, calling *Invoke* on a delegate does the same thing.

Using *Delegate::Combine* is a pain because it returns a *Delegate* pointer that you have to cast to the delegate type that you are combining. The C++ compiler allows you to combine two delegates with the += operator, as the following code shows:

```
MyDelegate* d = new MyDelegate(0, &TestOne::StaticMethod);
d += new MyDelegate(0, &TestTwo::StaticMethod);
d += new MyDelegate(0, &TestThree::StaticMethod);
```

This code is equivalent to the previous code and is far more readable.

Invoking a multicast delegate is straightforward: you can call the *Invoke* method the compiler generates for you, or you can call the delegate object as if it is a method, which the compiler will convert to a call to *Invoke*. Because invoking the delegate is done through a single method call, only the return values from one method can be returned to the caller, and this value will be the values from the last method called by the delegate. This system is true of the method return value and any *out* parameters the method might have, as shown here:

```
__gc class Called
{
public:
   static int i;
   static int inc(){return ++i;}
};

__delegate int Incrementer();

void main()
{
   Incrementer* inc = new Incrementer(0, &Called::inc);
   inc += new Incrementer(0, &Called::inc);
   inc += new Incrementer(0, &Called::inc);
   Console::WriteLine(inc());
}
```

This code will print "3" because it is the return value from the third call to *Called::inc*. The method designer generally has a reason for providing a return value for a method, but here you have no choice. The invocation mechanism will throw away all return values except for the last one. Worse yet, if the delegate has an *out* parameter, each method called will write data back through the *out* parameter, which will then be overwritten by the next method call. If the call is cross-context, you will have the overhead of marshaling for data that you never see. There are two points to make about this system: first, you should review whether it makes sense to invoke a method that returns values via a multicast delegate; if it does make sense, your second option is to invoke the method in a way that allows you to get access to all the return values, as shown here:

```
IEnumerator* e = inc->GetInvocationList()->GetEnumerator();
while (e->MoveNext())
{
   Incrementer* i = dynamic_cast<Incrementer*>(e->Current);
   Console::WriteLine(i());
}
```

Delegates as Smart Function Pointers

Delegates are great because they encapsulate the method pointer and the object that is called, all in one object, which is one advantage they have over C++ pointer to member invocation. Their other main advantage is that they are type-safe. Consider this unmanaged code:

```
// typechecks.cpp
__nogc class TypeUnsafe
{
public:
   void f(int i){
      Console::WriteLine(S"f called with {0}", __box(i));}
   void g()     { Console::WriteLine(S"g called");}
};
```

We can call these instance methods like this:

```
typedef void (TypeUnsafe::* FUNC)();
TypeUnsafe* t = new TypeUnsafe;
FUNC f1 = reinterpret_cast<FUNC>(&TypeUnsafe::f);
FUNC f2 = &TypeUnsafe::g;
(t->*f1)();
(t->*f2)();
delete t;
```

I have declared a *typedef* to make the code a little easier to read. This pointer assumes that the method takes *no* parameters and has no return value. Through the wonders of *reinterpret_cast<>*, I can cast the pointer to *f* to this type, so when the *f1* variable is invoked, the method assumes that an integer will be on the stack, but the invoking code does not set up the stack in this way because *FUNC* indicates that the function has no parameters. As a consequence, the method will extract some meaningless value. In this case, the bug is fairly harmless, but you can imagine that such a bug could easily cause serious problems.

The problem is that I have used *reinterpret_cast<>* to turn off the type checks that the compiler will perform for me. There is no run-time check, so the method will be invoked even if, as is the case, it is incorrect to do so.

Now consider the following equivalent managed code:

```
// typechecks.cpp
__gc class TypeSafe
{
public:
   void f(int i){Console::WriteLine(S"f {0}", __box(i));}
   void g(){Console::WriteLine(S"g");}
};
```

```
__delegate void DelF(int);
__delegate void DelG();
```

I have defined two delegates, one that can be used to call *TypeSafe::f* and another that can be used to call *TypeSafe::g*. Now look at how these delegates can be used:

```
// typechecks.cpp
TypeSafe* t = new TypeSafe;
DelF* d1 = new DelF(t, &TypeSafe::f);
DelF* d2 = new DelF(t, &TypeSafe::g); // Will not compile
DelG* d3 = new DelG(t, &TypeSafe::g);
d1(42);
d3();
DelG* d4 = dynamic_cast<DelG*>(d1);
if (d4 != 0) d4();
```

The first point to make is that it is not possible to initialize a delegate with a method of the wrong type because the compiler checks to ensure that the types match. It is not possible to cast away this check. However, what you can do is cast between types, and here I have used *dynamic_cast<>* to perform a type check. In this case, the cast will fail and *d4* will be assigned to zero.

The preceding section showed an example of such a cast. If you call *Delegate::GetInvocationList*, the delegates are returned as an array of *Delegate* objects. The simplest way to invoke the delegate is to cast it to the appropriate delegate type. (Another option is to call *Delegate::DynamicInvoke*, but this means that you have to construct the parameter list as an array of *Object** pointers.)

Exceptions and Delegates

When you invoke a delegate, it is the runtime that calls the specified method. If that method throws an exception, the runtime will catch the exception in the context in which it was thrown. The runtime will rethrow the exception in the context in which the delegate was invoked. Thus, if the delegate is passed to a context other than the one in which it was created or if it is invoked asynchronously and the method throws an exception, that exception is serialized and passed back to the context that invoked the delegate and rethrown there.

If the delegate is multicast and if an exception is thrown by an invoked method, the runtime will stop the invocation and no other methods will be called. It is important that you are aware of this behavior, and in general, it is best to prevent any exceptions from leaking from the invoked method. The reason why I say this is because delegate invocation is disconnected in terms of the code that is involved. The class that invokes a delegate is usually written by a totally different developer than the developer who wrote the method code. Indeed, library code can use delegates as a notification mechanism and the client code might well be written by a totally different company. A multicast delegate could be composed of many delegates with different target objects and methods, so just because one of these methods throws an exception, should the entire invocation be aborted? The exception occurred in one method and other methods in the invocation list can be running in different AppDomains, so the other methods will be unaffected by the exceptional condition.

If you cannot guarantee the quality of the methods you are invoking through a multicast delegate, you can catch the exception yourself if you are willing to invoke each delegate in the multicast delegate, as shown here:

```
// del is a MyDelegate object.
IEnumerator* e = del->GetInvocationList()->GetEnumerator();
while (e->MoveNext())
{
   MyDelegate* d = dynamic_cast<MyDelegate*>(e->Current);
   try
   {
      // Invoke the delegate here.
      d();
   }
   catch (Exception* ex)
   {
      // Do something with the exception.
   }
}
```

An exception thrown because of an invalid argument might be a good reason to cancel the rest of the invocation (because it indicates that an error was traced from the calling code), but other than that it makes sense to continue the invocation.

Delegates and Interop

Some native APIs provide notifications through function callbacks. For example, the Win32 functions *::EnumDateFormatsEx*, *::EnumFontFamiliesEx*, *::EnumObjects*, *::EnumWindowStations*, and *::EnumWindows* are a few of the enumeration functions that will iterate through a list of items and call a user-defined callback function for each. In .NET, enumerations tend to be returned to the user via an array or a collection. For example, the *FontFamily* class in the *System::Drawing* namespace has a *static* property named *Families* that returns an array of *FontFamily* objects that represent each font family available on the system. In Win32, *::EnumFontFamilyEx* does the same thing through a callback.

The Win32 *::EnumWindows* API is interesting; it allows you to get the handle of each user interface (UI) window running on your system. (Windows 2000 and later can have UI-less windows, and these can be enumerated by repeatedly calling *::FindWindowEx* with *HWND_MESSAGE* as the parent window.) There is no .NET Framework class that returns this information, presumably because the class might be a security risk (by giving access to windows other than those used by the current application).

The following library assembly has a class named *EnumWin* that has a property named *WindowNames* that a user can access to get the names of the windows when the object was created:

```
// Compile with cl /clr /LD enumwin.cpp /link /noentry.
#using <mscorlib.dll>
using namespace System;
using namespace System::Collections;
using namespace System::Text;
using namespace System::Runtime::InteropServices;

public __gc class EnumWin
{
   __delegate bool WNDENUMPROC(IntPtr hwnd, IntPtr lParam);
   [DllImport("user32.dll")]
   static bool EnumWindows(WNDENUMPROC __gc* enumProc,
      IntPtr lParam);
   [DllImport("user32.dll")]
   static int GetWindowTextLength(IntPtr hwnd);
   [DllImport("user32.dll", CharSet=CharSet::Auto)]
   static int GetWindowText(IntPtr hwnd, StringBuilder* str,
      int max);
   bool GetInfo(IntPtr hwnd, IntPtr lParam)
   {
      int size = GetWindowTextLength(hwnd);
      StringBuilder* sb = new StringBuilder(size + 1);
      GetWindowText(hwnd, sb, sb->Capacity);
      GCHandle h = GCHandle::op_Explicit(lParam);
      ArrayList* arr = static_cast<ArrayList*>(h.Target);
      arr->Add(sb->ToString());
      return true;
   }
   String* names[];
public:
   __property String* get_WindowNames()[]
   {
      return names;
   }
```

```
    EnumWin()
    {
        ArrayList* arr = new ArrayList;
        GCHandle h = GCHandle::Alloc(arr);
        WNDENUMPROC* proc = new WNDENUMPROC(this,
            &EnumWin::GetInfo);
        EnumWindows(proc, static_cast<IntPtr>(h));
        h.Free();
        names = new String*[arr->Count];
        for (int i=0; i < arr->Count; i++)
        {
            names[i] = arr->Item[i]->ToString();
        }
    }
};
```

This code does not use the C runtime library (CRT), nor does it have any global native C++ objects, so it does not need the CRT start-up code, which is why I use the */noentry* linker switch. When *EnumWin* is created, the constructor creates an instance of the *WNDENUMPROC* delegate, passing it the member method *GetInfo*. This delegate is passed to *::EnumWindows*, which is called through platform invoke. *::EnumWindows* will call *GetInfo* for each window it can find. I want to record the title of each window, so in the *EnumWin* constructor, I create an *ArrayList*. I use this object because it will grow as items are inserted. I need to pass this object to *GetInfo*, which I can do through the second parameter of *::EnumWindows*, but because this call will mean that an object reference will be passed to native code, I need to ensure that the *ArrayList* is pinned. I perform the pinning using *GCHandle*. *::EnumWindows* blocks until all the windows have been enumerated, so at this point, the constructor will continue to run and create the string array with the strings in the *ArrayList*.

I have chosen to use platform invoke rather than IJW to call *::EnumWindows* because the declaration of the method allows me to provide marshaling information. If I used IJW, I would have to provide a prototype for *::EnumWindows* that matches the function in the import library. With platform invoke, I can provide the parameter types that I want (and any additional marshaling information) and the marshaler will marshal the managed types to the native parameters. The marshaler will take a pointer to a delegate, pin it, and then extract a function pointer. Note that this process is not the same as merely pinning the delegate because the delegate refers to a method called with the *__clrcall* calling convention, whereas the native code will expect one of the native calling conventions (most likely *__stdcall*). Instead, the marshaler will pass the native method a native thunk to the managed method.

This arrangement means that you can use the .NET platform invoke marshaler to convert a delegate to an unmanaged function pointer. Here is some code in a native DLL:

```
// Compile with:
// cl /LD thunklib.cpp.
extern "C" __declspec(dllexport) int Conv(int i)
{
   return i;
}
```

This code does nothing more than return the parameter it is passed. The code is compiled as a C++ DLL so that it can be used by a managed C++ source file using platform invoke.

```
// deladdr.cpp
// Declare a delegate.
__delegate void MyDelegate(int i);

// Link to our DLL.
[DllImport("thunklib.dll")]
extern "C" int Conv(MyDelegate __gc* del);
```

The *Conv* method is imported through platform invoke, and I have declared the parameter as a pointer to a delegate that I have declared. Platform invoke will convert the delegate to the unmanaged integer, and the function will simply return that integer.

Let's use this function. I can declare a class with a *static* method that can be called through the delegate, as shown here:

```
__gc class Managed
{
public:
   static void Callback(int i)
   {
      Console::WriteLine(__box(i));
   }
};
```

Next let's declare a *typedef* for an unmanaged function pointer that corresponds to the delegate and an unmanaged function that will be passed the delegate. Because the function is unmanaged, it is passed an integer that it converts by casting the integer to the function pointer.

```
typedef void (*FUNC)(int);
#pragma unmanaged
void Caller(int del)
```

```
{
   // Call back
   FUNC func = reinterpret_cast<FUNC>(del);
   func(42);
}
#pragma managed
```

Finally, here is the code that creates the delegate and passes it to the unmanaged function:

```
void main()
{
   MyDelegate __pin* del = new MyDelegate(0, &Managed::Callback);
   int d = Conv(del);
   Console::WriteLine(S"Address of delegate: {0:x}", __box(d));
   // Show that the delegate has been converted
   // to an unmanaged pointer.
   Caller(d);
}
```

Marshaling Delegates

All delegate classes are derived from *System::MulticastDelegate*. This class is marked with the *[Serializable]* attribute, and its base class, *Delegate*, implements *ISerializable*, which means that when marshaled, all delegates are passed by value using custom serialization. The *Delegate* class uses a private class named *DelegateSerializationHolder*, which serializes information about the delegate class, the targets held in the delegate, and the methods to be invoked.

If the delegate has a target object (that is, the method invoked is not *static*), the class of the target object must be serializable or marshal by reference. If the target object class is serializable, the object is serialized when the delegate is serialized, so the method will be executed in the same context as where the delegate is invoked. If the target object is marshal by reference, the reference will be passed to the context where the delegate is invoked, which means that the method will be invoked in the context where the target object was created. This process is summarized in Figure 3-2.

If the method to invoke is *static*, the method's class does not have to be serializable, so the method will always be invoked in the same context as where the delegate was invoked. However, in all cases, the assembly that has the method's class must be available to the assembly invoking the delegate because it is the assembly that deserializes the delegate that actually calls the method.

Because delegates are serializable, they can be passed to other contexts, to other AppDomains in the same process, or to other processes via .NET remoting. If the target objects are serializable, you can serialize a delegate to a file or to an object that is passed via Microsoft Message Queuing (MSMQ) to a disconnected object. This ability gives rise to the interesting situation of being able to invoke a delegate hours or days after the delegate has been created.

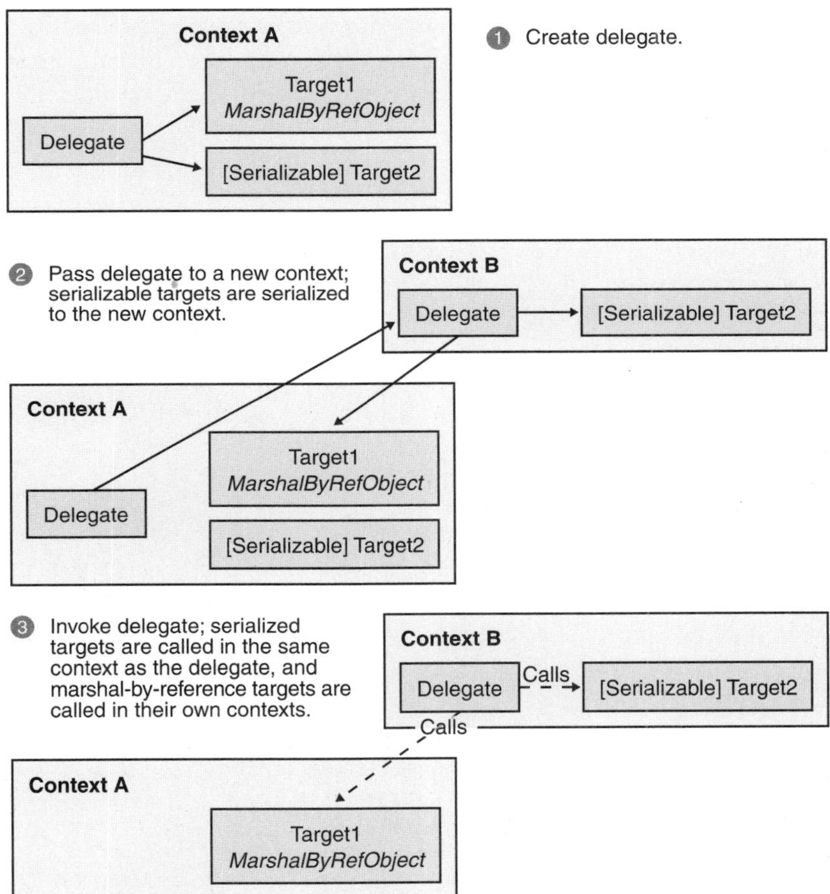

Figure 3-2 Passing delegates across context boundaries.

Asynchronous Programming

The .NET Framework was written with asynchronous programming in mind. Whenever you create a delegate, you have the choice of whether to invoke the delegate synchronously or asynchronously. The compiler will generate asynchronous methods to invoke the delegate, and the runtime will provide the implementation and the infrastructure for those methods.

The choice about whether a method is called asynchronously is made entirely by the caller. The same method is called for asynchronous and synchronous calls. The called code does not know how it is called and is not written with the calling mechanism in mind. When client code calls a method asynchronously, it calls *BeginInvoke* to start the method call and the .NET Framework calls the specified method on another thread. From this point onward, there is nothing that the client can do to cancel the call.

Parameters and Asynchronous Delegates

In general, .NET *__gc* types are passed to methods through pointers and hence are passed by reference; *__value* types are usually passed to methods by value but can be passed by reference if a pointer is passed to the *__value* type. For synchronous calls, by reference means that data can be passed to a method and returned from the method through the parameter; the parameter is *in/out*. With asynchronous calls, "by reference" for a non- *__gc* type might mean that the parameter is an *in* parameter or an *in/out* parameter, depending on the type of the pointer.

Consider the following code:

```
public __delegate int CallMe(Int32 inParam, Int32* inoutParam);
```

The compiler will generate a class that looks like this (in pseudo C++):

```
__gc __sealed class CallMe : public MulticastDelegate
{
public:
   CallMe(Object* obj, int meth);
   virtual Int32 Invoke(Int32 inParam, Int32* inoutParam);
   virtual IAsyncResult* BeginInvoke(
      Int32 inParam, Int32* inoutParam,
      AsyncCallback* cb, Object* state);
   virtual Int32 EndInvoke(Int32* inoutParam, IAsyncResult* ar);
};
```

The last two methods are used for asynchronous calls. The compiler has determined which parameters are *in* parameters and which are *in/out* parameters by the level of indirection: for *__value* types, if a pointer is used, the parameter is an *in/out* parameter; for a *__gc* type, if a pointer to pointer is used, the parameter is an *in/out* parameter. Thus, in this example, the first delegate parameter is a *__value* type and is not a pointer, so it is an *in* parameter and appears only in *BeginInvoke*, whereas the second delegate parameter is a *__value* type and is passed through a pointer, so the compiler treats it as an *in/out* parameter and it appears in both *BeginInvoke* and *EndInvoke*.

C++ code typically uses C++ references for *in/out* parameters. However, don't be tempted to use these references on managed code because the C++ compiler will treat them as *in* parameters when generating the delegate class. This behavior is the opposite of what you would expect. Furthermore, be careful about using C++ primitive types. Consider these two delegates:

```
__delegate void Pass_Int32Ptr(Int32*);
__delegate void Pass_intPtr(int*);
```

I have already shown these two delegates, and I made the point that the parameter to *Pass_intPtr* is a *__nogc* pointer, whereas the parameter to *Pass_Int32Ptr* is a *__gc* pointer. The delegate classes generated by the compiler will treat the parameter to *Pass_Int32Ptr* as an *in/out* parameter as you would expect, but it will treat the parameter to *Pass_intPtr* as an *in* parameter. Again, this behavior is the opposite of what you expect. So I will repeat the warning I gave earlier: when you declare a delegate that has a pointer to non-*__gc* types, it is important to explicitly declare the pointer type.

The *[Out]* attribute can be used to give a hint to the runtime that you do not intend to pass a value in through a parameter; however, it is ignored by the compiler when generating a delegate class. Here's an example:

```
__delegate void OutDel([Out] Int32* outParam);
```

The invocation methods generated by the compiler look like this:

```
virtual void Invoke([Out] Int32* outParam);
virtual IAsyncResult* BeginInvoke([Out] Int32* outParam,
   AsyncCallback* cb, object* state);
virtual void EndInvoke([Out] Int32* outParam, IAsyncResult* ar);
```

The first parameter of *BeginInvoke* is marked as *[Out]*, which makes no sense whatsoever.

These are the rules for declaring the parameters of delegates:

- Don't use C++ reference parameters.
- Don't use C++ primitive types; it is safer to use .NET Framework primitive types.
- Always explicitly specify the pointer type for *__value* types.
- Don't use *[Out]*.

Calling Delegates Asynchronously

To initiate the asynchronous delegate invocation, you call *BeginInvoke* and pass the *in* parameters and *in/out* parameters. The runtime will select a pool thread and use this thread to make the invocation, and then *BeginInvoke* will return. When the delegate invocation has completed, you call *EndInvoke* to obtain the return value and the value of the *in/out* parameters. Of course, this process is relevant only for single-cast delegates.

BeginInvoke returns a pointer to *IAsyncResult*. This interface pointer is for the asynchronous call object created by the runtime to handle the asynchronous call. The asynchronous call object is an instance of the *AsyncResult* class, but usually you will only need to access the members of the *IAsyncResult* interface. When *BeginInvoke* returns, the delegate invocation is unlikely to have completed. You access the asynchronous call object to determine when the call has completed. There are several ways to do this.

```
// For the delegate: __delegate void MyDelegate();
MyDelegate* del = new MyDelegate(new CallObject, &CallObject::CallMe);
IAsyncResult* ar = del->BeginInvoke(0, 0);
while (!ar->IsCompleted) DoSomeTask();
del->EndInvoke(ar);
```

This code starts the delegate call and then polls for completion by accessing the *IsCompleted* property. If the call has not completed, *DoSomeTask* performs some idle time processing.

The asynchronous call object also has a synchronization object that will be set when the call is completed, as shown in this example:

```
IAsyncResult* ar = del->BeginInvoke(0, 0);
while (!ar->AsyncWaitHandle->WaitOne(100, false)) DoSomeTask();
del->EndInvoke(ar);
```

This code is equivalent to the previous code in many respects. The difference is that it will wait for the synchronization object to signal and if the synchronization object does not signal after 100 milliseconds (ms), *WaitOne* will return *false* and *DoSomeTask* will be called.

Here is a concrete example: imagine that you want to get a list of all the files in a folder and in its child folders sorted by file size. The following class will do just this:

```
// sortfiles.cpp
public __gc class SortedFiles : public IComparer
{
public:
   __property FileInfo* get_Items()[]
   {
      return static_cast<FileInfo*[]>(
         m_list->ToArray(__typeof(FileInfo)));
   }
```

```
    // This method is used during the sorting process.
    int Compare(Object* x, Object* y)
    {
       FileInfo* fx = static_cast<FileInfo*>(x);
       FileInfo* fy = static_cast<FileInfo*>(y);
       if (fx->Length == fy->Length) return 0;
       if (fx->Length > fy->Length) return 1;
       return -1;
    }
    // Create instances through a static method so that we can
    // use it with a delegate.
    static SortedFiles* GetFiles(String* s)
    {
       return new SortedFiles(s);
    }
protected:
    ArrayList* m_list;
    SortedFiles(String* strRoot)
    {
       m_list = new ArrayList();
       // First just get all the files.
       Fill(strRoot);
       // Now sort into file size order.
       m_list->Sort(this);
    }
    void Fill(String* s)
    {
       // First add the files in the current directory.
       DirectoryInfo* di = new DirectoryInfo(s);
       FileInfo* files[];
       try
       {
          files = di->GetFiles();
       }
       catch(UnauthorizedAccessException* ex)
       {
          // We have tried to access a folder that we don't
          // have access to.
          return;
       }
       // Add each file to our list.
       IEnumerator* items = files->GetEnumerator();
       while (items->MoveNext())
       {
          FileInfo* fi = static_cast<FileInfo*>(items->Current);
          m_list->Add(fi);
       }
```

```
        // Now go through the subdirectories and recursively
        // call Fill() to add their files.
        DirectoryInfo* dirs[] = di->GetDirectories();
        items = dirs->GetEnumerator();
        while (items->MoveNext())
        {
            DirectoryInfo* di =
                static_cast<DirectoryInfo*>(items->Current);
            Fill(di->FullName);
        }
    }
};
```

If I pass the root of a disk to this class, the process is likely to take a while, so I want this class to operate asynchronously and provide some visual feedback that the process hasn't simply crashed. Here's one way to do this:

```
// sortfiles.cpp
#using <mscorlib.dll>
using namespace System;
using namespace System::Collections;
using namespace System::IO;

#using <system.windows.forms.dll>
#using <system.dll>
using namespace System::Windows::Forms;

// Defined elsewhere
__gc class SortedFiles;
// Class to provide feedback
__gc class Progress : public Form
{
    ProgressBar* pb;
public:
    Progress()
    {
        Width = 200;
        Height = 20;
        FormBorderStyle = FormBorderStyle::None;
        TopMost = true;
        StartPosition = System::Windows::Forms::
                            FormStartPosition::CenterScreen;
        pb = new ProgressBar;
        pb->Width = Width;
        pb->Height = Height;
        this->Controls->Add(pb);
    }
```

```
   void Increment()
   {
      if (pb->Value >= pb->Maximum) pb->Value = pb->Minimum;
      pb->PerformStep();
   }
};

__delegate SortedFiles* GetFiles(String* s);

void main()
{
   String* args[] = Environment::GetCommandLineArgs();
   if (args->Length == 1) return;
   Progress* p = new Progress;
   p->Show();
   GetFiles* gf = new GetFiles(0, &SortedFiles::GetFiles);
   IAsyncResult* ar;
   ar = gf->BeginInvoke(args[1], 0, 0);
   while (!ar->AsyncWaitHandle->WaitOne(100, false))
   {
      p->Increment();
   }
   SortedFiles* sf = gf->EndInvoke(ar);
   p->Hide();

   FileInfo* fi =
      static_cast<FileInfo*>(sf->Items[sf->Items->Count-1]);
   Console::WriteLine(S"{0}\\{1} is {2}",
      fi->DirectoryName, fi->Name, __box(fi->Length));
}
```

The *Progress* class is a captionless form that contains a single progress bar that is incremented at 100 ms intervals. Because I cannot tell how long this action will take, I cannot set a maximum value. Instead I leave this value at the default of 100 and the step will be left at 10, so after about a second, the progress bar will have reached the maximum. At this point, I set the value back to the minimum value and start the process again. When *ar->AsyncWaitHandle* is signaled, the creation of the *SortedList* has completed and we can access the object. The last item in the array will be the largest file.

Now consider this usage of delegates:

```
IAsyncResult* ar = del->BeginInvoke(0, 0);
DoSomeTask();
ar->AsyncWaitHandle->WaitOne();
del->EndInvoke(ar);
```

In this version, the delegate is invoked and then *DoSomeTask* is called. When this method returns, the thread needs the results from the delegate, so it calls *WaitOne* with no parameters, which will simply block the calling thread until the synchronization object signals that the delegate call has completed. Now consider this:

```
IAsyncResult* ar = del->BeginInvoke(0, 0);
DoSomeTask();
del->EndInvoke(ar);
```

Here I call *BeginInvoke* to start the asynchronous call, and then I call *DoSomeTask* to run some code while the delegate is invoked. After this method has completed, I call *EndInvoke*. In this example, I do not check to ensure that the delegate has completed, but this is not a problem because *EndInvoke* will block until the delegate call completes and then it will perform cleanup before returning any values returned from the delegate call. If you use *EndInvoke*, the call to the synchronization object is unnecessary, but I think that it is better to make the call to the synchronization object because it makes it clear that the thread is blocked until the method has completed.

In all these examples, the *EndInvoke* method is called on the same thread that called *BeginInvoke*, and it is passed the *IAsyncResult* interface of the asynchronous call object. If the delegate does not return any values (as in these examples), you can omit the call to *EndInvoke*.

The final way you can handle when the asynchronous call has completed is to use the last two parameters of the *BeginInvoke*. These are a delegate and a state object. The delegate looks like this:

```
__delegate void AsyncCallback(IAsyncResult* ar);
```

A method used to initialize this *AsyncCallback* will be called when the asynchronous delegate completes, and it will be passed the interface on the asynchronous call object. However, the important point is that this method will be called on the same thread that was used to make the actual call on the asynchronous delegate, rather than the thread that is used to invoke the delegate.

```
// logfiles.cpp
__gc class Logger
{
   StreamWriter* sw;
public:
   Logger(String* s)
   {
      if (File::Exists(s)) File::Delete(s);
      sw = new StreamWriter(File::OpenWrite(s));
   }
```

```
   void Close()
   {
      if (sw) sw->Close();
      sw = 0;
   }
   ~Logger()
   { Close(); }
   void LogData(IAsyncResult* ar)
   {
      AsyncResult* obj = static_cast<AsyncResult*>(ar);
      GetFiles* gf = static_cast<GetFiles*>(obj->AsyncDelegate);
      SortedFiles* sf = gf->EndInvoke(ar);
      for (int i = sf->Items->Length-1;
         i > sf->Items->Length-6 && i >= 0; i--)
      {
         FileInfo* fi = static_cast<FileInfo*>(sf->Items[i]);
            sw->WriteLine(S"{0}\\{1} is {2}",
               fi->DirectoryName, fi->Name, __box(fi->Length));
      }
      sw->Flush();
   }
};
```

The *Logger* class is created based on a text file. The *LogData* method has the signature of *AsyncCallback*, so it can be used to create a delegate that can be passed to *BeginInvoke*. When the asynchronous call completes, *LogData* is called; the method needs to obtain the results from the asynchronous call, so it gets access to the asynchronous call object and then gets access to the asynchronous delegate through the *AsyncDelegate* property. Once it has the *SortedFiles* object, the *LogData* method can log the information required.

However, this code has a few problems. Consider one way to call it:

```
Progress* p = new Progress;
p->Show();
GetFiles* gf = new GetFiles(0, &SortedFiles::GetFiles);
Logger* log = new Logger(S"results.txt");
AsyncCallback* acb = new AsyncCallback(log, &Logger::LogData);
IAsyncResult* ar;
ar = gf->BeginInvoke(Environment::GetCommandLineArgs()[1], acb, 0);
while (!ar->AsyncWaitHandle->WaitOne(100, false))
{
   p->Increment();
}
p->Hide();
// Do some other work.
log->Close();
```

I have been careful about the *Logger* class by giving it a destructor. I have also added a method named *Close* so that I can explicitly release the resources when I know that they are no longer needed. The problem with this code is that there will be a race condition between the thread that runs this code and the thread that makes the asynchronous call and calls *LogData*. The effect of this race will be that when the asynchronous method has completed, the *while* loop will complete and the file will be closed before *LogData* has completed its work. The point is that the *AsyncWaitHandle* synchronization object will be signaled *before* the callback is called. If you want to use both the synchronization object and the callback delegate, you should use some other synchronization to ensure that resources are used in the order that you expect.

You can take another approach. Consider this adjusted version of the *Logger* class:

```
__gc class Logger
{
public:
   static void LogData(IAsyncResult* ar)
   {
      StreamWriter* sw =
         static_cast<StreamWriter*>(ar->AsyncState);
      AsyncResult* obj = static_cast<AsyncResult*>(ar);
      GetFiles* gf = static_cast<GetFiles*>(obj->AsyncDelegate);
      SortedFiles* sf = gf->EndInvoke(ar);
      for (int i = sf->Items->Length-1;
         i > sf->Items->Length-6 && i >= 0; i--)
      {
         FileInfo* fi = static_cast<FileInfo*>(sf->Items[i]);
            sw->WriteLine(S"{0}\\{1} is {2}",
               fi->DirectoryName, fi->Name, __box(fi->Length));
      }
      sw->Close();
   }
};
```

This time *LogData* is a *static* method and the file is accessed through the *IAsyncResult::AsyncState* property. In this case, I know that the *StreamWriter* object will not be used by any other thread after *LogData* is called, so I can close the file when then method completes. The callback delegate is used like this:

```
String* strPath = Environment::GetCommandLineArgs()[1];
String* s = S"results.txt";
if (File::Exists(s)) File::Delete(s);
StreamWriter* sw = new StreamWriter(File::OpenWrite(s));
sw->WriteLine(S"searching {0}", strPath);
```

```
GetFiles* gf = new GetFiles(0, &SortedFiles::GetFiles);
AsyncCallback* acb = new AsyncCallback(0, &Logger::LogData);
IAsyncResult* ar = gf->BeginInvoke(strPath, acb, sw);
sw = 0;
// Do other work.
```

The thread that calls this code can initialize the *StreamWriter* object and use the object before passing it to the asynchronous call object by calling *BeginInvoke*. At this point, I release my reference on the *StreamWriter* object so that this thread cannot use it and so that the .NET object is not kept longer than it is actually needed. Again, it is worth pointing out that if you pass an object as the final parameter to *BeginInvoke* and you want to access this object in the asynchronous call thread and in the calling thread, then you will need to use some additional synchronization.

Asynchronous Calls and Exceptions

Consider this code:

```
__gc class Called
{
public:
   void CallMe()
   {
      throw new Exception(S"oops");
   }
};
__delegate void Del();
void CallIt()
{
   Del* d = new Del(new Called, &Called::CallMe);
   d->BeginInvoke(0, 0);
}
```

Called::CallMe throws an exception, but *CallIt* will run fine. As far as it is concerned, no exception has been thrown. When you think about it, the reason is obvious: *BeginInvoke* is used for *in* and *in/out* parameters, but the exception comes from the method that was called, so it is effectively an *out* parameter. This code will catch the exception:

```
void CallIt()
{
   Del* d = new Del(new Called, &Called::CallMe);
   IAsyncResult* ar = d->BeginInvoke(0, 0);
   ar->AsyncWaitHandle->WaitOne();
   try
```

```
    {
       d->EndInvoke(ar);
    }
    catch(Exception* e)
    {
       Console::WriteLine(S"caught exception: {0}", e->ToString());
    }
}
```

If you think it is important that you handle exceptions thrown by the method and called asynchronously, you must call *EndInvoke*, even if the method has no return values. It is interesting to look at the stack trace dumped in the exception handler in this example. This stack trace will show the state of the stack in the thread where the exception was thrown *and* the stack where the delegate was invoked. This trace shows that .NET remoting sinks are used even if the asynchronous call is made in the same AppDomain.

One pattern you might consider is fire and forget. In this case, your intention is to inform connected code that some event has occurred, but you do not want to know the reaction of the connected code to the notification nor are you interested in whether the connected code throws an exception when it receives the notification. To do this, the notifier calls *BeginInvoke* so that the notification is performed on a separate thread, and the notifier omits the call to *EndInvoke*. Of course, the asynchronous call object will still get any return values and exceptions thrown by the code that receives the notification. If this process involves a call across AppDomain boundaries, you will be marshaling data that you will not use. You can tell the runtime that this code will not generate any return values by marking it with the *[OneWay]* attribute. If such code generates an exception, the exception will be eaten by the runtime and it will not be propagated to the calling code.

The thread that makes the asynchronous call can itself throw an exception, and this exception could cause the thread to terminate before the asynchronous method call has completed. This exception does not affect the asynchronous method call; the call will complete as expected.

Asynchronous Calls and the .NET Framework Class Library

You can declare a delegate for any method, which means that you can invoke any method asynchronously. You can even call .NET Framework classes asynchronously. However, closer inspection of the .NET Framework class library shows that a few classes already have methods that look like they support asynchronous calls. For example, the *FileStream* object is used to give stream access to a file (or a pipe), and you have the choice of accessing the object synchronously (as shown in the following code) or asynchronously:

```
// Open the file.
FileStream* fs = File::Open(S"file.dat", FileMode::Open);
// Read 10,000 bytes from the file.
Byte b[] = new Byte[10000];
fs->Read(b, 0, b->Length);
// Now do something with the data.
fs->Close();
```

You can also access the file asynchronously, as shown here:

```
// Open the file.
FileStream* fs = File::Open(S"file.dat", FileMode::Open);
// Read 10,000 bytes from the file.
Byte b[] = new Byte[10000];
IAsyncResult* ar = fs->BeginRead(b, 0, b->Length, 0, 0);
// Do some other work.
fs->EndRead(ar);
// Now do something with the data.
fs->Close();
```

This code looks like you have accessed the *FileStream* object through a delegate, but these methods are implemented on the *FileStream* class and not on a separate delegate class. If you choose, you could declare a delegate to do this:

```
__delegate int FileReader(Byte arr[], int offset, int count);
```

So have the .NET Framework designers decided to add these asynchronous methods to save you the effort of declaring a delegate? No. When you call a method asynchronously through a delegate, the runtime will use a separate pool thread and pass the delegate to that thread where it will be invoked. In effect, you have a separate thread where the method is called synchronously, and the asynchronous aspect is that the thread that invoked the delegate can access the asynchronous call object at any time to determine whether the call has completed and whether it has access to the results.

Under the covers, *FileStream* is implemented by the Win32 file APIs. The Win32 file APIs can be called asynchronously by passing *FILE_FLAG_OVERLAPPED* to the Win32 *::CreateFile* function and then providing an *OVERLAPPED* structure for *::ReadFile* and *::WriteFile*. The *OVERLAPPED* structure has members to indicate the location in the file that you want to access, and it has an event that will be signaled when the access has completed. This arrangement means that you can queue up multiple accesses to the same file by calling *::ReadFile* or *::WriteFile* multiple times each with a different instance of *OVERLAPPED*. Win32 asynchronous file access has been fine-tuned by the Windows developers, and clearly it makes sense to use this code rather than to reimplement a new asynchronous mechanism over the top of the synchronous file access. This is why *FileStream* has asynchronous methods: they use the native mechanisms to read data from the file asynchronously.

Only a few classes in the .NET Framework have asynchronous methods. The *FileStream* class is a good example, but in addition, there are classes that use sockets (*Socket*, *NetworkStream*, *Dns*, and various Http classes) and the *MessageQueue* class. In all of these cases, there is a native asynchronous mechanism that can be used: *Socket* is based on WinSock 2, which can read/write to a socket through *::WSARecv* and *::WSASend* synchronously or asynchronously; and message queuing, by definition, is loosely coupled.

In all of these cases, it is the object that has made provision for asynchronous calls. In general, this behavior is not the case for .NET asynchronous calls, where the called object should be unaware whether it is called synchronously or asynchronously. When you write your own types, you should follow the general .NET pattern and allow the caller to determine whether the method should be called asynchronously. The examples I showed earlier are the exception, where the asynchronous methods can be implemented more efficiently than by relying on the default asynchronous architecture (*FileStream* and sockets), or where the design of the object might mean that it should not be called synchronously.

Managed Events

When code invokes a delegate, the chain of methods contained in the delegate is called. If the delegate has only *in* parameters, you can view the invocation as being a notification from the code that called the delegate to the code that implements the methods in the delegate that something has happened, as shown in this example:

```
__delegate void Completed(int x);
__gc class Calculator
{
public:
   void Calculate(int operand, Completed* OnCompleted)
   {
      // Do some calculation.
      operand *= 2;
      OnCompleted(operand);
   }
};
```

Here a caller will create an instance of *Calculator* and call *Calculate* to do some complicated calculation. When that calculation has completed, the method informs its caller by calling the delegate passed to the method. Of course, the great thing about delegates is that there could be more than one target, so there can be more than one object that depends on the results of *Calculate*.

A delegate is just an instance of a class that derives from *MulticastDelegate*, which means that a delegate can be a field in a class, as shown here:

```
__delegate void Completed(int x);
__gc class Calculator2
{
protected:
   Completed* OnCompleted;
public:
   Calculator2(Completed* d) : OnCompleted(d) {}
   void CalculateSomething(int operand)
   {
      // Do some calculation.
      operand *= 2;
      OnCompleted (operand);
   }
};
```

Here the class is initialized with a delegate, and whenever the method is called, it will inform the clients by invoking the delegate. The delegate field is made *protected* because it makes no sense for code outside the class to initiate the notification, but it does make sense for derived classes to be able to initiate the notification.

This mechanism—a class being initialized with a delegate and then being able to invoke the delegate to notify clients—is so useful that .NET has formalized it as a .NET event. An event is a metadata device. When you add an event to a class, you are informing the compiler to add metadata to the class that indicates that instances can raise the event. Because an event is metadata, an event can be a member of an interface, which makes a lot of sense because interfaces describe behavior and the fact that a class can raise an event is certainly a behavior worth noting. Of course, to be able to raise an event, a class needs to have a delegate field (to hold the delegates that will be called) and methods to add and remove delegates; the class raises the event by invoking the delegate. If you do not provide these members yourself, the compiler will add default members for you.

The change to the class to raise notifications through an event is straightforward, as the following code shows:

```
__delegate void Completed(int x);
__gc class Calculator3
```

```
{
public:
   __event Completed* OnCompleted;
   void CalculateSomething(int operand)
   {
      // Do some calculation.
      operand *= 2;
      OnCompleted(operand);
   }
};
```

This class no longer needs to have a constructor to initialize the event because the compiler will add some methods to initialize the event, which I will come to in a moment. In most cases, you will want to make the event public. The reason is that the event is part of an object and is a mechanism for users of the object to register their interest that they want to be notified when an event occurs; making the event *public* means that external code can perform this registration. The compiler will add three methods to this class. Two of then are *public*: *add_OnCompleted* and *remove_OnCompleted*, and the third is *protected*, *raise_OnCompleted*. In addition, the compiler will add a *private* delegate field, the *add_* method adds a delegate to this field, the *remove_* method removes a delegate from this field, and the *raise_* method invokes the multicast delegate. As with delegates, the compiler allows you to use the += and -= operators, which will call the *add_* and *remove_* methods, respectively.

If you look at the MSIL code for these compiler-generated methods, you will see that the compiler has marked them with the *synchronized* attribute. When the runtime sees this attribute, it will attempt to get a synchronization lock for the object, and only when the runtime gets this lock will it be able to execute the method. This lock can be held only by a single thread, so only one thread can call one of the event methods at any time, which prevents the situation of one thread trying to add (or remove) a delegate while another thread is trying to raise the event.

I mentioned in Chapter 1 that you can write your own *add_*, *remove_*, and *_raise* methods and mark them with the *__event* keyword to indicate that the compiler should generate the relevant metadata, as shown here:

```
__gc class Calculator4
{
   Completed* d;
protected:
   __event void raise_OnCompleted(int i){d(i);}
public:
   __event void add_OnCompleted(Completed* c){d += c;}
   __event void remove_OnCompleted(Completed* c){d -= c;}
```

```
   void CalculateSomething(int operand)
   {
      // Do some calculation.
      operand *= 2;
      OnCompleted(operand);
   }
};
```

This scheme allows you to provide custom code to store an event's delegate and to invoke it. One situation in which you will want to do this is if your class supports many events. In Chapter 4, I will show you such an example with the *Control* class. This class can generate 57 events; if each event is implemented through a delegate field, this would mean 57 fields, but most code will provide handlers for only a handful of events, which means that most of these fields will be unused. The *Control* class (and other classes that derive from *Component*) solve this issue by providing custom event methods that store the delegates in a single field of the class *EventHandlerList*. This collection class allocates memory only for the events that have handlers.

The .NET Framework and Events

Windows is event-based: something happens and the system will place a message about the event in the appropriate window's message queue. The Windows C API is a pull model: it is your responsibility to pump the message queue for messages and act upon them. As you will see in Chapter 4, the Windows Forms library is a push model and is based on .NET events. Your code registers its interest in a particular event (for example, a window resizing) by providing a delegate for an event handler method. When the event occurs, the .NET Framework will invoke the event and your handler will be called.

Most Windows Forms events will be of the type *EventHandler*, shown here.

```
public __delegate void EventHandler(
   Object* sender, EventArgs* e);
```

The other event delegates look similar to this delegate. The main difference is the last parameter, which is used to pass information about the event. The interesting point is that all of these delegates return *void* and that the parameters are treated as *in* parameters. The code that generates the event is not interested in your code's reaction to the event. Windows messages sometimes require action—for example, the *WM_SIZING* message is sent to a window when its size is changing. This message is sent a pointer to a *RECT* structure that has the size of the drag rectangle that the user is requesting, and you can change this size by altering the values in the *RECT* structure. In the Windows Forms framework, the equivalent is to handle the *Resize* event; however, this event is the *EventHandler* delegate and the *EventArgs* class does not contain any information, so when you get this event, you have to explicitly ask for the size and then change it accordingly.

This process is typical of Windows Forms event handling: your code is informed that something has happened, and it is up to your code to make any necessary changes. Windows Forms event handling is not always better than Win32 message handling. As you will see in Chapter 4, explicitly handling the *WM_SIZING* message gives better results than handling the *Resize* event. But I'll wait until then to show you what I mean.

Some .NET Framework events will have an event argument derived from the *EventArgs* class. For example, the *Control::KeyDown* event is a *KeyEventHandler*:

```
public __delegate void KeyEventHandler(
   Object* sender, KeyEventArgs* e);
```

KeyEventArgs derives from *EventArgs* and is used to pass information about the key that was pressed and whether the keypress was combined with another key (such as Shift or Ctrl). The argument is used to pass information pertinent to the event, but no more information than that. If the event source is your class (which is typical for Windows Forms code), you can get additional information through the members of your class.

The delegates for .NET Framework events always have a first parameter that is the *this* pointer of the object that generated the event. This means that you can make the event handler a *static* member, or it can be a member of a class other than the sender of the event. You can use the *sender* parameter to access the sender object. .NET supports only single inheritance, so you cannot have separate event handler classes and derive from each class that has an event handler that you want to use (for example, look at how ATL adds support for interfaces through *Impl* classes). However, because you have the *sender* parameter, you can have separate handler objects as members of your form class. I will go into more depth about this topic in the next chapter.

Unified Event Model

The code that I have shown so far for using an event in a class has a separate declaration of the delegate. In many cases, this arrangement will make sense because the delegate could be used for other events. However, there might be cases when the delegate is used *only* for this particular event in this particular class. In this case, it makes sense to declare the delegate as a *public* nested member of the class. The C++ compiler gives you a mechanism where you can associate the delegate with a class that has the event, and does this with a simple declaration: the Unified Event Model.

Take a look at this class:

```
// unified.cpp
__gc class Calculator5
{
public:
   __event void OnCompleted(int operand);
   void CalculateSomething(int operand)
   {
      // Do some calculation.
      operand *= 2;
      OnCompleted(operand);
   }
};
```

The event declaration in the class does not specify a delegate. In fact, the declaration of *OnCompleted* is both an inline declaration of the delegate and the event based on the delegate. At compile time, the compiler will generate a nested delegate class (named *__Delegate_OnCompleted*) and the necessary members for the event. You can use the *[event_source(managed)]* C++ attribute on the class as a visual reminder that the compiler will generate code for you but it is not required. *[event_source()]* is not a .NET attribute, and you can use this attribute in code that has not been compiled with */clr*. Native code can use either *com* or *native* as the parameter to *[event_source()]* to generate event source classes that will generate COM connection point events or events based on C++ function callbacks. Three types of events can be generated with the same syntax, and this is the reason for the name Unified Event Model.

You can use the */Fx* compiler switch to see the code generated by the compiler. If your file is named file.cpp, */Fx* will generate an additional file named file.mrg.cpp. The generated class looks like this:

```
// Class generated by the compiler in the mrg file
__gc class Calculator5
{
public:
   Calculator5() { OnCompleted = 0; }
   void CalculateSomething(int operand)
   {
      // Do some calculation.
      operand *= 2;
      OnCompleted(operand);
   }
```

```
   __delegate __gc
       class __Delegate_OnCompleted
         : public System::MulticastDelegate
   {
   public:
      __Delegate_OnCompleted(Object*, IntPtr);
      virtual void Invoke(int operand);
      virtual IAsyncResult* BeginInvoke(
         int operand, AsyncCallback*, Object*);
      virtual void EndInvoke(IAsyncResult*);
   };
   __Delegate_OnCompleted* OnCompleted;
   void add_OnCompleted(Calculator5::__Delegate_OnCompleted* eh)
   {
      OnCompleted =
         static_cast< Calculator5::__Delegate_OnCompleted*>
            (Delegate::Combine(OnCompleted, eh));
   }
   void remove_OnCompleted(Calculator5::__Delegate_OnCompleted* eh)
   {
      OnCompleted =
         static_cast< Calculator5::__Delegate_OnCompleted*>
            (Delegate::Remove(OnCompleted, eh));
   }
   void raise_OnCompleted(int i1)
   {
      if (OnCompleted != 0)
      {
         OnCompleted->Invoke(i1);
      }
   }
   __event void OnCompleted(int operand);
};
```

Be wary about the code generated by */Fx* because it is not the actual code that is compiled. This is apparent when you look at the declaration of *raise_OnCompleted*. This class implies that this method is *public*, but if you look at the IL in the assembly, this method is actually declared as *family*; that is, it is a *protected* member. Furthermore, you will see that there will be an *__event* member added to the class. This is nonsense because there are already implementations of the event methods. I suspect that the code that generates the .mrg file has read the metadata for the generated code, seen that there is an *.event* directive, and added the *__event* member to show that this metadata exists.

Of course, the name of the delegate has been generated by the compiler, so it makes the code that adds a delegate to the event look a little ugly, as shown here:

```
Calculator5* c = new Calculator5;
c->OnCompleted += new Calculator5::__Delegate_OnCompleted
                      (new Inform, &Inform::NotifyMe);
```

The C++ compiler provides a mechanism to allow you to create a delegate and add (or remove) this delegate from the event. This process is carried out with two new keywords: *__hook* and *__unhook* (and optionally, a C++ attribute named *[event_receiver(managed)]*). The event handler class looks like this:

```
// unified.cpp
__gc class Inform
{
public:
   void CallMe(int i)
   { Console::WriteLine(S"called with {0}", __box(i)); }
   void HookUp(Calculator5* p)
   { __hook(&Calculator5::OnCompleted, p, &Inform::CallMe); }
   void Unhook(Calculator5* p)
   { __unhook(&Calculator5::OnCompleted, p, &Inform::CallMe); }
};
```

The *CallMe* method is the event handler, and the *__hook* code will generate a delegate identified by the first parameter, initialize it with the *this* pointer of the current object and the method specified by the last parameter, and then add this delegate to the event field of the object indicated by the second parameter. The compiler will generate a class that looks like this:

```
// Generated by the compiler
__gc class Inform
{
public:
   void CallMe(int i)
   {Console::WriteLine(S"called with {0}", __box(i));}
   void HookUp(Calculator5* p)
   {
      (p)->add_OnCompleted(
         new Calculator5::__Delegate_OnCompleted(
            this, &Inform::CallMe));
   }
   void Unhook(Calculator5* p)
```

```
    {
        (p)->remove_OnCompleted(
            new Calculator5::__Delegate_OnCompleted(
                this, &Inform::CallMe));
    }
};
```

If you look in the .mrg file, you will see that the *HookUp* and *Unhook* code will also contain the *__hook* and *__unhook* statements that generated the code. I have not shown them here to make the code in this book easier to read (and because the generated code is merged with the code that it is generated from, which produces a mish-mash that is not proper C++). When you use the *__hook* and *__unhook* keywords within a class, you do not need to specify the fully qualified name of the handler method. The compiler will use the name of the enclosing class by default, as shown here:

```
// unified.cpp
void HookUp(Calculator5* p)
{
    __hook(&Calculator5::OnCompleted, p, &Inform::CallMe);
}
```

Using this code is quite straightforward, as the following code shows:

```
Calculator5* c = new Calculator5;
Inform* i = new Inform;
i->HookUp(c);
c->CalculateSomething(42);
i->Unhook(c);
```

There is another form of *__hook* and *__unhook* that takes an additional parameter that is the target object that will be added to the delegate. If you use this version, these keywords don't have to be used in a class method.

```
// unified.cpp
Calculator5* c2 = new Calculator5;
Inform* i2 = new Inform;
__hook(&Calculator5::OnCompleted, c2, &Inform::CallMe, i2);
c2->CalculateSomething(42);
__unhook(&Calculator5::OnCompleted, c2, &Inform::CallMe, i2);
```

The handler method can be a static method, in which case you pass a zero as the last parameter to *__hook* and *__unhook*. You can use *__hook* and *__unhook* on an event source class that does not use the Unified Event Model, so for this class:

```
__gc class Ticker
{
public:
```

```
    void Tick(Object* sender, ElapsedEventArgs* e)
    {
        Console::WriteLine(S"Tick: {0}", __box(e->SignalTime));
    }
};
```

You can provide this method as the handler for the *System::Timers::Timer* class's *Elapsed* event.

```
Timer* timer = new Timer(1000);
__hook(&Timer::Elapsed, timer, &Ticker::Tick, new Ticker);
timer->Start();
System::Threading::Thread::Sleep(5000);
timer->Stop();
__unhook(&Timer::Elapsed, timer, &Ticker::Tick, new Ticker);
```

This code will allow the timer to tick for 5 seconds before telling it to stop.

Finally, the C++ compiler also supports the *__raise* keyword to raise an event.

COM Events

There was one part of COM interop that I did not cover in Chapter 2 because it is more pertinent here: COM events. COM events are interface based; function pointers cannot be marshaled by COM, but interfaces can. An interface can have more than one method, so if a class can handle events from the interface, it must handle *all* events on the interface. This restriction is one of the responsibilities imposed on you by interface programming: you cannot implement just part of an interface; the code will simply not compile. For this reason, many developers use *dispinterface*s for event interfaces because although the handler needs to handle *IDispatch*, the handler can choose which members of the *dispinterface* to implement. A *dispinterface* is not a COM interface (it is just a named implementation of *IDispatch*), so there is no contract to fulfill.

This aspect of COM events—that they are interface based—conflicts with .NET events, and predictably this incompatibility is handled by TlbImp and TlbExp, which will generate delegates from event interfaces and interfaces from delegates.

Handling COM Events in .NET

A COM object specifies the event interface that it will call when an event occurs as a *[source]* interface in the type library, as shown in this example:

```
[ uuid(96578D1F-8202-4882-99FA-2F6743FCF1C1)]
dispinterface IEvents
```

```
{
properties:
methods:
   [id(1)] void  EventOne();
   [id(2)] void  EventTwo([in]BSTR bstr);
};
[ version(1.0),
  uuid(BFBE1B63-769F-480b-A797-8421537A2A34) ]
coclass Src
{
   interface ISrc;
   [default, source] interface IEvents;
};
```

When this type library is run through TlbImp, it will add the items shown in Table 3-1.

Table 3-1 Items Generated by TlbImp for a Class with a *dispinterface* Source Interface

Item	Type	Description
IEvents	Interface	Managed version of the event interface
IEvents_Event	Interface	Delegate-based version of the event interface
IEvents_EventOneEventHandler	Delegate	Delegate for the first member of the event interface
IEvents_EventTwoEventHandler	Delegate	Delegate for the other member of the event interface
IEvents_EventProvider	Class	Does the actual work of accessing connection point objects and advising
IEvents_SinkHelper	Class	Associates a delegate with a connection point

When an object connects to a COM object that can generate events, it first queries for *IConnectionPointContainer*. It then asks this interface for the connection point for the event interface, and then finally it calls *IConnectionPoint::Advise*, passing the handler that implements the event interface and receiving back a cookie for the connection.

The implementation of the event interface is provided by the *IEvents_SinkHelper* class, which has a delegate field for each member of the event interface, and it is this delegate that is invoked when the handler event interface method is called. This class also has a field for the cookie that associates the handler object with the connection point.

As I mentioned in Chapter 2, TlbImp will generate a managed class for the COM coclass. This class has the *[ComSourceInterfaces]* attribute that identifies the event interface. This class derives from the managed version of the coclass interfaces and *IEvents_Event*, which is an interface with the .NET events equivalent to the members of the COM event interface. This class does not have any implementation. The methods are marked with *runtime managed internalcall*, which means that the runtime provides an implementation. The runtime can handle the COM interfaces, but the implementation of the handlers for the event interfaces is a different matter. *IEvents_Event* looks like this:

```
[ComVisible(false),
   ComEventInterface(__typeof(IEvents),
      __typeof(IEvents_EventProvider)]
public __gc __interface IEvents_Event
{
   __event IEvents_EventOneEventHandler EventOne;
   __event IEvents_EventTwoEventHandler EventTwo;
}
```

The *[ComEventInterface]* attribute identifies the class that acts as the bridge between the runtime and the COM connection point object, in this case, *IEvents_EventProvider*. This class has a field that holds the *IConnectionPointContainer* of the COM object, the *IConnectionPoint* for the event interface, and an *ArrayList* holding the sink objects. When you add a delegate to the coclass, the runtime calls the event method's *IEvents_EventProvider add_* event methods. This process will create an *IEvents_SinkHelper* object and pass it to *IConnectionPoint::Advise*, which will return a cookie that is stored in the *IEvents_SinkHelper* object along with the delegate. Thus, the *IEvents_SinkHelper* object associates a delegate with the cookie to the connection to a COM object. The *add_* method adds this object to the *ArrayList* so that it can be accessed later. When a delegate is removed, you want to break the connection to a connection point in the COM object. The *remove_* method looks up the appropriate *IEvents_SinkHelper* object in the *ArrayList* and passes the cookie to *IConnectionPoint::Unadvise* to break the connection.

Figure 3-3 shows how connection points are implemented in managed code.

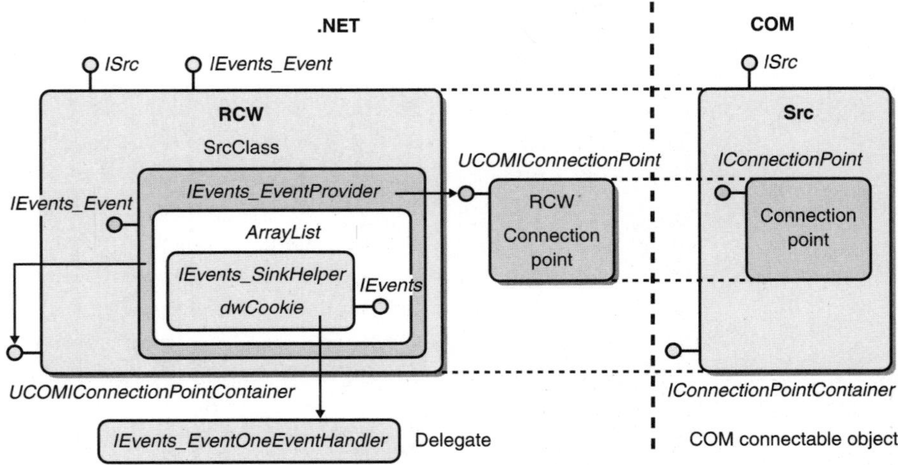

Figure 3-3 Implementation of connection points in managed code

Handling .NET Events in COM

To make your .NET objects accessible to COM clients with the COM Callable Wrapper (CCW), you must register the assembly using RegAsm. The CCW will implement *IConnectionPointContainer* so that COM clients can connect to the object. Consider this code:

```
// mansrc.cpp
// I don't want these in the type library.
[ComVisible(false)] public __delegate void EventOne();
[ComVisible(false)] public __delegate void EventTwo(String*);

[ GuidAttribute("C966757E-7F36-45c4-A791-D900EB882F8B"),
  InterfaceType(ComInterfaceType::InterfaceIsIDispatch) ]
public __gc __interface IManEvents
{
   [DispId(1)]void OnEventOne();
   [DispId(2)]void OnEventTwo(String*);
};

[ GuidAttribute("66B3A3C5-61CF-4a8a-88A7-A1CC6D538F80") ]
public __gc __interface IManSrc
{
   void DoSomething();
};
```

```
[ GuidAttribute("8515BCB4-C73F-433b-A0BA-7F8AE9FCF19E"),
   ComSourceInterfaces(__typeof(IManEvents)) ]
public __gc class ManSrc : public IManSrc
{
public:
   __event EventOne* OnEventOne;
   __event EventTwo* OnEventTwo;
   void DoSomething()
   {
      Console::WriteLine(S"called managed object");
      OnEventOne();
      OnEventTwo(S"Something happened");
   }
};
```

I have created an interface that has two methods. This interface is the managed version of the COM event interface. So that TlbExp will identify the event interface as the source interface for the CCW, the managed class has the *[ComSourceInterfaces]* attribute. If you omit this custom attribute, the CCW will not know which source interfaces (and hence, events) should be available through connection points.

The names of the methods on the event interface are the names of the event members in the class. This naming is important because it is how .NET hooks up a client sink object to the delegates in the managed class. The COM code will have sink objects that implement the COM version of *IManEvents*. They do not need to have access to the delegates, so I have marked them as *[ComVisible(false)]*.

The TlbExp tool will generate a type library that looks like this (but I have edited it a little to make it easier to read):

```
[ uuid(CD55FCB3-5A8A-3019-900C-74A7C025109E), version(1.0) ]
library ManSrc
{
   importlib("mscorlib.tlb");
   importlib("stdole2.tlb");
   dispinterface IManEvents;
   interface IManSrc;
   interface _ManSrc;
   [ uuid(C966757E-7F36-45C4-A791-D900EB882F8B), version(1.0) ]
   dispinterface IManEvents
   {
   properties:
   methods:
```

```
      [id(1)] void OnEventOne();
      [id(2)] void OnEventTwo([in] BSTR bstr);
   };
   [ uuid(66B3A3C5-61CF-4A8A-88A7-A1CC6D538F80),
      version(1.0), dual, oleautomation ]
   interface IManSrc : IDispatch
   {
      [id(0x60020000)] HRESULT DoSomething();
   };
   [ uuid(8515BCB4-C73F-433B-A0BA-7F8AE9FCF19E), version(1.0) ]
   coclass ManSrc
   {
      [default] interface _ManSrc;
      interface _Object;
      interface IManSrc;
      [default, source] dispinterface IManEvents;
   };
   [ uuid(58794410-0083-347B-9E33-8A0B6DC73CAC),
      hidden, dual, oleautomation ]
   interface _ManSrc : IDispatch { };
};
```

Apart from the mention of *_Object* (the COM version of the "class" interface for *System::Object*), this code looks just like the type information that would be provided for a COM object that can generate events via connection points. I won't go into the details about writing a client with C++; instead, here's a client in Visual Basic Scripting Edition (VBScript) that you can run using the Windows scripting host:

```
' useman.vbs
' Sink handler
sub obj_OnEventOne()
   WScript.Echo "called me"
End sub

Dim obj
Set obj = WScript.CreateObject("ManSrc")
WScript.ConnectObject obj, "obj_"
obj.DoSomething
```

If you want to call your .NET objects using the Windows scripting host, be aware that wscript.exe and cscript.exe are located in %system_root%\System32—that is, they are not in the same folder as your assembly. Fusion will throw an error with this code because it will look only in the current folder for an assembly, and wherever you invoke the Windows scripting host, this will be %systemroot%\System32. To get around this issue, you can use */codebase* when you call RegAsm or you can add the assembly to the GAC.

In general, if you register an assembly with RegAsm, you know that some of the types will be used by COM clients. If this is the case, it makes sense to put in a little effort to add attributes to make the class easier to use by the COM client.

Writing Multithreaded Code

One of the situations in which you'll come across delegates is when you're writing multithreaded code because you'll provide the thread procedure through a delegate. Multithreading presents many problems to users mainly through the misuse, or the lack of, synchronization. In this section, I'll outline how threads are managed and how you can access them safely.

Managed Threads

The *System::Threading* namespace has the various classes that you will use to write multithreaded code. Of particular interest is the *Thread* class. This class allows you to create managed threads, and although the documentation does not explicitly say so, it is easy to use the performance monitor to see that when you create a managed thread, an operating system thread is created. However, this detail is an implementation detail and there is no direct mechanism that you can use to wrap a managed thread object around an existing operating system thread.

Creating a managed thread is straightforward, as shown here:

```
// counter.cpp
__gc class Counter
{
   int count;
public:
   Counter(int c) : count(c){}
   // Count down in 1-second increments.
   void Countdown()
   {
      for (int i = count; i > 0; i--)
```

```
      {
         Console::WriteLine(i);
         Thread::Sleep(1000);
      }
      Console::WriteLine(S"Blast Off!");
   }
   static Thread* CreateCounterThread(int i)
   {
      return new Thread(
         new ThreadStart(new Counter(i), &Counter::Countdown));
   }
};
```

The *Thread* class is initialized with an instance of the *ThreadStart* delegate; this delegate has no parameters and no return value. This code creates an instance of a managed thread, but it does not start the thread. (I will explain how to do this task later in this section.) In this example, I have shown how you can provide initialization information for the thread procedure: as member variables of the target object in the delegate. This technique is fine because I am passing a *__value* object. You might have problems if the data is passed by reference, but I will come back to this problem later in this section.

The *System::Diagnostics* namespace has a class named *ProcessThread*; however, this class is for operating system threads, not managed threads. You can get information about the operating system threads in the current process through the *Process::Threads* property, shown here:

```
// counter.cpp
IEnumerator* e =
   Process::GetCurrentProcess()->Threads->GetEnumerator();
while (e->MoveNext())
{
   ProcessThread* t = static_cast<ProcessThread*>(e->Current);
   Console::WriteLine(S"thread: {0:x8}",
      __box(reinterpret_cast<int>(static_cast<void*>(t->StartAddress))));
}
```

This code will list the *operating system* threads running in the process, and in the current version of the .NET runtime this list will include the managed threads created through the *Thread* class. The *Thread* class encapsulates many of the things that you will do with a thread, but it is worth pointing out that *Thread* is sealed, so you cannot derive from it. Table 3-2 gives a summary of the members of this class.

Table 3-2 ***System::Threading::Thread* Members and the Equivalent Functions in Win32**

Thread	Win32 Equivalent	Description
Abort	*TerminateThread*	Stop the thread.
AllocateDataSlot, AllocateNamed-DataSlot, FreeNamedDataSlot, Get-Data, GetNamedDataSlot, SetData	*TlsAlloc, Tls-GetValue, Tls-SetValue, TlsFree*	Create a data slot that holds data specific to a particular thread.
ApartmentState	No equivalent	The COM apartment type.
CurrentContext	No equivalent	The .NET context (read-only).
CurrentCulture	*GetThreadLocale*	The culture for formatting items.
CurrentPrincipal	*OpenThreadTo-ken, GetTokenIn-formation*	Get the security principal.
CurrentThread	*GetCurrent-Thread*	The thread that is executing the code.
CurrentUICulture	No equivalent	Culture used for obtaining UI resources.
GetDomain	No equivalent	Get the AppDomain where the thread is running.
GetDomainID	No equivalent	Identifier for the current AppDomain.
Interrupt	No equivalent	Wake a thread that has gone into long-term sleep.
IsAlive	*WaitForSingleOb-ject*	Test to see if a thread is still alive (read-only).
IsBackground	No equivalent	Test to see if it is a background or foreground thread.

Table 3-2 *System::Threading::Thread* Members and the Equivalent Functions in Win32 *(continued)*

Thread	Win32 Equivalent	Description
IsThreadPoolThread	No equivalent	Test to see if the thread is in a thread pool (read-only).
Join	*WaitForSingleObject*	Wait for the thread to finish.
Name	No equivalent	Name of the thread.
Priority	*Get/SetThreadPriority*	Thread priority.
ResetAbort	No equivalent	Cancel a request to terminate the thread.
Resume	*ResumeThread*	Resume a suspended thread.
Sleep	*Sleep*	Sleep for a specified time.
SpinWait	No equivalent	Spins in a loop the specified number of times. Each loop is a no-op.
Start	No equivalent	Starts a newly created thread.
Suspend	*SuspendThread*	Suspend a thread.
Thread constructor	*CreateThread*	Create a new thread.
ThreadState	No equivalent	Get information about the current state (read-only).

At any time, you can call the *static* property *Thread::CurrentThread* to get access to the managed thread that is running the current code.

```
Thread* t = Thread::CurrentThread;
Console::WriteLine(S"This thread is \'{0}\'", t->Name);
Console::WriteLine(S"current culture {0}", t->CurrentCulture);
Console::WriteLine(S"priority {0}", __box(t->Priority));
```

The name of the thread is usually unset. It is a read/write property, so you can give a thread a name, which is useful for diagnostic purposes. The thread name is truly thread specific, so you can regard this as one way to pass thread-specific data to a thread.

```
// counter2.cpp
__gc class Counter
{
public:
   // Count down in 1-second increments.
   static void Countdown()
   {
      int count = Int32::Parse(Thread::CurrentThread->Name);
      for (int i = count; i > 0; i--)
      {
         Console::WriteLine(i);
         Thread::Sleep(1000);
      }
      Console::WriteLine(S"Blast Off!");
   }
   static Thread* CreateCounterThread(int i)
   {
      Thread* t = new Thread(
         new ThreadStart(0, &Counter::Countdown));
      t->Name = __box(i)->ToString();
      return t;
   }
};
```

Of course, this technique has its limitations.

If you want to return data from a thread, you will need to use a member variable because the thread procedure does not return a value. Here's one example:

```
// factorial.cpp
__gc class Factorial
{
   __int64 m_value;
public:
   __property __int64 get_Value() { return m_value; }
   Factorial(__int64 v)
   {
      if (v > 24) throw new ArgumentException(
         S"parameter must be between 1 and 24");
      if (v <= 0) throw new ArgumentException(
         S"parameter must be between 1 and 24");
      m_value = v;
   }
   void DoWork()
```

```
    {
        __int64 result = 1;
        __int64 limit = m_value;
        m_value = 0;
        for (int i = 1; i < limit; i++)
        {
            result *= i;
        }
        m_value = result;
    }
};
```

This code implies that you'll create an instance of *Factorial* and pass the value to calculate to the constructor. This code can be called like this:

```
// factorial.cpp
Factorial* f = new Factorial(24);
Thread* t = new Thread(new ThreadStart(f, &Factorial::DoWork));
t->Start();
// Calculation occurs.
t->Join();
Console::WriteLine(S"Result = {0}", __box(f->Value));
```

Every thread is created in the *Unstarted* state, so you have to call *Start* to start the calculation. On a uniprocessor machine, the calculation will actually occur when the new thread is scheduled to run—in this case, if the calculation is longer than the time given to the thread to run, another thread could have access to the *Factorial* object before the calculation has completed. On a multiprocessor machine, the new thread could be scheduled to run on another processor, which increases the possibility of another thread being able to access the *Factorial* object before the calculation has completed. In this code, I allow the new thread to complete its work by calling *Thread::Join*, which will block the current thread until the new thread has finished.

```
// factorial2.cpp
__gc class Factorial
{
    __int64 m_value;
    ManualResetEvent* event;
public:
    __property __int64 get_Value()
    {
        event->WaitOne();
        return m_value;
    }
    Factorial(__int64 v)
```

```
    {
        if (v > 24) throw new ArgumentException(
            S"parameter must be between 1 and 24");
        if (v <= 0) throw new ArgumentException(
            S"parameter must be between 1 and 24");
        m_value = v;
        event = new ManualResetEvent(false);
    }
    void DoWork()
    {
        __int64 result = 1;
        __int64 limit = m_value;
        m_value = 0;
        for (int i = 1; i < limit; i++)
        {
            result *= i;
        }
        m_value = result;
        event->Set();
    }
};
```

In this version, a manual reset event is used for interthread communication. The event is created unsignaled, and *WaitOne* will block until the event becomes signaled. The property accessor calls *WaitOne*, so the calling thread will block until *DoWork* has completed and calls *Set*. I will return to synchronization objects later in this chapter in the section "Synchronization Objects."

```
// factorial2.cpp
Factorial* f = new Factorial(operand);
Thread* t = new Thread(new ThreadStart(f, &Factorial::DoWork));
t->Start();
// NB I do not have to call Join()
Console::WriteLine(S"Result = {0}", __box(f->Value));
```

Earlier, I showed the *static Sleep* method, which is called with a 32-bit integer or a *TimeSpan* object. If an integer is used, it represents the sleep time in milliseconds. This method is *static* because it can be called only on the current thread; if you want to tell another thread to stop working, you can call the *Suspend* method. There are two main differences between the two methods. First, the thread that calls *Sleep* knows where it is going to start to sleep, but when a thread calls *Suspend*, it does not know what code the called thread is executing, so the runtime takes over and finds a "safe" point where it is safe to suspend the thread (that is, the garbage collector is happy about the action). The other main difference between the two is that a suspended thread can be told to start working by calling *Resume*; there is no direct way to get a thread to restart at the point where it started sleeping.

The *Sleep* method can be passed a value of zero to tell the system that the thread has completed its work for the current timeslice and to allow the system to allow another thread to do some work. The thread can also be told to sleep for *Timeout::Infinite*, which means that the thread will sleep forever. In fact, a sleeping thread can be told to wake up, but it is not as clean as a suspended thread being told to resume. Another thread can call *Interrupt*, which will cause the *ThreadInterruptedException* to be thrown in the sleeping thread. Thus, a thread can go into a deep sleep and catch this exception and take it as an indication to do some work.

```
void Interruptable ()
{
   while (true)
   {
      try {Thread::Sleep(Timeout::Infinite);}
      catch(Exception*){}
      DoWork();
   }
}
```

In this code, the thread goes to sleep in a guarded block and catches the exception that will be thrown when the sleep state is interrupted. At this point, the thread can do some work before going back to sleep and waiting to be interrupted again.

The final thread method I want to cover here is the *Abort* method. This method can be called by another thread, which will cause *ThreadAbortException* to be thrown. This exception is special because although you can handle it in a *catch* clause, this handler is not sufficient to stop the thread from aborting because after the *catch* handler has finished, the thread will still abort. To prevent this thread from aborting the *catch* handler, your catch handler can call *ResetAbort*. (The code needs *ControlThread* permission to do this.) However, it rarely makes sense to do this. If a thread has been told to abort, you should take this as a very heavy hint that the thread should finish as quickly as possible.

Thread States

I mentioned that all managed threads are created in an *Unstarted* state. A thread can be in 10 different states, and you can test the current state through the

ThreadState property. The various states are summarized in Table 3-3. These are bitmasks, and a thread can be in more than one state at any one time.

Table 3-3 ***System::Thread*** **States**

State	Description	Thread Method
Aborted	The thread has aborted.	
AbortRequested	The thread has been told to abort; *ThreadAbortException* is raised in the thread.	Abort
Background	The thread is running in the background.	
Running	The thread is running.	Start
Stopped	The thread has stopped.	
StopRequested	The thread has been told to stop.	
Suspended	The thread has been suspended.	
Suspend-Requested	The thread has been told to suspend.	Suspend
Unstarted	The thread object has been created but not started.	Thread constructor
WaitSleepJoin	The thread is blocked.	*Join*, *Sleep*, or *Wait* on a synchronization object

Foreground and Background Threads

A .NET thread can be a foreground thread or a background thread. The difference is that a foreground thread will keep a process alive, whereas a background thread will not. For example, assuming the *Counter* class I showed you earlier (in the section "Writing Multithreaded Code"), can you imagine what will happen here?

```
void main()
{
   Thread* thread = Counter::CreateCounterThread(100);
   thread->Start();
}
```

Once the *Start* method has been called, the *main* method will complete, and you would imagine that this completion would mean that the process will finish. In fact, it doesn't; the reason is that by default *Thread* objects are created as foreground threads, so although the main thread has finished its work, the *Counter* thread will still be working and will continue to work until it decides it has completed.

Now consider this:

```
void main()
{
   Thread* thread = Counter::CreateCounterThread(100);
   thread->IsBackground = true;
   thread->Start();
}
```

This code explicitly makes the thread a background thread, so after *main* completes, the process will finish, even though the *Counter* thread might not have finished.

Thread Local Data

If you pass a *__gc* object to another thread, two threads will have access to the same object—the thread where the object originated and the thread where the object was passed. You can use synchronization objects to synchronize access to the data members, but this scheme does assume that you want all threads to have access to the same data. Threads can have thread local data—that is, multiple threads can have access to the same variable, but each thread will have different values for the data. This system is equivalent to the Win32 concept of thread local storage.

Thread local data uses local data slots. You can either allocate named or unmanaged data slots through the *Thread* class. Consider this class:

```
// tls.cpp
__gc class MyThread
{
public:
   String* str;
   void Proc()
   {
      Thread* t = Thread::CurrentThread;
      if (str == 0)
         str = t->Name;
      Console::WriteLine(str);
   }
};
```

I can use this class like this:

```
// tls.cpp
MyThread* obj = new MyThread;
for (int i = 0; i < 5; i++)
{
   Thread* t = new Thread(new ThreadStart(obj, &MyThread::Proc));
   t->Name = i.ToString();
   t->Start();
}
```

I have created a single instance of *MyThread* and passed it to five threads. When the thread procedure runs, it checks to see whether the *str* field has been assigned, and if not, the procedure uses the name of the thread. With this version of *MyThread*, the first thread to run will assign *str* to a value of *0* and after that each call to *Proc* will use the same value because each call shares the same value. Thus the output of this code will be 0 five times.

To use thread local data, you have to allocate a data slot. Consider this new version of the class:

```
// tls.cpp
__gc class MyThread2
{
public:
   LocalDataStoreSlot* lds;
   MyThread2()
   {
      lds = Thread::CurrentThread->AllocateDataSlot();
   }
   void Proc()
   {
      Thread* t = Thread::CurrentThread;
      if (t->GetData(lds) == 0)
         t->SetData(lds, t->Name);
      Console::WriteLine(t->GetData(lds)->ToString());
   }
};
```

The constructor allocates an unmanaged data slot and stores it in the field *lds*. After the slot is stored, a thread can get the value specific to this thread by calling *GetData* and can write this value with *SetData*. When each thread first calls this code, it will get a zero from *SetData* because the data slot for the thread will be clear. As a consequence, this code will print 0 to 5 on the console.

A data slot can be named, which means that you do not need to hold a *LocalDataStoreSlot* object. You can allocate a named data slot by calling *AllocateNamedDataSlot*, passing the name of the data slot. Any thread can get access to the data slot by calling *GetNamedDataSlot*, as shown here:

```
// threads.cpp
__gc class MyThread3
{
public:
   void Proc()
   {
      Thread* t = Thread::CurrentThread;
      LocalDataStoreSlot* lds = t->GetNamedDataSlot(S"my name");
      if (t->GetData(lds) == 0)
         t->SetData(lds, t->Name);
      Console::WriteLine(t->GetData(lds)->ToString());
   }
};
```

The system maintains an internal table that associates names with data slots. *GetNamedDataSlot* uses this table to return the data slot associated with the name. If you call *GetNamedDataSlot* and the name does not exist, the method will allocate a data slot. This table is a global table, so when you have finished with a name, you should call *FreeNamedDataSlot* to remove the name from the table. Named data slots can be accessed on any thread.

A *static* field in a class is shared between all instances of the class, whatever thread those objects are accessed on. The *[ThreadStatic]* attribute preserves part of the meaning of *static*, in that each instance of the class on a particular thread will have access to the same value; however, there will be a separate shared data member for each thread. Consider this class:

```
// threads.cpp
__gc class SharedData
{
   static int i;
   String* name;
public:
   SharedData(String* s) : name(s) {}
   String* ToString()
   {
      return String::Format(S"{0} {1}", name,
         __box(Interlocked::Increment(&i)));
   }
   static void Proc()
```

```
    {
        SharedData* s1 = new SharedData(S"one");
        SharedData* s2 = new SharedData(S"two");
        Console::WriteLine(s1->ToString());
        Console::WriteLine(s2->ToString());
    }
};
void main()
{
    for (int i = 0; i < 5; i++)
    {
        Thread* t = new Thread(new ThreadStart(0,
            &SharedData::Proc));
        t->Start();
    }
}
```

In this example, the *SharedData* class has a static member and an instance member. The *ToString* method will print out the value of both members, but it also increments the *static* integer value (using the thread safe *Interlocked::Increment*). If you run this code, you will get results similar to the following:

```
one 1
two 2
one 3
two 4
one 5
two 6
one 7
two 8
one 9
two 10
```

The reason is that there will be a single static variable for *all* objects created on all threads. If you add the *[ThreadStatic]* attribute to the member *i*, you will get this result:

```
one 1
two 2
one 1
two 2
one 1
two 2
one 1
two 2
one 1
two 2
```

The reason for this behavior is that now there will be a static member for each *thread*, so the *static* member will be incremented to a maximum of 2 because on each thread, *SharedData::ToString* is called only twice.

Threads and Exceptions

Exceptions are thread based. This is an important point. Remember that exceptions are serializable, so they can be considered as an additional return value from every method. The only way to persuade the runtime to ignore an exception is to mark the method as *[OneWay]*, and this strategy works only when .NET remoting is used. However, when you start a thread, that thread has the responsibility to run the code. When the thread has finished its work (when it is aborted or the thread procedure has finished), there is no return value and no code to accept this return value. (By definition, a thread is a separate unit of execution and thus can be treated as an independent entity.)

Look at this code:

```
__gc class MyThread
{
public:
   void Proc()
   {
      throw new Exception(S"bye, bye");
   }
};
void main()
{
   Thread* t = new Thread(new ThreadStart(new MyThread,
      &MyThread::Proc));
   try
   {
      t->Start();
      // Not necessary, but let's block this thread anyway.
      t->Join();
   }
   catch(Exception* e)
   {
      Console::WriteLine(e->ToString());
   }
}
```

Even though the main thread uses exception handling, the process will still be terminated due to an unhandled exception. The exception can be caught only by the thread that threw the exception with one (ahem) exception:

if an exception is not handled, it will be passed to the AppDomain, which will pass the exception through to the *UnhandledException* event, as shown here:

```
__gc class Catcher
{
public:
   static void Unhandled(Object* sender,
      UnhandledExceptionEventArgs* e)
   {
      Console::WriteLine(S"Handled exception:");
      Console::WriteLine(e->ExceptionObject->ToString());

   }
};
void main()
{
   AppDomain* ad = AppDomain::CurrentDomain;
   ad->UnhandledException +=
      new UnhandledExceptionEventHandler(0, &Catcher::Unhandled);
   Thread* t = new Thread(new ThreadStart(new MyThread,
      &MyThread::Proc));
   t->Start();
   // Give the other thread some time to work.
   Thread::Sleep(2000);
   Console::WriteLine(S"normal shutdown");
}
```

Both the main thread and the new thread run in the same AppDomain. When an exception is thrown in a thread running in the AppDomain and it is not caught by the thread where it is thrown, the exception will be passed to the unhandled exception event handler. The thread that generated the exception will be shut down, but all the other threads and the AppDomain will be unaffected. So, in this example, the process will be shut down normally. This behavior works only for the first AppDomain that the system creates.

The main thread is treated slightly differently than the other threads; if the main thread throws an exception that is not handled, the unhandled exception event handler will be called, but only after the JIT debugger handling is informed (if this is turned on). I will give more details about this process in Chapter 7.

The runtime will pass all exceptions to the unhandled exception event handler except the *ThreadAbortException*; this exception will always be handled by causing the targeted thread to abort. It never "leaks" out of the thread.

It is good practice to make sure that you handle all exceptions thrown in your thread code—if only by using a *try/catch* block in your thread procedure, and/or by implementing an unhandled exception event handler to ensure that the user never sees the unhandled exception dialog box presented by the system. It is also a good idea to reset any synchronization objects held by the thread that is about to die so that any other threads waiting on these objects will not be permanently blocked. This brings me to the subject of synchronization objects.

Synchronization Objects

The .NET Framework has several classes that allow you to synchronize execution between threads. Some of these are similar to the synchronization objects in Win32; others provide more functionality. Most synchronization objects derive from the abstract class *WaitHandle*, and the three important members of this class are the instance method *WaitOne* and the static members *WaitAll* and *WaitAny*. *WaitOne* is like the Win32 ::*WaitForSingleObject* in that it will block until the handle has become signaled or a timeout occurs. The timeout can be expressed as a 32-bit integer with the time in milliseconds or as a *TimeSpan* object. The other two members are used when you have more than one waitable object. Both of these *static* methods take an array of waitable objects, and the method will block until the timeout occurs, or if one object signals for *WaitOne*, or if all of the objects have signaled with *WaitAll*.

The classes that derive from *WaitHandle* are *AutoResetEvent*, *ManualResetEvent*, and *Mutex*. The first two are similar to the Win32 event kernel object. The object can be created in a signaled or an unsignaled state, and a thread can change the signaled state by calling *Set* or *Reset*. More than one thread can wait on a single event. The difference between the two types of events is how these waiting threads are released when the event is signaled. When a *ManualResetEvent* is signaled, all threads waiting on the event will be released from the wait state. When an *AutoResetEvent* is signaled, only one thread is released from the wait state and then the event will be automatically made nonsignaled. To release the other waiting threads, the event has to be signaled the appropriate number of times. Note that if you have a uniprocessor machine, you will have to allow the other threads to have the opportunity to be released from the wait state.

```
// waiting.cpp
__gc class WaitingThread
{
public:
   AutoResetEvent* e;
   WaitingThread (){ e = new AutoResetEvent(false); }
   void Proc()
   {
      // Wait until event signals.
      e->WaitOne();
```

```
      Console::WriteLine(S"{0} released",
         Thread::CurrentThread->Name);
   }
};

void main()
{
   WaitingThread* x = new WaitingThread;
   int i;
   for (i = 0; i < 10; i++)
   {
      Thread* t = new Thread(new ThreadStart(x,
         &WaitingThread::Proc));
      t->Name = __box(i)->ToString();
      // Thread starts, but waits on the event.
      t->Start();
   }

   for (i = 1; i < 11; i++)
   {
      Console::WriteLine(S"{0}th time Set has been called",
         __box(i));
      x->e->Set();
   }
}
```

If you run this code as it stands on a uniprocessor machine, you will find that not all of the threads will be released. The reason is that the second *for* loop might execute several loops before the main thread's timeslice has been completed to give another thread the opportunity to run. It is only when a thread has been released from a wait state that the event will become unsignaled, so if *Set* is called 5 times before any other thread is allowed to run, still only one thread will be released. The solution is to insert a call to *Thread::Sleep(0)* after the call to *Set*. This call will tell the system to reschedule the current thread and ignore the remaining time left in the current timeslice. This solves the problem in this example, where we know that there will be a thread waiting for the event to be signaled.

The other *WaitHandle* is the *Mutex*, which is similar to the Win32 mutex kernel object in that only one thread can own the mutex at any one time. *Mutex* objects are global objects, in the respect that any process on a single machine can have access to a mutex. Furthermore, .NET *Mutex* objects are based on Win32 mutexes, so you can get access to a named Win32 mutex, or a Win32 process can have access to a named .NET *Mutex*. The *Mutex* constructor has four overloads; two allow you to create unnamed objects (and hence they can be used only in the current process), and the other two allow you to create a named mutex. In the following code, a *Mutex* object is created and the current thread has "ownership":

```
Mutex mutex = new Mutex(true);
// Pass this mutex object to other threads.
// Do stuff with shared objects that should only be accessed
// by a single thread at a time.
// Now allow another thread to access the shared objects.
mutex->ReleaseMutex();
// One other thread now owns the mutex.
```

A thread requests the ownership of a mutex by calling a *Wait* method, for example, *WaitOne*. This call will block until the thread gains ownership of the mutex, and after the thread has finished its work on the shared objects, the thread relinquishes its ownership by calling *ReleaseMutex*.

You can use a *Mutex* to protect data that could be accessed by multiple threads, as shown here:

```
// mutexes.cpp
__gc class Data
{
   int x;
public:
   Mutex* m;
   Data(){m = new Mutex(false);}
   void Proc()
   {
      m->WaitOne();
      int i = x++;
      Console::WriteLine(S"{0} has the mutex {1}",
         Thread::CurrentThread->Name, __box(i));
      // Allow another thread to try to access the shared data.
      Thread::Sleep(500);
      m->ReleaseMutex();
   }
   // Other public methods that access the instance data and
   // are protected by the mutex
};
```

You can even use a mutex in the property accessors, as this code shows:

```
// mutexes.cpp
__property int get_Count()
{
   int i;
   m->WaitOne();
```

```
    i = x;
    m->ReleaseMutex();
    return i;
}
__property void set_Count(int val)
{
    m->WaitOne();
    x = val;
    m->ReleaseMutex();
}
```

Such property accessors will prevent more than one thread accessing the data. However, there is a problem. Imagine that you have multiple threads trying to read the property. It makes no sense to lock access to the property in this case because the value will not change. You might decide to remove the protection from the *get_* accessor, but this action will not protect you from the situation when another thread tries to write to the property because the write action might not be completed before another thread tries to read the property.

To protect you in this situation, the .NET Framework supplies the *ReaderWriterLock* class. This class will allow multiple reader threads to access the lock but only when there are no writer threads.

```
ReaderWriterLock* wrl;
Data() { wrl = new ReaderWriterLock(); }
__property int get_Count()
{
    int i;
    wrl->AcquireReaderLock (Timeout::Infinite);
    i = x;
    wrl->ReleaseReaderLock();
    return i;
}
__property void set_Count(int val)
{
    wrl->AcquireWriterLock (Timeout::Infinite);
    x = val;
    wrl->ReleaseWriterLock();
}
```

In these examples, the thread synchronization objects are rather overkill for a 32-bit integer. The *Interlocked* class has *static* methods that allow you to increment and decrement 32-bit and 64-bit integers and to assign 32-bit integers, single-precision real numbers, and objects in an atomic way.

If you have many lines of code within an object that logically should be executed together by only one thread at a time, you could use a mutex to protect this code. Another option is to use the *Monitor* class, which has *static* members that take an object. The *Monitor::Enter* method will block until the lock for the object that is passed as a parameter is released. The lock is released by calling *Monitor::Exit*.

Thread Pool

Threads are expensive objects. The following code, when run on a machine with 512 MB of memory, will throw an *OutOfMemoryException* exception when 1970 threads have been created:

```
for (int i = 0; i < 10000; i++)
{
   Thread* t = new Thread(new ThreadStart(0, &Code::Proc));
   t->Start();
}
```

Win32 has a memory limit of 4 GB; 2 GB are addressable by user-mode code.[4] By default, when an operating system thread is created, it will get 1 MB of stack, so I guess 1,970 threads means that the 2-GB limit has been reached. Unfortunately, there is no way that you can specify the stack space used by a managed thread. When this exception was thrown, I was relieved—yes, I really was. The reason is that in the past I have run similar tests with native C++ and have found that Win32 will attempt to create all the threads that I have requested. This attempt will result in Windows NT paging virtual memory back and forth between physical memory and the page file, which will result in lots of disk activity and eventually the UI will freeze. .NET has spared me this problem before it gets out of hand.

Threads are a great idea insofar as they allow you to divide your code into logical tasks, but you must avoid creating large numbers of threads. The maximum number of threads you can safely create depends on how much memory you have and how much memory your code will use. Restricting the number of threads that you have can complicate your code as you try to decide which thread should perform the work. One way to solve this issue is to use a thread pool, and the .NET Framework provides you with a thread pool class.

Contrast the following code with the previous code:

```
for (int i = 0; i < 10000; i++)
{
   ThreadPool::QueueUserWorkItem(new WaitCallback(0,
      &Code::Proc2));
}
```

---

4. Windows 2000 DataCenter has a 3Gb limit for user mode code.

This code will run fine, and no exception will be thrown. The first time you call *QueueUserWorkItem*, the thread pool will be created, and each time you call this method, the request will be queued. The system maintains the thread pool, and in times of stress (for example, in this loop), the system will increase the size of the pool, but it will throttle the number of threads to a maximum figure. You can get the maximum number of threads in the pool by calling *GetMaxThreads*, and you can get the number of threads that are currently available for work by calling *GetAvailableThreads*. If a pool thread is idle for some (undisclosed) amount of time, the system can terminate threads and allow the pool to shrink to conserve resources.

The threads in the thread pool are created as background threads, which means that if the other foreground threads (including the main thread) complete before all the requests have completed, the process will die. You can make the pool thread a foreground thread in the method called by the *WaitCallback* delegate if the action is important, but because the pool thread can be reused, it makes sense to return the thread back to a background thread once the method has completed. Furthermore, the pool thread is created with *Normal* priority, and again you can change the priority if the action is particularly important or unimportant.

QueueUserWorkItem is passed an instance of the *WaitCallback* delegate:

```
public __delegate void WaitCallback(Object* state);
```

This method takes a reference to some object that you can use to pass data into, or receive results from, the procedure executed by the pool thread. Because the code that calls *QueueUserWorkItem* does not have access to the thread that does the actual work, it is not possible to determine when that work has completed. If you rely on a result that will come from the method executed by the pool thread, you will have to set up some interthread communication. For example, you could create an unsignaled event object and pass it as the *state* object or as a member of the object that is the target of the delegate. In both cases, the method can indicate when it has completed its work by setting the event, as shown here:

```
__gc class Code
{
public:
   void Proc(Object* o)
   {
      // Do some complex calculation.
      Value = 42;
      ManualResetEvent* ev = static_cast<ManualResetEvent*>(o);
      ev->Set();
   }
   int Value;
};
```

```
// Code that uses the thread pool.
Code* obj = new Code;
ManualResetEvent* ev = new ManualResetEvent(false);
ThreadPool::QueueUserWorkItem(
   new WaitCallback(obj, &Code::Proc), ev);
// Do some work while we wait for the result.
ev->WaitOne();
Console::Write(S"result = {0}", __box(obj->Value));
```

As you can see, this overload of *QueueUserWorkItem* takes the *event* object as the last parameter.

Synchronized Contexts

If a class is context-bound (the class derives from *ContextBoundObject*, which includes all classes derived from *MarshalByRefObject*), it can be marked with *[Synchronization]* to specify whether access to the object is synchronized. This attribute is declared in the *System::Runtime::Remoting::Contexts* namespace, but note that there is a similar named attribute in *System::EnterpriseServices* that controls synchronization with respect to COM+ contexts.

If you specify that synchronization is required, only one thread at a time can access instance methods and fields. All calls from other threads will block. Here's an example:

```
// syncctx.cpp
__gc class Data : public ContextBoundObject
{
public:
   void Proc()
   {
      Console::WriteLine(__box(DateTime::Now));
      // Simulate some other work.
      Thread::Sleep(1000);
   }
};
```

This code prints out the time and then does some other work, which I have simulated by calling *Sleep*. You could call this class from multiple threads in code like this:

```
// syncctx.cpp
Data* data = new Data;
for (int i = 0; i < 5; i++)
{
   Thread* t = new Thread(new ThreadStart(data, &Data::Proc));
   t->Start();
}
```

The results will show that the five threads appear to call the *Proc* method at the same time, and the only indication that the *Sleep* call was made is a slight pause after the last time is printed at the console. The reason is that the threads are called in parallel. If you add this line to the declaration of the class:

```
// syncctx.cpp
[Synchronization((Int32)SynchronizationAttribute::REQUIRED)]
__gc class Data {};
```

you will find that the time will be printed with a second interval between each time a line is printed. The reason is that the attribute tells the runtime that whenever there is an access from another thread, the runtime will attempt to access a lock for the object. There is only one lock, so if another thread has this lock, the requesting thread is blocked until the lock becomes available. In this example, the lock is applied until the *Proc* method has completed.

There are four values that you can use in the constructor for *[Synchronization]*; these are *static* fields of the class and are shown in Table 3-4. To keep the compiler happy, you have to ensure that you give the complete name of the class (*SynchronizationAttribute*) and you have to cast the field to an *Int32*.

Table 3-4 The Values That Can Be Passed to the Constructor of *[Synchronization]*

Member	Value	Meaning
NOT_SUPPORTED	1	No synchronization will occur.
SUPPORTED	2	If the object is used in a context that has synchronization, every access will be synchronized.
REQUIRED	4	Every access will require synchronization; the class can be created in an existing synchronized context.
REQUIRES_NEW	8	Every access will require synchronization; the object will always be created in a new context.

These values appear to be bitmasks, but they are not. You can apply only one of these on a class. The reason there are four values is that you can specify whether the class will be used in the same context as its creator (*NOT_SUPPORTED*, *SUPPORTED*, and *REQUIRED*, if the creator has a synchronized context), and you can indicate whether synchronization will occur (*REQUIRED*, *REQUIRES_NEW*, and *SUPPORTED* if the calling context is a synchronized context) through one value.

Another way to get the same effect is to use the *[MethodImpl]* attribute in the *System::Runtime::CompilerServices* namespace. As the name suggests, this namespace is intended only for writers of compilers, but it has some nice tools, one of which is the *[MethodImpl]* attribute that is used to give additional information (*MethodImplOptions*) to the runtime about a method. One of the values you can pass tells the runtime that the method is synchronized, as shown here:

```
// syncctx2.cpp
__gc class Data
{
public:
   [MethodImpl(MethodImplOptions::Synchronized)]
   void Proc()
   {
      Console::WriteLine(__box(DateTime::Now));
      // Simulate some other work.
      Thread::Sleep(1000);
   }
};
```

There are two important differences between this class and the previous one: first, the attribute is applied to the method and not the class, and second, the class does not have to derive from *ContextBoundObject*. The effect is the same as before: the method can be accessed only by one thread at a time.

Summary

.NET is type-safe. If it were not, malicious code could manipulate your code to do things that you do not want it to do. This type safety is also applied to making indirect calls to methods through pointers, and to do this, the .NET Framework provides a type called a *delegate*. However, delegates are far more than just a mechanism to allow you to make indirect calls on methods: they are the main mechanism that allows you to call methods asynchronously, and they are vital for declaring the code that will be called in multithreaded code. Microsoft .NET formalizes notifications through delegates using metadata called events. Windows GUI is event based, and this is the subject of Chapter 4.

4

User Interface Development

The Microsoft .NET Framework has classes that allow you to develop graphical user interface (GUI) applications. Drawing code is based on a new technology named *GDI+*, and as the name suggests, this technology extends Microsoft Windows GDI facilities. Windowing code is based on a technology named *Windows Forms*. In this chapter, I will describe both the GDI+ and Windows Forms libraries and explain how they work and how to use them.

Developing Windows Forms with C++

Among the assemblies of the .NET Framework is a native DLL named *gdiplus.dll*,[1] which contains the new object-oriented graphics code named *GDI+*. The API is unmanaged and is based on C functions exported from the DLL. Microsoft Visual Studio .NET provides unmanaged C++ classes, and the .NET Framework provides managed classes to access GDI+. You will find the managed classes in the System.Drawing.dll assembly. As the name suggests, GDI+ builds upon the Windows graphics device interface (GDI) and provides tools to draw on graphics devices. The graphics device that you are most likely to use is a window. The .NET Framework provides you with a managed window object called a *form*. The way that you use this form and its properties has very strong parallels with unmanaged Visual Basic forms.

1. This DLL is also distributed as part of Windows XP.

If you do Windows development with C++, you will most likely use the Windows SDK directly or, more likely, the Microsoft Foundation Class Library (MFC). MFC is an unmanaged application framework and is based on the document/view model. This library is still part of Visual C++ .NET. MFC has been extended in version 7 to have closer integration with the Active Template Library (ATL), and it has new classes for the new Windows XP controls. You can continue to develop in MFC with Visual Studio .NET; do not think that you have to port your code to Windows Forms.

Windows Forms is only for managed development, and compared to MFC, it is definitely a version 1 product. Windows Forms provides no support for the management of documents, nor does it provide any application framework features. Windows Forms provides only the basic infrastructure to create forms and to create controls as part of those forms; you have to write all the other code to connect the controls. MFC is an application framework, so it has support to link the associated items on menus and toolbars. When you highlight a menu item, the MFC framework will add the item's descriptive text to the status bar. With Windows Forms, you can add a menu and a status bar to a form, but you have the responsibility to check for the selection of a menu item and then add the description to the status bar.

Frameworks such as MFC allow you to provide multiple views of documents of your data. MFC has framework support to load and save these documents and to select an appropriate view of the data. Windows Forms is not an application framework. Windows Forms is the basic SDK for managing controls and drawing in device contexts, and you have to write the code to manage documents and views of your data. The .NET Framework has built-in support for serialization of objects, so you can compose your documents from multiple objects, serialize those objects, and save them to or load them from storage (most likely a file). Furthermore, Windows Forms also has support for the OLE features of embedded and linked objects, including copying objects to the clipboard as a data object and drag and drop. However, you have to write the code to render such objects.

In short, the .NET Framework class library has all of the low-level facilities that you can use to write a fully fledged document-based application, but it has none of the convenience of more mature frameworks, so you have to write your own application framework classes. Regard the .NET Framework much in the same way as a 1990s developer regarded the Windows SDK, and hope that Microsoft will be working on an application framework.

The main namespaces and assemblies used for GUI development are summarized in Table 4-1.

Table 4-1 The Main GUI Namespaces and Assemblies in the .NET Framework

Namespace	Main Assembly	Description
System::ComponentModel	*system, system.windows.forms*	Building blocks used for components and component containers
System::ComponentModel::Design	*system, system.design*	Basic classes for providing design-time support for components and controls.
System::Drawing	*system.drawing*	Basic access to GDI+
System::Drawing2D	*system.drawing*	Classes for 2D and vector graphics drawing
System::Drawing::Design	*system.design, system.drawing*	Design-time support for drawing elements.
System::Drawing::Imaging	*system.drawing*	Support for Windows metafiles
System::Drawing::Printing	*system.drawing*	Classes for rendering images on a hard copy device
System::Drawing::Text	*system.drawing*	Classes for rendering text
System::Resources	*mscorlib, system.windows.forms*	Classes to create, store, and use culture-specific resources
System::Windows::Forms	*system.windows.forms*	Classes for Windows controls, form-based windows, and common dialog boxes, and also has classes to handle mouse and keyboard input
System::Windows::Forms::Design	*system.design, system.windows.forms*	Design-time support for forms.

Components and Containers

Every discussion of .NET GUI development must start with a discussion about components. Forms and controls are *Component* based: a UI class is derived from *Component*, and a UI element that can contain other UI elements will be a *Component* container. UI elements are based on scarce system resources.[2] When you have finished with such an item, you must dispose of it as soon as

2. As you will see later, when you create a control, you will get a new Windows handle. The Windows Forms library makes no attempt to conserve Windows handles like, for example, so-called "windowless" ActiveX controls do.

possible to allow the .NET Framework to release the UI resource. The reason for this disposal is that .NET does not support so-called deterministic finalization. Objects are finalized when the garbage collector decides it is right to do so. Thus, you are responsible for determining when a resource is no longer used by a top-level window and then taking the action to release the resource. (A parent control will dispose of its child controls.)

Disposable Objects

The .NET Framework provides an interface named *IDisposable*, which should be implemented by all classes that hold resources. The interface looks like this:

```
public __gc __interface IDisposable
{
   void Dispose();
};
```

When a class implements *IDisposable*, the class user knows that instances of the class hold a resource. The resource must be released as soon as possible, so the user knows that when she has finished using an instance of the class, she should call *IDisposable::Dispose*. A class that implements *IDisposable* should also implement a finalizer (in C++ terms, this means that the class should have a destructor) to release the held resource in the unlikely event that the user did not call *Dispose*.

```
// resholder.cpp
__gc class MyResourceHolder : public IDisposable
{
   HANDLE resourceHandle;
public:
   MyResourceHolder()
   {
      resourceHandle = ObtainNativeResource();
   }
   virtual void Dispose()
   {
      if (resourceHandle != 0)
         ReleaseNativeResource(resourceHandle);
      resourceHandle = 0;
      GC::SuppressFinalize(this);
   }
   virtual ~MyResourceHolder()
   {
      Dispose();
   }
   // Methods that use the resource
};
```

This class shows the typical pattern to implement if you have a class that uses an unmanaged resource: the constructor obtains the resource and caches the handle, and *Dispose* releases the resource. Even though interface methods and destructors are always *virtual*, I have explicitly used the *virtual* keyword to remind you of this fact, which becomes important when you consider derived classes.

When you call *Dispose*, the object is disposed of. This disposal means that the object is still alive, but the resource it holds is no longer initialized. The user could still call one of the methods that use the resource. To prevent this action from calling an API with an invalid handle, *Dispose* zeros the resource handle. It is the responsibility of the object methods to ensure that they check to see whether an object has been disposed of and to handle this possibility appropriately by throwing the *ObjectDisposedException* exception.

The destructor needs to release the resource so it too calls *Dispose*. When *Dispose* has been called, it makes no sense to call the method another time, so *Dispose* calls *GC::SuppressFinalize* to prevent the runtime from queuing the object for finalization (and calling the destructor code). If you implement a class with *IDisposable*, the class can be used with the C# *using* clause, as shown here:

```
// C#
MyResourceHolder res = new MyResourceHolder();
using (res)
{
   // Use object here
} // MyResourceHolder::Dispose() will be called
res = null;
```

If you use this class with C++, you must call *Dispose* explicitly, as the following code shows:

```
// C++
MyResourceHolder* res = new MyResourceHolder;
try
{
   // Use object here
}
__finally // Use finally so that Dispose is always called.
{
   IDisposable* d = dyanamic_cast<IDisposable*>(res);
   if (d != 0) d->Dispose();
}
res = 0;
```

We know that the class supports *IDisposable*, so the cast is unnecessary; however, I have shown the cast to indicate how to make the code more generic. Disposable classes are quite a responsibility. As you have seen, the *Dispose* method must be called by the user of an instance of the class. If you derive from a disposable class, you have the responsibility of disposing the resources you use in the new class.

```
// childres.cpp
__gc class ChildHolder : public MyResourceHolder
{
public:
   // Methods that use the resource obtained by the parent class
   virtual void Dispose()
   {
      // Release child resources here.
      MyResourceHolder::Dispose();
   }
};
```

I mentioned earlier that interface methods and destructors are called virtually. Here is where that fact comes into play: Because the parent has a destructor, instances of this class will also be finalized, and when this finalization happens, the finalizer on the child class will be called first (which calls the child destructor) and then the parent finalizer will be called (calling the parent destructor). The parent destructor calls *Dispose* virtually, thus *ChildHolder::Dispose* is called, which then calls *MyResourceHolder::Dispose*. If the user remembers that the class is disposable and calls *Dispose* on a child instance, *ChildHolder::Dispose* is called first, followed by *MyResourceHolder::Dispose*. Note that there is no need to call *GC::SuppressFinalize* in the child version of *Dispose* because this method is called in the parent version of *Dispose*. You should not implement a destructor on the child because *GC::SuppressFinalize* will turn off finalization for the base part of the object and not for the child. Hence the child destructor will be called by the finalization thread, which will dispose of the child object twice.

The .NET Framework uses another pattern, which is followed by many classes, such as *Control*, *EventLog*, and *FileStream*. This pattern assumes that a class holds on to both managed and unmanaged resources. Unmanaged resources must be explicitly released; managed resources will be implemented by classes that have finalizers, so the resource will be released when the object that contains the resource is itself finalized. If such a container class is disposed of, the caller is making the assertion that all resources should be released at that point, so both managed and unmanaged resources should be released. If an instance of a container class is finalized, the object will die and the references it holds will die too—in this case, the object must still explicitly release its unmanaged resources, but it can ignore the managed resources because they will be garbage collected and finalized soon after the container object is finalized.

A container object that has both managed and unmanaged resources should have a *protected* method that looks like this:

```
protected:
   virtual void Dispose(bool disposing);
```

The parameter is passed a value of *true* if the object is being disposed of; that is, the object will exist for some indeterminate amount of time after the method is called. In this situation, you must release both managed and unmanaged resources. A *false* value for this parameter means that *Dispose* has been called when the object was being finalized, so there is no need to release managed resources. An object that implements this version of *Dispose* will call it in *IDisposable::Dispose*, passing a parameter of *true*, and will call the following method in the destructor passing a parameter of *false*:

```
// manreshold.cpp
__gc class MyOtherResHolder : public IDisposable
{
   HANDLE resourceHandle;
   FileStream* fs;
public:
   MyOtherResHolder()
   {
      resourceHandle = ObtainNativeResource();
      fs = File::OpenWrite(S"Data.dat");
   }
   virtual void Dispose()
   {
      Dispose(true);
      GC::SuppressFinalize(this);
   }
   virtual ~MyOtherResHolder()
   {
      Dispose(false);
   }
   // Methods that use the resources
protected:
   virtual void Dispose(bool disposing)
```

```
   {
      if (disposing) fs->Close();
      if (resourceHandle != 0)
         ReleaseNativeResource(resourceHandle);
      resourceHandle = 0;
   }
};
```

As you can see, the *protected* version of *Dispose* will close the *FileStream* object only if the method is called when the object is being disposed of. If you derive a class from *MyOtherResHolder*, you have two choices. If the derived class does not have any managed or unmanaged resources, it does not have to implement *Dispose* or have a destructor. Because the base class implements *IDisposable*, a user can call *IDisposable::Dispose* to dispose of the parent class's resources. Because the parent class has a finalizer if *Dispose* is not called, the parent's destructor will be called when the finalizer is called. If the derived class has managed or unmanaged resources, these resources must be released at the appropriate time. In this case, the derived class need implement only the protected version of *Dispose*, as shown here:

```
// manreshold.cpp
__gc class OtherChildHolder : public MyOtherResHolder
{
public:
   OtherChildHolder()
   {
      // Obtain child managed resources.
      // Obtain child unmanaged resources.
   }
protected:
   virtual void Dispose(bool disposing)
   {
      if (disposing)
      {
         // Release child managed resources.
      }
      // Release child unmanaged resources.
      MyOtherResHolder::Dispose(disposing);
   }
};
```

Now imagine that you have a container class, that is, a class that has fields that are instances of other classes. If those field classes are disposable, the container class must also be disposable.

```
// rescont.cpp
__gc class Container : public IDisposable
{
   MyResourceHolder* res1;
   MyResourceHolder* res2;
public:
   Container()
   {
      res1 = new MyResourceHolder;
      res2 = new MyResourceHolder;
   }
   virtual void Dispose()
   {
      Dispose(true);
      GC::SuppressFinalize(this);
   }
   ~Container()
   {
      Dispose(false);
   }
protected:
   virtual void Dispose(bool disposing)
   {
      if (disposing)
      {
         res1->Dispose();
         res2->Dispose();
      }
   }
};
```

Again, the destructor must call *Dispose* on the disposable objects that it holds. Of course, the coding is far easier if the disposable objects are held in a container, in which case you can simply iterate through the items in the container.

Components

If a disposable object is used with one of the Visual Studio .NET designers, the object's class should implement *IComponent*. This interface looks like this:

```
public __gc __interface IComponent : public IDisposable
{
   __property ISite* get_Site();
   __property void set_Site(ISite*);
   __event EventHandler* Disposed;
};
```

The interface derives from *IDisposable*, as you would expect, and it has an event that is invoked when the component is disposed of. If you have another component that depends on this component, the dependent component can add a delegate to the event. When the dependent component is informed that the component has been disposed of, the dependent component can release its reference to the disposed of component. In addition, the interface has a read/write property that gives access to an *ISite* interface that is implemented on the site where the component is being used, as shown in this code:

```
public __gc __interface ISite : public IServiceProvider
{
   __property IComponent* get_Component();
   __property IContainer* get_Container();
   __property bool get_DesignMode();
   __property String* get_Name();
   __property void set_Name(String*);
};
```

The interface has four properties, three of them read-only. The site itself is a component, so you are able to have nested components and sites. A component is used as part of some other object. The component can have a UI (such as a *TextBox* control), or it might not have a UI (such as an *EventLog*). The component site might or might not be a UI element (such as a *Form*).

Visual Studio .NET provides designers for UI elements and non-UI elements. Designers show a RAD image of the solution that you are developing. If you are developing a form with a designer, then you will be able to see the controls that you are adding to the form. The designer allows you to move the controls and configure their properties. If you are developing a UI-less solution—the IDE calls this a *component*—then you will be able to see the other UI-less components that you are using and use the IDE to change their properties.

However, designers are available only with C# and Visual Basic .NET. The reason is that a designer needs to generate code that corresponds to the components that are shown on the designer surface, and crucially, the designer also needs to be able to parse code. There are definitions in the *System::CodeDom* and *System::CodeDom::Compiler* namespaces, and there are actual implementations of the code generators in the *Microsoft::CSharp* and *Microsoft::VisualBasic* namespaces (which are implemented in the microsoft.visualbasic and system assemblies), but the *Microsoft::VisualC* namespace (in the microsoft.visualc assembly) is notably devoid of any *CodeDom* classes. The current version of Visual Studio .NET does not include a *CodeDom* code generator or parser for C++, so there is no designer support for C++. Having said that, it is important to look at the support for designers because the components you will develop might well be used by other languages that do have designer support.

When a component is being used by a designer, the *ISite::DesignMode* property will return *true*. You might decide to change the behavior of your component in design mode—for example, you might be developing a component that accesses a specific hardware device, and at design time, that device might not be available, so your component could provide a simulation instead.

Notice that the *ISite* interface derives from *IServiceProvider*, as shown here:

```
public __gc __interface IServiceProvider
{
   Object* GetService(Type*);
};
```

This interface is a problem, as I mentioned in Chapter 2 (in the section "Calling Win32 APIs Using IJW"), because it has the same name as a COM interface that is included when you include windows.h, and if you want to use both the COM and .NET interfaces, you can access the .NET interface only using its fully qualified name. The idea behind this interface is that a component can provide several services, so you can access these services by calling *GetService* and passing the type object of the service that you require. The service could be implemented by the component, or it could be implemented by another, separate object.

The Visual Studio .NET designers and the UI items such as the property window are components, and they provide services through *IServiceProvider*. For example, if you want to provide a property editor for a specific control, you provide a class derived from *UITypeEditor* and mark the control class with the *[Editor]* attribute. The editor class implements a method named *EditValue* that is passed the *IServiceProvider* of the property window, and you use this interface to get the *IWindowsFormsEditorService* to specify whether the property is edited using a separate dialog (*ShowDialog*) or through a drop-down list box (*DropDownControl* and *CloseDropDown*). *IServiceProvider* looks like quite a useful facility, but it has an inherent weakness: *GetService* takes a *Type* object, so you can use the services on a component only if you know the services that it supports. There is no way to ask a component to list its services.

A component could be one of many components at a site. These components will be held by a component container that implements *IContainer*:

```
public __gc __interface IContainer : public IDisposable
{
   __property ComponentCollection* get_Components();
   void Add(IComponent*);
   void Add(IComponent*, String*);
   void Remove(IComponent*);
};
```

This interface has one property—a collection of components—and the other members are used to add or remove components from the container. The container that holds the components has to be disposable, which makes sense because the components that it holds are disposable. *ComponentCollection* is a read-only class, so a container that implements this interface will hold the components in some other collection (which will be operated on by the interface *Add* and *Remove* methods) and then implement the *Components* property by initializing a new instance of *ComponentCollection* with an array of *IComponents*.

Writing Components

The current version of Visual Studio .NET does not support designers for C++, but a component written with C++ can be used in a designer for another language. If the component is a UI component, it should derive from *Control* or *UserControl*. These classes provide an implementation of *IComponent*, so you do not have to worry about providing your own implementation. If you are writing a UI-less component (examples of UI-less components are the *EventLog* and the *PerformanceCounter* classes), you can provide your own implementation of *IComponent* or use an implementation from the .NET Framework.

If the component is context bound—that is, if you pass a reference to the component to another context—a call to the component will always be executed in the original context. Then the best option is to use the implementations of *IComponent* provided by the .NET Framework. The *Component* class derives from *MarshalByRefObject* and hence should be the base class for components that are context-bound objects. The framework class *MarshalByValueComponent* is used as the base class for components that are context agile and hence are marshaled by value. If you derive from either of these classes, your component should provide two constructors: a parameterless default constructor and a constructor that takes an *IContainer*. The component should add itself to the container.

In addition to the properties of *IComponent*, the *Component* and *MarshalByValueComponent* classes also implement *IServiceProvider*. These classes also have *DesignMode* and *Container* properties so that if your component is a site, you can use these properties to implement *ISite*. These two classes also implement the version of *Dispose* that takes a *bool* parameter; the method is implemented like this:

```
// Implementation in Component; MSIL converted to C++ with some
// changes made for clarity
protected virtual void Dispose(bool disposing)
{
   if (disposing)
```

```
    {
        Monitor::Enter(this)
        try
        {
            if (this->Site != 0 && this->Site->Container != 0)
                this->Site->Container->Remove(this);
            if (this->Events != 0)
            {
                EventHandler* event;
                event = __try_cast<EventHandler*>
                    (this->Events->Item[Component::EventDisposed];
                if (event != 0)
                    event->Invoke(this, System::EventArgs::Empty);
            }
        }
        __finally
        {
            Monitor::Exit(this)
        }
    }
}
```

The first point to make about this code is that because the *Component* class does not know the fields in the derived class, it cannot dispose them. Thus, if you have managed or unmanaged resources in your class, you must override this method. The second point to make is that the code checks to see whether the *Site* property has a valid value, and if it does, this method removes the current component from the site's container. You can see that the *ISite* interface is used for communication between a component and its site, so if you override this method, it is important that you call the base class in your override.

The final point to make is that the code raises an *EventHandler* event, but look at how the code does this. The *Component* class provides custom *add_* and *remove_* event methods that store the event delegates in a property named *Events*:

```
protected:
    __property EventHandlerList* get_Events();
```

This property is *protected*, so only derived classes can access it. The delegate for the *Disposed* event is added to the *EventHandlerList* field with a key, and the *Dispose* method uses the key to obtain the delegate. The *EventHandlerList* class contains a linked list of a private class named *ListEntry*, which contains a delegate and a key to identify the link. The key is an *Object*, and the *EventHandlerList* class does a simple identity check on the key when searching for an entry. (This arrangement conserves memory; if a string were used instead, memory would be allocated for all the characters as well as for other members of the string object.) The *Component* class has a *static* object named *EventDisposed* that is used for the key.

The reason for using *EventHandlerList* is not immediately obvious from this code, but it becomes apparent when you consider a class derived from *Component* that implements many events, such as *Control*. The *Control* class is the base class for all controls and forms, and it can generate 57 different events. If each of these events were added to the *Control* class using the *__event* keyword on a delegate field, the class would have 57 fields to hold the multicast delegates and 171 methods (an *add_*, *remove_*, and *raise_* method for each event). These 57 fields represent a large amount of memory, and this arrangement is wasteful if the user of the control provides event handlers only for a handful of events. Instead, *Control* implements each event with three methods: an *add_* method, a *remove_* method, and a raise method with the name of *On<Event>*, where *<Event>* is the event name. The *add_* and *remove_* methods are added as metadata to the event, but the *On<Event>* method is not added to the metadata, so to raise the event, you have to call this method explicitly.

Take, for example, the *Click* event:

```
// Implementation of the Click event, C++ converted from MSIL
public:
   __event void add_Click(EventHandler* value)
   {
      this->Events->AddHandler(Control::EventClick, value);
   }
   __event void remove_Click(EventHandler* value)
   {
      this->Events->RemoveHandler(Control::EventClick, value);
   }
protected:
   virtual void OnClick(EventArgs* e)
   {
      if (this.CanRaiseEvents)
      {
         EventHandler event;
         event = __try_cast<EventHandler*>
                  (this->Events->get_Item[Control::EventClick]);
         if (event != 0) event->Invoke(this, e);
      }
   }
```

The event obtained from *Events* is cast using the MSIL *castclass* operator, which is equivalent to the C++ *__try_cast<>* operator. The check to see if the variable is zero is redundant because if the cast fails an exception will be thrown. The class has only one field for all of the events, the *EventHandlerList* used by the *Events* property (the *private CanRaiseEvents* property is not implemented with a field). The memory used by the *EventHandlerList* field will increase as you add handlers for the events, but you can feel assured that you have only as much memory as you require.

The astute reader will notice that the delegate is obtained from the *EventHandlerList* field using a member named *EventClick* as the key, which implies that there will be 57 such objects. Doesn't this behavior mean that *Control* actually uses *more* memory than if the events were implemented with delegate fields? This arrangement is not the case because *EventClick* is a *static* member, so you get the overhead of these keys only once in an assembly. All other instances of *Control* will use the same objects.

Controls and Forms

The *Control* class is the base class of all UI items in the Windows Forms library; *Control* derives from *Component*, and it implements *ISynchronizeInvoke* and *IWin32Window*. *ISynchronizeInvoke* has methods that allow you to invoke a delegate on the thread where the control is running. UI items are context bound, and any graphical action must be performed on the same thread as the thread where the *Control* was created. The *IWin32Window* interface has a single read-only property that returns the Windows handle of the control.

The *Control* class is not *__abstract*, but there is little point in creating an abstract class because there will not be any code to draw the control's UI. I will return to how to draw a control's UI later in this chapter in the section "Using GDI+." Instead, you should derive a class either directly or indirectly from *Control*. Table 4-2 shows the base classes in the Windows Forms library. These classes provide functionality exhibited by one or more UI controls: containing a list box or a spinner, having a buttonlike behavior, or being a container for other controls.

Table 4-2 Control Base Classes in the Windows Forms Library

Base Class	Description
ButtonBase	Basic functionality for button controls, such as *Button*, *CheckBox* and *RadioButton*.
ContainerControl	A control that can contain child controls, one of which will have the focus. This control has handler code for mnemonics. This control is the base class for *Form*, *PropertyGrid*, *UpDownBase*, and *UserControl*.

Table 4-2 Control Base Classes in the Windows Forms Library *(continued)*

Base Class	Description
ListControl	Base class for controls that show a list: *ListBox* and *ComboBox*.
ScrollableControl	Base class for controls that contain controls and can have scroll bars, *ContainerControl* and *Panel*.
ScrollBar	Base class for controls that represent scroll bars, *HScrollBar* and *VScrollBar*.
TextBoxBase	Base class for controls that contain text, *TextBox* and *RichTextBox*.
UpDownBase	Base class for a control that has a spinner control, *DomainUpDown* and *NumericUpDown*.
UserControl	Base class for composite controls that are based on other controls.

All of the classes in Table 4-2 are abstract except *ContainerControl*, *ScrollableControl*, and *UserControl*, but you are unlikely to want to create instances of these classes.

Forms as Control Containers

The *Form* class is derived from *Control*. A form is also a container of controls, so when you add a control to a form, you do so through a call to the *Controls* property of the form, as shown in the following code:

```
__gc class MyForm : public Form
{
public:
   MyForm()
   {
      Button* btn = new Button;
      btn->Width = 100; btn->Height = 50;
      this->Controls->Add(btn);
   }
};
```

The *Controls* property gives access to an instance of the *Control::ControlCollection* nested class. The collection is of controls needed by *Form*'s layout manager. When the form is disposed of, the *Form* object knows the controls that it contains. When a *Form* object's *Dispose* is called this method will go through the collection of *Control* objects and dispose of each one. This means that you do not have to dispose of the controls on a form in the form's *Dispose* method.

If you use non-*Control* components, these will not be added to the control collection, so you have to ensure that these components are disposed of when the form is disposed of. To perform this disposal, you should add a *Dispose* method to your form, but be sure that you call the parent *Dispose* method, as shown here:

```
__gc class MyForm : public Form
{
   EventLog* log;
public:
   MyForm()
   {
      log = new EventLog(S"Application");
   }
protected:
   void Dispose(bool disposing)
   {
      if (disposing) log->Dispose();
      Form::Dispose(disposing);
   }
};
```

If you have numerous components, you can add a *Container* private member to hold the components and tell this container to dispose of the components it holds.

```
__gc class MyForm : public Form
{
   EventLog* log;
   System::ComponentModel::Container* components;
public:
   MyForm()
   {
      components = new System::ComponentModel::Container;
      log = new EventLog(S"Application");
      components->Add(log);
   }
protected:
   void Dispose(bool disposing)
   {
      if (disposing)
         components->Dispose();
      Form::Dispose(disposing);
   }
};
```

Notice that I have to give the fully qualified name of the *Container* class even if I use *using namespace* for the namespace of this class. This is an illustration of a very irritating feature of the Windows Forms library—the designers of many of the classes have given some properties names that are the same names of types in the .NET Framework. The *Form* class is derived indirectly from *Component*, and *Component* has a property named *Container*. So if I create an instance of the *Container* class, the compiler does not know whether I mean the class or the base class member. The only way to resolve this issue is to use a fully qualified name for the class. I guess the original designers used these names because they were unaware of this name clash issue: properties are implemented with get and/or set methods, so these names are different from the class names. This problem is identified through the rather irrelevant error C2065.

The Windows Forms designer for C# and Visual Basic .NET will add a component container and a *Dispose* method similar to the one I have shown here, but curiously, when you add components using a designer, they are not added to the container. This behavior means that the components are not disposed of until the garbage collector calls the finalizer of the form, and this makes the *Dispose* method useless. When you trust the design of your code to a RAD designer, you always run the risk—as in this case—of producing useless code.

Components do something; that's why you use them. You might get the component to perform some action by explicitly calling its methods, or the component might be attached to some system resource that generates data that the component passes onto your code through events. You are most likely to create a component in a form's constructor (or the constructor of any component container), but at this point, your form will not be completely constructed, so it will not be able to handle any events correctly.

A component that generates events in this manner can implement *ISupportInitialize*. This interface has two methods: *BeginInit* and *EndInit*. The form will call *BeginInit* to initialize the component but to indicate that the form is not ready to handle events. The form is able to hook up event handlers to the component, reassured that the handlers will not be called. At the end of the form's constructor, the form will be initialized and ready to handle events. At this point, the form can call *EndInit* to indicate that the component can start generating events.

A component container has no control over how a component generates an event. The component could create a thread that monitors some hardware devices and then generate an event when some hardware action occurs. Can a component container handle events generated on another thread? In many cases, the answer is yes as long as the event handler method protects thread-sensitive code and data from multithreaded access. However, some component containers are context bound, and others (such as controls and forms) should be accessed only on the thread on which they were created. This restriction is why *Control* implements *ISynchronizeInvoke*, as shown here:

```
__gc __interface ISynchronizeInvoke
{
   __property bool get_InvokeRequired();
   IAsyncResult* BeginInvoke(Delegate*, Object*[]);
   Object* EndInvoke(IAsyncResult*);
   Object* BeginInvoke(Delegate*, Object*[]);
};
```

A component that implements this interface indicates through the *InvokeRequired* property whether the component can be called on a thread other than the thread that created the component. If *InvokeRequired* is *true*, the component cannot be accessed directly by other threads and those threads must call the invocation methods on *ISynchronizeInvoke*, which guarantees that the delegate will be invoked on the thread where the component was created.

Take the *FileSystemWatcher* class, for example. As the name suggests, this class watches a folder for changes (file creation, deletion, or renaming) and then generates appropriate events. Instances of this class use a *ThreadPool* thread to do the watching, and the events will be generated on this thread pool thread. This arrangement means that even if you create a *FileSystemWatcher* in the constructor of a form (and hence on the same thread as the form), the events will be generated on another thread. If the event generation results in a direct call to a form method, the method will be called by a thread other than the one to which the form is bound. The event is actually generated by a method named *On<Event>*, where *<Event>* is the event name (for example, *OnCreated*). This method checks to see whether the event should be generated on the thread pool thread or on another thread. This check is performed by accessing a member property named *FileSystemWatcher::SynchronizingObject*, which is an *ISynchronizeInvoke* interface. If this member is zero, it means that the event handler object is happy to be called by any thread, and so the event is invoked on the thread pool thread. If the member is nonzero, the method tests *ISynchronizeInvoke::InvokeRequired* and if it is *true*, the method calls *ISynchronizeInvoke::Invoke*, which will call the event handler on the thread to which the *SynchronizingObject* is bound.

If you have a component that implements *ISynchronizeInvoke*, it means that the component is thread bound and so its methods must be invoked on a specified thread. If that thread-bound component uses a component that has a

SynchronizingObject member, you should initialize the property with the thread-bound component. Note that a component that has a *SynchronizingObject* member will merely pass the event delegate to the component that implements *ISynchronizeInvoke*. Such a delegate can have targets other than the synchronizing component, but it makes little sense to marshal those methods through to the synchronizing component. In essence, when you have this intimate connection between a synchronizing component and a component that has a *SynchronizingObject* member, it is best to ensure that the event-generating object has delegates only to the synchronizing component.

Building GUI Applications

Think back to the days of developing native C++ code for Windows. Now answer this question: What is the difference between a console application and a GUI application? Your first answer could be that the entry point for a console application is *main*, and for a GUI application, it is *WinMain*, but isn't it also true that you can call your entry point anything you like as long as you inform the linker? Yes, that is true, so your second answer to this issue is that the parameters of the entry points are different for console and GUI applications. But this really isn't the essence of how console and GUI applications differ. Actually, the original question is a trick question because the answer is in the question: the difference is that a console application needs a console to run, while a GUI application doesn't need one because, well, the application draws its own graphical user interface.

You indicate the type of the application by using the linker switch */subsystem*. For a console application, you use */subsystem:console*, and for a GUI application, you use */subsystem:windows*. This switch instructs the linker to add an appropriate flag to the PE header so that when the Windows loader loads the application, it can determine whether it needs to use an existing console (or create one if the application is not started from the command line) or whether the application will provide its own window.

The .NET assembly manifest also has a flag to indicate the type of application. This flag is the *.subsystem* directive. For a console application, it has a value of 0x2, and for a GUI application, it has a value of 0x3.[3] There are two ways to set the value for the *.subsystem* directive. The first way is to use the */subsystem* linker switch. If you use */subsystem:windows*, your entry point must be

---

3. Perhaps it is unsurprising that these values are the same as used in the PE header to indicate these application types.

called either *WinMain* or *wWinMain*, depending on whether you are compiling an ANSI or a UNICODE entry point. In both cases, the CRT will be initialized. If you use */subsystem:console*, you can call the entry point anything you like by using the */entry* linker switch (with the proviso that you do not use *WinMain* or *wWinMain*), but if you want to use the CRT, you have to call the entry point *main* or *wmain*. The other way of determining the application type is implicit in the previous discussion: if your entry point is *main* or *wmain*, the compiler will assume that the application is for the console, and if the entry point is *WinMain* or *wWinMain*, the compiler will assume that the application is a GUI application.

For example, this code will show a message box, but if you start it using Windows Explorer, you'll also get a console window:

```
// Compile with cl /clr cons.cpp.
#using <mscorlib.dll>
#using <system.windows.forms.dll>
void main()
{
   System::Windows::Forms::MessageBox::Show(
      S"Console application");
}
```

On the other hand, the following code will create a GUI application:

```
// Compile with cl /clr gui.cpp
#using <mscorlib.dll>
#using <system.windows.forms.dll>
int __stdcall WinMain(unsigned, unsigned, char*, int)
{
   System::Windows::Forms::MessageBox::Show(S"GUI application");
   return 0;
}
```

Why am I saying this? Well, occasionally there are advantages to having a console associated with a GUI application. For example, a very basic debugging technique is to sprinkle your code with *Console::WriteLine* statements to give indications of the current state of the application. If your application does not have a console, the output has nowhere to go. I will describe more effective ways to provide trace statements in Chapter 7, but it is important to note that the .NET Framework libraries have no knowledge whether you will use them in a console or a GUI application, so any output they produce will go to the console. This code will invoke JIT debugging:

```
void main()
{
   throw new Exception(S"Error");
}
```

If you tell the Just-In-Time Debugging dialog box that you do not want to start a debugger, the runtime will rather helpfully print the following code at the command line:

```
Unhandled Exception: System.Exception: Error
   at main()
```

Later in this chapter (in the section "Exceptions"), I will show that the Windows Forms library will provide a dialog to show exception information. However, if you dismiss this dialog and continue to run the application, you lose the exception information (because there is no attached console for the dump of the exception to go to). With a GUI application, you have to use some other mechanism to trace the uncaught exception.

Before leaving the subject of the GUI entry point, it is worth mentioning the use of COM in GUI applications. In .NET applications, you can use COM objects through COM interop, and this means that the managed thread must be initialized in a COM apartment. Managed GUI applications can also access COM objects, and in some cases it is not apparent that COM is being used. For example, GUI-managed applications can be hosts for ActiveX controls and they can use drag and drop. (See the sections "Controls and ActiveX Interfaces" and "Drag and Drop" later in this chapter for more about these topics.)

All messages sent to a Win32 window must go through a message queue, which as the name suggests, synchronizes the messages so that they are handled in the order that they are placed in the queue. A message queue is thread based, so a window must access the queue using that specific thread. If this thread performs some lengthy task, it will not be pumping the message queue and hence system messages sent to update the window's UI will not be handled. Such a lengthy task could be accessing a COM object—in particular, if the object is in another process or on another machine—so COM provides a mechanism to allow the message queue to be pumped for UI messages while waiting for a COM method call to complete. A single-threaded apartment (STA) thread uses a Windows message queue to synchronize access to the apartment, and this includes the notification that a COM call has completed. While an STA is pumping the message queue for such a notification, it could receive—and handle—UI messages from the system.[4]

4. This mechanism only handles a subset of UI messages, but it does help prevent a window from appearing to have stopped responding.

There is no default synchronization to code in a multithreaded apartment (MTA), so if you make a UI thread an MTA thread it means that while a COM call is active, the thread will be blocked and will not pump the message queue. In essence, all UI threads must be initialized in an STA if the thread is to make any COM calls. By default, when a managed thread first makes a COM call, the runtime will initialize the thread into an apartment. However, the default apartment type is the process's MTA. If your application has even the slightest risk of using COM, you *must* initialize the main thread (the thread that calls *Application::Run*; see the next section) in an STA. You can do this through the *[STAThread]* attribute:

```
[STAThread]
int __stdcall WinMain(unsigned, unsigned, char*, int)
{
   // GUI code
   return 0;
}
```

Using GDI+

A GUI application by definition has a GUI supplied by a window. You can provide information through a GUI in two general ways: through controls, which are child windows that have a user interface, and by drawing an image. Drawing images is the purpose of the GDI+ library, and I will cover the basics in this section. Controls are covered by the Windows Forms library, which I will delay for the section "Controls and Forms."

You can use the GDI+ library from unmanaged C++ as well as managed C++. Visual Studio .NET is provided with classes that are wrappers around the functions exported from the gdiplus.dll file, and if you intend to perform managed development with GDI+, it is worth reading the documentation for the unmanaged library as well as the documentation for the managed library. The classes in the *system.drawing* assembly (in the *System::Drawing*, *System::Drawing::Drawing2D*, *System::Drawing::Imaging*, *System::Drawing::Text*, and *System::Drawing::Printing* namespaces) are managed wrappers around the GDI+ library.

So that you can try out some of GDI+ classes, I need to briefly tell you how to get a window that you can draw upon. A stand-alone window is a *Form* that derives from the *Control* class and inherits from it the *Control::Paint* event.

```
protected:
   virtual void OnPaint(PaintEventArgs*);
public:
   void add_Paint(PaintEventHandler*);
   void remove_Paint(PaintEventHandler*);
```

As I mentioned earlier, the *add_* and *remove_* methods add and remove a delegate from a private *EventHandlerList* field, and the *OnPaint* method raises the event. The *OnPaint* method is called when the native window on which the control is based receives the Win32 *WM_PAINT* message. Thus you can view the *OnPaint* method as the *WM_PAINT* message handler, and because its role is to raise the *Paint* event, you can also regard it as the bridge between the Win32 message-based event system and the .NET delegate-based event system.

If you know that no code is going to add a *Paint* handler delegate, you can simply override the *OnPaint* method. If you think that code might add a *Paint* handler delegate, you can still override the *OnPaint* method but you have to be sure that you call the base class method. Here's the code to draw a cross on the form:

```
// basicform.cpp
__gc class TestForm : public Form
{
protected:
   void OnPaint(PaintEventArgs* args)
   {
      Graphics* g = args->Graphics;
      g->DrawLine(Pens::Black,
                  0, 0,
                  ClientSize.Width-1, ClientSize.Height-1);
      g->DrawLine(Pens::Black,
                  0, ClientSize.Height-1,
                  ClientSize.Width-1, 0);
      Form::OnPaint(args);
   }
};
```

I will describe the *Graphics* object in more detail later, but it is worth pointing out that I have not paid any attention to the clipping rectangle (the invalid region that needs to be updated), so if you resize this window, you will find that the cross will be drawn a little skewed. Again, I'll return to these issues later.

The entry point for this assembly looks like this:

```
// basicform.cpp
int __stdcall WinMain(unsigned int, unsigned int, char*, int)
{
   Application::Run(new TestForm);
   return 0;
}
```

The *Run* method is the equivalent to the message loop in a Win32 application. The final point I need to make concerns the assemblies that the application will need. As you will expect, the application needs to use types in mscorlib.dll and in system.windows.forms.dll; however, because this code uses some GDI+ commands, it also needs to reference system.drawing.dll. There is one final assembly that you need to be aware of. The *Forms* class derives from *Component*. This class is in the *System::ComponentModel* namespace and is implemented in the system.dll assembly. In general, if you do any work with Windows Forms, you will need to reference these four assemblies:

```
// basicform.cpp
#using <mscorlib.dll>
#using <system.dll>
#using <system.drawing.dll>
#using <system.windows.forms.dll>

using namespace System;
using namespace System::Drawing;
using namespace System::Windows::Forms;
```

Graphics Class

The *PaintEventArgs* sent to a paint handler contains a *Graphics* object. This object is equivalent to the device context that Win32 code uses when it draws graphics. The *Graphics* object even has a *static* method, *FromHdc*, that you can use to create a *Graphics* object from a Win32 device context, and an instance method *GetHdc* that will return the encapsulated device context. Note that a device context is a system resource, so if you call *GetHdc*, you will also need to call *Graphics::ReleaseHdc*. Furthermore, because a *Graphics* object caches a device context, the *Graphics* object must be disposed of when it no longer being used.

Normally, you would obtain the *Graphics* object from the *PaintEventArgs* passed to *OnPaint* or to a *Paint* event handler (which, of course, is called by *OnPaint*). This *Graphics* object will be created by another method higher up in the call stack, and this method will ensure that when the stack is unwound, the *Graphics* object will be disposed of. You can also get a *Graphics* object by calling *Control::CreateGraphics*. If you do this, it is your responsibility to dispose of the object.

```
void OnClick(EventArgs* args)
{
   Graphics* g = CreateGraphics();
   // Generate a color from the mouse position.
   Color col = Color::FromArgb(MousePosition.X & 0xff,
                               MousePosition.Y & 0xff,
                               (MousePosition.X * MousePosition.Y)
                               & 0xff);
   g->FillRectangle(new SolidBrush(col), ClientRectangle);
   g->Dispose();
}
```

The *Graphics* object encapsulates the device context where the drawing will occur, and it also has the methods to do that drawing. Table 4-3 is a summary of the drawing methods in the *Graphics* class. It is interesting that there are two methods for drawing shapes such as rectangles and ellipses, one to draw the outline, and another to draw the interior. This arrangement is in contrast to Win32, where a single function is used to draw the outline and the interior of a shape; in Win32, you draw an outline by using a null brush, and you draw a shape without an outline with a pen the same color as the brush used for the interior.

Table 4-3 Members of the *Graphics* Object Used to Draw on a Device Context

Method	Description	Win32 Equivalent
DrawArc	Draws an arc	*Arc*
DrawBezier	Draws a Bezier spline	*PolyBezier*
DrawBeziers	Draws a series of Bezier splines	*PolyBezier*
DrawClosedCurve	Draws a closed cardinal spline	*PolyDraw*
DrawCurve	Draws a cardinal spline	none
DrawEllipse	Draws the outline of an ellipse	*Ellipse*
DrawIcon	Draws an icon to fill a rectangle	none
DrawIconUnstretched	Draws an icon without stretching	*DrawIconEx*
DrawImage	Draws an image to fill a rectangle	*StretchBlt*
DrawImageUnscaled	Draws an imaged without stretching	*BitBlt*
DrawLine	Draws a line between two points	*LineTo*
DrawLines	Draws a series of connected lines	*Polyline*
DrawPath	Draws the outline of a path	*StrokePath*
DrawPie	Draws the outline of a pie	*AngleArc*
DrawPolygon	Draws the outline of a polygon	*PolyDraw*

Table 4-3 Members of the *Graphics* Object Used to Draw on a Device Context *(continued)*

Method	Description	Win32 Equivalent
DrawRectangle	Draws a rectangle outline	*Rectangle*
DrawRectangles	Draws a series of rectangles	none
DrawString	Draws a string	*DrawTextEx*
FillClosedCurve	Fills the interior of a closed cardinal spline	none
FillEllipse	Fills the interior of an ellipse	*Ellipse*
FillPath	Fills the interior of a path	*FillPath*
FillPie	Fills the interior of a pie	*Pie*
FillPolygon	Fills the interior of a polygon	*Polygon*
FillRectangle	Fills the interior of a rectangle	*Rectangle*
FillRectangles	Fills the interiors of a series of rectangles	none
FillRegion	Fills the interior of a region	*FillRgn*

When you draw on a device context using the Win32 drawing functions, you first have to prepare the device context by *selecting* the pen, brush, font, or bitmap that you want to use during the drawing, which means that you can perform several drawing actions using, for example, the same pen. In contrast, the drawing methods of *Graphics* are passed the appropriate *Pen*, *Brush*, *Icon*, or *Image* object that will be used only for that method call. If you want to perform another drawing action using the same pen, you need to pass that method the same *Pen* object. Furthermore, as you draw in a Win32 device context, the last point is retained, for example *::LineTo* or *::PolyBezierTo*; such information is not retained in the *Graphics* object.

Coordinate Structures

When you draw using a *Graphics* object, you have to specify where the drawing will occur. Some drawing methods draw between two points (for example, *DrawLine*). In this case, you supply the positions with Cartesian points. You can supply the positions with either integer or floating point values, as individual coordinates or through *Point* or *PointF* structures, as shown here:

```
g->DrawLine(Pens::Black, Point(0, 0), Point(100, 0));
g->DrawLine(Pens::Black, PointF(100.0f, 0.0f),
   Point(100.0f, 100.0f));
g->DrawLine(Pens::Black, 100, 100, 0, 100);
g->DrawLine(Pens::Black, 0.0f, 100.0f, 0.0f, 0.0f);
```

These lines will draw a square 100 by 100 units.

Most *Graphics* methods will draw within a rectangle, and in this case, you can either give the position and size of the rectangle as four integers or four floats, or you can use a *Rectangle* object. *Rectangle* and *Point* objects are useful because you can perform certain operations on them. Table 4-4 gives a summary of these operations for *Point* and *Rectangle*; *RectangleF* has operations similar to *Rectangle*, but curiously, *PointF* has no operations. *Rectangle* and *Point* have static members that convert from the floating point version.

Table 4-4 Coordinate Operations for the Integer Versions of *Point* and *Rectangle*

Method	Description
Point::Offset	Translate the point.
Rectangle::Inflate	Change the size of the rectangle so that the center remains in the same place. A positive number increases the size; a negative number decreases the size. The actual inflation is twice as large as the value you specify.
Rectangle::Offset	Translate the rectangle.
Rectangle::Intersect	Get a rectangle that is the intersection of two other rectangles.
Rectangle::Union	Get a rectangle that will fully contain two other rectangles.

The *Rectangle::Inflate* method is interesting; this method will change the size of a rectangle, increasing it or decreasing it. The value you specify for the inflation in a direction is half the actual transform because the inflation is applied on both edges in that direction so that the center remains in the same place.

```
// A rectangle at (0, 0) which is 100 units wide
// and 100 units high
Rectangle rect(0, 0, 100, 100);
Console::WriteLine(rect.ToString())
// Prints {X=0,Y=0,Width=100,Height=100}
// Deflate the rectangle.
rect.Inflate(-10, -20);
Console::WriteLine(rect.ToString())
// Prints {X=10,Y=20,Width=80,Height=60}
```

Here the 100 by 100 rectangle is deflated by 10 in the x-direction (so this deflation will take off 10 units from the distance between the center and both the left edge and the right edge) and 20 in the y-direction (so 20 units are taken off the distance between the center and both the top edge and the bottom edge). The rectangle structures also have methods to determine whether a point or a rectangle is contained in its area (*Contains*), or if part of its area intersects with another rectangle (*IntersectsWith*).

Coordinate Transforms

In the earlier discussion, I was careful to use the term *units* rather than a specific unit such as *pixel*. The coordinates that you specify are named *World units*. Before GDI+ performs a graphics action, the *Graphics* object performs two transforms on the coordinate to determine how the coordinate refers to the device. The first transform is named the *World transform*, and it is specified by the *Graphics::Transform* property. This property is a *Matrix* object that represents a 2D matrix and a vector translation. I will not go into the mathematics here, but basically, a rotation, a stretch, or a skew operation on a 2D shape can be specified by a 2 by 2 matrix. A translation—moving a shape—cannot be represented by a matrix operation because it is simply an offset added to the x-coordinate and y-coordinate of the shape being transformed. You can set the *Graphics::Transform* property directly, or you can use methods on the *Graphics* object. If you set them yourself, either you can provide the values directly through the *Matrix* constructor or you can use the transform methods on this class.

One use for the *Transform* property is to change the coordinate axes that are used by the *Graphics* object. The default origin is the upper-left corner of the graphics object, and the default direction of the x-axis is from left to right. For the y-axis, it is from top to bottom. This arrangement is the same as for Win32 device contexts.

The following code draws two axes 100 units long, as shown in Figure 4-1:

```
g->DrawLine(Pens::Black, 0, 0, 0, 100);
g->DrawLine(Pens::Black, 0, 0, 100, 0);
```

Figure 4-1 Two axes drawn using the default transforms. The y-axis goes from the upper-left corner to the lower-left corner.

If you would prefer to have the y-axis going from bottom to top, you have to use two transforms. The first transform is to mirror on the x-axis so that points below the x-axis appear above it. However, because the x-axis is originally along the top edge, all the points above the x-axis will be outside of the client area. To remedy this problem, a translation will have to be applied to move all points down the screen. In this example, I move the x-axis down by the height of the client area, as shown in Figure 4-2.

```
g->Transform = new Matrix(1, 0, 0, -1, 0,
   ClientRectangle.Height-1);
g->DrawLine(Pens::Black, 0, 0, 0, 100);
g->DrawLine(Pens::Black, 0, 0, 100, 0);
```

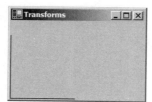

Figure 4-2 The two axes transformed so that the y-axis goes from the lower-left corner to the upper-left corner.

The interesting thing about this transform is that you only set it once; after that, all drawing actions on this specific graphics object are subject to the transform. In the preceding code, I know that the transform that mirrors points on the x-axis is represented by the four integers (1, 0, 0, -1). The final two integers are the translation. I could use the following code instead:

```
Matrix* m = new Matrix;
m->Reset();
m->Scale(1, -1);
m->Translate(0, 1-ClientRectangle.Height);
g->Transform = m;
```

It is important that you assign *Transform* to the *Matrix* after you have set this object. The reason is that the property *get_* method will obtain the matrix from GDI+ and return a *copy*, so the transform will be applied to the copy rather than to the actual matrix. These lines of code are equivalent:

```
// Illustrating why property access is not always a good thing;
// don't do this.
// This code...
g->Transform->Reset();
g->Transform->Scale(1, -1);
g->Transform->Translate(0, 1-ClientRectangle.Height);
// ...is the same as this code
Matrix* m;
m = g->Transform; m->Reset();
m = g->Transform; m->Scale(1, -1);
m = g->Transform; m->Translate(0, 1-ClientRectangle.Height);
```

It is a pity that the Windows Forms library makes such an extensive use of properties because often code that looks like it should work doesn't work the way you would expect. For example, this code looks obvious:

```
this->ClientSize.Width = 100;
this->ClientSize.Height = 100;
```

The *Form::ClientSize* property gives the width and height of the client area of a form (the area excluding the border and caption). The code looks like it should change the size of the form so that the client area is 100 by 100 units. However, it does not change the physical window. The reason is that these calls represent the following property method calls:

```
this->get_ClientSize().get_Width = 100;
this->get_ClientSize().get_Height = 100;
```

The code to resize the window occurs in the *set_ClientSize* property method, which has not been called in this code. Instead, you have to write this code:

```
this->ClientSize = new System::Drawing::Size(100, 100);
```

Notice that to use the *Size* class I have to give the fully qualified name because *Control* has a property named *Size*. Let's go back to the working code I gave earlier:

```
Matrix* m = new Matrix;
m->Reset();
m->Scale(1, -1);
m->Translate(0, 1-ClientRectangle.Height);
g->Transform = m;
```

The mirror action is achieved by multiplying the y values by -1 (the call to *Scale*); however, note that the translation is now negative. The reason is that because I have set the mirror transform, this transform will be applied to the parameters of the translation. Also be aware that the order that the transforms are applied is important; a mirror followed by a translation is not the same as the same translation followed by the same mirror.

The *Graphics* class also has methods that you can apply to the transformation:

```
g->ScaleTransform(1, -1);
g->TranslateTransform(0, 1-ClientRectangle.Height);
```

This code avoids the problem I mentioned earlier with the property access to the *Transform* member because these methods do the transform directly on the GDI+ structure that holds the transform. However, the advantage of creating a *Matrix* object is that it can be created once in the constructor and cached as a field, so in the paint methods, you only need to assign the *Graphics::Transform* object to this cached field without having to perform the transforms each time.[5]

I said that there were two transforms that are performed by GDI+. The transform represented by *Graphics::Transform* is named the *World transform,* and it transforms the World units to Page units. The other transform is the *Page transform,* and it transforms the Page units to Device units, that is, the actual pixels used by the graphics device. The Page transform is a scaling and involves two properties of the *Graphics* class: *Graphics::PageUnit* and *Graphics::PageScale*. The Page units are simply multiplied by the *Graphics::PageScale*. The *Graphics::PageUnit* is a little more complicated because you use it to identify the units that you have used so that the Page transform must determine the scaling factor from your units to the device units depending on the resolution of the device.

---

5. Note that the transform should be created in the *Resize* handler because only during the *Resize* handler will you know the size of the client area to be able to perform the translation.

The values that you can use for *Graphics::PageUnit* are given in Table 4-5. The default unit is *GraphicsUnit::Pixel*.

Table 4-5 Values in the *GraphicsUnit* Enumeration

Enumeration	Size of Unit
Display	Same as Pixel for video devices, 1/100 inch for printers
Document	1/300 inch
Inch	1 inch
Millimeter	1 millimeter
Pixel	Single pixel
Point	1/72 inch
World	Nontransformed units

Clipping Regions

Earlier I gave this code for the paint message handler:

```
// basicform.cpp
void OnPaint(PaintEventArgs* args)
{
   Graphics* g = args->Graphics;
   g->DrawLine(Pens::Black,
               0, 0,
               ClientSize.Width-1, ClientSize.Height-1);
   g->DrawLine(Pens::Black,
               0, ClientSize.Height-1,
               ClientSize.Width-1, 0);
   Form::OnPaint (args);
}
```

If the form is sizable, this method will be called whenever the form is resized. As the name suggests, the form is the area where drawing will occur; any drawing outside of this area will be clipped. In this example, the idea is to draw across from corner to corner, so if the size of the form changes, the entire cross should be redrawn. To change the clip rectangle, you can tell the framework that the entire client area ought to be redrawn. Here is one way to do this:

```
// clipform.cpp
   TestForm()
   {
      Resize += new EventHandler(this, &TestForm::Resized);
   }
```

```
protected:
   void Resized(Object*, EventArgs*)
   {
      Invalidate();
   }
```

In this case, I have decided to provide the *Resize* event handler through a delegate rather than by overriding *OnResize*, which allows the *Resize* event to be handled by several other handlers. The clipping area is actually a *Region*, which does not have to be rectangular. This area can be accessed through the *Graphics::Clip* property. The *Invalidate* method is overloaded and can be passed a *Region* that indicates the area that should be updated. The overloaded version I have called here will make the entire client area invalid. When you call any of the *Invalidate* methods, the *Paint* event is raised. In general, if the state of your *Control* changes so that the visual image will also change, it is best to redraw the *Control* by invalidating it. If your image is complicated (for example, a fractal image), you will find that your application will have better performance if you draw only in the clip region because the drawing you do outside of this region is simply ignored.

Finally, it is worth mentioning that the *Form* class has a property named *ResizeRedraw*, and if this property is set to *true*, the entire *Form* will be invalidated when the *Form* is resized.

Colors

Pens and brushes will have a color. The framework provides several classes to allow you to choose the color to use. A color is made up of four values each varying between 0 and 255: the red, blue, and green components and an alpha component. The alpha component is effectively the *transparency* of the color, so a color that has an alpha value of 0 is totally transparent and will not be seen. The *Color __value* type has a property for each of these four values. These are named *R*, *G*, *B*, and *A*, but these properties are read-only. To create a *Color* with specific values, you use the *static* methods named *FromArgb*, as shown here:

```
// Create a red, partially transparent color.
Color c = Color::FromArgb(128, 255, 0, 0);
```

You can also create a color object of a named color; the *Color* class has 141 named colors, which are *static* properties, and each property corresponds to a member of the *KnownColor* enumeration. If you use a named color, you can get the actual name of the color in a string variable, as the following code shows:

```
Color red = Color::Red;
String* strName = red.Name;
unsigned char redValue = red.R;
```

The *KnownColor* enumeration also has some values for colors used by the system—for example, *ActiveCaption*, which can be determined only at run time, and *Color*, which provides a method, *FromKnownColor*, that will determine at run time the value of the specified color. However, only a limited number of the named system colors are in *Color*; to get the complete range, you use a class named *SystemColors*.

Pens

When you draw on a surface, you need to specify the *Pen* and/or the *Brush* to use. A *Pen* is used to draw lines, and it is used for the outline of shapes. *Pen* is a generic class that has properties for the color and width, as well as information about how two lines drawn with the pen are joined together. Furthermore, pens can be used to draw dashed lines, and the *Pen* class has properties to specify the type of the dash and the length of the dashes. When a pen is used, it is assumed that it has a circular tip with the diameter given by the width of the pen. You can change the tip through a transform, and the *Pen* class has a *Transform* property and transform methods. When the pen is used, the transform is applied (ignoring the translation part of the transformation). Because a transformation can include a stretch (*Pen::ScaleTransform*), the *Pen::Width* property does not necessarily reflect the actual width of the pen.

Here is how to create a red pen:

```
Pen* redPen = new Pen(Color::Red);
```

The width of the pen will be determined by *Pen::Width*, *Graphics::PageUnit*, and *Graphics::PageScale*. The default width is one page unit, so if the page units are set to *GraphicsUnit::Inch* (and the scale is set to 1), you'll get a very thick line! For convenience, the framework also supplies a class named *Pens* that has a *static* member for each of the named colors in *Color* and a class named *SystemPens* that has a pen for each of the foreground colors in *SystemColors*. *Pens* would suggest that there will always be 140 or so pens in your application, so isn't this an excessive use of system resources? Well, as you will see in a moment, you get only as many pens as you actually use.

You can specify the dashed property of a pen through *Pen::DashStyle* (one of the *DashStyle* enumerations) and *Pen::DashOffset*, to give the dash spacing. You can also provide a custom dash pattern through *Pen::DashPattern*, which is an array of floats where alternative elements give the length of the dash and the length of the space between dashes. By default, a pen is solid across its width, but you can make the line be drawn as a series of parallel lines by providing a value for *Pen::CompoundArray*. Again, this property is an array of floats, but in this case, the alternate values give the proportion of the width that will be filled or clear. For example, if you want a pen that appears hollow with the center 50 percent empty, you could do this:

```
// pens.cpp
Pen* hollow = new Pen(Color::Black, 10);
// Fill the first quarter, leave half empty,
// and fill the last quarter.
float lines __gc[] = {0.0, 0.25, 0.75, 1.0};
hollow->CompoundArray = lines;
// use pen
hollow->Dispose();
```

By default, the end of a line drawn with a pen will be square, but you can use the *Pen::EndCap* and *Pen::StartCap* to specify one of the *LineCap* values, or you can provide your own cap style with *Pen::CustomEndCap* and *Pen::CustomStartCap*. These properties take a *CustomLineCap*, which is a class that is constructed from a *GraphicsPath*, which I will come to later. However, the framework does provide a derived class named *AdjustableArrowCap* that you can use to give the width and height of the arrow used for the end cap, as shown here:

```
// pens.cpp
// Black pen, 5 units wide
Pen* arrow = new Pen(Color::Black, 5);
// The end is an arrow, twice the width of the pen, and the
// length is also twice the width of the pen.
arrow->CustomEndCap = new AdjustableArrowCap(2, 2);
// use pen
arrow->Dispose();
```

Finally, it is worth mentioning that a pen is based on a system resource, so if you create a pen, it makes sense to dispose of the pen when you have finished using it. However, be careful what you do. Take a look at this:

```
Pen* pen1 = Pens::Black;
Pen* pen2 = new Pen(Color::Black);
```

Doesn't this mean that these two pens are the same? After all, they are both black with default values for the other properties. Well, no. This difference is highlighted if this code is in a *Paint* handler and you try to dispose of *pen1*. You will find that the code will work fine the first time the handler is called, but the second time it is called you will get an exception. The reason is that

Pens::Black is a *static* property member. The first time the property is accessed, the pen will be created and placed in a *Hashtable* specific for the current thread. (This object is stored in a data slot.) On subsequent accesses, the pen will be extracted from the *Hashtable*. There is no way that you can get access to the *Hashtable*, so you cannot remove the entry. Hence, if you dispose of a pen that is in the *Hashtable*, a reference to the disposed-of object will remain in the *Hashtable*. Then, when you try to access the pen, you will access a disposed-of object.

This design of *Pens* (and *SystemPens*) means that you get only as many pens as you use, and these pens are only created once—when you first use the pen—and disposed of when the application finishes. However, because the members of *Pens* and *SystemPens* return a *Pen* object, there is no obvious indication that you should not dispose of the pen. If you create a pen yourself (as I did earlier with *pen2*), you *should* dispose of the pen when you have finished with it. This requirement is why I cautioned you earlier.

Brushes

Brushes are used to fill areas, and typically they are used for background fills. The *Brush* class is abstract and is the base for all the other brush classes, shown in Table 4-6. The *Brushes* and *SystemBrushes* classes are the brush equivalent of *Pens* and *SystemPens*: they contain static properties for named and system colors, and the brushes are created only on the first access when they are stored in a *Hashtable*.

Table 4-6 The *Brush* Classes in *System::Drawing* and *System::Drawing::Drawing2D*

Class	Description
Brushes	Contains static properties, each a *SolidBrush* of a named color.
HatchBrush	A brush based on a hatch pattern made up of a foreground color and a background color.
LinearGradientBrush	A brush with a linear gradient between two colors.
PathGradientBrush	A brush that is used to fill a *GraphicsPath*. The gradient is from the center of the path outwards.
SolidBrush	A brush with a single, solid color.

Table 4-6 The *Brush* Classes in *System::Drawing* and *System::Drawing::Drawing2D* *(continued)*

Class	Description
SystemBrushes	Contains static members. Each is a *SolidBrush* with a color used by the system.
TextureBrush	A brush that is based on an image. The area filled with this brush will have one or more copies of the image.

As with pens, brushes encapsulate system resources, so it is important to dispose of a brush when you no longer need it. Do not dispose of the brushes you obtain from *Brushes* and *SystemBrushes*.

The various gradient brushes are new to GDI+. They allow you to fill an area so that it graduates from one color to another, as shown here:

```
// brushes.cpp
LinearGradientBrush* brush;
brush = new LinearGradientBrush(Point(0, 0), Point(255, 0),
                                Color::Red, Color::Green);
g->FillRectangle(brush, 0, 0, 255, 50);
brush->Dispose();
```

This code (in a *Paint* handler) will draw a rectangle 255 units wide and 50 units high graduating from red at the left to green at the right (and hence, a rather mucky brown in the center).

Bitmaps

The *Image* class is the base for *Bitmap* and *Metafile*. *Image* has basic properties for the size of the image and the palette that will be used to draw it. More interesting are the methods of *Image*: these methods allow you to create an *Image* object from a file (or some other *Stream* object) and to save the image to a file. *Image* objects are also custom serializable, so you can serialize them and store them in some other type of persistent storage.

The *Bitmap* class can be based on an existing bitmap saved to a file or accessible through a stream, or it can be created as an empty bitmap of a specified size. The image file formats that are supported are given as properties of the *ImageFormat* class, and the class supports the most common image formats, including BMP, GIF, JPG, and TIFF. Because a bitmap can be created from a stream, a stream can be part of an assembly manifest, and you can simply pass the *Stream* obtained from a call to *Assembly::GetManifestResourceStream* to the *Bitmap* constructor.

```
// resform.cpp
__gc class ResForm : public Form
{
public:
   ResForm()
   {
      String* strName;
      strName = String::Concat(
                 RuntimeEnvironment::GetRuntimeDirectory(),
                 S"\\system.windows.forms.dll");
      Assembly* assem = Assembly::LoadFrom(strName);
      Stream* stm = assem->GetManifestResourceStream(
         S"System.Windows.Forms.ComponentModel.OrderImages.bmp");
      Bitmap* bmp = new Bitmap(stm);
      BackgroundImage = bmp;
   }
};
```

The *OrderImages.bmp* bitmap is an embedded resource in the *system.windows.forms* assembly. Once you have an initialized *Bitmap*, there are two ways that you can show it on a control: you can draw it with *Graphics::DrawImage*, or you can make the image the *BackgroundImage* of the control. If you choose to make the bitmap the background image, the bitmap will be copied repeatedly to completely fill the client area of the form. The set method for the *BackgroundImage* property checks the image that is passed to initialize the background and if the image is different from the current background image the set method will call *Invalidate* so that the form is redrawn with the new image. If the control has child controls (for example, if it is a *Form*), when the control is updated its child controls will also be informed that the background image has changed. *DrawImage* has many overloads that allow you to draw the bitmap at its original size, stretched in a rectangle, transformed to a parallelogram, or drawn with its colors adjusted. These actions can be performed on the whole bitmap or on a part of the bitmap.

You can change a bitmap, but the only drawing method *Bitmap* supplies is *SetPixel*. However, you can create a *Graphics* object from a *Bitmap*, which means that you can perform off-screen drawing and then render the bitmap.

```
// drawoff.cpp
// First draw 500 dots at random positions in a form's Paint handler,
// and then get the size of the client area.
Rectangle rect = ClientRectangle;
// Use a 10-unit border around the image.
rect.Inflate(-10, -10);
if (rect.Width > 0 && rect.Height > 0)
```

```
{
   // Create the bitmap
   Bitmap* bmp = new Bitmap(rect.Width, rect.Height);
   Random* rand = new Random;
   // Draw the dots.
   for (int i = 0; i < 500; i++)
      bmp->SetPixel(rand->Next(rect.Width),
                    rand->Next(rect.Height),
                    Color::Black);
   // Draw a rectangle within the bitmap.
   Graphics* grfx = Graphics::FromImage(bmp);
   grfx->DrawRectangle(Pens::Black, 0, 0,
      rect.Width-1, rect.Height-1);
   // Render the image on the form.
   // Graphics* g has been initialized elsewhere.
   g->DrawImage(bmp, rect);
   grfx->Dispose();
   bmp->Dispose();
}
```

There is no facility in .NET to initialize a *Bitmap* from a window, presumably for security reasons to prevent people from writing screen scraping programs. If you do want to get a bitmap image from the device context of a window, you will have to use *::BitBlt* through IJW or platform invoke.

Cursors

A *cursor* is the image used to indicate the current mouse position. A *Control* has a cursor property so that when the mouse is moved over the *Control*, the system will change the mouse cursor to the *Control*'s cursor. Your *Control* can also change the cursor at run time. Another situation in which you will use a cursor is if you use drag and drop. When you drag from one window, the cursor will change to the drag cursor you specify, and when the cursor moves over a drop target window, the cursor will change to indicate whether the item can be dropped and if so, whether the item is moved or copied.

A cursor can be created from a file or a stream. Typically, you will have a cursor embedded as a resource, so you can obtain a stream to the resource through *GetManifestResourceStream*, as shown in this example:

```
__gc class MainForm : public Form
{
public:
   MainForm()
```

```
    {
        Assembly* assem = Assembly::GetExecutingAssembly();
        this->Cursor = new System::Windows::Forms::Cursor (
            assem->GetManifestResourceStream("cursor.cur"));
    }
};
```

This code assumes that the file cursor.cur has been bound as a managed resource to the assembly. (I'll show you how in the section "Managed Resources" later in this chapter.) The *Cursor* class can be initialized only with a .cur file; it cannot be initialized with an animated cursor (.ani) file.

The *Cursors* class contains *static* properties; however, these properties are handled in a different way than the properties of *Pens* or *Brushes*. On the first call to each property *get_* method, the appropriate system cursor is accessed and wrapped by a managed *Cursor* object. This *Cursor* object is stored in a *private* field so that on subsequent calls to the property *get_* method the field is returned. One of these cursors is a *WaitCursor*, so before you start some lengthy operation that might freeze the UI, it is worth changing the cursor to the wait cursor, assuming, of course, that you remember to return it back to the original cursor after the operation has completed.

```
System::Windows::Cursor* cur = this->Cursor;
this->Cursor = Cursors::WaitCursor;
DoLengthyOperation();
this->Cursor = cur;
```

Icons

There are three uses for icons. First, they are small image files, so you might want to use them as bitmaps. Indeed, the *Bitmap* class can be initialized with an icon. Second, each window will have a small icon as the system menu (in the left corner of the caption bar). In both of these cases, the icon is wrapped by a managed class named *Icon*. Finally, each PE file can have an icon; this can be a large icon or a small icon. The large icon (32 × 32) is shown when Windows Explorer is set to large icon view. When you put a shortcut to the application on the desktop and when you Alt-Tab, the large icon is shown in the task switch window. The small icon is used when you use the small icon, list, or detailed view in Windows Explorer.

These icon files can be created with the Visual Studio .NET resource editor, but the binding of the icon to the PE file is done in a different way for icons used for forms and icons used for PE files. If an icon is to be used for the PE file, it will have to be an unmanaged resource, compiled using the resource compiler, rc.exe, and bound with the linker. If an icon is to be used to initialize an *Icon* object, it will have to be accessed through a stream or in an .ico file. Such a managed object can be in the manifest (as I have shown earlier with bitmaps), or it can be compiled as a serialized item in a *ResX* resource. I will return to the various types of managed resources later in this chapter in the section "Compiled Managed Resources."

Text and Fonts

The *Graphics* object can be used to draw strings with the *DrawString* method. Each of the overloads of this method takes the string, a font, a brush to fill the drawn string, and an indication of the position to draw the string. The location can be a point or a rectangle, and you can also provide a *StringFormat* object that gives information about text alignment, line spacing, tab stops, and how strings are truncated.

Text will be drawn using a font. When you create a control, the framework will initialize the *Control::Font* property to a default font, so the simplest way to print a string is to use this font:

```
// Graphics* g initialized somewhere else
g->DrawString(S"Test string", this->Font,
   Brushes::Black, 10.0, 20.0);
```

Notice that the position of the string, whether given as a point or a rectangle, is given as floating point numbers rather than integers. Perhaps this system reflects the fact that much of text alignment will be performed using nonpixel units such as points or inches.

When you draw strings in a control, it is important to use the *Font* property because RAD tools will have access to this property and will provide a value. If you are developing a form, it will be your decision about which font to use, and often the standard font will not be suitable. The *Font* property is an object of the *Font* class. You can initialize this object several ways, but the most natural way is to supply the name of the font and the point size, as shown here:

```
// Graphics* g initialized somewhere else
System::Drawing::Font* font =
   new System::Drawing::Font(S"Arial", 12);
g->DrawString(S"Test string", font, Brushes::Black,
   10.0, 20.0);
font->Dispose();
```

This text will appear in a method of a class derived from *Control*. Because *Control* has a property named *Font*, the code has to use the fully qualified name. Note that a *Font* object is based on a system resource, so you have to make sure that you dispose of it when you have finished with it.

To position a string, you will want to know how much space the string takes when it has been drawn. To determine this space, you can call *Graphics::MeasureString*:

```
// strings.h
Graphics* g = args->Graphics;
String* str = S"Test string";
System::Drawing::Font* font =
   new System::Drawing::Font(S"Arial", 12);
// Get the size of the string
SizeF sizeStr;
sizeStr = g->MeasureString(str, font);
// Calculate a rectangle in the center of the form that will
// contain the string.
RectangleF rect = RectangleF::op_Implicit(this->ClientRectangle);
rect.X = rect.X + (rect.Width - sizeStr.Width)/2;
rect.Y = rect.Y + (rect.Height - sizeStr.Height)/2;
rect.Size = sizeStr;
g->DrawString(str, font, Brushes::Black, rect);
font->Dispose();
```

Of course, you have to ensure that the values you use to initialize a *Font* object correspond to an actual font installed on your machine. The framework will attempt to find a font that best fits the properties you specify, but it is often better to check at run time whether the fonts are installed. Fonts of a similar type will be members of a font family, which you can obtain through an instance of the *FontFamily* class. The families that are accessible in a *Graphics* object can be obtained through the static *FontFamily::GetFamilies* method, and once you have selected an appropriate *FontFamily* object, you can provide it to a *Font* constructor along with other information that will better identify the font you want.

Graphics Paths

A graphics path is a collection of lines and curves and thus allows you to create complicated outline shapes. You create graphics paths using the *GraphicsPath* class. This class has methods similar to those of the *Graphics* class. The difference is that you add an instruction to draw a line or a shape rather than actually draw the shape. These instructions can be played back later through the *Graphics::DrawPath* and *Graphics::FillPath* methods. A graphics path might be open or closed, and to close a path, you call the *GraphicsPath::CloseFigure* method, which will simply draw a line between the start and end points. A region can be created from a *GraphicsPath*, in which case an open graphics path will be closed automatically.

GraphicsPath has a *Transform* method, which you can use to supply a *Matrix* object and a *Warp* method so that the class can distort the image, through the array of floating point values passed as a parameter.

Regions

I have mentioned already that when you draw in a control, you draw in the current clipping *Region*; however, there are other uses for *Region* objects. A region is made up of *GraphicsPath* objects and rectangular regions, and a region is used to specify an area where you can draw. You can also create a region based on other regions: either the union of two regions (*Union*), the intersection of them (*Intersect*), the area occupied by either region but not both regions (*Xor*) or the region occupied by one region but not by the other (*Exclude* and *Complement*).

```
// regions.cpp
__gc class MainWindow : public Form
{
public:
   MainWindow()
   {
      this->FormBorderStyle = FormBorderStyle::FixedDialog;
      System::Drawing::Region* reg;
      reg = new System::Drawing::Region(this->Bounds);
      Rectangle rect(0, this->Height/3, this->Width/2,
         this->Height/3);
      reg->Exclude(rect);
      this->Region = reg;
   }
};
```

This code will create a form that is rectangular but has a central portion excluded. The *Region* property of a form defines the area where you can draw. The results of this code can be seen in Figure 4-3.

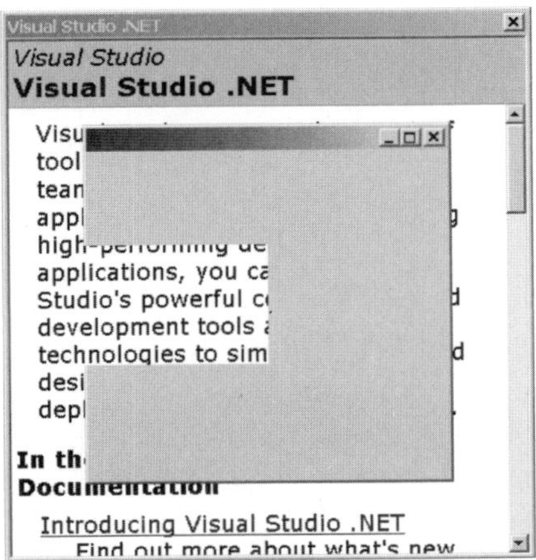

Figure 4-3 The results from defining the region for a form.

Controls and Forms

The Windows Forms library contains the classes used to develop controls and forms. A control is a UI element that can paint itself and can contain other forms. However, a control cannot be created on its own; it must be part of a control container. In this respect, a control is analogous to an ActiveX control or a Win32 child window. Controls typically have *Control* or *UserControl* as the immediate base class, although you can derive from any of the existing controls in the Windows Forms library.

A form is a control container, and it can paint itself. Unlike a control, a form can be created as a stand-alone window. Typically, forms derive from *Form* (which is a child class of *Control*), but you can extend an existing form by deriving from its class. Forms are very much like Visual Basic 6 forms, which is presumably where the name originates. Indeed, you will find that some obscure Visual Basic features that are hardly relevant to .NET have been carried over to Windows Forms (for example, *Control* has a *Tag* property and *Form* has a *Load* event). These features have endured to facilitate the porting of Visual Basic 6 code to Visual Basic .NET.

Controls and forms are based on windows (they each have a *Handle* property that gives access to the *HWND*, which I'll return to in the next section, "Where's the *WndProc*?"), but they are quite unlike Win32 windows to program. You do not have to register a Windows class nor do you have to write a Windows procedure. The *Form* class does all of that for you and translates Windows messages into .NET events. This behavior is another case in which forms are very much like Visual Basic 6 and are very different from traditional Win32 Windows programming. Indeed, you will find that it is a far from straightforward task to convert Windows SDK C++ code or MFC code to Windows Forms. If you have unmanaged GUI code, it is far better to leave it as unmanaged code, where you have some guarantee that it will work.[6]

Where's the *WndProc*?

Windows Forms technology is built over Win32 windows. When you write pure Win32 SDK code, you create a window by passing the name of a Windows class to *::CreateWindowEx*. The Windows class is either registered by the system (these are the standard Windows controls) or the class is a custom window registered by you. The Windows class is essentially a description of the window's behavior, and the most important part of the Windows class is the address of the Windows procedure (*WndProc*) that will handle the messages the window receives.

When you create a *Form* or a *Control*, what you see is a Win32 window. Windows forms, as you know, are event-based. These events look suspiciously like managed versions of Windows messages, and indeed they are. So how does a Windows message get translated to a Windows Forms event?

The *Form* class is derived from *Control*, which has the code for creating the Win32 window. The *Control* class has a nested class named *ControlNativeWindow*, and there is an *assembly* access field of this class named *Control::window*. The constructor of the *Control* class initializes the *ControlNativeWindow* with the *this* pointer of the *Control* object, so the native control has access to the managed control. This initialization is all that happens when you create a control—no Win32 window is created.

Of course, a window is no use unless it is visible. I do not want to sound too philosophical, but if you cannot see the window, how do you know that it exists? Turning this logic on its head, when you make a window visible, you have to have an existing window, so the *set_Visible* property method is the key method for creating the native window. The first time that *set_Visible* is called, a Win32 Windows class is registered and a window is created.

ControlNativeWindow derives from a class named *NativeWindow* that has interesting code. To make the window visible, *set_Visible* needs to access the native window handle, and on the first call to *Control::get_Handle*, the property method will see that the native window handle is zero and create the handle.

---

6. I would also make this recommendation to Visual Basic 6 programmers: don't be tempted to create ported code by porting your Visual Basic 6 code to Visual Basic .NET. By definition, ported code runs in an environment other than where it was designed to work. However, I am not a Visual Basic programmer, so I do not suppose any Visual Basic programmers will listen to me.

This process involves various calls that end up in a call to *NativeWindow::CreateHandle*, passing an instance of *CreateParams*, which comes from the *Control::CreateParams* property and which has information about the style of the window to create. This method looks something like this:

```
// C++ generated from MSIL
virtual void NativeWindow::CreateHandle(CreateParams* cp)
{
   // Other code
   WindowClass* wc = WindowClass::Create(cp->ClassName,
      cp->ClassStyle);
   Monitor::Enter(wc);
   IntPtr hMod = GetModuleHandle(0);
   IntPtr hWnd = CreateWindowEx(..., wc->windowClassName,
      ..., hMod, ...);
   // Other code
   Monitor::Exit(this);
}
```

WindowClass is a nested class declared in *NativeWindow*. The constructor is passed the name of the class to create and the style of the window. If this code is called to create a custom control, the class name will be zero, in which case the *Create* method generates a Windows class of the following form:

```
<windowsformsversion>.<windowclassname>.app.<appdomainID>
```

Here *<windowsformsversion>* is the version of Windows Forms that is installed and currently is the string *WindowsForms10*. The *<windowclassname>* is the string *Window.* suffixed with the style of the window class (for example, *Window.8*), and *<appdomainID>* is the unique ID for the current AppDomain.

Here is an example Windows class name generated for a *Form*:

```
WindowsForms10.Window.8.app1
```

Once *Create* has generated a class name, it uses this name to register the Windows class and it passes *WindowClass::Callback* as the Windows procedure of the class. This procedure is just a temporary Windows procedure that is called when the window is first created with the call to *CreateWindowEx*, as shown here:

```
// C++ generated from MSIL
public IntPtr Callback(IntPtr hWnd, int msg, IntPtr wparam,
   IntPtr lparam)
```

```
{
   ::SetWindowLong(hWnd, GWL_WNDPROC, this->defWindowProc);
   this->targetWindow->AssignHandle(hWnd);
   return this->targetWindow->Callback(hWnd, msg, wparam,
      lparam);
}
```

This code is passed the Windows handle of the Win32 handle that has just been created. *NativeWindow::targetWindow* is the *ControlNativeWindow* that called *WindowClass::Create*. In effect, this code stores the native Windows handle of the Win32 window that was created (remember, this code is called because *Control::get_Handle* was called), and it replaces the registered Windows procedure for this window with the method pointer stored in *WindowsClass::defWindowProc*, which is the message handler code that will be called. If *Control* does not handle a message, *WindowClass::RegisterClass* will assign this method pointer to the Win32 function *::DefWindowProcA*.

However, *AssignHandle* does a little more than this.

```
// C++ generated from MSIL
void NativeWindow::AssignHandle(IntPtr handle,
   bool assignUniqueID)
{
   // Other code
   this->handle = handle;
   this->defWindowProc = ::GetWindowLong(handle, GWL_WNDPROC);
   if (this->WndProcShouldBeDebuggable)
      this->windowProc = new WndProc(this, &NativeWindow::DebuggableCallback);
   else
      this->windowProc = new WndProc(this, &NativeWindow::Callback);
   // Other code
   ::SetWindowLong(handle, GWL_WNDPROC, this->windowProc);
   // Other code
}
```

This code stores the handle, obtains the Windows procedure (which *WindowClass::Callback* had assigned to *::DefWindowProcA*), and stores the Windows procedure as the default Windows procedure. Then the code subclasses *again,* but this time it sets the Windows procedure either as *DebuggableCallback* or *Callback* depending on whether a debugger is attached. *NativeWindow::Callback* and *NativeWindow::DebuggableCallback* follow the same procedure. The difference is that *Callback* has exception handling so that at run time, exceptions are not thrown when handling a message. Here is the version without the exception handling:

```
IntPtr NativeWindow::DebuggableCallback(
   IntPtr hWnd, int msg, IntPtr wparam, IntPtr lparam)
{
   Message* manMsg = Message::Create(hWnd, msg, wparam, lparam);
   this->WndProc(manMsg);
   if (msg == WM_NCDESTROY) this->ReleaseHandle(false);
   return manMsg->Result;
}
```

This code creates a managed message object initialized with the parameters of the method and then calls the *ControlNativeWindow::WndProc*, which does some handling for mouse messages and then calls *ControlNativeWindow::OnMessage*:

```
virtual void OnMessage(Message* m)
{
   this->control->WndProc(m);
}
```

This method calls *Control::WndProc* on your control. *WndProc* essentially has a switch that tests for Windows messages and calls an appropriate member method. *Control* has many methods of the form *Wm<MSG>*, which will call *DefWndProc* either before or after processing the message. This arrangement ensures that if you do not provide an event handler in your derived class, default message handling will be performed.

The processing of the message can be straightforward or complicated depending on the particular message. For example, *WmPaint* creates a *PaintEventArgs* by calling the Win32 *::BeginPaint* and extracting the device context and the invalidated area. The calls to the *Wm<MSG>* methods will end up in a call to the appropriate *On<MSG>* method that will generate the managed event. For example, *WmPaint* calls *PaintWithErrorHandling*, which will call *OnPaint*.

The *Form* class is a control container. Remember that when you create a control instance with the *new* keyword you are not actually creating the control window. The control is created when it is told to show itself. You do not create controls on their own; they have to be added to a control container, such as a *Form*. *Form* has a property named *Form::Controls* that is a *Control::ControlCollection*. A *Form*'s window is created when *set_Visible* is first called. This call will result in the windows of the controls in the *Controls* collection being created. Remember that when you create a control object, you do not create the underlying Win32 window, but you do initialize it with layout information. This means that the *ControlCollection* contains the information of the child controls and their properties. This information is essentially the same information you'll find in a dialog template in a Win32 application.

The *WndProc* method is a *protected virtual* member of *Control*, so you can override it in your class. Note that because the *Wm<MSG>* methods are responsible for the default message handling, it is vital that you call the base class implementation of *WndProc* in your override. For example, the caption bar of a window is used to drag a window around the desktop. If you set the *ControlBox* property of the *Form* to *false*, the form will not have a caption, so you will not be able to move the window.[7] To remedy this you can override the *WndProc* to test for *WM_NCHITTEST*, which the system will send to the window to test to see whether a mouse click is in the client area or in the non–client area. If you return *HTCAPTION* to this message, you indicate that the position clicked is in the caption bar and hence you'll get the caption bar behavior of being able to drag the window. In the following code, I return this value for the entire window, so any location can be used to drag the window:

```
// captionless.cpp
#define HTCAPTION 2
#define WM_NCHITTEST 0x84

__gc class CaptionlessForm : public Form
{
public:
   CaptionlessForm(){ControlBox = false;}
protected:
   void WndProc(Message* m)
   {
      if (m->Msg == WM_NCHITTEST)
      {
         m->Result = HTCAPTION;
         return;
      }
      Form::WndProc(m);
   }
};
```

The *Message* class is a value type, but because the *WndProc* does not return a value, the parameter is passed by reference through a pointer, so the return value is returned through *Message::Result*.

A *Form* looks very much like a dialog box. Indeed, the class has two methods, *ShowDialog* and *Show*, that allow you to show a form as a modal or a modeless dialog box. If you use *Show*, you can hide the form with the *Hide* method or toggle the *Visible* property. Indeed, you can start your Windows Forms application with code such as this:

7. Removing the caption bar also means that you'll not have a close button. To close such a window you can use Alt-F4.

```
void main()
{
   Form* frm = new Form;
   frm->ShowDialog();
}
```

Under the covers, *ShowDialog* and *Application::Run* call the same method, *Application::ThreadContext::RunMessageLoop*. This method starts the Win32 message loop.

Standard Windows Controls

The most prevalent of the classes in the *System::Windows::Forms* namespace are those that wrap existing Win32 controls and common controls. I will not go into great detail about how to use these classes; there are many good texts that will explain how to program them.[8] Instead, I will explain how these classes relate to the Win32 controls that they wrap. Take, for example, the *Label* class, which is used to add a label to a form, what a seasoned Win32 developer would call a *static control*. As you can imagine, this class derives from *Control* and overrides methods to provide implementations for this specific control type, and the static constructor initializes the identifiers used for the new events, properties, and state members.

But how does the implementation tell the system to create an instance of the Win32 static control? The answer lies in the *CreateParams* property, which is used to supply the parameters to the *NativeWindow::CreateHandle* method, which I mentioned earlier when I talked about creating a control. The *Label* class has the following implementation:

```
// C++ generated from MSIL
protected:
   virtual Label::CreateParams* get_CreateParams ()
   {
      // First get the base class version
      CreateParams __gc * params = Control::CreateParams;
      params->ClassName = S"STATIC";
      if (this->OwnerDraw)
      {
         params->Style = params.Style | 13;
         params->ExStyle = params.ExStyle & 0xffffefff;
      }
```

8. The most authoritative text is Charles Petzold's *Programming Microsoft Windows with C# (Microsoft Press, 2002)*.

```
        params->Style = params->Style;
        BorderStyle border = this->BorderStyle;
        switch (border - 1)
        {
        case 0:
           params->Style = params->Style | 0x800000;
           break;
        case 1:
           params->Style = params->Style | 0x1000;
           break;
        }
        if (!this->UseMnemonic) params->Style =
           params->Style | 0x80;
        return params;
    }
```

The important point is that the class name is set to *STATIC* when *CreateParams* is called by *Control::CreateHandle*, so the appropriate control is created.

Exceptions

If an exception is thrown when a form or a control is created, the exception will be passed to the code that attempted to create the object. Once the Windows handle is created, exceptions on this thread will be handled by the *Application::OnThreadException* method that raises the *Application::ThreadException* event. If this event is not assigned to a delegate, the method will create an instance of *ThreadExceptionDialog*, which will show the exception and will allow you to continue the application or abort it. I will talk more about handling exceptions in Chapter 7, but in general, you should not allow a system-generated exception dialog box to be shown to a user. Such a dialog box is of great advantage to a developer, but the average user will not have a clue what to do. Thus, you should provide an event handler to handle the exception, as shown here:

```
// winexcept.cpp
__gc class MyForm : public Form
{
public:
   MyForm(){ Click+=new EventHandler(this, &MyForm::MyClick); }
   void MyClick(Object* sender, EventArgs* args)
   {
      throw new Exception(S"Don\'t click me!");
   }
```

```
    static void Handler(Object* sender,
        ThreadExceptionEventArgs* args)
    {
        MessageBox::Show(args->Exception->ToString(),
            S"Thread Exception");
    }
};

int __stdcall WinMain(unsigned, unsigned, char*, int)
{
    Application::ThreadException +=
        new ThreadExceptionEventHandler(0, &MyForm::Handler);
    Application::Run(new MyForm);
    return 0;
}
```

When you click on this form, it will throw an exception. This exception will be caught by the system and passed to the *MyForm::Handler* method. If the form is running under the debugger, your event handler will not get the thread exception event. Instead, the exception will be passed to the debugger, which can place a break point where the exception was thrown.

Events, Properties, and Status

The *Control* and *Form* classes have .NET events for all the common events that will happen to a window. The *Control* class holds all the event delegates in an instance of *EventHandlerList* so that your *Control* takes up only as much memory as is required for the events that you actually handle. When you change the position or the size of a *Control*, it will generate a *Layout* event. When you add a control to a control container, the *Layout* event will be sent to the control container. The event looks like this:

```
__delegate void LayoutEventHandler(
    Object* sender, LayoutEventArgs* e);
```

The *LayoutEventArgs* object passes information about the control and the property on the control that has changed. Layout information is used by the layout manager (an instance of the private nested class *LayoutManager*) to handle controls that are docked or anchored to the container. A docked control is created by specifying a docking edge. The layout manager will ensure that the control will be docked to the edge and will fill the available space in the container in the orthogonal direction. An anchored control is created by specifying an anchored edge. When the container is resized, the layout manager will ensure that the control remains the same distance from the anchored edge.

During construction of a form, you will be adding several controls and changing their layout information, but it makes little sense for the layout manager to process this information. You can inform the control container to ignore layout events by calling *SuspendLayout*. When all controls have been created, you can tell the layout manager to perform its magic by calling *ResumeLayout*.

Control and *Form* have many properties. These properties either return information that is set by the system (for example, the *ClientRectangle* property), or they can be used to affect the behavior of the item (for example, the *Visible* property). These items also have state that is not associated with a property—for example, the control style is accessed through *GetStyle* and changed through *SetStyle*. If each property represented storage (a field) in the *Control*, the control would take up a lot of memory. Instead, the *Control* and *Form* classes have fields only for the data that is required and without which the object cannot be used (for example, the *controlStyle* field used by *GetStyle* and *SetStyle*). There are other properties that require storage, but these properties can be considered as optional. For example, *Control::Name* gives a name to a control, which you can use to identify an instance; however, to make a completely reliable comparison of two *Form* objects, you should use *Object::ReferenceEquals* so that the *Name* property is treated as optional. There is no field for this property; instead, it is stored in a collection of type *PropertyStore*, which is an associated container. The key that is used to identify the property in the container is an integer that is a *static* member of *Control* (for example, *Control::PropName*, the convention is for the variable to be prefixed with *Prop*). These keys are initialized in the static constructor for *Control* through *PropertyStore::CreateKey*, which merely returns an incremented static variable. Here is the code for the *Name* property:

```
String * get_Name()
{
   String* str;
   str = (String*) this->Properties->GetObject(
      Control::PropName);
   if (str == 0 || str->Length == 0)
   {
      if (this->Site != 0) str = this->Site->Name;
      if (str == 0) str = S"";
   }
   return str;
}

void set_Name(String* value)
{
   if (value == 0 || value->Length == 0)
```

```
    {
        this->Properties->SetObject(Control::PropName, 0);
        return;
    }
    this->Properties->SetObject(Control::PropName, value);
}
```

The *Properties* property returns the property store for this object.

The *Form* class, and other classes derived from *Control*, also have state properties. These properties indicate state such as whether the form is active (*Form::Active*) or whether it is topmost (*Form::TopMost*). All of these state members are characterized by the fact that they are Boolean values. If a *bool* was used to indicate each of these items, your program would waste a great deal of memory because a *bool* is stored as a byte, even though only one bit is used. The solution here is to use a class in the *System::Collection::Specialized* namespace named *BitVector32*. As the name suggests, instances contain just 32-bits of memory, so the total space taken up by all items in it cannot exceed this value. To use this class, you indicate which portion of the 32 bits will be used by creating *BitVector32::Section* objects. A *Section* is effectively a count of the number of bits required and the position of each in the *BitVector32*. Once you have a *Section*, you can get or set a value through the *BitVector32::Item* property, passing the *Section*. Classes such as *Form* have *Section* objects as static members so that the overhead of these members occurs once for all instances of the class. The class has an instance member of *BitVector32*, so potentially, 32 *bool* values could be represented by a single 32-bit *BitVector32*.

Controls and ActiveX Interfaces

If you look at the *Control* class with ILDASM, you'll see that in addition to the managed interfaces I have mentioned already (*IComponent*, *IDisposable*, *ISynchronizeInvoke*, and *IWin32Window*), this class implements several COM interfaces. The *System::Windows::Forms* namespace has a class named *UnsafeNativeMethods* that contains managed versions of the most common COM interfaces. The *Control* class implements the following COM interfaces:

- *IOleControl*
- *IOleObject*
- *IOleInPlaceObject*
- *IOleInActivePlaceObject*
- *IOleWindow*
- *IViewObject*

- *IViewObject2*
- *IPersist*
- *IPersistStreamInit*
- *IPersistPropertyBag*
- *IPersistStorage*
- *IQuickActivate*

The methods on these interfaces are actually delegated to a property named *ActiveXInstance*, which is an instance of a nested class named *ActiveX-Impl*. As a consequence, you can use a .NET control in an unmanaged application such as an MFC dialog or a Visual Basic 6 form.

```
// ctrls.cpp
public __gc class Ctrl : public Control
{
public:
   Ctrl() { Text = "Ctrl class"; }
protected:
   virtual void OnPaint(PaintEventArgs* args)
   {
      Graphics* g = args->Graphics;
      g->DrawRectangle(new Pen(ForeColor),
         0, 0, Size.Width-1, Size.Height-1);
      StringFormat* format = new StringFormat;
      format->Alignment = StringAlignment::Center;
      format->LineAlignment = StringAlignment::Center;
      g->DrawString(this->Text, this->Font,
         new SolidBrush(ForeColor), RectangleF(Point(0, 0),
            this->Size),
         format);
      Control::OnPaint(args);
   }
};
```

The *Ctrl* class merely draws a rectangle within its border and draws its *Text* property in the center. If this class is compiled into an assembly named *Ctrls* that has a strong name, you can run RegAsm.exe on the assembly to register the control as a COM object. If you have an MFC application with a dialog box, you can add a control to the dialog box by right-clicking and selecting Insert ActiveX Control. This command will show the Insert Object dialog box created with *OleUIInsertObject* with the *IOF_SHOWINSERTCONTROL* | *IOF_SELECTCREATECONTROL* flags. However, this command will not show your control. The reason is that this dialog box will show the objects registered in *HKCR\CLSID* with specific keys, and RegAsm.exe does not add those keys.

As I explained in Chapter 2, RegAsm.exe will add an entry to *HKCR\CLSID* for each public class it finds in the specified assembly. To this entry, RegAsm.exe adds the *InprocServer32* key, the *ProgID* key, and the *Implemented Categories* key. The category that the control implements is shown here:

```
{62C8FE65-4EBB-45e7-B440-6E39B2CDBF29}
```

This key is named *.NET Category* and indicates that the class is a .NET class. The *OleUIInsertObject* dialog box will look for a class that has the *Control* and *Insertable* subkeys.[9] It is a pain (and error-prone) to edit the registry by hand. The solution is to provide a registration method to add these keys (and an unregistration method to remove these keys when the control is unregistered). RegAsm.exe will call your registration method when it is registering your control. These methods are *static* members of a class and can take either a *Type* or a *String* parameter. RegAsm.exe knows which method to call because the registration method is marked with *[ComRegisterFunction]*, and the unregister method is marked with *[ComUnregisterFunction]*.

```
// ctrls.cpp
using namespace Microsoft::Win32;
using namespace System::Runtime::InteropServices;

namespace Ctrls {
public __gc class Ctrl : public Control
{
public:
   Ctrl() { Text = "Ctrl class"; }
   [ComRegisterFunction]
   static void Register(Type* t)
   {
      String* strKey = S"CLSID\\{";
      strKey = String::Concat(strKey,
                  Marshal::GenerateGuidForType(t).ToString());
      String* newKey = String::Concat(strKey, S"}\\Control");
      Registry::ClassesRoot->CreateSubKey(newKey);
      newKey = String::Concat(strKey, S"}\\Insertable");
      Registry::ClassesRoot->CreateSubKey(newKey);
   }
   [ComUnregisterFunction]
   static void Unregister(Type* t)
```

9. The Office applications will only allow you to insert controls that have an *Insertable* key in the *Prog ID* key in the root of *HKCR*.

```
    {
        String* strKey = S"CLSID\\{";
        strKey = String::Concat(strKey,
                    Marshal::GenerateGuidForType(t).ToString());
        String* delKey = String::Concat(strKey, S"}\\Control");
        Registry::ClassesRoot->DeleteSubKey(delKey);
        delKey = String::Concat(strKey, S"}\\Insertable");
        Registry::ClassesRoot->DeleteSubKey(delKey);
    }
// Other methods
};
}; // namespace Ctrls
```

This code uses the registry classes in the *Microsoft.Win32* namespace, so you have to have the appropriate *RegistryPermission* security permissions for this code to succeed. As you can see, the registration method obtains the GUID for the type using *GenerateGuidForType*, and so that this control has the standard ProgId format, I have put this class in a namespace called *Ctrls*. (The version-independent ProgID for this control will be *Ctrls.Ctrl*.)[10]

The .NET Framework also allows you to use ActiveX controls on a form. To use these controls, you have to import the controls with COM interop. A control must derive from *Control*, so it is not sufficient just to run TlbImp.exe on the ActiveX control's COM type library. Instead, the Framework provides a tool named aximp.exe. This tool creates two assemblies, one for COM interop and another that provides a control wrapper around these imported classes. The wrapper derives from *AxHost*, which implements the client site interfaces that a container needs to implement to be a container for an ActiveX control. Thus, each ActiveX control that you import through aximp.exe will have its own ActiveX control container.

After you have imported an ActiveX control, all you need to do to use it on a form is use the wrapper class. The tool aximp.exe will generate a name for the wrapper class that is the control name given in the type library prefixed by *Ax* (so the wrapper for *MyCtrl* will be *AxMyCtrl*).

Control Handles

Managed controls are based on Win32 windows. I explained earlier that the window is created when the control is first made visible. Now take a look at this code:

---

10. As a tip: if you have opened an MFC project and opened a dialog (with the dialog editor) that contains an assembly registered with regasm you should shut down this instance of Visual Studio.NET before recompiling that assembly. Merely closing the MFC project solution is not sufficient.

```
// hundred.cpp
#define INCR 10
__gc class MainForm : public Form
{
public:
   MainForm()
   {
      Location = System::Drawing::Point(0,0);
      Size = SystemInformation::WorkingArea.Size;

      int xInc = this->Width / INCR;
      int yInc = this->Height / INCR;

      for (int x = 0; x < INCR; x++)
      {
         for (int y = 0; y < INCR; y++)
         {
            Ctrl* ctrl = new Ctrl;
            ctrl->Text = String::Format(
               S"{0:x}", __box(reinterpret_cast<int>(
                           static_cast<void*>(ctrl->Handle))));
            ctrl->Width = xInc;
            ctrl->Height = yInc;
            ctrl->Left = x * xInc;
            ctrl->Top = y * yInc;
            this->Controls->Add(ctrl);
         }
      }
   }
};
```

The *MainForm* class creates 100 instances of the control that I showed earlier. If you run this code and look closely, you will see that each of these controls has a different Windows handle, and as a consequence, it takes a short while to construct the form. Sadly, this delay takes us back to the bad old days of Visual Basic 3. In those days, when you ran a Windows application, you knew whether it had been written in Visual Basic 3 or C/C++ by the speed of the user interface: If you could see the UI build itself control by control, you knew the application was written in Visual Basic 3. If the UI built itself instantaneously, you knew the application was written in C or C++.

The ActiveX control programmers recognized that creating lots of controls in a container would be a problem, so ActiveX controls could be written to be *windowless*. This type of control informs its container that it will not create a window handle, and instead, the container passes the control a portion of the container's window. .NET controls are not created as windowless; they are always created with their own Windows handle.

Thus, you should make sure that you limit the number of controls on your forms. If your form visibly redraws itself (as in the previous example), you should try to reduce the number of controls on the form. If you have several controls of the same type, it might be a good idea to rewrite a single control class that does the same work. Because Windows Forms uses Windows handles in such an inefficient way, I would advise you against building controls based on other .NET controls.

Drag and Drop

The *Control* class supports OLE drag and drop. This operation is supported by two nested classes (*Control::DropSource* and *Control::DropTarget*) and a public class named *DataObject*. These classes provide a bridge between the managed control and OLE drag and drop: it is COM that provides the drag-and-drop support, so the thread must be initialized to run in an STA (either with the *[STAThread]* attribute or explicitly through *Thread::ApartmentState*). You are able to drag any items from any control, but you need to initiate the drag. For example, you might decide that when the user clicks on a control, drag and drop should be started, and to initiate the drag, you call the *DoDragDrop* method, as shown here:

```
// dragndrop.cpp
__gc class DragSource : public Form
{
public:
   DragSource()
   {
      MouseDown += new MouseEventHandler(this,
         &DragSource::MouseDownHandler);
   }
   void MouseDownHandler(Object* sender, MouseEventArgs* args)
   {
      DoDragDrop(S"Data", DragDropEffects::Copy);
   }
};
```

Here the data object is the string *Data*. I have decided that the drag-and-drop operation will be *Copy*. If the operation is *Move*, you will have to perform some action to remove the source object from the drag source. You cannot drag any object; the object must implement *ISerializable* or *IDataObject*. The framework provides an implementation of *IDataObject* as the *DataObject* class. When you initiate the drag and drop operation, the object is copied to the clipboard, and when the object is dropped, the target obtains the object from the clipboard. The clipboard stores *formatted* objects—that is, there is an indication of the type of data that is stored, so you can request the data object to be extracted as the appropriate format. The *DataObject* class allows you to copy data to and from the clipboard.

In the previous example, the *DoDragDrop* method has to deduce the data type, and for a *String** pointer, the data is stored as a *CF_TEXT* and as a format named *System.String*. In general, a data object will be stored with the name of the type of the object; strings and bitmaps are exceptions because there are standard clipboard formats available. If you want to control the formats put on the clipboard for either a drag-and-drop operation or for a clipboard copy operation, you can create a *DataObject* and copy the drag and drop object into the data object using the *SetData* method. This method has a parameter that you can use to specify the data format, so it allows you to copy data in a format other than the serializable format that .NET knows about. Often, the clipboard format will involve generating a binary representation of the object, and to perform this task, you can use the *MemoryStream* class in the *System::IO* namespace. This class is serializable, and it holds binary data. You can call *SetData* several times to add more than one format to the data object.

To be able to drop an object on a control, you have to set its *AllowDrop* property to *true*. The property accessor method will call the Win32 *::RegisterDragDrop*, passing it an instance of *Control::DropTarget*. The rest of the drag-and-drop operation is carried out using events, and these events are summarized in Table 4-7.

Table 4-7 Drag-and-Drop Events in the *Control* Class

Event	Description
DragDrop	Raised when the drag-and-drop operation has completed. Use this event to obtain the data object.
DragEnter	Raised when you drag an object over a control's bounds. Use this event to indicate the drag-and-drop operation that can be performed with the data object.
DragLeave	Raised when you drag an object out of a control's bounds
DragOver	Raised as you drag an object over a control. Use this event to provide some visual feedback of the drag-and-drop operation.
GiveFeedback	Raised during a drag-and-drop operation and allows you to provide visual feedback.

When an object is dragged over a control, you will first get the *DragEnter* event; as you continue to drag over the control, you will get the *DragOver* event until the cursor moves out of the bounds of the control, at which point, you will get the *DragLeave* event. The main use of *DragEnter* is to indicate what can be done with the object.

```
// dragndrop.cpp
void EnterCtrl(Object* sender, DragEventArgs* args)
{
   if (args->Data->GetDataPresent(S"System.String"))
      args->Effect = DragDropEffects::All;
}
```

The *DragEventArgs* class has property members that you can check to see the data that is being dragged and the position of the mouse cursor. These properties are read-only except for *Effect*, which is read/write. You use this property to indicate whether the item can be dropped, and if the data object is dropped, whether it is copied or moved. In this example, I test the data object to see whether the data is a *System::String*—notice that the format uses a dot as the resolution operator—and if so, the data can be copied or moved.

When the object is dropped, the control will get the *DragDrop* event. This event also has a *DragEventArgs* parameter, but this time, you should consider the properties as being read-only. The *AllowedEffect* will give the drag and drop effects allowed by the source, and *Effect* will be drag and drop effects allowed by the target. The *KeyState* property indicates whether the Ctrl or Shift key is pressed. The *Data* member is an *IDataObject* that you can use to get the object that is being dropped. *IDataObject::Formats* will return an array of strings with the formats in the data object. *IDataObject::GetDataPresent* will test to see whether a specific data format is in the data object, and finally, *IDataObject::GetData* will get the dropped object in the specified format.

```
// dragndrop.cpp
void Drop(Object* sender, DragEventArgs* args)
{
   String* str;
   str = dynamic_cast<String*>(args->Data->GetData(
      S"System.String"));
   if (str != 0)
   {
      Graphics* g = this->CreateGraphics();
      Point p(args->X, args->Y);
```

```
        p = this->PointToClient(p);
        g->DrawString(str, this->Font,
            Brushes::Black, p.X, p.Y);
        g->Dispose();
    }
}
```

The *DragEventArgs::X* and *DragEventArgs::Y* properties are in mouse coordinates, so to convert to client coordinates, I use *Control::PointToClient*. If the data is in a format other than a serialized .NET object, you will need to know the details of that format. You can obtain the data through a *MemoryStream* object and access the individual bytes that make up the serialized form of the dropped object.

Superclassing

Superclassing is a term used in Win32 to describe the mechanism where you take an existing Windows class and extend it to create another class. You can then create instances of this new class, and they will exhibit the new behavior. In Win32 terms, you superclass a window class by obtaining the original (registered) Windows class by calling *GetClassInfo*. You then create a new Windows class, with a new *WndProc* containing message handlers. You use the *WndProc* of the class you are superclassing as the default message handler of your new class, and you can also call this procedure in some of your message handlers. Thus, the default code to handle messages is the class you are superclassing, and you add extra code to this implementation.

This process is essentially the same as deriving from a class. In C++ terms, the class you are superclassing is the base class. If you do not override a base class implementation, the base class method is called. If you do override a base class method, you have the option of either replacing this base class method totally or providing implementation in addition to the base class.

It will come as no surprise that if you want to create a control (or a form) with a behavior similar to an existing control, all you have to do is derive from that control's class and add the extra functionality.

```
public __gc class Ctrl : public Button
{
protected:
    virtual void OnPaint(PaintEventArgs* args)
    {
        Button::OnPaint(args);
        Graphics* g = args->Graphics;
        g->DrawEllipse(new Pen(ForeColor),
            0, 0, Size.Width-1, Size.Height-1);
    }
};
```

This code derives from the standard button class and adds extra functionality to the *OnPaint* method that draws an ellipse.

A final point to make concerns *subclassing*. Subclassing is another term that Win32 SDK programmers use and it involves taking an existing window (*not* a class to a window) and replacing its *WndProc* with a custom procedure that can replace or augment the control's behavior. .NET is type-safe, so in terms of .NET classes, it is not possible to take an object of one type and cast it to an unrelated type. Although *Control* has a method named *FromHandle* that appears to do the necessary action—create a .NET control from a *HWND*—it will work only if the handle refers to a .NET control (and is obtained through the *Control::Handle* property).

Standard Forms

Win32 has a library named comdlg32.dll that defines the Windows classes for standard dialog boxes such as the file open dialog or the color picker dialog box. *System::Windows::Forms* has classes (shown in Table 4-8) that wrap these common dialog boxes. Note that there is no folder picker dialog box, such as the Win32 *::SHBrowseForFolder*. However, this lack of a folder picker dialog class is not a problem because all you need to do is call *::SHBrowseForFolder* through IJW.

Table 4-8 Standard Dialogs in the Windows Forms Library and the Equivalent Win32 Common Dialog Boxes

Class	Win32 Equivalent	Description
ColorDialog	*ChooseColor*	Choose a color from standard colors or a color swatch.
FontDialog	*ChooseFont*	Chose a font from those installed on the system.
OpenFileDialog	*GetOpenFileName*	Select a file to open.
PageSetupDialog	*PageSetupDlg*	Set up printer properties.
PrintDialog	*PrintDlgEx*	Start a print operation.
SaveFileDialog	*GetSaveFileName*	Select the location to save a file.

The classes in Table 4-8 are derived from *CommonDialog*, which is derived from *Component*. *Form* is not used. These classes mirror the Win32 common dialog boxes, which raises the question of why you would want to use these rather than using the Win32 dialogs directly. The main advantage you get with these classes is that their authors have applied code access security (discussed in Chapter 5), so that only code with a specific permission can call the code. Thus, an assembly method can show a *OpenFileDialog* only if the assembly has the *FileDialogPermission* granted to it. If your code calls the Win32 API directly (*::GetOpenFileName*), no check is performed as to whether your assembly is allowed to open files with this dialog (although clearly NTFS access checks will be performed when you try to open a file).

To show a standard form, you create an instance of the class, set various properties according to the type of the dialog box, and then call *ShowDialog*, as shown here:

```
OpenFileDialog* file = new OpenFileDialog;
file->ShowDialog();
```

The *CommonDialog::ShowDialog* method goes into a modal loop and then calls *OpenFileDialog::RunDialog*, which calls the appropriate Win32 common dialog box function.

Event Handling Strategies

.NET only allows classes to derive from a single base class. This arrangement restricts your options somewhat for developing a class hierarchy. Native C++ allows you to use multiple inheritance, which means that you can have base classes that perform some specific implementation. For example, you could have a class that handles keystrokes and another that handles mouse movements; such base classes could use downcasts to get access to child class members.

In .NET, you can simulate this handling using containment, as shown in the following example:

```
// cont.cpp
__gc class KeyPressHandler
{
   Control* parent;
public:
   KeyPressHandler(Control* p) : parent(p){}
   void KeyPressed(Object* sender, KeyPressEventArgs* args)
   {
      // Handle the keypress, and access form through parent.
   }
};
__gc class MyForm : public Form
{
```

```
   KeyPressHandler* kp;
public:
   MyForm()
   {
      kp = new KeyPressHandler(this);
      KeyPress += new KeyPressEventHandler(kp,
         &KeyPressHandler::KeyPressed);
   }
};
```

In this simple example, I have an extra class named *KeyPressHandler* that will have common code that can be used by other classes. In this case, the *MyForm* class creates an instance of the class and passes its *this* pointer to the object. *MyForm* then uses this object as the handler for the *KeyPressed* event. Because the *KeyPressHandler* object is a field, it can expose members that the *MyForm* class can use to alter the event handling behavior at run time.

Also be aware that handling a Windows message via an event might not be the best option. Take a look at this class:

```
// restsize.cpp
__gc class RestrictedSize : public Form
{
public:
   RestrictedSize()
   {
      this->Resize += new EventHandler(this,
         &RestrictedSize::ResizeMe);
      this->Width = 200;
   }
   void ResizeMe(Object* sender, EventArgs* args)
   {
      if (this->Size.Width > 200)
         this->Size = System::Drawing::Size(200,
            this->Size.Height);
   }
};
```

The intention is that the *Resize* event is used to restrict the width so that it cannot be changed to a value more than 200; the height can be changed to any value. However, because this method handles the *Resize* event, the window already has been resized before the size is reduced back to 200. As a consequence, you will see a flickering of the window in the brief time between when the *Resize* event is raised and when the width is changed. The solution to this problem is to handle the Win32 *WM_SIZING* message, as shown here:

```
protected:
   void WndProc(Message* m)
   {
      if (m->Msg == WM_SIZING)
      {
         RECT* rect = reinterpret_cast<RECT*>(
                          static_cast<void*>(m->LParam));
         if ((rect->right - rect->left) > 200)
         {
            rect->right = rect->left + 200;
            m->Result = IntPtr(1);
            return;
         }
      }
      Form::WndProc(m);
   }
```

The whole point about the *WM_SIZING* message is that you are informed—before the form is sized—about the new size. This new code will allow you to restrict the width of the forms without the annoying flicker obtained in the previous version. Windows Forms does not always provide the best solution, but at least you will be assured that you have the option of reverting to a Win32 solution.

Using Windows Header Files

The final issue I want to address in this section is the use of the Win32 header files If you plan to call Win32 code through IJW, you will want to use windows.h and other Windows headers. I have already addressed the issues of name clashes and problems with the preprocessor; however, there are deeper issues that you will have to address. Take a look at this code:

```
#using <mscorlib.dll>
#include <windows.h>
#include <commctrl.h>
#pragma comment(lib, "comctl32.lib")

int __stdcall WinMain(HINSTANCE, HINSTANCE, char*, int)
{
   InitCommonControls();
   HIMAGELIST hList;
   hList = ImageList_Create(16, 16, ILC_COLOR, 0, 1);
   // Other code
   return 0;
}
```

This code does not do anything, but it is the sort of code that you might see in the entry point of a GUI application. I have decided that I want to use managed types, so I have compiled this code with */clr*. There are no name clashes nor are there any preprocessor issues. However, when you run this code, it will throw an exception. If you change the entry point to *main* and start this from a command line, you will get the following dump of the exception:

```
Unhandled Exception: System.TypeLoadException: Could not
 load type _IMAGELIST from assembly Test, Version=0.0.0.0,
 Culture=neutral, PublicKeyToken=null.
   at main()
```

The weird thing is that if you use ildasm.exe to look at your assembly, you will see that neither *HIMAGELIST* nor *_HIMAGELIST* is defined. The problem is that commctrl.h defines *HIMAGELIST* like this:

```
#ifndef HIMAGELIST
struct _IMAGELIST;
typedef struct _IMAGELIST* HIMAGELIST;
#endif
```

Because this code defines a *struct* with no members, the compiler adds nothing to the assembly, but it still uses this type. The consequence is that the type loader sees that the code uses a type that does not exist and throws an exception. The solution to this problem is to define the *struct _HIMAGELIST* by hand before I include commctrl.h.

```
struct _IMAGELIST{};
```

Now the assembly will compile and it will have a type named *_HIMAGELIST* defined, so the type loader will be happy. This problem only appears to be related to *HIMAGELIST* and *HTREEVIEW*, and with the current version of the compiler, this solution is the only one available.

Using Managed Resources

The PE file format has a section named .rsrc for resources. These resources can be one of the standard resource types (one of the *RT_* prefixed symbols as documented in the Platform SDK, for example, *RT_ICON*, *RT_MENU* or *RT_STRING*), or they can be a binary resource that only your application knows about (*RT_RCDATA*). The resources will be arranged in the resource section of the PE file within a resource directory. (This directory is documented in winnt.h.) To construct this directory, you use a resource script (.rc file) and compile this script with the resource compiler (rc.exe). The resulting .res file will be linked to the final PE file by the linker. The Win32 *::FindResourceEx* function is passed the module handle of a loaded PE file that contains the resource, the identifier of the requested resource, and the type of the resource (an *RT_* symbol). The API will then search through the resource section of the specified PE file for the resource directory and locate the resource. The return value can then be used by *::LoadResource* to get an *HGLOBAL* that you pass to *LockResource* to finally get a pointer to the resource.[11]

In general, if your assembly uses only .NET code, you will not need Win32 resources (with the exception of the icon resource for the file); if your code uses Win32 code through IJW, you might need to have Win32 resources. Visual Studio .NET supports Win32 resource files for managed projects, and the resource compiler will edit the resource script appropriately. The exception is as I have given earlier: Windows Explorer will use the first Win32 icon it can find in the PE file as its icon. *First* means the icon resource with the lowest resource ID, or if the resources have names rather than numeric IDs, the first alphabetically. (Resources with string IDs are considered to be before resources with numeric IDs.) Typically, you will want to have at least one Win32 icon (and hence a resource script) in your project for this purpose.

Assemblies and Win32 Resources

You have to be careful of managed and unmanaged version resources clashing. I will go into more details about this in Chapter 5 when I cover .NET versioning. However, in this chapter, I will explain the problem from the point of view of resources. Win32 resources use the *VERSIONINFO* resource type to provide information about a file, but .NET uses custom attributes given in the *System::Reflection* namespace. These attributes are compared and summarized in Table 4-9. For the *VERSIONINFO* column, the items in all caps are members of *VERSIONINFO*, and the items in mixed case are members of the *StringFileInfo* block.

11. There is often a more straightforward way to access a resource, such as *LoadIcon*, but this method is the most generic and will work with all resource types.

Table 4-9 Win32 and .NET File Versioning

Attribute	VERSIONINFO	Description
[AssemblyCompany]	*CompanyName*	Your company's name
[AssemblyConfiguration]	*FILEFLAGS*	Information about the type of build
[AssemblyCopyright]	*LegalCopyright*	Your company's copyright
[AssemblyCulture]	no equivalent	The culture that the assembly was built for
[AssemblyDefaultAlias]	no equivalent	Friendly name for the assembly
[AssemblyDescription]	*FileDescription*	Description of the assembly
[AssemblyFileVersion]	*FileVersion*	Version of the file
[AssemblyFlags]	no equivalent	Information about how to load the assembly
[AssemblyInformationalVersion]	*Comments*	Additional information not used by the runtime
[AssemblyProduct]	*ProductName*	Name of the product that this assembly is a part of
[AssemblyTitle]	no equivalent	Title of the assembly
[AssemblyTrademark]	*LegalTrademark*	Your company's trademark
[AssemblyVersion]	*FILEVERSION*	Assembly version, used by the runtime

The *[AssemblyVersion]* attribute is important to the runtime and provides information that becomes part of the full name of an assembly. The equivalent member of *VERSIONINFO* is the *FILEINFO* member. Note, however, that although there is a logical connection between the two, there is no physical connection, so you can provide a different value for the managed file version and the unmanaged file version. Unfortunately, there is no simple solution to this problem. You have to manually change both versions when you change the version number.

Managed Resources

.NET resources are not stored in the PE .rsrc section; they are stored in the .data section along with the IL and metadata of the assembly. .NET resources can be added, compiled, or uncompiled. An uncompiled resource can be linked to your file with the */assemblyresource* linker switch. For example, if you have a .txt file with some text, it can be linked as a .NET resource with this command line:

```
cl /clr textreader.cpp /link /assemblyresource:text.txt
```

This command will add a managed resource named text.txt to the manifest:

```
.mresource public text.txt
{
}
```

To read this resource, you have to use the *Assembly::GetManifestResourceStream* method:

```
// textreader.cpp
#using <mscorlib.dll>
using namespace System;
using namespace System::IO;
using namespace System::Reflection;

void main()
{
   Assembly* assem = Assembly::GetExecutingAssembly();
   Stream* stm;
   stm = assem->GetManifestResourceStream(S"text.txt");
   StreamReader* sr = new StreamReader(stm);
   Console::WriteLine(sr->ReadToEnd());
   sr->Close();
}
```

GetManifestResourceStream returns a stream, and you can use the *Read* method to read the data as a byte array. Because I know that the resource is printable text I have used *StreamReader*, which will read the stream and convert the data to managed strings.

Note that the */assemblyresource* will embed a resource in an assembly. Compare this to the assembly linker tool, al.exe and the C# compiler, which both give you the option of embedding or linking resources to an assembly. You do not have this option with link.exe.

Compiled Managed Resources

You can also compile resources using the managed resource compiler resgen.exe. If a resource is compiled, you can use the classes in *System::Resources* to get access to the items in the resource. Compiled resources make the most sense for string table resources, but if you are willing to do the work, you can also add binary resources.

Here's a very simple resource file:

```
#this file is called data.txt
one=First Item
two=Second Item
three=Third Item
```

To compile this file, you use resgen.exe. This tool can take an input file with the extension of .txt or .resx (I'll return to this type in a moment) and output the compiled resources in a file with the extension .resources. This tool will also decompile compiled resources; if the input file is a .resources file, resgen will output the original source. Once you have compiled the resource, you link it to the assembly with the */assemblyresource* linker switch as before.

You can read a compiled managed resource in several ways. The first way is to get access to a stream to the resource in the manifest and use the *ResourceReader* class, as shown here:

```
Assembly* assem = Assembly::GetExecutingAssembly();
Stream* stm;
stm = assem->GetManifestResourceStream(S"data.resources");
ResourceReader* reader = new ResourceReader(stm);
IDictionaryEnumerator* e = reader->GetEnumerator();
while (e->MoveNext())
{
   String* key = static_cast<String*>(e->Key);
   String* value = static_cast<String*>(e->Value);
   Console::WriteLine(S"{0}={1}", key, value);
}
reader->Close();
```

The *ResourceReader* implements *IResourceReader* interface. The main method is the *GetEnumerator* function that allows you to iterate through the values sequentially. However, the function does not support random access. To retrieve specific values, you need to use a *ResourceManager*, as the following code shows:

```
ResourceManager* man;
man = new ResourceManager(S"data", assem);
Console::WriteLine(man->GetString(S"one"));
```

The *ResourceManager* is most useful for localization, which I will cover in a later section. The resource manager is initialized with the name of the assembly that has the neutral culture resource, but because this example does not have localized resources, this essentially means the assembly with the resource. The resource manager needs to know the resource to load, which is the purpose of the first parameter; the resource manager assumes that resources have an extension of .resources, so in this example, the resource manager will look for a resource in the manifest named data.resources.

After you have created a resource manager, you can ask the manager for a named resource. There are two overloaded methods to do this querying, *GetString* and *GetObject*. In this example, the resources are strings, so I have used *GetString* with the name of the string item to return. This code will return the string *First Item* because I have requested the *one* string.

The resource manager is based on a resource set. The resource set determines the class that will be used to read the resource. You can determine the resource set being used by the resource manager through *ResourceManager::GetResourceSet*. This method returns a *ResourceSet* pointer, and you can call *ResourceSet::GetDefaultReader* to get the *IResourceReader*. If you want to change the resource reader (or for that matter, the resource writer), you have to derive a class from *ResourceSet* and pass this class to the constructor of *ResourceManager*.

Resources can also be specified through XML files, as shown here:

```
<?xml version="1.0" encoding="utf-8"?>
<root>
  <!-- Header information about the version of the resource format
       and the classes used to read and write the resources -->
  <resheader name="resmimetype">
    <value>text/microsoft-resx</value>
  </resheader>
  <resheader name="version">
    <value>1.3</value>
  </resheader>
  <resheader name="writer">
    <value>
      System.Resources.ResXResourceWriter,
      System.Windows.Forms, Version=1.0.3300.0, Culture=neutral,
      PublicKeyToken=b77a5c561934e089
    </value>
  </resheader>
  <resheader name="reader">
```

```
    <value>
      System.Resources.ResXResourceReader,
      System.Windows.Forms, Version=1.0.3300.0, Culture=neutral,
      PublicKeyToken=b77a5c561934e089
    </value>
  </resheader>
  <!-- The resource data -->
   <data name="one">
      <value>First Item</value>
   </data>
   <data name="two">
      <value>Second Item</value>
   </data>
   <data name="three">
      <value>Third Item</value>
   </data>
</root>
```

This data is the bare minimum resource file. You will often find that .resx files will also have a schema. This data can be compiled with resgen.exe, which will generate a .resources file that can be linked to the final assembly. You can use the *ResourceManager* to read the compiled resource. So what is the advantage of using a .resx file rather than a .txt file? The advantage is that you can provide type information in .resx files that the resource reader will use to interpret the data.

```
<data name="background"
      type="System.Drawing.Color, System.Drawing,
         Version=1.0.3300.0,
         Culture=neutral,
         PublicKeyToken=b03f5f7f11d50a3a">
   <value>Green</value>
</data>
```

The *type* attribute gives the type of the data; in this case, it is *Color*; notice that I had to split this string over several lines to fit the format of this book. However, resgen expects the string to occupy a single line. The *ResourceManager* will read the appropriate section and then convert the value to the specified type.

```
// resdata.cpp
ResourceManager* man = new ResourceManager(S"data", assem);
Color __box* c = static_cast<Color __box*>(
                    man->GetObject(S"background"));
Console::WriteLine(c->ToString());
```

If the data type is a binary type, it has to be stored in the .resx file as a base64 encoded serialized object. The serialization can be done with either the *BinaryFormatter* or *SoapFormatter* and then encoded with *Convert::ToBase64String*. The *ResXResourceWriter* will generate the serialized objects with *BinaryFormatter* and *ResXResourceReader* will read objects serialized with *BinaryFormatter* or *SoapFormatter*. You indicate which formatter has been used through the *mime-type* attribute of the *<data>* tag, as shown in Table 4-10.

Table 4-10 Mime Types and the Formatters That Are Used

Mime Type	Formatter
application/x-microsoft.net.object.binary.base64	*BinaryFormatter*
application/x-microsoft.net.object.soap.base64	*SoapFormatter*

ResourceManager also has a *static* method named *CreateFileBased-ResourceManager*. This method takes two strings and a *Type*. The *Type* specifies the *ResourceSet* to use, and the two strings give the name of a folder to search and the base name of the resource. If the data.resx file is compiled to data.resources, the resources can be obtained through the resource manager obtained from the following code:

```
ResourceManager* man;
man = ResourceManager::CreateFileBasedResourceManager(
   S"data", S".", 0);
```

The *ResourceManager* class can also be initialized with a type, which allows you to associate a resource with the type that will use it. This constructor will create a resource name from the type name by appending .resources so that *MyNamespace::MyForm* has resources in *MyNamespace.MyForm.resources*. (Double colons are replaced by periods.) However, the resource manager actually goes one step further than this because it takes into account the locale where the code is running and uses this information to search for a localized resource, which leads us to localization.

Localization

We live in a global world of localized cultures. Not only is it good manners to provide localized versions of your application, but it also makes good business sense: people prefer to use software that is easy to use, and an application in a different language can hardly be described as being easy to use.[12]

Every thread has a culture. You can obtain this culture through the *Thread* properties *CurrentCulture* and *CurrentUICulture*. The first of these properties

12. Language is just one part of a culture. A few years ago, I bought a programming book and could read only the first 20 pages. The reason was that the author decided to use a baseball analogy throughout his description of network programming, and to an Englishman like me, this made the entire text incomprehensible.

returns a *CultureInfo* that describes the current culture used to format dates and numbers (obtained through the *CultureInfo::DateTimeFormat* and *CultureInfo::NumberFormat* properties). When a thread starts, this property is initialized from the locale obtained by calling *::GetUserDefaultLCID*. *CurrentUICulture* is used by the *ResourceManager* class and is first obtained by calling the Win32 *::GetUserDefaultUILanguage*. Both of these properties are read/write so you can change the current culture.

```
Thread::CurrentThread->CurrentUICulture =
   new CultureInfo(S"en-GB");
```

The *CultureInfo* class is initialized with a culture name in RFC1766 format. This name can be a culture—with a language and a region ID, in this case, UK English—or it can be a language identifier (for example, *en* for English).

Earlier I showed that compiled resources can have associated culture-specific or language-specific values, as shown in this example:

```
<!-- en resources -->
<data name= "btnStop">
   <value>Stop Search</value>
</data>
```

To use this data, you could name the compiled resource file with a culture identifier and then either embed this resource in your assembly or provide the resource as a stand-alone .resources file. At run time, you could then access *CurrentThread->CurrentUICulture*, and through the *CultureInfo::Name* property, you could access the name of the locale of the current machine and use this name to load the appropriate resource through *GetManifestResourceStream* or load the appropriate .resources file.

In fact, you do not have to go to all of this effort because *ResourceManager* will do this task automatically for you. The name of a managed resource follows this format:

```
<base name>.<culture>.resources
```

Here *<base name>* is the name that I have used so far when initializing the *ResourceManager* object, *<culture>* is the RFC1766 culture name, and for a neutral resource, this name (and the preceding period) can be omitted. An EXE assembly should be culture neutral and have the neutral culture resources bound to it. So if you are creating an assembly named *assem* with a resource named *MyResources*, the assembly will have a managed resource bound to it named *myresources.resources*.

The culture-specific resources should be bound to library assemblies that are culture-specific but have the same short name derived from the neutral assembly's short name. This arrangement is likely to cause a problem because the Windows file system cannot distinguish between such assemblies that have the same short name. To get around this problem, the culture-specific assemblies should be in subfolders named according to the culture.[13] Thus, the *MyResources.en-US.resources* resource should be in a library assembly named assem.resources.dll in a subfolder named *en-US*, and the *MyResources.en.resources* resource should be in a library assembly also named assem.resources.dll but this will be in a subfolder named *en*.

The assemblies that contain culture-specific resources contain no code and are named *satellite* assemblies. The name comes from the fact that they are associated with a culture-neutral assembly with the same resource name. You use the assembler linker tool, al.exe, to create a satellite assembly, as shown here:

```
al /embed:MyResources.en-US.resources /culture:en-US
   /target:library /out:assem.resources.dll
```

The assembly has the name of the *assembly* that it is associated with rather than the resource base name.

At run time, you can load the culture-specific resource using a resource manager, as the following code shows:

```
ResourceManager* man;
man  = new ResourceManager(
   S"MyResources", Assembly::GetExecutingAssembly());
```

The resource manager will obtain the current culture, and using this information, it will look for a satellite resource, that is, an assembly with the same short name as the specified assembly in a subfolder with the name of the current culture. If the satellite cannot be found (or the satellite does not have the culture-specific resource), the resource manager will attempt to load the culture-neutral resource. It is worth mentioning here that if you have problems with satellite assemblies, the Fusion log viewer is an invaluable tool because it tells you the names of the assemblies that the runtime is attempting to load.

If I build an assembly named assem.exe with the culture-neutral resource *MyResources.resources*, build a satellite assembly assem.resources.dll with the U.S. English resource *MyResources.en-US.resources*, and run assem.exe on a U.S. English machine, then the satellite assembly will be loaded and the resource manager will use the U.S.-specific resources. For any other locale the

13. Chapter 5 will look at placing assemblies in the global assembly cache, but for satellite resource assemblies, this subfolder naming scheme will be used.

culture-neutral resources will be loaded. I can force the runtime to load the U.S. resources by changing the current culture with the following code:

```
Thread::CurrentThread->CurrentUICulture =
   new CultureInfo(S"en-US");
ResourceManager* man;
man  = new ResourceManager(
   S"MyResources", Assembly::GetExecutingAssembly());
```

I will give examples of assemblies with satellite resources in Chapter 6, where I will illustrate how to use Visual Studio .NET build events and Makefile projects to create satellite assemblies in appropriate folders.

Summary

Win32 PE applications can be console applications and associated with a console window, or they can be GUI applications that run in their own window (or indeed, no window at all). When you compile your application, you should indicate whether the application is a console or GUI application through a linker switch or through the entry point of the application.

Your application, or a library assembly code used by an application, will need to create windows and draw on those windows. The managed code to create forms is the Windows Forms library, and the code to draw on windows is the GDI+ library. Both libraries are based on native Windows code, and you can interop your managed windowing code with Win32 code.

Your managed code might use resources, and these can be managed resources (compiled or uncompiled resources), or they can be unmanaged resources. Resources are important for localization and for versioning of your assemblies. These issues of versioning and localized cultures developed further in the following two chapters.

5

Systems Programming

From the chapters you have read so far, you will be aware that Microsoft Visual C++ .NET is the .NET systems programming language. C++ gives you the facility to do things that are not possible to do in other languages supported by the .NET Framework. If you are the sort of person who wants complete control, Visual C++ .NET is the language for you.

In this chapter, I will go into more depth about how .NET works and how you can configure it for your code. I will address the systems concepts of how assemblies are implemented and how to get information about the types that are implemented in assemblies. I will explain how assemblies are configured and how you can get configuration information. I will also explain how code access security protects your code and the implications of writing assemblies in C++ on code access security. Finally, I will show the unmanaged API for accessing the runtime and explain how you can use it.

Assemblies

Assemblies are the units of deployment, versioning, and security in .NET, and in this chapter, I will cover each of these issues. Assemblies can be made up of more than one file, but all code will be contained in the Microsoft portable executable (PE) files. Assemblies have to contain metadata (which is vital to how .NET works), and each code file in an assembly will have metadata. One file in the assembly will have information about all the other files in the metadata in a section named the *manifest*. This file, the one that contains the manifest, is your central point for investigating how assemblies work and the information that they contain.

Portable Executable Files

Code that executes on Windows is stored in a file format known as *portable executable*, which is an extension of the Common Object File Format (COFF). The PE file format is shown in Figure 5-1. A PE file consists of headers containing flags about the file and sections that contain code and data. For historical reasons, all PE files have an MS-DOS header that has a small amount of x86 code that will run under MS-DOS and print out the message *This program cannot be run in DOS mode*. The MS-DOS header can be identified by the two bytes *MZ*[1] at the beginning of the file. The four bytes at location 0x3c within the MS-DOS header are the offset of the PE header from the beginning of the file.

The PE header is made up of two structures, the COFF header and the PE header, and starts with a 4-byte signature, which is *PE* followed by 2 NUL bytes. The 20-byte COFF header contains information about the type of the machine that the file should be run on, the time and date that the file was created, and the characteristics of the file, which indicate things such as whether the file is a DLL or an EXE. The COFF header also gives the number of sections that are in the PE file.

The PE header immediately follows the COFF header, and the size of the PE header is a field in the COFF header. The PE header contains information about the version of the linker that was used, the size of the code and data sections, the versions of the target operating systems and subsystems, and various other flags. The PE header is 96 bytes followed by the data directory. (The size in the COFF header is the size of the fixed fields plus the size of the data directory.) The data directory contains sixteen 8-byte entries (although the data directory can obtain a different number of entries, current tools generate only 16 entries), where each entry is a relative virtual address (RVA) of the relevant table and the size of the table. An RVA is the location of the item when the file is loaded in memory relative to the load address of the file.

The values in the PE header can be viewed with the DUMPBIN tool using the */headers* switch. (This tool is just a stub for the linker with the */dump* switch.) DUMPBIN calls the COFF header *file header values*, and it calls the PE header *optional header values*. The current version of DUMPBIN also describes the fifteenth data directory as the *COM descriptor directory*; however, this description is likely an artifact from the various names that were used for .NET before the current name was chosen. The ECMA specification calls the fifteenth data directory the *CLI header*, and confusingly, you can obtain this information with the */clrheader* switch to DUMPBIN. The CLI header gives the RVA for the managed resources and the metadata directory. The managed resource directory holds the resources that you have added to your assembly through the linker */assemblyresource* switch. The CLI header also gives the minimum version of the runtime required to run

1. These are the initials of Mark Zbikowski, one of the original architects of MS-DOS.

the assembly, but curiously, this version is given as 2.0. I guess the reason for this odd versioning is that .NET was known as COM+ 2.0 during the early part of its development.

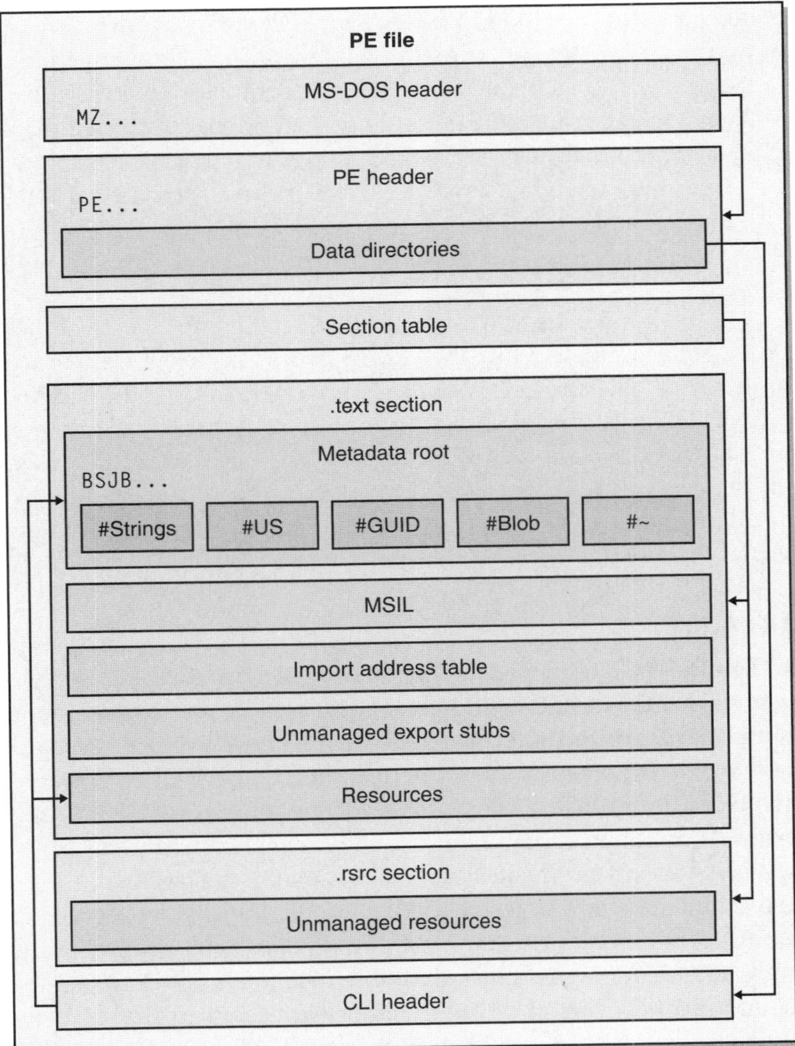

Figure 5-1 The PE file format

Immediately after the PE header is a section table that has 40 bytes for each entry. (The COFF header gives the total number of sections.) *Section* is the name of a part of the PE file that can contain either code or data. The section table indicates the name of the section, its size and position in the PE file, and whether the section contains code or data. If the section contains code, the entry in the section header indicates whether the code is readable or writable. Sections in PE files will be located at linker determined alignments. At run time, sections are *always* loaded at page boundaries. This combination of read/write characteristics and the fact that they are loaded at page boundaries implies that the main purpose of a section is to provide the basic information required by the Win32 virtual memory APIs.

Section names generated by Microsoft compilers always start with a period, but if you define your own sections with *#pragma data_seg* (for example, to declare a shared data section), you can use any name you want. Section names have a maximum of eight characters, and names longer than this will be truncated. Furthermore, they are not necessarily NUL terminated: the entry in the section table is *exactly* 8 bytes. The DUMPBIN */headers* switch gives this information for each section.

The PE header also gives the address of the entry point of the PE file. This code is simply a JMP to either the *_CorExeMain* or *_CorDllMain* function exported from mscoree.dll. This DLL is statically imported by all .NET modules and is the only .NET file that is copied to your machine's system directory. mscoree.dll is a shim DLL that forwards calls to the appropriate .NET system DLL (mscorwks.dll or mscorsvr.dll; see the section "Initializing the Runtime" later in this chapter).

All that I have described here is true of executable and library assemblies and of .NET module files.

Metadata Directory

One field in the CLI header is the RVA for the metadata directory, which gives access to all the metadata used by the assembly. The metadata directory starts with the string *BSJB* and has information about the version of the metadata and the version of the .NET Framework (as a string) that was used to create the assembly (documented as the *IMAGE_COR20_HEADER* structure in corhdr.h). After the header, the directory has information about the metadata streams that are used in the assembly. A metadata stream is a table holding information used by your code. The Microsoft intermediate language (MSIL) code in your types uses metadata tokens to identify elements that can be held in metadata (such as type names, member names, and user strings). A metadata token identifies which stream the metadata is held in and the location of the metadata in the stream. The various metadata streams that can be generated by the C++ compiler are given in Table 5-1.

When your code is compiled, the compiler will generate a metadata directory in the .obj file, and when the assembly is created, the linker will amalgamate the metadata directories from the various .obj files in your project. The compiler will add entries to the #~ stream for metadata items such as class definitions, class members, and references to externally defined classes. The actual names of these items are stored in the *#Strings* stream. You can see the entries that are stored in these streams by turning on the display of tokens in ILDASM. You turn on the display of tokens using the */tokens* switch, or using the */advanced* switch and selecting Show Token Values from the View menu.

Table 5-1 Metadata Streams

Stream	Description
#~	Optimized stream of the metadata tables*
#Blob	Holds internal metadata binary objects
#Guid	Holds GUIDs
#Strings	Holds the names of metadata items
#US	*User Strings*, holds user-defined strings

* .NET also defines a stream called #-, which is a non-optimized stream of metadata tables. Current tools only generate the optimized stream.

Metadata tokens identify both the stream and the location of the item in the stream. The top byte identifies the metadata table (one of the *CorTokenType* enumerated types documented in the corhdr.h). All of these tables except *mdt-String* can be found in the *#~* stream; the *mdtString* items are located in the *#US* stream. The lower three bytes of tokens for items in the *#~* stream give the record ID (RID) of the item in the stream. In contrast, the lower three bytes of tokens for items in the *#US* stream are an offset from the beginning of the stream of the item. For example, the code

```
Test* t = new Test;
String* str1 = S"Test1";
String* str2 = S"Test2";
```

will generate the following MSIL:

```
newobj instance void Test/* 02000003 */::.ctor() /* 06000008 */
stloc.2
ldstr "Test1" /* 70000001 */
stloc.1
ldstr "Test2" /* 7000000D */
stloc.0
```

The string *Test1* is stored as the first item in the *#US* stream. (All streams are indexed from 1.) The string is stored as a Unicode string (0xa bytes long) prefixed with the length of the entire entry. Metadata uses a compressed format for the length of the string so that strings with a short length will use a single byte for the length, which is the case for the *Test1* string: it has a length of 0x0b (0xa + 1). This layout means that the second string in the *#US* stream will be at location 0xd, which is the reason that the string *Test2* has the token 0x7000000d (a top byte of 0x70 is a user string). Here is the actual data held in the *#US* stream:

```
71c8 00 00 00 00 00 0b 54 00  ......T.
71d0 65 00 73 00 74 00 31 00  e.s.t.1.
71d8 00 0b 54 00 65 00 73 00  ..T.e.s.
71e0 74 00 32 00 00 00 00 00  t.2.....
```

The class *Test* is defined in this assembly, and it is the third definition, whereas the constructor is the eighth method defined in the assembly.

The definition of a type will be accessed through the #~ stream. I won't go into the fine details of how to obtain the definition of the type because the type is documented in the ECMA specification, which you can find in the Program Files\Microsoft Visual Studio .NET\FrameworkSDK\Tool Developers Guide\docs\Partition II Metadata.doc file. The various definitions that you can have in an assembly will be accessed through a table. The current specification defines 35 different tables and the format of those tables. The header to the #~ stream contains a 64-bit bit mask where each bit specifies whether a corresponding table is used in the assembly. The header is followed by an array of 32-bit integers giving the number of entries in each of the tables. This data is then followed by the actual table.

The metadata table for each type of metadata is different, so each entry for the *Module* table has 10 bytes, and each entry for the *TypeDef* table (used to give information about type definitions) has 20 bytes. The ECMA specification contains the schema for each table. A type definition contains an index into the *#Strings* stream for the name of the type and the namespace. The definition also gives an index into the *Field* and *Method* tables for the fields and methods implemented by the type. Each entry in the *Field* table has the RVA of the implementation of the method (the MSIL for the method).

Reading Metadata

The physical layout of assemblies and metadata is documented in the ECMA specification. The ECMA specification also documents the format of each IL opcode, so if you choose, you can write unmanaged (or managed) code to read an assembly, get information about the types implemented in the assembly and the types that the assembly uses, and dump the IL of those types. Of course, this process would be rather tedious, so Microsoft has provided two APIs to get access to metadata: reflection and the unmanaged metadata API.

The reflection API is a high-level managed API. It presents a logical view of metadata and is accessible from any .NET language. Reflection is concerned with metadata—the description of types—so it does not give access to MSIL. However, the API does allow you to invoke a method of a type, as shown in the following code:

```
// reflinvoke.cpp
String* str = S"Hello";
Type* t = str->GetType();
Type* params[] = new Type*[0];
// Get the overload of ToUpper that has no parameters.
```

```
MethodInfo* mi = t->GetMethod(S"ToUpper", params);
// Invoke the method. We know that the return value is a String*.
String* str2 = static_cast<String*>(mi->Invoke(str, 0));
Console::WriteLine(str2);
```

The unmanaged API is far closer to the physical layout of metadata in the PE file. This API is documented in the Tools Developers Guide supplied with the .NET Framework SDK (the Metadata Unmanaged API.doc and the Assembly Metadata Unmanaged API.doc files in the Program Files\Microsoft Visual Studio .NET\FrameworkSDK\Tool Developers Guide\docs directory) and is provided through COM objects. The interfaces and CLSIDs for these objects are declared in cor.h, and the types and enumerations used to describe metadata are declared in corhdr.h. The .NET Framework SDK comes with an example named *metainfo* that shows how to use these interfaces. This tool is also useful for probing into how metadata is stored in assemblies. The */heaps* switch for *metainfo* dumps the entries in the *#Strings*, *#US*, and *#Blobs* streams, and it will give information about the metadata tables that are present in the #~ stream. The */raw* switch will dump the entries in each table in the #~ stream and the schema of each table. Some of the entries in a metadata table will be an index into one of the other streams or into another table, but the information provided by this tool gives you enough information to determine the items in the assembly.

The metadata API is straightforward to use. The first stage is to access the metadata dispenser object, as shown here:

```
// dumptypes.cpp
IMetaDataDispenserEx* pDispenser;
CoCreateInstance(CLSID_CorMetaDataDispenser, NULL,
   CLSCTX_INPROC_SERVER, IID_IMetaDataDispenserEx,
   (void**)&pDispenser);
```

This is the gateway to the other metadata APIs. There are three metadata interfaces: *IMetaDataImport* and *IMetaDataAssemblyImport* and the lower-level interface *IMetaDataTables*. These are implemented by a separate object named the *scope* object, as the following code shows:

```
// dumptypes.cpp
IMetaDataImport* pImport;
pDispenser->OpenScope(strFile, 0,
   IID_IMetaDataImport, (LPUNKNOWN*)&pImport);
```

The *OpenScope* method returns an interface for an assembly in a file, and there is a version that returns the interface for an in-memory assembly. You can request *IMetaDataImport*, *ImetaDataAssemblyImport*, or *IMetaDataTables* from this method because they are all implemented on the scope object. You can get information about an individual item through its metadata token. The methods on *IMetaDataImport* will use the token to locate the item in the appropriate table in the #~ stream. You can get a token for an item either by requesting the item by name or by enumerating the items of a particular type. If you use an enumerator, you must free it once the enumeration has completed. When you have a token, you can call a method to get information about the specified object. Here is an example:

```
// dumptypes.cpp
HRESULT hr;
HCORENUM hEnum = 0;
mdTypeDef typeDefs[5];
ULONG count = 0;
do
{
   hr = pImport->EnumTypeDefs(&hEnum, typeDefs,
           sizeof(typeDefs)/sizeof(mdTypeDef), &count);
   for (ULONG idx = 0; idx < count; idx++)
   {
      ULONG size = 0;
      // Get the size of the name.
      pImport->GetTypeDefProps(typeDefs[idx], 0, 0, &size, 0, 0);
      LPWSTR strName = new WCHAR[size];
      DWORD flags;
      mdToken baseClass = 0;
      pImport->GetTypeDefProps(
         typeDefs[idx], strName, size, 0, &flags, &baseClass);
      LPCWSTR strType = TypeOfType(pImport, flags, baseClass);
      // If the class is nested, get the full name by
      // repeatedly accessing the name of the encloser class.
      if (IsTdNested(flags))
      {
         LPWSTR strEncloser = 0;
         mdTypeDef nestedType = typeDefs[idx];
         while (true)
         {
            // Get the token of the enclosing class.
            mdTypeDef encloser;
            pImport->GetNestedClassProps(nestedType, &encloser);
            LPWSTR str = GetTypeName(pImport, encloser);
            if (strEncloser == 0)
               strEncloser = str;
            else
            {
               // Prefix the name with the enclosing class.
               LPWSTR strTemp;
               strTemp = new WCHAR[lstrlen(strEncloser)
                                 + lstrlen(str) + 3];
               wcscpy(strTemp, str);
               wcscat(strTemp, L"::");
               wcscat(strTemp, strEncloser);
               delete [] strEncloser;
               delete [] str;
               strEncloser = strTemp;
            }
            // See if the encloser class is a nested class.
            pImport->GetTypeDefProps(
                        encloser, 0, 0, 0, &flags, 0);
```

```
            if (!IsTdNested(flags)) break;
            nestedType = encloser;
         }
         wprintf(L"%s %s::%s;\n",
               strType, strEncloser, strName);
         delete [] strEncloser;
      }
      else
         wprintf(L"%s %s;\n", strType, strName);
      delete [] strName;
   }
} while (count > 0);
if (hEnum) pImport->CloseEnum(hEnum);
```

EnumTypeDefs is called repeatedly until the enumeration is exhausted. The first time that the method is called it is passed zero as the first parameter. A handle to the enumeration is returned, and this handle is passed to *EnumTypeDefs* on subsequent calls. The method will attempt to fill the array with tokens and return the count of tokens that were returned. After the enumeration has completed, *CloseEnum* is called to clean up resources allocated for the enumeration.

For each token, I call *GetTypeDefProps* to get information about the type. This method can return the name, a token for the base class of the type, and a flags value that will return one of the values from the *CorTypeAttr* enumeration. The corhdr.h file defines various macros to check for various flags in this enumeration, and I will concentrate on just two flags (*tdInterface* and *tdClass*) and three macros (*IsTdInterface*, *IsTdClass*, and *IsTdNested*). If the class is nested within another class, the *IsTdNested* macro will return *true*, and to get the token of the enclosing class, you can call *GetNestedClassProps*. Because classes can be nested to multiple levels, I loop until I get to the top-level class.

EnumTypeDefs will return tokens of *__value* and *__gc* types; *__value* types can be classes or enums, and *__gc* types can be classes or interfaces, so the code needs to determine which of these four types the token refers to. The *tdInterface* flag is a nonzero flag that makes the positive assertion that the type is an interface. The *tdClass* flag is zero, so you check to see whether a type is an interface; otherwise, it is a noninterface type. However, there is no flag for value types or enumerations. The only way to check for these is to test the base class for the type. This test is the purpose of the *TypeOfType* method that I have defined, as shown here:

```
// dumptypes.cpp
LPCWSTR TypeOfType(IMetaDataImport* pImport, DWORD flags,
   mdToken baseClass)
{
   static LPCWSTR types[] =
   {
      L"__gc __interface",
      L"__gc class",
      L"__value class",
```

```
        L"__value enum"
    };
    int type = 0;
    if (!IsTdInterface(flags))
    {
        LPWSTR name = GetTypeName(pImport, baseClass);
        if (name != 0)
        {
            if (wcscmp(name, L"System.ValueType") == 0) type = 2;
            else if (wcscmp(name, L"System.Enum") == 0) type = 3;
            else type = 1;
            delete [] name;
        }
    }
    return types[type];
}
```

Here I use a static array of the types that you can have in .NET. If *IsTdInterface* returns true, the type is an interface. Otherwise, the method obtains the base class name and uses this to determine whether the type is an *enum*, a *__value* type, or a *__gc class* type.

The *GetTypeName* method returns the name of the base type. This process is a little more complex than calling *GetTypeDefProps* because *GetTypeDefProps* returns the properties of a type defined in the current scope, but the base class type might have been defined in another assembly, in which case you do not want to get the properties of a type *definition*, but of a type *reference*. Here is my implementation of *GetTypeName*:

```
// dumptypes.cpp
// This method returns a string allocated with the C++ new
// operator, so you must delete the value when you have finished
// with it.
LPWSTR GetTypeName(IMetaDataImport* pImport, mdToken baseClass)
{
    ULONG size = 0;
    LPWSTR name = 0;
    pImport->GetTypeDefProps(baseClass, 0, 0, &size, 0, 0);
    if (size == 0)
    {
        // Since the size is zero, we attempt to see if the token is
        // a type reference.
        pImport->GetTypeRefProps(baseClass, 0, 0, 0, &size);
        // Interfaces return a NUL character as the base class name
        // when they have no base interface.
        if (size > 1)
        {
            name = new WCHAR[size];
            pImport->GetTypeRefProps(baseClass, 0, name, size, 0);
            return name;
        }
        else
        {
```

```
            // There is no name.
            return 0;
        }
    }
    else
    {
        // The token is a type definition.
        name = new WCHAR[size];
        pImport->GetTypeDefProps(baseClass, name, size, 0, 0, 0);
        return name;
    }
    return 0;
}
```

Once you have a token to a type definition, you can get access to the members of the type. *EnumMembers* will return the methods and fields, or you can call *EnumMethods*, *EnumFields*, *EnumProperties*, or *EnumEvents* to get the specific members of the type. If the type implements interfaces, you can call *EnumInterfaceImpls* to get the tokens of these interfaces. Interfaces are the only types in .NET that do not have to have a base class. However, *GetTypeDefProps* will return a non-NULL token for the base class, and the name from this base class will be the single NUL character. This is why I test for this situation in *GetTypeName*.

The source code for this chapter has a screen saver that will print the types exported from all the assemblies in the .NET Framework folder. This screen saver is an unmanaged application and uses the unmanaged APIs that I have described here.

Assembly Format

An assembly contains a manifest, which is essentially a repository for information about the files that constitute the assembly, the resources it holds, the security permissions it requires, and the assemblies that the current assembly is statically linked to. The manifest is contained in a PE file, either a DLL or an EXE. This DLL is the file that you specify in a *#using* statement.

An assembly is made up from one or more *modules*. A module contains code and is a mechanism for the .NET runtime to load only the code that is actually being executed. I will go into more depth about building multimodule assemblies in Chapter 6. However, it is worth pointing out that you will rarely want to create an assembly with more than one module. Indeed, the .NET Framework assemblies are all single-module assemblies. There are two main situations in which you will want to have more than one module. The first case is when you have a library with types that you use frequently and types that you will rarely use. In this case, you can put the rarely used types in a separate module. When the assembly is loaded, the module with the frequently used types will be loaded, and the other module will be loaded into memory only in the rare situation in which the types it defines are referenced. The other situation in which you will use multiple modules is when the assembly is designed to be downloaded from another machine. You can put types that are likely to need updates in a separate module, and when you update a module, only this module will be downloaded. However, as you will find out in the section “Verifiable Code,” the C++ compiler cannot be used to create assemblies that are intended to be downloaded because the .NET loader will refuse to load such an assembly sourced from another machine.

Each module will have metadata containing information about the types that the module implements and the assemblies that it references. One module will contain the manifest. In addition to information about the types that this module implements and the assemblies it references, the manifest contains metadata about the other modules in the assembly and information about the assembly. You can view the manifest with ILDASM, but note that this tool identifies the tables of type definitions and assembly references as MANIFEST even if the module does not contain an assembly manifest.

Two important pieces of information in an assembly manifest are the security permissions required by the assembly (which will be covered in the section “Security” later in this chapter) and the complete name of the assembly. Because an assembly can be made up of more than one file, there must be some mechanism to name the entire assembly. When you build an assembly, you will get one or more PE files. The PE file that contains the manifest supplies the short name of the assembly; all assemblies have a short name. In addition, an assembly can have metadata to indicate the version, the culture, and a public key of the publisher of the assembly. The full name of an assembly is a combination of these four: the short name, version, culture, and public key. The version, culture, and public key for an assembly are provided through custom attributes.

Version

The version of an assembly is supplied through the *[AssemblyVersion]* attribute. The version is supplied as the parameter to this attribute as a string in this format:

<major>.<minor>.<build>.<revision>

Each part of the version string is a number, and each number is separated by a period. There is a major and a minor version, a build number, and a revision. You *must* provide the major version, and the rest can be regarded as optional and will be assumed to be zero if you do not specify them. If you provide an asterisk for the build, the compiler will generate the build number by calculating the number of days since the year 2000 from the build date, and then the compiler will generate the revision number by calculating the number of seconds from midnight module 2 from the build time. This mechanism means that each time an assembly is compiled, the build and revision are changed. If the assembly has a strong name (see the section “Assembly Strong Name” later in this chapter), the runtime will create the complete name of the referenced assembly using the version stored in the referring assembly. If the runtime cannot find an assembly with this *exact* name,[2] you will get a *FileLoadException*. The problem with using * within *[AssemblyVersion]* is that if the assembly is a library assembly and has a strong name, you have to compile the assemblies that use the library every time you recompile the library. Of course, you might decide to recompile the library because the public interface of the types exported from the assembly (that is, the public members of public types) has changed, so the users of the library must be recompiled to take advantage of the new public interface. If only the *implementation* of those types has changed, it should be unnecessary to recompile the users of the library.

Furthermore, when you use the *[AssemblyVersion]* attribute in a C++ file, the compiler will change the *.ver* metadata attribute, but it does not change the *VERSIONINFO* unmanaged resource in the final assembly. Because you have two versions to keep synchronized, it makes no sense to rely on the compiler to provide the values for the build and revision. For all of these reasons, I recommend that you do not use * in the version string for the *[AssemblyVersion]* attribute.

If you have multiple source files for your project, you should use *[AssemblyVersion]* in only one file; if you have this attribute in more than one source file, the linker will notice this duplication, issue a warning, and use the version in the .obj file that was last passed to the linker.

The .NET Framework also provides an attribute named *[AssemblyFileVersion]*, but this attribute has no effect on the assembly version. The compiler will add metadata for the attribute as a custom attribute. The compiler *does* read the attribute, and it will validate the value passed to the attribute to ensure that this string contains only numbers and periods. The parameter to *[AssemblyFileVersion]* is a string in the form *major.minor.build.revision*, but you can omit parts of the string except for *major*. Similar to the assembly version, the value passed in *[AssemblyFileVersion]* is not automatically used to update the *VERSIONINFO* unmanaged resource. You will have to manually synchronize the managed and unmanaged versions.[3]

Culture

The culture for an assembly is especially important for a library assembly that is used as a satellite assembly. The culture is also useful for library assemblies in general, but it is of no use for an EXE assembly because an EXE assembly should be culture neutral, and if it needs a localized resource, an EXE should use a satellite assembly. For this reason, the C++ compiler will issue an error

2. You can change this behavior with a configuration file. See the section "Locating Assemblies" later in this chapter.

3. I do this with a script that obtains the relevant files from Visual SourceSafe, changes the versions, and then checks the files back in. At each milestone in the development cycle, I can run the script for all the assemblies in the project and set the managed and unmanaged version to the same value.

when you attempt to add a culture to an EXE assembly. You add a culture to a library assembly through the *[AssemblyCulture]* attribute and pass the culture identifier to the constructor.

Assembly Strong Name

You give an assembly a strong name by providing a public/private key pair. When the assembly is built, the compiler will read the files that constitute the assembly and generate a hash for each one. This hash is added to the manifest of the assembly so that the .NET loader can check to see whether the file has changed when it is loaded. The default hash algorithm is SHA-1, but you can change the algorithm with the *[AssemblyAlgorithmId]* attribute. The options are given by the *AssemblyHashAlgorithm* enumeration, either SHA-1 or MD5.

Once the compiler has created the manifest, the compiler will create a hash (always using SHA-1) from the entire PE file that contains the manifest, and it will sign this hash with the private key that you provide. The hash and the public key are stored in the assembly (in a location that is not hashed) so that when an assembly is loaded, the loader can generate a hash and compare this hash with the signed hash in the assembly. If the two do not agree, the file has been tampered with and the loader will not load it. Note that the signing occurs on the file with the manifest; if an assembly has other modules, the hash of the module is not signed.

To create a public/private key pair, you run the sn.exe tool. This tool can create a key pair in a file, or it can put the key pair in a cryptographic container. Typically, you will only ever want to run this utility once to create the publisher key pair for your company. You can then use the same key pair for every assembly that you produce that has a strong name. Because you will only ever need one key pair, it makes sense to install this key pair into a cryptographic container so that the key pair will be available from any folder on your machine. It is a two-step process to put a key pair in a container. The first step is to generate a key pair in a file, as shown here:

```
sn -k RTG.snk
```

The file RTG.snk will contain the key pair. This file can then be installed in a key container—a part of the key database that contains all the key pairs (exchange and signature key pairs) belonging to a specific user—with the following:

```
sn -i RTG.snk RTG
```

The key pair in the file will be installed into the container named RTG. Each cryptographic service provider on your machine has a *key database* that is used to store persistent keys. There is a machine-wide database and a user-specific database. You can use the *-m* switch on *sn* to specify which database to use, and you can use the *-m* switch to check the current setting. (The machine key database is stored in the \Documents and Settings\All Users\Application Data\Microsoft\Crypto\RSA\MachineKeys folder, and the per-user database is stored in\Documents and Settings\<*User*>\Application Data\Microsoft\Crypto\RSA\<*SID*>, where <*User*> is the user's name and <*SID*> is the user's SID.)

To apply a strong name to an assembly, you use the *[AssemblyKeyFile]* or *[AssemblyKeyName]* attribute. The former is passed the name of the file that holds the key; the latter is passed the name of the crypto key container. You can view the public key that is added to the assembly using ILDASM, and you'll find that there is a metadata entry named *.publickey* that lists the key. It is interesting that the C++ compiler also adds a custom attribute for both of these even though this is unnecessary.

The public key is typically 600 bytes or so and is a key component of the strong name. However, if the name of an assembly contained the entire public key, the name would be extremely long, so instead of using the public key in the strong name, .NET uses a 64-bit hash of the public key named a *public key token*. The .NET Framework SDK exports functions from mscoree.dll to generate key pairs and public key tokens. These functions are prototyped in strongname.h, as shown in this example:

```
// Create a key pair.
LPBYTE key;
ULONG sizeKey;
StrongNameKeyGen(NULL, 0, &key, &sizeKey);
// Do something with the key pair.

// Create a token from the key pair.
LPBYTE token;
ULONG sizeToken;
StrongNameTokenFromPublicKey(key, sizeKey, &token, &sizeToken);

// We know that the token is 64 bits.
wprintf(L"\n%02x%02x%02x%02x%02x%02x%02x%02x\n",
   token[0], token[1], token[2], token[3],
   token[4], token[5], token[6], token[7]);

// Free the buffers used by the API.
StrongNameFreeBuffer(token);
StrongNameFreeBuffer(key);
```

The strong name APIs return buffers allocated by the API; you must free these buffers by calling *StrongNameFreeBuffer*. There are functions in strongname.h to install key pairs in a key container, to extract a public key from an assembly, to perform tasks, such as hash blobs of data and files, and to verify a signed manifest file. Clearly, the *sn* tool is implemented using these functions (and you can verify this by running the DEPENDS utility on mscoree.dll).

Assembly Configuration

One of the goals of .NET is to simplify application deployment. Microsoft calls this process *XCOPY deployment* because the implication is that you can simply copy the application (using Windows Explorer, or indeed, the command-line XCOPY command) to copy the application files to the target machine. Related to XCOPY deployment is *DEL uninstallation*. The idea is that when you want to remove an application from your system, you merely delete the files. Of course, not all applications can be installed and uninstalled in this way (applications that are Windows Services are an example), but the situation is certainly better than in the days before .NET. One area where Microsoft has made improvements to facilitate XCOPY deployment is in configuration.

In the early days of Windows, the preferred configuration technique was to use INI files: an application could store its settings in a global INI file named win.ini or in a private file. The API you use to read INI files is dated, and the format of these files is rather restrictive. Because these settings were file-based, while one application was writing to the INI file, the application had a lock on the file, so other applications could not have access.

To get around these problems, newer versions of Windows provide a hierarchical database named the *registry*. The actual underlying technology of this database is hidden from you through the API. However, access to the registry is more sophisticated than mere file access; it is a multiuser system where two threads can access different parts of the registry at the same time. Registry keys can have access control lists, so you can control who has access to a key. The API also has a simple mechanism to have global settings for all users (*HKEY_LOCAL_MACHINE*, commonly abbreviated HKLM) and to allow you to have settings specific to the current user (*HKEY_CURRENT_USER*, or HKCU). (If you have an account with sufficient privileges, you can even access the registry on another machine, which means that administrators have less distance to walk when administering machines.)

The problem with the registry comes in two forms: configuration and bloat. When an application is installed on a machine, the installation program must add values for the application into the registry to allow the application to run. Unless you have privileged knowledge about the values that the application needs, you have no choice but to use the installer program, which means that XCOPY deployment is not possible. When you remove an application, you also have to remove the registry entries, which brings me to bloat. Even if your applications do uninstall themselves properly, the registry is a hungry beast and will grow with time until its size reaches a user-specified setting, at which point you will get a dire warning from the system telling you to increase the registry size.[4]

The .NET Framework introduces a new configuration system. XML is ubiquitous in the .NET Framework, and it will come as no surprise to learn that the .NET Framework uses XML files to hold configuration information. It is interesting that Microsoft appears to have performed a U-turn with configuration files and has gone back to the old days of providing a user-readable file for each application, rather than a central repository. In this section, I will describe how configuration files are used and explain some nice configuration file features, but bear in mind that configuration files do not solve the issue of multiple threads accessing a single file locked by another thread writing to the file. The .NET configuration file API essentially ignores this issue by treating the files as read-only by applications. Furthermore, there are no per-user configuration files, so if you have an application that can be used by several users on the same machine, you will have to find another mechanism to save per-user settings.

Configuration Files

Each configuration file is an XML file and has the extension *.config*. The root element in a configuration file is named *<configuration>*; the other elements in a configuration file are defined by the configuration file schema and can be extended. Your machine will have configuration files for security and for applications. For applications, there will be a single, centralized file named *machine.config* that has configuration settings used by all applications. In addition, each application can have a configuration file that has a name in the form *<app>*.config, where *<app>* is the EXE file for the application, so an application named MyApp.exe will have a configuration file named MyApp.exe.config. You can also have files to configure .NET remoting, but these files are loaded in a different way than application configuration files, as I will explain in the section "Remoting" later in this chapter.

When you read a configuration section, you will get an amalgamation of the settings in the application file and the machine's configuration file. If there is a setting with the same name in both files, the application file setting takes precedence. Under the covers, when a configuration section is requested and it is found to exist in the application configuration file or the machine.config file, the setting is cached in a *Hashtable*. This mechanism reinforces the statement that I made earlier: configuration files are read-only because changes that are made while the application is running are not guaranteed to be readable by the application.

4. One situation where bloat is an issue is with COM object registration. The bloat associated with COM object registration is such an issue for the developer that I have gotten into the habit of adding a special value to the main key of my COM objects when built for DEBUG. I can then clean the registry at any time by running a utility that looks for the special value and then deletes the key and its subkeys.

Note that configuration files are for *applications*; you cannot have a configuration file for a library assembly. ASP.NET uses library assemblies, so to get around this restriction, ASP.NET applications have configuration files named *web.config* in the Web application's folder. This is all I will say about web.config files because this book is not about ASP.NET.

When you develop an application, you will find the application configuration file useful because there are settings that you can make to configure debugging options. (I will give details in Chapter 7.) Configuration files are also useful for deployed applications. There are two main scenarios: user configuration settings and run-time settings. User configurations settings are whatever you choose to use, and typically you will put these in the *<appSettings>* section of the file. (See the next section, "Application Settings".) Configuration files also have settings that are read by the runtime. You do not have to do anything to get the runtime to read the settings; the runtime will automatically load your configuration file and look for the values that it requires.

By default, Visual Studio .NET does not allow you to manage configuration files for C++ projects (although it does for C# projects). In Chapter 6, I will show how to use build events to manage configuration files. Common configuration file sections that you can have in an application configuration file are given in Table 5-2. Note that the capitalization used in the section name is important; if you use a different capitalization, the system will throw a configuration exception.

Table 5-2 Common Configuration File Sections

Section	Description
<appSettings>	Custom configuration settings
<configSections>	Allows you to extend configuration files
<runtime>	Information about garbage collection, assembly binding, and probing
<startup>	Information about the version of the runtime that the application requires
<system.diagnostics>	Settings for tracing applications
<system.net>	Configuration settings for the *System.Net* classes that allow you to use sockets
<system.runtime.remoting>	Configuration settings for remote objects and remoting channels
<system.web>	Configuration settings for ASP.NET applications

Application Settings

You can supply application settings in a configuration file through the *<appSettings>* section. Remember, the application regards these sections as read-only. The user of an application provides the application settings. Essentially, this section can be regarded as equivalent to command-line switches. Here is an example configuration file:

```
<!-- MyForm.exe.config -->
<configuration>
   <appSettings>
      <add key="BackColor" value="RED"/>
      <add key="Height" value="100"/>
      <add key="Width" value="200"/>
   </appSettings>
</configuration>
```

It is important to point out that these pairs are key-value pairs and *not* name-value pairs. Just about every exception I have ever received from using the *<appSettings>* section has been because I have used *name* instead of *key*. (The confusion occurs because other sections in configuration files are name-value pairs.) The few exceptions that I have had that have not been caused through using *name* have been caused because I have used the wrong capitalization in the section names.

There are several ways to read these settings. The simplest way is to use a class named *AppSettingsReader* in the *System::Configuration* namespace. This class has a single method named *GetValue* that is provided the name of the setting and the type. The method will read the setting and attempt to convert the value from a string to the type you specify by calling the *Parse* method on the target type. In this example, I want to specify a color but the *Color* class does not have a *Parse* method, so I specify that the setting is read as a string and I do the conversion myself:

```
// myform.cpp
Form* frm = new Form;
AppSettingsReader* reader = new AppSettingsReader;
String* strColor = static_cast<String*>(
   reader->GetValue(S"BackColor", __typeof(String)));
frm->BackColor = Color::FromName(strColor);
Int32 __box* width = static_cast<Int32 __box*>(
   reader->GetValue(S"Width", __typeof(Int32)));
frm->Width = *width;
Int32 __box* height = static_cast<Int32 __box*>(
   reader->GetValue(S"Height", __typeof(Int32)));
frm->Height = *height;
Application::Run(frm);
```

This code reads the *BackColor* setting as a string and then uses the *FromName* method to create a color from a known color name. This color value is then used for the background color of the form. The code also reads the *Width* and *Height* settings, but because *Int32* does have a *Parse* method, the code can allow *GetValue* to do the conversion.

The other way to read values in the *<appSettings>* section is to read the entire section in one go and access these settings through a collection, and to perform this task, you use the *Configuration::AppSettings* static property. The *<appSettings>* section, like many sections in a configuration file, has nested sections, and to help you read these, the .NET Framework defines collection classes (which I will cover in the section "Configuration Section Handlers" later in this chapter).

```
// myform2.cpp
Form* frm = new Form;
AppSettingsReader* reader = new AppSettingsReader;
String* strColor =
   ConfigurationSettings::AppSettings->Item[S"BackColor"];
frm->BackColor = Color::FromName(strColor);
String* strWidth =
   ConfigurationSettings::AppSettings->Item[S"Width"];
frm->Width = Int32::Parse(strWidth);
String* strHeight =
   ConfigurationSettings::AppSettings->Item[S"Height"];
frm->Height = Int32::Parse(strHeight);
Application::Run(frm);
```

Configuration::AppSettings is a *NameValueCollection*, which has an indexer property. You pass the name of the setting as the parameter to the *Item* property, and it will return back a string. Even if the setting is for a type that has a *Parse* method (as in this case with *Width* and *Height*), you still have to explicitly convert from a string.

You can also have an *<appSettings>* section in the machine.config file that will hold global settings used by all applications. At run time, you will get a combination of the settings from machine.config and from your own application configuration file. This arrangement means that your application might inherit settings from machine.config that the user does not want the application to receive. To remove an individual item, you can use the *<remove>* tag in the application configuration file; to remove all the settings inherited from the machine.config file, you can use the *<clear>* element.

If you have many items in your configuration file, you might decide it would be better to split the file into two files. You can do this operation with the *<appSettings>* section by providing a *file* attribute to the tag:

```
<configuration>
   <appSettings file="otherSettings.xml">
      <add key="BackColor" value="RED"/>
   </appSettings>
</configuration>
```

The system reads the application settings in the application configuration file first, followed by the settings in the file you specify. If any settings are replicated, the values given in the file specified by the *file* attribute will take precedence. For this example, the extra file would look like this:

```
<!-- otherSettings.xml -->
<appSettings>
   <add key="BackColor" value="GREEN"/>
   <add key="Height" value="100"/>
   <add key="Width" value="200"/>
</appSettings>
```

Notice that the root of this file is *<appSettings>*. The application will create a green form because the value in this file will be used instead of the value provided by the application configuration file. Although this facility is of some use, I can see that it could have been even more useful. For example, if I could give the name of an environment variable for the file, I would have a very simple mechanism to provide per-user settings through the *%USERNAME%* variable. Sadly, the mechanism does not work this way.

Diagnostic Switches

The *<system.diagnostics>* section has several values that you can use to determine how debugging actions and tracing occurs in your application, and I will defer discussion of these until Chapter 7. However, it is interesting to take a look at one of the sections, *<switches>*. If you have a need for an integer value in a configuration file, you can put it in the *<switches>* section and read the value directly using a class derived from *Switch*. This class is abstract, and the .NET Framework provides an implementation named *BooleanSwitch* that interprets the value as either true or false. The documentation in MSDN says that you should enable tracing or debugging in your application to use switches. However, you can safely ignore this advice because the runtime makes no check. Using *BooleanSwitch* is simple: in the configuration file, you add a *<switches>* section, as shown here:

```
<!-- Bool.exe.config -->
<configuration>
   <system.diagnostics>
      <switches>
         <add name="Value" value="1"/>
      </switches>
   </system.diagnostics>
</configuration>
```

Notice that this setting is a name-value pair. You provide the name of the switch to the constructor of *BooleanSwitch*, and curiously, you also provide a description of the switch, as shown in the following code:

```
// bool.cpp
BooleanSwitch* value = new BooleanSwitch(S"Value",
   S"description");
if (value->Enabled) Console::WriteLine(S"Enabled");
else Console::WriteLine(S"Not enabled");
```

The description parameter is ignored by the .NET Framework, and I guess this behavior is left over from an earlier version of this class developed during the beta cycle of the Framework classes.[5] If the switch does not exist in the configuration file or if it has a value of zero, the switch is considered not to be enabled, so the *Enabled* property returns false. Otherwise, the property will be true. The property is read/write, which would suggest that you could use this property to write to configuration files. Alas, this is not the case; the set method of the property is used for another purpose. *BooleanSwitch* derives from *Switch*, which has a protected virtual method named *OnSwitchSettingChanged*. The set method of *Enabled* calls *OnSwitchSettingChanged*, which does nothing in both *BooleanSwitch* and *Switch*. However, you could derive your own class from *BooleanSwitch* and implement *OnSwitchSettingChanged*, which performs some action when the switch is changed programmatically.

Indeed, you can derive a class from *Switch* to read a value from the configuration file. *Switch* has a property named *SwitchSetting* that will read the switch with the name passed to its constructor. This property is a 32-bit integer.

Remoting

The remoting section holds many values that are used to configure .NET remoting. I won't go into the details here because to do so would require a complete description of .NET remoting and contexts.[6] However, it is interesting to note that remoting sections are not automatically read by the system. Instead, you have to explicitly call *RemotingConfiguration::Configure* and pass the name of the file that contains these configuration sections.

Startup

An application can indicate that it runs under a specific version of the runtime through the *<requiredRuntime>* element in a configuration file, as shown here:

```
<configuration>
   <startup>
      <requiredRuntime version="v1.0.3705.0"/>
   </startup>
</configuration>
```

The runtime checks the major and minor version given in the configuration file. If the specified version of the runtime is not installed on the machine, the application will not be loaded.

---

5. The beta versions of this class also allowed you to set a switch as an environment variable or in the registry, but the release version only supports configuration files.

6. And there is no better source for such a description than my book *Developing Applications with Visual Studio .NET* (Addison Wesley, 2002), ISBN 0-201-70852-3.

Configuration Section Handlers

The machine.config file can be found in the CONFIG folder in the .NET Framework system folder (in the %systemroot%\Microsoft.NET\Framework\<*version*> folder, where <*version*> is the version of the .NET Framework that you have installed). This file contains a description of all the sections that you can include in a configuration file in a section named <*configSections*>. I will explain this section in more detail in the next section ("Custom Configuration Sections"); however, I want to point out here that these settings indicate the name of a handler that will be used to read the section. For example, here is the value for the <*appSettings*> section:

```
<!-- machine.config -->
<configuration>
   <configSections>
      <section name="appSettings"
         type="System.Configuration.NameValueFileSectionHandler,
            System, Version=1.0.3300.0, Culture=neutral,
            PublicKeyToken=b77a5c561934e089"/>
   </configSections>
</configuration>
```

This value indicates that the handler for this section is *NameValueFileSectionHandler* in the *System::Configuration* namespace. As I mentioned earlier, this handler is misnamed because it reads key-value pairs. This class is poorly documented in the MSDN library, which merely says: "This type supports the .NET Framework infrastructure and is not intended to be used directly from your code." However, this type, and the other handlers in the *System::Configuration* namespace, should have been documented better if only to give a clue as to the type of collection that is used to hold the configuration sections that they handle.

The terse documentation in the MSDN library is right in one respect: you do not use these classes yourself; instead, you use a class named *ConfigurationSettings*. This class has a static method named *GetConfig* to which you pass the name of the section that you want to read. This method will return an instance of the collections identified in Table 5-3.

Table 5-3 Collections for .NET Framework Configuration Section Handlers

Handler	Collection
DictionarySectionHandler	*System::Collection::Hashtable*
DiagnosticsConfigurationHandler	*System::Collection::Hashtable*
IgnoreSectionHandler	
NameValueFileSectionHandler	*System::Collection::Specialized::NameValueCollection*

Table 5-3 Collections for .NET Framework Configuration Section Handlers *(continued)*

Handler	Collection
NameValueSectionHandler	*System::Collection::Specialized::NameValue-Collection*
SingleTagSectionHandler	*System::Collection::Hashtable*

I have not given a collection for the *IgnoreSectionHandler* class because as the name suggests, when *GetConfig* is asked to read a section with this type, a NULL pointer will be returned. The implication is that the section is not intended to be read using *GetConfig*.

As an example of using *GetConfig*, you can get access to the *<system.diagnostics>* section with the following code:

```
// sections.cpp
Hashtable* h;
h = static_cast<Hashtable*>(
   ConfigurationSettings::GetConfig(S"system.diagnostics"));
IDictionary* d =
   static_cast<IDictionary*>(h->Item[S"switches"]);
IEnumerator* e = d->Keys->GetEnumerator();

while (e->MoveNext())
{
   Console::WriteLine(S"switches[{0}] = {1}",
      e->Current, d->Item[e->Current]);
}
```

When this code calls *GetConfig*, the method will create an instance of the *DiagnosticsConfigurationHandler* class, which will read the specified section and return a *Hashtable* containing the items. The *<system.diagnostics>* section can have nested collections. The *Hashtable* class implements *IDictionary*—that is, it is an associative container, so I can access the *Item* property to get a specific item. In this case, I access the *<switches>* collection, which returns another *IDictionary* interface that I can use to iterate over all the items in the section.

If you look through the *<configSections>* section in machine.config, you will see that there are some sections that are declared with *<sectionGroup>* rather than *<section>*. Such sections have nested sections, and the *<sectionGroup>* element allows you to identify the section handler. As you can see with *<appSettings>*, a section can have a single handler even though it has nested sections, but in this case, the handler provides a collection with all the data. The *<sectionGroup>* element allows you to provide collections better suited to the nested section.

The *<sectionGroup>* element does not have a type associated with it, so there is no handler and you cannot pass the name of the group to *GetConfig*. Instead, you have to pass the group name and section within that group concatenated with a /. For example, to get the *<webControls>* section within the *<system.web>* section group, you call:

```
Hashtable* h = static_cast<Hashtable*>(
   ConfigurationSettings::GetConfig(S"system.web/webControls"));
```

Custom Configuration Sections

You can create your own configuration section handlers. To do so, you should create a class that implements *IConfigurationSectionHandler* and add entries to the configuration file to identify the new section handler. For example, the following configuration file defines a new section named *<appData>*, which I intend to use for my own application data. *<appData>* is a group, but I have defined just one child section named *<window>* that is handled by a class within the assembly named *WindowConfig*[7]:

```
<!-- dynamicForms.exe.config -->
<configuration>
   <configSections>
      <sectionGroup name="appData">
         <section name="window"
                  type="WindowConfig,dynamicForms" />
      </sectionGroup>
   </configSections>

   <appData>
      <window Name = "mainForm" Text = "Test Window"
              Width = "400" Height = "150"
              FormBorderStyle = "FixedDialog">
         <controls>
            <control class = "TextBox" Name = "txt"
               Multiline = "true" Dock = "Top" Height = "50" />
            <control class = "Button" Name = "btn"
               Dock = "Bottom" Height = "50" Text = "Press Me" />
         </controls>
      </window>
   </appData>
</configuration>
```

In this configuration file, I declare an *<appData>* section with a child *<window>* section. *<window>* is used to describe a form that contains controls. The *<window>* tag has attributes for the form, and these attributes conveniently have the same name as properties of the *Form* class. To declare the controls that go on the form, I use a section named *<controls>* that is a collection of *<control>* elements. The *<controls>* and *<control>* tags are not mentioned in the *<configSections>* because they do not have a specific handler. It is the responsibility of *WindowConfig* to parse this data. The *<control>* element describes a control in the *System::Windows::Forms* namespace, the *class* attribute

7. This class is in the global namespace. If the class was in a named namespace, I would have to give the complete name, including the namespace using a period as the scope resolution operator.

is the name of the control class, and the other attributes are names of properties of the *Control* class.

The *WindowConfig* class implements *IconfigurationSectionHandler*, which has a single method named *Create*:

```
Object* Create(Object* parent, Object* ctx, XmlNode* sec);
```

This method is passed the XML of the section that it is to parse in the final parameter. In my case, this will be the *<window>* element. The other parameters are not relevant in this discussion. The *Create* method should parse the XML and then return the configuration object that is returned from the *GetConfig* method. Note that there is no indication of the type of the object that will be returned from this method. It would have been nice if the designers of the .NET Framework had added an extra attribute to *<section>* for a developer to provide the type of the configuration object. Instead, you have to call *GetConfig* and use *Object::GetType* to determine the type. My implementation of *Create* will read the items in the <window> section and use it to construct a *Form* object. Here is the code:

```
// dynamicForms.cpp
// This is the handler class for the custom section.
// It creates a window based on the items in the config file.
public __gc class WindowConfig :
   public IConfigurationSectionHandler
{
public:
   // Create a new Form object based on the
   // data in the config file.
   Object* Create(Object* parent, Object* ctx, XmlNode* sec)
   {
      // Make sure that we are passed an XML node from the file.
      // If sec is zero, we cannot create a form.
      if (sec != 0)
      {
         // Make sure that we are passed the <window> section.
         if (!sec->Name->ToLower()->Equals(S"window")) return 0;

         Form* frm = new Form;
         // Initialize the form's properties with the items
         // passed as attributes of the main node.
         InitProperties(sec, frm);

         // Get the <controls> collection so that we can create
         // the controls on the form.
         XmlNode* controls = sec->Item[S"controls"];
         if (controls != 0)
         {
            // We need to get a display name of
            // system.windows.forms so that we can pass
            // this information to CreateInstance.
            Assembly* swf = frm->GetType()->Module->Assembly;
```

```
            try
            {
               // Iterate through all of the <control> nodes.
               IEnumerator* en = controls->GetEnumerator();
               while (en->MoveNext())
               {
                  XmlNode* control =
                     static_cast<XmlNode*>(en->Current);
                  // Each node must have a class name.
                  if (control->Attributes->ItemOf[S"class"] == 0)
                     continue;

                  // Create the specified control.
                  ObjectHandle* oh;
                  String* strCtrl = String::Concat(
                     S"System.Windows.Forms.",
                     control->Attributes->
                     ItemOf[S"class"]->Value);
                  oh = Activator::CreateInstance(swf->FullName,
                     strCtrl);
                  Control* ctrl =
                     dynamic_cast<Control*>(oh->Unwrap());

                  // Initialize the properties of the control
                  // from the <control> node attributes.
                  InitProperties(control, ctrl);

                  // Add the control to the form.
                  frm->Controls->Add(ctrl);
               }
            }
            catch(Exception*){/* do nothing */}
         }

         return frm;
      }
      return 0;
   }
private:
   // This is used to initialize the properties of a control
   // using the attributes in a node.
   void InitProperties(XmlNode* node, Control* ctrl);
};
```

This method parses the XML passed through the *sec* parameter. I won't go into the fine details of how to use the .NET Framework XML classes. Instead, I will focus on what the code does with the data. The first action is to create the form, so the code first checks to ensure that the XML refers to the *<window>* section and then creates a form passing this object and the XML to a member function named *InitProperties*, which will parse through the element's attributes and use these to initialize the properties on the *Form* object. I will show *InitProperties* in a moment.

Next the code obtains the *<controls>* element, and for each one, it creates a control. Because *Create* does not know the type of control to create, it has to create instances dynamically through *Activator::CreateInstance*. I use the overloaded version of this method that has two strings: the name of the assembly that contains the type and the name of the type. The name of the assembly must be the full name of the *system.windows.forms* assembly. Because the *Form* class is in this assembly, I can get the assembly object with this line:

```
Assembly* swf = frm->GetType()->Module->Assembly;
```

The full name of the assembly is returned through the *Assembly::FullName* property. *Activator::CreateInstance* also needs the full name of the type, which I create by prefixing the control name with *System.Windows.Forms.*, using a period as the separator. *Activator::CreateInstance* returns an *ObjectHandle*, and I can get the actual object by calling *Unwrap* and then casting to *Control*. I can then initialize this object with *InitProperties* before adding it to the form's *Controls* collection.

InitProperties looks like this:

```
// dynamicForms.cpp
private:
   void InitProperties(XmlNode* node, Control* ctrl)
   {
      // Iterate through all the attributes.
      IEnumerator* en = node->Attributes->GetEnumerator();
      while (en->MoveNext())
      {
         XmlNode* attr = static_cast<XmlNode*>(en->Current);
         PropertyInfo* pi;
         // See if the control has a property with the same name.
         // Note that the capitalization used in the config file
         // must be exactly right.
         pi = ctrl->GetType()->GetProperty(attr->Name);
         if (pi != 0)
         {
            // Enumerated values cannot be converted from strings
            // using the Convert class.
            if (pi->PropertyType->IsEnum)
            {
               // Initialize the property.
               Object* val = Enum::Parse(
                  pi->PropertyType, attr->Value);
               pi->SetValue(ctrl, val, 0);
            }
            else
            {
               // Initialize the property.
               Object* val = Convert::ChangeType(
                  attr->Value, pi->PropertyType);
               pi->SetValue(ctrl, val, 0);
            }
         }
      }
   }
```

In this code, I iterate through all the attributes of the XML node. I use the name as the name of the control's property, and the value of the attribute as the value of the property. Once I have the property name, I use reflection to get information about the property, including its type. So that I can set the property, I need to convert the string value given in the configuration file to the actual type of the property. If the property takes a type other than an enumerated type, I can use *Convert::ChangeType*. For enumerated values, I have to use *Enum::Parse*.

Using this handler is simple, as shown here:

```
Form* frm = static_cast<Form*>(
   ConfigurationSettings::GetConfig(S"appData/window"));
if (frm != 0)
   Application::Run(frm);
else
   MessageBox::Show("No form in config file");
```

Because the *<window>* section is a child section, I use *appData/window* as the name of the section.

Writing to Configuration Files

The configuration file API is essentially a read-only API, which is a pity because you cannot programmatically change settings set via a user interface and have these persisted for the next run of the application. Of course, configuration files are just XML files, so you can use the .NET Framework XML classes to change the file. The *System::Data::DataSet* class provides a convenient way to do this because it presents the XML data in the form of a database. Here is a class that will do this work:

```
// write.cpp
__gc class ConfigWriter : public IDisposable
{
public:
   DataSet* data;
   bool bChanged;
   ConfigWriter()
   {
      data = new DataSet;
      data->ReadXml(
         AppDomain::CurrentDomain->SetupInformation->
         ConfigurationFile);
      bChanged = false;
   }
   void ChangeValue(String* name, String* value)
   {
      if (data == 0)
      {
         throw new ObjectDisposedException(
            S"data", S"Dataset object is disposed");
      }
      DataTable* dt = data->Tables->Item[S"appSettings"];
      if (dt != 0)
```

```
        {
            DataRelation* add;
            add = dt->ChildRelations->Item[S"appSettings_add"];
            if (add != 0)
            {
                // Iterate through each <add> looking for Value.
                DataTable* addTable;
                addTable = static_cast<DataTable*>(add->ChildTable);

                IEnumerator* e = addTable->Rows->GetEnumerator();
                bool bSucceeded = false;
                while (e->MoveNext())
                {
                    DataRow* dr = static_cast<DataRow*>(e->Current);
                    String* val =
                        static_cast<String*>(dr->Item[S"key"]);
                    if (val->Equals(name))
                    {
                        // Set the value.
                        dr->Item[S"value"] = value;
                        bChanged = true;
                        bSucceeded = true;
                        break;
                    }
                }
                if (!bSucceeded)
                    throw new ArgumentException(
                        String::Concat(S"Cannot find ", name));
            }
            else
            {
                throw new ConfigurationException(
                    S"cannot find <add> section");
            }
        }
        else
        {
            throw new ConfigurationException(
                S"cannot find <appSettings> section");
        }
    }
    void Flush()
    {
        if (data == 0)
        {
            throw new ObjectDisposedException(
                S"data", S"Dataset object is disposed");
        }
        if (bChanged)
        {
            data->AcceptChanges();
            data->WriteXml(
                AppDomain::CurrentDomain->SetupInformation->
                ConfigurationFile);
```

```
        }
    }
    void Dispose()
    {
        Flush();
        if (data != 0) data->Dispose();
        data = 0;
    }
};
```

There are a few points to be made about this class. The class is based on a disposable resource, so it should also be disposable. Therefore, the class keeps a Boolean member that determines whether a change has been made, and if so, the *Flush* method will write the data to the configuration file. The constructor of this class opens the *DataSet* object using the configuration file. The name of this file is taken from the name of the default name for the current application domain. The *ChangeValue* method can be called to change any value in the *<appSettings>* section. First this method obtains the table named *appSettings* from the dataset, and then it checks to see whether there is a child table for all the *<add>* elements. To do this, it looks for a child relation named *appSettings_add*. If there is a child relation with this name, there will be a table where each row is an *<add>* element, and each column of these rows will be an attribute of the *<add>* element. The code simply checks the *key* column to see whether the element is the one that has been requested, and then the code changes the *value* column to the appropriate value. If the specified element does not exist, the class throws an exception. I was tempted to handle this situation by creating a new element with the suggested values. However, there is a bug in the *DataTable* class, so a new row is added to the child relation outside of the *<appSettings>* element. The source code for this chapter shows an alternative solution that uses the *System::Xml* classes to write to a config file that can add new elements.

Here is some code that uses the *ConfigWriter* class to keep a count of how many times the application has been run:

```
void main()
{
    AppSettingsReader* reader = new AppSettingsReader;
    int i = *static_cast<Int32 __box*>(
        reader->GetValue(S"RunCount", __typeof(Int32)));
    i++;
    Console::WriteLine(S"This is run number {0}", __box(i));

    ConfigWriter* writer = new ConfigWriter;
    writer->ChangeValue(S"RunCount", i.ToString());
    writer->Dispose();
}
```

Bear in mind that the *DataSet* class has to parse the XML and this task does take a while. So although it is possible to write to configuration files, the message is clear: .NET configuration files were designed as read-only files.

Per-User Configuration Files

There is no mechanism to tell the runtime to read a configuration setting based on the currently logged-on user. I regard this as a serious deficiency in the configuration file API because without such a facility, all users will get the same settings. You might decide that only certain users should get particular features, or you might decide that you want to persist user settings such as the last file loaded by a word processing application. In this situation, the registry API excels: all you need to do is create a key under the *HKEY_CURRENT_USER* hive, and the API will determine the current user and store the data in a registry file specifically for that user.

So how do you do this in .NET? There are several ways, and I will outline a few. The most obvious is to use the registry classes in the Microsoft.Win32 assembly to access the *HKEY_CURRENT_USER* hive. However, this strategy breaks the idea of XCOPY deployment and DEL uninstallation because if you copy the application to another machine, you will not copy its configuration settings, and if you delete the application, its settings will still remain in the registry.

You can obtain the currently logged-on user by reading the *USERNAME* environment variable, as shown here:

```
String* strUser = Environment::GetEnvironmentVariable(S"USERNAME");
```

You could use this to create a configuration file with a name derived from the *USERNAME* variable. Under the covers, the configuration system appears to give some hope of specifying a configuration file other than the one derived from the application name. The *AppDomain* class has a read-only property named *SetupInformation* that is an *AppDomainSetup* object. The *SetupInformation* class has a read/write property named *ConfigurationFile* that gives the full path to the application configuration file. (I used this property in *ConfigWriter* in the previous section.) Having the *ConfigurationFile* property read/write would imply that you could change this property and then create an *AppSettingsReader* object based on this new file. Sadly, you cannot do this operation because each *AppSettingsReader* object is actually created from the static *ConfigurationSettings::AppSettings* property, and *AppSetings* reads its values from the file determined by *ConfigurationSettings::GetConfig* the first time it is called. *GetConfig* obtains the configuration name from the current application domain and caches these values in a private member for future use. *GetConfig* is called by the runtime when an application is started, so from that point onward, the name of the application configuration file has been cached and cannot be changed. Your only option is to read in the values from a custom configuration file by reading the XML, with the *DataSet* class or with the *XmlDocument* class, as shown in this code:

```
AppDomainSetup* setup =
   AppDomain::CurrentDomain->SetupInformation;
String* strUser =
   Environment::GetEnvironmentVariable(S"USERNAME");
String* strConfig;
```

```
strConfig = String::Concat(setup->ApplicationBase,
   strUser, S".config");
DataSet* config = new DataSet;
config->ReadXml(strConfig);
// Read the per-user settings.
```

If you perform this operation, you do not get the advantage of the merging of configuration data. So if you determine that the per-user configuration file does not have a specific setting, you will have to explicitly check the application configuration for the setting to see whether there is a default value for all users. You could get around this problem by merging the XML for the section from the per-user configuration file, the application configuration file, and machine.config, but the details about how to perform this task are beyond the scope of this book.

The advantage of the scheme I outlined above is that you can store the configuration file in the same folder as the application so that you preserve the idea behind XCOPY deployment and DEL uninstallation.

Another way to provide per-user configuration settings would be to add per-user sections to the application configuration file, as shown in this example:

```
<configuration>
   <users>
      <user name="Richard">
         <lastDoc>chapter5.doc</lastDoc>
      </user>
      <user name="Ellinor">
         <lastDoc>accounts2002.doc</lastDoc>
      </user>
   </users>
</configuration>
```

There are several disadvantages to this solution. Here are two. The first problem is that the *<users>* section needs to have a section handler to allow you to access the settings, so you need to write this class (and a corresponding class to write values to the appropriate section). Second, the settings for all users are stored in the same file. This means that if I copy the application and its configuration file to another machine, I get the settings for all users even if the only user on the new machine is me.

Versioning and Fusion

One of the goals of .NET is to solve the problem of DLL Hell. To a certain extent, if everyone plays by the rules, DLL Hell would never occur; however, few people know what the rules are and fewer still follow them.[8] COM tried to

8. Put succinctly, the rules are that if you update a library, you should only add functionality. You should not remove or change functionality used by older applications. If you cannot guarantee this behavior, you should ensure that your library does not replace earlier versions and cannot be loaded by older applications.

solve this problem by basing versioning on absolute names of interfaces and classes with the implied rule that a new implementation means a new name (CLSID) for the implementation, but again, people broke that rule.

Windows introduced the idea of redirection files, empty files with the same name as the application file but with the extension .local, which indicated to the system to load DLLs from the local folder before following the *LoadLibrary* search algorithm. This system protects against loading the wrong version of a DLL, but it does not protect against replacing a DLL with a newer, incompatible version. To protect against this incompatibility, Windows introduced the idea of *protected* and *shared* DLLs. When a DLL is registered as shared, a reference count is maintained in the registry. When an installer installs an application that uses this DLL, the installer can update the reference count, and when the application is uninstalled, the reference count is decremented. Such a DLL is removed only when the count falls to zero. Also, during installation, the installer can check the version of the existing shared DLL and replace the DLL if the installer has a newer version. Windows also protects its own system DLLs by maintaining a copy of the official version. If you attempt to replace a system DLL, Windows will revert to the cached copy. Only a service pack can change a system DLL.

All of these facilities help to patch up a system that is suffering from DLL Hell, but they are essentially retrograde solutions applied after it became clear that a problem existed. The .NET Fusion technology is Microsoft's attempt to solve the problem by designing versioning and location rules into the system so that you have rules to prevent the wrong library being loaded but you also have the flexibility to change the rules if necessary.

Fusion comes with a tool named the Fusion Log Viewer (fuslogvw.exe). If Fusion cannot find a library, you can use the Fusion Log Viewer to see the search paths and the files that Fusion attempts to use, and from this, you can make an informed choice about how to solve the issue. Once you have fixed and run an application, the .NET Framework will store details about the application and the libraries it uses in an ini file in the folder

```
\Document and Settings\<User>\Local Settings
   \Application Data\ApplicationHistory
```

where <*User*> is the currently logged-on user. This file is an INI file, but you should not read it directly. Instead, the .NET Framework setup will install a Microsoft Management Console (MMC) snap-in named Microsoft .NET Framework Configuration. To view the working versions of an application, you select the Applications node from the tree view and then select Fix An Application from the view pane. This action will give a list of all the .NET applications that you have ever run. You can select a particular application, and the tool will list date ranges when the application was run without assembly load problems as well as Application SafeMode, which is the original version of the assemblies that the application was first built and tested with.

You can select one of these settings, and the tool will write values in the application's configuration file to indicate the specific version of the library assembly that the application uses, and from this point onward, the application will use only those versions. You can edit the configuration file by hand to change these settings at a later stage, and if this configuration works, it will represent another entry in the Fix An Application dialog box. I will explain how to do this in the section "Locating Assemblies" later in this chapter.

Private Assemblies

As the name suggests, library assemblies are intended to be used by other assemblies. Libraries can be *shared* or *private*. A shared assembly can be used by more than one application, and I will explain how this sharing is achieved in the next section. A private assembly is used only by the application in its folder (or immediate parent folder, as I'll explain in a moment). This arrangement means that if multiple applications use the same private library, there will be multiple copies of that library on your hard disk, but it does mean that the applications will have the library that they were built to use.

A private assembly can have any name that you choose, and it does not need a strong name. The private assembly is located in the same folder as the application that uses it, or in a subfolder. This subfolder has either the same name as the short name of the assembly, or it has the name of the culture of the assembly, or it is a subfolder mentioned in the *privatePath* attribute of the *<probing>* section of the application configuration file (as explained in the "Locating Assemblies" section later in this chapter). So, if you build an assembly named utils.dll with a culture of "en-GB," the assembly's PE file can be in the application folder (*AppDomain::BaseDirectory*), in a folder named *utils*, or in a folder named *en-GB*.

Shared Assemblies

Shared assemblies are stored in a special folder on your hard disk named the *global assembly cache* (GAC). Figure 5-2 shows the GAC on my machine. In general, the GAC appears as a folder named *assembly* under the %SYSTEMROOT% folder of your machine. This folder is actually a namespace extension provided by shfusion.dll. You are not expected to view the actual folder structure, but if you are interested, you can navigate the GAC through the command line.

The namespace extension actually gives a list of assemblies in the GAC and assemblies in the native image cache. (The Type column lists "native images" for these assemblies in the native image cache.) Assemblies can be in either or both of these locations. The native image cache contains assemblies that have been PreJITted, as I'll explain in the next section ("PreJITted Assemblies").

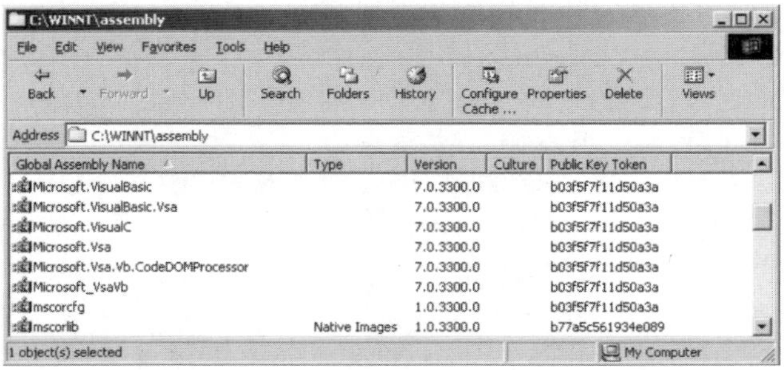

Figure 5-2 The global assembly cache

The GAC contains only shared assemblies, and any installer application run under the Administrators account can install an assembly in the GAC. If the GAC was simply a FAT32 or an NTFS folder, this installation could cause a potential problem because the name of the PE file is not sufficiently unique to prevent an installer copying over an existing library. The GAC is actually a series of folders. Figure 5-3 shows the format of the GAC when I disable the Fusion namespace extension.[9] The *assembly* folder has a folder named *GAC*, and immediately below the *GAC* folder is a folder that has the short name of each assembly in the GAC. Within each of these subfolders are folders that are named according to the version, culture, and public key token of the assembly. The most important of these is the public key token: an assembly must have a strong name if it is to be put in the GAC.

There are several ways to configure assemblies in the GAC. You can use the gacutil utility to add and remove assemblies; you can use the *-i* switch and the *assembly filename* to add an assembly and the */u* switch with the *full name* of the assembly to remove the assembly from the GAC. The Microsoft Installer can also add assemblies to the GAC, and you can use the namespace extension. (You can drag and drop an assembly to install it, or use the delete context menu to remove an assembly.)

The *assembly* folder in the namespace extension also shows a subfolder named *Download*. This folder contains assemblies that have been downloaded from other machines. In the section "Verifiable Code" later in this chapter, I will explain that you cannot write such assemblies with managed C++.

9. To do this, use the command line to navigate to %systemroot%\assembly, then use *attrib* to remove the SHR attributes on Desktop.ini, and then rename this file to something else. Remember to rename the file and apply the SHR attributes after you have finished examining the folder structure.

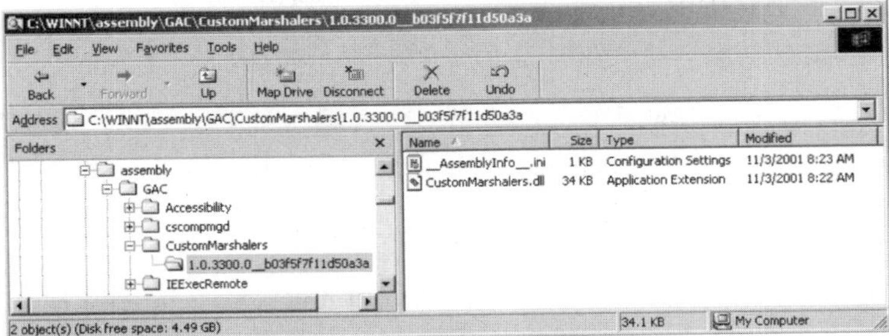

Figure 5-3 The global assembly cache shown with the namespace extension disabled

PreJITted Assemblies

The shell extension (Figure 5-2) gives the short name, the version, the culture, and the public key token of the assemblies that are installed. There is also a column named *Type*. This column indicates whether the assembly is MSIL or has been PreJITted. In Figure 5-2, you can see that the mscorlib assembly has been PreJITted because the Type column has the phrase *Native Images*. A PreJITted assembly is one where the entire assembly has been run through the JITter so that all the MSIL has been compiled to native code and then saved to a special area of your hard disk called the *Native Image Cache*. Figure 5-4 shows the Native Image Cache in Windows Explorer with the Fusion namespace disabled. You can PreJit your own assemblies with the tool ngen. When you run this tool, it will JIT-compile the assembly and then install the JITted assembly in the native image cache. The native image cache can hold more than one version of the PreJITted assembly, but unlike the GAC, you do not need to provide a strong name for the assembly.

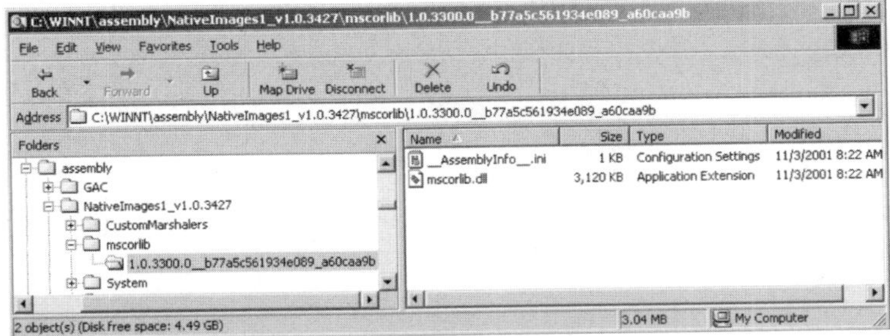

Figure 5-4 The Native Image Cache shown with the namespace extension disabled

PreJITted assemblies do not contain the metadata tables held by MSIL assemblies: ILDASM will show only the manifest for a PreJITted assembly.

However, this limitation is not a problem because you use the non-PreJITted assembly in *#using* statements, and at run time, the .NET Framework will locate the relevant PreJITted assembly in the native image cache, or if the Framework cannot find the right library, it will resort to JITting the non-PreJITted assembly. This strategy means that a machine that has a PreJITted assembly will also have the non-PreJITted assembly, so you cannot use this scheme to hide the implementation of your code. Figure 5-2 shows that mscorlib is PreJITted, but the assembly that you refer to in *#using* statements is the assembly in the .NET Framework system folder.

The reason for PreJITting is to make the initial loading of an assembly faster. However, once loaded into memory, a PreJITted assembly is unlikely to have any performance gain over code in a non-PreJITted assembly.

Locating Assemblies

Assemblies are loaded in two ways, dynamic or static. A dynamically loaded assembly is obtained through a call to *Assembly::Load*, and although this mechanism gives great flexibility, it also requires more work than static loading because you have to use the *Activator* class to create objects rather than the managed *new*. *Assembly::Load* requires that you provide the full name of the assembly. You can also provide partial information about the assembly using *Assembly::LoadWithPartialName*; however, this strategy can make the load process slower, and you do not get the benefit of versioning.

When you use the *#using* statement, you indicate that you want to statically link to the assembly. The compiler will add the complete name of the assembly to the manifest of the referring assembly, which includes the short name, the version, the culture, and if it has a strong name, the public key token. Whether an assembly is statically or dynamically loaded, it is subject to Fusion probing.

Probing is the name for the mechanism that Fusion uses to locate an assembly. The first thing that Fusion does is check to see whether the assembly has a strong name. If the assembly has a strong name, .NET versioning can be used, so Fusion determines the version of the assembly. This information will be specified in the manifest of the referring assembly (or the *AssemblyName* if the assembly is dynamically loaded), but it can be changed through the application's configuration file. The relevant section is *<assemblyBinding>* within the *<runtime>* section, as shown in the following code:

```
<configuration>
   <runtime>
      <assemblyBinding>
         <dependentAssembly>
            <assemblyIdentity name="myAssem"
                PublicKeyToken="c4c3b887dbc8b8c1"/>
            <bindingRedirect oldVersion="1.1.0.0"
                newVersion="1.2.0.0"/>
         </dependentAssembly>
```

```
        </assemblyBinding>
    </runtime>
</configuration>
```

For each assembly that you want to provide binding information, you have to have a *<dependentAssembly>* element. The name of the assembly is given in the *<assemblyIdentity>* element. This name does not have a version because that information is given by the *<bindingRedirect>* tag. This entry indicates that version 1.2.0.0 is installed on the machine, but when an application that requires version 1.1.0.0 of the assembly runs, the runtime will load the newer version instead. If the assembly is shared, there might be a publisher policy file (discussed in the next section, "Publisher Policy Files") that can override both the version given in the referring assembly's manifest or in the application file.

Fusion now has the complete name of the assembly and can test to see whether the assembly has already been loaded. If the assembly is loaded, the loaded version will be used. Otherwise, Fusion starts the process of locating the assembly. If the assembly has a strong name, it could be a shared assembly, so the next step performed by Fusion is to check the GAC. If the assembly is not in the GAC, Fusion treats the assembly as a private assembly and attempts to determine the private assembly's location.

The first check Fusion makes is the codebase. A dynamic loaded assembly can specify this location through the *AssemblyName::Codebase* property or through *Assembly::LoadFrom*.[10] A static-bound assembly can be loaded from a location other than the default location (another folder or a URL) through the *<codeBase>* element in the application configuration file (or a policy file). When you specify a codebase folder, it must be a subfolder of the application folder. You cannot specify a global folder. This reinforces the fact that the only way that you can share an assembly is to put the assembly in the GAC.

Once the codebase has been checked, Fusion will check the current folder (*AppDomain::BaseDirectory*), a subfolder with the short name of the library assembly, or a subfolder with the name of the library assembly's culture. If the library assembly cannot be located in these folders, Fusion will check to see whether there is a *<probing>* element in the application configuration file. This element can have an attribute named *privatePath* that is a list of subfolders, and Fusion will check these folders (and if the library has a culture, a folder with the culture name) for the assembly.

If all these checks fail, Fusion cannot find the assembly and it will throw an exception. You can then use the Fusion Log Viewer to look at all the tests performed and why they failed. When you are developing a shared assembly, you are likely to build the assembly frequently. To test such an assembly, you'll

---

10. Also, a *Codebase* can be added to the registry entry for an assembly called through COM interop with the */codebase* switch of RegAsm.

have to install the assembly in the GAC each time you rebuild it. This process can be tedious, so the Framework offers a solution with the *DEVPATH* environment variable. You put the path to the directory that contains the assembly in *DEVPATH* and then add the *<developmentMode>* to machine.config.

```
<!-- machine.config -->
<configuration>
   <runtime>
      <developmentMode developerInstallation="true"/>
   </runtime>
</configuration>
```

I will return to this issue again in Chapter 7.

Publisher Policy Files

Earlier I said that only executable assemblies have a configuration file. That is not completely true because a shared library assembly installed can have a publisher policy file. This file is a resource-only assembly. The resource is an XML file in the format of a configuration file that is linked (not embedded) to the assembly. The difference between a policy file and a config file is that the resource in a policy file is associated with a library assembly, contains information pertinent to applications using the library, and is used to identify version redirects or a codebase. The resource-only assembly is installed into the GAC, so it must have a strong name. The linker cannot be used to create the policy file because it will only embed resources, and a publisher policy file must have a linked resource. Instead, you use the assembly linker tool, *al*:

```
al /linkresource:myAssem.config /version:1.0.0.0
   /keyfile:mykey.snk /out:Policy.1.0.myAssem.dll
```

The name of the policy file has three parts:

```
Policy.<version>.<assembly>.dll
```

Policy indicates to the runtime that this is a policy file, *<assembly>* gives the short name, and *<version>* is the major and minor version of the assembly to which the policy file refers. Thus, the example applies to the versions of myAssem that have a major and minor version of 1.0.

Security

Security is hugely important. Every project design should start with security considerations, and only after the security permissions required by the code have been decided should you consider designing the code.

The Windows NT security model is based on security accounts possessing a security token and secured objects (files, named pipes, synchronization objects, and so on) possessing an access control list (ACL). The token gives access to a unique security ID (SID), and an ACL contains a list of SIDs that have access, or are denied access, to the secured object. Windows NT security checks are performed on principals, and principals have a SID, which allows authentication to be performed (a mechanism in which a principal is checked to ensure it is who the principal says it is). Many Win32 APIs access secured objects (for example, *::CreateFile* to access an existing file), and the API will automatically perform an access check on the object's ACL using the current access token to see whether the principal has access to the object. These access checks are performed automatically; the developer does not have to provide additional code. Much of Windows NT security programming involves maintaining ACLs on secured objects and allowing Win32 to perform access checks. The Win32 API allows you to programmatically access security, but the process is rather arcane and obscure, and as a consequence, most designs rely on using the default security. Finally, COM+ provides role-based security, which brings security into the domain of Visual Basic programmers.

.NET security is implemented using Windows NT security and provides code to perform access checks and role-based security. However, .NET security goes one step further than this because .NET security also provides code access security (also referred to as evidence-based security), whereby access checks are performed on the call stack rather than on the principal.

Code Access Security

Access checks on principals are fine as long as you know what the code is about to do. When you run an application, Windows will attach your access token to the process so that when the application attempts to access a secured object, the access check (and auditing, if enabled) will be performed using your access token. If you have administrator's access to your machine, any code that you run will have administrator's access. Do you know the resources that each application on your machine tries to access? Are those accesses legitimate? Should a screen saver, for example, have access to your address book and be able to send e-mail? If the screen saver runs under your account, there is no mechanism in Windows to prevent the screen saver from sending spam to all the contacts in your address book.

This issue becomes even more important when you run code in DLLs. When you load a DLL—either statically or dynamically—the code in the DLL is treated the same as the code in the application from a security point of view. If the DLL code attempts to access a secured object that your account has access to, the DLL code will also have access. If you cannot guarantee the integrity of the code, it is clearly a risky action to allow the DLL to run under your account. You cannot specify that all code in a specified DLL should be run with a different access token than the one used by the process that loads the DLL. A process can impersonate another account on a thread (for example, one with lower privileges), as long as the process is run under an account that is allowed to perform impersonation. You could ensure that the DLL is called only on this impersonating thread, but if the thread needs to call code outside of the suspect DLL, that code will be called under the impersonating token and your code could suffer.

COM provides some protection because a DLL server can be run under a surrogate process. Such a surrogate can be assigned a Windows identity that provides the access token for the surrogate process, so this process can be a low privileged account. However, using a surrogate process requires interprocess communications, which presents a performance issue, and the technique cannot be used for ActiveX controls, which have to be loaded in process.

Code access security[11] in the .NET Framework solves this issue by applying the access checks on the code within the stack trace. Classes and methods can have a security permission attribute to indicate that the code requires specific permissions to run. Code in a method can also explicitly demand a permission. When such a check is performed, code access security will perform the access check for each method within the stack trace until the access check fails, or until all methods have been checked.

Assemblies are the unit of security. When your code requests a permission and that permission is granted, it will be granted based on the *evidence* of the assembly and such a permission is granted to the assembly. The evidence can include any information that you choose, but by default includes information about the origin of the code. From the evidence, code access security assigns the code to one of the *code groups* defined in the security configuration files. A code group defines the permissions that the code will be given. Typically, the machine administrator manages code groups and permission sets that the code groups will obtain through the Microsoft .NET Framework Configuration MMC snap-in. The *System::Security::Policy* namespace also has classes to programmatically manipulate the security policy files.

The significant point is that these checks are performed on all code further up in the call stack,[12] so if your trusted code calls a library method which then calls a .NET Framework class to perform some action that requires permissions, code access security will check all the code in the stack. If the library was downloaded from the Internet and the permission that is requested is not allowed for code in the code group for downloaded code, the permission will not be granted, even if your trusted code has sufficient privileges.

You know what your assembly can do, so you can specify that the assembly has code that requires specific permissions. If an attempt is made to load your assembly by code that does not have the permission, the load will fail. To

---

11. For a more complete appraisal of code access security, see Keith Brown's article, "Enforce Code Access Rights with the Common Language Runtime," MSDN Magazine, February 2001 (*http://msdn.microsoft.com/msdnmag/issues/01/02/CAS/CAS.asp*).

12. Code in the call stack that has the specified permissions can call *CodeAccessPermission::Assert* to stop the check from propagating to code higher in the call stack.

specify that your assembly requires specific permissions, your code can add the *[SecurityPermission]* attribute to the assembly, providing information about the permissions that your assembly requires. Every assembly that you compile with the C++ compiler will have this attribute[13]:

```
[assembly: SecurityPermission(SecurityAction::RequestMinimum,
                              SkipVerification=true)];
```

This line indicates that the minimum permission that will be required is to skip verification of the code. I will cover verification in the section "Verifiable Code" later in this chapter, but note that C++ .NET code is not verifiable, and as a consequence, it can be called only by code in the code groups that are able to skip verification—which by default means only code that originates on the local machine. This limitation means that you cannot use C++ to write .NET code that will be accessed from another machine or downloaded from another machine. You can read the permission set for an assembly by passing the name of the assembly file to the permview tool.

You can also apply access permissions to classes and to methods. If the caller does not have the correct permission when calling such a method, or a member of an object of such a class, then a security exception will be thrown. Furthermore, a method can specifically demand a permission by creating a permission object and calling the *Demand* method. *Demand* will cause a stack walk to check that the code further up the stack has the relevant permission, thus allowing you to perform fine-grain code access checks.

There are classes in the *System::Security::Permissions* namespace (as well as *System::Diagnostics* and *System::ServiceProcess*) for determining the permissions for various common actions, such as accessing the file system, the registry, and user interface API. These classes are shown in Table 5-4. These permissions are supplied both as a class that you can call in your code and as attributes.

The *SecurityPermission* class and attribute allows you to demand permissions for various .NET actions such as creating and manipulating *AppDomain* objects, configuring .NET, extending remoting, skipping verification, and calling unmanaged code. These actions are specified as members of the *SecurityPermissionFlag* enumeration.

One interesting attribute that you will find in the *System::Security* namespace is *[SuppressUnmanagedCodeSecurity]*. When managed code makes a call through to unmanaged code, the runtime will demand the *SecurityPermissionFlag::Unmanaged* permission. In some code—particularly C++ code that makes calls through IJW—there might be many managed/unmanaged transitions, which will involve multiple stack walks with a corresponding detrimental

13. If you look at the manifest of an assembly, you'll see a *.permissionset reqmin* directive and an XML permission set that has the *SkipVerification* permission.

effect on performance. The *[SuppressUnmanagedCodeSecurity]* attribute indicates that the demand for the *Unmanaged* permission occurs only once, when the code is first JIT-compiled, and the demand is suppressed for subsequent calls to the unmanaged code. The C++ compiler will add this attribute to all the thunks that it generates for IJW.

Table 5-4 Common Code Access Security Permission Classes

Class	Description
DirectoryServicesPermission	Determines the permissions to read, write, delete, and browse items in directory services
EnvironmentPermission	Determines the permission to read and write environment variables
EventLogPermission	Determines the permissions to read and write to logs, and to create sources and logs
FileDialogPermission	Determine the permissions to show the Open and Save file dialog boxes
FileIOPermission	Determines the permissions to read and write files, append files, and traverse directories
IsolatedStorageFilePermission	Determines the permissions to access isolated storage
PerformanceCounterPermission	Determines the permissions to read, write, and create performance counter categories
ReflectionPermission	Permissions concerning whether the code can use Reflection to access protected and private members of a type
RegistryPermission	Determines the permissions to read, write, and create entries in the registry
SecurityPermission	Determine various permissions concerned with managed code
ServiceControllerPermission	Determines the permissions to connect to or control Windows services
SiteIdentityPermission	Ensures that callers are from a specific Web site
StrongNameIdentityPermission	Ensures that callers have a specific strong name
UIPermission	Determines the permissions to draw and access user inputs from windows, and access the clipboard
UrlIdentityPermission	Ensures that callers are from a specific URL
ZoneIdentityPermission	Ensure that callers are from a specific Internet Explorer Zone

Role-Based Security

The .NET Framework also gives access to principals. You can define your own principal type, but you are more likely to use the .NET Framework classes that give access to Windows principals. You can access the identity of the current principal through the static *WindowsIdentity::GetCurrent* property, shown here:

```
Console::WriteLine(S"The principal is {0}",
   WindowsIdentity::GetCurrent()->Name);
```

The *WindowsPrincipal* class has a property that is an *IIdentity* pointer, which is an instance of the *WindowsIdentity* class. The *WindowsPrincipal* is intended to check to see whether the current principal is within a particular *role*. A role is a description of the type of actions that an account can perform. *WindowsPrincipal* treats security groups as roles, so *IPrincipal::IsInRole* tests a principal for membership of a group.

```
WindowsPrincipal* p = new WindowsPrincipal(
   WindowsIdentity::GetCurrent());
if (p->IsInRole(WindowsBuiltInRole::Administrator))
{
  // Do some administrative task.
}
```

You can also use roles in code access security through the *PrincipalPermission* class and the *[PrincipalPermission]* attribute. These types will test the permissions against the principal for the current thread. By default, the *Thread::CurrentPrincipal* will not be set, so you have to set this property yourself. After you have done that, you can use either the attribute or demand the permission through the class, as the following code shows:

```
__gc class Secret
{
public:
   [PrincipalPermission(SecurityAction::Demand,
                        Role="BUILTIN\\Administrators")]
   void SpecialAction();
};
void main()
{
   WindowsPrincipal* p;
   p = new WindowsPrincipal(WindowsIdentity::GetCurrent());
   // Set the thread principal to the principal based on the
   // windows identity.
   Thread::CurrentPrincipal = p;
   // Demand a permission to do some action.
   PrincipalPermission* perm;
   perm = new PrincipalPermission(S"MACHINE_A\\Richard",
                                  S"BUILTIN\\Administrators");

   try
```

```
    {
        perm->Demand();
        // Do something that only Richard can do.
    }
    catch(Exception*) { }

    // Create the secret object.
    Secret* secret = new Secret;
    try
    {
        // Do something that only Administrators can do.
        secret->SpecialAction();
    }
    catch(Exception*) { }
}
```

In this action, I demand just one permission; however, I can demand more than one permission through a *PermissionSet* object that essentially acts as a container for permission objects. Demanding a permission set is likely to be more efficient than demanding individual permissions.

Be careful about demanding permissions because a demand (either explicitly or through an attribute) will cause a stack walk and if you are calling a .NET Framework class to perform some action, it too might demand some permission. For example, there is no point in demanding the *FileIOPermission* before accessing one of the .NET Framework IO classes because they will also demand the same permissions, so a stack walk will be performed twice. An example where demanding the *FileIOPermission* is useful is if you have some object that does many file actions in its methods, and you could demand the *FileIOPermission* in the constructor so that if the permission cannot be accessed, the object will not be created. If the demand in the constructor succeeds, the object can be created and you know that when a *System::IO* class demands the same permissions the demand will succeed. Because the constructor has already confirmed that a demand will succeed, your object's methods could call *Assert* so that demands for permissions will not propagate further up the stack.

Verifiable Code

.NET is type-safe, so to call a type member, the MSIL will have the metadata of the type and the member. MSIL is stack-based, and .NET compilers that generate the MSIL should construct the stack correctly before calling a type member. When your code is loaded by the runtime, the code is verified to see that it is type-safe and also that the code does not do anything else that is unsafe, such as access unmanaged memory or get direct access to the managed heap through an interior pointer. If the code fails this verification, it will not run in trusted situations. Furthermore, the code has to have the *SkipVerification* security permission request to run at all. All assemblies created by the C++ compiler have this security permission request.[14]

Code that is downloaded from another machine must be verifiable before it can be run. Clearly, allowing non-verifiable code to run on your machine is not desirable because the code could bypass .NET security and type safety, access managed memory, and manipulate the stack. Code that is not verifiable will not be loaded if its source is another machine. This means that you cannot use C++ to write assemblies intended to be loaded from another machine.

Unmanaged .NET Services API

Many parts of the .NET Framework are exposed to external code. Clearly, if you want to get information about the runtime or affect how the runtime works, this task should be done from outside the runtime, from non-.NET code. The .NET Framework SDK contains definitions of COM interfaces and objects that give access to the runtime. The header files that contain these definitions are shown in Table 5-5.

Table 5-5 Framework SDK Header Files

Header	Description
cor.h	Main header file for the metadata APIs
cordebug.h	Main .NET debugger interfaces
corerror.h	Definitions of the HRESULTs that can be returned from the runtime
corhdr.h	Definitions of the metadata structures
corhlpr.h	Helper functions
corprof.h	Profiling interfaces
corpub.h	Access to the list of running .NET processes
corsvc.h	Services for .NET debuggers
corsym.h	API to read and write debugging symbols
gchost.h	Gives access to statistics about the garbage collector
iceefilegen.h	API for generating .NET files
icmprecs.h	Access to the .NET data storage layer
ivalidator.h, ivehandler.h	API to validate .NET files
mscoree.h	Main header file for hosting the runtime
strongname.h	Header for the APIs to generate strong names.

14. The .NET Framework provides a tool named *peverify* that you can use to check whether an assembly has type-safe code. Even C++ assemblies that do not perform unsafe actions will fail verification with peverify.

Enumerating Managed Processes

The corpub.h header contains interfaces that allow you to get a list of the managed processes running on your machine and the application domains in those applications. This task involves standard COM programming using COM enumerator interfaces.

```
// processes.h
#include <objbase.h>
#include <stdio.h>
#include <corpub.h>
#pragma comment(lib, "ole32.lib")
#define NAME_LEN 256

void main()
{
   CoInitialize(0);
   HRESULT hr;
   // Get the COR process publisher object.
   ICorPublish* pub;
   hr = CoCreateInstance(__uuidof(CorpubPublish), 0,
                         CLSCTX_INPROC_SERVER,
                         __uuidof(pub), (void**)&pub);
   if (SUCCEEDED(hr))
   {
      // Enumerate the managed processes.
      ICorPublishProcessEnum* pEnum;
      hr = pub->EnumProcesses(COR_PUB_MANAGEDONLY, &pEnum);
      if (SUCCEEDED(hr))
      {
         ICorPublishProcess* processes[5];
         ULONG fetched = 1;
         while(pEnum->Next(5, processes, &fetched) == S_OK
               && fetched > 0)
         {
            // Get information about each process.
            for (ULONG i = 0; i < fetched; i++)
            {
               WCHAR name[NAME_LEN];
               ULONG32 size = 0;
               // Get the file name.
               processes[i]->GetDisplayName(NAME_LEN,
                  &size, name);
               if (size > 0)
               {
                  wprintf(L"name = %s\n", name);
               }
               // Get the process ID.
               unsigned pid;
               processes[i]->GetProcessID(&pid);
               wprintf(L"\tprocess id = %ld\n", pid);
               // Enumerate the application domains.
               ICorPublishAppDomainEnum* pEnumDomains;
```

```
                hr = processes[i]->EnumAppDomains(&pEnumDomains);
                if (SUCCEEDED(hr))
                {
                    ICorPublishAppDomain* appDomains[5];
                    ULONG aFetched = 1;
                    while (aFetched > 0 &&
                             pEnumDomains->Next(5,
                                appDomains, &aFetched) == S_OK)
                    {
                        // Get information about each domain.
                        for (ULONG j = 0; j < aFetched; j++)
                        {
                            WCHAR name[NAME_LEN];
                            ULONG32 size=0;
                            appDomains[j]->GetName(NAME_LEN,
                                &size, name);
                            if (size > 0)
                            {
                                wprintf(L"\t\tname = %s\n", name);
                            }

                            appDomains[j]->Release();
                        }
                    }
                    pEnumDomains->Release();
                }
                processes[i]->Release();
            }
        }
        pEnum->Release();
    }
    pub->Release();
  }
  CoUninitialize();
}
```

The *CorpubPublish* object implements the *ICorPublish* interface, which you can use to get information about a single managed process or to get access to an enumerator (*ICorPublishProcessEnum*) to iterate through all the managed processes. Information about a managed process is obtained through *ICorPublishProcess*, which allows you to get the file name of the process and its Windows process ID. Once you have a process ID, you can pass it to the Win32 *::OpenProcess* function to get a process handle and then get other information about the process using Win32 process functions.[15]

The *ICorPublishProcess* interface also allows you to enumerate the application domains in a process and from each one get the name and ID of the *AppDomain*.

15. Christophe Nasarre describes these APIs in his article "Escape from DLL Hell with Custom Debugging and Instrumentation Tools and Utilities," MSDN Magazine, June 2002 (*http://msdn.microsoft.com/msdnmag/issues/02/06/debug/debug.asp*).

Getting Information About the Garbage Collector

The runtime is represented by an object named the *CorRuntimeHost* (which is defined in mscoree.h). This object implements the *IGCHost* interface, which you can call to get information about the garbage collector.

```
// gc.cpp
ICorRuntimeHost* pHost;
CorBindToRuntimeEx(0, 0, 0, __uuidof(CorRuntimeHost),
                            __uuidof(pHost), (void**)&pHost);
UseTheRuntime(pHost);
IGCHost* pGC;
pHost->QueryInterface(__uuidof(pGC), (void**)&pGC);
COR_GC_STATS stats;
memset(&stats, 0, sizeof(stats));
stats.Flags = COR_GC_MEMORYUSAGE|COR_GC_COUNTS;
pGC->GetStats(&stats);
printf("GC called explicitly %ld times\n",
       stats.ExplicitGCCount);
printf("committed %ld kB\n", stats.CommittedKBytes);
printf("reserved %ld kB\n", stats.ReservedKBytes);
printf("generation 0 has %ld kB\n",
       stats.Gen0HeapSizeKBytes);
printf("\tcollections: %ld\n",
       stats.GenCollectionsTaken[0]);
printf("generation 1 has %ld kB\n",
       stats.Gen1HeapSizeKBytes);
printf("\tcollections: %ld\n",
       stats.GenCollectionsTaken[1]);
printf("generation 2 has %ld kB\n",
       stats.Gen2HeapSizeKBytes);
printf("\tcollections: %ld\n",
       stats.GenCollectionsTaken[2]);
printf("large object heap has %ld kB\n",
       stats.LargeObjectHeapSizeKBytes);
pGC->Release();
```

The preferred way to get access to the runtime is through a call to *CorBindToRuntime* because this API allows you to specify the version of the runtime to load and provides some optimization flags. In this example, I have passed zero for all the options, which indicates that default values will be used. (This is equivalent to calling *::CoCreateInstance* to get the run-time object.) I will explain these parameters in the next section, "Hosting the .NET Runtime."

In this example, I call the user function *UseTheRuntime* that will call some .NET code and then I dump the garbage collection statistics. *IGCHost::GetStats* is passed an instance of *COR_GC_STATS* through which statistics about the garbage collector are returned. This parameter is *in/out*, and you have to initialize the *Flags* member to indicate which statistics you require. The *IGCHost* interface also allows you to configure the garbage collector, and of these methods, perhaps the least dangerous to call is *Collect*, which allows you to explicitly tell the garbage collector to perform a collection on a specific generation or on all generations.

Hosting the .NET Runtime

The .NET Framework SDK also contains code to allow you to host the .NET runtime.[16] This hosting means that you can create application domains, load types into those domains, and then execute them. Examples of processes that host the .NET runtime are the ASP.NET worker process that is called by IIS to run ASP.NET applications, and Internet Explorer when it is requested to host a .NET control on an HTML page.

Hosting the .NET runtime is only one way to access .NET types from unmanaged code. You can also do the same thing with COM interop, or you can simply compile your unmanaged C++ application as a managed application (with the */clr* switch) and import the .NET types with *#using*. You will decide to host the runtime if you want to have greater control over how application domains are created and the version of the runtime, or if you want to have closer integration and receive events from the runtime.

Hosting the runtime is straightforward, but calling .NET code is not a trivial task because effectively you have to use an equivalent of the .NET Reflection API through COM automation compatible interfaces. I can handle COM interfaces, but when I have to handle the overhead of *IDispatch*, *VARIANT*, and *SAFEARRAY* from C++, I start to wonder whether the benefits are worth the effort. If you want to call more than one object or more than one method on an object, it is far better to use another solution. However, if you want to call a single entry point method on an assembly, the pain of calling automation interfaces is worth the effort.

Initializing the Runtime

The first task to perform is to initialize the runtime. .NET allows side-by-side installation of the runtime; that is, you can have more than one version of the runtime installed on a machine. An application can indicate that it runs under a specific version of the runtime through the *<requiredRuntime>* element in a configuration file. More than one version of the runtime can execute on a machine at the same time. *CorBindToRuntimeEx* takes the version of the runtime as a string to its first parameter. This string is in the following format:

```
v<major>.<minor>.<build>
```

An example is *v1.0.3750*. In other words, this string is in a similar format to the naming convention used for the .NET Framework system folder. If you pass a NULL for this parameter, the most recent version of the runtime will be

16. For more details, see "Microsoft .NET: Implement a Custom Common Language Runtime Host for Your Managed App," Steven Pratschner, *MSDN Magazine*, March 2001, which you can read at *www.msdn.microsoft.com/msdnmag/issues/01/03/clr/clr.asp*.

loaded. You can fill a string with the most recent version of the .NET runtime by calling *CorGetVersion*. The second parameter is called the *build flavor* and can be *wks* or *svr*. This parameter indicates whether you want to load the workstation or server version of the runtime (mscorwks.dll or mscorsvr.dll). If you pass NULL for this parameter, you will get the workstation build. If you have a uniprocessor machine, you will always get the workstation build.

The third parameter of *CorBindToRuntimeEx* is an optimization flag. For a uniprocessor machine, this flag will allow you to determine whether assemblies are loaded into every application domain, or if they are treated as being *domain-neutral*. If assemblies are loaded into each application domain and your process has more than one application domain, this strategy can increase the memory footprint of the process. However, if assemblies are domain-neutral, a separate copy of static data must be made for all application domains, and this duplication can slow performance.

CorBindToRuntimeEx is passed the CLSID of the run-time object and the interface that you require. Table 5-6 lists the interfaces that you can request. (These are documented in mscoree.idl.)

Table 5-6 Runtime Object Interfaces

Interface	Description
ICorConfiguration	Allows you to provide callbacks so that your code is informed when certain thread events occur and when the virtual memory limits have been exceeded
ICorRuntimeHost	Allows you to start or stop the runtime, and to manipulate application domains
IDebuggerInfo	Determines whether a debugger is attached
IGCHost	Gets statistics about and configures the garbage collector
ICorThreadPool	Gets access to the .NET thread pool
IValidator	Validates .NET files

Typically, you will request the *ICorRuntimeHost* so that you can start the runtime and get access to an application domain, as shown here:

```
HRESULT hr;
ICorRuntimeHost* pHost;
hr = CorBindToRuntimeEx(0, 0, 0, __uuidof(CorRuntimeHost),
                        __uuidof(pHost), (void**)&pHost);
if (SUCCEEDED(hr))
{
   pHost->Start();
   RunCodeInAppDomain(pHost);
   pHost->Stop();
   pHost->Release();
}
```

The user function *RunCodeInAppDomain* will obtain an application domain and use it to load and execute the user code. There are several methods on *ICorRuntimeHost* for getting access to an application domain. The first method is *GetDefaultDomain*, which as the name suggests, is the first domain in the runtime and is created automatically when the runtime starts in the process. If you prefer, you can create your own application domain, and there are two ways to do this: in a single action, or in a two-step call. *CreateDomain* will create a domain with a specific name and return an interface on that domain. *CreateDomainSetup* will return a pointer to an *IAppDomainSetup* that you can use to set parameters for the domain and then pass this object to the *CreateDomainEx* to create the application domain. Finally, you can enumerate all the existing domains by calling methods on the *ICorRuntimeHost* interface—you do not get a separate enumerator object.

The methods that return an application domain actually return an *IUnknown* interface. There is no application domain interface defined in mscoree.idl. Indeed, the application domain set-up parameters are also passed to *CreateDomainEx* through an *IUnknown* pointer. The *IAppDomainSetup* interface is also notable by its absence in mscoree.idl. The application domain is accessed through a pointer to the *_AppDomain* interface. These two interfaces are described in the *mscorlib.tlb* type library, and this is where the fun begins.

The *_AppDomain* interface is a COM version of the class interface for the *System::AppDomain* class, so you can use the documentation in the Framework SDK to determine the parameters for the methods. However, the first question is: which method should you call? The problem arises because interfaces in .NET can be overloaded, but in COM they cannot, so when interfaces are exported to COM from .NET, overloaded methods are renamed. For example, there are seven overloads of the *AppDomain::Load* method, and these overloads appear in the *_AppDomain* COM interface as methods *Load*, *Load_2*, … *Load_6*. You have to use OLEView to look at the signatures of these methods to determine which method you intend to call.

You get a description in the type library for *_AppDomain* because this class is marked with the *[ClassInterface]* attribute to indicate that it is *ClassInterfaceType::AutoDual*. However, this behavior is not the default, and you are discouraged from using this attribute value on your own classes. The default is not to provide a definition for a class interface for COM and only to support late binding. Take, for example, the *_Module* interface (the class interface of the *System::Reflection::Module* class). The type library gives this:

```
[ odl, uuid(D002E9BA-D9E3-3749-B1D3-D565A08B13E7),
  hidden, oleautomation ]
interface _Module : IDispatch {};
```

There is no indication of the methods implemented on this interface. "But," you say, "you always have the option of using the documentation for the

Module class." Yes, you do, but what about overloaded methods? To be absolutely sure, you have to write code to access the type information that is generated dynamically for the *Module* object (*IDispatch::GetTypeInfo*) and check for a method that has the same parameter types and with a name the same as you expect, or with an underscore and a number. This process is all rather messy.

To make even trivial calls to .NET Framework library classes requires lots of C++ simply to make the automation calls. This is why I said earlier that if you want to call more than an entry point function, you should consider some other method of accessing the runtime from unmanaged code. IJW, of course, is your perfect C++ solution.

Summary

The more .NET code you write, the more you realize that there is more to the .NET Framework than scripting together Web controls on an ASP.NET page or controls on a form. The .NET Framework has been built from the bottom up to be secure, flexible, and fully configurable. In this chapter, I have given details of how assemblies are implemented in PE files and how metadata is stored in those files and accessed through the unmanaged API. I have also shown how applications are configured and some of the great things you can do, as well as some of the deficiencies in the current design.

6

Building Code with Visual C++ .NET

Visual C++ .NET is more than just a compiler and a linker; it is a whole development environment, a collection of tools and libraries. Although you can develop applications with the command-line tools—compiling each file through a batch file—if you have a project with more than a handful of files, it starts to become inconvenient to wait for all files to be built when just one file has changed. You can take advantage of the *nmake* tool to compile only those files that have changed, but *nmake* make files are far from intuitive to create. In this situation, you really do need a visual tool to develop your code, which is where the Visual Studio .NET integrated development environment (IDE) comes in.

In this chapter, I will describe how to use the IDE to develop your code and how to use the various tools the IDE provides. I will also explain the managed C++ projects that you can develop, and at the end of the chapter, I will give examples of solutions that you will commonly create.

Visual Studio .NET IDE

The Visual Studio .NET IDE provides all the tools to manage projects. Through context menus, you can provide dependency information, and through property pages, you can specify the build tool to use to compile a source file. The various tools that you can use are available through the main IDE menu, through toolbars and context menus. Because some menus have nested levels of submenus, it would be cumbersome for me to describe the exact location of each tool. Luckily, there is a simpler way to invoke these tools because the IDE provides an extensibility model that allows you to invoke the IDE tools through *commands*. Before I describe the IDE, I have to explain what a command is.

Commands

The Visual Studio .NET IDE exposes its functionality through COM objects. This arrangement means that you can write macros and Visual Studio Add-ins to extend the functionality of the IDE, and you can also access these objects through the Command window. The Command window has two modes: command mode and immediate mode. Immediate mode is used to get information about variables during a debugging session, which I will cover in Chapter 7. As the name suggests, the command mode allows you to execute commands. When you first open the Command window (through the View, Other Windows menu), it will be in command mode. You can tell if you are in command mode because the prompt will be a greater-than symbol (>). If you type the command *immed*, the window will switch to immediate mode and there will be no prompt. When you are in immediate mode, you can switch back to command mode by typing *>cmd*. The > symbol is important because it temporarily puts the Command window into command mode so that the window can execute the command *cmd* to switch to command mode. If you omit the > symbol, the Command window will treat whatever you type as an expression to execute. While in immediate mode, you can execute any command by typing the > symbol and then the command name, and after the command has completed, you will be returned to immediate mode again.

Command mode supports IntelliSense, so when you start typing, the window will present a drop-down list box with the commands that fit the text you are typing. (See Figure 6-1.) Notice that the lower-right corner of the list box shows that it is resizable (indicated by the diagonal lines in the corner), so you can resize the list box by dragging this corner. As with all IntelliSense list boxes, you can scroll up and down the list with the mouse or the keyboard and select the command that you require. IntelliSense is perhaps a bit of a misnomer in this context because it rather dumbly fills the list box with all the commands that look like the command you are typing. It does not check whether those command are relevant in the current context, so often you will find that when you select a command, you will get an error saying that the command is not available. All of the IDE menu items are available through commands in the Command window, but note that when you pull down a menu, the items that are not relevant in the current context are disabled; thus, there is information to indicate which commands are relevant. It is a pity that the IntelliSense author did not use the same information.[1]

There are two broad types of commands that you can execute, *DTE commands* and *aliases*. DTE stands for Design-Time Environment and is accessible through the DTE object. (I'll return to this object in the section "The DTE

---

1. Each command is represented by an *EnvDTE::Command* object that has an *IsAvailable* property.

Object" later in this chapter.) DTE commands are actions that you can perform in the IDE, as shown in this example:

```
File.OpenFile
```

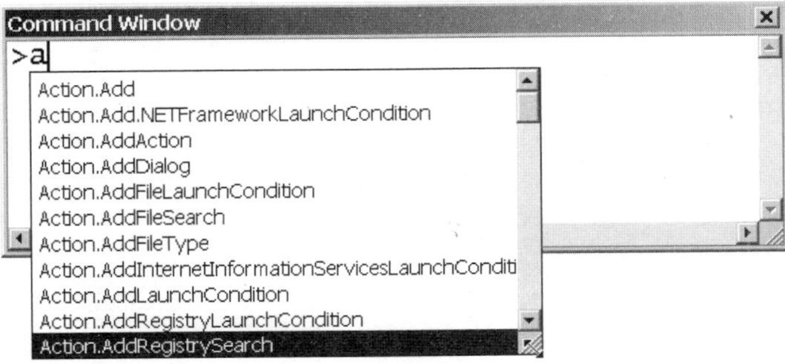

Figure 6-1 IntelliSense in the Command window

This command will show the Open File dialog box. This command makes it look like there is a *File* object (or a *File* class; the C# and Visual Basic .NET dot operator is sloppy in that respect) with a method named *OpenFile*. In fact, this is not the case. The dot does no more than separate *File* from *OpenFile*; the entire name of the command is *File.OpenFile*. The naming comes from the menu item that gives access to the command, so *File.OpenFile* is accessed by going to the File menu, selecting the Open submenu, and then selecting the File menu item. Here's a good visual hint: if you cannot see a menu named Query, you cannot execute any command that starts with the *Query.* text (in other words, the text "Query" followed by a period). Table 6-1 gives a description of the various command prefixes.

Throughout this chapter and Chapter 7, I will use the command name when I refer to a Visual Studio .NET window.

Some commands will show a window or manipulate the currently selected UI item, and other commands take parameters. For example, the *File.OpenFile* command without any parameters will show the Open File dialog box, but if you give a parameter, the command will open the specified file. IntelliSense helps here. The word completion facility will search for the file that best fits the characters that you have typed. So, if you type

```
File.OpenFile i
```

IntelliSense will give a list of all the files and folders starting with *i*. This command can take another parameter that specifies the editor to use to edit the file. If you do not give an editor name, the default editor for the file will be used. For example, if you load a file with the .ico extension, the icon will be loaded into the Resource Editor. If you want to load this file in the Binary Editor, you can use a command such as this:

```
File.OpenFile myIcon.ico /e:"Binary Editor"
```

Table 6-1 Command Menu Identifiers

Menu Identifier	Command Descriptions
Action	Use in setup projects to specify the actions that can be performed when installing or uninstalling an application.
Analyzer	Manipulate a Visual Studio Analyzer project.
Build	Build a solution or a project, and access the Configuration Manager.
Data	Generate datasets from data sources.
Database	Access and manipulate a database connection open in Server Explorer.
Debug	Start or stop a debug session, step through code, and view memory, variables, and other statistics.
Diagram	Generate database diagrams used to establish relationships between tables.
Edit	Manipulate text in the editor, move the insertion point, and find and replace text.
File	Open and save files and solutions; add projects to solutions; print files and access source control.
Format	Format controls in a dialog in the Resource Editor.
Frames	Manipulate framesets in the Frameset Editor.
Help	Access dynamic help and MSDN in the Microsoft Document Explorer.
Image	Manipulate cursors, icons, and bitmaps.
Insert	Add items to an HTML page in the HTML Editor.
Macros	Execute macros.
Project	Manipulate projects: add items and specify build order and dependencies.
Query	Edit a query in a database project.
Schema	Edit an XML schema with the XML Schema Designer.
Styles	Edit a style sheet.
Table	Manipulate tables in an HTML page.
Tools	Access external tools and customize toolbars, Server Explorer, and the Toolbox.
View	Specify visible windows.
Window	Manipulate visible windows.
XML	Validate XML and create a schema from XML.

Some commands have similar names, and this similarity can cause confusion. For example, *Debug.Threads* will show the Threads window, but the

Debug.ListThreads command will print out a summary of the currently running threads in the Command window.

In some cases, there are commands that do the same thing, for example, *View.ToolBox* and *toolbox*. The former command fits into the pattern that I have already described: this command will select the ToolBox menu item from the View menu. The *toolbox* command is an *alias* for the *View.ToolBox* command; you can view the aliases and the commands for which each is an alias by using the *alias* command. In some cases, aliases are simply shorthand for a command. For example, *of* has far fewer letters to type than the command *File.OpenFile* for which it is an alias. In other cases, the alias has specific parameters. For example, the command *StopFind* is an alias for *Edit.FindInFiles /stop*. You can define your own alias using the *alias* command, as shown here:

```
alias binLoad File.OpenFile /e:"Binary Editor"
```

The *binLoad* alias should be used with a file name, and this file will be loaded with the Binary Editor. The system saves alias definitions in a file named aliases.ini in a subfolder of the VisualStudio folder under your Documents And Settings folder. (The aliases are written to this file when you shut down the IDE.)

One alias that is useful is the *shell* alias (*Tools.Shell*), which will run the process that you specify. The process can be started as a separate window, so the following command will show the contents of the current folder in a Windows Explorer window[2]:

```
shell explorer .
```

If the process is a command-line process, you can redirect the output to either the Command window (using the */c* switch) or the Command pane of the Output window (using the */o* switch). The following command will list the help for the command-line C++ compiler in the Command window[3]:

```
shell /c cl /help
```

Finally, you can also execute commands from the Find drop-down list box on the Standard toolbar. Normally, you use this feature to search for text in the currently open document (by typing the text and then pressing the Enter key or F3), but if you type the > symbol, you can give the name of a command. So, if you type *>File.OpenFile* in the Find list box, you will get the File Open dialog box rather than having to search the document for the text *>File.OpenFile*. If you decide that you would like to search the current document for the text *>File.OpenFile*, you have to use the Find dialog box (accessed through the *Edit.Find* command), or you could type the following in the Find list box:

```
>Edit.Find >File.OpenFile
```

---

2. This command passes the parameter to the shell, and since the default process is Explorer, you can get the same effect by omitting *explorer* in this example.

3. This assumes that the path to the C++ compiler is in the system *PATH* environment variable.

Projects, Solutions, and Configurations

Visual Studio .NET uses projects and solutions to manage your code. A project has an output, so you use projects to build DLLs, EXEs, or MSI (Microsoft Installer) files. A solution contains projects; the solution can have a single output, or it can have multiple outputs. C++ projects are described by XML files with the extension .vcproj. Because this file is XML, you can read it with a simple text editor such as Notepad. Such a project file contains the dependency and build tool information for each source file. Visual Studio 6 had an option to export a project as an *nmake* make file; however, this feature is missing in Visual Studio .NET. Solutions are described by files with the extension .sln. These files are also text files, but they have a proprietary format.

Solutions and projects have one or more configurations. A project configuration has specific build properties, and by default, the wizards will usually give you a Release build and a Debug build configuration. You can supply any build tool values in the configuration through the project property pages. Because the project property pages allow you to include and exclude files from a build, you can use project configurations to compile different files in the project. (But note that project dependencies are configuration independent.) Some properties that are accessible through the project property pages are used by the build tools (for example, the C++ compiler). You can provide these settings for each individual file, or you can set them on the project. If such a property is set on the project, it becomes the default value. For example, you can set the preprocessor symbols that will be defined for each file in the project, and you can also define additional preprocessor symbols on a per-file basis.

Solutions also have configurations, and these have the same names as the project configurations. However, and rather confusingly, you can use the solution property pages to identify the *project* configuration on a per-project basis that will be used for a particular *solution* configuration. I will explain these property pages further in the section "Managing Configurations" later in this chapter.

When you use Visual Studio .NET with an open solution, you will get some additional nonessential files in the solution and project folders. These files hold optional information and will be created if they do not exist. There are three files to consider: the solution options file (.suo), the no-compile browser file (.ncb), and the resource editor file (.aps). The solution options file holds information about the files that you had open and your position in those files when the solution was last saved. This feature is useful for you, because at the end of a day all the information about your workspace will be saved, and when you load the solution the next day, you will get the same files open at the same positions that you used the previous day. This information is unlikely to be useful for a coworker, so if you copy a solution to transmit to a colleague, it makes little sense to copy the .suo file.

When you load a resource script (.rc), the IDE Resource Editor will create a compiled version of the script in the .aps file. This arrangement means that the Resource Script Editor does not have to parse the resource script in subsequent editing sessions, but during a build, the resource script is always used to create the final output's resources. The compiled version of the resource script, .aps, is used to load resource information quickly in the Resource Editor and can always be regenerated from a resource script.

The no-compile browser file contains information about the classes that you have used in your project and information used for statement completion. The no-compile browser file can get quite large, and it will be generated if Visual Studio .NET cannot find one in the solution folder. There is a school of thought that says that .ncb files can take time to build afresh, but I take the opposite view that disk space (and download time, if a project is sent to me) is more important than the time it takes to re-create a no-compile build file.

Thus, I usually delete the .suo, .ncb, and .aps files when I have completed work on a solution. I don't put these files under source control, and if I send a solution to a coworker, I *always* exclude these files.

Creating Projects and Solutions

Creating a solution with Visual Studio .NET is as simple as running the New Project dialog box (*File.NewProject*). This dialog box allows you to select the location for the solution and to select the first project type. By default, the dialog will name the solution after the first project and put the .sln file in the project folder. If you want to create a multiproject solution, it is better to separate the solution and project files. To do this task, you should click on the More button and check the Create Directory For Solution check box. This option allows you to specify the name for the solution folder, and the project folder will be created as a subfolder. If you have existing projects, these can be added to a solution through *File.AddExistingProject*. You can create a blank solution through the Visual Studio Solutions category of the New Project dialog box or through *File.NewBlankSolution*.

Solution Explorer

Visual Studio .NET offers two views on your solution, one based on the files in the projects and the other based on the types that you have defined. Solution Explorer shows the files in your solution, and Class View shows the types. Each view is a tree view control with an entry for each project in the solution. Solution Explorer also has an additional entry named *Solution Items* for items that have been added to the solution rather than to an individual project. In addition, if you open a file that is not part of any project in your solution, this file will be shown in a folder in Solution Explorer named *Miscellaneous Files*.[4] When you close a solution, the current contents of the Miscellaneous Files folder (in other words, the nonsolution files open in the workspace) will be saved in the solution so that when you open the solution, the miscellaneous files will be opened too. When there are no miscellaneous files, the Miscellaneous Files folder will not show in Solution Explorer. You can indicate that the Miscellaneous Files folder is used as a most recently used folder for nonsolution files. You enable this option through the workspace properties (*Tools.Options*) by specifying how many files are saved in the Miscellaneous Files folder. By default, this value is set to zero.

Each project in the Solution Explorer view has "folders" that categorize your files. By default you'll get three folders (shown in Table 6-2) for the code files, headers, and resource files. You can put any type of file into any folder; the build process is not affected by the Solution Explorer folders. Each folder has a filter. When you add a new file to a project through the Add Class (*Project.AddClass*) or Add New Item (*File.AddNewItem*) dialog boxes, the filter will be used to determine which folder the file should be added to. If a new file is of a type not covered by any filter, the file will be added to the top level of the project entry.

Table 6-2 Filters for Default Folders in Solution Explorer

Folder	Filter
Source Files	cpp;c;cxx;def;odl;idl;hpj;bat;asm
Header Files	h;hpp;hxx;hm;inl;inc
Resource Files	rc;ico;cur;bmp;dlg;rc2;rct;bin;rgs;gif;jpg;jpeg;jpe;r

There is no connection between the folders in Solution Explorer and folders on the hard disk (unlike C# or Visual Basic .NET projects). Indeed, you can add files from any location (including other machines) to a Solution Explorer folder. When you add a file to a Solution Explorer folder, the file is not moved; you are merely adding information about the file to the folder. This behavior means that you can share a file between solutions, and it also means that if you remove a file from a folder, the physical file is unaffected. If you want to delete a file (or rename it), you have to do this with an external tool such as Windows Explorer.

When you open a file from Solution Explorer, the IDE will check the file association to determine the editor to use. The IDE provides several editors, and you can add an association for an external tool. The mechanism to do this

4. If you do not see this folder, it is disabled. To enable this folder, go to the Environment, Documents property page of the *Tools.Options* dialog box and check Show Miscellaneous Files In Solution Explorer.

task is not immediately obvious: you have to show the Open dialog (*File.OpenFile*) and then click on the down arrow button next to the Open button. This action will show a drop-down menu, and from this menu, you can select Open With. This command shows the Open With dialog box (shown in Figure 6-2), and through this dialog, you can select one of the IDE's editors or add your own editor. The Add button allows you to specify the path to an editor and give a friendly name that will be used in the Open With dialog box. Be careful about what you use for the friendly name because it is the same name that you will use with the *File.OpenFile /e* switch, so it is best to give a short, but obvious name. (For example, typing the name of the default editor, */e:"Source code (Text) Editor"* is very tedious; it would have been better to have named it simply *Text Editor*.) If you open a file with an external editor, you will get a separate window. If the solution is under source control, you will have to check the file out of source control first; otherwise, the file will be opened as read-only.

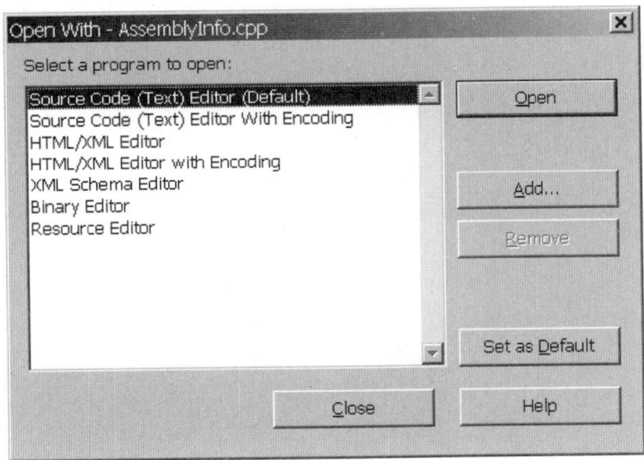

Figure 6-2 The Open With dialog box showing the default Visual Studio .NET editors

You can add new folders to your project, which will be added to your .vcproj file. You can use the Properties window (*View.PropertiesWindows*) to change the properties of a folder. As I have mentioned already, the filter property is used to determine which folder a new file will be added to. In addition, you have properties to determine whether files added to the folder will be parsed to provide information for Class View (*Parse Files*) and whether the files will be subject to source code control (*SCC*). Folders can also be nested.

You can add files to a folder in one of several ways: you can use the context menu of the folder, you can use items on the File or Project menu (the *File.AddExistingItem* command is available through both menus), or you can use drag and drop, either from another folder or from Windows Explorer.

Unfortunately, the Open File dialog box shown by the *File.AddExistingItem* command does not use the filter set for the folder. Be aware that within a project a file can be in only one folder.

Files within a folder also have properties. The starting place to look is the Properties window, which will give the name and the location of the file. This window also has a property named *Content* that indicates whether the file is considered as "content" as part of the output of the project. When a project is deployed, all the outputs of the project—the compiled output and the content files—will be copied to the deployment location. Rather confusingly, files can also have property pages. To show a property page, you can select the Properties item from the context menu for the file (*View.PropertyPages*) or you can click the Property Pages button on the Properties window. This window will have a page named *General,* which indicates the tool to use to build the file and whether the file is included in the build for the current configuration. If Excluded From Build is set to Yes, the file will not be compiled; if this property is set to No, the build tool will be used.

Table 6-3 lists the tool that will be used for various files. You can change the build tool through the Tool property (which will list only the five options in Table 6-3), in which case you need to click the OK button of the dialog box to get the property pages for the specified tool. For each build tool in Table 6-3, I have given the name of the property pages; you will find that the project will also have property pages for the build tool. The project property pages provide build tool settings that are the default for all appropriate files in the project, and the file property pages are used to specify the settings for a specific file. Note that some file types will be listed as having a Custom Build Tool when you might think that there is a suitable build tool available. For example, header files (.h) will be listed as Custom Build Tool rather than C/C++ Compiler Tool. When you think about it, the reason is obvious: header files are not compiled because they are always included in a C or C++ file; however, Solution Explorer does not have enough intelligence to indicate this fact.

Table 6-3 Build Tools

File Extension	Build Tool	Property Pages
.c, .cpp. .cxx	C/C++ Compiler Tool	C/C++
.rc	Resource Compiler Tool	Resources
.wsdl	Web Service Proxy Generator	Web References
.idl	MIDL Tool	MIDL
All other files	Custom Build Tool	Custom Build Step

Class View

Visual Studio .NET can also show your solution in Class View (*View.ClassView*). Again, this window is a tree view control, and you will get a top-level item for each project; however, you will not have the equivalent of Miscellaneous Files or Solution Items. Class View will show all the classes in your project, and there are also containers named *Global Functions And Variables* and *Macros And Constants*. You cannot add folders to this view. Class View has three main purposes. First, it is a browsing and navigation tool to help you find definitions of code in your project. Second, Class View allows you to access properties specific to a type. Finally, Class View gives access to various wizards that you can use to change your code. I will address the browsing uses in this section, I will cover wizards in the section "Code Wizards" later in this chapter, and I will cover item properties in the section "Editing Code" later in this chapter.

The type browsing facility of Class View is particularly useful in large projects when classes can be defined in many files. When you add a file to a Solution Explorer folder that has the *Parse* property set to True, the file will be parsed and the types are added to the relevant folders in Class View. If you double-click on a type or a member of a type in Class View, the file containing the implementation will be loaded and the insertion point is placed on the item. If the declaration and implementation are in different files, you can use the context menu to select either the declaration (in the header) or the definition (in the .cpp file).

A class entry in Class View will list all its members. Interestingly, for unmanaged classes, the destructor is listed with the destructor name (such as *~MyClass*), but for managed classes, the destructor is listed as *Finalize* even though the compiler explicitly refuses to allow you to define a method named *Finalize* on your class. Class View also gives an item named *Bases And Interfaces* that lists the base classes and interfaces implemented by the class. If the source of the base class is available through a file in a folder with *Parse* set to True, you will be able to browse the base class members too.

To get more information, you can use the Object Browser (*View.ObjectBrowser*), shown in Figure 6-3. This tool can be used to browse items (classes and functions) in your solution and also to browse other files that contain type information. Such files include browser files (.bsc), type libraries, and assemblies. In Figure 6-3, I am browsing the current project and the classes in the mscorlib assembly. To browse these files, you have to select Selected Components from the Browse list box and then select the Customize button (*Tools.CustomizeObjectBrowsingScope*). This action allows you to select files that contain type libraries and assemblies. If you want to load a .bsc browser file, you have to use the Open File dialog box (*File.OpenFile*).

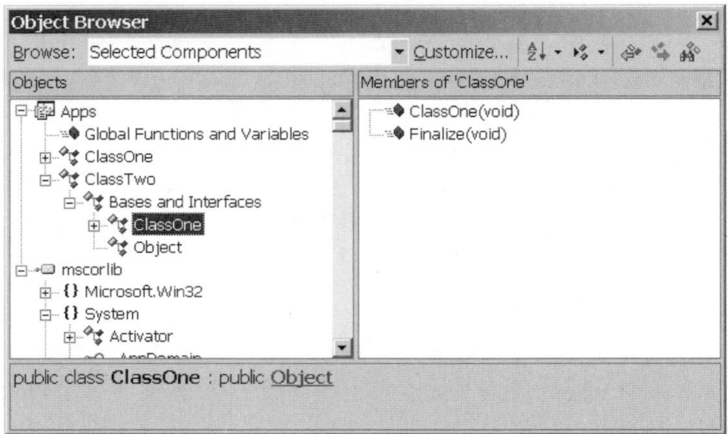

Figure 6-3 The Object Browser

Object Browser and Class View allow you to search for the use of a type or a type member. This feature is accessible through the Find Symbol dialog box (*Edit.FindSymbol*) or through the Quick Find Symbols context menu item (to search for the selected item). The Find Symbol Results window (*View.FindSymbolResults*) lists where in your solution the symbol is used. Note that to be able to search your own project for the use of a specified symbol you have to generate browser files (.bsc). This setting is not enabled by default, and to enable it requires two changes. First, you have to go to the Browser Information page of the C/C++ property pages (*Project.Properties*) and change Enable Browse Information to Include All Browse Information. This setting will create browser information files (.sbr) for all source files, but to combine these files into a single source browser file (.bsc), you also have to go to the General page of the project property pages and change the Build Browser Information property to Yes.

Resource View

As I mentioned in Chapter 4, an assembly can have both managed and unmanaged resources. Resource View is available in both managed and unmanaged projects, but it shows *only* unmanaged resources. Managed resources are not maintained through resource scripts, so there is no need for a specific resource script editor and so Resource View is not used for managed resources. Resource View has a tree view where the top level items are the projects in the solution and beneath each project entry are the resource scripts in each project.

Resource View parses the .rc file when you first load the file. After you have finished making changes, Resource View writes to the .rc file. This behavior means that the resource script has the specific format recognized by Resource View, and you should not attempt to change the script by hand. If you have a specific need to add unmanaged resources to the assembly that are not handled by the Resource Editor, you have to perform this task through the context menu. The context menu for a resource file in Resource View has the menu items Resource Includes (*Edit.ResourceIncludes*) and Resource Symbols (*Edit.ResourceSymbols*). Resource Includes allows you to specify the name of the file that contains symbols for the items in the resource script that can be edited by Resource View. (By default, this file will be resource.h.) Resource Includes also allows you to specify header files, which the Resource View cannot edit (by default, this list will be one file, afxres.h), and Resource Includes allows you to specify resource script entries. (By resource script entries, I mean any item that can go in a .rc file; the entries that you type will be added verbatim to the resource script.)

When you add new unmanaged resources to a project, Resource View assigns a symbol for the resource. You can use the Properties window to change the symbol for an item, either to provide a new symbol name or to use a symbol from one of the included header files (included through Resource Includes). If you use a new symbol, the definition of the symbol will be added to the symbol header file (by default, resource.h). If you rename a symbol, the original symbol will remain in the symbol header file. You should not edit the symbol header by hand, so to clean up these extra symbols, you use the Resource Symbols dialog box (*Edit.ResourceSymbols*).

Visual Studio .NET has editors for the resources that you will use most often. There is an Image Editor for cursors, icons, bitmaps, and toolbars; a Dialog Box Editor; an HTML Editor for Web pages; an editor for VERSION_INFO resources; an editor for editing unmanaged menus; and editors for string tables and accelerator tables. These editors are used when you double-click on a resource in Resource View. If your project has managed resources, the resource editors will be used for those too (in particular, the Image Editor and the HTML Editor).

Solution Properties

Solutions have properties that are accessible through the Properties window and the solution property pages. (This window is shown by the *Project.Properties* or *View.PropertyPages* command when the solution is selected.) The Properties window is essentially a summary of the solution properties. Not all of the solution property pages are specific to a solution; confusingly, the property pages mix the solution pages with a page that really should be in the general options for Visual Studio .NET (*Tools.Options*). I'll start by describing the real solution property pages.

The solution property pages are mainly concerned with manipulating configurations. The Startup Project page allows you to specify which project is the start-up project. When you debug a solution, the output from the start up project is started under the debugger. A solution can have more than one start up project because you can debug more than one process at a single time. (For more details, see Chapter 7.) If you choose to have more than one start up project, you have the option of determining whether the output is started under the debugger, started stand-alone, or ignored during a debugging session.

If you have more than one project in a solution, some projects might depend on the outputs of others. For example, if you have a solution with a library assembly and an executable assembly that uses the library, you will more than likely statically link to the library, so the compiler needs metadata to make the calls (which the compiler gets through the *#using* statement) and the linker needs the metadata to generate the assembly's manifest. This arrangement means that the library must be built before the executable, and if the library source changes and has to be rebuilt, the executable must be rebuilt too. Thus, the executable depends on the library, and the executable must be built after the library.

The Project Dependencies property page allows you to identify the dependencies between projects. It has one checked list box with all the projects other than the project being configured. You use the drop-down list box at the top of the property page to identify the project whose dependencies you want to alter. Once you have selected a project, you then check the projects that it depends on. The dependencies define the order that projects are built, and you can view this order through the Build Order tab of the Project Dependencies dialog box (through the project or solution context menu).

The next solution property page is named *Debug Source Files*. As the name suggests, this page allows you to specify the location of the source files for the libraries that you use. By default, this page will have the locations of the source files for the CRT, MFC, and ATL, but you can add paths to the location of your own libraries. When you debug your solution and step into a library method, the debugger will search the folders that you give for the file specified in the library's program database (.pdb).

The final property page really should not be on this dialog. It is named *Debug Symbol Files*. As the name suggests, this page is used to give the paths that will be searched for symbol files (.dbg or .pdb) for system libraries. If you have the symbols for your operating system installed, I urge you to add the path to those symbols. Although you will not have access to the source code for the operating system, the symbols allow you to locate which operating system function has thrown an exception, which gives you more information about how to determine what caused the problem. I will cover symbol files in more detail in Chapter 7.

Symbols are also provided with the .NET Framework SDK. Note that symbols are not provided for the class library. The Framework SDK provides symbols for the DLLs that have native (but not ngen-created) code. So there are symbols for files such as mscoree.dll and mscorwks.dll. If you are likely to write code to access the functions exported from such DLLs (for example, if you want to use the strong name APIs), it makes sense to add these symbol files to your symbol file path. These symbols can be found in the Symbols folder under the FrameworkSDK folder.

I said that these are *not* solution settings because when you add a symbol path through this dialog, the path will be available to *any* solution. Thus, it would have been better to put this property page in the IDE options available through *Tools.Options*.

Project Properties

Most of the configuration that you will perform will be through the project property pages. However, unlike solutions, the Properties window is not a mere summary of the properties; it has one property that is not available elsewhere: Policy File. A policy file has the extension .tdl and contains XML descriptions of the actions that can be performed on the project. A policy file can be used to identify the items that can be added to a project, the help that can be shown, and items in the toolbox. The idea is that an administrator can define a policy file for the type of project that developers in a team are working on, and the policy file assures that no developer is able to add facilities that are not supported by the policy. A more complete description of policy files is beyond the scope of this book.

The project's property pages (when the project is selected, *Project.Properties* or *View.PropertyPages*) give access to the parameters that will be passed to the various tools used to perform the build (shown in Table 6-4). The IDE performs project maintenance, manages dependencies, and determines the build tools to use for the various file types. The *nmake* utility is not used. One of the advantages of using the IDE to perform the build is that it will produce a summary Web page at the end of the build with a complete description of the actions that have been performed. This file is named *BuildLog.htm* and is copied to the output directory. This file lists the current environment variables, the command lines passed to the build tools, and the outputs from the build tools, which means that you have complete information about a build, which helps you to identify the problem if a build fails.

I will cover the settings for the compiler and linker for managed projects in later sections of this chapter. (See "Compiler Switches" and "Linker Switches.") The Custom Build Step and Build Events categories allow you to identify a custom tool that will be run at a particular point during the build process. (See the section "Build Steps" later in this chapter.)

In this section, I will describe only one property page, the General property page (Figure 6-4). This page is used to provide general settings for the project configuration; these are settings that affect the whole project. The first two properties are the Intermediate Directory and the Output Directory. The Intermediate Directory property takes the outputs of the pre-link tools such as the C++ compiler and the resource compiler, and the Output Directory property has the outputs of the linker and the browser make utility. The values that you enter here will be available to other properties through the *$(IntDir)* and *$(OutDir)* macros. By default, these properties are the same and are a folder under the project folder with the name of the configuration, but you can provide any name you want and can even include environment variables. These properties are useful if you want to have a general output directory for all the projects in a solution. (See the sections "Multiassembly Solutions" and "Multimodule Solutions" later in this chapter.)

Table 6-4 Project Property Page Categories

Property Page Category	Build Tool
C/C++	C++ compiler, cl.exe
Linker	The linker, link.exe
Resources	Resource compiler, rc.exe
MIDL	IDL compiler, midl.exe
Browse Information	The browse information maintenance utility, BscMake.exe
Build Events	Custom
Custom Build Step	Custom
Web References	The Web proxy generation tool, sproxy.exe for unmanaged projects, wsdl.exe for managed projects
Web Deployment	The Web deployment tool, VCDeploy.exe

The other two properties on this page that I ought to mention are the Character Set and Use Managed Extensions properties. As the name suggests, the Use Managed Extensions property determines whether the */clr* switch is passed to the compiler. However, do not assume that to compile a project as a managed project all you have to do is set this property because some of the compiler switches are incompatible with the */clr* switch. Furthermore, the project property pages even allow you to set switches that are incompatible with the */clr* switch. It would have been nice if the Use Managed Extensions property was a "master switch" that determined which switches you can set with the Project Properties dialog box.

The Character Set property determines whether the project will be built for Unicode or the Multi-Byte Character Set (MBCS). The value of this property determines which version of MFC and ATL static-link libraries will be used, and it also defines appropriate manifest symbols. The Character Set property specifies default values for the project.

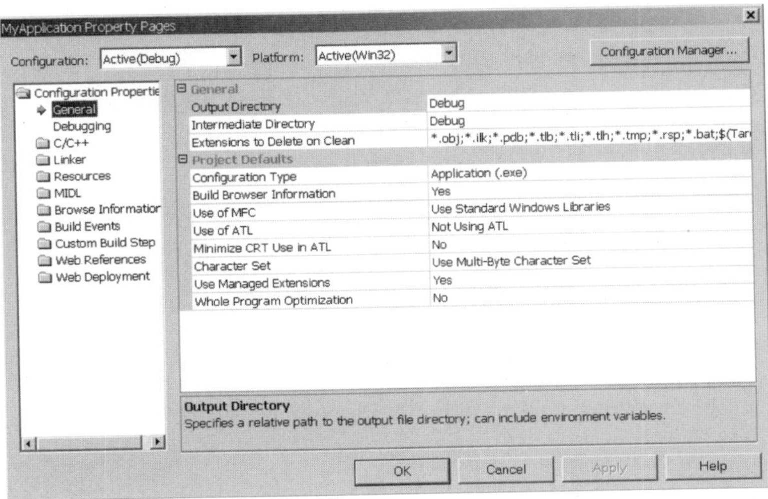

Figure 6-4 The General property page

When you edit a property, you will usually get either a combo box or a drop-down list box in the grid. For properties that can have only specific values, you will get these in a drop-down list box. For other properties, such as the output file name or preprocessor symbols to define, you will get a combo box. You can type the value in the edit control of the combo, or you can select <Edit…> from the list box, and you will get a dialog box to help you edit the value. Figure 6-5 shows the dialog box used to edit the name of the output folder for a project (on the Project.Properties dialog box, select Output Directory from the General page). The dialog has a Macros>> button; if you click this button, you will see Visual Studio .NET macro definitions. Macros are used in project properties using the same format as *nmake*, that is, *$(macroname)*, where *macroname* is the macro that you want to use. So, for example, in Figure 6-5, you can see that the C++ files are installed in a folder named *$(VCInstallDir)*.

If the property you are editing can take a list of items (for example, preprocessor symbols), you should separate each item with a semicolon. Don't add a space because this space will be treated as part of the item. So, if I want to define the TRACE and STRICT preprocessor symbols, I enter the following information for the Preprocessor Definitions on the Preprocessor C/C++ page:

```
TRACE;STRICT
```

Figure 6-5 Editing a project's output folder name with the Visual C++ macros visible

Managing Configurations

When you build a solution, you have to identify the solution configuration to build. A solution configuration has information about the project configurations that will be used to build each project in the solution. A project configuration contains the properties that you have set through the project property pages. By default, you will get two configurations, Debug and Release, that have project settings to compile with and without debugging information.

The IDE provides a tool named the *Configuration Manager* (*Build.ConfigurationManager*), which you can use to manage *solution* configurations (shown in Figure 6-6). This dialog has a grid that lists the projects in the solution, and it allows you to specify which project configuration will be used for each project in the solution for a specified solution configuration. The Active Solution Configuration allows you to specify the solution configuration that you want to edit, and the Configuration Manager will fill the grid with the current project configurations. You can also use this dialog to specify whether a particular project is built when the solution configuration is built.

The Configuration Manager also allows you to add new configurations. To add a solution configuration, you select <New…> from the Active Solution Configuration list box. This option shows the New Solution dialog box that will allow you to create either a new solution configuration or both a solution configuration and a configuration for each project. The New Solution Configuration dialog box has a check box named Also Create New Project Configuration(s); if you select this check box, a configuration with the same name will be created in the solution and in each project. If you uncheck this box, only a solution configuration will be created. If you create project configurations through the New Solution Configuration dialog box, the configurations will apply only to the current projects. If you add another project to the solution, the project will get only the default Debug and Release configurations. If you want to have a project configuration that corresponds to a solution configuration for the new project, you have to add that configuration by hand.

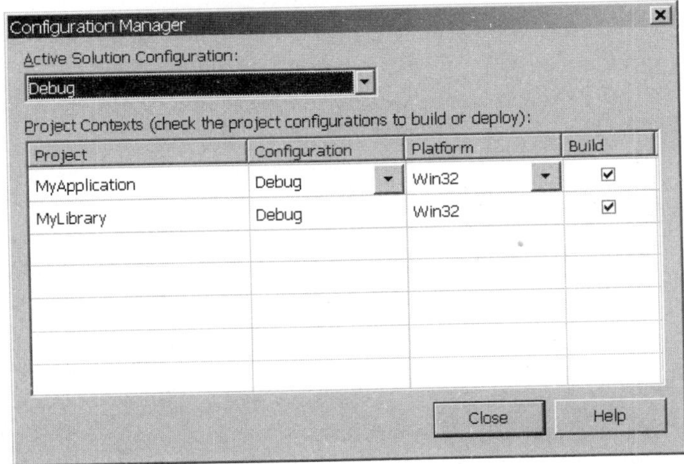

Figure 6-6 The Configuration Manager

To add a new project configuration, you select <New…> for the configuration of a project in the Configuration Manager (shown in Figure 6-7). This option will show the New Project Configuration dialog box, which looks the same as the New Solution Configuration dialog box; indeed, this dialog also has a check box named Also Create New Solution Configuration(s), so you have the choice of creating just a project configuration or both a project and a solution configuration with the same name.

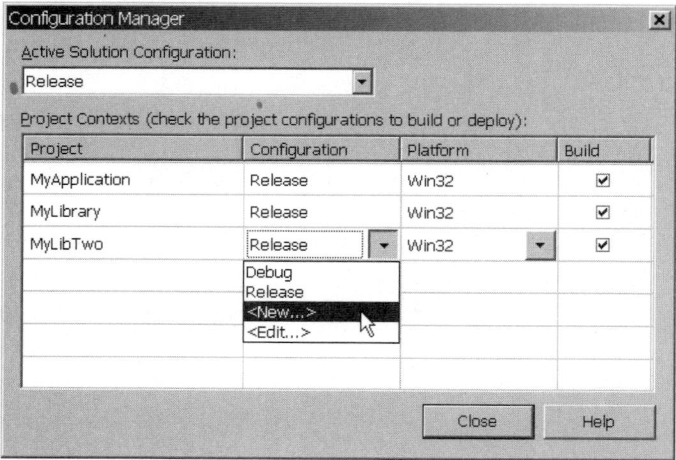

Figure 6-7 Adding a new project configuration through the Configuration Manager dialog box

Visual Studio .NET Options

Visual Studio .NET also has general properties that are specific to C++ builds but will be applied to all C++ solutions. You can access these properties through the *Tools.Options* dialog box in the Projects category. The VC++ Build page allows you to specify the C++ file extensions, whether the BuildLog.htm file will be generated, and whether build timings will be shown. The VC++ Directories page is more interesting; this page is used to identify the folders that will be searched, and the search order, for the build tools, the header files, the static-link libraries, the source files for code completion, and the assemblies that are used in the *#using* statement. The values that you give on this page will apply to *all* C++ solutions, and I think this is where the page for symbol files should have been shown. Note that the values on this page are different to the equivalent environment variables, *PATH*, *INCLUDE*, *LIB*, and *LIBPATH*. However, if you prefer Visual Studio .NET to use the environment variables, you should start it with the */useenv* switch. (See the section "Visual Studio .NET Command Line" later in this chapter.) If you use this switch, you will find that the VC++ Directories page will have the values of the *PATH*, *INCLUDE*, *LIB*, and *LIBPATH* variables when the IDE was started. This page stores the settings in the registry, so if you change these environment variables, the search paths will be unaffected, and if you change the search paths through this page, the environment variables will be unaffected.

Editing Code

The main reason you will want to use Visual Studio .NET for developing your code is the tools that it offers to manage your project, which I have covered in the previous sections. The next most important reason is the Visual Studio .NET text editor. The Visual Studio .NET editor is integrated with the Visual Studio .NET help system and with IntelliSense, so you can get information about the classes and methods that you want to use and you get code completion.

Text Editor

The Visual Studio .NET text editor is essentially Notepad on steroids: it offers no-nonsense editing of text, but in addition, it gives you tools that make your work much easier. The first big change that you get over Notepad is that the status bar will indicate where in the source file the insertion point is located. You get the current line position, character position, and column number.[5] This information, of course, is important when you have a list of warnings and errors from a build, but as I will mention in Chapter 7, if you double-click on an error in the Output pane, the caret will be moved automatically to the source of the error.

The text editor also supports code coloring. The text editor knows the type of the document that you are editing (it gets this from the extension of the file), and as you type text, it checks to see what the text is used for. For example, the editor checks to see whether the text is a language keyword, a comment, a literal string, or an identifier (class name, class member, or a variable), and it will assign the text to the appropriate color. This feature is a useful check as you type because you will be able to see from the syntax coloring whether the compiler will treat the text as a keyword.

You can edit the colors that will be used through the Fonts And Colors page of the Environment category in the Options dialog box (*Tools.Options*). This page allows you to set the colors and fonts used for the text editor and various other windows in the IDE and for the printer. The Display Items list box gives the various types of text that you can apply a color to. One of these types is named *User Keyword*. The coloring that you specify for this item will be applied to any text that you give in a file named *usertype.dat*. This text file has one keyword per line, and it should be saved in the same folder as DevEnv.exe. When the IDE first loads, it reads the usertype.dat file, so for any changes to take effect, you have to restart the IDE.

The text editor also performs code highlighting. If you type text that should occur in pairs, the text editor will highlight the two sections of text when you type the second of the pair. For example, if you type a closing parenthesis,

5. One of the most important updates in Windows XP was that Notepad was given a status bar with these facilities. If you are unsure about whether to upgrade to Windows XP, I hope that this change will finally make up your mind that upgrading is worth the bother of Windows Activation.

the text editor will highlight this symbol and the corresponding opening parenthesis. The text editor will count nested parentheses, so this feature will allow you to avoid mismatching them. This feature works for parenthesis, braces, C-style comments (*/** and **/*), quotes (" and "), angle brackets (< and >), square brackets, keywords that occur in pairs (*if* and *else*), and the preprocessor directives for conditional compilation.

Depending on the size of the font you select, you will find that at some point you will exceed the width of the current editor window. The default action is for the window to scroll horizontally as you add more text, but you can change the text editor setting (*Tools.Options* dialog box, Text Editor, C/C++, General page) to enable word wrap. This setting will wrap code so that it always fits the current window, by moving code to the next line. Word wrap is useful for reading code, but it should not be used for editing code because it overrides some of the formatting that the editor can supply. The same options page also allows you to enable virtual space. This facility will be familiar to Microsoft Word users. Virtual space allows you to insert text at any point in a source file beyond the end of an existing line. Once virtual space has been enabled, you simply click at the location where you want to insert text—such as the middle of a blank line—and the editor will pad out the space between the text and the old end of the line with spaces. I find virtual space useful for adding inline comments.

Formatting Code

Formatted code is more readable than unformatted code. As you type code, the text editor will apply formatting to your code. The text editor options (*Tools.Options*, Text Editor, C/C++) has several pages to specify how code is formatted. There is one page that allows you to set whether the tab key inserts spaces or a tab character and how code should be indented. You have three options: either you have to format the code yourself with spaces and tabs (None), or when you press the Enter key, the insertion point will be aligned with the text on the preceding line (Block), or the text editor will use formatting rules to determine how to indent code (Smart).

I usually set my format settings to indicate that the tab key inserts spaces. This makes it easier for me to format text, but if I load code written by another developer or code that has been generated by the code wizards, this code can contain tab characters. The text editor allows you to see which characters have been used for white space (*Edit.ViewWhiteSpace*), and you can indicate that it should replace spaces with tab characters (*Edit.TabifySelection*) or replace tab characters with spaces (*Edit.UntabifySelection*). You can even indicate that the editor should remove the white space at the end of a line (*Edit.DeleteHorizontalWhiteSpace*). This tool is more complicated than it first appears because the first time you apply it on a line that has white space, it will replace tabs with a single space and it will replace multiple spaces with a single space. The net effect is to have single spaces between each word. If you use this tool on a line with only single spaces, it will remove all of them. If you select more than one line of code, you can choose to delete the lines that do not contain code (*Edit.DeleteBlankLines*).

The final facility that I should mention here is the block commenting feature (*Edit.CommentSelection*). This command will comment selected lines with the C++ comment character (//), which is useful for commenting out blocks of code because the text editor also offers an uncomment command (*Edit.UncommentSelection*) that will remove the comment character. Note that this feature works only with C++ comments; it does not work with C-style multiline comments (/* */).

Navigating Code

A large source file presents problems to navigating code. The text editor gives you several tools that make navigating easier. The first tool occurs at the top of the text editor for source files and headers that are part of your project. Here you will find two drop-down list boxes. The left-hand box lists class names, and the right-hand box lists the members of the selected class. This facility appears to have been added to the text editor to keep Visual Basic programmers happy (Visual Basic .NET shares the text editor) because the editor is similar to the text editor in Visual Basic 6. As a consequence, this feature is not quite as useful as it might seem to be because the members list box does not distinguish between overloaded methods. Class View is a far more effective way to navigate code.

Another way to navigate through code in a large source file is to use the keyboard arrow keys to scroll. These are largely as you would expect: the arrow keys move one line at a time, and the Page Up and Page Down keys move a screen at a time. There are other key sequences too: on the default keyboard mapping, Ctrl+Home will move the caret to the beginning of the file and Ctrl+End will move to the end of the file. Furthermore, Ctrl+Page Up will move the caret to the top of the screen, Ctrl+Page Down will move the caret to the bottom of the screen, and Ctrl with the left or right arrow keys will move the caret left or right one word at a time. When you use the arrow keys to scroll up or down, the caret will move through the text. If you use the Ctrl key with the up or down arrow, the caret will stay in the same position in the text and the text will scroll. In both cases, if the caret position moves out of the current screen, the caret will be moved through the text so that it appears at the top or the bottom of the screen (depending on the direction you are scrolling).

If your mouse has a wheel, you can use this wheel to scroll the code, and if you have a third mouse button (or a wheel), clicking the button or wheel turns on autoscrolling so that the scroll speed can be adjusted by moving the mouse forward or backward. Autoscrolling works only in one direction—from the start to the end of the document. It does not work in the horizontal direction, so if you have a source file with long lines, it makes sense to turn on word wrap before using autoscrolling.

Of course, if you know the name of the class member, you can always search for it. The Visual Studio .NET IDE gives you three ways to do this task: Find (*Edit.Find*), Find In Files (*Edit.FindinFiles*), and incremental search (*Edit.IncrementalSearch*, but as you will see, you will not be able to execute this command from the Command window). The Find dialog box (shown in Figure 6-8) allows you to search the current file or the files opened in the current project. The search will start from the current caret position, so you can specify that the search is performed upwards or downwards. The dialog allows you to search for part or all of a specified word or through the Use drop-down list box, to provide a regular expression or a simplified version of regular expressions that is named *Wildcards*. In Figure 6-8, I am searching for the expression *?his*; this expression will search for any word that starts with a single character followed by the three characters *his*.

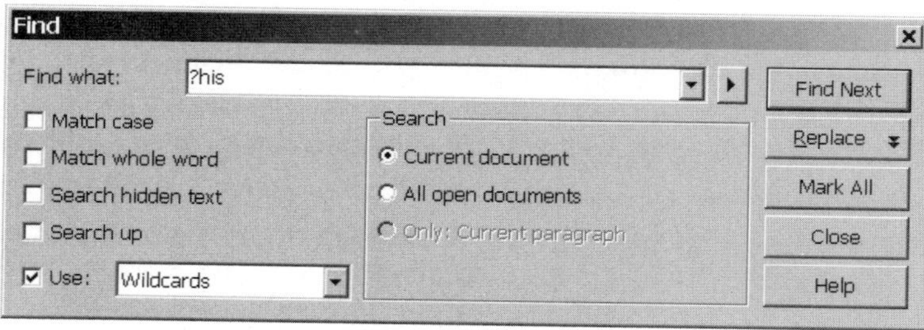

Figure 6-8 The Find dialog box

The Find dialog box is modeless, so each time you click the Find Next button, the search will pause on the next word that is found. If you click the Mark All button, a bookmark will be placed against all the matches. The Standard toolbar has a combo box named *Find*, which is a quick way to search the current document.

Next to the Find combo box on the Standard toolbar is the Find In Files button, which will show the Find In Files dialog box. This dialog allows you to search a specific file, a file that fits a particular pattern, or the files in a path. The path can be the current solution, or you can browse for a folder on your hard disk, on a file share, or all of these: the browse dialog allows you to select more than one path.

If you specify a folder to search, you can indicate that subfolders are searched too. This process can take a long time, so the Find In Files dialog box also has a Stop button (*Edit.StopSearch*). When the search has completed, the results will go to the Find window. There are two Find windows, named *Find*

Results 1 and *Find Results 2*, and the Find In Files dialog box has a check box that you can use to indicate which Find window will be used. When the search has completed, you can double-click on any of the results and the IDE will load the file and position the caret at the location of the text that was found.

These two dialogs can also be used to replace text. When you click the Replace button, an extra edit box will be shown that you can use to supply the replacing text. If the search string is a regular expression, you can provide an expression for the replacing text. You have two options: either you can go through each found text individually and check manually whether the replacement should be made, or you can click Replace All to make all changes in one go. With the Find In Files dialog box, you have to be careful with Replace All because a lot of files could be affected and, because the files are not loaded into the IDE, you cannot undo the changes.

You can also search through a document using an incremental search. Once initiated by pressing Ctrl+I, you provide the search word character by character, and the incremental search will find the first word that fits the characters that have been typed. You can then continue to search for these characters by pressing Ctrl+I again, or you can provide more search characters, and incremental search will look for the first word that matches all of these characters.

Finally, you can navigate text blocks through the *Edit.GotoBrace* command. The default keyboard mapping for this command is Ctrl+}. To use this command, you have to select text that starts a text block and then call the command. The text block can start with a brace, a parenthesis, a square or an angled bracket, a single or double quote, a preprocessor directive used to identify a code block (*#if*, *#ifdef*, or *#ifndef*), or C++ keywords that occur in pairs (for example, *if* and *else*).

Outlining

By default, outlining is not enabled, but you can enable it with the *Edit.CollapsetoDefinitions* command. This command will collapse blocks of code, showing just the first line. You can tell that a block of code has been collapsed by the plus symbol (+) to the left of the code block. If you click the + symbol, the code block will be expanded. Outlined code blocks can be nested so that when a namespace is expanded, it will show classes collapsed; when a class is expanded, it will show methods collapsed; and when a method is expanded, it will show comments and *if* and *while* blocks collapsed. The various code blocks that can be used in outlining are shown in Table 6-5.

An expanded code block will show the code within the block. The first line of the code block will have a minus symbol (–) next to it, and clicking on this symbol collapses the code block. When a code block is collapsed and you hover the mouse over the ellipsis, a ToolTip will appear with as much of the code block as can be fitted into the ToolTip.

Table 6-5 Outlining

Code Block	Collapsed View
Blocks of comments	*/**/*
Namespaces	*namespace* name and ellipsis
Classes	Class name and ellipsis
Functions	Function signature and ellipsis
Mixed blocks of code	*[ ]*

IntelliSense

I have already mentioned that the text editor will check the text that you type and will use this to apply syntax coloring. The checks that are performed extend far beyond mere cosmetics. From the text that you type, the text editor will gain information for the following tools:

- **Dynamic help** Topics that might be of help will be shown in a separate window.
- **IntelliSense** For the complete names of a type, IntelliSense will list the members of the type.
- **Code completion** From a partial name of a type, or type member, code completion will attempt to determine the complete name or will give a list of possible names.

  For example, if you type

```
int testVar;
test
```

in the text editor, the text editor can guess that you are about to type *testVar*. You can use code completion (Alt+Right Arrow, *Edit.CompleteWord*) to allow the text editor to complete the word. If there is more than one possibility for the text, a list box will appear with all possible names in this context, even those that are not applicable. The best match will be selected. If you type a complete name, IntelliSense will be able to give you options about the item. Here is an example:

```
Console::
```

This text is a complete class name, so IntelliSense will show a list box with all the members of the *Console* class. You can then scroll through the list box (or type more characters of the name) and select the member that you want to use. If you type the name of a method, IntelliSense will show the parameters of the method in a ToolTip, and as you type a parameter, the appropriate item in the ToolTip is highlighted. If the method is overloaded, the ToolTip will show an up and down arrow that you can use to select the appropriate overload.

One nice feature is that when you select items in a list box generated by IntelliSense, a ToolTip will appear with the name of the namespace and the file (assembly or source file) where the item is implemented. Furthermore, if the item has a comment on the same line as the item or on the line above, the comment will also be shown in this ToolTip.

Code Wizards

Visual Studio .NET has many wizards to generate code, I will cover the project wizards (*File.NewProject*) in the section "Project Types" later in this chapter. In this section, I will cover the wizards provided to add code and edit existing code.

Both Solution Explorer and Class View have a context menu item named *Add Class* (*Project.AddClass*). The Add Class wizard exists mainly for unmanaged code; most of the class types are ATL or MFC. The only class type that is vaguely relevant to .NET is the Generic C++ Class, but this wizard adds a native class to your code and it does little work. The wizard will add a header to your project (and optionally, a .cpp file), and it adds a class that can be derived from a base class. To be honest, this wizard does very little and it has some annoying quirks. Although it adds the header to your project, it does not add a *#include* for the header anywhere in the project, and the wizard assumes that all class names begin with a C and that the class source files have the same name as the class, so it removes the initial C to determine the name of the header file. If you have a class named *Customer*, the header created by this wizard will be named *ustomer.h*. You can specify the name of the header file that you want created, but to be honest, I never remember this limitation and usually end up having to rename the file with Windows Explorer, which expends as much effort as the wizard attempts to save. It is best to ignore this wizard and use *File.AddNewItem* to add a blank header to your project.

Class View has two wizards that you can use to alter an existing class, the Add Member Function wizard (started with the *Project.AddFunction* command) and the Add Member Variable wizard (started with the *Project.AddVariable* command), but these save you little effort. For a managed class, most of the items on the Add Member Variable wizard are disabled, which means that you merely have controls to enter the name, type, access, and a comment for the variable. Again, you might as well edit the class by hand.

The Add Member Function wizard provides a few more facilities; it allows you to build up the parameter list, name, access level, and return type (as shown in Figure 6-9). However, the types provided in the Parameter Type combo box do not offer any managed types, nor do you have the opportunity to apply attributes to either the function or its parameters. Again, you will expend less effort if you add the function to the class by hand. Finally, it is worth pointing out that there is no wizard to indicate that a class implements an interface, nor one to add support for events or properties. The support for managed classes in Class View is so poor that it really is not worth bothering with them.

The Properties window fares slightly better, but you really should use it only to view information about a class rather than use it to change a class. Consider the following managed class[6]:

```
[Obsolete("Don't use this class")]
__gc class MyClass
{
  public:
};
```

Figure 6-10 shows the properties of this class.

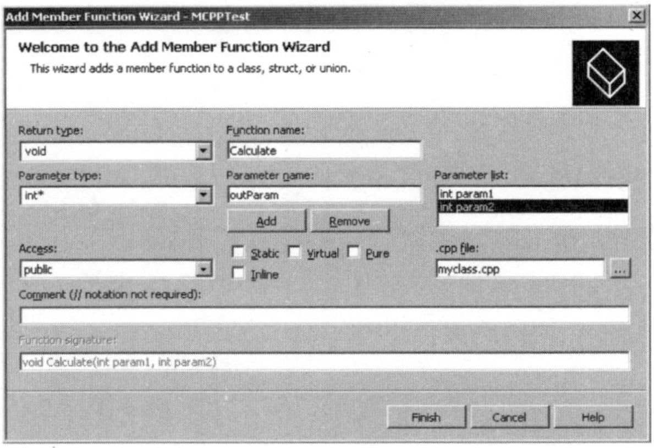

Figure 6-9 The Add Member Function wizard

The Properties window gives a list of the attributes applied to the class, and although you can change the existing parameters, you cannot use the Properties window to add a new parameter to an attribute. The class parameters look over-engineered; a class can be *__gc*, *__value*, or neither, but it cannot be both, so it seems odd to have two Boolean properties *IsManaged* and *IsValue*, where it would be far better to have an enumerated property instead. The reason is that these properties are not really intended for you to change. (You can change them, and the Properties window does ensure that these two properties are never both true.) They are actually part of the Visual Studio .NET automation model (members of the *VCCodeClass*) and are intended to be used by custom Visual Studio .NET Add-ins.

The Properties window gives you information about a class, but it will not allow you to make any changes to the class other than trivial changes. Although

6. Note that you do not have to escape a single quote when it is used in a string used to initialize an attribute.

the Properties window has an Events button, the window does not list the events that you can handle by the class, so if you want to develop a *Form*, you are on your own. Indeed, I have found that if I change a class through the Properties window, occasionally, the class and the Properties window get out of synch. In such a situation, the only remedy is to close down the solution, delete the no-compile browser file (.ncb), and reload the solution. The Properties window was clearly a nice idea, but one that was not developed for C++ classes.

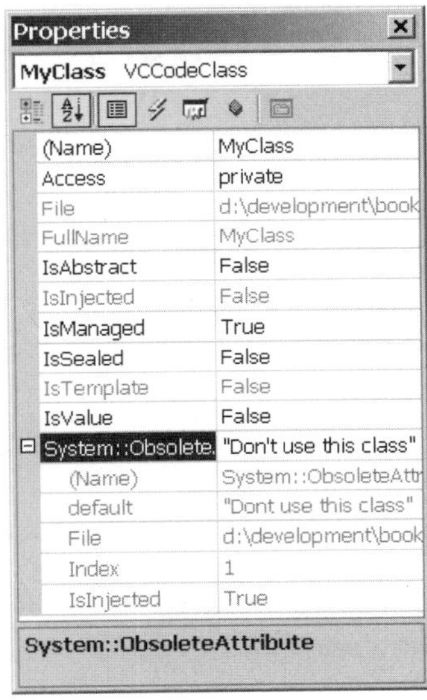

Figure 6-10 The Properties window showing the properties of a class

Visual Studio .NET Command Line

When you start Visual Studio .NET from the command line, you actually start a command-line process named *DevEnv.com*. This process parses the command line, and if the command-line parameters are correct, it passes them to the GUI executable DevEnv.exe. If you start Visual Studio .NET from the Start menu, you will start DevEnv.exe directly.[7] The common command-line switches are summarized in Table 6-6.

The command-line build switches allow you to build, clean, rebuild, or deploy a solution (or a project) from the command line. If you omit one of these switches, the solution will be loaded in the IDE. Remember that although the *nmake* tool is provided as part of Visual C++ .NET, it is not used when building solutions with the IDE because solutions and project files use a totally

7. Compare the results from typing **devenv.com /?** and **devenv.exe /?** at the command line.

different format to store dependency and build information. You can pass the name of a solution or a project file to DevEnv. If you give the name of a solution file, all of the projects in the solution will be built. Whether you decide to pass a solution or a project file, you have to give the name of the configuration to build, as shown in this example:

```
devenv MySolution.sln /build Debug
devenv MySolution.sln /build Debug /project TestProject
```

The first of these two lines will build all of the projects in the MySolution.sln file using the Debug solution configuration. The second line builds the Debug solution configuration of the TestProject project. These two commands are straightforward; however, take a look at the this line:

```
devenv MySolution.sln /build Debug /project TestProject
   /projectconfig "Debug|Win32"
```

Table 6-6 Visual Studio .NET Command-Line Switches

Switch	Description
/build	Build either a project or a solution of a specified configuration.
/clean	Clean a project or a solution of a specified configuration.
/command	Execute the command.
/deploy	Deploy a project or a solution of a specified configuration.
/fn	The name of the font to use.
/fs	The size of the font to use.
/mdi	Use the MDI interface.
/mditabs	Use the tabbed window interface.
/out	Write build output to the specified file.
/project	Use with */build* to specify a particular project to build.
/projectconfig	Use with */project* to specify a particular configuration.
/rebuild	Clean and then build a project or solution of a specified configuration.
/run	Build a project or solution of a specified configuration through the IDE, and then run the startup project.
/runexit	Build a project or solution of a specified configuration through the IDE and then exit.
/useenv	Use the paths specified by the *PATH*, *INCLUDE*, *LIB*, and *LIBPATH* environment variables.

In this case, the TestProject is built, but this time I specify the *project* configuration as well. This is not the name of the configuration that you see in the configuration manager, but the amalgamation of the configuration and the platform. In this case, I want to build the Debug configuration for the Win32 platform. Because this name uses a pipe symbol, I have to use quotation marks on the command line. Otherwise, the command-line processor will assume that I am trying to pipe output to a process named *Win32*.

If you use the */out* switch, the output which would have gone to the IDE Output window will be sent to the file you specify. If you use */out* with */build*, */rebuild*, */clean*, or */deploy*, the output will be to the file and to the command line. If you use the */run* or */runexit* switch, the IDE will be started, the solution will be loaded and built, and then the output of the startup project will be run. If you use */out* with either of these switches, the output generated during the run (which included information about the symbols that were loaded) will also go to the specified file. However, this output is not the same as the build log file. Indeed, by default, the build log file will still be generated.

Finally, the */command* switch allows you to start the IDE to run a specified command and then leave the IDE running. For example, you can start the IDE and show the New Project dialog with the following line:

```
devenv /command File.NewProject
```

Unfortunately, the processing of the command line is not too clever. If the command takes parameters, you have to give the entire command in quotation marks, as shown here:

```
devenv /command "Edit.FindinFiles include /lookin:. /ext:*.cpp"
```

This will search for the text *include* in all .cpp files in the current directory. Calling commands such as this from the command line is of limited use because the command string cannot have nested strings, so for example, I cannot search for the text *#define UNICODE*.

The DTE Object

Although the IDE has some managed elements (the Properties window is an instance of the *PropertyGrid* class in the *System::Windows::Forms* namespace), it is largely an unmanaged application with COM as the glue that holds everything together. Indeed, the COM objects in the IDE have been developed with ATL. I know this because if I load DevEnv.exe into the IDE (the default view for an executable is a view of the unmanaged resources in the file), I can see that the executable contains several ATL .rgs registration scripts (a resource named REGISTRY).

The IDE is accessed through a COM object with the ProgID of *VisualStudio.DTE.7*. The registry entry of this object is interesting. The coclass registration has an inproc server entry *and* a local server entry. The local server entry gives DevEnv.exe, the IDE process, as the COM server. This information is what you would expect because the DTE object is the IDE. The inproc server registration gives the name of the EnvDTE assembly and specifies that the class is *EnvDTE.DTEClass*. If you look at this assembly with ILDASM (the assembly can be found in the .NET system folder), you will see that *DTEClass* looks something like this:

```
[
   CoClass("EnvDTE.DTEClass"),
   GuidAttribute("04A72314-32E9-48E2-9B87-A63603454F3E")
]
public __gc __interface DTE : public _DTE
{
   // Other members
};
[
   ClassInterface(ClassInterfaceType::None), DefaultMember("Name"),
   GuidAttribute("3C9CFE1E-389F-4118-9FAD-365385190329"),
   TypeLibType(TypeLibTypeFlags::FAppObject
              | TypeLibTypeFlags::FCanCreate
              | TypeLibTypeFlags::FPreDeclId)
]
public __gc class DTEClass
   : public _DTE, public DTE
{
   // Other members
};
```

Guess what? The GUID of *DTEClass* is the GUID of *VisualStudio.DTE.7*. So this information means that when you create an inproc *VisualStudio.DTE.7*, you get an instance of the .NET object *DTEClass* through COM interop, which accesses the local server *VisualStudio.DTE.7* object through COM interop. I would hope that .NET COM interop marshaling will optimize away the unnecessary transitions from COM to .NET to COM.

The *DTE* object has almost 40 properties and a handful of methods. The main reason for this object is to give access to all the other objects in the IDE. The COM interface is a dispinterface, so it has been designed to be scripted. You can write a script in one of a multitude of automation-aware languages, but you are most likely to want to access the IDE object model from code that runs within the IDE as a macro or as a Visual Studio .NET Add-in.

Here is an example of scripting the *DTE* object with a VBScript script that you can run from the command line:

```
' Run with cscript dumpcommands.vbs.
Dim msdev
Set msdev = WScript.CreateObject("VisualStudio.DTE.7")
Dim command
For Each command in msdev.Commands
   If command.Name <> "" Then
      WScript.Echo command.Name
   End If
Next
```

The *Commands* property is a collection of *Command* objects, and this example will list at the command the names of all the commands supported by the IDE. You can also execute commands through the *ExecuteCommand* method, as shown here:

```
' Run with cscript find.vbs.
Dim searchFor
WScript.Echo "Type search text"
searchFor = WScript.StdIn.ReadLine

Dim msdev
Set msdev = WScript.CreateObject("VisualStudio.DTE.7")
' Get the current folder path.
Dim fso
Set fso = CreateObject("Scripting.FileSystemObject")
' Create the parameters for the command.
Dim str
str = searchFor & " /lookin:" & Chr(34)
str = str & fso.GetFolder(".").Path & Chr(34)
str = str & " /ext:*.cpp"
msdev.ExecuteCommand "Edit.FindinFiles", str
' Show IDE with the find results.
msdev.MainWindow.Visible = True
WScript.Sleep 5000
```

In this code, I use the VBScript *ReadLine* method to get a line of text from the user. This text is then appended to the parameter that is passed to the *Execute-Command* method. After the search is made, the script makes the IDE visible. The object will be destroyed at the end of the script, and this will shut down the IDE, so I get the script to sleep for 5 seconds to give the user the opportunity to see that there are some results.

The Visual C++ 7 Libraries

When you install Visual Studio .NET on your machine, the install program will install various libraries. In this section, I want to describe these libraries and explain where you can find them. I will use the Visual C++ macros to specify locations on your hard disk. With the release of Visual Studio .NET, Microsoft has decided to reorganize the include and library folders. Table 6-7 shows the folders used by the standard folders. The most important change is that the headers for the CRT and C++ standard library are located in a separate folder from the folders used for the Platform SDK.

Table 6-7 Visual C++ Libraries

Folder	Description
$(FrameworkSDKDir)	Contains samples, documentation, and library files for the Framework SDK. Some of the samples have Visual Studio .NET solutions; others use make files. The include and lib folders contain the SDK files for metadata and accessing the runtime object.
$(FrameworkSDKDir)\Tool Developers Guide	Contains samples that show how to access the runtime from C++, how to write a profiler, and how to write a basic .NET compiler. This folder tree also has the ECMA specification.
$(VCInstallDir)\atlmfc	Contains the headers, static-link libraries and source files for the combined ATL and MFC libraries.
$(VCInstallDir)\crt	Contains the source code for the C runtime library.
$(VCInstallDir)\include $(VCInstallDir)\lib	Contains headers and static-link libraries for the C runtime library, the C++ standard library, and other libraries specific to Visual C++ .
$(VCInstallDir)\PlatformSDK	Contains the headers and static-link libraries for the Platform SDK, which includes the Windows SDK.

Project Types

Solutions are containers for projects. When you create a project through the New Project dialog box, the IDE will also create a solution for the project. You can load a project without loading a solution (*File.OpenProject* and select a .vcproj file), but when you load a project without loading a solution, the IDE will look in the project folder for a solution file with the same name as the project file, and if it cannot find this solution file, the IDE will search any solution file to see if it references the project file. If the IDE cannot find a saved solution for the project, it will create a new solution file. A project will always be loaded into the IDE within a solution.

If you intend to develop a solution with more than one project, it is best to create a folder hierarchy with each project in a subfolder within the solution folder. If you forget to create this folder hierarchy when you create the first project, you can do it at a later stage by creating a blank solution, copying the project folders into the solution folder, and then using *File.AddExistingProject* to add the projects to the solution. Once you have created a solution, you can add new projects to the solution through the Add New Project dialog box (*File.AddNewProject*). This dialog is the same as the New Project dialog box except that it has no options to determine the name or location of the solution. Table 6-8 shows the C++ projects that are shown in the New Project and Add New Project dialog boxes. I have indicated which of these projects are managed. For the Makefile Project, I have said *possibly* because whether the project is managed depends on the contents of the make file.

The unmanaged projects typically give you options about the code that you want the wizard to create. Previous versions of Visual Studio took the attitude of "why have several project wizards when you can combine them all into one?" The worst example of this was the Win32 Project Wizard, which allowed you to create unrelated items such as EXEs, DLLs, and static-link libraries through a single wizard, while ignoring important options such as support for the CRT, the C++ Standard Library, and the character set used by the code. Furthermore, this wizard did not even give you the option of creating a Windows Service. This wizard still exists in Visual Studio .NET.

The new C++ project types in Visual Studio .NET take a different approach. The attitude seems to have swung in the completely opposite direction and appears to be "why have one project wizard when we have space for lots of them in the New Project dialog box?" This change has resulted in silly situations such as the one that occurs with ATL Server projects: you have a wizard to create ATL Server Applications *and* Web Services and another wizard to create just ATL Server Web Services. The latter is just the former with a few check boxes checked—I think that most people are capable of checking a box marked Create As Web Service.

The other main difference that you find with the new projects in Visual Studio .NET (the ATL Server projects are an exception) is that the designers have decided that you as the developer have no useful input in the process of creating a project. The managed C++ projects follow this approach, and they will always create a one-size-fits-all project for you. This arrangement necessarily means that the wizard generates the barest of bare-bones code. Depending on your point of view about code wizards ("I always delete wizard-generated code because the code that I write is always better" or "all I do is stitch together the code generated by the wizard"), this arrangement might appear to you to be a good thing or a bad thing. If you habitually delete wizard-generated code, one reason could be that the wizard is not creating code appropriate to your work, but solace is at hand because Visual Studio .NET allows you to create your own project wizards (Custom Wizard). Of course, you could always be right that the code you write is better than machine-generated code. In the following sections, I will explain just the managed projects.

Table 6-8 Visual C++ .NET Project Types

Project Type	Managed?	Description
ATL Project	No	EXE or DLL COM Server
ATL Server Project	No	Web Service or Web Application ISAPI extension
ATL Server Web Service	No	Web Service ISAPI extension
Custom Wizard	No	Creates a Visual Studio .NET project wizard
Extended Stored Procedure Dll	No	Extension DLL containing SQL Server stored procedures
Makefile Project	Possibly	
Managed C++ Application	Yes	Managed console application
Managed C++ Class Library	Yes	Library assembly
Managed C++ Empty Project	Yes	An empty project; you decide what type of assembly the project should create
Managed C++ Web Service	Yes	Managed Web Service
MFC ActiveX Control	No	DLL COM Server containing controls
MFC Application	No	EXE application
MFC DLL	No	MFC extension DLL
MFC ISAPI Extension	No	ISAPI extension DLL
Win32 Project	No	DLL, static-link library, GUI, or console application

Managed Applications

The Managed C++ Application project wizard creates a project for an EXE assembly. The main C++ file looks like this:

```
#include "stdafx.h"

#using <mscorlib.dll>
#include <tchar.h>
```

```
using namespace System;

// This is the entry point for this application.
int _tmain(void)
{
   // TODO: Please replace the sample code below with your own.
   Console::WriteLine(S"Hello World");
   return 0;
}
```

There are several points to make about this code. The first is that the file includes tchar.h and has *_tmain* as the entry point. The tchar.h header file has definitions for the various *_t* prefixed symbols with conditional compilation that give either the Unicode or ANSI CRT functions, depending on whether the *_UNICODE* symbol is defined. One of these definitions is for the *_tmain* symbol, which will be defined as either *wmain* or *main*. The implication is that you can compile the code for either Unicode or ANSI. However, the project wizard gives two project configurations, Debug and Release, both of which have the Character Set project property set to Use Multi-Byte Character Set. If you would prefer to have a Unicode build, you should change this setting to Use Unicode Character Set or you can create a new configuration based on each of the Debug and Release configurations and configure these to compile as Unicode.

The next point is that *_tmain* is the managed entry point, and the first thread created for the project will run this function. Recall from Chapter 2 that TlbImp will generate .NET classes to help you call COM objects through COM interop. If you call these classes in *_tmain*, what COM apartment will the COM object run? By default, the runtime will initialize the thread in the process's MTA apartment when a COM object is first used, and this process is what will happen in this code. If you know that the objects you will create will be STA objects, you will save yourself some marshaling by making the main thread run in an STA. If your process is GUI, you must make the first thread run in an STA so that COM synchronization occurs through the process's message loop. To make the main thread run in an STA, you need to apply the *[STAThread]* attribute, as shown here:

```
[STAThread]
int _tmain(void)
```

The next point to make about this file is the inclusion of stdafx.h. This inclusion means that the project is configured to use precompiled headers. Precompiled headers are useful when you have headers that are likely to be used by all the source files in your project but will not be changed during your development cycle. (Windows.h is the canonical example.) I will return to this issue in the section "Precompiled Headers" later in this chapter.

The project will also have a file named *AssemblyInfo.h*, which looks like this with the comments removed:

```
#include "stdafx.h"

#using <mscorlib.dll>

using namespace System::Reflection;
using namespace System::Runtime::CompilerServices;

[assembly:AssemblyTitleAttribute("")];
[assembly:AssemblyDescriptionAttribute("")];
[assembly:AssemblyConfigurationAttribute("")];
[assembly:AssemblyCompanyAttribute("")];
[assembly:AssemblyProductAttribute("")];
[assembly:AssemblyCopyrightAttribute("")];
[assembly:AssemblyTrademarkAttribute("")];
[assembly:AssemblyCultureAttribute("")];

[assembly:AssemblyVersionAttribute("1.0.*")];

[assembly:AssemblyDelaySignAttribute(false)];
[assembly:AssemblyKeyFileAttribute("")];
[assembly:AssemblyKeyNameAttribute("")];
```

This code looks very suspiciously like the author of the wizard has been playing "me too" with the author of the C# project wizards because this code is an exact translation from the AssemblyInfo.cs file that is added to C# projects. The code even has the same comments about versioning and the correspondingly unpleasant effects from using * in the *[AssemblyVersion]* attribute.

It doesn't make much sense to have attributes without values. Indeed, I would have expected the project wizard to make some intelligent guesses at the values for these attributes. (For example, *[AssemblyCompany]* could be assigned the same value that you gave as your Organization when you installed Visual Studio .NET.) This file certainly feels like a version 1 attempt.

In Chapter 5, I described how you can configure how a process works through a configuration file. However, the IDE does not support configuration files as part of a project, but it is quite simple to add a config file to a project and set the custom build properties. Here is what to do: First create a new folder in the project, and set its properties so that *Parse* is set to False—this step is not required, but because config files do not contain anything that will be shown in Class View, there is no point in parsing them. You can then create a file named *app.config* and add this file to the folder that you created. Next open the property pages for this file, and from the Configuration drop-down list box, select All Configurations and then set the properties according to Table 6-9.

When you perform a build, the IDE will compare the timestamp on the file app.config with the timestamp on the file mentioned in the Outputs property, and if the timestamp of app.config is later, the build command will be performed. By using the macros, the same settings can be used for all configurations. *$(OutDir)* will be the name of the output directory where the executable will be created. The name of the executable is given by *$(TargetFileName)*, so the configuration name is the name of the executable file appended with .config.

Table 6-9 Properties for a Config File

Property	Value
Command Line	copy /y app.config "$(OutDir)\$(TargetFile-Name).config"
Description	Copying $(TargetFileName).config
Outputs	$(OutDir)\$(TargetFileName).config
Additional Dependencies	<leave empty>

Managed Class Libraries

The Managed C++ Class Library project type creates the code for a library assembly. Yet again you have a file named *AssemblyInfo.cpp* and the support files for precompiled headers. Unlike the Application project, there is a reference to the mscorlib assembly in the stdafx.h file. The main difference between this project type and the application project type is that there is no file with an entry point. (Library assemblies do not need entry points.) Instead, you will have a .cpp and a header file for the library classes, as shown in this example:

```
// MyLibrary.h
#pragma once
using namespace System;

namespace MyLibrary
{
   public __gc class Class1
   {
      // TODO: Add your methods for this class here.
   };
}
```

Of course, your first task is to change the name of the class from *Class1* to something more appropriate. This is the file that the wizard generates for a library project named *MyLibrary*, and it is interesting to note that the wizard has departed from the usual file-naming convention: the header file is usually named after the class rather than the namespace. Yet again a C++ wizard is following the behavior of a C# wizard.

Obviously, a library does not run on its own; you have to load it into a process. This restriction becomes most apparent when you want to debug the library. The debugging properties for a library project allow you to specify the process that will load the library (details are given in Chapter 7), but note that in most cases, the library will be statically bound (that is, you have mentioned the library in the process with a *#using* statement). This arrangement means that the process must be built with the specific version of the library. Thus, the process *depends* on the library.

Furthermore, if the library is a private library, the library must be in the same folder as the process (or in a subfolder). Whether the library is shared or not, the compiler must be able to resolve the *#using* statement in the process source code so that the compiler can access the metadata of the library. There are several strategies that you can use, and I'll address these in the section "Multiassembly Solutions" later in this chapter.

Managed Object Files and Modules

Assemblies have at least one module, but they can contain more than one module. The New Project dialog box does not have a project for creating .NET modules as part of an assembly, but it is quite trivial to create this type of project. To create this type of project, you should create a library project and specify that the output is a .NET module by going to the Linker category of the project's property pages and on the Advanced page, changing the Turn Off Assembly Generation property to Yes. The convention in .NET is that modules should have the extension of .netmodule (it is not a mandatory convention), so you should also go to the General page of the Linker category and change the Output File property so that the output file has this extension.

A .NET module cannot be used on its own; it *must* be part of an assembly. This restriction means that you should also have a project that creates an assembly that uses the module, and because the linker requires the module when it builds the assembly, the assembly project depends on the module project. The module must be in the same folder as the assembly, which means that you have to configure your solution so that you have a common output folder for the module and assembly. I will explain how to perform this task in the section "Multimodule Solutions" later in this chapter.

The C++ compiler will compile each source file to an object file (.obj) with the */clr* and */c* switches (compile, don't link); you will get an object file with managed code. The compiler will add to the .obj file information about the metadata streams that the linker will merge into the final module. If you dump the object file with dumpbin, you will see that the file has a section named *.cormeta* that contains the metadata streams. (Use the switches */section:.cormeta /rawdata* to see this.) In general, if you want to share code, you will prefer to do this sharing through a library, but there are occasions when you will want to provide private utility classes to make available to more than one assembly. The IDE does not provide a managed project type that is not linked, but because by definition an object file comes from a single .cpp source file, you do not need the IDE's source file management. You will provide such utility classes through a compiled .obj file if you think that your users will not be interested in the actual implementation of those classes. If this is not the case, you should provide the source through an include file (.h or .inl).

Makefile Projects

If you have special build requirements, you can use the Visual Studio .NET Makefile project. The name is misleading because the project does not create a make file for the *nmake* utility. You can add *any* source file to this project and use *any* build tool, so you can choose to use *nmake* if you want. The Makefile project uses a wizard with a user interface. This simple wizard has four fields, described in Table 6-10.

Table 6-10 Makefile Project Wizard's Options

Field	Description
Build command line	The command line that will be called when the project is built.
Output	This property is not used; your make file commands define the output.
Clean command	The command line to "clean" the project. Use this command to delete outputs and intermediate files.
Rebuild command line	The command to rebuild the project; essentially perform the clean command before performing the build command.

For example, you could define a file named *makefile* with an *all* target that has the actions to build the project and a *clean* target to clean the project. You can then use *nmake* as the build tool and give *nmake* as the build command,[8] *nmake clean* to clean the project and *nmake /a* to rebuild the project.

The project wizard creates three folders with *Parse* set to True: Source Files, Header Files, and Resource Files. These folders have the same filters as for any other C++ project. However, these folders are really only cosmetic because the IDE does not check the timestamp of these files against the compiler output like it does for other C++ projects because this is the responsibility of your build tool. Thus, if you want files to be compiled only when they have changed, you should use *nmake* as the build tool.

8. If you invoke *nmake* without the name of a make file, it will automatically look for a make file with the name *makefile*.

Managed Web Services

The Managed C++ Web Service project is a port of the C# ASP.NET Web Service project, so you will find that most of the files in the project are direct copies. One example is the Global.asax file, which gives information to ASP.NET about the class that will handle application-level or session-level events. If you are writing the Web service in C#, the source files reside on the Web server. You have the option of providing code in a script as well as in a compiled assembly. When the Web service is accessed for the first time (or if the script has changed), the C# in the script will be compiled. This option requires CodeDOM support for the language. In C#, you can also provide code in a separate file, called the *code-behind file*. In addition, code can be provided as a compiled assembly. The assembly is located in a folder named *bin* in the IIS virtual directory for the Web Service project.

There is no CodeDOM support for C++, so you cannot provide C++ in the script file or in a code-behind file, but the Global.asax file generated by the wizard contains a reference to a code-behind file (Global.asax.h). This reference makes no sense whatsoever because when ASP.NET parses Global.asax, it will not be able to find the specified code-behind file, and even if it could, it would not be able to compile it. As a consequence, these items are ignored by ASP.NET, so there is no need for them to be there. (I'll explain the steps in a moment.) A further example that Managed C++ Web Service projects are a mere port from C# is that the header files contain C#-style XML comments (which start with the /// comment). XML comments are used only by the C# compiler.

Before you can write a Web service, you have to clean up the files generated by the wizard. You should delete the *CodeBehind* attribute from Global.asax. The wizard creates a namespace with the name of the project, and it adds a class for the Web service named *Class1*. The rationale is that your Web service project could contain several Web services. However, the name of the header and .cpp files is used for the name of the *namespace*, and this would suggest that if you add another class, it should be in a different namespace. Instead, I prefer the normal C++ convention of naming the header and .cpp file after the *class*. To do this through the New Project wizard, you have to give the project the name of the class; otherwise, you have to change the name of the files by hand. In the following example, I assume that I have just one Web service class, so I have named the project after the name of the class.

The first change is to Global.asax. After the wizard has finished, it will look like this:

```
<%@ Application Codebehind="Global.asax.h" Inherits="GetTime.Global" %>
```

Edit it so that it looks something like this:

```
<%@ Application Inherits="MyServices.Global" %>
```

As I have already mentioned, the class will be called *Class1*. This is far from satisfactory, so you should rename it to something that reflects your Web service and then edit the .asmx file created by the wizard for your Web service. This is the code generated by the wizard:

```
<!-- GetTime.asmx -->
<%@ WebService Class=GetTime.Class1 %>
```

Change this to the following:

```
<!-- GetTime.asmx -->
<%@ WebService Class=MyServices.GetTime %>
```

This Web service is named *GetTime*, and it simply returns a string with the current time. Here is my implementation of the Web service, where I have highlighted the changes:

```
// GetTime.h
#pragma once
#using <System.Web.Services.dll>
using namespace System;
using namespace System::Web::Services;

namespace MyServices
{
   [WebService(Namespace="http://www.myserver.com/webservices/")]
   public __gc class GetTime
   {
   public:
      [WebMethod]
      String __gc* Time()
      {
         return DateTime::Now.ToString();
      }
   };
}
```

The project wizard will not add the *[Web Service]* attribute for you to supply the default XML namespace for the Web service. As a result, when you first call the Web service (by requesting the GetTime.asmx file) from the Web server, you will get a Web page saying that you are using http://tempuri.org/ as the namespace. The wizard will derive your Web service class from *WebService*. This derivation is not necessary unless you want to use the ASP.NET facilities that this class offers: session state, user authentication, or access to the actual HTTP request.

The most important code here is the *[WebMethod]* attribute. This attribute indicates that the method can be called as a Web service method, and it also indicates that ASP.NET will generate a description for the method in WSDL (Web Service Description Language). To view the WSDL for a Web service, you call the Web service page with WSDL as a parameter, as shown here:

```
http://:www.myserver.com/GetTime/GetTime.asmx?WSDL
```

When you build the project, the Web service will be deployed on the target machine. This behavior is a consequence of the lack of support for code-behind. When you build the project, it is built in the local folder used by Visual Studio .NET, and this folder will not be the same as the folders used by ASP.NET. The files that are deployed will have the *Content* property set to True in the Properties window. The files that are deployed are listed in Table 6-11, where *<project>* is the name of the project.

Table 6-11 Deployed Files for Web Service Projects

File	Description
Global.asax	ASP.NET application file that indicates the code that will handle application-level events
<project>.asmx	File containing the Web service's processing directives
<project>.dll	Assembly containing the Web service
<project>.vsdisco	Web service dynamic discovery file containing information that ASP.NET will use to search for discovery information
Web.config	Configuration file for the Web service

Note that the assembly is a library, which is loaded into its own application domain in the ASP.NET worker process (aspnet_wp.exe). I mentioned in the Chapter 5 that configuration files are for processes and cannot be used by libraries. ASP.NET is the exception to this rule, but note that the configuration file is always named *Web.config*.

When the Web service is deployed (I'll mention how in a moment), folders are created in the virtual directory for the IIS extension for the Web service. Web service discovery allows a user to get information about a Web service. ASP.NET supports dynamic discovery so that at run time, ASP.NET will search for assembly files and use reflection to determine the Web methods that are exposed from those assemblies. The .vsdisco file contains information that ASP.NET uses to search for this information. The wizard-generated file contains information about the folders that are *not* searched for information.

When you build a Web Services project, the files that have changed will be deployed to the Web server.[9] You can also manually deploy the project through the Deploy context menu item (*Build.Deploy*). Deployment is performed by a separate tool named *vcdeploy*, which is also used by unmanaged ATL Server Web projects. This tool is not documented, but you can get an idea of what it

9. This information is not completely accurate; there appears to be a bug so that deployment only occurs if assembly has been rebuilt. If you change one of the other content files, you have to manually deploy the project.

will do by looking at the input file that it takes. After you have deployed a project, take a look at the build summary file, BuildLog.htm, and you will see that the IDE has created an XML file that looks something like this:

```
<?xml version="1.0" encoding="Windows-1252"?>
<ATLSINSTSETTINGS>
   <WEBHOSTNAME>localhost</WEBHOSTNAME>
   <VIRTDIRNAME>GetTime</VIRTDIRNAME>
   <VIRTDIRFSPATH>c:\inetpub\wwwroot\GetTime</VIRTDIRFSPATH>
   <APPISOLATION>0</APPISOLATION>

   <APPFILEGROUP>
      <!-- Other entries deleted for clarity -->
      <APPFILENAME>
         <SRC>c:\GetTime\GetTime.asmx</SRC>
         <DEST>GetTime.asmx</DEST>
      </APPFILENAME>
      <APPFILENAME>
         <SRC>c:\GetTime\Web.config</SRC>
         <DEST>Web.config</DEST>
      </APPFILENAME>
      <APPFILENAME>
         <SRC>c:\GetTime\Debug\GetTime.dll</SRC>
         <DEST>bin\GetTime.dll</DEST>
      </APPFILENAME>
   </APPFILEGROUP>
</ATLSINSTSETTINGS>
```

The first point to make regards the name of the main element, *<ATLSINSTSETTINGS>*: this name implies that the tool was originally developed for ATL Server projects. There are two groups of elements here. The first group gives information about the Web server, and I'll return to this in a moment; the second group is the collection *<APPFILEGROUP>*, which identifies the files to be deployed. Each *<APPFILENAME>* entry is a file in the project with the *Content* property set to True. The child elements give the path to the file that is to be copied and the relative path where the file will be copied.

The project's property pages have a category named *Web Deployment* that has the properties that the IDE uses to generate the XML file to pass to vcdeploy. This category allows you to indicate the name of the virtual directory, but it does not allow you to indicate the machine where the application will be deployed, which will always be the local machine. Because this tool is also used by ATL Server projects, there are settings that are not applicable to Managed C++ Web Service projects. ASP.NET assumes that the assembly will be in a subfolder named *bin*, so do not be tempted to change the Relative Path property. Also, ASP.NET applications will be hosted by the ASP.NET worker process, so the Application Protection property (the *<APPISOLATION>* element) is irrelevant.

Finally, it is important to point out that the deployment performed by vcdeploy is intended for the development phase of your project. Visual Studio .NET provides a project named *Web Setup Project* that you can use to create an MSI (Microsoft Installer) file that contains the assembly and content files. When you deploy your final project, you should deploy it through Microsoft Installer.

Web Service Clients

There is no specific project type for Web service clients because you can use Web services in any of the other project types. However, there are two different tools used to add the code to a project to access Web services, one for managed projects, and another for unmanaged projects. I will cover managed projects first.

The Solution Explorer context menu has an item called Add Web Reference (*Project.AddWebReference*). This menu item will show the Add Web Reference dialog box, which allows you to browse for the WSDL for a Web service. In the Address combo box, you should type the URL that will return the WSDL. For an ASP.NET project, this will be either the .asmx file, or the .asmx file with the WSDL parameter, like this:

```
http://localhost/GetTime/GetTime.asmx?WSDL
```

Once this tool has located the WSDL, you can click on the Add Reference button and the tool will store the WSDL in a file and add the file to the project. The build rule for this file (expressed on the property pages) indicates that the file will be compiled with the Web Service Proxy Generator (wsdl.exe).[10] For the preceding *GetTime* example, the following commands will be executed when the Web reference is first added to the project and when the project is built:

```
wsdl /nologo /l:cs /out:"GetTime.cs" "GetTime.wsdl"
csc /t:module /nologo /o+ /debug- /out:"GetTime.dll" "GetTime.cs"
copy "GetTime.dll" "Debug\GetTime.dll"
```

The *wsdl* tool will create the code that can be compiled to an assembly to access the Web service. This tool will *not* generate managed C++, so C# is chosen as the language (*/l:cs*); however, this option is not configurable, and it does not appear on the property pages for the WSDL file. The C# is compiled to a .NET module (*not* an assembly) and then copied to the configuration out folder. Again, these steps are not configurable; there are no project properties or build events that specify these actions. It is a pity that you cannot configure these settings because the extension of the module will be .dll and not the conventional .netmodule. (Although the WSDL file's property page indicates the output name

---

10. Interestingly, this property page indicates that the Generated Proxy Language is Managed C++, but this tool cannot create C++.

that will be generated, the name that you supply will be ignored, so there is no way to change the module extension.)

Add Web Reference also adds a header file to the project called WebService.h, which looks like this:

```
#using <System.DLL>
#using <GetTime.dll>
#using <System.Web.Services.DLL>
#using <System.Data.DLL>
```

There are two points that should be made about this file. The first point concerns the line importing the metadata from the module GetTime.dll. This line indicates that you can use the Web service classes in this file, or any file that includes it. However, since the wizard did not know in which file you want to use the Web service, you have to add an appropriate *#include* line by hand. Also, although the GetTime.dll module is part of the assembly you are compiling, the linker is not informed of this (that is, */assemblymodule* is not used; see the section "Linker Switches" later in this chapter). The reason is that if you use *#using* with a module, the compiler will automatically assume that you want to add the module to the assembly, so the linker will oblige without explicitly being told to add the module.

The second point to make about this header file is the assemblies that are referenced. The module uses the system and system.web.services assemblies, so the references to these are required. The module does *not* use the system.data assembly, and I can see no reason why the wizard adds this reference.

You can add a reference to an unmanaged C++ client. Again, you do this through *Project.AddWebReference*, which will add a WSDL file to the project. This time the property pages for the WSDL file are correct. The Generated Proxy Language is given as Native C++, and the values that you enter on these property pages are used by the build tool. The tool that is used is called sproxy.exe. The command line that will be generated for the GetTime Web service looks like this:

```
sproxy.exe GetTime.wsdl /out:"GetTime.h" /nologo
```

The header file generated by this tool is added to the project and contains ATL code to access the Web service. Because this code used by the Microsoft XML parser through COM, you have to make sure that in an unmanaged project you initialize a COM apartment before you use the generated class.

Comment Web Pages

The Tools menu has a command named *Build Comment Web Pages* (*Tools.BuildCommentWebPages*). If you look this up in the online help, you will see a note that says:

> *Currently, only C# supports the code comment syntax required for code comment Web reports. Additional languages might also support code comment syntax at a later date.*

This information is misleading because it implies that you can use only *Tools.BuildCommentWebPages* for C# projects. In fact, you can use this command on C++ projects; you just lose some of the fine details offered by C# XML comments. This tool parses source code; it does not require that the source is built. The tool will generate HTML pages that list each namespace and give the classes and functions defined. Classes and functions not defined in a namespace will be given in a namespace named *Global*. Each element that the tool finds will have a Web page with a description of the item. To provide a description, you should give one or more lines of comments before the item in the source code. The only exceptions are comments for parameters and the return value, for which you should use the XML-like tags *<param>* and *<returns>*, as shown in this example:

```
// This is a widget object.
__gc class Widget
{
   // The widget state.
   int i;
public:
   // Create a widget with default values.
   Widget();
   // Calculates the widget value.
   // <param name="j">The parameter.</param>
   // <returns>The calculated value of the widget</returns>
   String* Value(int j);
};
```

Note that these comments use the C++ comment symbol (//). You do not use the C# XML comments symbol (///). The comment tool will create the table shown in Figure 6-11. This table lists the members of the class, and each member is a hyperlink to a page that describes the member. The note that I quoted earlier is partially true because as you can see from the screen shot, the Description column for the *Value* function contains the description of the function and its parameter and return value, which is not what you would expect. These are intended for the page for the function. However, it is a fairly trivial task to edit the HTML generated by the *Tools.BuildCommentWebPages* tool to create a comment page.

Thus, although the *Tools.BuildCommentWebPages* tool is not intended for C++ projects, it goes 95 percent of the way to producing useful comment pages. With a little work to tidy up the results, you can create good-looking documentation for your libraries.

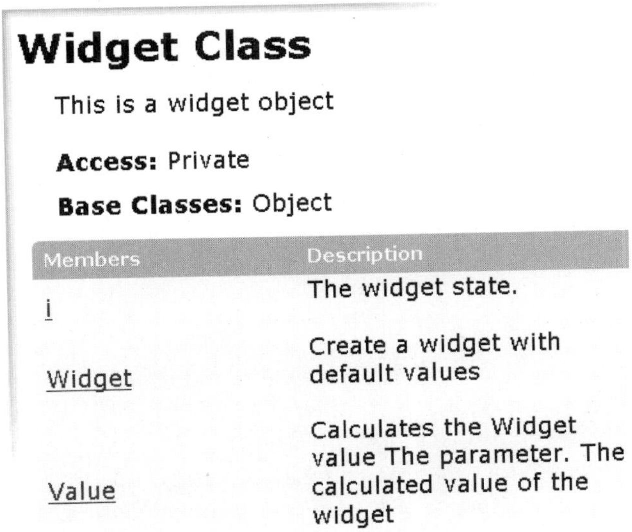

Widget Class

This is a widget object

Access: Private

Base Classes: Object

Members	Description
i	The widget state.
Widget	Create a widget with default values
Value	Calculates the Widget value The parameter. The calculated value of the widget

Figure 6-11 Comment page for the *Widget* class

Compiling Code

The project property pages allow you to specify the switches for the various C++ build tools. In this section, I describe the build tool switches that are specific to compiling managed code. In general, to compile code to an assembly, you have to reference the metadata in the source files with *#using* and you have to pass the */clr* switch to the compiler. There are some switches that are incompatible with */clr*, and I will mention some of these. The categories for the C++ compiler and linker both have a page named *Command Line* that gives a summary of the command-line switches that will be passed to the tool at build time. If the property pages do not have a property for a switch that you want to use, you can use this page to add the switch. It is also worthwhile to point out here again that the BuildLog.htm file lists the command-line switches that were used to invoke the tool at build time; you can use this to help determine if a failed build was due to the tool options you used.

Compiler Switches

The most important compiler switch for .NET code is */clr*. In the project settings, this switch is set through the Use Managed Extensions property on the General page. When you pass */clr* to the compiler, it will define the *_MANAGED* symbol. This symbol means that you can have files shared between managed and unmanaged projects and use conditional compilation to call .NET Framework classes only when the code is compiled in a managed project. Note that this symbol is set according to the *mode* of the compiler rather than according to the type of the code being compiled. Consider this code:

```
#pragma unmanaged
void NativeCode()
{
#ifdef _MANAGED
#pragma message("/clr has been used")
#endif
}
#pragma managed
```

If this code is compiled with the */clr* switch, the function will be compiled to native x86 because I have used the *unmanaged* pragma, but the message will still be sent to the output window because the compiler was passed the */clr* switch. The */clr* switch assumes that the source file has managed (or *__value*) classes that use the new keywords. However, these keywords *are* compatible with the */Za* (Disable Language Extension) switch.

The */clr* switch has an option named *noAssembly* (the capitalization is important); however, you cannot use this option on the project properties page. This option is used when the C++ compiler is called to compile and link in one invocation to create a module, as shown here:

```
cl File.cpp /clr:noAssembly /LD /FeFile.netmodule
```

Modules have to be created using the */LD* switch, and by convention, the file has the extension .netmodule (hence the reason for the */Fe* switch). Modules do not have an assembly manifest, and this option is usually selected by passing the */noassembly* switch to the linker. (The */clr:noAssembly* switch tells the compiler to pass the linker the */noassembly* switch.) The IDE always compiles and links in two separate invocations (the compiler is passed the */c* switch), so */clr:noAssembly* is not relevant to files compiled through the IDE.

I mentioned in Chapter 1 that all files compiled with */clr* ought to access the metadata in the mscorlib.dll assembly file with a *#using* statement. In fact, you can omit this statement as long as you use the */FU* switch to identify this assembly file, as shown in the following line of code:

```
cl File.cpp /clr /FUmscorlib.dll
```

You can use the */FU* switch more than once on a command line. This switch is accessible through the project property pages on the Advanced C/C++ page. In general, I prefer to provide the *#using* statement in source files, but if the compiler gives me the C2065 error message one too many times (because I have forgotten to provide a *#using* statement), I find it therapeutic to call the compiler telling it FU.

While on the subject of *#using*, I ought to mention how the compiler locates the metadata files. You can use an absolute path in the *#using* statement, or you can provide a search path for the compiler to use. There are two ways to perform this task. The first is to provide the search path temporarily through the */AI* switch. This switch should be called for each folder path that you want to provide. In the IDE, you provide these values through the Resolve #using References property on the C/C++ General page. The advantage of setting this through the IDE is that you can use Visual Studio .NET macros, as I'll explain in the sections under the heading "Examples of Common Solutions" at the end of this chapter.

If you have shared libraries that you will use often, it is a pain to have to provide the path to these through */AI* for every project you create. Instead, you can use the Reference files directories (through the *Tools.Options*, Projects, VC++ Directories property page). For command-line projects, you can get the same effect by setting the *LIBPATH* environment variable. Note that the compiler automatically checks these directories; the IDE does not pass them to the compiler through the */AI* switch.

The output of the compiler is an object file, but you can also use compiler switches to indicate that additional output files should be created. The most interesting of these is the */FA* switch to generate assembly code listing (the Assembly Output property on the Output Files C/C++ property pages). When you use */FA* with */clr*, the output will be MSIL rather than x86 assembly. It is useful to use */Fas*, which will show the IL and the original source code.

It is important to point out that managed projects do not support Edit And Continue (Debug Information Format property on the General C/C++ page), and that if you are using the CRT, you must link with the multithreaded version of the library (Runtime Library property on the Code Generation C/C++ page).

Precompiled Headers

If you do not use the */FU* switch, each file that has managed code ought to have access to the metadata in the mscorlib assembly, and your code might also need to access metadata in other assemblies. One way to provide this access is to have a single header file used by all source files in your project and place the common *#using* statements in there. The convention is to name this common header file stdafx.h. Of course, if that header file references many header files or has many *#using* statements, it could take a prolonged length of time for the preprocessor to parse all the files for each source file. This is the reason for precompiled headers: the header file is processed just once and a memory snapshot is taken and stored on the hard disk as a .pch file. This file is loaded when the compiler processes a file that includes stdafx.h and saves time to process the header.

It makes sense to put common *#using* statements in the stdafx.h file because it centralizes this code. However, note that for the mscorlib assembly, the compiler will place only information about common types in the precompiled header, so when the compiler compiles other files, it will still have to access the mscorlib assembly. Also note that metadata is easier for the compiler to process than the data in header files, so you are unlikely to gain much time during a build by having *#using* statements in the precompiled header.

Linker Switches

The linker also has switches for managed code. Two go hand-in-hand, the */noassembly* and */assemblymodule* switches. The */noassembly* switch is used to create a module, that is, a file without an assembly manifest. This switch is accessed through the Turn Off Assembly Generation property on the Advanced Linker property page. A module cannot be used on its own. It must be part of an assembly, and there are two ways to add a module to an assembly. I have already mentioned the first way: if you reference a module through *#using*, the module is implicitly added to the assembly. However, I prefer the second, more explicit way: to use the Add Module To Assembly property (*/assemblymodule*) on the Input Linker page.

Another linker switch that you can use is */noentry*, which is accessed through the Resource Only DLL property on the Advanced Linker property page. This switch is useful for library assemblies and modules. A library assembly does not have a .NET entry point, and if the library or module does not use the CRT (or have global C++ objects), there is no need to have a Win32 entry point either.

The only other .NET-specific linker switch is */assemblyresource*. This switch is used to add a .NET resource to the final output. This linker switch adds the resource to the metadata of the assembly. There are two ways to get a resource added to an assembly: as a noncompiled resource, or as a resource compiled through ResGen. The IDE does not have direct support for using ResGen, and I'll show you the steps of how to use this utility in the section "Projects That Use Resources" later in this chapter. The output of ResGen is a .resources file, and this file should be added to the Embed Managed Resource File property on the Linker Input page. You can also add resources that are not compiled, and to do this task, you simply provide the name to the list in the Embed Managed Resource File property. Resources can only be embedded; you cannot link them as separate files. Also, there is no support in the resource property pages to treat a resource as a managed resource. Although a resource file has a Content property on its Properties window, this property refers to deploying the file during Web deployment and is not interpreted as indicating that the resource file is content as part of the assembly. Furthermore, it would have been nice if the Embed Managed Resource File property editor gave a list of the resources that are part of the project, but sadly, it does not do this, so you have to remember the names of the resources in the project.

Optimization

Release builds have optimizations turned on. The default is the */O2* compiler switch, which optimizes for the fastest code.[11] In the IDE, compiler optimizations are accessed through the Optimization C/C++ property page. The Optimization property is a general switch that you can use to optimize for the fastest code or the smallest code, and the compiler will use appropriate optimization switches. If you want to fine-tune the optimization, you can set the Optimization property to Custom and then set the other properties on the page. Assemblies can be optimized with any of the compiler and linker optimization switches except one, whole program optimization (*/GL* compiler switch, */LTCG* linker switch), so the Whole Program Optimization property on the General project property page should always be set to No.

Build Steps

The Solution Explorer and Class View context menus have Build, Rebuild, Clean Link, and Deploy for projects; solutions have Build, Rebuild, Clean, and Batch Build; and files merely have a Compile item. The Build (*Build.BuildSelection* and *Build.BuildSolution*) option will compile only those files that have changed, Clean (*Build.CleanSelection* and *Build.CleanSolution*) will delete all outputs and intermediate files. Rebuild (*Build.RebuildSelection* and *Build.RebuildSolution*) will compile all code, this command is essentially the same as Clean followed by Build. The project Link command (*Build.Link* when a project is selected) and the file Compile command (*Build.Compile*) do not check to see whether the source file has changed since the action was last performed; they force the link or compile.

When you rebuild a solution, all projects in the solution will be built. You can use the Solution configuration to indicate that particular projects should not be built. If you want to temporarily remove a project from the build process, you can do so by unloading the project (*Project.UnloadProject*). This option is accessible only through the Project menu. (It is not o n the context menu.) If

11. However, as John Robbins mentions in his Bugslayer column for MSDN magazine, October 2000, (*http://msdn.microsoft.com/msdnmag/issues/1000/Bugslayer/Bugslayer1000.asp*), an application optimized for size will often run faster than one optimized for speed because the number of page faults will be less.

you rebuild a solution with one of the projects unloaded, you will get a message in the Output window saying:

```
Error: Cannot access data for the desired project since
       it is in a zombie state.
```

The zombie project is merely ignored, and the build process will continue with the next project. When you have decided that you want to build the project as part of the solution, you can reload the project through the context menu (*Project.ReloadProject*).

The project property pages allow you to add custom commands within the build process. These are accessed through two categories on the property pages dialog box: Build Events and Custom Build Step. The Build Events category defines three build events: Pre-Build Event, Pre-Link Event, and Post-Build Event. Thus, the build order is as follows:

1. Command defined in the Pre-Build Event.
2. Compile the source files.
3. Command defined in the Pre-Link Event.
4. Link the project.
5. Command defined in the Custom Build Step.
6. Command defined in the Post-Build Event.

The IDE ignores the outputs of the commands entered on the Build Events category. The Custom Build Step has an Outputs property that must not be left empty. (If it is, the step will be ignored.) However, the IDE does not check the timestamp on the output. When the project is built (that is, when one of the source files changes or when you perform a rebuild), the Custom Build Step is always performed.

Examples of Common Solutions

So far in this chapter, I have shown you the basic building blocks that you will use to create your solutions. I have shown you the projects provided by Visual Studio .NET, the options that you can use on the build tool, and how to specify these options using configurations. In this final section, I will describe how to develop real-life managed solutions with Visual Studio .NET.

Multiassembly Solutions

If you develop a library solution, you will need to have an application assembly to test the code. In many cases, you will want to develop an application and the library assemblies it uses in a single solution. The problem with using library assemblies is that the metadata must be available to the compiler when the compiler builds the application so that information about the library can be added to the application's manifest. This limitation means that the application assembly must be last in the build order, and to set this order, you should select the solution in Solution Explorer and select Project Dependencies (*Project.ProjectDependencies*). On this dialog, select the application project from the Project drop-down list and then check the library projects it uses from the Depends On list box.

When you run the application, Fusion has to be able to find the library assembly. If the library is private, either the library is in the same folder as the application assembly or you use some mechanism to indicate that it is in another folder.

Specifying a Search Order

If the compiler has a problem finding the metadata for a library assembly, why not use the *LIBPATH* environment variable, the compiler switch */AI*, or the Reference files property (through *Tools.Options*)? Indeed, these options will solve the problem of locating metadata, but they do nothing to help Fusion to find the library at run time. Also, note that when the IDE is started, it reads the environment variables. If you start the IDE with */useenv*, it will initialize the references path with the *LIBPATH* variable but only at that point in time. If you change any environment variable after the IDE has started, you have to restart the IDE to pick up the new value.

If you do not provide Fusion with information about where to find the library, you will get an exception thrown in *mainCRTStartup* (crt0.c) of type *FileNotFoundException*, which will mention the name of the assembly that Fusion cannot find. To get further information, you can run the Fusion Log Viewer (fuslogvw).

One way to provide assembly location to Fusion is to use the *DEVPATH* environment variable. You can set this variable to a single path, and when Fusion starts its probing for an assembly, it will use this path first before processing the application configuration file or searching any subfolders. This solution is suitable only when you have a single library assembly in a project because you can specify only a single path. When I use this solution, I usually set the environment variable at the command line and then start the IDE from the same command line. This way I know that the environment is only temporary. If I set this via the control panel, I would run the risk of the environment variable being used by another project (or indeed, when any .NET application is started).

The way that the *DEVPATH* variable is used is a little odd. First, the runtime assumes that the last character is a backslash, and it removes this character before, well, adding another backslash and the name of the library. The runtime does not check to see whether the last character actually is a backslash, so if you set the variable to

```
C:\Dev\Debug
```

which you know contains a library named myLib.dll, the runtime will attempt to locate

```
C:\Dev\Debu\myLib.dll
```

This “feature” has caught me several times because I have to check the Fusion log very carefully to see that the *g* in Debug is missing. The other odd behavior of Fusion’s treatment of the *DEVPATH* variable is that if you supply the path in quotes, Fusion will append the path to the process’s Appbase (in other words, the current folder). So, I could type the following at the command line:

```
set DEVPATH="C:\Dev\Debug\"
```

If I now start the IDE from the command line, open the solution in C:\Dev, and try to run the output, the IDE will fail to start the process with the following lines in the Fusion log:

```
LOG: Appbase = c:\Dev\Debug\
LOG: DEVPATH = c:\Dev\"C:\Dev\Debug\
LOG: Unable to find assembly in DEVPATH location:
     c:\Dev\"C:\Dev\Debug\myLib.DLL.
```

I suspect part of the problem is that the runtime does not check the last character of the path in *DEVPATH*, but I cannot see the rationale of appending this path to what appears to be a cut down version of Appbase.

Finally, before you can use *DEVPATH*, you have to add the following code to the machine.config file:

```
<runtime>
   <developmentMode developerInstallation="true" />
</runtime>
```

To be honest, I find *DEVPATH* fragile to use. It is too dependent on fixed paths, and it is not associated with the solution, so if I copy a solution to another machine (out of shared source control, for example), I have to determine yet again the paths to use. Thus, I rarely use *DEVPATH* when developing multiassembly projects.

Using a Common Output Folder

In my opinion, the best solution to this problem is to maintain a common output folder for all the projects in the solution. (You can see this solution with the MultiMod example in the source code for this chapter.) I usually provide a separate folder named *bin* under the solution folder and then have subfolders under this folder for each of the solution configurations. To set up this arrangement, I need to provide a Pre-Build Event and edit the project properties.

The first step is use the solution's build order (*Project.ProjectBuildOrder*) to determine the project that will be built first. For this project, open the property pages and select All Configurations from the Configuration drop-down list box. Then set the Pre-Build Event to

```
if not exist "$(SolutionDir)bin" md "$(SolutionDir)bin"
```

For each project in the solution that has an assembly output, open the property pages for All Configurations, go to the Linker General page, and set the Output File to

```
$(SolutionDir)bin/$(OutDir)/<file>
```

where *<file>* is the name of the file including its extension. In other words, you prefix the command that is already there with *$(SolutionDir)bin/*. Note that the linker is quite relaxed about using slashes in paths. Indeed, you can mix slashes and backslashes. Some tools are not so relaxed. One such tool is the command-line copy, which I mentioned in Table 6-9 for managing configuration files in a project. If you have a configuration file in a multiassembly solution, you need to change the command to copy the file to include your new output directory. (See Table 6-12.)

Table 6-12 Properties for a Config File in a Multiassembly Solution

Property	Value
Command Line	copy /y app.config "$(SolutionDir)bin\$(OutDir)\$(TargetFileName).config"
Outputs	"$(SolutionDir)bin\$(OutDir)\$(TargetFileName).config"

Next you need to give the compiler the path to find the metadata. To do this task, you should open the property pages for the application assembly, select All Configurations, and on the C/C++ General page, change the Resolve #using References to

```
$(SolutionDir)bin\$(OutDir)
```

The final task is to allow the debugger to find the .pdb files associated with the assemblies (see Chapter 7). This step is not strictly necessary because when an assembly is built, the path to the .pdb is put in the file, but logically, the .pdb is an output, so it should be copied to the output folder. To perform this task, you should open each project's property pages for All Configurations,[12] and in the Linker Debug page, change the Generate Program Database File property to

```
$(SolutionDir)bin/$(OutDir)/$(ProjectName).pdb
```

Now when you build the solution, you will get the output files in a subfolder with the configuration name under the bin folder and the intermediate files in a subfolder with the configuration name under each project folder. You will be able to run the solution under the debugger and from the command line.

Multimodule Solutions

A multimodule solution has the same problems as a multiassembly solution: you have to make sure that the compiler can find the metadata for the modules when you reference them, and the best solution to this problem is to use a common output folder as I explained earlier. The MultiMod example in the source code for this chapter shows the steps that I will describe here.

In addition, you have to provide projects that create modules rather than assemblies. To do this task, you should create a Managed C++ Class Library for all modules. (If the assembly you are creating is an application, the module that contains the assembly manifest should be a Managed C++ application.) Then, for all modules except the module that contains the assembly manifest, you should go to the Linker Advanced page for All Configurations, change the Turn Off Assembly Generation property to Yes, and on the General page, change the output file name so that it has the extension .netmodule.

Once you have done this, you should go to the project that has the assembly manifest, and on the Linker Input page, add the name of the module in the Add Module to Assembly property. This name should be the full path to the module, as shown in this example

```
$(SolutionDir)bin/$(OutDir)/ModOne.netmodule
```

where *ModOne* is the name of the module. If you have more than one module, you should add them to this property and separate each with only a semicolon. (Do not use a semicolon and a space.)

Projects That Use Resources

Adding unmanaged resources to a project is straightforward: you select Add Resource from the Solution Explorer context menu, and the IDE will add a

12. As you'll see in Chapter 7, there are some advantages to be gained in generating symbols for release builds.

resource script (.rc) and symbol header file (resource.h) to the project. Adding a managed resource is a little more work. If the resource is not compiled, you merely have to add the resource file name to the Embed Managed Resource File on the Linker Input property page.

If the resource is compiled, the Embed Managed Resource File needs the name of the .resources file created by the ResGen utility. For example, to add a string resource to an assembly, you should add a .txt file to your project and open the All Configurations property pages. Set the Custom Build Step Command Line to

```
resgen $(InputFileName) $(IntDir)/$(InputName).resources
```

Here *$(InputFileName)* will give the name of the text file, and *$(InputName)* is the name without the .txt extension. Unfortunately, you cannot use macros to add the compiled file to the managed resources list, so you have to use the actual name. If *$(InputFileName)* is strings.txt, add the following line to the Embed Managed Resource File property:

```
$(IntDir)/strings.resources
```

The ResGen utility also takes an XML file as an input. As I mentioned in Chapter 4, the format of these files is hardly memorable, so you should either copy a .resx file from another project or use the following trick. The ResGen utility will convert input files (.txt or .resx) to .resources files *and vice versa*. So you can do this:

```
resgen strings.txt strings.resources
resgen strings.resources strings.resx
```

The first line creates the .resources file, and the second line creates the XML file with the schema and the data that was given in strings.txt. You can then add the .resx file to your project. The IDE has an XML editor, and I find it more useful to use XML view than Dataset view. If you want to add a binary resource to a .resx file, you will have to do this by hand because there are no tools provided to obtain the encoded serialized form of a binary file. The only solution is to create a temporary C# forms project and use that.

Solutions That Have Satellite Assemblies

Recall from Chapter 4 that applications use satellite assemblies for locale-dependent resources. A satellite assembly is associated with an application assembly, but the application assembly does not depend on the satellite because the application should have culture-neutral resources to fall back on if the localized resource cannot be found. For an application assembly in a file named *ResApp.exe*, the satellite assembly is named *ResApp.resources.dll*. This file must be built as a resource-only library and have a culture. Because all satellites have the same name, they can be distinguished only by their location, so a satellite must be installed in a subfolder with the name of the culture.

All of this information means that you cannot use the Managed C++ Class Library project and instead you have to use the assembly linker tool (al.exe). To build using this tool, you have to add a Makefile project to your solution and ensure that the output is installed in the correct folder. The source code for this chapter has an example (Resources) that shows how this type of building can be done.

Summary

You can develop applications using Notepad to edit the source code, the command-line tools to compile the code, and *nmake* to control the build process, but the process is tedious. The Visual Studio .NET IDE does all this work for you and more. It provides tools to edit your code, to browse and search for specific words, and to control the dependencies and build process. The IDE also provides wizards to create initial code for you, but as I have explained in this chapter, two of these wizards are important: the projects to create managed applications and library assemblies. However, these projects are just the bare bones, so if you want to do anything slightly more complicated, you have to customize the projects yourself. In this chapter, I have explained how to use the project and solution options to develop multiassembly applications and multimodule assemblies, and I have shown how to develop assemblies that have managed resources.

Of course, when you are developing an application, you always need to test that it works, and this task involves running the code under a debugger, which is the subject of the Chapter 7.

7 Debugging

Every code needs debugging at some point during its development. Initially, you will need to debug while you are developing your algorithm: you might need to test that the algorithm is working correctly, or you can use a debugger for code coverage—testing to see how often code is called. You might also find bugs when your code is unit or system tested, or you might get a bug reported by an end user. When you get a bug report, you have to decide where the error occurs and what situation causes the problem. Thus, your life will be far easier if the original code is written with debugging in mind—in particular, checking return values, tracing values, and reporting errors.

Once you have located the error, you need to set up a debug session to test the code and to determine how to fix the code. To do this debugging, you will need to single-step through the code and watch how variables change, and perhaps even change some variables yourself. Your code can use native code through interop or through It Just Works (IJW), in which case you will want to step between the .NET and native worlds testing all of your code. Your application might be distributed over several machines, in which case you will want to be able to debug code on remote machines.

In this chapter, I describe how to use the debugging tools in Microsoft Visual Studio .NET and how to make your code more debuggable. The .NET Framework has classes that you can use to trace intermediate results and to assert that values are correct. I will describe how these classes work, how you can use them, and how to improve them. When you install Visual Studio .NET, you will have several debuggers. The most useful are those built into the IDE because these integrated tools allow you to seamlessly debug both native and JIT-compiled code. I will explain how to use these debuggers and the associated tools that can supply you with additional information about the process you are debugging. Finally I will explain how to debug code across thread boundaries, across application domain boundaries, and in other processes on the same or on a remote machine.

Writing Code for Debugging

No developer assumes that his code will have a bug. Can you imagine a candidate at an interview freely admitting that his code will have bugs? But no one is infallible, so it is far better to admit to yourself that your code inevitably will have bugs and then to add code that enables the compiler to find those bugs or allows the bugs to be picked up during testing. If you write your code with debugging in mind, you will save yourself an immense amount of effort when your first bug is reported.

Debuggable Code

Your first line of defense against bugs is the compiler. Perhaps the most useful keyword in C++ is *const* because it allows you to specify how a parameter or a variable will be used, and the compiler ensures that the parameter or the variable is used as you intend. Consider this code:

```
void PrintName(const wchar_t* strName)
{
   _putws(strName);
   wcscpy(strName, L"no name");
}
```

The method signature specifies that the string the parameter points to will not be changed in the method. When you build the project, the compiler will issue an error that the data pointed to by *strName* will be changed by the call to *wcscpy*. (The compiler cannot convert from *const wchar_t** to *wchar_t**.)

Now consider the equivalent code in managed code:

```
void PrintName(String* strName)
{
   Console::WriteLine(strName);
   strName = S"no name";
}
```

On the surface, this code looks as if the string can be altered in the method. However, instances of *System::String* are immutable, so the assignment changes the string pointer, not the original contents. (The pointer will be passed on the stack, the assignment will not affect the original string pointer passed in the call, and the value on the stack will be cleared when the method returns.) The parameter is effectively an *in* parameter; that is, any changes to the parameter will not be returned to the calling code.

If the method signature is for a method that will be called through interop, it is useful to make explicit the fact that the data will not be changed so that the marshaler will know that it will not need to return data.

```
[DllImport("myDll.dll")]
extern void PrintName([In] String* strName);
```

The immutability of *System::String* ensures that code cannot inadvertently change values. However, consider this class:

```
__gc class Counter
{
public:
   int count;
   Counter(int c) : count(c) {}
   String* ToString()
   { return String::Format(S"Counter is {0}", __box(count)); }
   // Other members omitted
};
```

Now look at the following method that takes an instance as a parameter:

```
void Count(Counter* counter)
{
   while (true)
   {
      if (counter->count = 5) break;
      // Do something with counter.
      Console::WriteLine(counter->count);
      counter->count--;
   }
}
```

Can you see the bug here? For every *Counter* that is passed to this method, the *while* loop will end immediately and the *count* member will be changed to 5. The reason is that I have used an assignment operator instead of the equality operator. If the parameter is changed to *const Counter**, the compiler will detect that the assignment is being performed and will issue the error "l-value specifies a *const* object," that is, you cannot change a *const* object.[1] When the

1. There are two further points to be made about this code. First, you should not make fields public, the check on the value of the object's state should be performed using a method member of *Counter*. The second point is that the assignment/equality bug can be caught by the compiler by placing the literal value on the left hand side; this will not catch the bug when non literal values are compared.

compiler sees the *const* keyword in this context, it will modify the parameter with the following IL:

```
modopt([Microsoft.VisualC]Microsoft.VisualC.IsConstModifier)
```

However, the compiler performs the check that the parameter is treated as a *const* object, so the runtime should not need to know this information. Indeed, if *Count* is a member of a public class and the parameter is marked as *const*, the method can still be called by code written in languages other than C++.

Note also that you can use the C++ *const_cast<>* operator to remove the *const*-ness of a pointer. The *IsConstModifier* modifier means nothing to the runtime, so the IL for *const_cast<>* merely takes the *const* variable and calls it as if it were a non-*const* variable. From a C++ point of view, you clearly must have a good reason to cast away a pointer's *const*-ness.

In a similar way, you can declare objects as being *const* to prevent them from being modified or passed to methods that can modify them, and again, the compiler, not the runtime, performs the test. You cannot apply *const* to a method, so the code

```
const Counter* c = new Counter(50);
Console::WriteLine(c->ToString());
```

will cause the compiler to issue an error that it "cannot convert the *this* pointer from a '*const Counter*' to a '*Counter &*'" in order call the *ToString* method. For an *__nogc* class, this error can be removed by applying *const* to *ToString* to indicate that the method does not change the object, so the method can be safely called through a *const* pointer. With a *__gc* class, you cannot remove the error in this manner; instead, you have to cast away the *const*-ness of the pointer before passing it to *WriteLine*, as shown here:

```
Console::WriteLine(const_cast<Counter*>(c)->ToString());
```

This casting will remove the error, and although it requires extra code, the casting results in no extra IL because as I mentioned earlier, *const* is used only by the compiler, not by the runtime. The *const* keyword is extremely useful to get the compiler to perform checks for you, but it involves writing extra code. As always, you have to expend more effort to ensure that your code will be safe.

Finally for this section, I cannot stress enough the importance of writing code that is readable. Comments are vital because they document the purpose of the code and the expected inputs and outputs. If you comment your code well, when you return to the code months later, you will be able to start debugging immediately. The Visual Studio .NET IDE helps here with the commands to comment and uncomment sections of text in the editor (*Edit.CommentSelection*, *Edit.UncommentSelection*), so you can type your comments as if they are text in a word processor and then turn them into a comment with a single command.

Dividing your code into procedures is also important and outlining (which I mentioned in the section "Outlining" in Chapter 6) helps to order what you see in the text editor. Try to avoid writing methods that have hundreds of lines of code. If you section your code into procedures, you can more effectively determine the expected inputs and outputs and use assertions to ensure that these conditions are met at run time. Furthermore, if you use short procedures, the code will be JIT-compiled and will start to execute quicker than an equivalent monolithic method. This advice is particularly true if a method contains sections that will be executed infrequently. Placing such code in a separate method ensures that the code will be JIT-compiled only when it is first called, and because this occurs infrequently, the JIT-compilation of the method might never occur, so you get a performance benefit. Determining the code that is executed infrequently involves profiling, which I will return to in the section "Profiling" later in this chapter.

.NET Conditional Code

The *System::Diagnostics* namespace has an attribute named *[Conditional]*, which indicates that code with the attribute should be used only when the appropriate symbol is defined. This attribute is not the same as conditional compilation because the code that has the *[Conditional]* attribute will be compiled into the final assembly. The intention of the attribute is to indicate to the compiler that the code can be *called* only when the specified symbol is defined. If the symbol is not defined, the intention of the attribute is that the compiler should ignore the statements that call the conditional method, as shown in this example:

```
// conditional.cpp
__gc class Test
{
public:
   [Conditional("TEST")] void TestOnly(){}
   void Always(){}
};
```

This code indicates that the *Always* method can be called irrespective of the symbols that are defined when the code is compiled, whereas the *TestOnly* method should be called only in builds where *TEST* has been defined. The problem with this code is that the *[Conditional]* attribute has no effect whatsoever on the C++ compiler.[2] This arrangement means that the code

```
#undefine TEST
Test* test = new Test;
test->TestOnly();
```

will actually call the *TestOnly* method even though I have explicitly made sure that the *TEST* symbol is not defined. You should be extremely careful about checking for code that has the *[Conditional]* attribute (several classes in the .NET Framework SDK use this attribute), and for such a method, you should manually add conditional compilation, as shown in the following code:

```
Test* test = new Test;
#ifdef TEST
test->TestOnly();
#endif
```

Clearly, if you are going to regularly call methods that have the *[Conditional]* attribute, you will have your code cluttered with conditional compilation. To make your code far more readable, you should get the preprocessor to do the work through a macro, as shown here:

```
// conditional.cpp
#ifdef TEST
#define TESTMETHOD(p) p->TestOnly()
#else
#define TESTMETHOD(p) __noop
#endif
```

The *__noop* intrinsic indicates that the call should be ignored. Now you can use the *TESTMETHOD* macro in your code, and the preprocessor will call the method only if the *TEST* symbol is defined.

```
Test* test = new Test;
TESTMETHOD(test);
```

Other than making your code more readable, the advantage with this approach is that you can centralize your conditional compilation macros in one header file, and more important, it shows that you have had the discipline to check for *[Conditional]* methods. One final point: it is worth reminding you that in debug builds, the C++ compiler defines the *_DEBUG* symbol but it does not define the *DEBUG* symbol.

---

2. It is one of the few features where I will admit that the C# compiler has done things right: the C# compiler will compile only calls to code without the *[Conditional]* attribute and code where the symbol specified by *[Conditional]* has been defined.

Tracing Code

When an error occurs in your code, the first task is to locate the errant code. If the error causes an exception to be thrown, you have a starting point in your code from which you can backtrack to try and locate the original source of the error. If the bug causes your code to run without an exception but causes your code to return incorrect results, you have a more difficult task because the bug could potentially be anywhere in your code.

Tracing values allows you to output method parameters, intermediate values, and return values, as well as to indicate the execution flow. You can use this information to compare the traced output with test data and then use this comparison to locate the method that has the incorrect code. Furthermore, you can use asserts to ensure that you are immediately informed whenever important values are not right. You then have the opportunity to run the errant code under a debugger.

Once you have a strong candidate for the source of the bug, you have the issue of stepping through the code to determine where the problem lies in your algorithm. I will explain stepping through code using the debugger in the section "Stepping Through Code" later in this chapter; however, I have to point out that in some situations single-stepping is not practical. Such a situation is when the error occurs within a loop and the error is a culmination of many iterations; if you single-stepped through all of the loops, you would have a very tedious time. The debugger will allow you to break when a variable has a specific value or when a certain number of loops have been run, but it is often simpler to trace the value of the variable that has the problem and then watch how the value changes, thus determining when the problem occurs.

Tracing involves generating a string with information that you might need to isolate problems in the code and then reporting that string in a way that allows the string to be read at a later stage. The information that you report is fairly useless if it does not contain information to locate where the information was generated. Therefore, it is usually useful to include information, such as the source file and the line number, or the assembly, class, and method name, along with the traced information. It is often better to use the source file and the line number because this information will allow you to locate the problem within the source file. Furthermore, if this information appears within the Output pane in Visual Studio .NET, you can load the source file and place the caret at the position of the problem merely by double-clicking on the line in the Output pane. The format that you should use to get this behavior is shown in this code:

```
source_file (line_number, character_position): message
```

Here, *source_file* is the name of the file, which can be a full path to the file; if just the name of the file is used, the current project directory will be searched. The pair, *line_number* and *character_position*, gives the location of the problem, and when you double-click on the report in the Output pane, the caret will be moved to this position. You can leave out the character position (which is the format that the C++ compiler uses for its error and warning messages), in which case the caret will be placed at the beginning of the line. The string after the colon is used to describe the problem, and when you double-click on the error report, this string will be shown in the status area of Visual Studio .NET.

If your application is composed of several assemblies, it might be a good idea to put the assembly name in the reported message. If you use the full name (which includes the version, culture, and public key token of the assembly), you will find that the string that identifies the assembly might clutter up the Output pane. In this case, you can use just the short name of the assembly and use some code to dump the full name of the assemblies as they are loaded, as shown in this example:

```
// traceassem.cpp
// Static member
void App::AssemblyLoaded(Object* sender, AssemblyLoadEventArgs* args)
{
   // Example uses WriteLine(); to get this information sent to the
   // Output pane; use Trace::WriteLine() as described later.
   Console::WriteLine(S"Loaded {0}", args->LoadedAssembly->FullName);
}

// In the entry point of the main assembly
AppDomain::CurrentDomain->AssemblyLoad +=
   new AssemblyLoadEventHandler (0, &App::AssemblyLoaded));
```

The full name of an assembly includes its short name (that is, the name of the file that contains the assembly manifest but without the extension), so you should be able to use these messages to identify the assembly. In the preceding code, I have printed the assembly name to the command line. I will show how to get this information into the Output pane in a moment.

If the application involves the interaction between several processes on the same machine or distributed over several machines, the messages that are being reported must be collected in a way that allows them to be collated and analyzed together. If these messages are collected on the machine where they are generated, you have the issue of synchronizing the messages when they are collated. This arrangement means that the clocks on the target machines must be accurately synchronized. On the other hand, a single machine can be used to record the messages, but this arrangement means that network traffic will increase significantly and performance will suffer. The Windows NT event log can be used in both ways: you can log messages on the machine where they are generated, in which case you will need to compare event logs from several machines, or you can nominate a single machine, and all processes in the application can log messages to that machine.

The simplest method to report an event is to use the *::OutputDebugString* Win32 API. As the name suggests, this function sends the specified string to the output debug stream. Internally, this function uses *::RaiseException* to generate a structured exception with the undocumented code 0x40010006, passing the length of the string and the string as the exception parameters and indicating that the exception is continuable.[3] So, in the following code, the call to *::OutputDebugString* and *::RaiseException* do the same thing[4]:

```
// Unmanaged C++
LPCSTR str = "Test String\n";
OutputDebugString(str);
LPCSTR args[2] = {reinterpret_cast<LPCSTR>(strlen(str)), str};
RaiseException(0x40010006, 0, 2,
   reinterpret_cast<const DWORD*>(args));
```

If the process that generated the string is being debugged, the string will be passed synchronously to the debugger when the process calls the Win32 API *::WaitForDebugEvent*. If the process is not being debugged, the system handles the exception by placing the string and the process ID of the process that generates the message in a shared memory section through a memory mapped file named *DBWIN_BUFFER*. Because this file is shared by all processes reading from and writing to this shared memory, the access is controlled by two events: *DBWIN_BUFFER_READY* and *DBWIN_DATA_READY*.

The upshot is that whatever mechanism is used to read the message, the code that does the reading is coupled to the code that generates the message. The thread that generates the message will block until the process that reads the message has completed the read, so if the reading code is not efficient, the reading code can cause the generating process to run exceptionally slow or even to hang. If your process is multithreaded and you use *::OutputDebugString* in each thread, these events will also synchronize your threads, which is not an effect that you would expect.

---

3. I found this out by writing some unmanaged C++ code that uses *::OutputDebugString*. I ran this code under the Visual Studio .NET debugger, and when I came to the *::OutputDebugString* statement, I single-stepped in the Disassembly window. The NT symbols showed me that *::OutputDebugString* called *::RaiseException*.

---

4. I have shown this code as native C++. The reason is that the .NET Framework does not provide a mechanism to raise a native exception. The nearest possible method is *Marshal::ThrowExceptionForHR*, but this method does not take a string parameter, so although the exception is handled (you do not see the unhandled exception dialog box), it is useless because you cannot provide the message.

Thus, you *should not* trace messages through *::OutputDebugString* in release builds that will be executed under normal circumstances. Tracing is often useful in release builds, but it has to be explicitly turned on, perhaps through a command-line switch or through a config file. By default, C# projects define the *TRACE* symbol in release builds, which, as you will see in the next section, means that tracing through the *System::Diagnostics::Trace* class is enabled. Trace messages are handled by *trace listeners*, and one of the default listeners reports the message via *::OutputDebugString*, so if the C# developer is not aware of this issue, he will effectively allow his release builds to be coupled to the debug stream monitor that the user chooses to run. This action is dangerous and is an example of simplifying builds to the point of affecting the performance of the process.

.NET Tracing

The .NET Framework class library provides classes in the *System::Diagnostics* namespace to handle tracing. Effectively, .NET tracing involves two types of classes: a writer class and a listener class. There are two writer classes, *Trace* and *Debug*. These classes have their methods marked with the *[Conditional]* attribute, the intention being that if the *TRACE* symbol is defined, the *Trace* methods can be called, and if the *DEBUG* symbol is defined, the *Debug* methods can be called. As I mentioned earlier, these methods will be available *even if* the appropriate symbol is not defined. This arrangement means that if you have to use C++ conditional compilation with the *Write* and *WriteLine* methods of *Debug* and *Trace*, your code will be cluttered, which limits the usefulness of these classes. One possibility is to use the alternative methods, *WriteIf* and *WriteLineIf*. These methods take a *Boolean* parameter, and the message will be reported only if this parameter is *true*. You can obtain this value from a config file or perhaps define a global *bool* whose value is *true* only when the appropriate symbol is defined, as shown in this example:

```
#ifdef TRACE
bool g_bTrace = true;
#else
bool g_bTrace = false;
#endif
// In your code
Trace::WriteLineIf(g_bTrace, S"This is a message");
```

Although this code places the conditional compilation in just one place—to determine the value of the *bool* global variable—this arrangement still means that a check is performed when the trace messages are required. You can get rid of this check by using a macro that is conditionally compiled, as shown here:

```
#ifdef TRACE
#define TRACEMSG Trace::WriteLine
#else
#define TRACEMSG __noop
#endif
```

It is a pity that the C++ compiler does not check for the *[Conditional]* attribute and compile the code only if the appropriate symbol is defined, as the C# compiler does. However, the *TRACEMSG* macro gives the same effect, and to be honest, I feel that the macro makes the code more readable because it makes it more obvious that the code is tracing a message.

The .NET Framework also provides a class named *Debugger*. I will return to this class later, but for this discussion, this class has a pertinent method named *Log*. This method does nothing if the process is not being debugged, but if the process is being debugged by the managed debugger, the method prints in the Output pane the message passed to the method.

The string passed to the *Debug* or the *Trace* class is passed to each entry in the *Listeners* collection created for each application domain. (Both classes use the same collection.) Each of these listener objects is an instance of a class derived from the *TraceListener* class, which has a *Write* and a *WriteLine* method. These methods record the message string to a location appropriate to the type of listener. Table 7-1 shows the trace listener classes provided by the .NET Framework.

Table 7-1 The .NET Trace Listener Classes in the *System::Diagnostics* Namespace

Class	Description
DefaultTraceListener	Logs messages to *::OutputDebugString* and to *Debugger::Log*; reports asserts through a modal message box, to *::OutputDebugString*, and to *Debugger::Log*
EventLogTraceListener	Logs messages and asserts to the Windows NT event log
TextWriterTraceListener	Logs messages and asserts to the *TextWriter* (a stream, a file, the console, or a custom *TextWriter*) passed to the constructor

I will return to the issue of asserts in the section ".NET Asserts" later in this chapter, but notice that *EventLogTraceListener* and *TextWriterTraceListener* treat failed asserts as merely a special kind of trace message. However, the *Default-TraceListener* class shows a modal dialog box for a failed assert. It is vital that code that can generate such a dialog box does not appear in release build code and especially vital for code that does not run in the interactive Window Station (so that no user can see the dialog box to be able to dismiss it).

You can get access to the listeners for your application domain by accessing the static *Listeners* property of either the *Trace* or *Debug* class, which returns a reference to an instance of *TraceListenerCollection*. This collection is read/write, so you can add and remove items as well as list the entries that it contains. So if you need to pass trace messages and failed asserts via a socket to another process, you could create the socket and use it to initialize a *TextWriterTraceListener* instance such as this:

```
NetworkStream* stm = new NetworkStream(mySocket);
StreamWriter* writer = new StreamWriter(stm);
TextWriterTraceListener* listener =
   new TextWriterTraceListener(writer);
Trace::Listeners->Add(listener);
```

If you have a special requirement for the tracing you intend to do, you can create your own tracing class derived from *TraceListener*. (You have to provide an overload for the abstract methods *Write(String*)* and *WriteLine(String*)*, and you must ensure that you initialize the inherited *Name* property to an appropriate value.)

The first time that code calls one of the *Trace* or *Debug* methods that write to the listeners for an application domain, the *Listeners* collection will be created, and by default, this collection will have an instance of *DefaultTraceListener* named *Default*. In addition, the system will view the configuration of the process to see if there is information about the *Listeners* collection. The configuration is contained in the *<system.diagnostics>* node. If this information is specified in the machine.config file, all processes will have the configuration, but note that the values in the process's configuration file take precedence. This node can contain a node named *<trace>* that has the trace settings. The *<trace>* node can contain a *<listeners>* node to which you can add or remove items, as shown in the following code:

```
<!-- tracing.exe.config -->
<configuration>
  <system.diagnostics>
    <trace>
      <listeners>
        <remove name="Default"/>
        <add name="txtListener"
            type=
              "System.Diagnostics.TextWriterTraceListener,
               System, Version=1.0.3300.0, Culture=neutral,
```

```
            PublicKeyToken=b77a5c561934e089"
          initializeData="Trace.log"/>
      </listeners>
    </trace>
  </system.diagnostics>
</configuration>
```

The first entry in the *<listeners>* node removes a named listener, in this case, the default listener, which means that the process using this config file will not log messages to the output debug stream. It makes sense to add this line to the config files of all your released processes so that if a developer inadvertently leaves a *Trace* or debug method call in the code, the call will be executed but will not result in *::OutputDebugString* being called. (Of course, this line can be removed for debug builds.)

The second entry adds a new listener to the *Listeners* collection. In this case, the listener is a *TextWriterTraceListener*, so the listener needs to be initialized with a value to indicate to the *TextWriter* the file in which the messages will be written. As you can see, this value is a single string and is used to call the *TextWriterTraceListener* constructor that takes a string—in other words, the string is the name of the log file. There is an inherent problem with initializing the *TextWriter* this way: if you have more than one application domain in which you trace messages, the *Listeners* collection in each domain will be initialized with the same data. In this case, the separate instances of *TextWriterTraceListener* will attempt to write to *Trace.log*. The first instance will place an exclusive lock on this file so that subsequent attempts to initialize the *Listeners* collection in another domain will fail with an exception in the configuration section handler. If logging to a file is your preference, it is better to derive from *TextWriterTraceListener* and use the constructor to create a log file unique to the application domain, as shown here:

```
// tracing.cpp
__gc class DomainSafeTextTrace : public TextWriterTraceListener
{
public:
   DomainSafeTextTrace()
   {
      Initialize(S"Trace.log");
   }
   DomainSafeTextTrace(String* str)
   {
      Initialize(str);
   }
protected:
   void Initialize(String* str)
```

```
    {
        this->Name = S"DomainSafeTextTrace";
        String* strFile;
        strFile = String::Concat(str, S".",
              AppDomain::CurrentDomain->FriendlyName);
        strFile = String::Concat(strFile, S".log");
        this->Writer = new StreamWriter(strFile, true);
    }
};
```

The first domain is named after the process, so if I use this class in a process named *Test.exe* and the config file provides *Trace* as the name of the tracing file, this class will create a file named *Trace.Text.exe.log*. If the process then creates an application domain named *Second_Domain*, a file named *Trace.Second_Domain.log* will be created. The source code for this chapter has two examples. Tracing.cpp uses *DomainSafeTextTrace* and identifies that this trace listener should be used with an entry in the config file. The other example, tracing2.cpp, uses a class similar to *DomainSafeTextTrace* that is designed to be added to the *Listeners* collection programmatically.

The *<trace>* node can have two attributes: *autoflush* and *indentsize*. These attributes correspond to the *AutoFlush* and *IndentSize* properties of *Trace*. If *AutoFlush* is set to *true*, the *Flush* method is called whenever a write is made through *Trace*. This behavior is especially useful if the entries in the *Listeners* collection are based on buffered streams (for example, those that are based on a file). If you do not use *AutoFlush*, you should manually call *Trace::Flush* before the application domain closes down. The *IndentSize* property specifies the size of indenting that will be used. Indenting helps you to format traced messages. For example, you might decide that it makes more sense to indent messages from method calls, as shown here:

```
void Test()
{
   Trace::Indent();
   Trace::WriteLine(S"In Test()");
   Trace::Unindent();
}
void main()
{
   Trace::WriteLine(S"In main()");
   Test();
}
```

This code will print "In main()" at column zero and then on the next line print In "Test()" at column number *IndentSize*. To set the *AutoFlush* and *IndentSize* properties of the *Debug* class, you should use the *autosize* and *indentsize* attributes of the *<debug>* node in *<system.diagnostics>*.

The various methods of *Trace* and *Debug* that allow you to write methods have an overloaded version that takes a second string; this string is the category. The category can be any value that you choose, and in the trace stream, you will find that the traced message will be prefixed with the category and a colon. Finally, there are also methods that take an *Object** pointer. These methods merely call *ToString* on the object and pass the resulting string to the method that takes a string.

These two classes are fine for basic tracing, but they do leave a lot for the programmer to do. The first issue is that *Write* and *WriteLine* take already formatted strings, so you cannot use a format string and variables to provide the values at run time for the placeholders in the format strings. These classes are sealed, so you cannot add new functionality by deriving a child class. Instead, you have to create a totally new class. Furthermore, since you cannot write code that uses the managed *varargs*, you have to use an array of *Object** and the *[ParamArray]* attribute, which simulates *varargs* for C# but does nothing for the C++ programmer. Another problem with these classes is that they do not have a "detail" level. The ATL trace macro (*ATLTRACE*) allows you to define a detail level so that at run time you can decide to trace messages at various detail levels. With *Debug* and *Trace*, all trace messages are generated, so you often have the problem of either generating too few messages and omitting important information or generating too many messages and having to filter through the messages after they have been collected.

Windows NT Event Log

The Windows NT event log is a wonderful facility in Windows NT, Windows 2000, and Windows XP. It is an efficient, persistent store of events. These events are accessible on the local machine, on a remote machine (if your account has the appropriate privileges), or through an exported file. This arrangement means that if you have a distributed application and something goes awry, you can copy the event log from the various machines that were involved in the application and examine the logs at your leisure on your own machine. Now comes the nice part: if these machines are located in different locales, the event log on each machine shows the events in the default language of the specific locale, but if you access the event on another machine in another locale (either by copying the exported event log file or by accessing the event log over the network), the event is formatted using the locale of the machine from where it is being viewed. This seems like magic, but in fact, it is quite straightforward.

When you log an event, you need a file (typically a DLL) called a *message resource file*. This file could be in your application, but typically it is a separate file because it should be installed on each machine where the events are to be read. The path to this file is registered with the system with a name called the *source name*.

The message resource file has Win32 resources of type *RT_MESSAGETABLE*. Each language that you will support will have a message table resource, and this resource essentially associates an event ID with a format string. The format string has the locale-specific message with placeholders (%1, %2, and so on) for values that are specific to each instance of the event. When the event is generated, the event log is given the source name, the event ID, and an array of strings that are used to fill the placeholders. The combination of these three allows the event log API to locate the right resource file for each event.

When you read an event from the event log, the API reads the source name, loads the resource file, determines the current locale, and finds the message table for that locale in the resource file. Finally, the API loads the format string and inserts the parameter strings into the placeholders. The process is slightly more complicated than what I've described here, but this overview is the essence of how the process works.

The most important aspect of this scheme is that as long as the message resource file is registered on each machine, you will always get the events formatted in the current locale. In addition, the format messages can be quite detailed, but because these messages are *not* stored in the event log, disk space is used efficiently where the events are stored and network time is reduced when the event log is accessed remotely.

The disk space aspect is important because there is less data to load when the event log first loads (so the event log starts much quicker). There is also less possibility of losing data. Event logs are limited to the size of the files used to store the events. When the file reaches this limit, messages in the event log will be overwritten. In normal operation, it might take many weeks to fill the event log, but the whole point about the facility is that you will need it at extraordinary times when something is failing catastrophically, which can involve logging many events.[5] Determining what caused an application to fail can be difficult, and it certainly does not help if events are lost. Storing format messages in a file other than the event log avoids this problem.

---

5. Note that you really should try to avoid such a situation occurring in your code. The event log should be used sparingly. However, you cannot guarantee that third-party code will follow such good practices.

If it sounds like I have a certain amount of affection and admiration for the event log, you are correct. Although some of the Win32 APIs for accessing the event log are somewhat arcane (they were originally designed for OS/2), they perform the job well. However, I have bad news for you: the .NET Framework classes for reporting events have debased the behavior of the event log to the point of making it just a little better than useless. I say this because the designers have decided to dispense with the use of message resource files. I suspect the reason is that the .NET classes were based on the code that appeared in unmanaged Visual Basic, which also dispensed with resource files. The .NET Framework puts the onus of localization on the code that *generates* the event and not on the code that reads the event. Thus, when you generate an event with *System::Diagnostics::EventLog*, you provide the string that will appear in *its entirety* in the event log. The .NET Framework does provide a message resource file, but the message table merely has 65,536 format strings that look like this:

```
%1
```

The problem with this approach is that the application logging the event will have to determine who will read the event. If the event will be read on the same machine where it is generated, the application will need to determine the language of the current machine. If the event will be read by another machine, the application will have to guess the locale of that machine. Because it is not possible to accurately guess the locale of the other machine, a suitable neutral language must be used, and invariably this will mean English. This default is fine for me because I speak only English, and I guess this is fine for those of you reading the English version of this book, but if your application is international, this behavior is bad manners at best, and at its worst, it is arrogant and also a possible source of errors.

If you want to avoid this problem, you must avoid using the *EventLog* class to report events and instead call the Win32 *::ReportEvent* method through interop or IJW. The code is pretty straightforward, and the only issue is converting a managed array of strings to an unmanaged array of string pointers. If you use interop, you can define a custom marshaler to do the conversion. If you use IJW, it is simple to create an unmanaged array and copy the data across the managed/unmanaged boundary, as shown in the following code:

```
// eventlog.cpp
__nogc class StringArray
{
   LPCWSTR* m_params;
   int m_length;
public:
```

```
    StringArray(String* strings[])
    {
       m_length = 0;
       m_params = NULL;
       if (strings != NULL)
       {
          m_length = strings->Length;
          m_params = new LPCWSTR [m_length];
          for (int i = 0; i < m_length; i++)
          {
             m_params[i] = (LPCWSTR)(LPVOID)
                Marshal::StringToHGlobalUni(strings[i]);
          }
       }
    }
    ~StringArray()
    {
       if (m_params != NULL)
       {
          for (int i = 0; i < m_length; i++)
          {
             IntPtr ptr = (LPVOID)m_params[i];
             Marshal::FreeHGlobal(ptr);
          }
          delete [] m_params;
       }
    }
    __declspec(property(get=GetLength)) const int Length;
    const int GetLength()
    {
       return m_length;
    }
    operator LPCWSTR*()
    {
       return m_params;
    }
};
```

This unmanaged C++ class takes a string array as a constructor parameter and converts the data in the array to an unmanaged array of string pointers. This unmanaged array is available through a conversion operator. The class is designed to be created on the stack, so the destructor of the class does the cleanup of the unmanaged resources. It can be used like this:

```
// eventlog.cpp
String* strings[] = { S"one", S"two" };
StringArray params(strings);
::ReportEvent(hEvt, 0, 0, evtID, NULL, params.Length,
   0, params, 0);
```

This code is managed. An instance of the unmanaged class is created on the stack and initialized with the managed string array; the constructor does the conversion to a *LPCWSTR* array. In the call to the Win32 *::ReportEvent*, the *StringArray::GetLength* method is called when the *Length* property is accessed, which is the purpose of the *__declspec(property)* modifier. Finally, when the object is passed as the eighth parameter to *::ReportEvent*, the conversion operator is called, which returns the unmanaged *LPCWSTR* array.

As I have mentioned, using a message resource file means that you can have Windows NT event messages that are correctly formatted in the Windows NT event viewer for the current locale. If you choose not to use the Windows NT event viewer, you can read the event messages using the *EventLog* class. Although this class is very poor at generating event messages (and I strongly urge you *not* to use it this way), it has excellent code to read event messages. Anyone who has used the Win32 *::ReadEventLog* and *::FormatMessage* APIs to read event messages will testify that these functions are far from ideal. The *EventLog* class has a property named *Entries* that is an *EventLogEntryCollection*. When you read this property, the next event is read and formatted for the current locale, whether the event was generated with *EventLog* or with *::ReportEvent*.

When you add an event, you specify a category value, a 16-bit value. The Windows NT event log viewer will search a category message resource file for the display string for the category. This file is essentially the same as an event message resource file, and the two can be combined. If the event log viewer cannot find the display string, it will show the category number. Yet again, this is another situation where the .NET Framework *EventLog* class is seriously deficient: there is no way that you can indicate a display string for a category.

To have the complete benefit of the event log, you have to register the source in the Windows NT registry. To do this, you have to create a key with the name of your source in

```
HKEY_LOCAL_MACHINE\CurrentControlSet\Services\Eventlog\Application
```

Within this new key, you must add two settings, a string value named *EventMessageFile* that has the path to the event message resource file, and a *DWORD* value named *TypesSupported* that is the combination of all the event log message types that can be generated. To perform this task in managed code, you need to use the classes in the *Microsoft::Win32* namespace, as shown here:

```
// eventlog.cpp
void Register(String* srcName, String* srcPath)
{
   RegistryKey* application;
   application = Registry::LocalMachine->OpenSubKey(
```

```
                S"SYSTEM\\CurrentControlSet\\Services"
                S"\\Eventlog\\Application", true);
   if (application != 0)
   {
      RegistryKey* src;
      src = application->CreateSubKey(srcName);
      if (src!= 0)
      {
         src->SetValue(S"EventMessageFile", srcPath);
         src->SetValue(S"TypeSupported", __box(7));
      }
   }
}
```

If you have descriptive strings for your categories, you should add a string setting named *CategoryMessageFile* that has a path to the category message resource file and a *DWORD* setting named *CategoryCount* that lists the number of categories that have a display string.

The message file should have the message table resource bound to it as a Win32 resource. The message table resource is created by the message compiler tool (mc.exe) from a message file (.mc). This tool will create binary resources—one for each language that is mentioned in the message file—and will generate a resource script (.rc) file that includes these resources. Typically, your makefile will have a build rule to compile .mc files with mc.exe, then compile the resultant resource script with the unmanaged resource compiler (rc.exe), and then link the resultant binary (.res) as an unmanaged resource to the output file. This file can be an assembly or an unmanaged DLL. It makes sense to add the registration code to the message resource file, and in the case of an unmanaged DLL, you can add this code to an exported function named *DllInstall*, as the following code shows:

```
HRESULT DllInstall(BOOL bInstall, LPCWSTR cmd);
```

The *DllInstall* function is called when you pass the DLL to regsvr32 with the *-i* switch. If the *-u* switch is also used, *bInstall* will be *FALSE* (uninstall the DLL); otherwise, it will be *TRUE*.

If the resource file is an assembly, you can add the registration code to an installer class. This class derives from *Installer* in the *System::Configuration::Install* namespace. The installer class should have the *[RunInstallerAttribute]* attribute set to *true*. The .NET Framework provides a tool named *installutil.exe* to which you pass the name of an assembly, and the tool then uses reflection to look for classes with the *[RunInstallerAttribute]* attribute set to *true*. Once the tool has found an installer class, it instantiates an instance and calls its *Install* method. If this method is successful, the tool will call the class's

Commit method; otherwise, it will call the *Rollback* method. Installer objects can be chained, and if one fails in its *Install* method, *Rollback* will be called on all the objects that have been run. Thus, you should call the *Register* method shown earlier within your custom installer class. You can create a deployment project through the Visual Studio .NET IDE that calls the installer class. Unfortunately, the documentation for installutil.exe indicates that this tool will not run an installer class written in managed C++. The workaround is to write a shim class in C# that calls your C++ code compiled into another module; because the installer class will be C#; installutil.exe will be happy.

Unfortunately, the Visual Studio .NET IDE does not recognize message files, which means that if you want to create message resource files (managed or unmanaged), you have to create a custom project in Visual Studio .NET. However, as I mentioned earlier, the advantages that you get from having correctly formatted messages in the Windows NT event log far outweigh the extra effort that you have to expend to create these resource files.

CRT Tracing

If you are likely to use the CRT or call other code that uses the CRT, you might well have code that generates trace messages through the CRT tracing mechanism. The Debug CRT libraries have a whole series of macros that start with *_RPT* or *_RPTF*; these macros call the *_CrtDbgReport* function, passing various parameters to the function. The output from *_CrtDbgReport* is either to the command line, a file, or a message box, and you call *_CrtSetReportMode* to specify the output destination. There is also another option: if you call *_CrtSetReportHook2*, you can provide your own reporting function. Your reporting function should have the following prototype:

```
int ReportHook(int reportType, char *message, int *returnValue);
```

When code using the CRT debugging API generates a report, it will give a report type, *_CRT_WARN*, *_CRT_ERROR_*, or *_CRT_ASSERT_*. This report type is passed as the first parameter to the report hook, so your code can perform different handling depending on the type of message that was generated. The actual message is sent as the second parameter. You can use these two pieces of information to decide whether to process the report. If you decide that you do not want to handle the report, you should return *FALSE* and *_CrtDbgReport* will be called; otherwise, return *TRUE*. The final parameter of the report hook should be treated as an out parameter and should be used to indicate what should happen after the hook function is called. The function should return *0* if no errors occurred (which is the case with trace messages), *1* if the debugger should be started, and *– 1* to shut down the process. From this discussion, you can see that it is possible to define a global function that will direct all trace messages to trace listeners, as shown here:

```
// assertcrt.cpp
int ReportHook(int reportType, char *message, int *returnValue)
{
   switch(reportType)
   {
   case _CRT_WARN:
      Debug::WriteLine(message);
      *returnValue = 0;
      break;
   case _CRT_ERROR:
   case _CRT_ASSERT:
      *returnValue = -1;
      Debug::Fail(message);
      break;
   }
   return TRUE;
}
```

Your entry point should identify the hook report function with the following code:

```
_CrtSetReportHook2(_CRT_RPTHOOK_INSTALL, ReportHook);
```

ReportHook will ensure that all trace messages are sent to the *Listeners* collection. I have also shown one way to handle assertions. However, the situation is not as simple as this, as you will see in the next section.

Assertions

Assertions are extremely useful in debug builds and are completely useless—even harmful—in release builds. You use an assertion to test that a condition required for the correct operation of your code is true, so if the assertion fails, you know that you have a source of a bug. Because a failed assertion is so important, you might choose to be informed immediately of the failure, typically through a modal dialog box. Clearly, it does your company's reputation little good to present to a user of your code a modal dialog box saying that the code has failed—if your code fails, I am sure that you would prefer the application to quietly slink away (and hope that the user blames some other code for the death of your application), rather than to boldly tell the user that the code has some horrendous bug that you thought could happen, and that, indeed, it has happened. Thus, assertions should be compiled away to nothing in release builds.

.NET Asserts

The .NET Framework provides assertions through the *Debug* and *Trace* classes. There are three overloaded *Assert* methods. The simplest takes a *bool*, which is the test that you want to perform. If this parameter is *false*, the assertion has failed and the user should be informed. The other two overloads have, respectively, an extra string parameter and an extra two string parameters. The first of these strings is a descriptive string that identifies the assertion that has failed. The final string is used for additional details about the assertion.

As with the tracing methods, the *Assert* methods are marked with the *[Conditional]* attribute. This attribute has *TRACE* for the methods in the *Trace* class, and it has *DEBUG* for the methods in the *Debug* class. As before, the C++ compiler will compile the calls to the *Assert* methods into your code whether or not these symbols are defined. Thus, you should not call these methods directly. Instead, you should define a macro similar to the *TRACEMSG* macro I mentioned earlier. Furthermore, under *no* circumstances should a call to *Debug::Assert* or *Trace::Assert* exist in your code in a release build, so to ensure that the calls occur only in debug builds, your assertion macro should be defined only if the symbol *_DEBUG* is defined (note the leading underscore).

```
#ifdef _DEBUG
#define ASSERT Debug::Assert
#else
#define ASSERT __noop
#endif
```

When the *Assert* method is called, the *Boolean* expression is evaluated, and if the result is *false*, the *Fail* method is called on each of the registered trace listeners. The *Trace* and *Debug* classes also have a *Fail* method, which will also call the *Fail* methods on the trace listeners, so you can fail the assert without even evaluating a *Boolean*.

Table 7-1 on page 431 gives the trace listener classes provided by the .NET Framework. The *DefaultTraceListener* does the most work, and I will describe this class in a moment. The *EventLogTraceListener* and *TextWriterTraceListener* classes inherit the *Fail* method from *TraceListener*, which merely concatenates the assert message and detailed description with a suitable header string identifying that an assertion failed. As you would expect, the *EventLogTraceListener* class adds this string to the event log as an entry, and the *TextWriterTraceListener* writes the string to the stream on which it is based. However, neither of these classes give any indication about where the assertion failed. If you decide to log failed assertions, you must indicate where the assertion failed because there is a bug in the .NET Framework class that prevents the automatic logging of where the assertion failed. In this situation, it is important to use the version of *Assert* that has two strings and use the second string to give the location of the assertion. I will describe how to obtain the location programmatically later in this section.

Only the *DefaultTraceListener* treats the assertion as requiring immediate attention. This class shows a modal dialog box with information about the assertion and hence the dialog box blocks the errant code. In addition, this class logs the assertion method to a log file and to the attached debugger. The *Fail* method for this class first checks the *Debugger* class to determine whether there is an attached debugger (and hence, logging is enabled), and if so, it sends the assertion message to the debugger by calling *Debugger::Log*. If no debugger is attached, this message is sent to the output debug stream with a call to *::OutputDebugString*. (Remember the comments that I made earlier in the section "Tracing Code" about using this Win32 function.) Next *Fail* checks to see whether a log file has been specified—the *DefaultTraceListener::LogFileName* property—and if so, *Fail* opens this file for append, adds the assertion failed message, and closes the file.

Finally *Fail* checks the *AssertUiEnabled* property to determine whether a modal dialog box should be shown. If this property is *true*, a modal dialog box is shown with the details of the assertion. I will have more to say about this dialog box in a moment. In all three cases (logging to the debugger, logging to the log file, and displaying the assert dialog box), the code obtains information about the current stack trace so that it can log the assertion location along with other information about the assertion. However, in version 1 of .NET, there is a bug in the *StackTrace* class (which I'll mention later) that results in an empty string being generated. Thus, no information is given about the location of the assertion, and as I mentioned before, you should provide this information in the detailed string parameter of *Assert*.

There is only one way to set the values of the *AsserUiEnabled* and *LogFileName* properties: through the config file. Although these properties are read/write, it turns out that the *get* method uses the value specified in the config file rather than the value passed through the set method, and if the process does not have a config file, a default value of *true* is used for *AssertUiEnabled* and an empty string is used for *LogFileName*. Because the config file is always used to get these properties, each instance of *DefaultTraceListener* has the same value for these properties. To set these properties, you need the <*assert*> node in the config file, as the following code shows:

```
<system.diagnostics>
   <assert assertuienabled="false" logfilename="asserts.log" />
</system.diagnostics>
```

Figure 7-1 shows the dialog box that is shown when an assertion fails. The top string is the message string, and the lower string is the *detailMessage* string.

Figure 7-1 Assertion dialog box generated by *DefaultTraceListener* when *AssertUiEnabled* is set to *true*

Now, ask yourself, if the button combination Abort–Retry–Ignore is so confusing, why didn't the designers of the *Trace* class merely change their captions to Quit–Debug–Continue rather than provide that extra information in the dialog box title? If the Abort–Retry–Ignore combination is not confusing, why bother with the title? It all seems to be rather sloppy programming to me. The reason why the assert dialog box shown in Figure 7-1 has these buttons is because it is a standard Win32 message box, and the code that displays the dialog box is equivalent to the following unmanaged C++ code:

```
// Unmanaged code equivalent
int ret;
ret = ::MessageBox(NULL, msg, caption,
   MB_ABORTRETRYIGNORE | MB_ICONHAND | MB_DEFBUTTON3);
switch (ret)
{
case IDABORT:
   ::ExitProcess(1);
   break;
case IDRETRY:
   ::DebugBreak();
   break;
case IDIGNORE:
   // Do nothing.
   break;
}
```

To be honest, the actual code that shows the assert dialog box is not much more complicated than this code. Instead of the Win32 *::ExitProcess*, the managed code calls the static *Application::Exit* to shut down the application. Note that the application gets shut down immediately, so if you have several *Trace* listeners registered for this process, you have to ensure that if you use the *DefaultTraceListener* class, it is the last one in the *Trace::Listeners* collection. Otherwise, none of the other trace listeners will be called when you select the Abort or Quit button. Instead of the Win32 *::DebugBreak* (which merely translates to an x86 *int 3* opcode), managed code calls methods on the *Debugger* class. This class acts as an interface to the managed debugger, and if the managed debugger is attached to the current process, the *Debugger::IsAttached* property will return *true*, in which case you can call *Debugger::Break* to make the debugger stop at the current position in the code. If the debugger is not currently attached, you can call *Debugger::Launch* to start it.

The designers of the *DefaultTraceListener* class[6] chose to call *::MessageBox* because *::MessageBox* is a system function and it has a predefined dialog box that most developers are familiar with. If the designers decided to create a *Form*-derived dialog box, the resultant assembly would have a dependence on *system.windows.forms.dll*. Code without assertions might not use this assembly, so there is no sense in adding the extra dependence. However, I still balk at the decision to give a key to the use of the buttons in the dialog box title—either the developer should learn what the buttons mean or the button's titles should be changed. If you regard the latter as the best course of action, the following example will interest you.

The source code for this chapter has a project named AssertDlg in the Assertions solution. Assemblies can have Win32 resources, so I decided to create a C++ managed library and add an unmanaged resource file. (In Solution Explorer, select the project, and through the context menu, select Add Resource.) After doing that, I added a dialog box template named *IDD_ASSERT* with the three buttons, which I labeled *Quit*, *Debug*, and *Ignore*. I gave these buttons the IDs *IDABORT*, *IDRETRY*, and *IDIGNORE*, respectively. Then I added a read-only edit box (*IDC_MSG*) and a picture box for the icon. To get the icon, I loaded user32.dll into Visual Studio .NET, located the icon used for *MB_ERROR*, and exported it. I then imported this icon into my project. Figure 7-2 shows an annotated view of this dialog box.

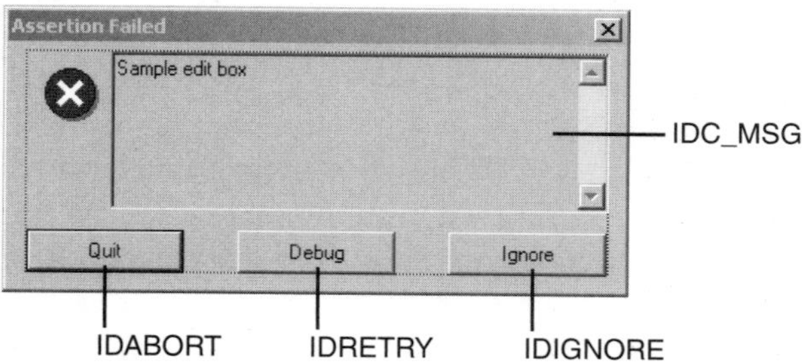

Figure 7-2 The Win32 resource template for the *IDD_ASSERT* dialog box

6. To be accurate, the code is actually in the private *System::Diagnostics::AssertWrapper* class, which is called by the *DefaultTraceListener* class through the private *TraceInternal* class.

To show this dialog box, I call the Win32 *::DialogBoxParam* function. This function creates a modal dialog box, but the function takes a dialog procedure parameter. I use the dialog procedure to initialize the dialog box and to handle the button clicks by merely closing the dialog box. In the initialization code, I fill the edit box with the assert message, the detailed description of the assertion, and details of where the assertion occurred. These strings have to be passed from managed code to the dialog procedure, so I have chosen to concatenate these strings together, convert the string to a native string, and pass it to *::DialogBoxParam* as the final parameter. This string is passed to the dialog procedure as the *LPARAM* parameter with the *WM_INITDIALOG* message. Here is the complete dialog procedure:

```
INT_PTR CALLBACK DialogProc(HWND hDlg, UINT msg,
   WPARAM wParam, LPARAM lParam)
{
   switch (msg)
   {
   case WM_INITDIALOG:
      {
         LPCWSTR strMsg = reinterpret_cast<LPCWSTR>(lParam);
         HWND msg = GetDlgItem(hDlg, IDC_MSG);
         ::SetWindowText(msg, strMsg);
         break;
      }
   case WM_CLOSE:
      EndDialog(hDlg, IDIGNORE);
      return TRUE;
   case WM_COMMAND:
      if (HIWORD(wParam) == BN_CLICKED)
      {
         EndDialog(hDlg, LOWORD(wParam));
         return TRUE;
      }
      return FALSE;
   }
   return FALSE;
}
```

As you can see, when the user clicks on one of the buttons, the ID of the button is returned through *::EndDialog* as the return value of *::DialogBoxParam*.

On the dialog box, I want to show the details of the assertion and details about where the location occurred. To perform this task, I use the *StackTrace* class. This class obtains a stack trace and allows you to step through the trace one frame at a time. The *FrameCount* property gives the total number of frames, and the *GetFrame* property returns the specified frame indexed from zero, thus the last frame should be *FrameCount – 1*. However, in .NET version 1, there is a bug in *StackFrame* that causes it to return one more stack frame than is actually in the trace, so *GetFrame(FrameCount – 1)* actually returns an uninitialized *StackFrame* object. Thus, you have to use *GetFrame(FrameCount – 2)* to get the last stack frame, as shown here:

```
StackTrace* st = new StackTrace(true);
// Get the frame that I require.
int frame = st->FrameCount - 2;
StackFrame* sf = st->GetFrame(frame);
// This is the source file.
String* strFile = sf->GetFileName();
// This is the line number.
int lineNo = sf->GetFileLineNumber();
```

This bug has gone unnoticed by the authors of the *DefaultTraceListener* class, which calls *GetFrame(FrameCount – 1)* and gets an uninitialized object. As a consequence, the location string that should appear on the Assert dialog box is empty, so there is no indication where the failed assertion occurs.

The dialog box is shown when an assertion fails, and as I have mentioned earlier, you can define your own trace listener class by deriving from *TraceListener*. In the following code, I have derived from *DefaultTraceListener* so that the new class inherits the other methods but overrides *Fail* to call my dialog box:

```
public __gc class FixedTraceListener
   : public DefaultTraceListener
{
public:
   void Fail(String* msg, String* detailed)
   {
      // Get the stack trace so that we can find out where the
      // assertion occurs.
      StackTrace* st = new StackTrace(true);
      int frame = st->FrameCount - 2;
      StackFrame* sf = st->GetFrame(frame);

      // Concatenate the strings.
      StringBuilder* sb = new StringBuilder();
      // Add the message to the string.
      if (msg != 0 && msg->Length > 0)
      {
         sb->Append(msg);
         sb->Append(S"\r\n");
      }
      else
```

```
        {
           sb->Append(S"Assertion failed");
        }
        // If there is a detailed description, add it.
        if (detailed != 0 && detailed->Length > 0)
        {
           sb->Append(detailed);
           sb->Append(S"\r\n");
        }
        // Now add details about where the assertion occurred.
        sb->Append(S"at line ");
        sb->Append(__box(sf->GetFileLineNumber()));
        sb->Append(S" in ");
        sb->Append(sf->GetFileName());

        // Convert to a native string.
        IntPtr str = Marshal::StringToHGlobalUni(sb->ToString());
        INT_PTR ret = IDIGNORE;
        // Create the dialog box; this call blocks until the
        // dialog box is closed.
        ret = ::DialogBoxParam(GetModuleHandle(L"AssertDlg.dll"),
                    MAKEINTRESOURCE(IDD_ASSERT), NULL, DialogProc,
                    (LPARAM)(LPVOID)str);
        // Free the converted string.
        Marshal::FreeHGlobal(str);
        // Perform the action the user requested.
        switch(ret)
        {
        case IDABORT:
           Environment::Exit(1);
           break;
        case IDRETRY:
           {
              if (Debugger::IsAttached)
                 Debugger::Break();
              else
                 Debugger::Launch();
           }
           break;
        case IDIGNORE:
           // Do nothing.
           break;
        }
    }
};
```

The *Fail* method creates the dialog box with *::DialogBoxParam*, which blocks until the dialog box is closed. The *switch* statement then tests the return value and performs an appropriate action, as I described earlier in this section. Take another look at the call to *::DialogBoxParam*, shown here:

```
ret = ::DialogBoxParam(GetModuleHandle(L"AssertDlg.dll"),
            MAKEINTRESOURCE(IDD_ASSERT), NULL, DialogProc,
            (LPARAM)(LPVOID)str);
```

The first parameter is the *HINSTANCE* of the module that has the resource. The module will be the assembly that contains the dialog procedure, and this *HINSTANCE* is obtained by calling *::GetModuleHandle*. Note that if I pass *NULL* as the parameter to this function, it will return the module handle of the *process* that loads the assembly, which is not what I want. Instead, I give the name of the assembly module (in this case, *AssertDlg.dll*). The name of the module has a .dll extension, which is in contrast to the short name of an assembly, which can have either .dll or .exe as the extension. (Fusion will attempt to find a file with either of these extensions.)

To use this class, you have to change the config file for the process that loads the library assembly. Here is the appropriate section, identifying the class in the AssertDlg.dll assembly:

```
<trace>
   <listeners>
      <add name="assertListener"
           type="FixedTraceListener, AssertDlg"/>
      <remove name="Default"/>
   </listeners>
</trace>
```

The source code for this chapter has a project named UseAssertions (part of the Assertions solution) that shows how to use this trace listener.

CRT Asserts

If you are likely to use code that calls the CRT, you are likely to have code that has CRT asserts. The CRT defines two macros, *_ASSERT* and *_ASSERTE*, and has a function named *assert*.

The *assert* function will report the assertion failure through a file stream (either a file or *stderr*) or to a modal dialog box, depending on the error reporting value set by calling *_set_error_mode*. The default is to print the assertion failure to *stderr* and then call *abort*, which will call *_CrtDebugReport*. Depending on how reporting is set up, you will get a report sent to a file, the command line, or a modal message box. The default mode is for *_CrtDebugReport* to use a message box, so *assert* appears to create both a message on the command line and in a message box.

If you use *_set_error_mode* to use a message box, you will get the familiar Abort–Retry–Ignore dialog box, so you get to choose whether to shut down the process. If you want to redirect assert failures generated by *assert* to a *TraceListener*, you have to ensure that *_set_error_mode* is set to *_OUT_TO_STDERR* so that *_CrtDbgReport* is called, and that *_CrtSetReportHook* is called to set a function that does the redirection. The *_ASSERT* and *_ASSERTE* macros call *_CrtDbgReport* with *_CRT_ASSERT* as the report type. *_ASSERTE* identifies the expression that failed, whereas *_ASSERT* merely identifies that there was a problem.

From the earlier discussion, it might be apparent that directing CRT assertions to trace listeners will involve defining a report hook function and registering it, as shown in the following code:

```
// assertcrt.cpp
_set_error_mode(_OUT_TO_STDERR);
_CrtSetReportHook2(_CRT_RPTHOOK_INSTALL, ReportHook);
```

I showed you the *ReportHook* function earlier in this chapter. This code has problems. The first problem occurs with handling *assert*; although we can successfully hook the assert through the *_CrtDbgReport* function, this function is called in *abort*, which means that whatever value the *ReportHook* function returns, the process is doomed to die. If your report hook function shows the Abort–Retry–Ignore dialog box from *DefaultTraceListener* and the user chooses Ignore, this selection will ultimately have the same affect as selecting Abort. (The only difference is that Ignore allows the CRT to abort the process, whereas in the case of Abort, *DefaultTraceListener* will close down the process.) You do have the advantage that the failed assertion will be sent to the logging files. If you use another trace listener, *assert(false)* will always abort the process after your listener has done its work, regardless of the value that you return from your report hook function. The Retry button is not much more help because although it starts the debugger, the breakpoint will be in your report hook function and all that you can do is look through the stack to see where the assertion failed before single-stepping through *abort* until it kills the process.

The *_ASSERT* and *_ASSERTE* macros respect the value returned from your report function. However, you now have the problem of determining what value to return. Recall that *DefaultTraceListener::Fail* returns *void* because it is just one of potentially several listeners that is called by the *Trace* or *Debug* class, so the listener has to determine the button that the user clicked and perform the appropriate action. There is no way that *ReportHook* can determine which button the user chose, so your code has to make a policy decision. In the code I gave in the "CRT Tracing" section earlier in this chapter, the assertion will always abort the process because I return a value of –1 from the hook function. So, if the user chooses Retry or Ignore, he will get back to the *ReportHook* function, after which the process will die. If you chose to return 1 from the hook function, the debugger will be started whether the Retry or the Ignore button is clicked. However, it is far better in this case to click Ignore because the managed debugger will be launched and the breakpoint will appear within the managed code, many stack frames away from the actual source of the assertion failure. In this situation, if you click the Ignore button, the CRT will ensure that the breakpoint occurs in the right place.

Symbol Files and Managed Code

Before you can debug code, you have to provide information for the debugger to interpret the stack to identify the method where the breakpoint is located, and the parameters and local variables to that method. This requirement is the reason for the generation of symbols, and although symbols are vital for debugging debug builds, symbols are not confined to debug builds because release builds can benefit from generating symbol files too.

Why would you want symbol files for release builds? The main reason is that if your code generates a fault when it has been released as a product, the symbol files will allow your clients to return more meaningful information to you. Clearly, if your code fails, your clients will not be too pleased, but if they have the symbol files at least they will be able to provide you with some information about what the problem is and where it has occurred. If your product is a library intended to be used by developers, you can assume that your clients will have the knowledge to return symbol information (perhaps through running your code under a debugger). If your code is for use by nondevelopers, you do not want to allow the raw exception to get to the user. You can write crash handler code as part of the assembly that catches exceptions before they reach the user and then uses symbols to determine where the exception occurred and save this information in a format that the user can transmit to you as part of a bug report.

However, because debugging symbol files have all the information about the stack, doesn't this give away all of your secrets? Well, if your code is all managed code, there are no issues here because users will be able to get most of the information they need about your code through .NET reflection anyway, and the stack will be set up according to .NET principles. However, currently there is no debugger that shows IL as it is being executed, so if a managed process throws an exception and a JIT debugger attaches, you will see x86 opcodes if no symbols are available, and you'll see opcodes annotated with the names of the functions if symbols are available.

If some of your code is native (linked in, for example, from static libraries), there is no type information available within the code. Furthermore, the code might have been optimized and some code could be inlined, and in other cases, the optimizer might even merge stack frames. Clearly, if code has been optimized, the debugger needs additional information to be able to reconstruct the stack according to how the source code is arranged. Symbol files have this information. Again, you might decide that you would prefer to limit the amount of information that is provided in the symbol files (principally information about local variables).

Both debug and release builds for managed C++ projects will create symbols. To change the settings, you should go to the Debug page of the Linker settings in the project's property pages (*Project.Properties*). Changing this property to *Yes* (or passing */DEBUG* on the linker command line) tells the linker to create debugging symbols in the program database (PDB), and the Generate Program Database File property (the */PDB* linker switch) allows you to specify the name of this file. The amount of information that is put into the PDB is determined by the setting you use for the Strip Private Symbols linker property (the */PDBSTRIPPED* linker switch) and the compiler's */Z* switch. The compiler settings are available through the Debug Information Format property on the General page, and Table 7-2 shows the compiler switches that determine the amount of information that is put into the PDB.

Table 7-2 Compiler Switches for Generating Symbolic Information for Managed Projects

Switch	Description
`/Z7`	Contains full symbolic information that is CodeView compatible
`/Zi`	Contains full symbolic information in PDB format

By default, */Zi* is used for debug builds of all managed C++ projects, but confusingly, it is used for release builds of EXE assemblies but not for release builds of library assemblies. Note that the C++ compiler also supports the */ZI* switch that adds full debugging information and enables edit and continue. However, this switch is not supported for managed projects, and the */Zd* switch, too, is incompatible with managed projects.

The */Zi* and */Z7* switches cause the *System.Diagnostics.DebuggableAttribute* attribute to be added to the assembly. This attribute affects how the runtime treats the code when JIT-compiling it; it indicates that the run-time optimizer should be turned off but that the runtime should track run-time information. The combined effect of this attribute is that there will be more information for the managed debugger, but performance will be affected even if the assembly is not being debugged. If you have native classes in your assembly, these will be marked with the undocumented *Microsoft::VisualC::DebugInfoInPDBAttribute* attribute to indicate that symbolic information was created for the type.

The compiler puts symbolic information in the .obj file when you use the */Z7* switch, but it creates a separate program database file for the */Zi* switch. By default, this file is named after the version of the compiler (that is, vc70.pdb), but you can change this name using the Program Database File Name property on the Output Files page (the */Fd* compiler switch). When the */DEBUG* switch is used with the linker, the linker collates the debug symbols from the .obj and .pdb files (if they exist) and creates a single .pdb file with the name of the project (the output name of the file generated by link.exe) or a file specified using the /PDB switch. Because the default setting for the managed C++ projects in Visual Studio .NET is */Zi*, you will get two .pdb files created when you compile a project: one named after the project and another named *vc70.pdb*. Only the .pdb file that is named after your project will actually be used.

The assembly-generated file will contain the full path to the .pdb file that was created, and the debugger will use this path to determine the name of the program database. If the debugger cannot find the PDB file in this path, it will look in the same directory as the file that it is debugging, and failing that, it will look in the path given in the Symbol Path property on the Debugging page of the project's property page. The solution Property Pages dialog also has a page to specify symbol paths (Debug Symbol Files on the Common Properties section), which will affect all projects in the solution.

When a debugger attaches to a process, it will get two important values in the CPU registers: the stack pointer and the instruction pointer. The instruction pointer will indicate where in the code the breakpoint has occurred, and with the use of information such as the map file (which can be generated during the build process but is clearly useful only if the breakpoint is within your process), you can manually determine which method the breakpoint lies on. However, this information is far from all that is required. The method could have been called by another method in your code, so you need the context of the call—which method called it. In addition, you need to have information about local variables, and if the method is part of a class, you need information about instance variables. All of this information is obtained through the stack.

The usual explanation is that each method occupies a stack frame pointed to by the stack pointer. (The EBP register points to the start of the stack frame.)

The return address and the function's parameters (including the *this* pointer for an object) are pushed onto the stack, and local variables usually occupy the following locations. However, the optimizer might remove the need for stack frames for some functions, so data called *Frame Pointer Omission* (FPO) records have to be generated in the symbol file to enable the debugger to correctly interpret these situations.

I mentioned the *StackTrace* class in the ".NET Asserts" section earlier in this chapter. This class relies on symbols, so consider this code:

```
// dumper.cpp
#using <mscorlib.dll>
#using <system.dll>
using namespace System;
using namespace System::Reflection;
using namespace System::Diagnostics;

__gc class Dumper
{
public:
   void Dump()
   {
      StackTrace* st = new StackTrace(true);
      for (int i = 0; i < st->FrameCount; i++)
      {
         Console::WriteLine(S"frame: {0} ", __box(i));
         StackFrame* sf = st->GetFrame(i);
         Console::WriteLine(S"\t{0} ({1}, {2})",
            sf->GetFileName(),
            __box(sf->GetFileLineNumber()),
            __box(sf->GetFileColumnNumber()));
         Console::WriteLine(S"\tNative: {0}",
            __box(sf->GetNativeOffset()));
         Console::WriteLine(S"\tMethod: {0} ({1})",
            sf->GetMethod()->Name,
            __box(sf->GetILOffset()));
      }
   }
};

void main()
{
   Dumper* dump = new Dumper();
   dump->Dump();
}
```

If you compile this code with symbols, using the command line

```
cl /clr /Zi dump.cpp
```

you should get an output like this:

```
frame: 0
   d:\development\test\symb\release\dump.cpp (12, 0)
   Native: 87
   Method: Dump (6)
frame: 1
   d:\development\test\symb\release\dump.cpp (29, 0)
   Native: 40
   Method: main (14)
frame: 2
    (0, 0)
   Native: 0
   Method: _mainCRTStartup (-1)
```

I initialized the *StackFrame* instance with *true* to indicate that I wanted file name and line number information. As you can see, this information is reflected in all the stack frames except the last one (frame 2), which is the bug I mentioned in the ".NET Asserts" section earlier in this chapter. If you compile the code without symbols (omit the */Zi* switch), the output will look like this:

```
frame: 0
    (0, 0)
   Native: 49
   Method: Dump (-1)
frame: 1
    (0, 0)
   Native: 18
   Method: main (-1)
frame: 2
    (0, 0)
   Native: 0
   Method: _mainCRTStartup (-1)
```

Thus, without symbols, you still have the method names. The *StackFrame* class uses *internalcall* methods to obtain information about the stack, so it is not possible to use ILDASM to determine how *StackFrame::GetMethod* works, but the fact that it returns a *MethodBase* instance would indicate that the function uses reflection rather than symbols.

The only other reliable information that you get from a stack trace without symbols is the offset returned by *GetNativeOffset*, which the documentation describes as "The offset from the start of the JIT-compiled code for the method being executed." Unless you know about the internal workings of the JIT compiler, it is difficult to determine the locations within the source code where the stack trace was generated using the native offset. Remember that the C++ compiler generates IL and this IL is JIT-compiled at run time, so one JIT compiler could create different code than another, and indeed, the same JIT compiler could create different code for different machines or even for different runs of the same code.

Turning on symbol generation by passing */DEBUG* to the linker also instructs the JIT compiler to track information (the *[Debuggable]* attribute), which clearly is influential in this respect. If you use the */PDBSTRIPPED* switch, the linker will generate a separate program database with just public symbols and FPO data. This information is not sufficient for *StackTrace*.

One final situation in which you will see symbol information is if there is an exception. Exceptions have a property named *StackTrace* that returns a string. The string is created by calling *Environment::GetStackTrace*, which constructs the string by calling the *StackTrace* class. Thus, if your assembly is distributed without symbols, you will get method names only in the *StackTrace* property but no information about source files or line numbers. One interesting point to bear in mind is that if you have a remote object that throws an exception, the exception will be serialized and passed to the client object that made the call, where an exception will be thrown. If the client object does not have symbols, there will not be any source file information in the exception's *StackTrace* property for the trace generated from the client side. However, if the remote object has symbols available, source file information will be returned back to the client through the serialized exception, so the client will have access to this information.

Making Code Easier to Debug

Although the compiler and the linker are the main sources for information used by the debugger, some other settings affect how .NET code is debugged. When code in an assembly is first used, the MSIL is JIT-compiled and the JIT compiler attempts to make the code as efficient as possible. I have already mentioned the *[Debuggable]* attribute, which the compiler adds to an assembly when you compile the code with symbolic information. The compiler applies this attribute to indicate that JIT tracking information is generated and the JIT compilation is not optimized. A release build does not have this attribute, but you can inform the JIT compiler to change its behavior by using an .ini file[7] with the same name as the application in the same folder, as shown here:

```
; myApp.ini for assembly myApp.exe
[.NET Framework Debugging Control]
GenerateTrackingInfo=1
AllowOptimize=0
```

The first value determines whether the JIT compiler creates information useful for a managed debugger; a value of 1 will generate this information. The second value specifies whether the JIT compiler will optimize the code it gen-

7. Yes, this is right: the file is an old-style Windows .ini file.

erates; a value of 0 turns off the optimizer. The preceding values should create JIT-compiled code that is easiest for managed debuggers to debug. Of course, there will be a drop in performance when you use these settings.

If you decide to use ngen when you deploy your assemblies, you have another problem. As I mentioned in Chapter 5, this tool will JIT-compile an assembly and install it into the native image cache. Managed debuggers expect assemblies to be MSIL so that they can be debugged. The ngen tool can add extra information to the native image that can allow the assembly to be debugged. To do this, you use the */debug* switch when you call ngen. If you do not use this switch, the runtime will use normal JIT compilation when the assembly is run under the debugger and will make appropriate debug information available to the debugger.

Using the Visual Studio .NET Debugger

When you install Visual Studio .NET, you get two GUI debuggers, the internal debugger of the IDE, which will allow you to do both managed and native debugging, and the CLR debugger (DbgCLR.exe), which will only debug managed code. The CLR debugger is essentially a cut down version of the IDE debugger and is provided as part of the .NET Framework SDK. In addition to these debuggers, Visual Studio .NET also has the command-line debugger, cordbg.exe. This debugger is an unmanaged application that calls the various objects exposed through COM interop to allow you to enumerate and attach to assemblies. If you are interested in writing your own debugger, you will be pleased to know that the source code for cordbg.exe is supplied as a sample in the .NET Framework SDK. (Look in the samples folder of the Tool Developers Guide.)

Locating Assemblies

The first issue with debugging managed applications is to ensure that the assemblies can be located. If your process uses library assemblies and these assemblies are part of your solution, you will have the source code and symbols for these libraries, so you will be able to single-step through the library code. However, you have to set up the IDE to allow Fusion to find these libraries. Recall how Fusion loads a .NET assembly: When Fusion has located an assembly's file, it reads the manifest to determine the library assemblies that are static bound. Fusion will then try to locate these assemblies, which includes searching the global assembly cache (GAC) and looking for the named assembly with the .dll and the .exe extension. Fusion will look for a subfolder with the name of the assembly and search that folder too. (Config files and publisher policy files affect the search order too, but I will ignore their effect in this discussion.)

If you have multiple projects in a solution, you will not get the paths that Fusion will expect. For example, if you have a solution with two projects, Main and Lib, where Lib is a library assembly used by Main, you are likely to get the folder arrangement shown in Figure 7-3. In this case, if you attempt to run the Main.exe assembly, Fusion will issue an error indicating that it cannot locate the library Lib.dll. (You can view the details with the Fusion log viewer.)

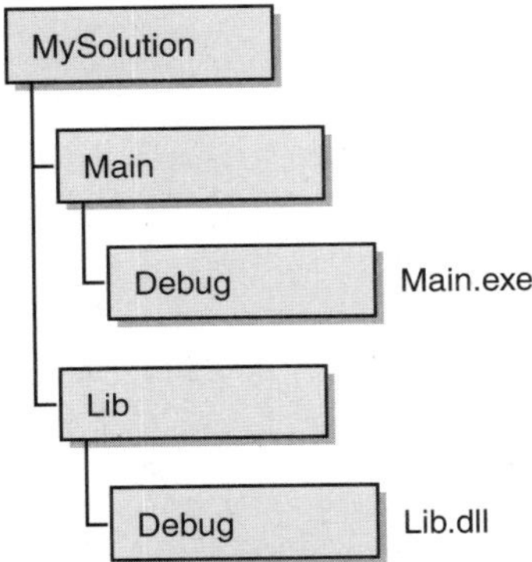

Figure 7-3 Typical folder arrangements for a solution

You might have used the */AI* compiler switch in your project settings for the Main project, but this switch only gives a path to metadata; it does not give a path to the location of the assembly at run time. There are several ways to solve this problem. I described the simplest way in Chapter 6 in the "Multiassembly Solutions" section: define a *bin* folder in your solution and direct all output to it. So, you can have a subfolder named *bin\Debug* for all outputs from debug builds and another folder named *bin\Release* for the outputs from release builds. This setting will ensure that all outputs from all projects are in the same folder so that when you run the main assembly in the solution, Fusion will be able to find the assemblies that it uses because by default it looks first in the current folder.

The .NET Framework also allows you to configure Fusion for debugging through the *DEVPATH* environment variable. When Fusion determines that the machine is used for development (which I will specify in a moment), it checks the folders mentioned in the *DEVPATH* variable for the assemblies that it is attempting to locate. Thus, in the preceding example, you could place the path MySolution\Lib\Debug\ in *DEVPATH*.

To indicate to Fusion that it should use *DEVPATH*, you should add the following code in the machine.config file:

```
<runtime>
   <developmentMode developerInstallation="true"/>
</runtime>
```

Of course, if you have multiple library assemblies in a solution, the *DEVPATH* can get cluttered, and you will need to remember to clean up the environment variable when you move on to another solution. For these reasons (and the reasons I mentioned in Chapter 6 in the "Specifying a Search Order" section), it is better to have a shared output folder, as I just mentioned.

The actual purpose of *DEVPATH* is for assemblies that would be located in the GAC when the assembly is deployed. If you are developing a shared assembly (an assembly with a strong name that will be installed in the GAC), you might find it a problem to remove the old version and install the new one every time that you change the assembly. In this case, you can add the assembly's folder to the *DEVPATH*, or (the better solution) you can change the output folder of the project to point to a folder that can be used as the output folders for other shared assemblies you are developing and put the path to this folder in the *DEVPATH* variable.

I mentioned in Chapter 6 that you can create multimodule assemblies, in which case the assembly will have one file that holds the manifest and one or more files that contain code and/or resources. These modules must be in the same code base as the manifest, so if you develop each module as a separate project, you should ensure that when you use the assembly the modules are in the same folder. In this case, you cannot use *DEVPATH* because Fusion will bind to the assembly (the module that has the manifest) and assumes that the other modules will be in the same location. Defining a single output folder for the entire solution will solve this issue.

Starting the Debugger

When you install Visual Studio .NET, the installer will create a Windows NT group named *Debugger Users*. Your account must be a member of this group or of the *Administrators* group to start the debugger. Most of the time, you will start the debugger through the IDE. However, sometimes you might decide to start the debugger through JIT debugging, so I will cover both cases here.

Debugging Through the IDE

When debugging through the IDE, you have two options: either you can attach to a running process, or you can start a process through a loaded solution. If you attach to a running process, the process can be on the current machine or on another machine. I will cover attaching to a running process in the "Attaching to a Running Process" section later in this chapter. Before you can debug an assembly, you have to ensure that each assembly can be loaded. If you have read through the "Locating Assemblies" section earlier in this chapter, you should not have any problems here.

You have two further options about starting a process through a solution. The first option is the most familiar to you: the solution will have source code, and the process will be an output of the project. In this case, you can start an instance of the process under the debugger through the Debug context menu of the project in Class View or Solution Explorer. (If the process is set to be the StartUp Project or if there is a single project in the solution, you can start the process from the Debug menu or through the keyboard shortcut key F5.) The second option you have is to start a process that is not part of the current solution. To do so, you add the executable using the *File.AddExistingProject* command. Once you have done this, you treat the executable as a project, so you can step into a new instance and you can set it as the Startup project. When the executable is run, you will be able to step through the source code, if the executable has symbols and the source code is available.

The IDE will allow you to debug more than one process at the same time. This ability is great news if you are designing an application that uses interprocess communication because you can run both processes in the same instance of the IDE. When you press the F5 key for the default keyboard mappings (*Debug.Start* command), the IDE starts the process from the start-up project. (I'll mention in a moment what happens if this is a library assembly.) You can configure more than one project to be the start-up project, and you can also specify what order the project outputs are started in. To do this configuring, you have to use the property pages of the solution and select the Startup Project page from Common Properties. The grid on this page lists all the projects in the solution, and the Action column in this grid lists three options: None, Start, and Start Without Debugging. Using the Start action will start the specified process and attach the debugger to it. You can use *Debug.ListPrograms* in the command window to verify that the processes have started. I regard these settings as an important property of the solution. Unfortunately, the designers of the IDE did not think so and persisted them in the solution options (.suo) file rather than the solution (.sln) file. The solution options file is not persisted when you put a solution under source control. As a consequence, when you get a solution out of source control, you must set the start-up order (or the start-up project) before you can debug the solution. I regard this as a bug in the IDE.

When you are debugging more than one process, you can switch between them by using the Debug Location toolbar, shown in Figure 7-4. The Program drop-down list shows the various programs that are being debugged, which is essentially the list you will get from the *Debug.ListPrograms* command. For the selected process, the Thread drop-down list gives the threads that are running in the process, which is the data that you will also see in the Threads window or through the *Debug.ListThreads* command. Finally, the Stack Frame drop-down lists the call stack for the selected thread, which is the same information that you will get from the Call Stack window or through the *Debug.ListCallStack* command.

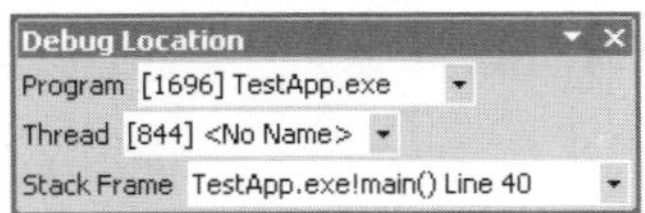

Figure 7-4 The Debug Location toolbar

There is another option that you should notice. When you start more than one process under the debugger, you can either treat the debugger as if there is a single thread of execution between the two applications, or you can allow the debugging to occur in both processes simultaneously. The IDE options (*Tools.Options*) Debugging pages lists an In Break Mode, Only Stop Execution Of The Current Process option on the General page. If this option is selected, the debugger will only break into the current process, so if you want to follow the action of making an interprocess communication, you will have to manually switch across from the source code of the process that makes the call to the source code that accepts the call and break into the process to allow the debugger to switch to the new process. You can then use the Run To Cursor command or the Continue (F5) command to run to the code that processes the interprocess call. If you deselect the In Break Mode option, you will be able to set breakpoints in each of the processes and wait for the breakpoints to be hit.

Debuggers can only debug processes, so if your project produces a library assembly (DLL), you have to nominate a process that will use the library. To do this task, you should use the project's property pages where the Debugging page has a property named *Command* that for an executable will be set to *$(TargetPath)*. For a library, this property should be set to the process that will use the library. While I am describing this property page, it is worth pointing out two other properties: *Working Directory* and *Command Arguments*. The process will be started in the folder that you give as the *Working Directory* property; if you do not give a value, the project folder (*$(ProjectDir)*) is used. Although this appears on the Debugging page, it is used as the current folder when you start without debugging (*Debug.StartWithoutDebugging*) and when you start the process under the debugger (*Debug.Start*). The values in the *Command Arguments* property will be passed to the command line of the specified process. If this process is one that you have written, you can obtain these arguments through one of the following mechanisms:

- If the process is a command-line process, the arguments will be available through the unmanaged *argv* parameter to *main*. The first item is the process name.
- If the process is a GUI, the unmanaged string parameter of *WinMain*, *lpCmdLine*, will be a concatenation of the arguments (but not the name of the process).
- The *Environment::CommandLine* property is a concatenation of the command-line arguments, including the name of the process.
- The *Environment::GetCommandLineArgs* method returns a *String** array with the arguments; the first one is the name of the process.

Attaching to a Running Process

If a process is already running, you can attach to that process through the *Debug.Processes* dialog box. (If you have a solution loaded, this command will be accessible through the Debug menu. Otherwise, it is on the Tools menu.) If your account is a member of the *Debugger Users* group or a member of the *Administrators* group, the Processes dialog box will list the processes running on the specified machine. I say, *the specified machine* because this dialog box is used to debug remote processes, as I will explain in the "Remote Debugging" section later in this chapter.

The Processes dialog box gives you the option of listing system (service) processes as well as nonsystem processes. However, if you are debugging a service, the dialog box is often of little use. The reason I say this is that services are often hosted by svchost.exe, and the dialog box merely lists the instances of this process and not the actual service that the instance is hosting. Similarly, COM+ applications hosted by dllhost.exe are merely shown as dllhost.exe and not as the actual COM+ application, which is a pity.[8]

Once you have identified the application that you want to attach to, you then have the option of specifying how to detach from the process. .NET allows you to detach from a process when you have finished debugging. If the process is native C++ and you are running on an operating system other then Windows

8. The information about the actual service that is run under svchost.exe is available; you can view this information with the ProcessExplorer utility from *www.sysinternals.com*.

XP, you have to run the Visual Studio .NET Debugger Proxy Service to be able to detach from a process. Windows XP has this facility built into the operating system.

Once you close the Processes dialog box, the appropriate debugger should be attached to the process and you should be able to set breakpoints in the source code for the process or the libraries used by the process. If you set a breakpoint and it shows a question mark glyph, the source code does not correspond to the process being debugged. There are two main causes of this problem. The first is if the source code is compiled to a DLL, the DLL might not have been loaded. (This is the case for unmanaged projects that use *LoadLibrary*, for managed and unmanaged projects that use COM, and for managed projects that access DLL methods through Platform Invoke.) Second, if you are debugging code hosted by dllhost.exe, you might have simply selected the wrong instance. The solution to this problem is to detach from the process and attach to another instance; continue this mechanism until the breakpoints are set correctly, indicating that you are debugging the right process.

JIT Debugging

When an exception occurs in a process, you will be informed by the system. JIT debugging is handled differently for managed and unmanaged code. If the code is unmanaged, the operating system determines what happens when an exception is thrown. If the code is managed, the exception will be caught by the runtime, which will then determine what should happen. The two mechanisms are separate and are controlled by different settings in the system registry.

If JIT debugging is enabled on your machine and the process is a native process, by default the system will give you a summary dialog box that identifies the exception and gives two buttons, OK and Cancel. Clicking the OK button will close down the process, and clicking the Cancel button will attach the debugger to the process to allow you to determine the source of the fault. JIT debugging of native processes is controlled by the following registry key:

```
HKEY_LOCAL_MACHINE\Software\Microsoft\Windows NT
\CurrentVersion\AeDebug
```

Table 7-3 shows the settings that will appear in the *AeDebug* key. This key has a setting named *Auto* that by default is 0, which indicates that the summary dialog box should be shown if a process generates a fault; thus the user is given the option as to whether to debug the process. If *Auto* is set to 1, the user is not given the option; instead, the debugger is always attached. The debugger process is identified in the *Debugger* setting. This setting has the path to the debugger and also the command line that identifies the process to debug (its process

ID) and the handle to an event object that is used to indicate to the system that the debugger has attached.

Table 7-3 Settings in the *AeDebug* Key

Setting	Description
Auto	Identifies whether the debugger will automatically attach to a process that generated an exception
Debugger	Command line to start the debugger
PreVisualStudio7Debugger	The debugger that was used before Visual Studio .NET was installed
UserDebuggerHotKey	This is the virtual key code of the hot key when the process is running under a debugger

The *UserDebuggerHotKey* setting identifies a "break" key to be used when a process is running under the debugger. This setting's value is a virtual key code of a key, and when you press the corresponding key, the system will cause a breakpoint (an *int 3* x86 opcode) to be generated. If you have installed Visual Studio .NET on the machine, you will also see the *PreVisualStudio7Debugger* setting that identifies the debugger that was used prior to installing Visual Studio .NET (usually the Dr. Watson utility). Visual Studio .NET will install the following as the debugger:

```
vs7jit.exe -p %ld -e %ld
```

The command-line parameters are the process ID of the process to debug and the value of an event handle. When a debugger has started, it should attach to the process by calling the Win32 *::OpenProcess* using the process ID. Once the debugger has attached, it can inform the system by setting the event. It does this simply by casting the event handle value to a *HANDLE* and then passing this value to the Win32 *::SetEvent* function.

The process vs7jit.exe presents the user with a dialog box showing the debuggers that can be used. The default option will be either the Visual Studio .NET IDE or DbgCLR.exe. If Visual Studio .NET is already running, the dialog box will also give you the option of using the running instance to attach to the process. The process vs7jit.exe will then start the debugger and pass it information about the process to debug. This information passing is not carried out through a command line like the *Debugger* setting in *AeDebug*. Instead, vs7jit.exe starts the selected debugger through COM. Both DevEnv.exe (the process for the IDE) and DbgCLR.exe have a command-line switch named */JITDEBUG* that is used to launch the process as a COM local server to perform JIT debugging. Once vs7jit.exe has launched the debugger, it gets access to an undocumented interface named *IDebugJIT2*, which vs7jit.exe presumably uses to pass information to the debugger to allow the debugger to attach to the process.

If a managed application throws an unhandled exception, the .NET Framework will catch the exception and allow you to debug the process. This process is carried out independently of the settings in *AeDebug*. The relevant registry key is as follows:

```
HKEY_LOCAL_MACHINE\Software\Microsoft\.NETFramework
```

This key has the settings shown in Table 7-4.

Table 7-4 The Registry Settings for the Managed Debugger

Setting	Description
DbgJITDebugLaunchSetting	This setting is used to indicate whether the user has the option about debugging.
DbgManagedDebugger	The command to start the managed debugger.

The *DbjJITDebugLaunchSetting* setting has the same purpose as the *Auto* setting in *AeDebug*: it allows you to specify whether the managed debugger automatically attaches to the process. If this setting has a value of 0, the user will see a modal dialog box specifying that an exception has occurred in a managed process. This dialog box has an OK to abort the process and a Cancel button to debug the process, the *DbgManagedDebugger* setting has the command to start the debugger. If *DbgJITDebugLaunchSetting* setting has a value of 1, a stack dump will be performed and the process will be terminated. Finally, if the value is 2, the managed debugger will be started automatically, without user intervention. When you install Visual Studio .NET, the managed debugger in *DbgManagedDebugger* will be vs7jit.exe, so whether you use 0 or 2 for *DbgJITDebugLaunchSetting*, you will always have the option of shutting down the faulted process without launching the debugger.

The IDE can debug both native processes and managed processes, so once it has been told to attach to a process, it presents the user with a dialog box asking the user which debugger to use.

As you can see, JIT debugging often presents the user with a plethora of dialog boxes. Although you can minimize the number of dialog boxes by changing the values in the *Auto* and *DbgJITDebugLaunchSetting* settings, you still have to negotiate the dialog box presented by vs7jit.exe and the IDE when it first starts. There are no options that you can set to make these processes assume default values.

You can use the IDE property pages through the *Tools.Options* command to change the JIT debugging settings. The relevant page is the Just-In-Time page in the Debugging category. This page lists the various debuggers that the

IDE implements, and you can use it to determine whether the debuggers will be used when a fault occurs in a process. This page edits the relevant registry setting, so if you uncheck the Native option, the IDE will replace the *Debugger* setting in *AeDebug* with the value in the *PreVisualStudio7Debugger* setting. Likewise, if you deselect the support for the common language runtime, the IDE will replace the value in the *DbgManagedDebugger* setting with the default value in a separate key also named *DbgManagedDebugger*. Sadly, this property does not affect the initial dialog box shown when the IDE is started up for JIT debugging.

Finally, the Machine Debug Manager (mdm.exe) is used when debugging processes. If you run this program with the */dumpjit* switch, it will present a dialog box with a summary of the settings in the *AeDebug* and *.NETFramework* keys.

The Exceptions Dialog Box

The Exceptions dialog box (*Debug.Exceptions*) allows you to configure how the IDE will treat exceptions. The dialog box categorizes exceptions according to whether the exception comes from the runtime, from the Win32 system, or from native C++, and for each exception, you can specify how the IDE treats an exception when it is first thrown and how it treats an exception if it is not handled by code. When a process is run under a debugger and an exception is thrown, the system will inform the debugger. This is called the *first-chance notification*. If the debugger does not handle the exception, the system looks for an appropriate exception handler. If it cannot find a handler, the debugger is informed again. This is known as the *last-chance notification*.

Through the Exceptions dialog box, you can specify that the debugger will break at that point or you can specify that execution will continue, which will allow the exception to be handled by a handler if one exists. If the exception is not handled, you can indicate how the IDE handles that, too: either break in the debugger or continue execution, which will most likely result in the process dying.

The dialog box shows the exceptions in a tree view. For .NET run-time exceptions, this view is nested according to the namespace of the exception. You have the ability to use this hierarchy when specifying how the IDE handles exceptions: you can specify a setting for the general type of exception, and the namespace (for a .NET exception), and specify that a specific exception uses the setting of its parent in the hierarchy. Although you can add your own exceptions to the dialog box, you cannot nest your exceptions according to the namespace similar to how the dialog box shows .NET Framework exceptions.

Debugging Processes

Once you have attached to a process, you can use the various tools in the IDE to view the stack, threads, variables, and memory, and to single-step through the rest of the process. In this section, I will outline how to use these tools during a debugging session.

Stepping Through Code

You have several options about stepping through code: you can single-step, you can run to a breakpoint, you can run to the cursor (caret), or you can change the execution point. The simplest of these options is to single-step (*Debug.StepOver*). The default keyboard layout assigns this command to the F10 key, and while you are in the text editor, the command allows you to single-step over a C++ statement. If that statement is a method call, you will execute the call in one step. If you want to step into the method call, you can press the F11 key (*Debug.StepInto*). If it becomes apparent to you that the method is large and that you do not want to single-step through all the method's statements, you can step out of the function to the point where you stepped into it by pressing Shift+F11 (*Debug.StepOut*). If you perform single-stepping in Disassembly view, then each statement will be an x86 statement—the Disassembly view shows x86 and not IL—which is useful if you are interested in the Win32 API calls that are being made.

If you have breakpoints set in your code, you can allow the process to run the debuggee process until one of these breakpoints is hit by pressing the F5 key (*Debug.Start*). There might be a situation in which the execution flow avoids these breakpoints, in which case, you can break into the process at whatever point the main thread is executing (*Debug.BreakAll*). This might well be deep into a Win32 API call, so you might have to walk up the stack to get back to some code that you recognize.

If you want to execute the next few statements, it is often overkill to set a breakpoint. Instead, what you can do is place the caret at the point in your code where you want to break and select Run To Cursor[9] (*Debug.RunToCursor*). Again, you have to be careful where you place the caret because you might place it at a point which will not be executed, in which case the process will merely run until it stops.

The final action that you can perform is to change the actual execution of the code. When a process is paused in break mode in the debugger, a yellow arrow will indicate the next statement that will be executed. As you single-step, this arrow will move. However, you can move this arrow yourself, skipping

9. Of course, this should be Run To Caret; the caret is the insertion point in the code, and the cursor indicates where the mouse is located.

some statements or re-executing others. This operation is illustrated in Figure 7-5, where the execution point is on the second line of the method, so *i* has been assigned a value of 4. I have selected the execution point in the indicator column and dragged it to the last line of the method. (I could also position the caret on the target line and select Set Next Statement from the context menu.) If I drop the execution point here, when I single-step, only the final line will be executed. The intervening lines concerning the variable *j* will be ignored. Thus, the method will return 4. In the figure, the upper arrow shows the current location of the execution point, and the cursor shows the position where the execution point will be moved to.

```
int Test()
{
   int i = 4;
   int j = 5;
   i += j;
   return i;
}
```

Figure 7-5 Moving the execution point with a drag-and-drop operation

Such an action is quite dangerous because you could skip over statements that return values that are used by subsequent statements. However, it can also be very useful. For example, if you have code that creates a file and periodically writes to it, and during a debugging session, you find that the file cannot be created, you can single-step through the code, and whenever there is a call to write to the file, you can move the execution point to the following statement. This action allows you to continue with the debugging session and delay until a later time the investigation of why the file failed to be created.

Setting Breakpoints

Breakpoints allow you to identify a particular piece of code as being worthy of further investigation. When you run the code under the debugger, it will run until a breakpoint is hit; execution will pause at the breakpoint. Break mode is important because many of the windows provided by the debugger only show useful results in break mode. There are essentially four ways to set a breakpoint. First, you can click in the indication area (the gray column on the left) in the text editor, which will toggle a breakpoint on the line. The second way is to place the caret on the line where you want to have the breakpoint and then press F9 (the *Debug.ToggleBreakpoint* command). In both cases, the debugger will allow breakpoints to be set only on lines that execute code, so you cannot place a breakpoint on a line that declares an uninitialized local variable. If you attempt to set a breakpoint on such a line in break mode, the breakpoint will be placed on the next acceptable line. If you do this when the code is not being debugged, the breakpoint will be moved when the debug session starts.

The third way to set a breakpoint is by means of code. How you set a breakpoint this way depends on whether you are writing managed code. In unmanaged code, you can use the inline assembler to insert an interrupt (*int 3*), and when the code reaches this point, you will get a structured exception. If you are running under the debugger, you will get an unhandled exception dialog box. Otherwise, you will get the opportunity to attach a debugger through JIT debugging. Clearly, using the inline assembler produces code that is not portable and is not a good .NET practice. However, you can still use this method in global functions that will compile under the managed compiler, and the compiler will replace the call with the IL *break* opcode. When you run the code without a debugger, you will get a structured exception and have the option of debugging the process. If the code is running under a debugger, the code will break at the line after the interrupt. You will not get the unhandled exception dialog box from the IDE.

Another way to get the same effect is to use the Win32 *::DebugBreak* function, which merely calls *int 3*. You can call this function in managed code through platform invoke or through IJW. However, a far better solution is to use the *__debugbreak* intrinsic. You can use this intrinsic in both managed and unmanaged code. If you use this intrinsic in unmanaged code, the compiler will add an *int 3*, but if you use this intrinsic in managed code, you will get the IL *break* statement. The intrinsic is effectively behaving as an inline IL assembler.

Note that all of these methods of adding a breakpoint in code should not be compiled into release builds. Thus, you should use conditional compilation to guarantee that the breakpoint is not in your release builds.

The final way to set a breakpoint is through the New Breakpoint dialog box (*Debug.NewBreakpoint*). This method gives you far more flexibility than the other methods I have mentioned. This dialog box has three tabs, Function, File, and Address.[10] The names imply how you indicate where you want a breakpoint to be set, by referring to a location in a source file or by indicating a specific function or an address. The Function and File tabs have edit boxes labeled Line and Character. However, the Character box is ignored by both tabs, and the Line edit box is ignored by the Function tab (which only supports placing breakpoints on the first line in a function).

---

10. There is also a Data tab that allows you to indicate a variable that will be watched. A break will occur in code that changes this variable. However, I have ignored it here because it is only applicable for unmanaged code.

The most flexible of the three is the Address tab. This tab allows you to give an address in the code. The actual format of this address is different for managed and unmanaged code. If your code is unmanaged, you can give the absolute address of the position in the code—you can use the MAP file for the process to determine the address of a function. For example, if you use an unmanaged static library through IJW, you might decide to put a breakpoint on code linked into your code by specifying the address, so if the MAP file has this entry:

```
Address          Publics by Value  Rva+Base      Lib:Object
0001:00015a70    _puts             00416a70 f    LIBCMTD:puts.obj
```

I could place a breakpoint in the *puts* function by putting the address 0x00416A70 in the Address edit box on the Address tab. The process loads at virtual address 0x00400000. If you have information about the source file or the DLL where a managed function is located, you can specify the address using the following syntax:

```
{function, source_file, binary}.line_number
```

You do not need all of the items here; you only need enough to identify the location where you want to break. Here are some examples:

```
{_putts, puts.c,}.41
{, puts.c,}.41
```

These examples both set a breakpoint at the beginning of the *puts* function. Note that the name of the function is *_putts*, which is the name conditionally defined for ANSI or Unicode. You can also set breakpoints in unmanaged DLLs, in which case you have to give the name of the DLL and the location within the DLL.

```
{,,mylib.dll}Func
```

In this case, the breakpoint will be set at the start of a function named *Func* exported from mylib.dll. If you have public-only dbg symbols, for example, those that are provided for the operating system, the name of the function should be prefixed with an underscore and appended with an @ character and the number of bytes that should be pushed on the stack, as shown here:

```
{,,kernel32.dll}_BaseProcessStart@4
```

In this example, I set a breakpoint on an undocumented Win32 function that is called by the system to start your process. Putting a breakpoint at this location will allow you to step through all the code that is called to set up the context for your process. You can tell whether you have entered the address correctly in the Address tab because when you start the process, the New

Breakpoint dialog box will replace the expression with the absolute address that corresponds to the expression.

Setting breakpoints in managed code is similar to setting them in native code, except that you have to remember that managed code is usually JIT-compiled at run time, in which case the actual location of the code will not be known until the code is run, and the location will vary between runs. The disassembly window will give the address as the offset from the beginning of the function, so setting a breakpoint in a function involves providing enough information to locate the function and an offset. The following line is the address of the breakpoint as entered in the Address tab:

```
System::Console::WriteLine + 0x00000000
```

This address will put a breakpoint on the first line of the *WriteLine* function in mscorlib.dll.

Be aware that when a DLL function is called through platform invoke, the DLL is dynamically loaded the first time the function is called. Thus, the breakpoint will not be resolved before this point.

When you use the Function tab to set a breakpoint, you must provide enough information for the debugger to identify the method, so you need to give the class and namespace. If you want to set a breakpoint on an overloaded method, you should also give the parameter list of the specific overload where you want the breakpoint set. If you do not give the parameter list, the New Breakpoint dialog box will determine the overloads of the method and will give you a dialog box to allow you to choose which one to use.

If you are debugging a loop and an error appears but only after several iterations, you will find it irritating to go through every iteration to get to the point where the error occurs. To get around this problem, you can set a *hit count*. In effect, the debugger keeps a count that the breakpoint has been reached but will only break when the hit count expression that you specify has been achieved. You can specify a value for the hit count, and the debugger can be instructed to break when the hit count is this value, when the hit count is a multiple of this value, or when it is greater than or equal to this value. In a similar way, you can also use the condition to give an expression that determines whether the debugger will break at the breakpoint. This condition can be the name of a variable, in which case the break will occur when the variable has changed, or you can give a *Boolean* expression and the break will occur when the expression is *true*.

The Call Stack Window

When you are in break mode, you can use the Call Stack window (*Debug.CallStack* command) to view the stack. The Call Stack window will use symbols and the values on the stack to determine the code that is being called, and it will interpret parameters passed to the method. For example, if I step into a call to *Console::WriteLine*, I can build up a stack that looks like this:

```
mscorlib.dll!System.IO.TextWriter::WriteLine(
   System.Object value = {System.Int32})
mscorlib.dll!SyncTextWriter::WriteLine(
   System.Object value = {System.Int32}) + 0x20 bytes
mscorlib.dll!System.Console::WriteLine(
   System.Object value = {System.Int32}) + 0x1c bytes
Test.exe!main() Line 52
Test.exe!mainCRTStartup()  Line 259 + 0x19
```

In the *main* function of Test.exe, I pass a single *int* to *Console::WriteLine* at line 52 in the source file. This value is passed to the version of *WriteLine* that takes a single parameter of type *Object**. Because this is a file in my project, the symbols are available, so the line number can be resolved. Note the format that the Call Stack window uses to identify functions. This format looks like a mixture of C++ (with :: as the scope operator) and C# (with . as the scope operator), but in fact, it is the format used by ILASM where the dot operator is used as the scope operator within namespaces and the double colon is used as the scope operator for class members.

The previous dump shows the case when you select all of the view options. If the methods in the view have many parameters, the view can get cluttered, so the context menu for the Call Stack window allows you to turn off display of byte offsets; line numbers; parameter names, values and types, and module names. You can also traverse through the call stack. When you double-click on an item, you will either see the source code for that method (if it is available) or you will get the disassembly for that code in the Disassembly view. The view will indicate the current execution point with a yellow arrow and the code that is being viewed with a green arrow.

When you are in break mode, all threads in the process are paused. You can switch to the Threads window and switch to another thread to view the call stack for that thread.

Disassembly

Whenever you step into code where source code is not available, you will see the Disassembly window. You will typically see this window when you set a breakpoint on an address (as I showed earlier). If you are stepping through source code and you come across a method for which you do not have source code, selecting Step Into will have no effect; it will be treated as Step Over. To step into such a method you need to switch to Disassembly view (*Debug.Disassembly*) and then proceed with single-stepping from that point.

The Disassembly view can show source code and line numbers in the source, symbol names, the address (with respect to the start of a method in managed code), and the actual bytes of the machine code; all of this information is configurable with the context menu. The window also has a toolbar, and you can use the Address combo box to type the name of a method; this method does not have to be in the current call stack, however, to see the disassembled code, you do need to have executed the method at some point. You can use either the dot operator or the :: operator as the scope resolution operator. However, if the method is overloaded, there is no way that you can indicate the particular version that you require.

If you chose, you can also perform disassembly from the Command window using the *Debug.ListDisassembly* command. This command will show the disassembly of the code at the current execution point and by default the next 8 bytes. You can use switches on this command to change the number of bytes to disassemble and to determine whether symbols and source code are shown.

Memory Window

The memory window is used to display a section of virtual memory. The IDE now supports four separate windows, which are accessed with the commands *Debug.Memory1* through *Debug.Memory4*. You can display any address that is mapped into your process. On the toolbar for the Memory window, there is a combo box named *Address* where you can type the address in hex, but you must remember to prefix the address with *0x*. In addition, you can also type symbol names, which means that in managed code, you can type the name of a method and actually see the location of the JIT-compiled code. (However, don't be tempted to type this absolute address in the Address box on the Disassembly window for managed code.) If you have unmanaged code, you can type the name of a pointer variable and the Memory window will show the contents at that memory. Unfortunately, if you pass the name of a pointer variable in managed code, the Memory window will not show the contents of that memory, but confusingly, if you give the name of an integer the Memory window *will* interpret the contents of the integer as a memory address and show the memory at that location, Thus, in this managed code:

```
int x = 0x100;
int __nogc* p = &x;
int y = reinterpret_cast<int>(&x);
```

If you type **x** in the Address box, you will get the memory at 0x100. If you type **p**, the debugger will not show you the actual memory location of the variable *x*; instead, it merely shows memory location 0x00000000. However, if you type **y**, which is the address of *x* cast to an integer, you will get the memory location of *x*. Of course, in managed code, you should never hold on to addresses of objects on the managed heap without pinning the object pointer first. So to investigate the internal data of a managed string, you should use code such as this:

```
String __pin* pStr = S"Test";
int y = reinterpret_cast<int>(pStr);
```

Once pinned, the address of the managed string can be safely accessed and then cast to an integer that can be shown in the Memory window.

The Memory window has a multitude of formatting options through the context menu. You can choose to view the data as string data (select No Data) either as ASCII or as Unicode; you can view it as one byte, two bytes, four bytes, eight bytes, 32-bit or 64-bit floating point with or without (No Text) an equivalent view in text. You can also specify how many columns will be shown on each line through the Columns box on the toolbar.

You can select data in the Memory window and copy it to the clipboard. The data is copied as *CF_TEXT*, rich text and other formats; *CF_TEXT* is the first format and includes all of the data that you selected in the window.[11] One powerful feature of the memory editor is that it allows you to change values, even of managed data. This ability means that you can change the internal data in an object, which is quite a risky thing to do unless you know *exactly* what you are changing.

You can also list memory in the Command window using the *Debug.ListMemory* command. This command will list the next 16 bytes at the execution point as bytes and characters. You can use switches to specify how many bytes and how this data is shown.

Watch Window

When you are debugging code, you are interested in two general issues, the execution flow and the value of variables. The execution flow can be determined by watching the Call Stack window, and the code shown in the Disassembly window or the source code. There are several ways that you can get the value of a variable. The debugger provides various Watch windows that will show variables pertinent to the window and also DataTips. When you hover the cursor over a variable within the source code, the debugger will show a ToolTip with the name of the variable and a summary of its value.

The Watch windows allow you to view the values of objects. The actual format of the data that is shown can be altered either by using format commands or

11. This is much better than the IDE's Binary Editor, which sadly only copies the binary data that you select and does not include the address or character representation of the data.

by providing a formatter object. I will come back to formatter objects in the "Formatting Watch Variables" section later in this chapter. Table 7-5 shows the various Watch windows, and in addition to these, you also have the Quick Watch dialog box (*Debug.QuickWatch*) that shows a variable and its members in a grid.

Table 7-5 The Watch Windows Provided by the Debugger

Watch Window	Description
Autos	The names of variables in the current statement and the previous statement
Locals	Stack variables
Registers	CPU registers
This	The *this* pointer of the current executing object
Watch1 to Watch4	Any variable you choose

The Autos, Locals, Registers, and This windows show you specific variables. You cannot add or remove variables, but you can change the values of the displayed variables. As you step through code, the values for the watched variables might change, and this change is shown by the value changing from black to red.

Each of the four Watch windows allows you to specify the variables that are shown, and each window also acts as an expression evaluator. Thus, you can type the following into the Name field of a Watch window:

```
"Hello".Length
```

and the value of the expression will be displayed as 5 in the corresponding Value field. Note that the syntax is C#; the expression evaluator will not understand S"Hello"->Length. You can also call static methods and global functions, as shown in this example:

```
String* GetGlobalString()
{
   return S"Hello from a global function";
}
__gc class Test
{
public:
   static String* GetString()
   {
      return S"Hello from a static method";
   }
};
```

If you type the following as the names of two variables in a Watch window grid, you will see the appropriate string as the value:

```
GetGlobalString()
Test::GetString()
```

The expression evaluator also allows you to create objects and will display the value of those objects, as shown here:

```
__gc class Creator
{
public:
   static Object* Create(String* s)
   {
      return Activator::CreateInstance(
         AppDomain::CurrentDomain->GetAssemblies()[0]->FullName,
            s);
   }
};
```

In this code, I assume that the first item in the array returned from *GetAssemblies* is mscorlib. The static method *Create* asks for an instance of the object passed as a parameter, so if you enter the following as the name of the watch variable, an instance of the *Debugger* class will be created:

```
Creator::Create("System.Diagnostics.Debugger")
```

The *Debugger* class is in the mscorlib assembly. If you pass the name of a class that does not exist in this assembly, the value that is shown will be the exception that is thrown. Similarly, if you try to create an object of a class that does not have a parameterless constructor, you'll see an exception.

The expression evaluator allows you to access array elements too.

```
__gc class MyData
{
public:
   static int GetData() __gc []
   {
      int i __gc[] = {0, 1, 2, 3};
      return i;
   }
};
```

If you use *MyData::GetData* as the name of the watch variable, you'll find that an integer array with your elements will be shown.

You can also call instance methods on existing objects. However, you should be careful because the method can change the state of the object, and furthermore, whenever you add a new variable to the Watch window, the expression evaluation is carried out on all expressions in the grid. Consider this class:

```
__gc class StringData
{
   String* m_s;
public:
   StringData(String* s):m_s(s){}
   String* Add(String* s)
   {
      m_s = String::Concat(m_s, s);
      return m_s;
   }
};
```

If you create an instance of this class in your code and then call *Add* through the variable name like this:

```
str.Add("more_data");
```

the instance in your code will have the string "more_data" appended to it, and whenever you add a new variable to the Watch window, the string "more_data" will be appended to the instance once more. You can also use operators on items, as long as the item supports the specified operator.

Immediate Mode

The Command window becomes very useful during a debug session. In the previous section, I mentioned various commands that you can give. Some of these commands will show windows (for example, *Debug.Threads*), whereas others will print out data to the Command window (for example *Debug.ListThreads*). In addition, while you are in break mode, you can put the Command window into immediate mode (the *immed* command; to get it back into command mode, type **cmd**). When you are in immediate mode, you can print out the values of variables, change the values of variables, and run code. For example, you can type the following

```
System::Math::Pow(2, 3)
```

which is the static method that returns the first number raised to the power of the second number, and the Command window will show 8.0.

The immediate mode will also show more complex data types, so using the example classes in the previous section, you can type *MyData::GetData* in immediate mode and the following will be printed out:

```
{Length=4}
    [0]: 0
    [1]: 1
    [2]: 2
    [3]: 3
```

In other words, the result is an array, and in the summary of the class, it prints out the value of the *Length* property, followed by each of the items in the array. Similarly, if you use the *Creator* class to create an instance of the *Debugger* class, the immediate mode will show this:

```
{System.Runtime.Remoting.ObjectHandle}
    System.MarshalByRefObject: {System.Runtime.Remoting.ObjectHandle}
    WrappedObject: {System.Diagnostics.Debugger}
```

The return value of the *Create* method actually returns an *ObjectHandle* instance, and *ObjectHandle* derives from *MarshalByRefObject*. *ObjectHandle* also has a single private field named *WrappedObject*, which is the actual object that was created, and in this case, the value is dumped in the Command window as the name of the class.

Formatting Watch Variables

In the earlier discussion on the Watch windows, I mentioned that objects are formatted in the grid. In fact, the DataTips and the immediate mode of the Command window also show formatted summaries of the objects that are printed out. These object summaries show either the name of the class or a formatted value; the Allow Property Evaluation In Variable Windows property on the General Debugger page of the IDE options (*Tool.Options*) determines which view is shown. (You have to restart the IDE for the change of the property to have an effect.)

The formatting rules that are shown in the object summary are given in .dat files in the Common7\Packages\Debugger folder. There are three such files in this folder: autoexp.dat has the rules for unmanaged projects, mcee_cs.dat has the rules for C# projects, and mcee_mc.dat has the rules for managed C++ projects. However, although there are two files for managed code, it appears that mcee_mc.dat is ignored and mcee_cs.dat is used for both C# and managed C++. Note that these rules are applied to the particular *project* type, so if you have an unmanaged class that you want to use in a managed project, the rules should be in mcee_cs.dat and not autoexp.dat.

These files are used by the debugger in conjunction with a formatter DLL. In terms of managed code, this formatter DLL is mcee.dll. For unmanaged code, you have the option of providing an extension DLL. The syntax for managed projects is straightforward: each line in mcee_cs.dat has an entry for a class that indicates how the fields should be shown. For example, this entry is the rule for *System::DateTime*:

```
; (Date is in US format, change to suit)
<System.DateTime>=<Month>/<Day>/<Year>
```

The class name and its members are shown in angle brackets, and the rule appears to the right of the equals sign and includes the literal / as a separator. When a *DateTime* object initialized to February 14, 2002 is added to a Watch window, the object's value is displayed as:

```
{2/14/02}
```

This display assumes that you have decided not to show integers as hexadecimals. Otherwise, using this default rule, you will see

```
{0x2/0xe/0x7d2}
```

which is far from useful. You can override this behavior by adding a format rule for the members, as shown here:

```
<System.DateTime>=<Month,d>/<Day,d>/<Year,d>
```

If you have already used a *DateTime* in your code, you will have to restart the IDE to get the new formatting rules. The *d* modifier indicates that the member will always be shown as a decimal. In addition, you can also use *h* for hexadecimal and *o* for octal. The *DateTime* value type has many data members, so against the name of the variable, you will see a tree view node that you can expand to see the other members; the rule just specifies the summary that is shown against the variable. If you choose, you can specify that the variable cannot be expanded. To specify this rule, you need to use the - modifier in the class name:

```
<System.DateTime,->=<Month,d>/<Day,d>/<Year,d>
```

Well, that's the theory. However, there seems to be a bug here too because turning off expansion also turns off the formatting rules, so you will not see any value for the object, just the class name.

It is also worth pointing out that when you give a formatting rule for a class, this rule is also used for the DataTips that appear when you hover the cursor over a variable in the source code editor.

If you call unmanaged code through Platform Invoke or through a static library with IJW, the native debugger will be used to step through your code. In this case, the types are defined in an *unmanaged project*, so the formatting rules should be in autoexp.dat. The syntax in this file is similar to the managed format files; the major difference is that the type name is given without angle brackets and that namespaces are identified with the :: operator. The other difference is that you get far more format modifiers and you can extend the expression evaluator using a DLL. This DLL is unmanaged and is loaded into the address space of Visual Studio .NET, so if your code throws an exception, this will affect the entire IDE.

Debugging Mixed Code

The IDE allows you to debug both managed and native code. The Debugging property page (*Project.Properties*) for a project allows you to specify the Debugger Type as one of Auto, Native, Managed, or Mixed. If you use Managed or Native, only that debugger will be used. If you have a managed project and set the debugger to be the managed debugger and then attempt to step into a native method, the debugger will treat the command as the Step Over command. This behavior happens even if you use the Disassembly window. For this reason, the Debugger Type property is usually set to Auto, which means that the IDE will determine the debugger to use from the code in the process. If you know that you will be debugging both native and managed code, you can select Mixed to get both debuggers.

When you single-step through source code under the managed debugger and you step into native code or COM code, the switch to the native debugger is seamless; you do not see any context changes. Correspondingly, when you step out of a native call back into managed code, you do not see the change from the native to the managed debugger. Indeed, if you single-step through the call from managed to native code, you will see that a call is made through to an address, and yet when you step into this call, you will stop at a totally different address. The native and managed debuggers clearly conspire to avoid allowing you to see the details of how the transition between managed and native code is performed. To a large extent, this transition is irrelevant because you are interested solely in the behavior of your code and not in the underlying plumbing of the infrastructure.

Debugging Multithreaded Code

Multithreaded code presents various problems to the debugger. In essence, when you are in break mode in the debugger, you see just one source file where the breakpoint has been hit, and there is a single thread of execution through which you are single-stepping. When you single-step a single-threaded application, you get the impression that the execution has slowed to an extremely slow rate. However, this is not the case with multithreaded applications. When in break mode, the other threads in the application will be suspended, and if the thread you are debugging depends on communication with these other threads, the behavior of the application will be affected.

Consider this class:

```
// multithread.cpp in the MultiThread project
__gc class ThreadProcs
{
```

```
public:
   AutoResetEvent* are1;
   AutoResetEvent* are2;
   ThreadProcs()
   {
      are1 = new AutoResetEvent(false);
      are2 = new AutoResetEvent(true);
   }
   void ProcOne()
   {
      while(true)
      {
         if (are1->WaitOne())
         {
            Thread::Sleep(100);
            Console::WriteLine(S"thread one");
            are2->Set();
         }
      }
   }
   void ProcTwo()
   {
      while(true)
      {
         if (are2->WaitOne())
         {
            Thread::Sleep(100);
            Console::WriteLine(S"thread two");
            are1->Set();
         }
      }
   }
};

void main()
{
   ThreadProcs* p = new ThreadProcs;
   Thread* one = new Thread(new ThreadStart(p, &ThreadProcs::ProcOne));
   one->IsBackground = false;
   Thread* two = new Thread(new ThreadStart(p, &ThreadProcs::ProcTwo));
   two->IsBackground = false;

   one->Start();
   two->Start();
}
```

The class defines two thread procedures that depend on two events. When the *are1* event is signaled, *ProcOne* runs and because the event is *autoreset*, the event will be unsignaled. The next time the thread calls *WaitOne* on this thread, it will block until the event has been set again. *ProcOne* waits a while before printing out a message to the console and then sets the *are2* event to allow the other thread to run before waiting on event *are1*. In effect, this code only allows one thread to run at a time.

If you place a breakpoint on the call to *Sleep* in both methods, you can watch how the debugger treats the events changing their signaled state. Because *are2* is created in a signaled state, the code will break first on the call to *Sleep* in *ProcTwo*, and because it is *autoreset*, the event will be unsignaled at this point. You will then be able to single-step through the code where the event *are1* is set, and finally *ProcTwo* will wait on *are2*. At this point, the debugger will see that the thread running *ProcTwo* is in a wait state, so it will give execution to the other thread, and because *are1* is now signaled, the breakpoint on *Sleep* in *ThreadOne* will be reached. Again, you will be able to single-step through this code, setting *are2* and then blocking on the call to wait on event *are1*, at which point the execution will be given over to the thread running *ProcTwo*.

This switching back and forth between threads can be a little confusing, but it illustrates that the debugger monitors the threads that are running and the communication that is occurring. In essence, there is a single thread of execution when you are single-stepping.

When a multithreaded application is in break mode, you can use the *Debug.Threads* command to bring up the Threads window to list the threads running in the process and the *Debug.ListThreads* command to print out the threads in the Command window.[12] You can also use immediate mode to call variables accessible to the code that the thread is running. Of course, you should be careful because in the preceding code, I could break in *ProcTwo* and call *this->are2->Set*—that is, I can set the event that the event will wait upon and screw up the thread synchronization.

You can also decide to debug another thread. To do this task, you should bring up the Threads window and select another thread by clicking on it, and then select Switch To Thread from the context menu. The debugger will show the execution point where it has been stopped in the selected thread, and you can then single-step. All other threads in the process will be frozen at this point, so if your code involves interthread communication, you will find that the code might not behave as you would expect.

---

12. Note that if you debug a managed application the list of threads is not the same as the number of OS threads running in the process.

Debugging Across Application Domains

If your application creates additional application domains, you might need to debug across application domains. The good news is that the debugger can step across application domain boundaries as if the call is the same as stepping into a method call. In some respects, cross-application domain calls can be less of an issue to debug than debugging multithreaded applications. The reason is that a process can have multiple application domains and yet only one thread of execution, so as long as object references are marshaled across the domain boundary (so that calls take into account the context differences between the domains), there is no synchronization issue, unlike multiple threads trying to access the same data.

```
// appdomains.cpp in AppDomains project
__gc class Other : public MarshalByRefObject
{
public:
   void CallMe()
   {
      Console::WriteLine(S"you have called {0}",
         AppDomain::CurrentDomain->FriendlyName);
   }
};

void main()
{
   AppDomain* ad = AppDomain::CreateDomain(S"Other domain");
   // Assume current assembly is the second one in the assembly array.
   String* str = AppDomain::CurrentDomain->GetAssemblies()[1]->FullName;
   Other* o = static_cast<Other*>(
                  ad->CreateInstance(str, S"Other")->Unwrap());
   o->CallMe();
}
```

In this code, the class *Other* is designed for interapplication domain calls. You can set breakpoints on code that runs in either of the application domains that are present when this process runs, so you can set a breakpoint on a line within *CallMe*. When a breakpoint is hit on a call to *CallMe*, the execution point will be moved to the method in the class and you can single-step through this method and step out of the method into the *main* method. However, a cursory glance at the stack trace when the execution point is in *CallMe* will indicate that there is much more going on. Cross-domain calls use .NET remoting, which means that a proxy for the *Other* object will be created in the default domain and the proxy will do the work of packaging up the request into a message to be sent via a channel to the actual object. Although this mechanism is optimized somewhat because the proxy and the object are within the same process, the net effect is the same as if the proxy and object were in different processes; that is, the code sets up sink chains to take into account the differences between the context between the proxy and object.

In contrast to the unmanaged/managed transition where the debugger hides the details of the context change, with cross-domain calls, you can see all the code that makes the context transition, and if you switch to the Disassembly window, you can see this code execute in its full glory.

Remote Debugging

The Visual Studio .NET debugger allows you to debug processes on another machine. There are two ways that the machines involved in the debugging can communicate, and the Processes dialog box distinguishes between the two by the transport that is used: TCP/IP and what it calls the Default protocol, which is DCOM. TCP/IP is only used for remotely debugging native code, whereas if you want to debug managed code, you must use the DCOM (Default) setting.[13]

The DCOM method of debugging uses a service called the *Machine Debug Manager*. The IDE communicates with this service using DCOM. This method is a secure way of connecting to the remote machine because you can use DCOM security to determine who can connect. When you install the remote debugging components, the installer will configure the Machine Debug Manager DCOM application to give launch and access permissions to accounts in the Debugger Users group. Thus, to enable another machine to debug processes on your machine, you must add the account of the interactive user that will run the IDE on that machine to the local Debugger Users account.

The TCP/IP remote debugging option is essentially the same as remote debugging in previous versions of Visual C++. To use this option, you have to install the Remote Debug Monitor, msvcmon.exe, on the remote machine, along with support DLLs. This tool is started on the command line and accepts connections from the client machine. If you remotely debug a native process using the DCOM protocol, you will actually use TCP/IP and the Remote Debug Monitor will be started automatically by the Machine Debug Manager (and it will be stopped when you detach or terminate the debugged application). In addition, when you select TCP/IP as the protocol, it is the Remote Debug Monitor that returns the list of processes on the remote machine, but the Available Processes grid on the Processes dialog box will show that all processes are Win32. If you select an application that is a .NET application, you will debug it as if it is a Win32 application. In other words, you will not be able to use the symbols for

13. I have heard it said that .NET would replace DCOM; well in this case, .NET requires the existence of DCOM!

the process and you will see the Win32 calls made by the runtime executing your JIT-compiled code. This exercise is interesting to do at least once, to see the code that the runtime calls, but it is of little use when trying to find bugs in your code.

Remote JIT Debugging

You might also decide to allow remote JIT debugging. To allow this debugging, you should run the Machine Debug Manager (mdm.exe) with the */remotecfg* switch. This switch causes the program to present a dialog box where you can specify that remote debugging is enabled. This dialog box also has a list box where you can add the names of machines that will be informed when an exception has occurred on the local machine and is caught by JIT debugging.

Be careful when you enable remote debugging because when an exception is thrown, you do not get a warning that the exception will be passed on to the other machine. In my opinion, JIT debugging on the machine that starts the debugger should have fewer dialog boxes, but JIT debugging across machine boundaries should at least have had a dialog box warning you that the exception is going to be handled by another machine. Therefore, it is safer to keep remote JIT debugging turned off and only enable it when you are about to start a debugging session. However, be aware that when you turn off remote JIT debugging by calling

```
mdm -remotecfg
```

and deselecting the option to enable JIT debugging, the Machine Debug Manager will turn off *all* JIT debugging on the local machine, so if you want to handle JIT debugging with the local copy of Visual Studio .NET, you have to enable local debugging through the Debugging category on the *Tools.Options* dialog box. It is a bit of a mess, but once you know what is going on, you soon get into the habit of turning JIT debugging on and off.

Remote Debugging from the IDE

When you debug a remote process, you have the option of having the project on the remote machine so that when you compile the code, the process will be on the correct machine, and the symbols for that process will be in there, too. (For .NET processes, the symbols must be on the remote machine.) However, you do have the associated problem that the source code will be on the remote machine, so the local machine must be able to have access to those files, perhaps through a UNC address. In this case, the local account must have permission to access the file on the remote machine, so you might have to use Windows Explorer to give members of the Debugger Users group access to the file. The other option is to have the project on the local machine and instruct the debugger to run the process on the remote machine. This option means that you can use the local project, but it causes problems due to code access security, which I'll mention in a moment.

Debugging code on a remote machine is straightforward. The issues that you need to address are: how do you start or attach to the remote process, and how do you single-step through it. If the process is installed on the remote machine, you can start that process and attach to it. The Processes dialog box (*Debug.Processes*) will list the processes on the remote machine, and if you are using the DCOM protocol, it will indicate whether the process is native (Win32) or .NET. You can use this dialog box to attach to a process. If the remote machine is set up for remote JIT debugging, when an unhandled exception occurs in a process on the remote machine, the client machine that was identified to mdm.exe will be contacted and vs7jit.exe will be run on the client, which gives the user on that machine the option of which debugger to use.

If the process's project is installed on the local machine, you can set values in the project's property pages to indicate that the process will run on another machine. These properties can be found on the Debugging page. The *Remote Machine* property indicates the name of the machine where the process should run, and the *Connection* property is used to indicate whether the process is local or whether TCP/IP or DCOM is used. Finally, *Remote Command* gives the command line that will start the process, which should be from the perspective of the remote machine. If the process is compiled and located on the local machine, you can use a UNC share name to the location of the process on the local machine. In this case, the remote machine will access the assembly from another machine, so there will be a code access security issue. The symbols must be available on the remote machine, so you will also have to set the *Symbol Path* property to point to the local machine.

The main issue that you will need to address when performing remote debugging is code access security. If you use the *Remote Command* property to indicate that the code that runs on the remote machine actually originates on another machine, you will have to set up code access security on the remote machine to all that code to run. If the code is accessed from another machine on the intranet, you can use the .NET Framework Configuration MMC snap-in to add a new code group under the machine's All_Code group, and for the membership condition, select the Local Intranet zone and then give FullTrust for the permission set.

Debugging .NET Remoting Applications

If you are debugging a .NET remoting application, initially you might decide to run the server on the same machine as the client. This way you can have the client and server projects in the same solution, and you will be able to single-step through the client code and hit breakpoints in the server code. Note that you have to run the server under the debugger to allow you to step into a remote method call. If the server is not running under the debugger and you step into a remote call, the debugger will not attach to the process and the request is treated as Step Over. Of course, if the server is running under the debugger, you can set breakpoints in the server code—even if the object is loaded through the <*service*> tag in a configuration file—and you will be able to step through the remote object code when the breakpoint is hit.

The whole point of .NET remoting is to run an object on another machine. This process is straightforward: all you have to do is ensure that you copy the assemblies, their symbols, and configuration files to the server machine. (You could access these from a share on the client machine, but again, you will have a code access security issue.) Then, in the server project's Debugging properties, you have to indicate that the server will run on the remote machine. To do this, the remote settings must be set to indicate that the *Connection* property is set to *Remote Via DCOM* and then you give the name of the remote machine and the location of the server with respect to the remote machine. Finally, you have to remember to change the client configuration file to access the remote object on the server machine. After you have done all of this, you will be able to step through code in the client and server just as if the server was running on the client machine.

Debugging Web Services

If the server is a managed Web service, the Debugging page should have the URL to the Web service's .asmx file as the HTTP URL. This setting will allow the debugger to attach to the Web service assembly, but you must be aware that the debugger will also start your Web browser with this URL, and as long as the Web browser runs, the debugger will be attached to the Web service. To finish your debugging session, you must close down the Web browser.

As with .NET remoting, you will not be able to step into a method in a client application and expect the debugger to step into the Web service method, but you can set breakpoints in the server code and see them hit when the client calls the Web service method. However, there are a few issues. The first issue is that when you change the Web service, you will have to manually deploy it to the remote server machine. (As I mentioned in the last chapter, there is no way to specify through the IDE the machine where the Web service should be deployed.) Next, be aware that when you add a Web reference to a managed project, the IDE adds the reference by generating a C# file with the information about the Web service, including the URL to the service. If you change the location of the Web service, you will have to ensure that the URL held by the Web service proxy is a URL to the new machine. The proxy object generated by wsdl.exe has *WebClientProtocol* as a base class. This class has a property named *Url*, which is the URL to the proxy. Thus, your Web service client should initialize this property before calling the Web service through the proxy.

Profiling

Visual Studio .NET does not provide a code profiler; however, the .NET runtime has built-in support for profiling, which means that you can write your own profiler, and the .NET Framework Tools Developers Guide has examples[14] illustrating how to write a profiler. The Tools Developers Guide contains comprehensive documentation for the API in a document called Profiling.doc in addition to comments in the corprof.idl file, which describes the profiling interfaces.

Essentially, a profiler is a COM object implemented in a DLL. This object should implement the *ICorProfilerCallback* interface, and it should be registered as an inproc server. Profiling is turned on with the help of two environment variables: *COR_ENABLE_PROFILING* and *COR_PROFILER*. If *COR_ENABLE_PROFILING* is set to 1, whenever a managed process is run, the profiler will be called. The runtime looks for the *COR_PROFILER* environment variable, which will have the CLSID (in registry format) of the profiler object.

ICorProfilerCallback is a rather large interface. It allows your profiler to be informed when profiling is starting or finishing (which is important because it allows the profiler to indicate the events that it is interested in), and it has methods for all the events that the runtime can use to inform the profiler, including events for creating and destroying application domains; loading assemblies, modules, and classes; JIT-compiling code; remoting events; handling exceptions; and making transitions between native and managed code. The interface is shown here:

```
[
   object,
   uuid(176FBED1-A55C-4796-98CA-A9DA0EF883E7),
   pointer_default(unique), local
]
interface ICorProfilerCallback : IUnknown
{
   // Startup/shutdown events
   HRESULT Initialize([in] IUnknown* pICorProfilerInfoUnk);
   HRESULT Shutdown();
```

14. There appears to be a bug in both examples when logging to a file. If you want to use these profilers, it is best to turn this option off by ensuring that the environment variable *DBG_PRF_LOG* is not set.

```
// Application domain events
HRESULT AppDomainCreationStarted(
   [in] AppDomainID appDomainId);
HRESULT AppDomainCreationFinished(
   [in] AppDomainID appDomainId,
   [in] HRESULT hrStatus);
HRESULT AppDomainShutdownStarted(
   [in] AppDomainID appDomainId);
HRESULT AppDomainShutdownFinished(
   [in] AppDomainID appDomainId,
   [in] HRESULT hrStatus);
// Assembly events
HRESULT AssemblyLoadStarted([in] AssemblyID assemblyId);
HRESULT AssemblyLoadFinished([in] AssemblyID assemblyId,
   [in] HRESULT hrStatus);
HRESULT AssemblyUnloadStarted([in] AssemblyID assemblyId);
HRESULT AssemblyUnloadFinished([in] AssemblyID assemblyId,
   [in] HRESULT hrStatus);
// Module events
HRESULT ModuleLoadStarted([in] ModuleID moduleId);
HRESULT ModuleLoadFinished([in] ModuleID moduleId,
   [in] HRESULT hrStatus);
HRESULT ModuleUnloadStarted([in] ModuleID moduleId);
HRESULT ModuleUnloadFinished([in] ModuleID moduleId,
   [in] HRESULT hrStatus);
HRESULT ModuleAttachedToAssembly([in] ModuleID moduleId,
   [in] AssemblyID AssemblyId);
// Class events
HRESULT ClassLoadStarted([in] ClassID classId);
HRESULT ClassLoadFinished([in] ClassID classId,
   [in] HRESULT hrStatus);
HRESULT ClassUnloadStarted([in] ClassID classId);
HRESULT ClassUnloadFinished([in] ClassID classId,
   [in] HRESULT hrStatus);
// JIT events
HRESULT FunctionUnloadStarted([in] FunctionID functionId);
HRESULT JITCompilationStarted([in] FunctionID functionId,
   [in] BOOL fIsSafeToBlock);
HRESULT JITCompilationFinished([in] FunctionID functionId,
   [in] HRESULT hrStatus, [in] BOOL fIsSafeToBlock);
HRESULT JITCachedFunctionSearchStarted(
   [in] FunctionID functionId,
   [out] BOOL *pbUseCachedFunction);
HRESULT JITCachedFunctionSearchFinished(
   [in] FunctionID functionId,
   [in] COR_PRF_JIT_CACHE result);
HRESULT JITFunctionPitched([in] FunctionID functionId);
HRESULT JITInlining([in] FunctionID callerId,
```

```
    [in] FunctionID calleeId, [out] BOOL *pfShouldInline);
// Thread events
HRESULT ThreadCreated([in] ThreadID threadId);
HRESULT ThreadDestroyed([in] ThreadID threadId);
HRESULT ThreadAssignedToOSThread(
    [in] ThreadID managedThreadId,
    [in] DWORD osThreadId);
// Client-side remoting events
HRESULT RemotingClientInvocationStarted();
HRESULT RemotingClientSendingMessage([in] GUID *pCookie,
    [in] BOOL fIsAsync);
HRESULT RemotingClientReceivingReply([in] GUID *pCookie,
    [in] BOOL fIsAsync);
HRESULT RemotingClientInvocationFinished();
// Server-side remoting events
HRESULT RemotingServerReceivingMessage([in] GUID *pCookie,
    [in] BOOL fIsAsync);
HRESULT RemotingServerInvocationStarted();
HRESULT RemotingServerInvocationReturned();
HRESULT RemotingServerSendingReply([in] GUID *pCookie,
    [in] BOOL fIsAsync);
// Transition events
HRESULT UnmanagedToManagedTransition(
    [in] FunctionID functionId,
    [in] COR_PRF_TRANSITION_REASON reason);
HRESULT ManagedToUnmanagedTransition(
    [in] FunctionID functionId,
    [in] COR_PRF_TRANSITION_REASON reason);
// Run-time suspension events
HRESULT RuntimeSuspendStarted(
    [in] COR_PRF_SUSPEND_REASON suspendReason);
HRESULT RuntimeSuspendFinished();
HRESULT RuntimeSuspendAborted();
HRESULT RuntimeResumeStarted();
HRESULT RuntimeResumeFinished();
HRESULT RuntimeThreadSuspended([in] ThreadID threadId);
HRESULT RuntimeThreadResumed([in] ThreadID threadId);
// GC events
HRESULT MovedReferences([in] ULONG cMovedObjectIDRanges,
    [in, size_is(cMovedObjectIDRanges)]
        ObjectID oldObjectIDRangeStart[],
    [in, size_is(cMovedObjectIDRanges)]
        ObjectID newObjectIDRangeStart[],
    [in, size_is(cMovedObjectIDRanges)]
        ULONG cObjectIDRangeLength[] );
HRESULT ObjectAllocated([in] ObjectID objectId,
    [in] ClassID classId);
HRESULT ObjectsAllocatedByClass([in] ULONG cClassCount,
```

```
      [in, size_is(cClassCount)] ClassID classIds[],
      [in, size_is(cClassCount)] ULONG cObjects[]);
   HRESULT ObjectReferences([in] ObjectID objectId,
      [in] ClassID  classId, [in] ULONG    cObjectRefs,
      [in, size_is(cObjectRefs)] ObjectID objectRefIds[]);
   HRESULT RootReferences([in] ULONG cRootRefs,
      [in, size_is(cRootRefs)] ObjectID rootRefIds[] );
   // Exception creation events
   HRESULT ExceptionThrown([in] ObjectID thrownObjectId);
   // Exception handler search events
   HRESULT ExceptionSearchFunctionEnter(
      [in] FunctionID functionId);
   HRESULT ExceptionSearchFunctionLeave();
   HRESULT ExceptionSearchFilterEnter(
      [in] FunctionID functionId);
   HRESULT ExceptionSearchFilterLeave();
   HRESULT ExceptionSearchCatcherFound(
      [in] FunctionID functionId);
   HRESULT ExceptionOSHandlerEnter([in] UINT_PTR __unused);
   HRESULT ExceptionOSHandlerLeave([in] UINT_PTR __unused);
   // Exception unwind events
   HRESULT ExceptionUnwindFunctionEnter(
      [in] FunctionID functionId);
   HRESULT ExceptionUnwindFunctionLeave();
   HRESULT ExceptionUnwindFinallyEnter(
      [in] FunctionID functionId);
   HRESULT ExceptionUnwindFinallyLeave();
   HRESULT ExceptionCatcherEnter([in] FunctionID functionId,
      [in] ObjectID objectId);
   HRESULT ExceptionCatcherLeave();
   // CLR->COM interop table events
   HRESULT COMClassicVTableCreated([in] ClassID wrappedClassId,
      [in] REFGUID implementedIID, [in] void  *pVTable,
      [in] ULONG   cSlots);
   HRESULT COMClassicVTableDestroyed(
      [in] ClassID wrappedClassId,
      [in] REFGUID implementedIID, [in] void *pVTable);
   HRESULT ExceptionCLRCatcherFound();
   HRESULT ExceptionCLRCatcherExecute();
}
```

It would have been easier to program the profiler object if the interface had been spilt into several interfaces, and it would make the code follow interface programming ethos.

The simplest way to write a profiler is to use ATL attributes. Here is the basic code:

```
// Compile with cl /LD profiler.cpp.
#define _ATL_ATTRIBUTES
#include <atlbase.h>
#include <atlcom.h>

#include <cor.h>
#include <corprof.h>

#include <stdio.h>

[module(dll, name="ProfilerLib")];

[coclass, uuid("1dbbf8c4-88a3-4b70-99a5-e1697f3b837b"),
 threading("free")]
class Profiler : public ICorProfilerCallback
{
   CComPtr<ICorProfilerInfo> m_pInfo;
public:
   HRESULT __stdcall Initialize(IUnknown* pICorProfilerInfoUnk)
   {
      puts("Profiler Initialized");
      pICorProfilerInfoUnk->QueryInterface(&m_pInfo);
      m_pInfo->SetEventMask(COR_PRF_MONITOR_JIT_COMPILATION);
      return S_OK;
   }
   HRESULT __stdcall Shutdown()
   {
      puts("Profiler Shutdown");
      m_pInfo.Release();
      return S_OK;
   }
// Other interface methods
};
```

ATL attributes make writing COM classes simple. The *[coclass]* attribute tells the compiler to generate a class factory and registration code, the *[module]* attribute tells the compiler to create the required COM DLL exported functions, and *[threading(free)]* adds registration and code support to make the class free-threaded. I have left out most of the methods of *ICorProfilerCallback*, but of course, there should be implementations of each.

The first point to make is that when a managed process is run, the registered profiler will be created in the process space of that managed process and the *Initialize* method will be called. The profiler has to indicate to the runtime which events it wants to receive by calling *ICorProfilerInfo::SetEventMask* and passing a bitmask. My profiler is only interested in JIT events, so I will provide special handling for the following three methods (the other interface methods are empty):

```
HRESULT __stdcall JITCompilationStarted(
   FunctionID functionId, BOOL fIsSafeToBlock)
{
   printf("starting to JIT-compile function \n", functionId);
   PrintFunctionName(functionId);
   return S_OK;
}
HRESULT __stdcall JITCompilationFinished(
   FunctionID functionId, HRESULT hrStatus, BOOL fIsSafeToBlock)
{
   printf("completed JIT-compiled function %ld ", functionId);
   PrintFunctionName(functionId);
   if (SUCCEEDED(hrStatus))
      printf("succeeded\n");
   else
      printf("failed with %08x\n", hrStatus);
   return S_OK;
}
HRESULT __stdcall JITInlining(
   FunctionID callerId, FunctionID calleeId,
      BOOL *pfShouldInline)
{
   printf("JIT inlining function %08x ", calleeId);
   PrintFunctionName(calleeId);
   printf("to function %08x ", callerId);
   PrintFunctionName(callerId);
   return S_OK;
}
```

I think it would have been far better if *ICorProfilerCallback* was split into several event interfaces because then *IUnknown::QueryInterface* would be used to determine whether the particular events were handled, and it would mean that I would not have to fill this class with a plethora of empty, useless methods.

The first two methods are called to indicate that JIT-compiling is about to start and then that the compilation has finished on a method. The third method indicates that a method will not be JIT-compiled in isolation but will be inlined as part of another method. I have decided just to print out the name of the method, but in your own profiler, you might decide to start a timer when the JIT-compilation starts and stop the timer when the JIT-compilation finishes to get an idea of how long JITting takes.

To indicate the method that is being JIT-compiled, these methods are passed a *FunctionId*, which is merely a *UINT_PTR*. To convert this *FunctionId* to the actual method name, I use a helper function named *PrintFunctionName*, as shown in the following code:

```
void PrintFunctionName(FunctionID id)
{
   mdToken tokMethod;
   CComPtr<IMetaDataImport> pImport;
   m_pInfo->GetTokenAndMetaDataFromFunction(
      id, IID_IMetaDataImport, (IUnknown**)&pImport, &tokMethod);
   HRESULT hr;
   ULONG nameLen = 0;
   hr = pImport->GetMethodProps(
         tokMethod, NULL, NULL, NULL,
         &nameLen, NULL, NULL, NULL, NULL, NULL);
   if (FAILED(hr))
   {
      puts("cannot get method name");
      return;
   }
    wchar_t* methodName = new wchar_t[nameLen];
   mdTypeDef tokCls;
   pImport->GetMethodProps(
      tokMethod, &tokCls, methodName, nameLen,
      &nameLen, NULL, NULL, NULL, NULL, NULL);
   nameLen = 0;
   hr = pImport->GetTypeDefProps(
      tokCls, NULL, 0, &nameLen, NULL, NULL);
   if (FAILED(hr))
   {
      puts("cannot get class name");
      delete [] methodName;
      return;
   }

   wchar_t* clsName = new wchar_t[nameLen];
   pImport->GetTypeDefProps(
      tokCls, clsName, nameLen, &nameLen, NULL, NULL);
      wprintf(L"%s.%s\n", clsName, methodName);
   delete [] methodName;
   delete [] clsName;
}
```

The significant thing about this code is that it calls the *ICorProfilerInfo* interface obtained when the runtime calls the *Initialize* method. The *ICorProfilerInfo* interface is yet another mega-interface that does all kinds of things. Again, I would prefer if the implementers of the .NET Framework had split *ICorProfilerInfo* into several interfaces. I cannot see why the implementers did not decide to do this splitting, especially because *Initialize* is passed an *IUnknown* pointer, so I am required to ask for the interface that I want to call.

ICorProfilerInfo has methods that allow you to convert from metadata tokens to the class and function identifiers used by *ICorProfilerCallback*; to get information about assemblies, modules, application domains, and threads; and to get metadata tokens about classes and functions so that you can get their names. In addition, *ICorProfilerInfo* has methods that can be called to cause a function to be JITted again, to cause the garbage collector to start a collection, to get the IL for a method, and even to replace the IL for a method that has not been JITted, and to indicate functions that are called when a method is about to be called and when the method has been called. Because these are such a diverse group of methods, they really should have been implemented on several different interfaces.

In *PrintFunctionName*, I call just *one* of these methods on *ICorProfilerInfo*: *GetTokenAndMetaDataFromFunction*, which returns the metadata token for the method that is JIT-compiled and a metadata interface that I can use to get the class and method name from this metadata token. For this I use methods on the *IMetaDataImport* interface (which I described in Chapter 5). *GetMethodProps* gets the name of the method and the metadata token of the class, whereas *GetTypeDefProps* returns the name of the class. Note that the class name returned by *GetTypeDefProps* is fully qualified with the namespace, but the resolution operator used is C# style; that is, a dot is used, so I have followed this style in my code.

For this simple assembly:

```
void main()
{
   Console::WriteLine(S"Simple Test");
}
```

I get this output:

```
Initialized profiler
starting to JIT-compile function 003753b0 .main
JIT inlining function 79b895a0 System.Console.WriteLine
to function 003753b0 .main
JIT inlining function 79b893e0 System.Console.get_Out
to function 003753b0 .main
completed JIT-compiled function 003753b0 .main
succeeded
Simple Test
Shutdown profiler
```

The profiling API is extremely powerful, but you have to be careful. In particular, the .NET Framework is free-threaded, which means that the *ICorProfilerCallback* interface might not be called on the same thread each time. This detail was overlooked by the writers of the example profilers and appears to be the source of the bug when logging profiler information to a file. Your profiler code is called by the .NET Framework, so you have to be very careful to ensure that the code is bug-free; otherwise, you might cause an error in the process being profiled. Furthermore, when you are profiling an application, be sure that you set the profiling environment variables only at the command line, and remember to clear the environment variables once you have finished profiling. This way the profiler will be called only when you decide it should be used. The C++ compiler uses managed code, so if you run it from a command line where you have set the profiler environment variables, you will get profiling information for the compiler.

Summary

In this chapter, I have given a comprehensive coverage of the tools that are available in Visual Studio .NET and in the .NET Framework to debug managed applications. C++ is well served in this area; indeed, there are areas where C++ is far better than any other .NET language for helping you to debug your application. In all cases, you have to take into account that your application can use native code. This issue is not great because Visual Studio .NET provides a native debugger, and the transition between managed and native debuggers appears seamlessly. Even if the native code runs on another machine, you can still treat the code as if it is managed, and the Machine Debug Manager will ensure that the appropriate code is run on the remote machine to facilitate native debugging.

It is also important to write your code in such a way that allows you to determine the source of an error. In this respect, C++ is both better than and yet deficient compared to other languages. It is deficient because the managed C++ compiler does not take the *[Conditional]* attribute into account, but it is trivial to use C++ conditional compilation to get the same affect. The diagnostics classes in the .NET Framework have their own problems, and C++ is the ideal language to improve these classes.

Appendix A

.NET Framework Libraries

The .NET Framework library replaces most of the C and C++ libraries that you are used to using to develop your code. Although you can still use the C runtime library (CRT) and the C++ standard library for existing code that you are recompiling for the .NET runtime, it makes sense when you create a new project to use the .NET Framework classes. In this appendix, I present in a series of tables the .NET Framework equivalent of the common CRT and C++ standard library routines. Sometimes there is no close match to a .NET Framework class, in which case I have not listed the CRT or standard library item. In other cases, I have listed the closest match, but you should always check the documentation carefully.

Strings

The main string classes are *System::String*, *System::Char*, and *System::Text::StringBuilder*. *String* objects are immutable and essentially contain an array of *Char*s. You use *StringBuilder* to manipulate a *Char* array, from which a *String* can be created.

Character Characterization

The *Char* class holds Unicode characters; however, for clarity in Table A-1, I give the Multi-Byte Character Set (MBCS) name of the CRT routine.

Table A-1 .NET *Char* Equivalents for CRT Character Routines

CRT Routine	.NET Equivalent
isalnum	*Char::IsLetterOrDigit*
isalpha	*Char::IsLetter*
iscntrl	*Char::IsControl*
isdigit	*Char::IsDigit*
islower	*Char::IsLower*
isxdigit	*Char::IsNumber*
ispunct	*Char::IsPunctuation*
isupper	*Char::IsUpper*
isspace	*Char::IsWhitespace*

String Routines

Again, .NET strings are Unicode. Note that *System::String* is immutable, so most of its methods return new strings. *StringBuilder* allows you to change the actual buffer, so this is more equivalent to the CRT routines. Also be aware that many CRT routines return pointers (for example, *strchr*), but the .NET equivalents return a character index (*IndexOf*), as shown in Table A-2.

Table A-2 .NET String Equivalents for CRT String Routines

CRT Routine	.NET Equivalent
sprintf	*String::Format*
strcat, strncat	*String::Concat*, *StringBuilder::Append*
strchr	*String::IndexOf*
strcmp	*String::Compare*, *String::CompareTo*
strcoll	*String::CompareOrdinal*
strcpy	*String::Copy*
strcspn	*String::IndexOfAny*
strftime	*DateTime::ToString*
strlen	*String::Length*
_strlwr	*String::ToLower*
strrchr	*String::LastIndexOf*
strstr	*String::LastIndexOfAny*
strtok	*String::Split*
_strupr	*String::ToUpper*

Data Conversion

.NET primitive types implement *IConvertible*, which means that a primitive type can be converted to other types. In addition, you can use *System::Convert*, which has static methods that allow you to convert between types. You convert a type to a string by calling the *ToString* method, as Table A-3 shows. This allows you to perform formatted conversion. I will explain this conversion further in the section “Formatted Output” later in this appendix.

Table A-3 .NET Conversion Methods for CRT Routines

CRT Routine	.NET Equivalent
atof, atoi, atol, strtod, strtol	Use the appropriate *Parse* method
_itoa, _itol, _ecvt, _fcvt, _gcvt, _ltoa	Use the appropriate *ToString* method

Files and I/O

.NET uses stream APIs for input and output. The *System::IO* namespace has the classes that can be used to access files and the general stream classes.

Stream I/O

The *File* class gives information about a file, and through static methods, it allows you to open files for read or write, as a binary file or as a text file. When a file is open in binary mode, a *FileStream* is returned; when a file is open in text mode, a *StreamWriter* or *StreamReader* method is returned. (Both of these objects are based on a *FileStream* object.) Table A-4 shows the equivalent *FileStream* for CRT stream I/O routines.

Table A-4 .NET *FileStream* Equivalents for CRT File Routines

CRT Routine	.NET Equivelant
fclose	*FileStream::Close*
feof	Compare *FileStream::Position* with *FileStream::Length*
fflush	*FileStream::Flush*
fopen	*File::Open*, *File::Create*, *File::OpenRead*, *File::OpenWrite*
fscanf	Pass *FileStream* object to *BinaryReader* constructor, and call *Read* methods
fseek	*FileStream::Seek*.
fprintf	Format string with *String::Format*, and write to stream with *FileStream::Write*
getc	*FileStream::ReadByte*
putc	*FileStream::WriteByte*
rewind	*FileStream::Seek*
setbuf	Wrap the stream with *BufferedStream*

Console I/O

The main class for console I/O is *System::Console*. This class has two static properties, *In* and *Out*, and exposes some methods as static members. Table A-5 shows .NET *Console* equivalents for CRT console I/O routines.

Table A-5 *Console* Equivalents for CRT I/O Routines

CRT Routine	.NET Equivalent
getchar	*Console::Read* *
gets	*Console::ReadLine*
printf	*Console::Write*, *Console::WriteLine*
putchar	*Console::Write*, or *WriteByte* on *Console::Out*
puts	*Console::WriteLine*
scanf	Pass *Console::OpenStandardInput* to *BinaryReader* constructor and call *Read* methods
sprintf	*String::Format*

* There is no direct equivalent in .NET because *Console::Read* will not return until the Enter key has been pressed.

Formatted Output

Methods that are used to format strings (for example, *String::Format* and *Console::WriteLine*) are passed a format string with placeholders. The placeholders are numbered—indexed from zero and corresponding to the parameters passed to the method—and the number is enclosed in braces. You can also supply format information in the placeholder, as indicated in Table A-6, where *n* is the placeholder number.

Table A-6 Available Placeholders for String-Formatting Methods

Placeholder	Description
{n:C}	Currency: the string has the currency symbol and the decimal places specified for the current culture.
{n:Dm}	Integer with *m* digits.
{n:Em}	Scientific format; *m* is the precision.
{n:Fm}	Fixed: *m* is the number of decimal places.
{n:Gm}	General format, fixed or scientific.
{n:Nm}	Number format: thousands are grouped with a culture-specific separator; *m* gives the number of decimal places.
{n:Pm}	Percentage format: the number is shown as a percentage with *m* digits after the decimal place.
{n:Rm}	Roundtrip format: the resulting string can be converted back to the number without loss of data.
{n:Xm}	Hex format: *m* gives the number of digits.

File Handling

Information about a file can be obtained through the *File* class and the *FileInfo* class. Table A-7 shows the .NET equivalents of these classes. File paths can be manipulated with the static methods on the *Path* class.

Table A-7 .NET File Handling Equivalents

CRT Routine	.NET Equivalent
_chsize	*FileStream::SetLength*
_filelength	*FileInfo::Length*
_fstat, _stat	*File::GetAttributes, File::GetCreationTime, File::GetLastAccessTime, File::GetLastWriteTime*
_fullpath	*Path::GetFullPath*
_makepath	*Path::Combine*
_mktemp	*Path::GetTempFileName*
remove, _unlink	*File::Delete*
rename	*File::Move*
_splitpath	Use static methods on *Path*

Directory Routines

The *Directory* class gives information about a folder and can be used to create and delete folders and get information about the current folder. Table A-8 shows the *Directory* class equivalents for CRT folder routines.

Table A-8 .NET *Directory* Class Equivalents for CRT Folder Routines

CRT Routine	.NET Equivalent
_chdir	*Directory::SetCurrentDirectory*
_findclose, _findfirst, _findnext	Use *Directory::GetDirectories* and *Directory::GetFiles*
_getcwd	*Directory::GetCurrentDirectory*
_getdrive	Pass *Directory::GetCurrentDirectory* to *Directory::GetDirectoryRoot*
_getdrives	*Directory::GetLogicalDrives*
_mkdir	*Directory::CreateDirectory*
_rmdir	*Directory::Delete*

Process and Environment Control

In .NET, threads are represented by the *System::Threading::Thread* class, and processes are represented by *System::Diagnostics::Process* class. The *System::Environment* class gives access to information such as environment variables, machine name, command line, and folder information. Table A-9 shows the .NET equivalents to the CRT routines for obtaining these types of information.

Table A-9 .NET Equivalents for Thread, Process, and Environment Routines

CRT Routine	.NET Equivalent
abort	*Environment::Exit*
assert	*Debug::Assert*, *Trace::Assert*
_beginthread	*Thread* constructor and *Thread::Start*
_endthread	*Thread::Terminate*
_execl, *_spawnl*	*Process::Start*
getenv	*Environment::GetEnvironmentVariables*

Time

The *System::DateTime* allows you to access the current time and to perform time manipulations. Time differences are returned as *System::TimeSpan* objects. The *System::Globalization::DateTimeFormatInfo* class has information used to format dates and times for a culture. The *CultureInfo::DateTimeFormat* property returns the format information for a specified culture. *DateTime::ToString* can be used to format a time for a culture. Table A-10 shows the .NET date and time equivalents to CRT date and time routines.

Table A-10 .NET Date and Time Equivalents for CRT Date and Time Routines

CRT Routine	.NET Equivalent
asctime, *ctime*, *_ftime*, *_strtime*, *_strdate*	Call *ToString* on *DateTime::Now*
clock	Get a *Process* object through *Process::GetCurrentProcess()* and call *TotalProcessorTime*
difftime	*DateTime::Subtract*
time	*DateTime::Now*

Containers

The *System::Collections* namespace contains the collection interfaces and common implementations. The *System::Collections::Specialized* namespace contains further collection classes. In the Table A-11, I have listed the .NET Framework classes that are the nearest match for the standard library container classes in terms of the behavior of adding and accessing items and whether the container is associative.

Table A-11 .NET Equivalents for C++ Standard Library Container Classes

C++ Class	.NET Equivalent
deque	*Array*
hash_map, hash_multimap	*HashTable*
hash_set, hash_multiset	*ArrayList*
list	*ArrayList*
map, multimap	*SortedList*
queue	*Queue*
set, multiset	*ArrayList*
stack	*Stack*
vector	*Array*

Appendix B

Further Resources

In this appendix, I list the tools and other resources that I find useful when I develop .NET code and when I investigate how .NET works.

Tools

While writing this book, I often needed to look into the assemblies produced by the C++ compiler and into the .NET Framework assemblies. In this section, I list the tools that I have found useful.

ILDASM

This tool is provided as part of the .NET Framework SDK. You can find it in the FrameworkSDK\Bin folder. This tool is a GUI application, but you can invoke it with command-line arguments, which means that you can change the registry so that ILDASM can be invoked through the context menu for an .exe, a .dll, or a .netmodule file. I use the */advanced* switch so that I get ILDASM in its full glory. Here is a script to add these values:

```
Windows Registry Editor Version 5.00
[HKEY_CLASSES_ROOT\exefile\shell]
[HKEY_CLASSES_ROOT\exefile\shell\Dissassemble]
[HKEY_CLASSES_ROOT\exefile\shell\Dissassemble\command]
@="ildasm /advanced %1"
[HKEY_CLASSES_ROOT\dllfile\shell]
[HKEY_CLASSES_ROOT\dllfile\shell\Disassemble]
[HKEY_CLASSES_ROOT\dllfile\shell\Disassemble\command]
@="ildasm.exe /advanced %1"
[HKEY_CLASSES_ROOT\.netmodule]
@="netmodulefile"
[HKEY_CLASSES_ROOT\netmodulefile]
[HKEY_CLASSES_ROOT\netmodulefile\shell]
[HKEY_CLASSES_ROOT\netmodulefile\shell\Disassemble]
[HKEY_CLASSES_ROOT\netmodulefile\shell\Disassemble\command]
@="ildasm /advanced %1"
```

Anakrino

This is a free decompilation tool written by Jay Freeman. You can get the latest release from *www.anakrino.org*. Anakrino allows you to decompile assemblies to C# or managed C++. By default, Anakrino lists the assemblies in the .NET Framework system folder in a tree view control that you can use to browse through the types and their members. This tool is invaluable in determining how a class works, but it really should be used in conjunction with ILDASM because Anakrino does not give access to all metadata.

MetaInfo

This tool is provided as a sample as part of the Tool Developer's Guide (which is part of the .NET Framework SDK). It gives you a raw view of the metadata in an assembly, in contrast to the logical view that is presented in ILDASM. If you are interested in developing code with the unmanaged metadata API, take a look at the source for this tool.

Rotor

This tool is also known by the rather uncatchy name of the Microsoft Shared Source CLI Implementation and can be downloaded from *http://msdn.microsoft.com/library/en-us/dndotnet/html/mssharsourcecli.asp*. Please pay attention to the license for this code. This tool is an implementation of the ECMA standards of a C# compiler and Common Language Infrastructure (CLI). The source code will compile and run on Windows XP and FreeBSD. The documentation says that "there are significant differences in implementation between this code and the code for Microsoft's commercial CLR implementation." Although I will not disagree with this statement in terms of the run-time DLLs, I can say that the .NET Framework classes that are provided in source form (in C#) look very similar to the decompilation obtained through Anakrino.

Rotor also contains the source code for various tools that you are used to using in the .NET Framework SDK: the IL assembler (ilasm.exe) and disassembler (ildasm.exe), the command-line debugger (cordbg.exe), the code access security command-line policy editor (caspol.exe), and the global assembly cache utility (gacutil.exe). Rotor also provides the source code for various compilers and build tools, so you get the assembly linker tool (al.exe), a C# compiler, and the source for nmake.exe. Finally, Rotor has the source for the main DLLs that constitute the .NET Framework, including code for Fusion, the JIT compiler, and the execution engine. If you want to get an idea of how garbage collection or JIT compilation can be implemented, this library will thrill you.

DUMPBIN

This tool is a shim around the linker. When you call *dumpbin*, you are actually calling *link /dump*. This tool is useful for investigating the format of PE files (.exe and .dll) and COFF object files (.obj), and the symbols they contain. The version provided with Visual Studio .NET (see VC7/bin) will also give information about the CLI Header.

PEDump

This tool is provided as part of Matt Pietrek's February 2002 article "Inside Windows: An In-Depth Look into the Win32 Portable Executable File Format" in *MSDN Magazine* (*http://download.microsoft.com/download/msdnmagazine/code/Feb02/WXP/EN-US/PE.exe*). PEDump does all that DUMPBIN does, but it does not depend on the linker tool.

DbgView

This tool shows you the strings passed to *OutputDebugString*. You can download the tool from *www.sysinternals.com*. When you run an application under the debugger, any debug strings (those passed to *Trace::WriteLine*) will show up in the Output window of Visual Studio .NET. This tool is useful on the occasions when you run an application that has debug messages without a debugger.

RegMon

This tool, also from *www.sysinternals.com*, will list the accesses made to the registry. It is useful to see the calls that are made to the registry because you can trace the COM objects that are created by the calls made to HKCR\Classes.

Tools Supplied with This Book

In some cases, I have had to write my own tools because I have not been able to find a suitable tool included with Visual Studio .NET or elsewhere.

Profiler

This tool is described in Chapter 7 and is a simple implementation of the profiling interface. The interesting thing about this tool is the ability to look at the types that are loaded when you start a .NET application. Again, this gives you some insight into how the runtime works.

HexDump

The Visual Studio .NET binary editor (*File.OpenFile /e"Binary Editor")* is great for scanning through a binary file to see if there are any undocumented command-line arguments (for example, the */nosplash* switch for DevEnv.exe) or just to look at the file structure. Unfortunately, when you copy a selection from this editor to the clipboard, the binary code is copied and not the formatted hex view. This limitation makes it useless for people like me to create hex dumps. The source code for this appendix has a small utility for dumping a file as hex to the command line; this utility is called *HexDump*.

DumpInterfaces

It is interesting to establish the interfaces that a COM class implements. This tool (supplied with the sample code) simply takes a ProgID or a CLSID, creates an instance of the object, and then calls *IUnknown::QueryInterface* for every interface registered in the system registry. It is crude, but it is surprising the information that you can obtain. The example uses ATL, so if you compile it at the command line, you have to ensure that your environment variables are set up correctly. (Run the *vcvars32.bat* batch file from the VC7\bin folder.)

Books

This is not a bibliography; it is a list of books that I think all .NET developers ought to read.

Inside Microsoft .NET IL Assembler by Serge Lidin (Microsoft Press, 2002), ISBN 0-7356-1547-0.

If you are ever likely to use ILDASM, you must read this book. If you are interested in metadata and how it is stored in assemblies, you must read this book.

Applied Microsoft .NET Framework Programming by Jeffrey Richter (Microsoft Press, 2002), ISBN 0-7356-1422-9.

Jeff is well known for his in-depth books about Windows—avoiding the fluff and getting to the metal. He has done the same thing here with the .NET Framework.

Programming Microsoft Windows with C# by Charles Petzold (Microsoft Press, 2002), ISBN 0-7356-1370-2.

Everyone must have at least one Petzold, and you might as well make it this one. This book covers the entire breadth of the Windows Forms and GDI+ libraries. Whatever you want to do in Windows Forms, you'll find out how to do it in this book.

Common Language Infrastructure, ECMA Specification.

You can find this specification in the Program Files\Microsoft Visual Studio .NET\FrameworkSDK\Tool Developers Guide\docs\Partition II Metadata.doc file. It is supplied in five documents covering the .NET runtime and the .NET Framework. As with all specifications, it is hard to read more than a few sections in a sitting, but these documents are invaluable to understand how .NET works.

Developing Applications with Visual Studio .NET by Richard Grimes (Addison-Wesley, 2002), ISBN 0-201-70852-3.

Buy this book so that I can pay my mortgage and have a place where I can write more books.

Index

Symbols and Numbers

A

B

D

M

N

O

P

S

T

U

W

X

Richard Grimes

In the 1980s, there was a graffito on a wall beneath the main lecture theater in the physics department at Nottingham University. This said: "Physics graduates have only two options: work for the defence industry or the software industry." (It is possible that the graffito is still there.) Richard Grimes graduated with an honours BSc in physics from Nottingham, but being ideologically opposed to the former option and finding that the latter lacked the challenges that he needed, he chose instead to defy the message of the graffito and go into research. He gained a PhD in semiconductor physics and then studied photothermal ionization and quantum effects in III-V semiconductors and II-VI semimagnetic semiconductors. After spending several years as a research scientist, Richard took time off to help bring up his newborn daughter, an endeavor that turned out to be the best-spent and most enjoyable nine months of his life. That was followed by a year as a computer trainer (the most unpleasant year of his life) and then almost four years as a software developer. With remarkable prescience, the graffito had clearly foretold his future.

During his time as a software developer, Richard started writing technical articles, and this undertaking led to his first book (on DCOM). The success of that book persuaded Richard to become an independent software developer and writer. He has since written several books on COM, MTS, COM+, and ATL—and more recently on .NET. He writes for various magazines, including *MSDN Magazine*, and was the .NET columnist for *Visual C++ Developers Journal* before its metamorphosis into *Visual Studio Magazine*. He also speaks regularly at conferences on Microsoft technologies, giving talks and workshops on topics related to .NET and C++.

Richard lives in the medieval town of Kenilworth in England with his wife and two children. For relaxation—and to break the occasional bout of writer's block—he enjoys working in his garden, where he grows fruit and vegetables. The only criterion for a plant to be included in his garden is that it has to be edible. Richard can be contacted on topics about C++ and .NET, or indeed, on the growing of fruit and vegetables, at *dotnet.dev@grimes.demon.co.uk*.

Drill Bits

The year was 1914, and the electric motor was still newfangled. Along came two bright young fellows, S. Duncan Black and Alonzo G. Decker, who saw its possibilities. They hooked one of the new motors up to a *drill bit*—a circular piece of metal with a chisel edge and cutting lips—and the world's first electric drill was born. It had a pistol grip and a trigger switch, and it made boring holes a snap, but it didn't really catch on until 20 years later when, in 1946, Black and Decker designed a model for consumers, and the tool took off. As usual, necessity was the mother of invention and the father of a highly successful company—a bit of wisdom you can drill home time and time again.*

At Microsoft Press, we use tools to illustrate our books for software developers and IT professionals. Tools very simply and powerfully symbolize human inventiveness. They're a metaphor for people extending their capabilities, precision, and reach. From simple calipers and pliers to digital micrometers and lasers, these stylized illustrations give each book a visual identity, and a personality to the series. With tools and knowledge, there's no limit to creativity and innovation. Our tagline says it all: The tools you need to put technology to work.

* From *The Great Tool Emporium* by David X. Manners (published by E.P. Dutton/Times Mirror Magazines, Inc., 1979)

The manuscript for this book was prepared and galleyed using Microsoft Word. Pages were composed by Microsoft Press using Adobe FrameMaker+SGML for Windows, with text in Garamond and display type in Helvetica Condensed. Composed pages were delivered to the printer as electronic prepress files.

Cover Designer:	Methodologie, Inc.
Interior Graphic Designer:	James D. Kramer
Principal Compositor:	Dan Latimer
Interior Artist:	Rob Nance
Copy Editor:	Holly M. Viola
Indexer:	Shane-Armstrong Information Systems

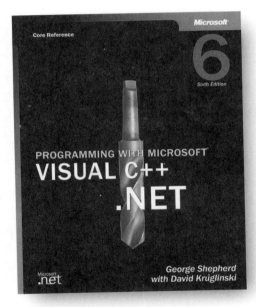

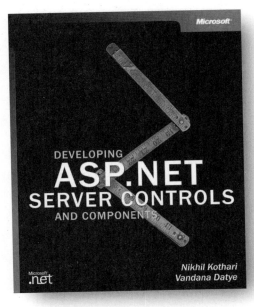

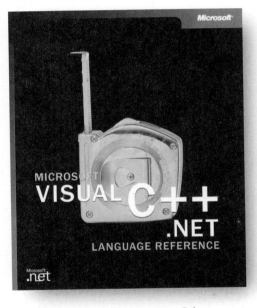

Proof of Purchase

Use this page as proof of purchase if participating in a promotion or rebate offer on this title. Proof of purchase must be used in conjunction with other proof(s) of payment such as your dated sales receipt—see offer details.

Programming with Managed Extensions for Microsoft® Visual C++® .NET

0-7356-1724-4

____

CUSTOMER NAME

Microsoft Press, PO Box 97017, Redmond, WA 98073-9830